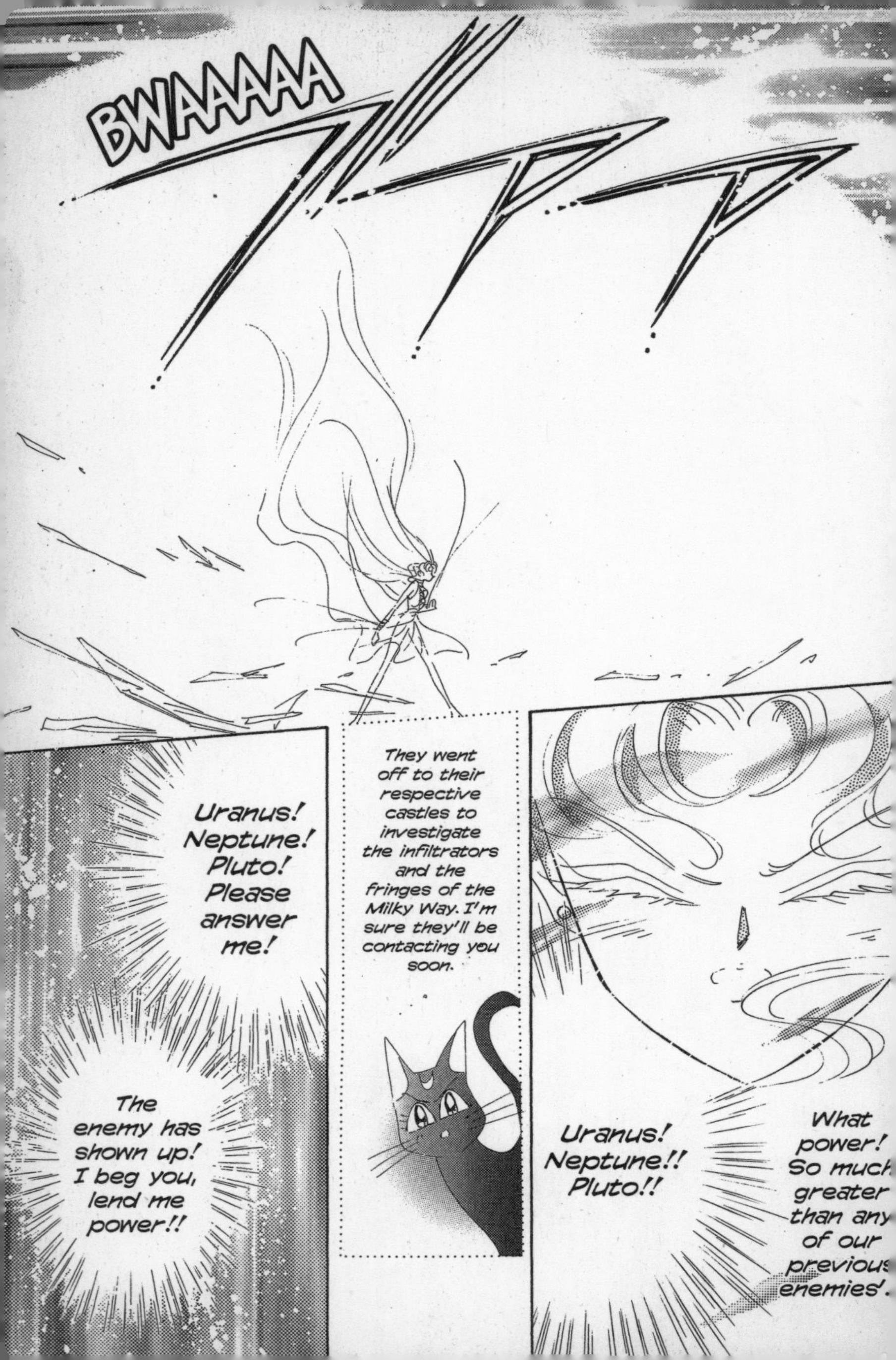
BWAAAAA
What power! So much greater than any of our previous enemies'.
Uranus! Neptune!! Pluto!!
They went off to their respective castles to investigate the infiltrators and the fringes of the Milky Way. I'm sure they'll be contacting you soon.
Uranus! Neptune! Pluto! Please answer me!
The enemy has shown up! I beg you, lend me power!!

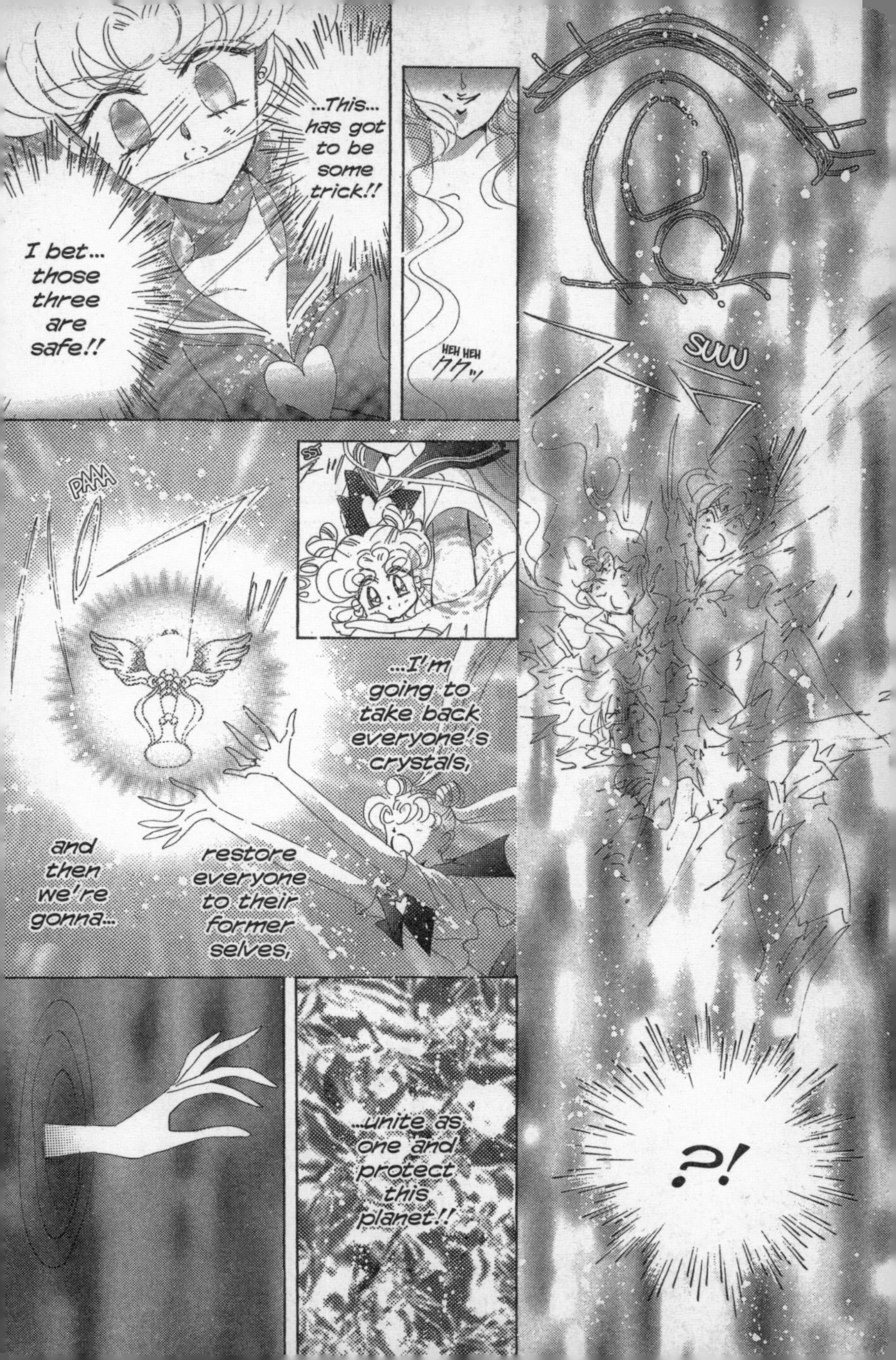
SUUU
?!
HEH HEH
ククッ
...This... has got to be some trick!!
I bet... those three are safe!!
SST
PAAA
...I'm going to take back everyone's crystals,
restore everyone to their former selves,
and then we're gonna...
...unite as one and protect this planet!!

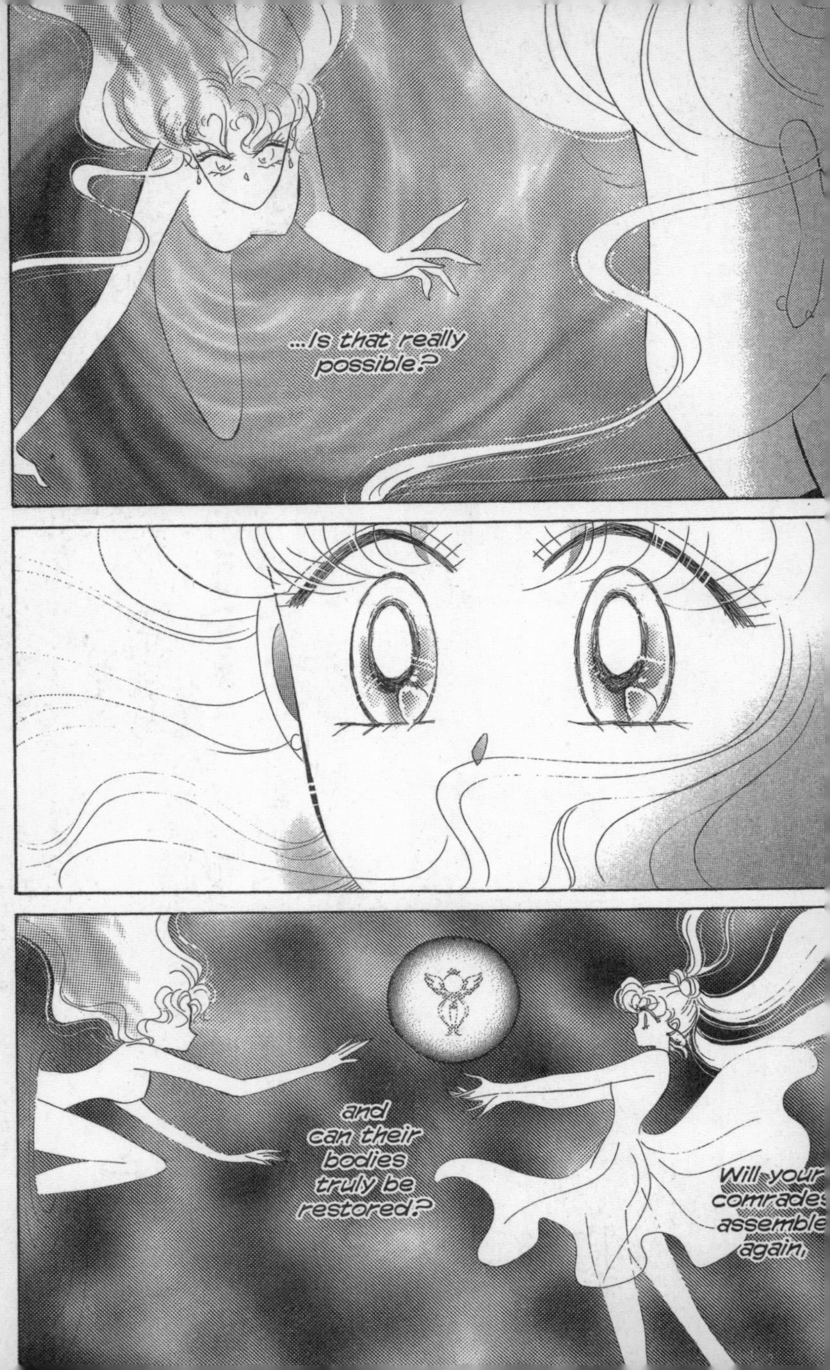
...Is that really possible?
Will your comrades assemble again,
and can their bodies truly be restored?

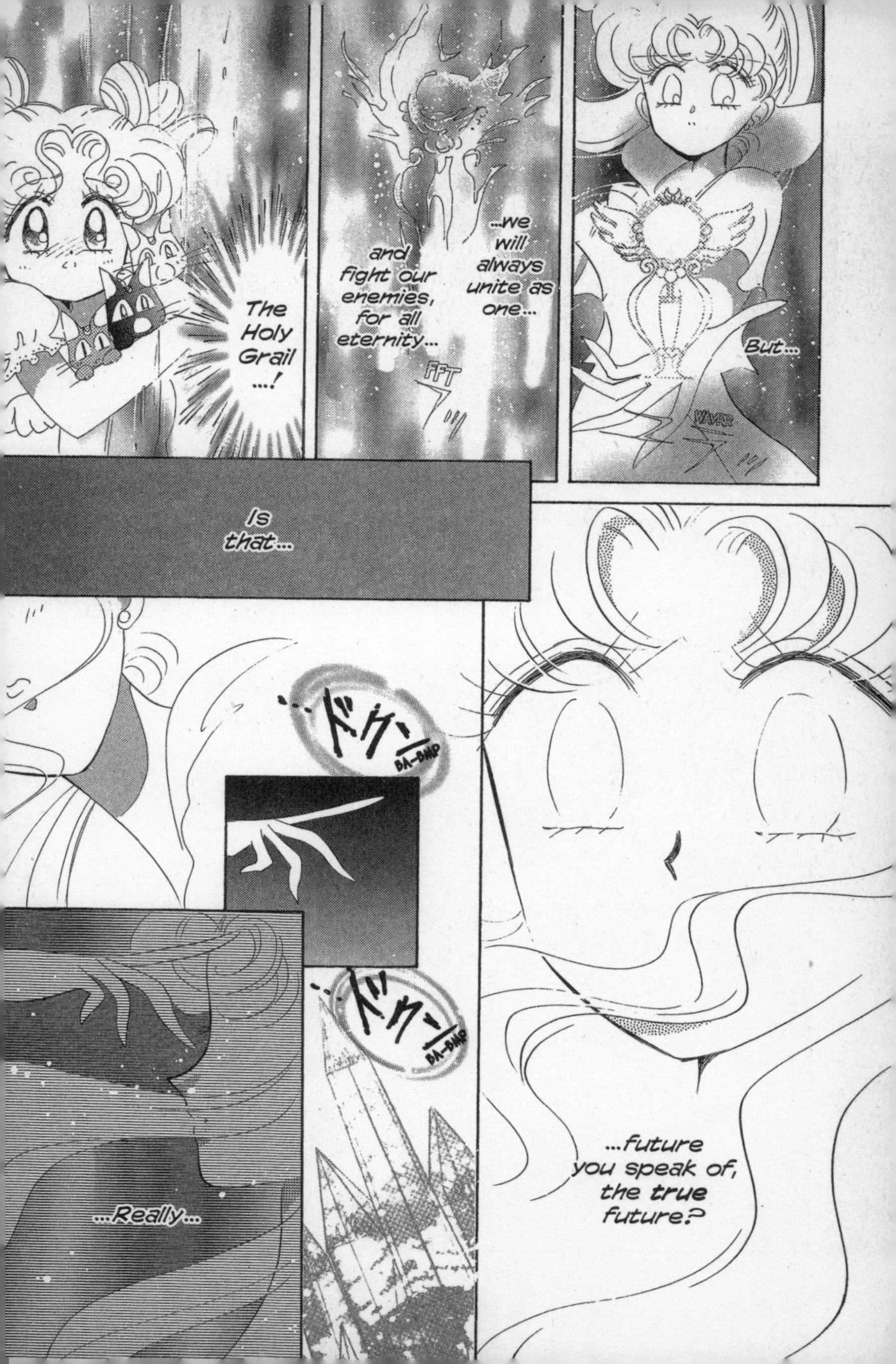

But...
WAVRR
...we will always unite as one...
and fight our enemies, for all eternity...
FFT
The Holy Grail ...!
Is that...
...future you speak of, the true future?
BA-BMP
BA-BMP
...Really...

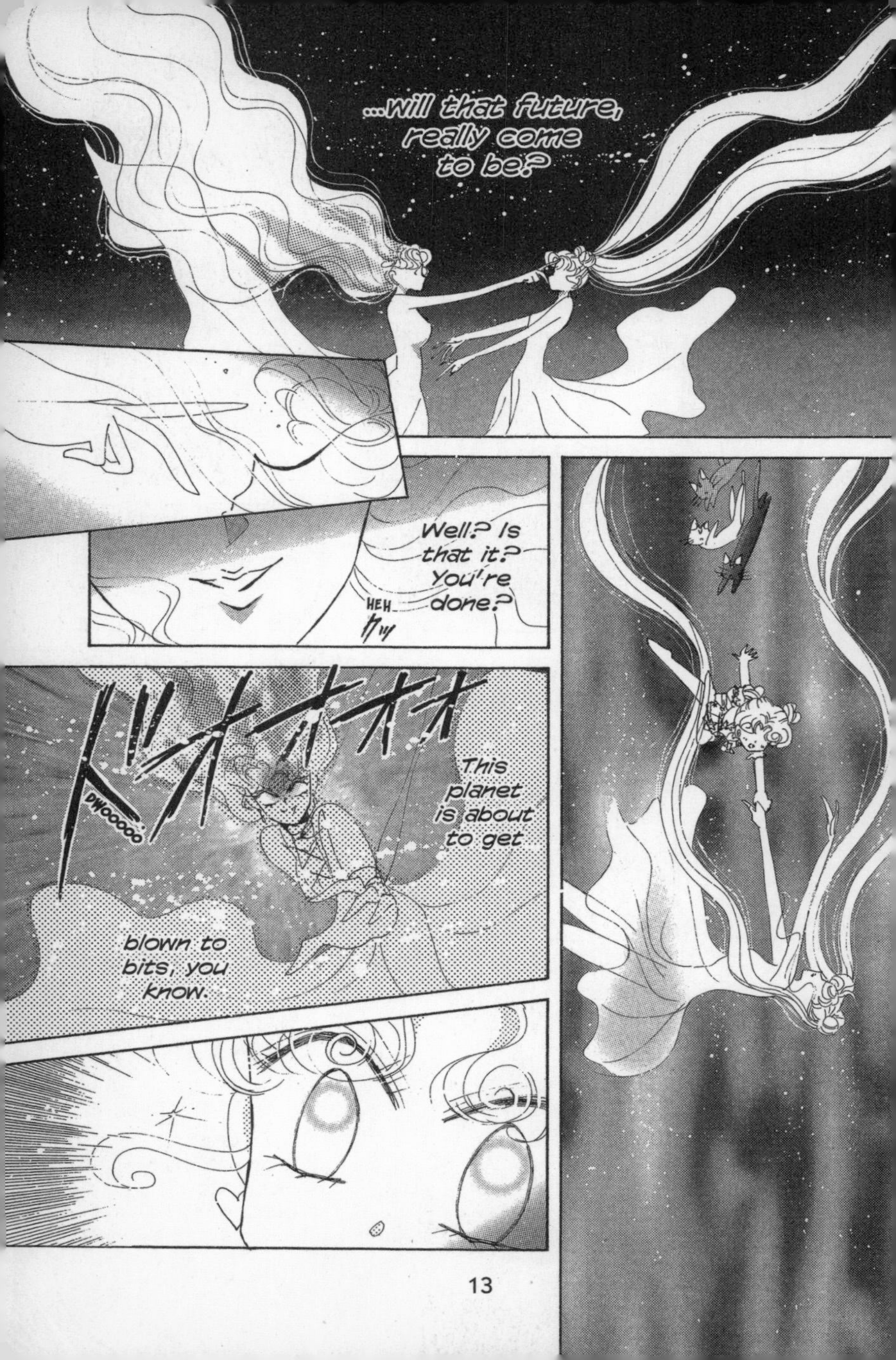
...will that future, really come to be?
Well? Is that it? You're done?
HEH
ケッ
ドッオオオオ
DWOOOOO
This planet is about to get
blown to bits, you know.

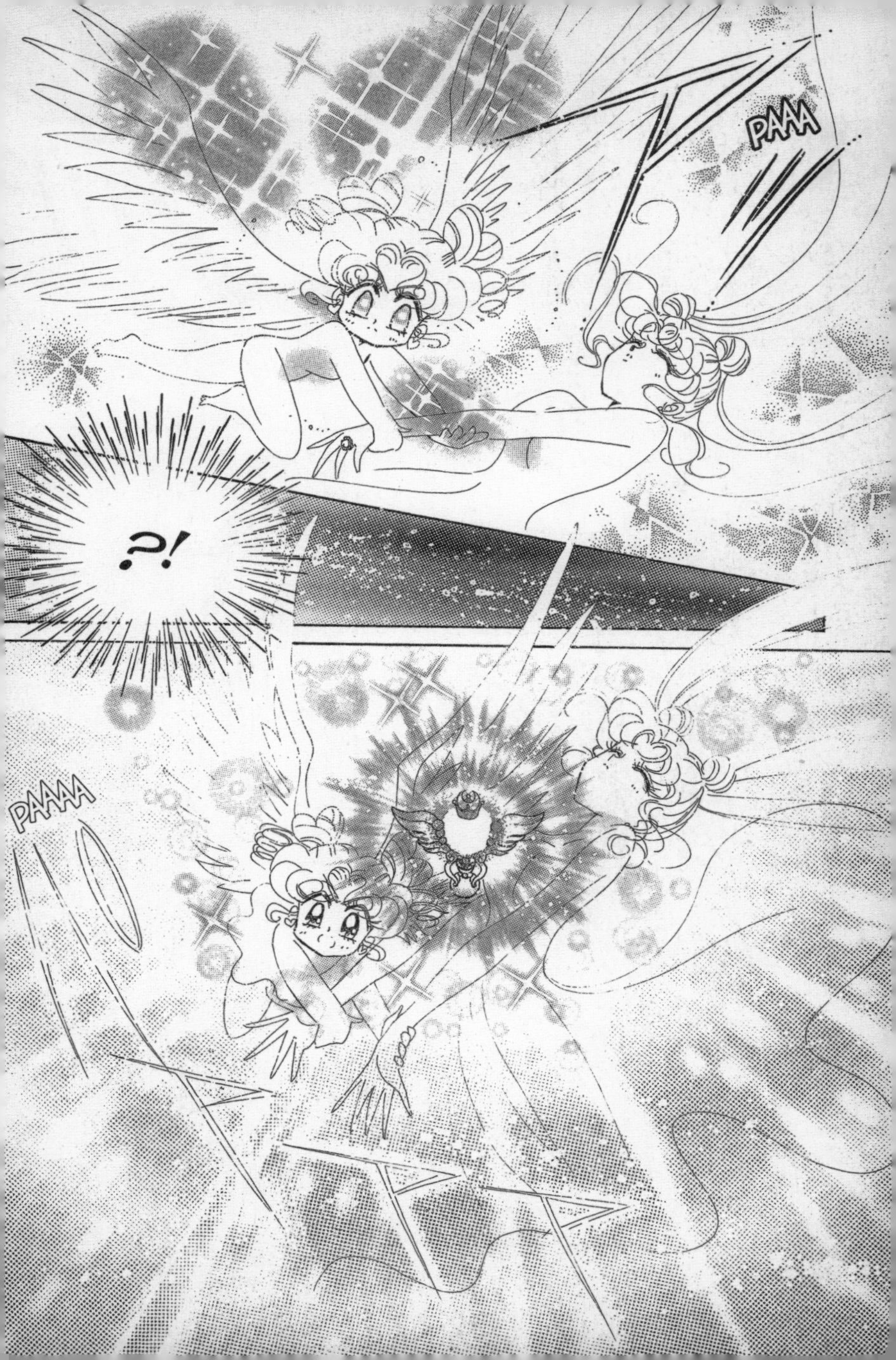
PAAA
?!
PAAAA

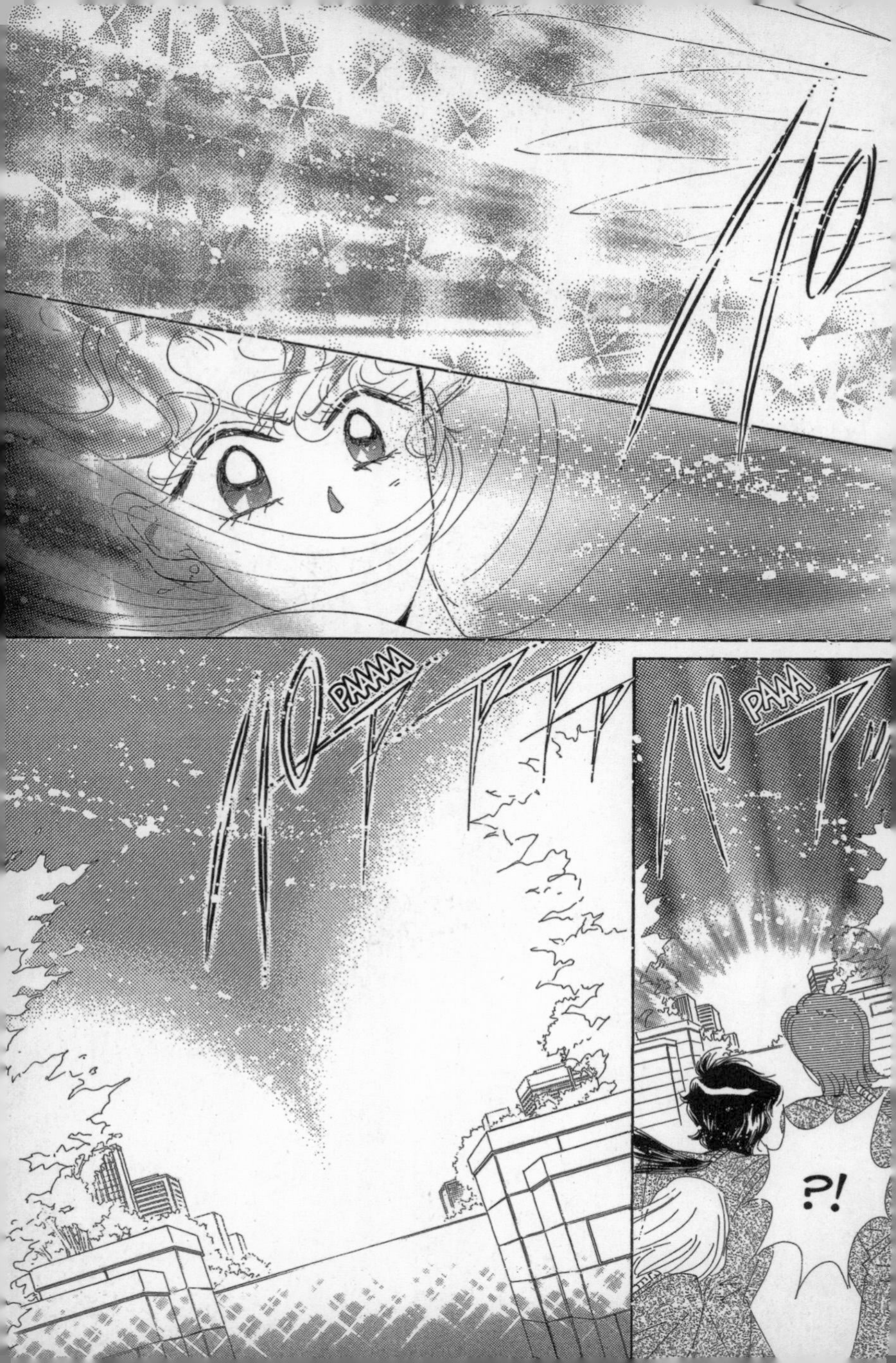
PAAA
?!
PAAAAA

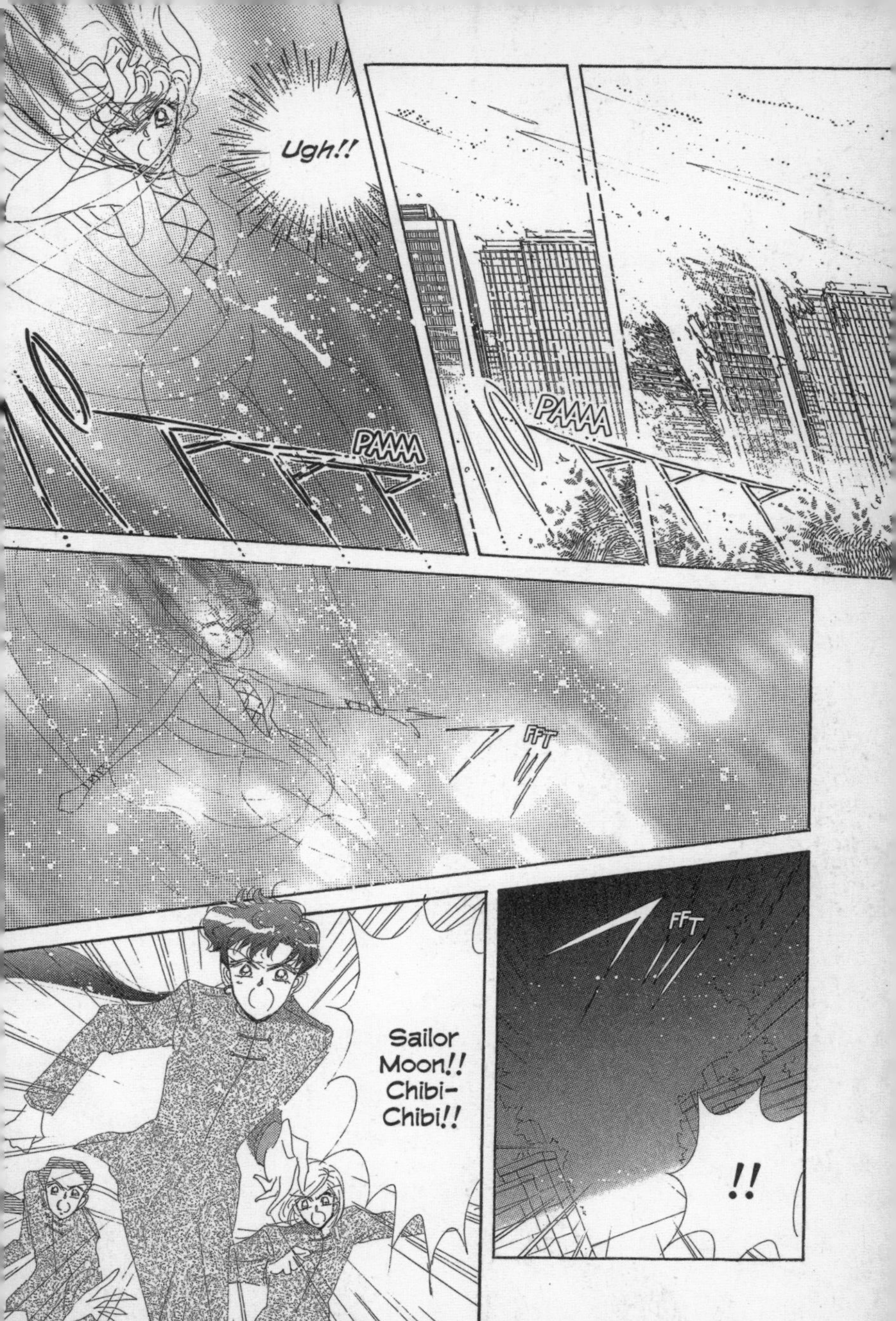
PAAAA
Ugh!!
PAAAA
FFT
FFT
!!
Sailor Moon!! Chibi-Chibi!!

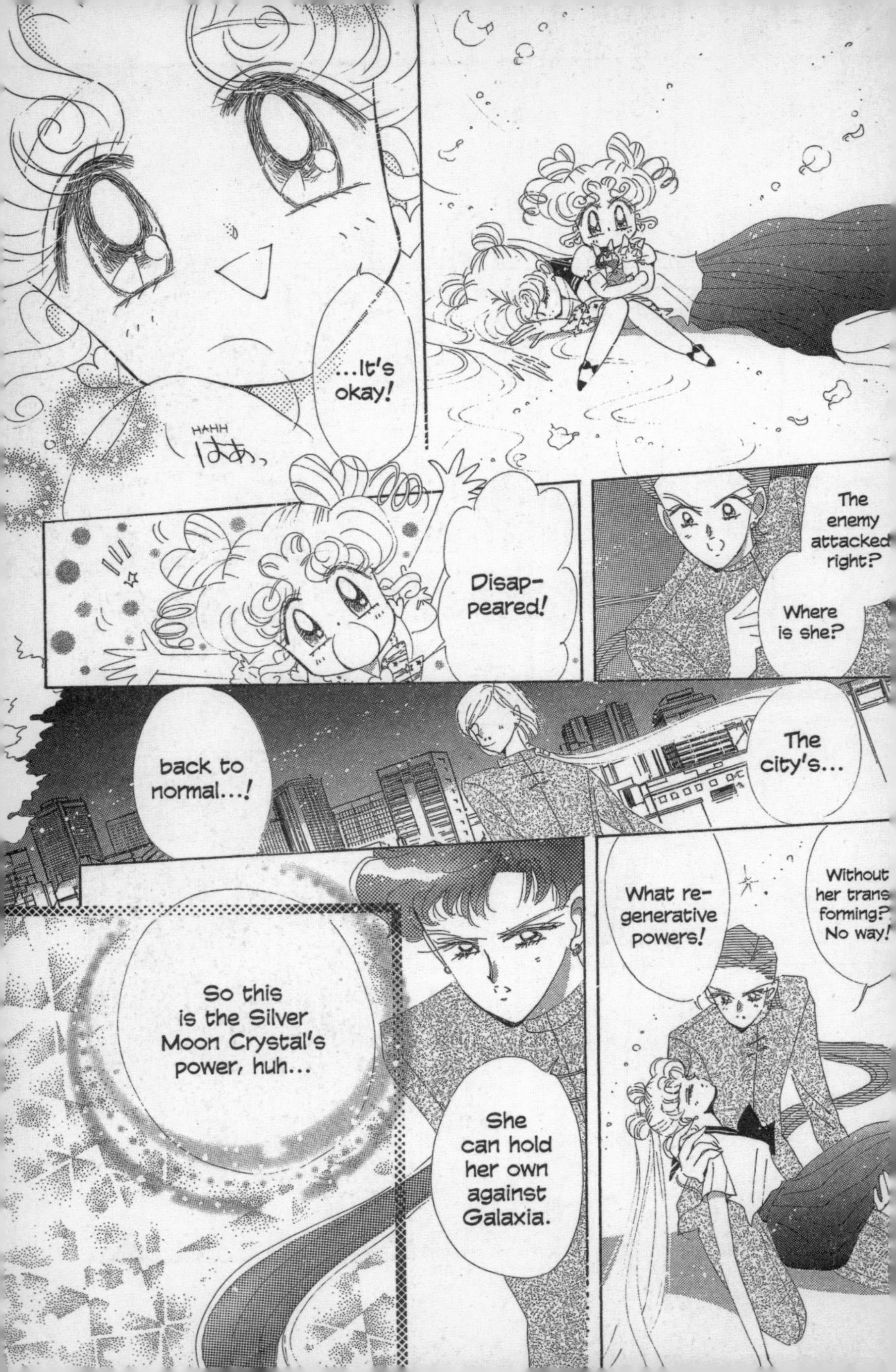

...It's okay!
HAHH
はあ
The enemy attacked right?
Where is she?
Disap-peared!
The city's...
back to normal...!
Without her trans forming? No way!
What re-generative powers!
So this is the Silver Moon Crystal's power, huh...
She can hold her own against Galaxia.

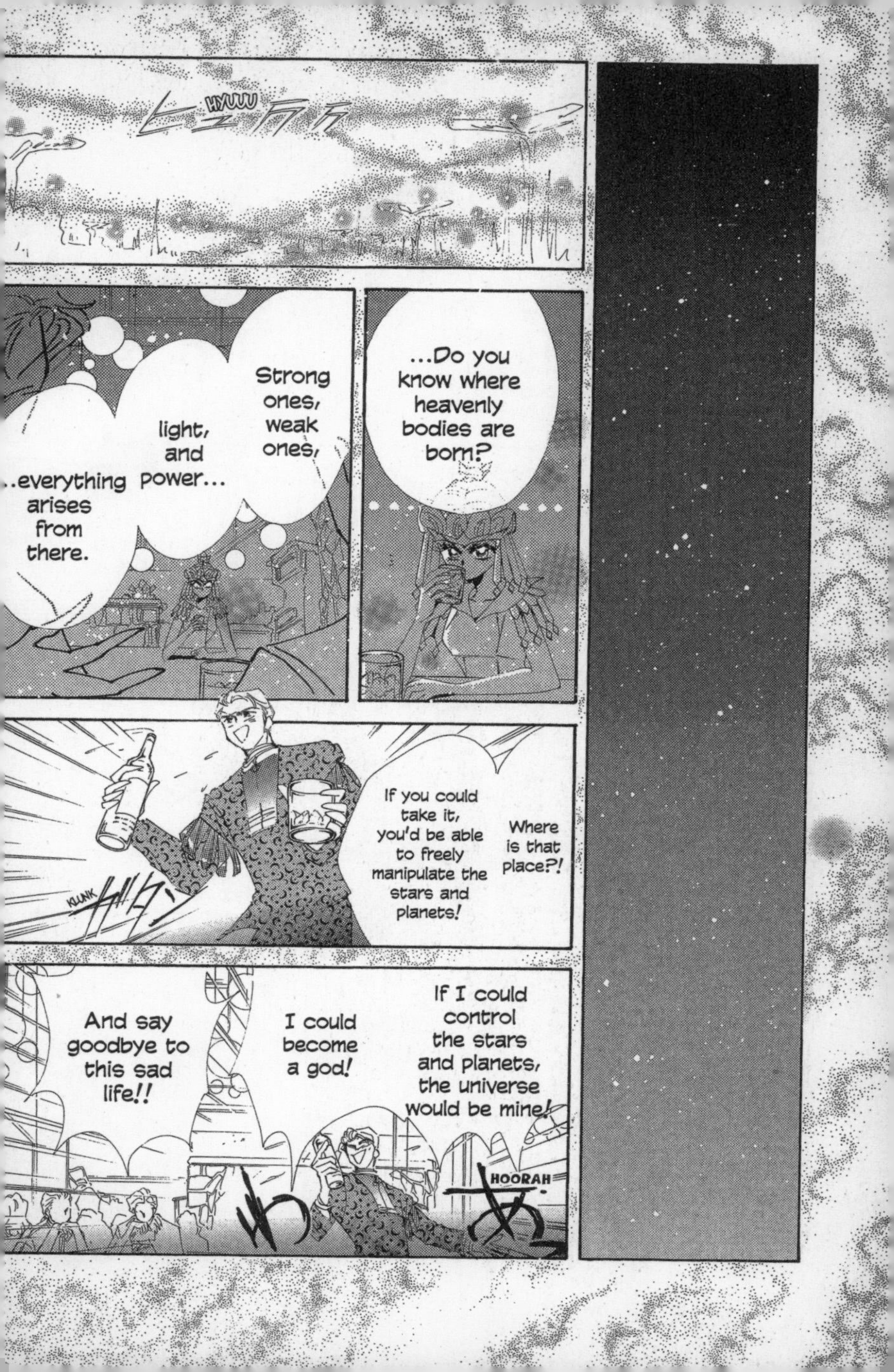
HYUUU
...Do you know where heavenly bodies are born?
Strong ones, weak ones,
light, and power...
..everything arises from there.
Where is that place?!
If you could take it, you'd be able to freely manipulate the stars and planets!
KLUNK
If I could control the stars and planets, the universe would be mine!
I could become a god!
And say goodbye to this sad life!!
HOORAH

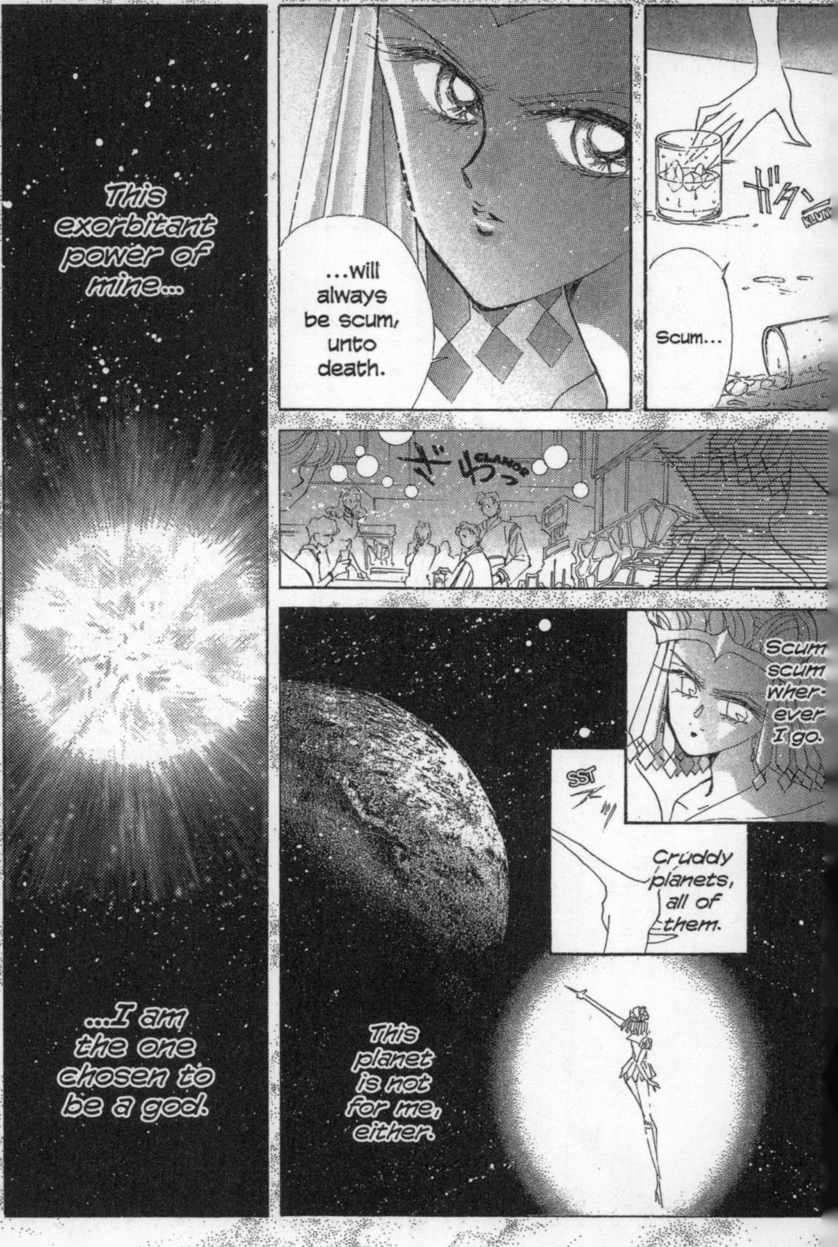
ガタン
KLUN
Scum...
...will always be scum, unto death.
ざわっ
CLAMOR
Scum, scum wherever I go.
SST
Cruddy planets, all of them.
This planet is not for me, either.
This exorbitant power of mine...
...I am the one chosen to be a god.

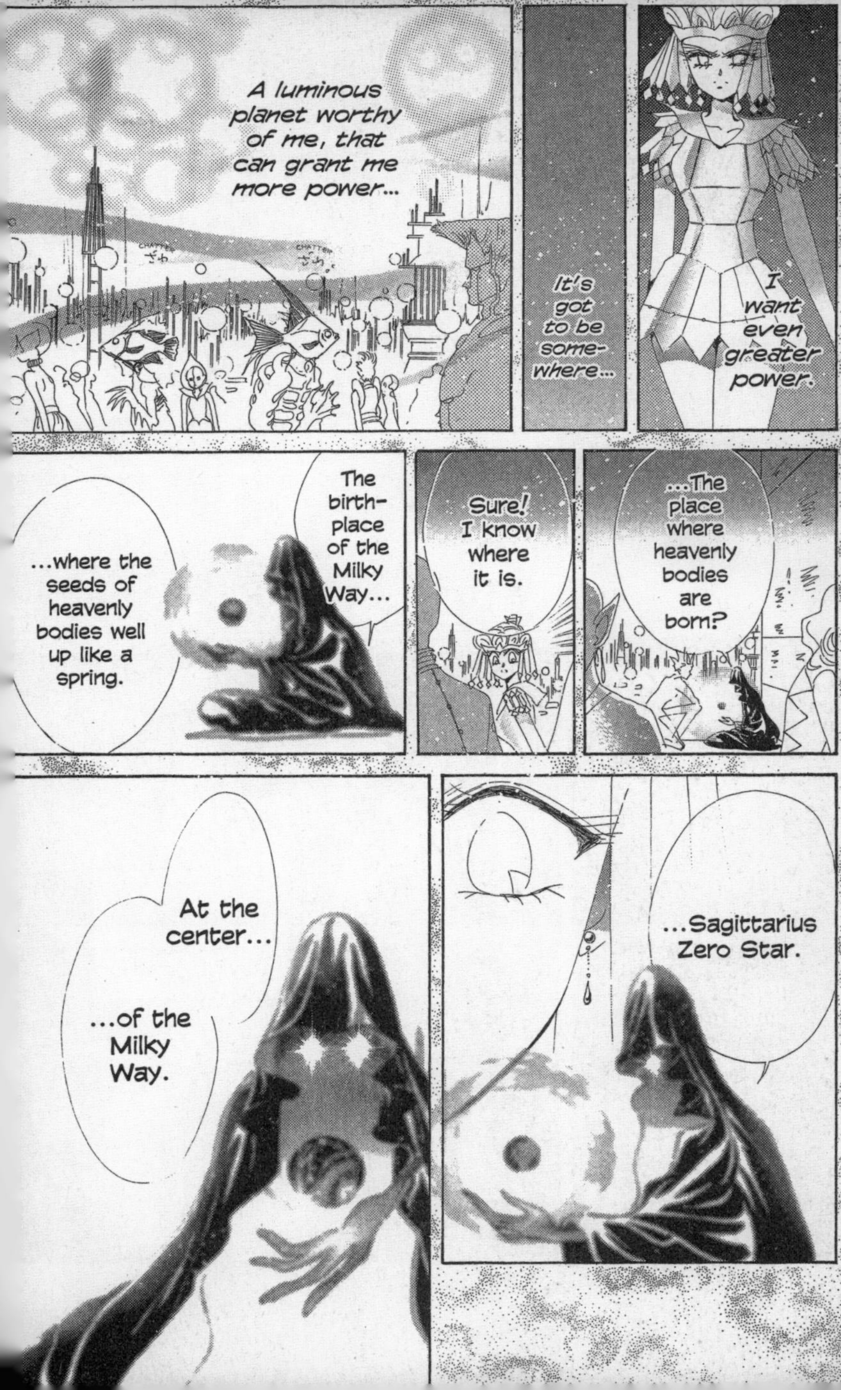
I want even greater power.
It's got to be somewhere...
A luminous planet worthy of me, that can grant me more power...
...The place where heavenly bodies are born?
Sure! I know where it is.
The birth-place of the Milky Way...
...where the seeds of heavenly bodies well up like a spring.
At the center...
...of the Milky Way.
...Sagittarius Zero Star.

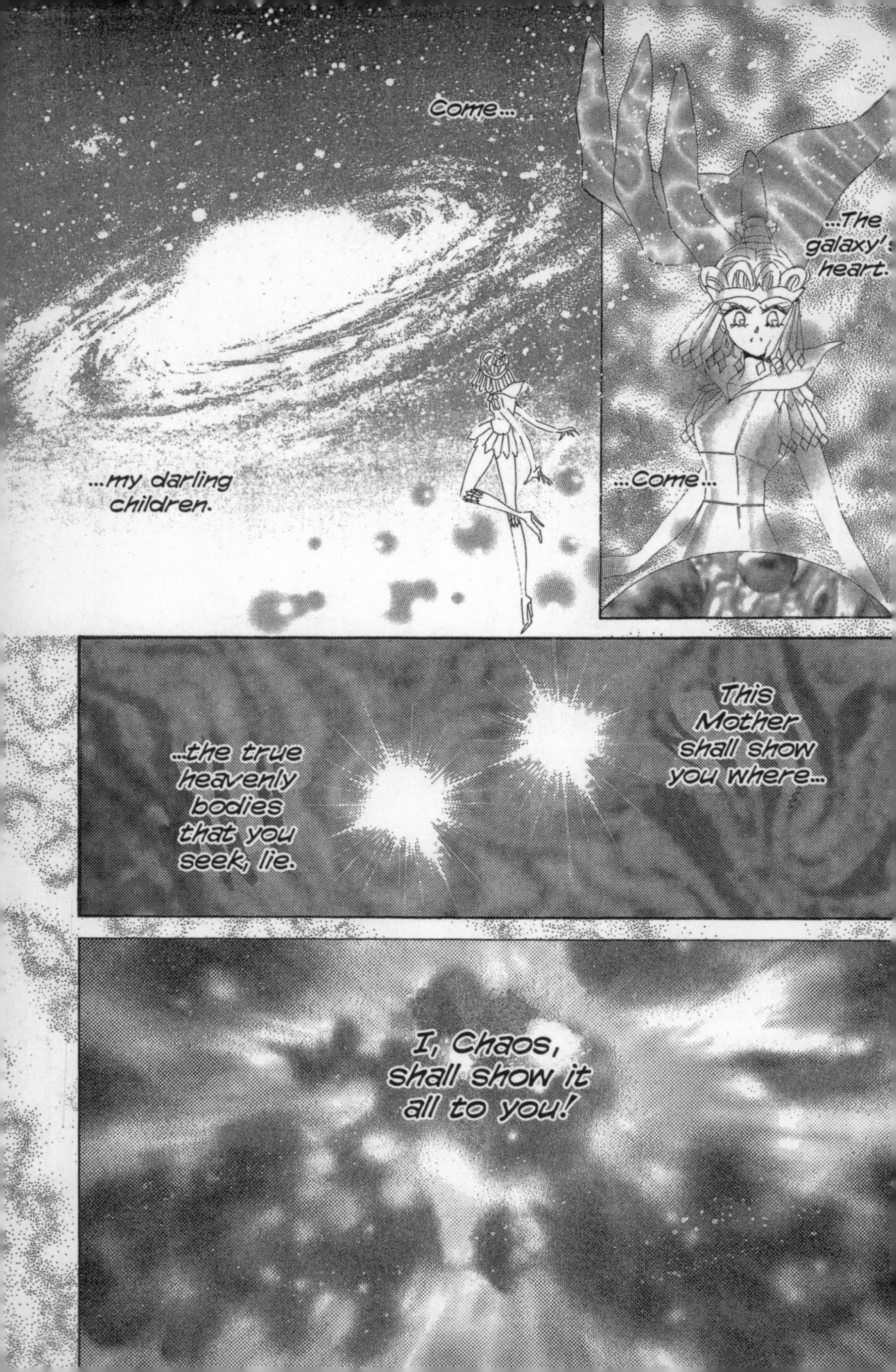
...The galaxy's heart.
...Come...
Come...
...my darling children.
This Mother shall show you where...
...the true heavenly bodies that you seek, lie.
I, Chaos, shall show it all to you!

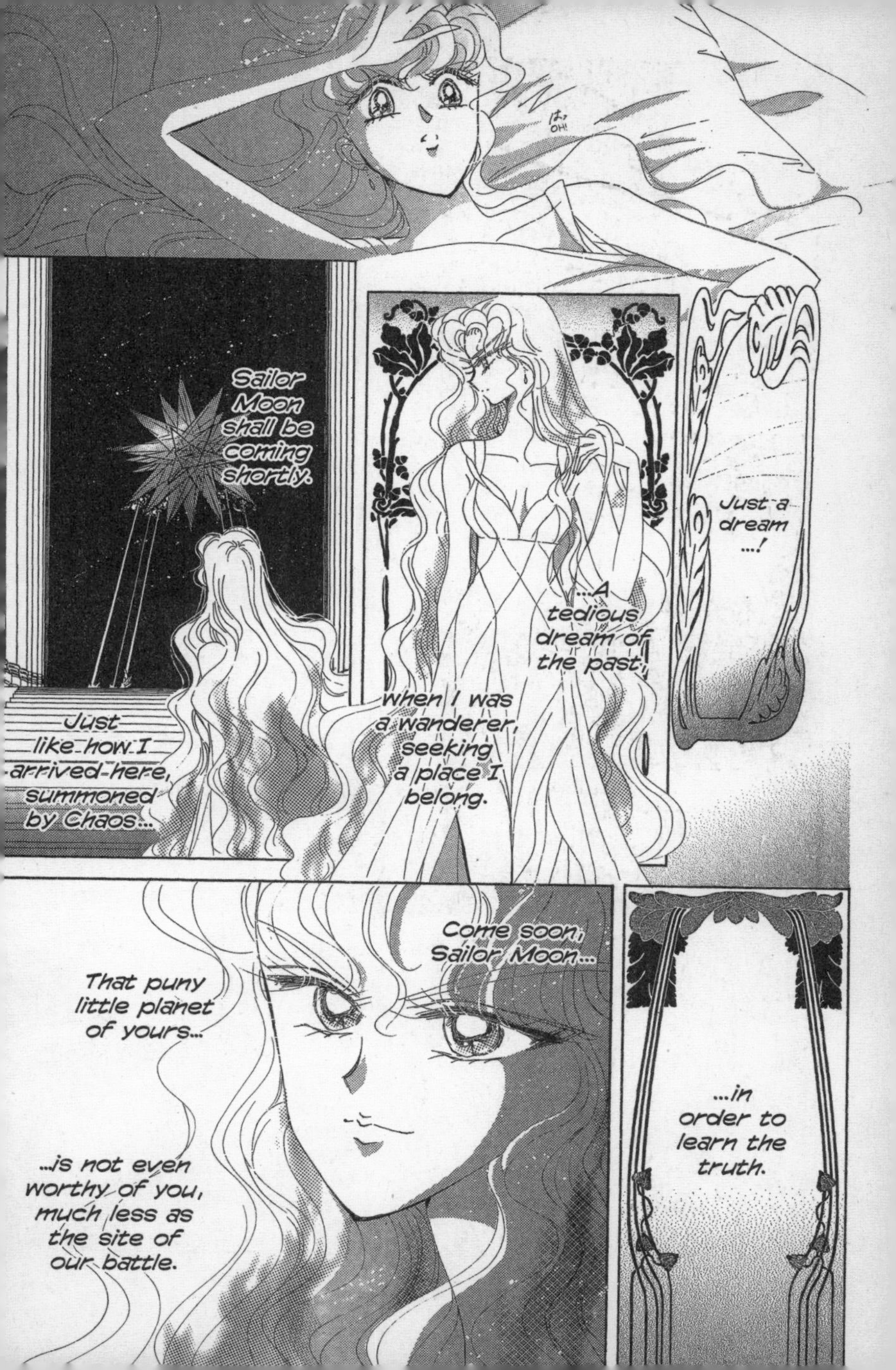
OH!
Just a dream ...!
...A tedious dream of the past,
when I was a wanderer, seeking a place I belong.
Sailor Moon shall be coming shortly.
Just like how I arrived here, summoned by Chaos...
...in order to learn the truth.
Come soon, Sailor Moon...
That puny little planet of yours...
...is not even worthy of you, much less as the site of our battle.

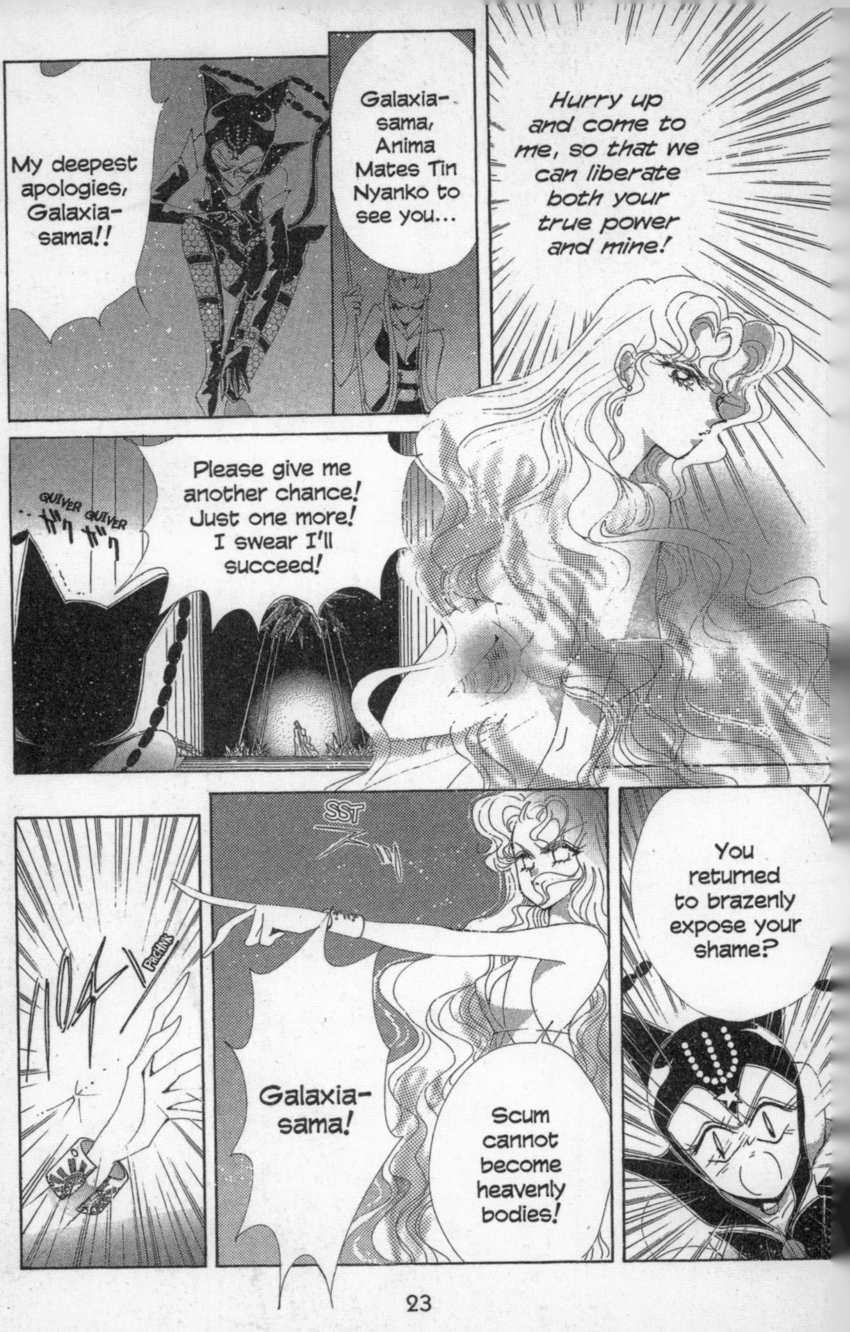
Hurry up and come to me, so that we can liberate both your true power and mine!
Galaxia-sama, Anima Mates Tin Nyanko to see you...
My deepest apologies, Galaxia-sama!!
Please give me another chance! Just one more! I swear I'll succeed!
QUIVER QUIVER
You returned to brazenly expose your shame?
SST
Scum cannot become heavenly bodies!
Galaxia-sama!
PACHINK

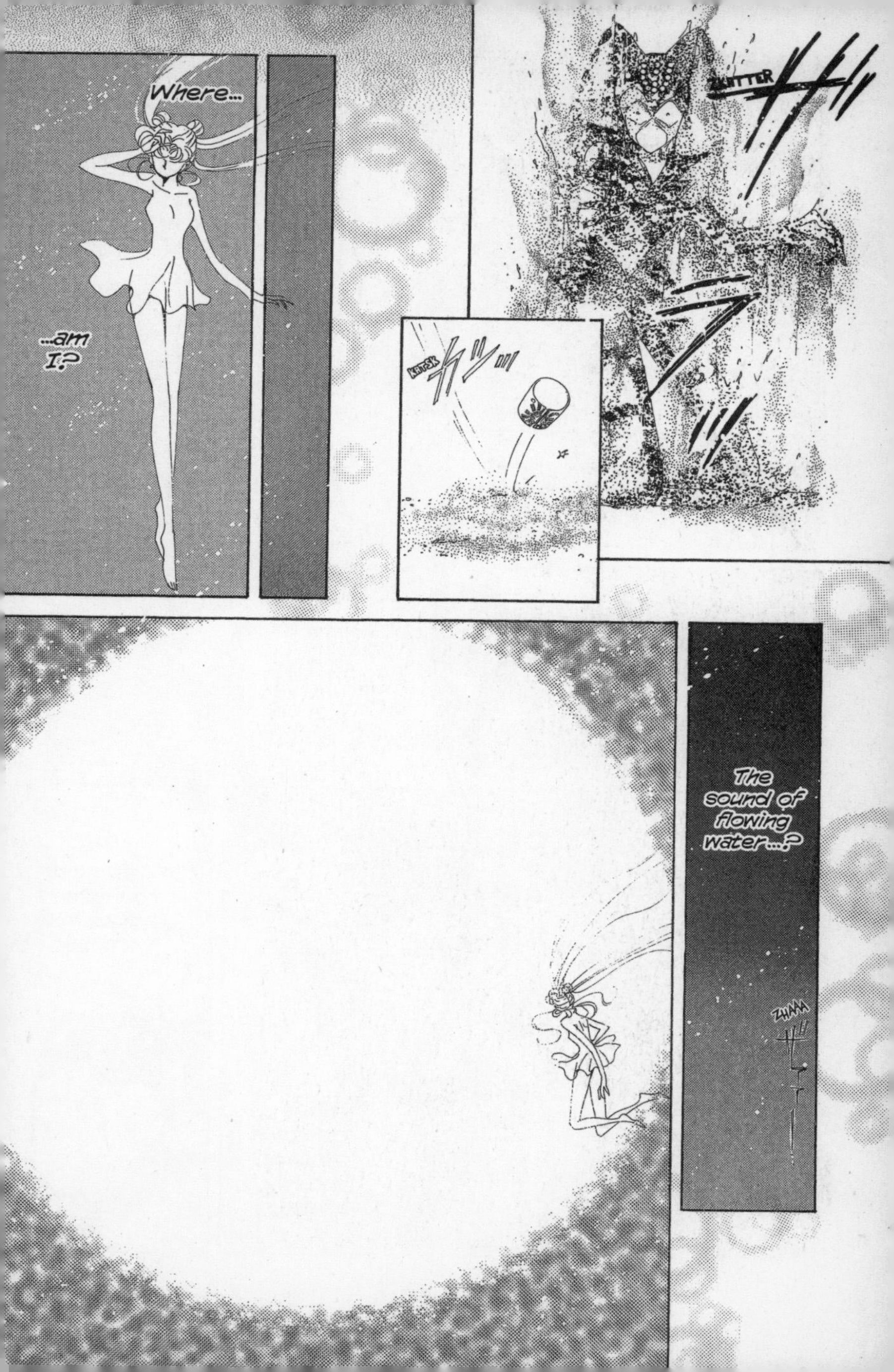
ZKITTER
KATSK
Where...
...am I?
The sound of flowing water...?
ZHAAA

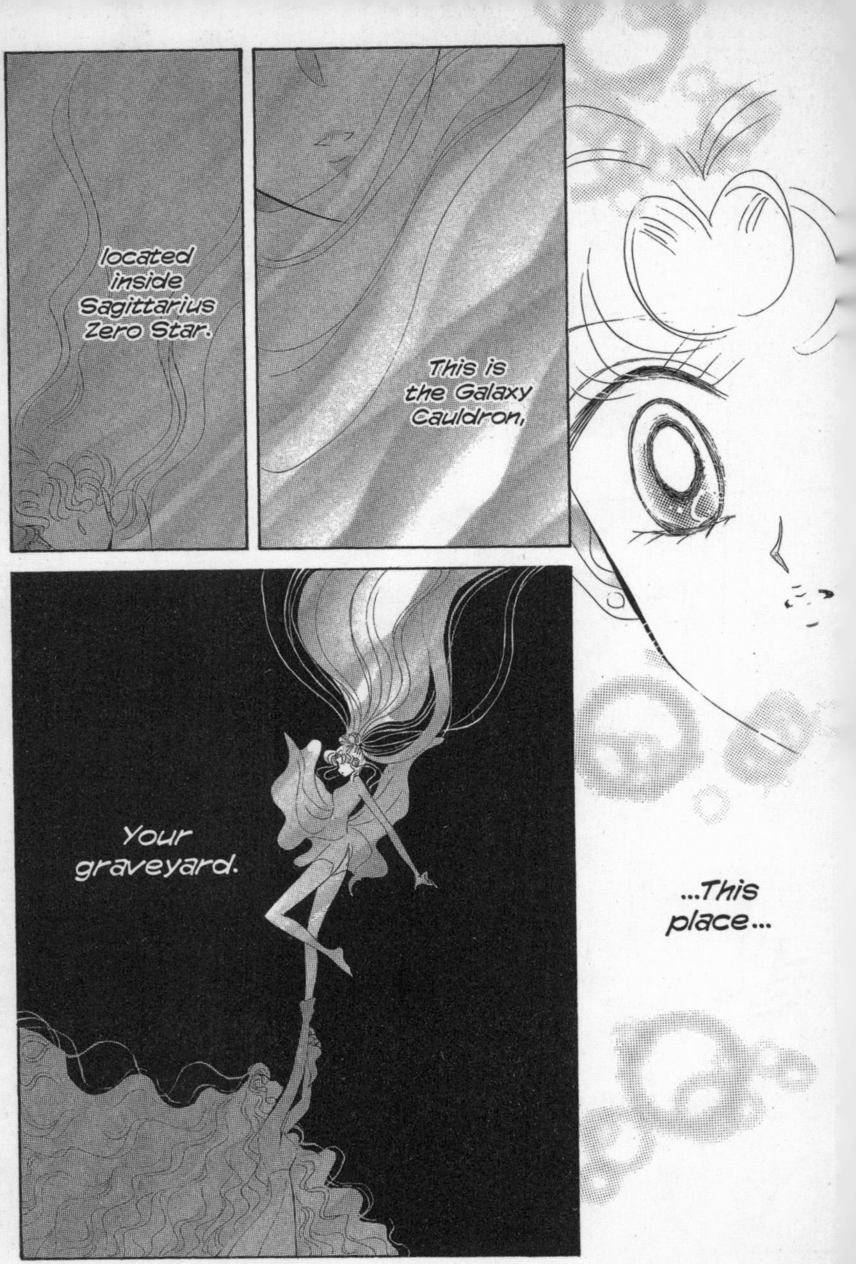
...This place...
This is the Galaxy Cauldron,
located inside Sagittarius Zero Star.
Your graveyard.

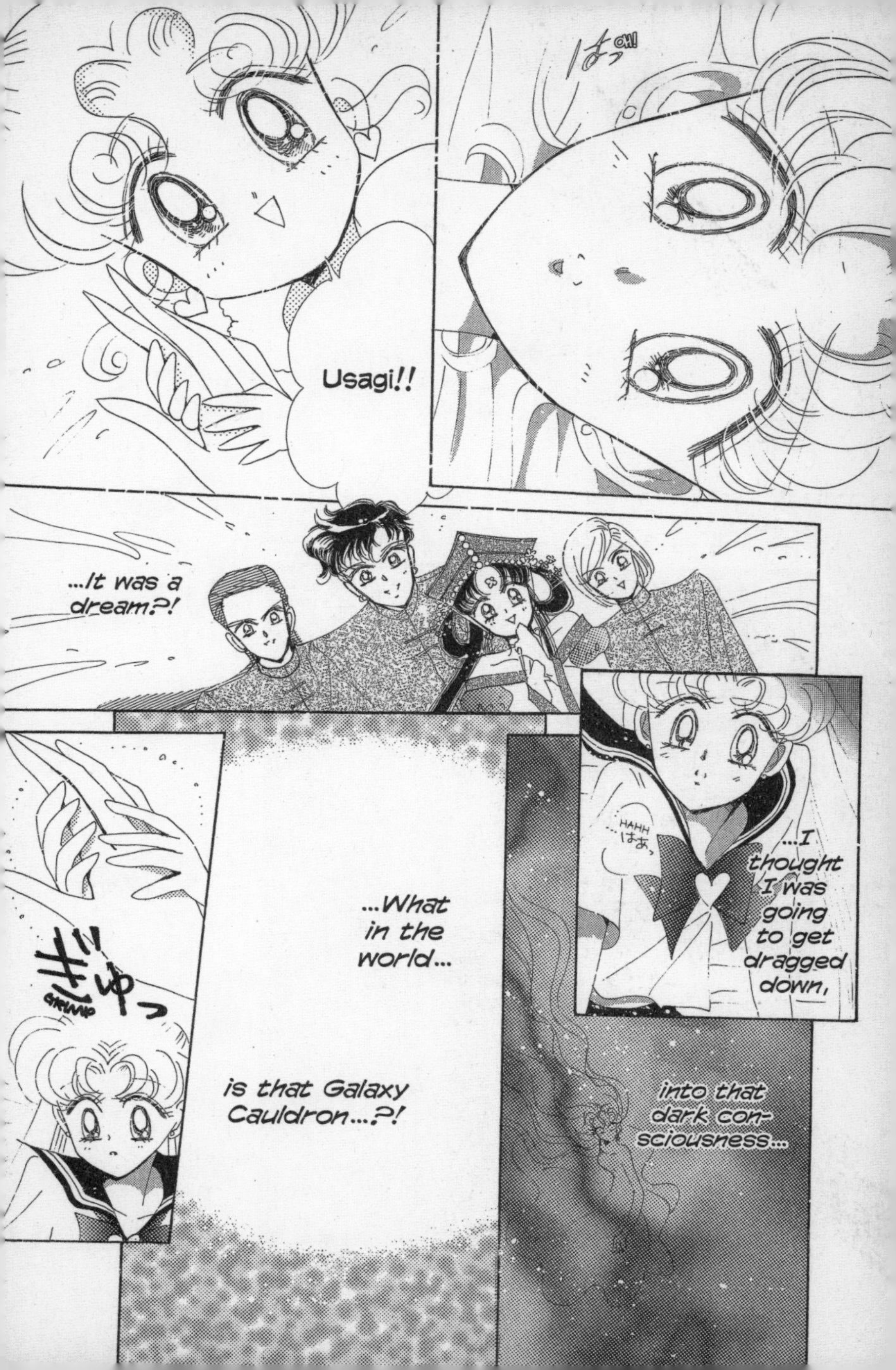

はっ
OH!
Usagi!!
...It was a dream?!
HAHH
はあっ
...I thought I was going to get dragged down,
into that dark consciousness...
...What in the world...
is that Galaxy Cauldron...?!
ぎゅっ
GRIMP

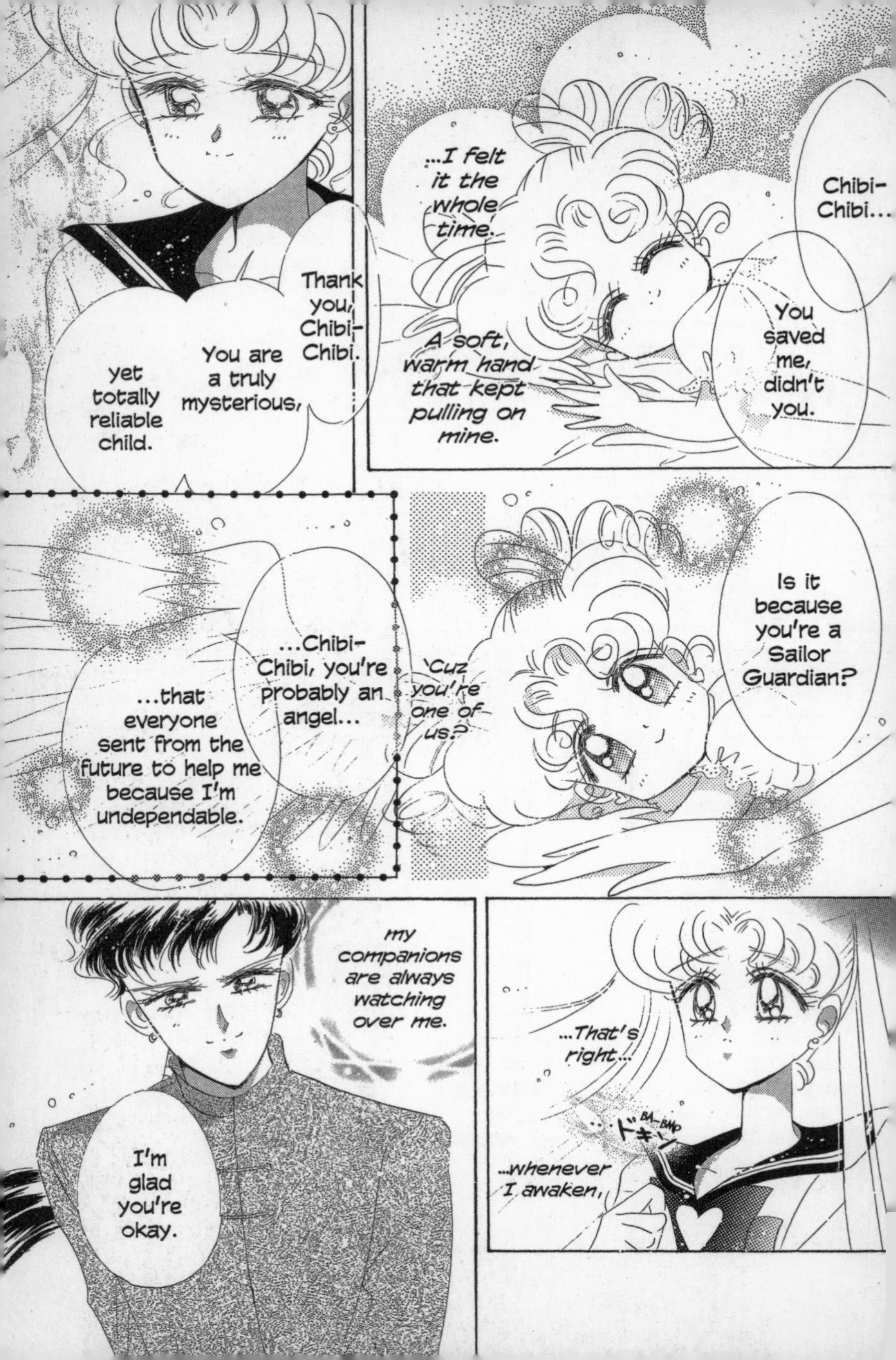
Chibi-Chibi...
You saved me, didn't you.
...I felt it the whole time.
A soft, warm hand that kept pulling on mine.
Thank you, Chibi-Chibi.
You are a truly mysterious,
yet totally reliable child.
Is it because you're a Sailor Guardian?
'Cuz you're one of us?
...Chibi-Chibi, you're probably an angel...
...that everyone sent from the future to help me because I'm undependable.
...That's right...
BA-BMP
...whenever I awaken,
my companions are always watching over me.
I'm glad you're okay.

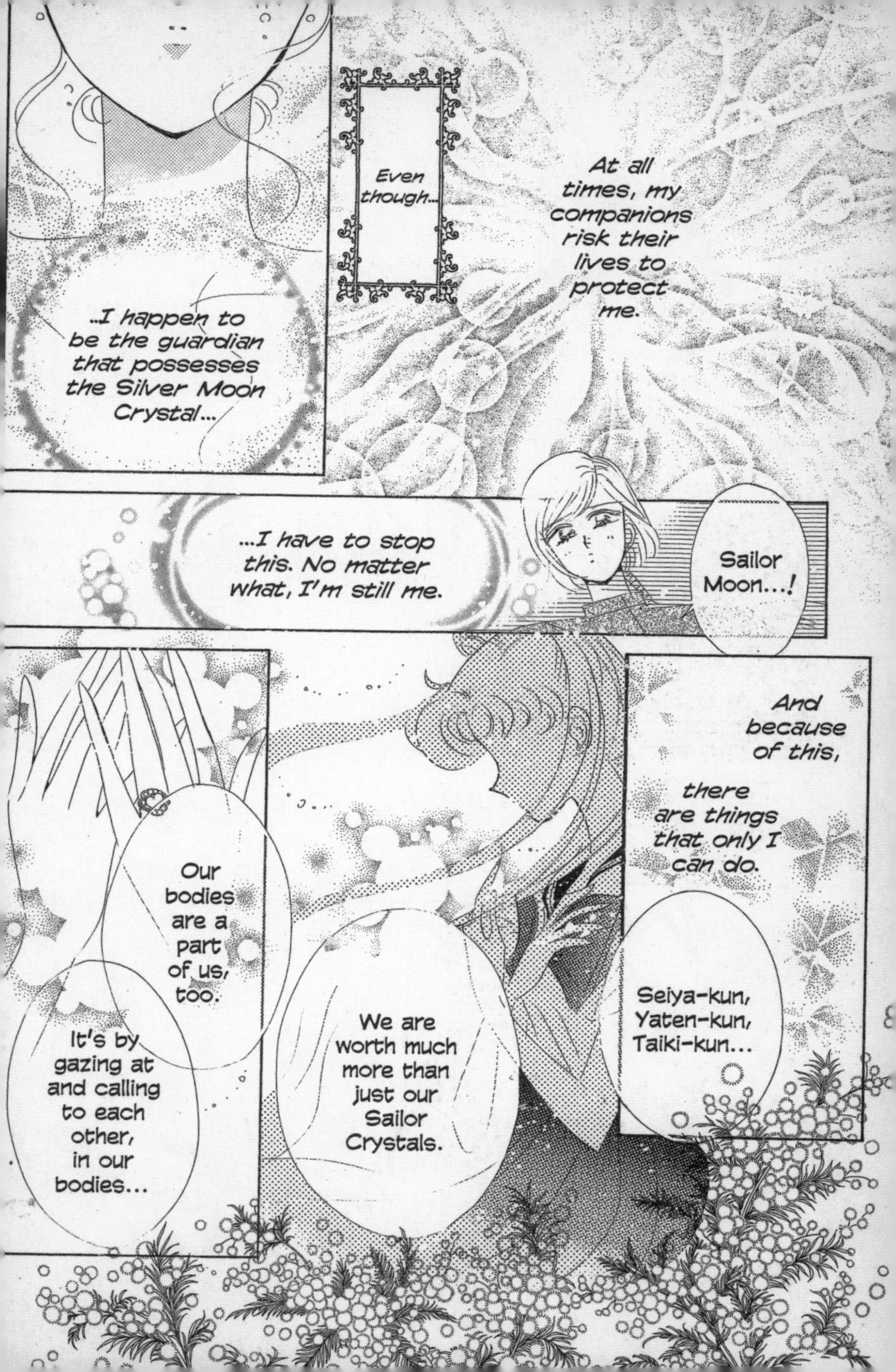
At all times, my companions risk their lives to protect me.
Even though...
...I happen to be the guardian that possesses the Silver Moon Crystal...
Sailor Moon...!
...I have to stop this. No matter what, I'm still me.
And because of this,
there are things that only I can do.
Seiya-kun, Yaten-kun, Taiki-kun...
We are worth much more than just our Sailor Crystals.
Our bodies are a part of us, too.
It's by gazing at and calling to each other, in our bodies...

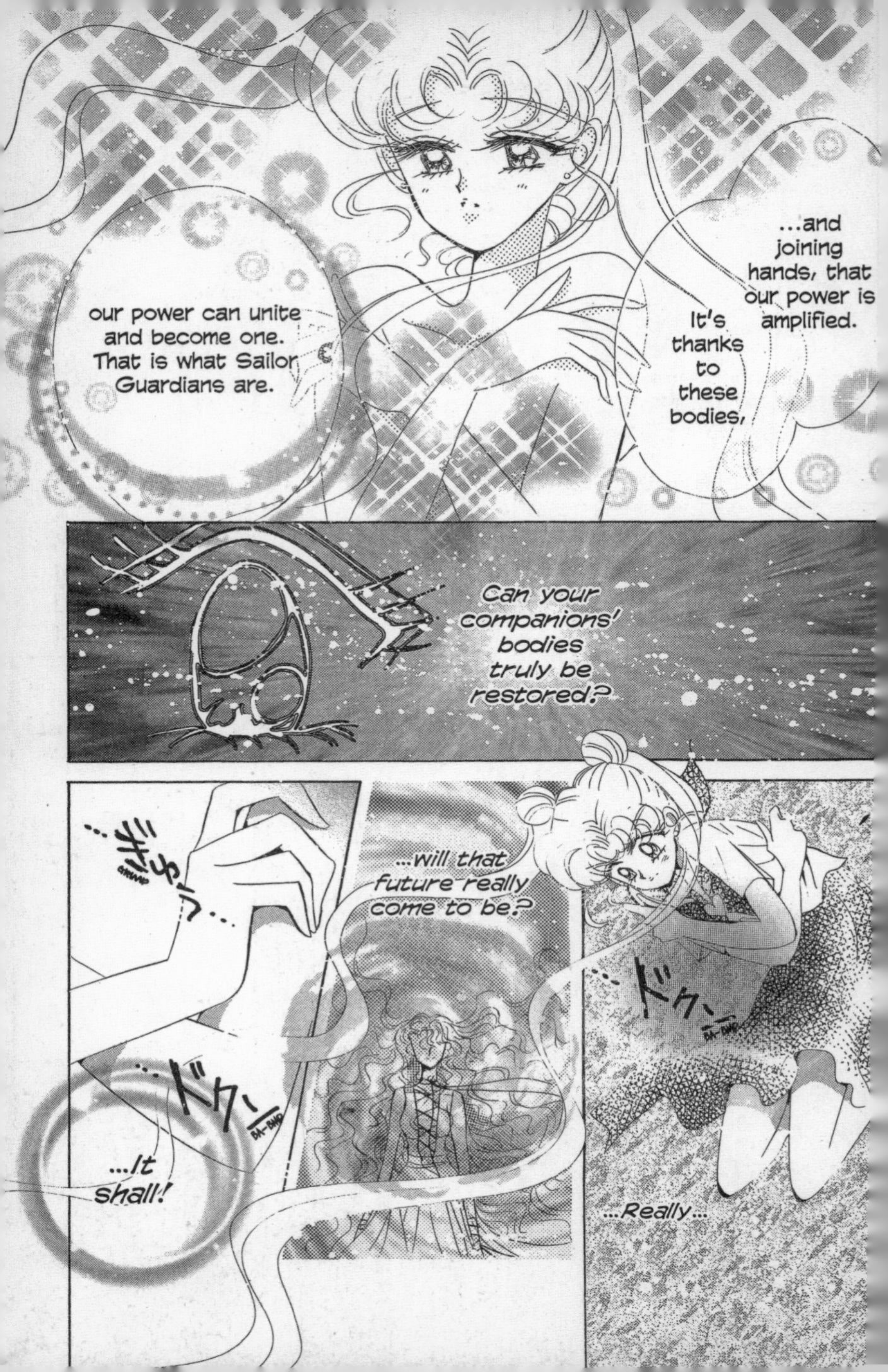

It's thanks to these bodies,
...and joining hands, that our power is amplified.
our power can unite and become one. That is what Sailor Guardians are.
Can your companions' bodies truly be restored?
...Really...
ドクン
BA-BMP
...will that future really come to be?
...It shall!
ドクン
BA-BMP

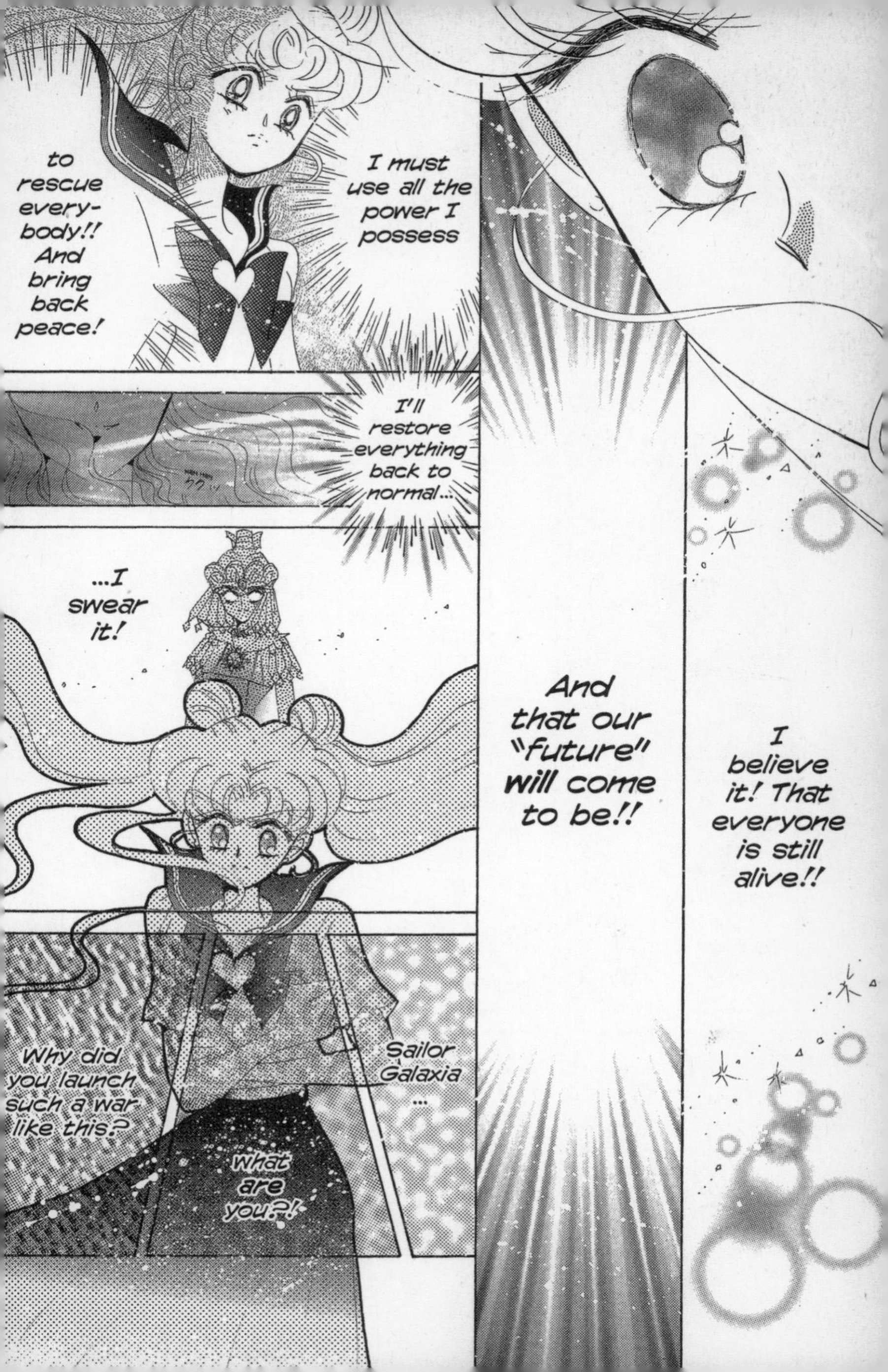
I believe it! That everyone is still alive!!
And that our "future" will come to be!!
I must use all the power I possess
to rescue every-body!! And bring back peace!
I'll restore everything back to normal...
...I swear it!
Sailor Galaxia ...
Why did you launch such a war like this?
what are you?!

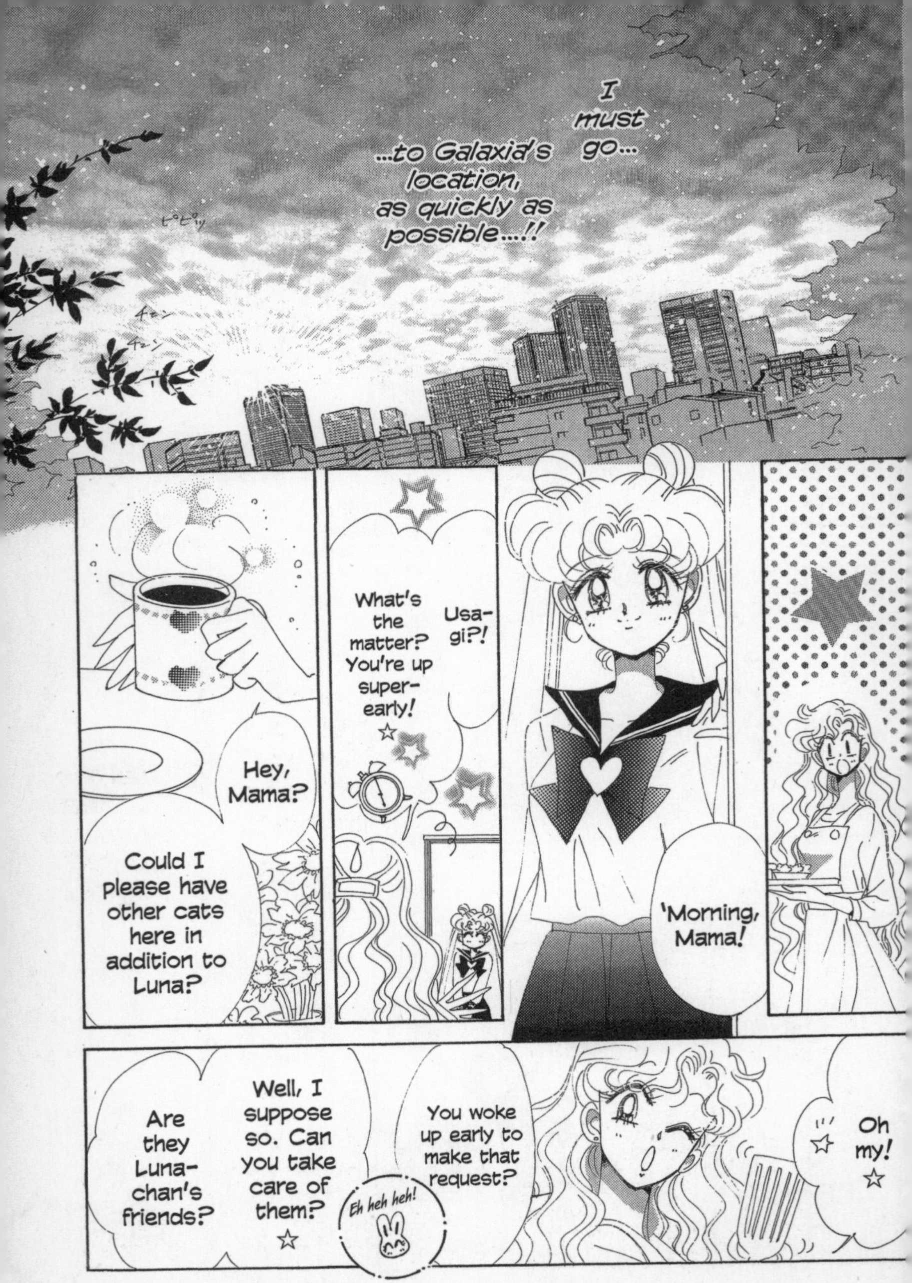
I must go...
...to Galaxia's location, as quickly as possible...!!
ピピッ
チュン
チュン
'Morning, Mama!
Usa-gi?!
What's the matter? You're up super-early!
Hey, Mama?
Could I please have other cats here in addition to Luna?
Oh my!
You woke up early to make that request?
Eh heh heh!
Well, I suppose so. Can you take care of them?
Are they Luna-chan's friends?

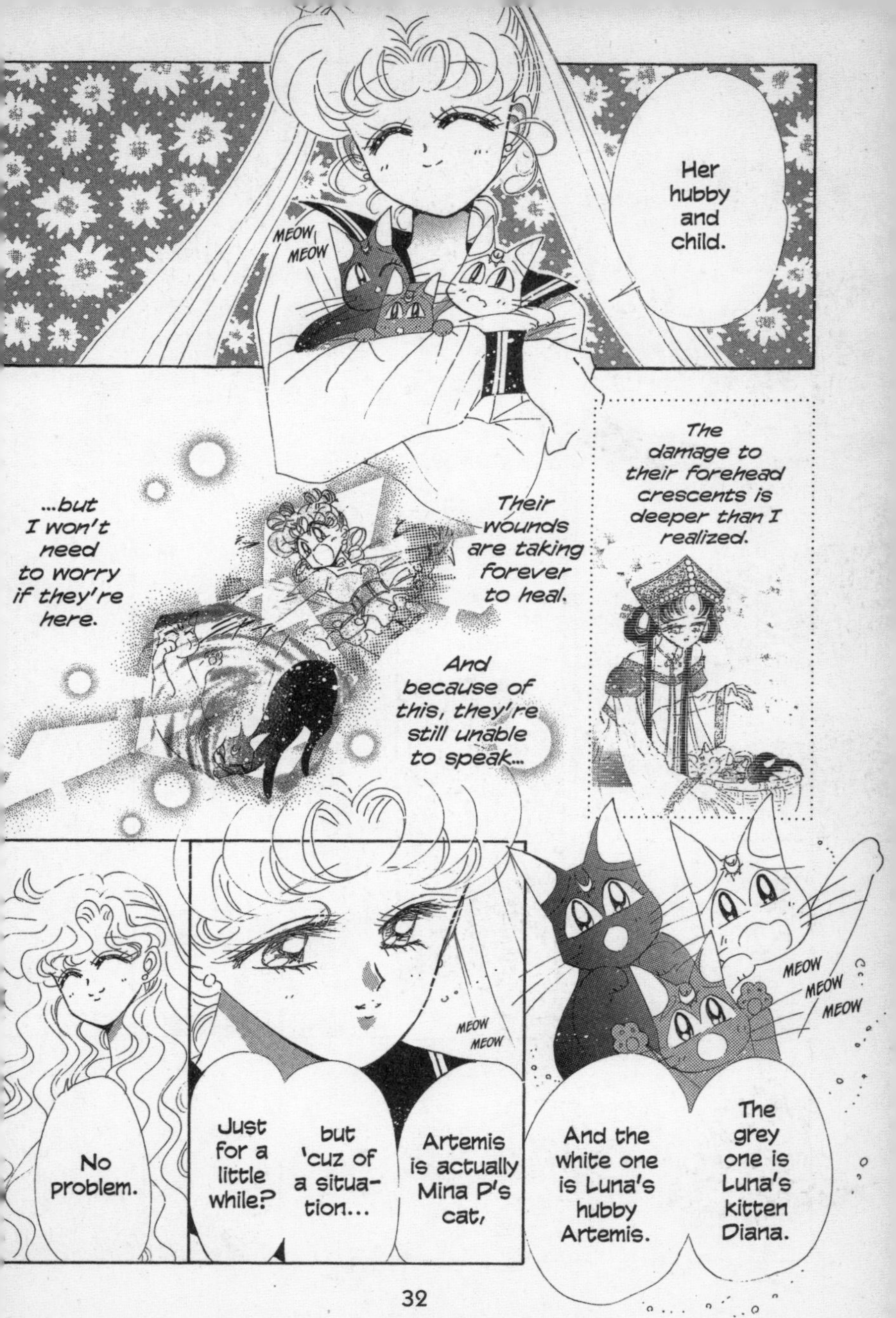
Her hubby and child.
MEOW MEOW
The damage to their forehead crescents is deeper than I realized.
Their wounds are taking forever to heal.
And because of this, they're still unable to speak...
...but I won't need to worry if they're here.
The grey one is Luna's kitten Diana.
And the white one is Luna's hubby Artemis.
MEOW MEOW MEOW
Artemis is actually Mina P's cat,
but 'cuz of a situation...
Just for a little while?
MEOW MEOW
No problem.

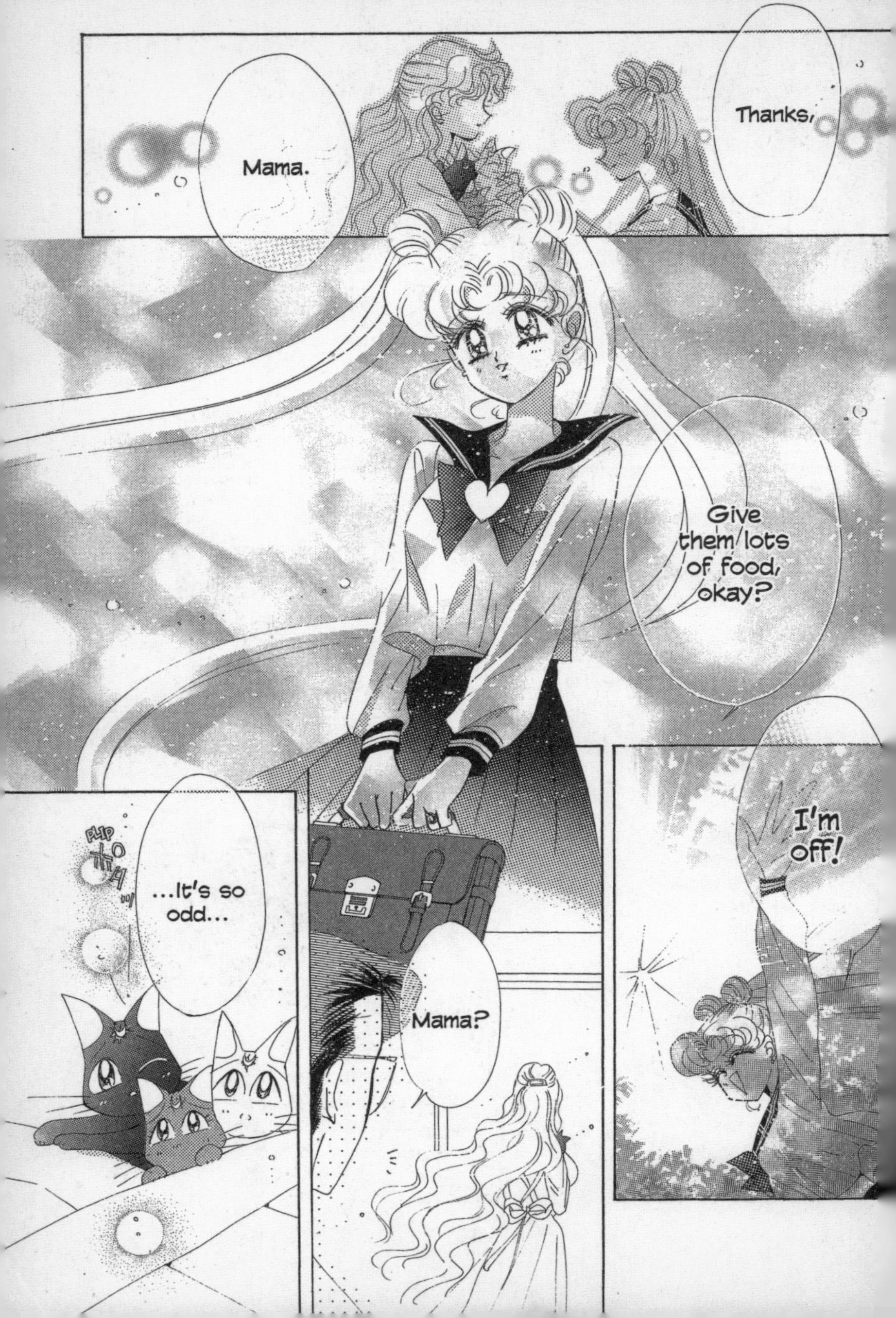
Thanks,
Mama.
Give them lots of food, okay?
I'm off!
Mama?
...It's so odd...

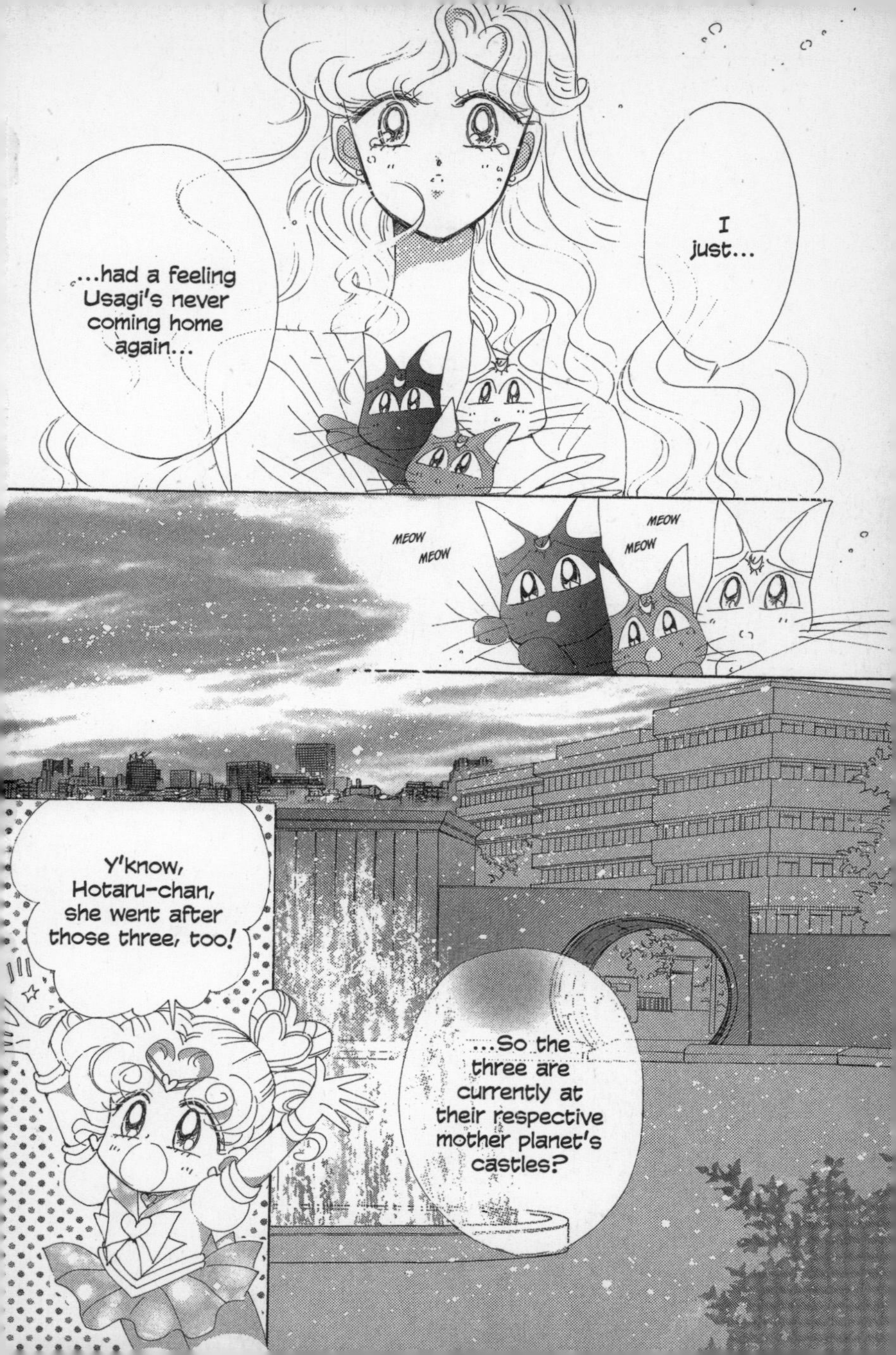
I just...
...had a feeling Usagi's never coming home again...
MEOW
MEOW
MEOW
MEOW
...So the three are currently at their respective mother planet's castles?
Y'know, Hotaru-chan, she went after those three, too!

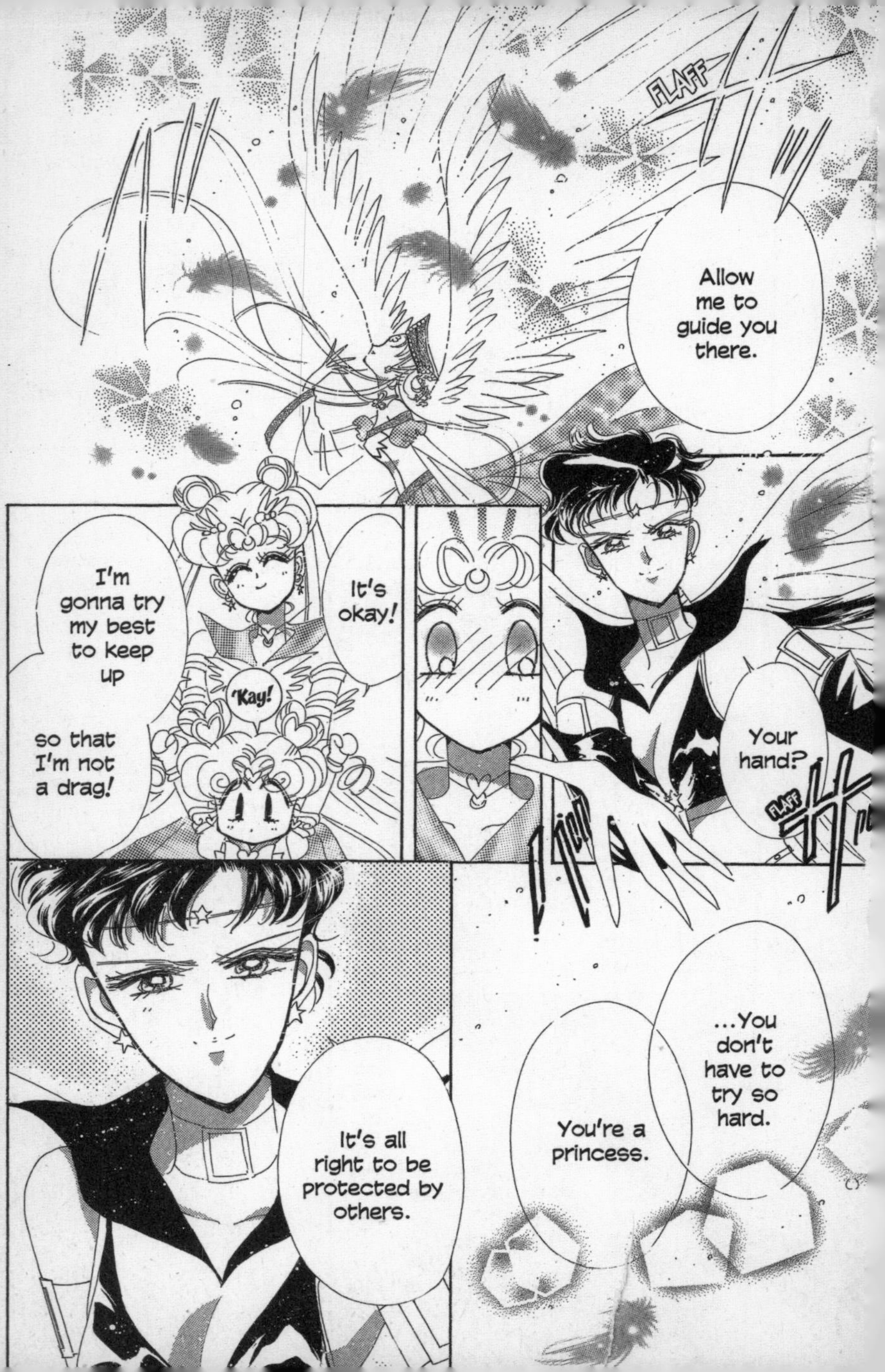
FLAFF
Allow me to guide you there.
Your hand?
FLAFF
It's okay!
I'm gonna try my best to keep up
'Kay!
so that I'm not a drag!
...You don't have to try so hard.
You're a princess.
It's all right to be protected by others.

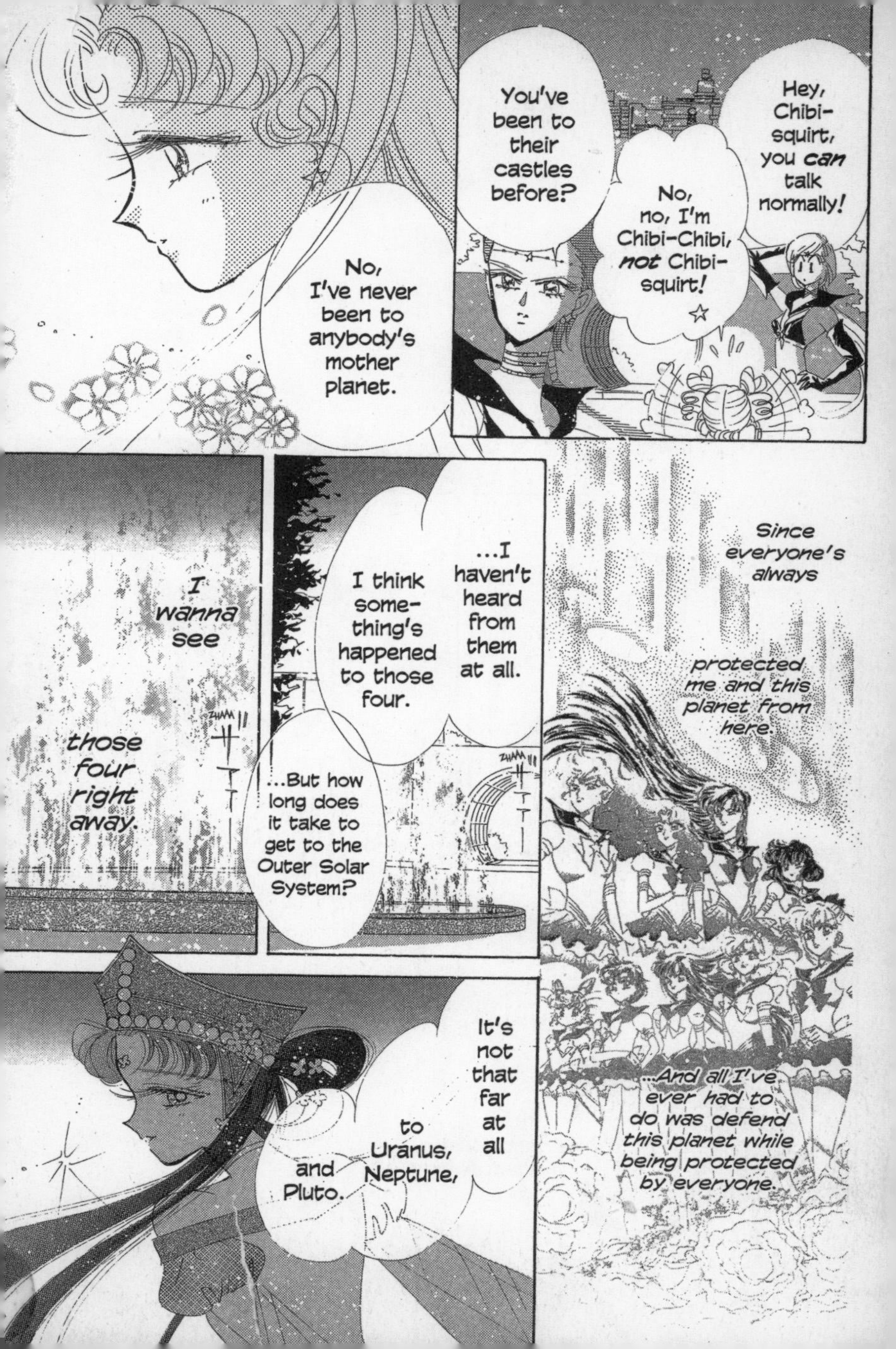
Hey, Chibi-squirt, you *can* talk normally!
No, no, I'm Chibi-Chibi, *not* Chibi-squirt!
You've been to their castles before?
No, I've never been to anybody's mother planet.
Since everyone's always protected me and this planet from here.
...And all I've ever had to do was defend this planet while being protected by everyone.
...I haven't heard from them at all.
I think some-thing's happened to those four.
...But how long does it take to get to the Outer Solar System?
I wanna see those four right away.
It's not that far at all to Uranus, Neptune, and Pluto.

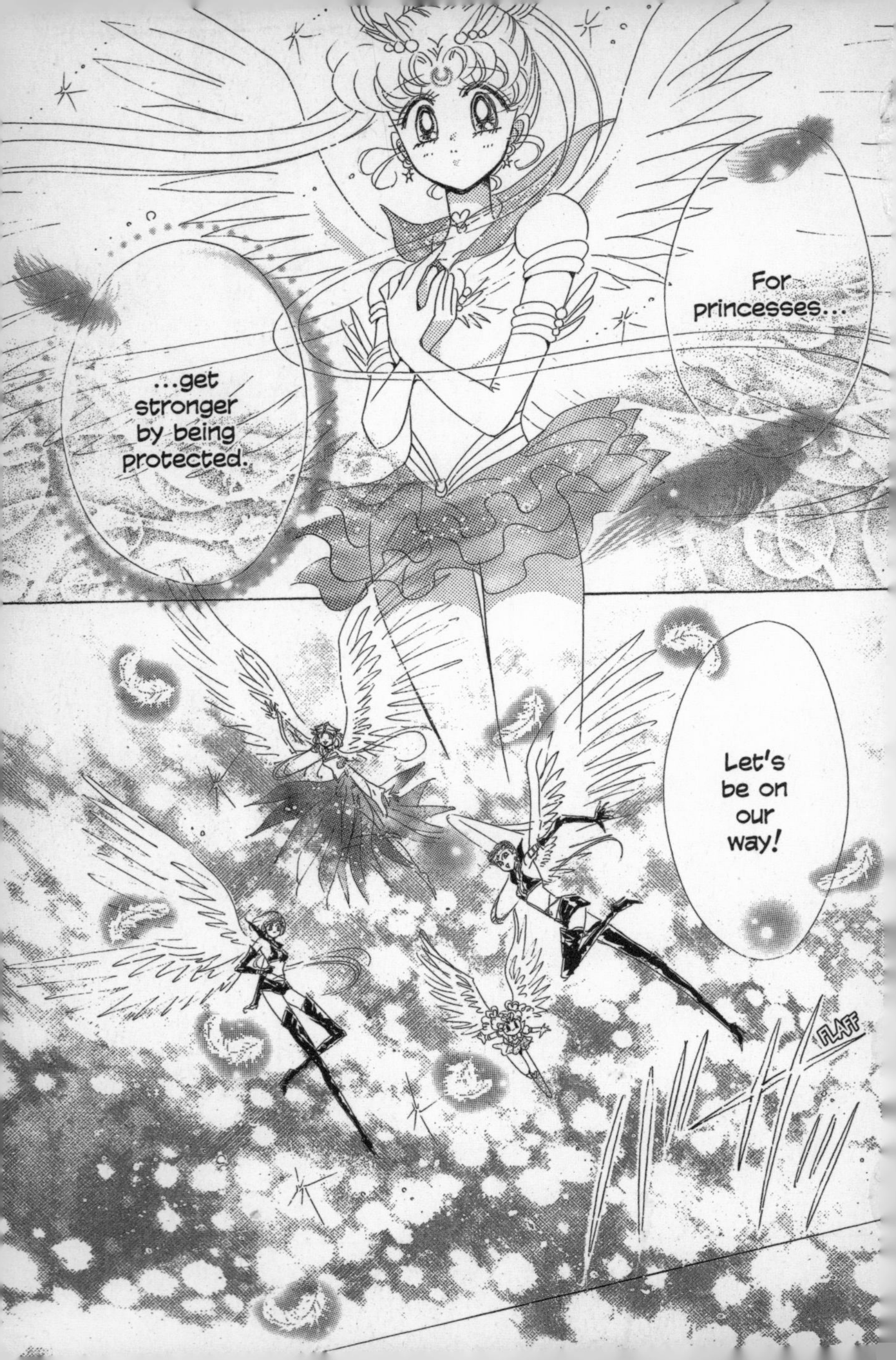
For princesses...
...get stronger by being protected.
Let's be on our way!
FLAFF

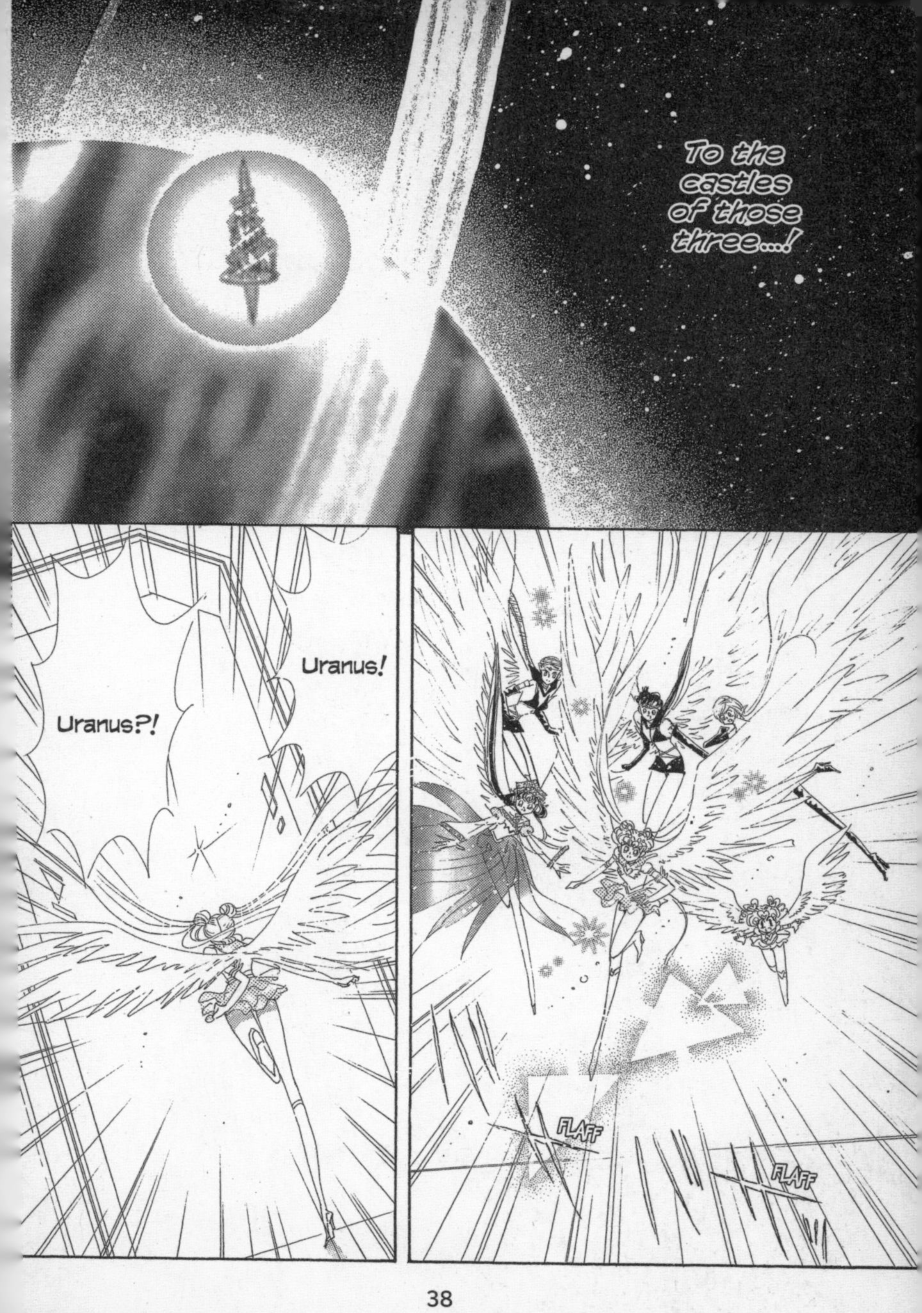
To the castles of those three...!
FLAFF
FLAFF
Uranus!
Uranus?!

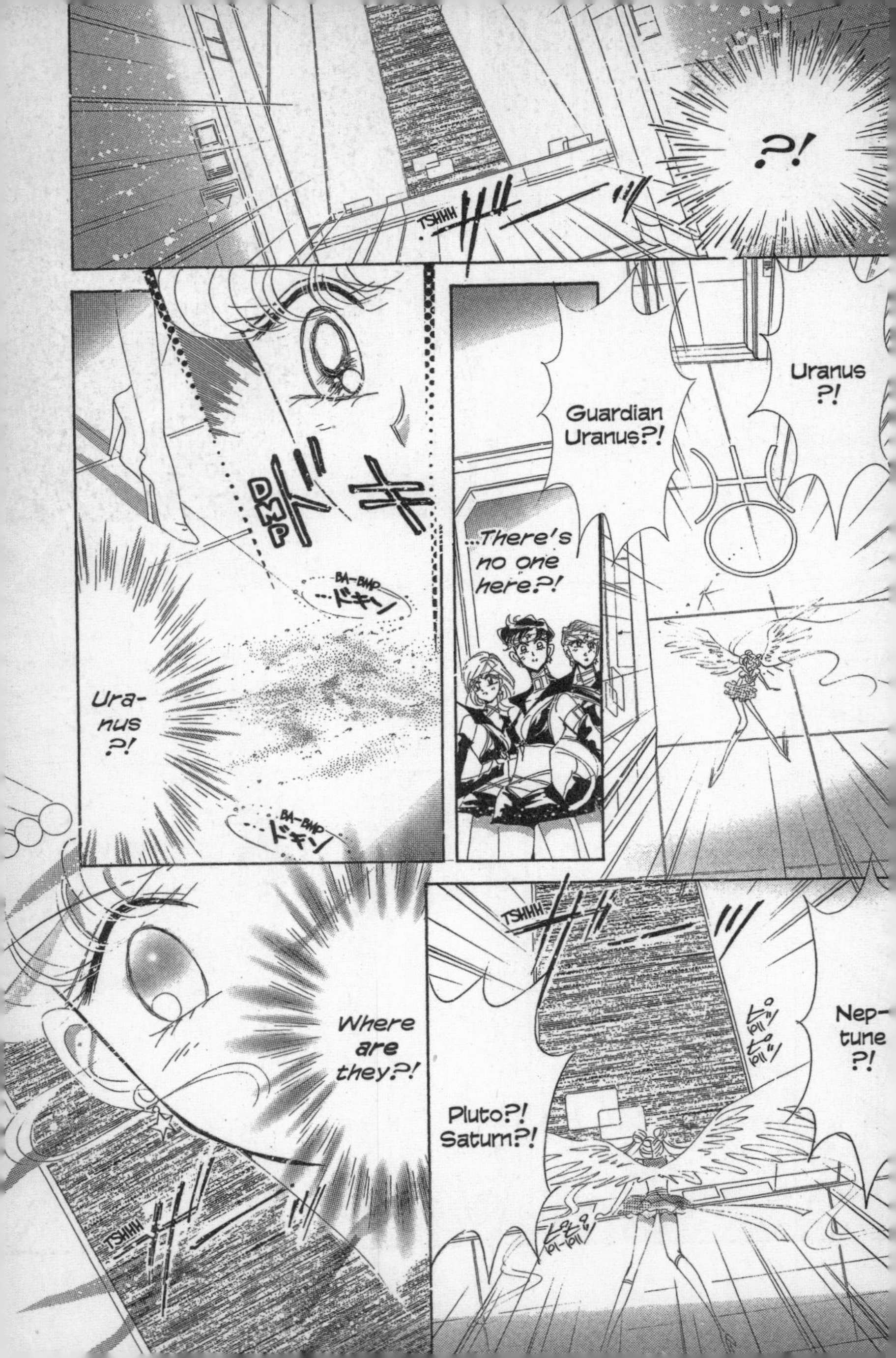
?!
TSHHH
Uranus ?!
Guardian Uranus?!
...There's no one here?!
DMP
BA-BMP
Ura-nus ?!
BA-BMP
Nep-tune ?!
TSHHH
Pluto?! Saturn?!
Where are they?!
TSHHH

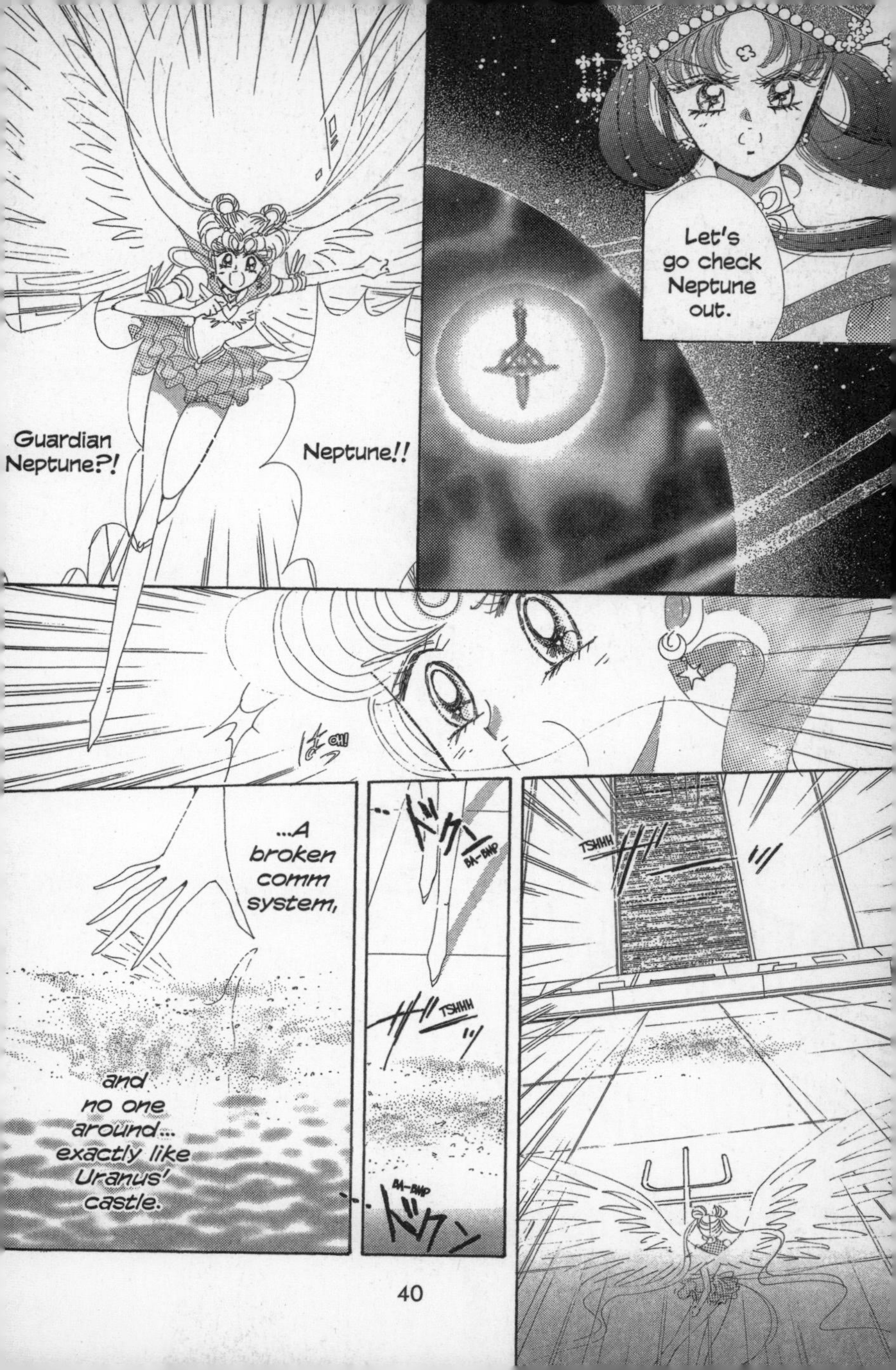
Let's go check Neptune out.
Neptune!!
Guardian Neptune?!
OH!
TSHHH
BA-BMP
TSHHH
BA-BMP
...A broken comm system,
and no one around... exactly like Uranus' castle.

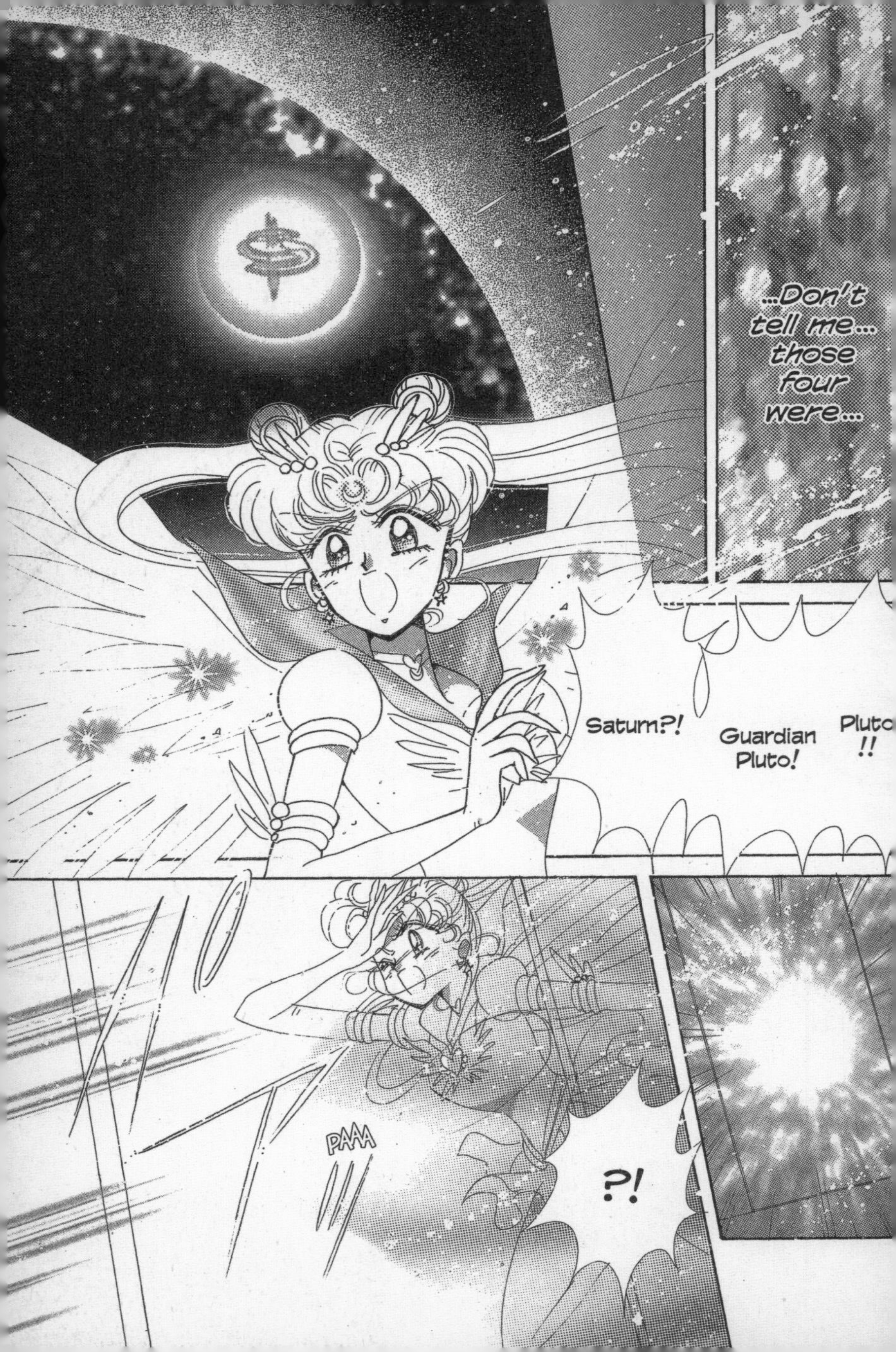
...Don't tell me... those four were...
Pluto !!
Guardian Pluto!
Saturn?!
?!
PAAA !!

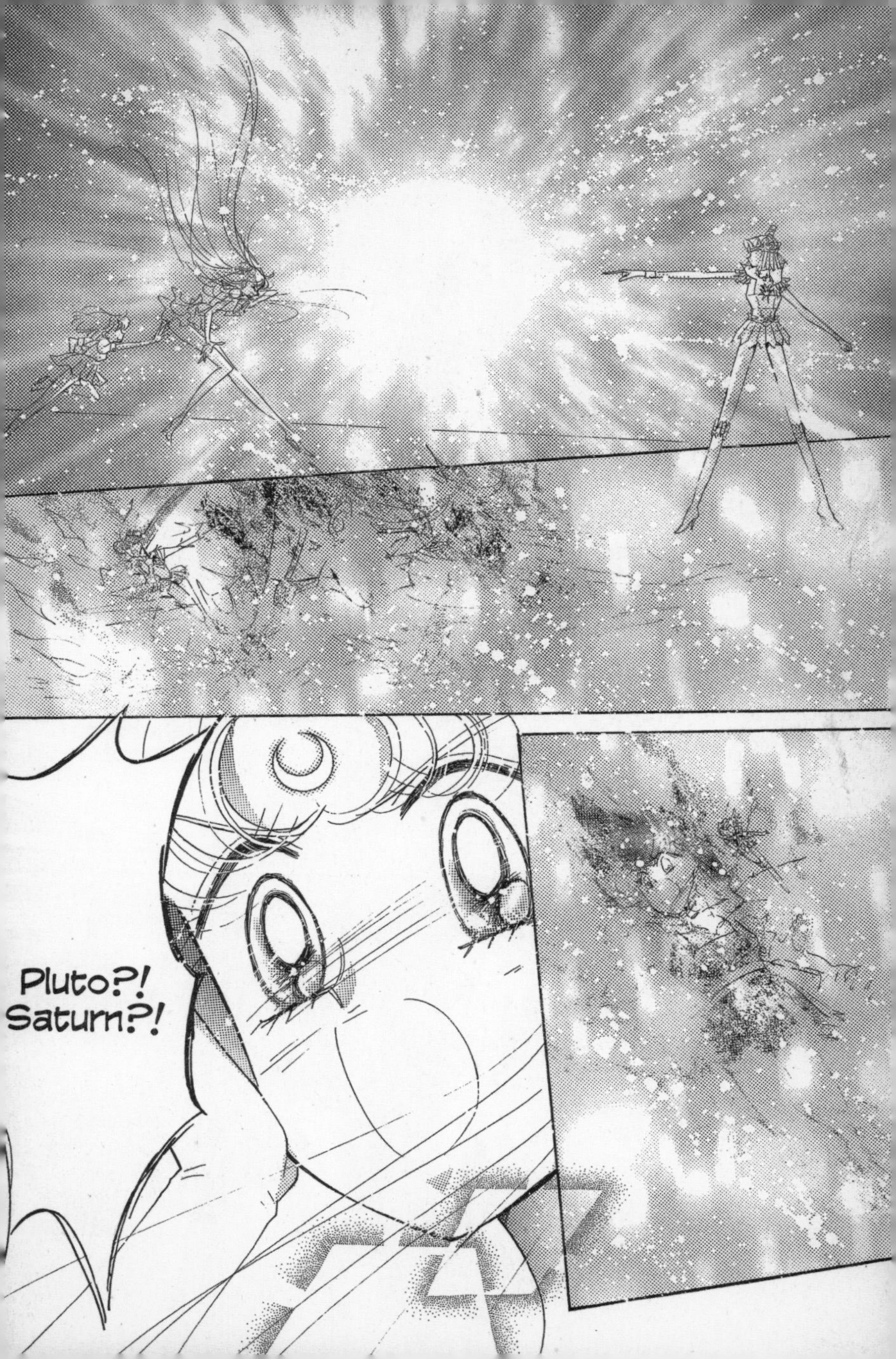
Pluto?!
Saturn?!

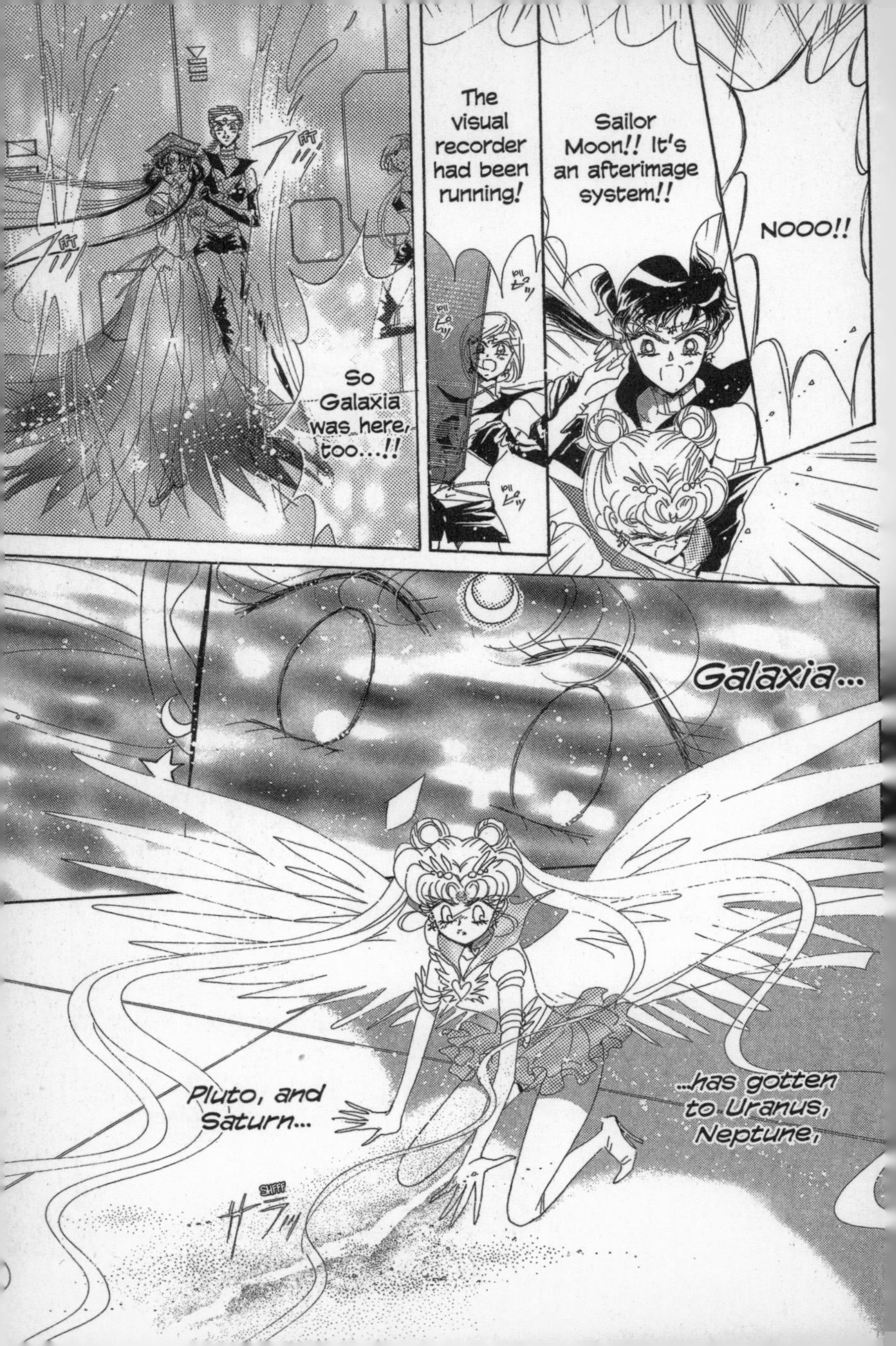
NOOO!!
Sailor Moon!! It's an afterimage system!!
The visual recorder had been running!
FFT
FFT
So Galaxia was here, too...!!
Galaxia...
...has gotten to Uranus, Neptune,
Pluto, and Saturn...
SHFFF

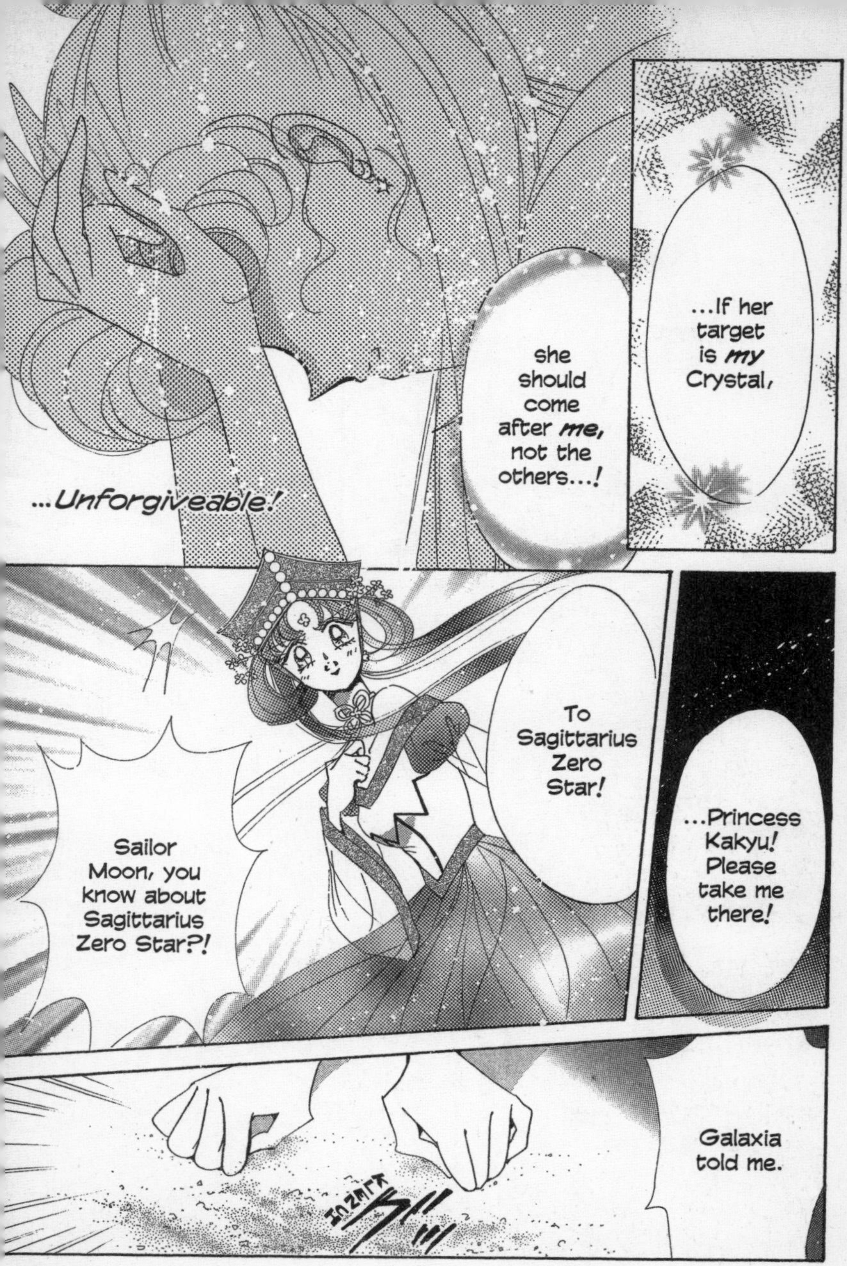
...If her target is *my* Crystal,
she should come after *me*, not the others...!
...*Unforgiveable!*
...Princess Kakyu! Please take me there!
To Sagittarius Zero Star!
Sailor Moon, you know about Sagittarius Zero Star?!
Galaxia told me.

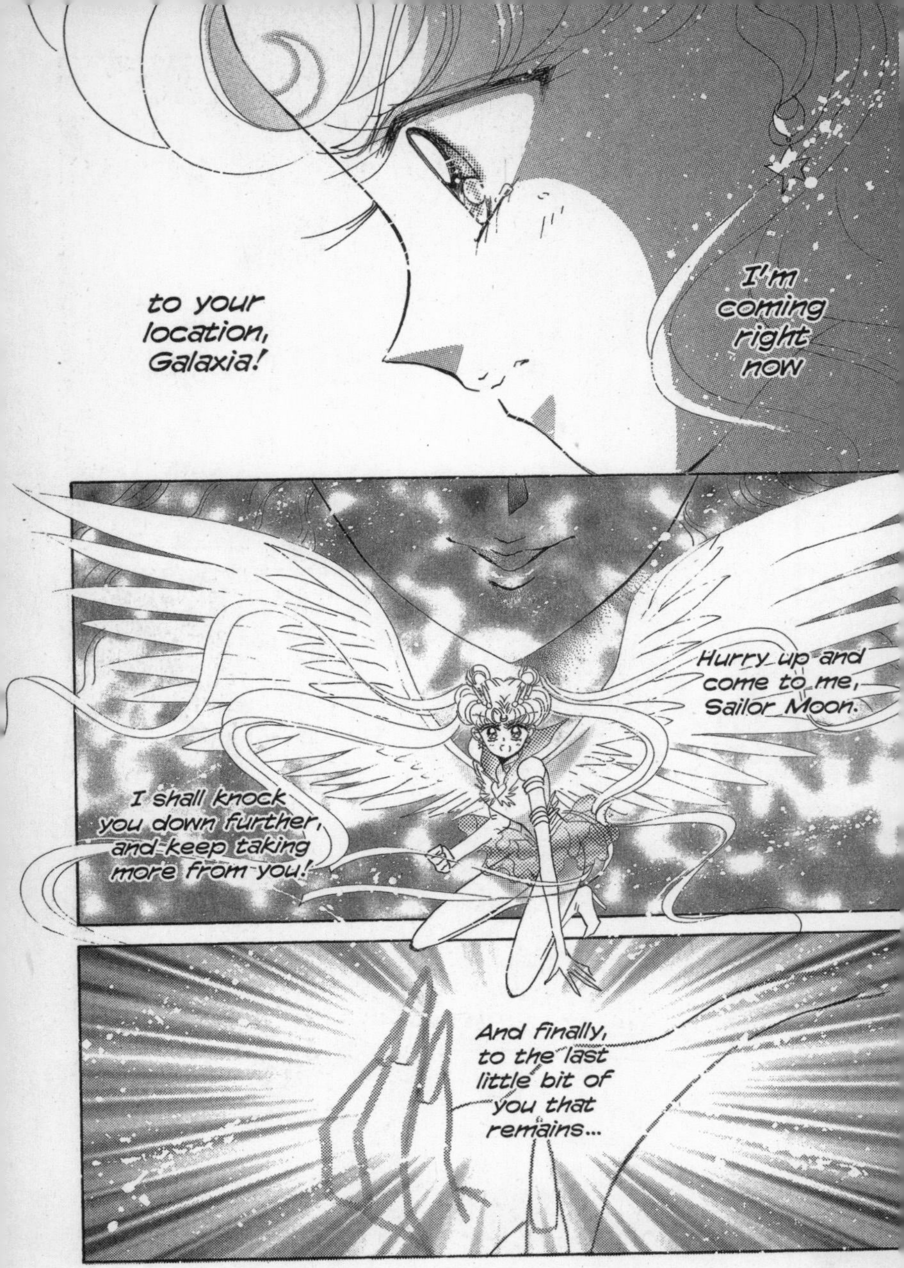
I'm coming right now
to your location, Galaxia!
Hurry up and come to me, Sailor Moon.
I shall knock you down further, and keep taking more from you!
And finally, to the last little bit of you that remains...

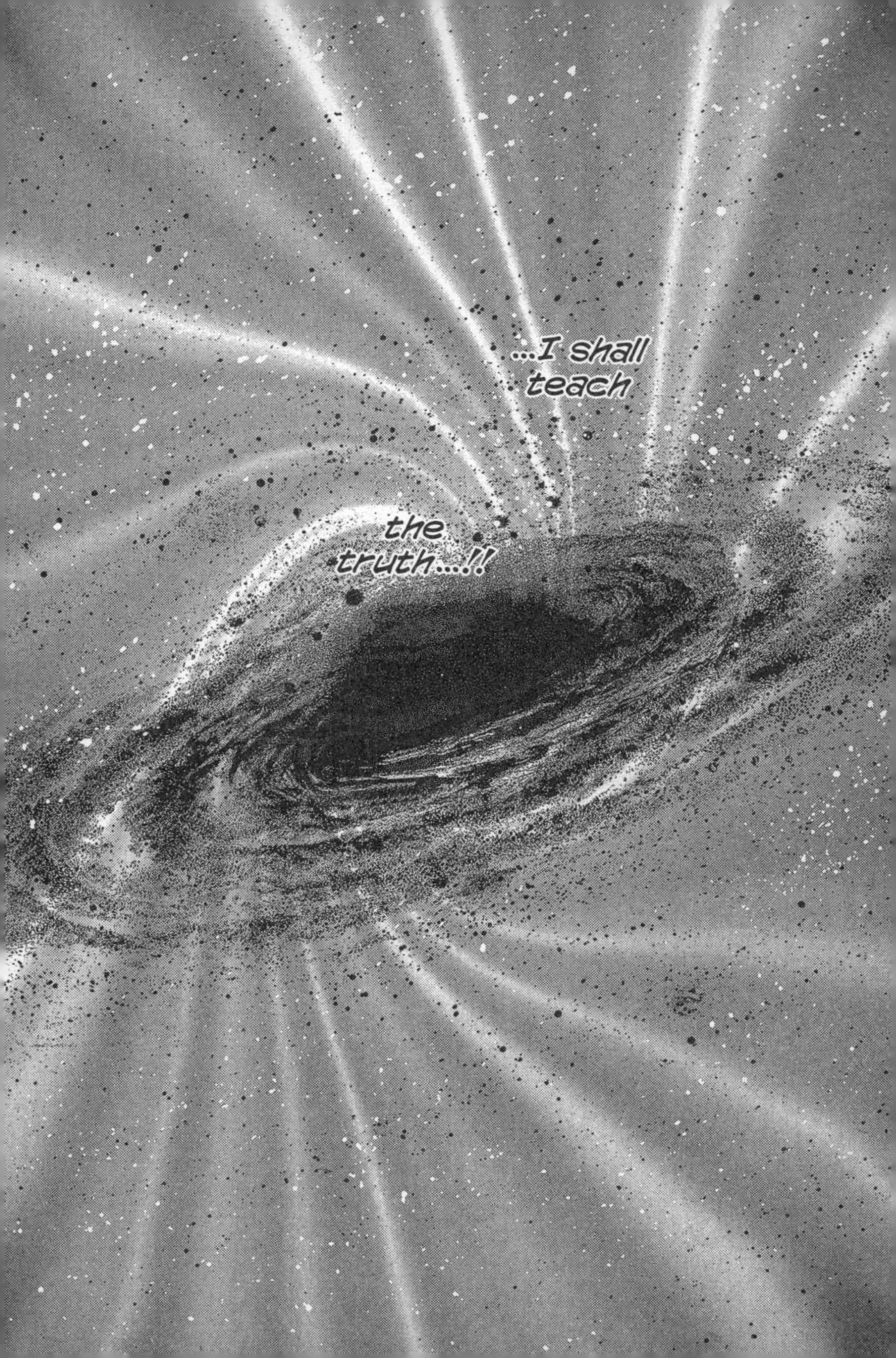
...I shall teach
the truth...!!

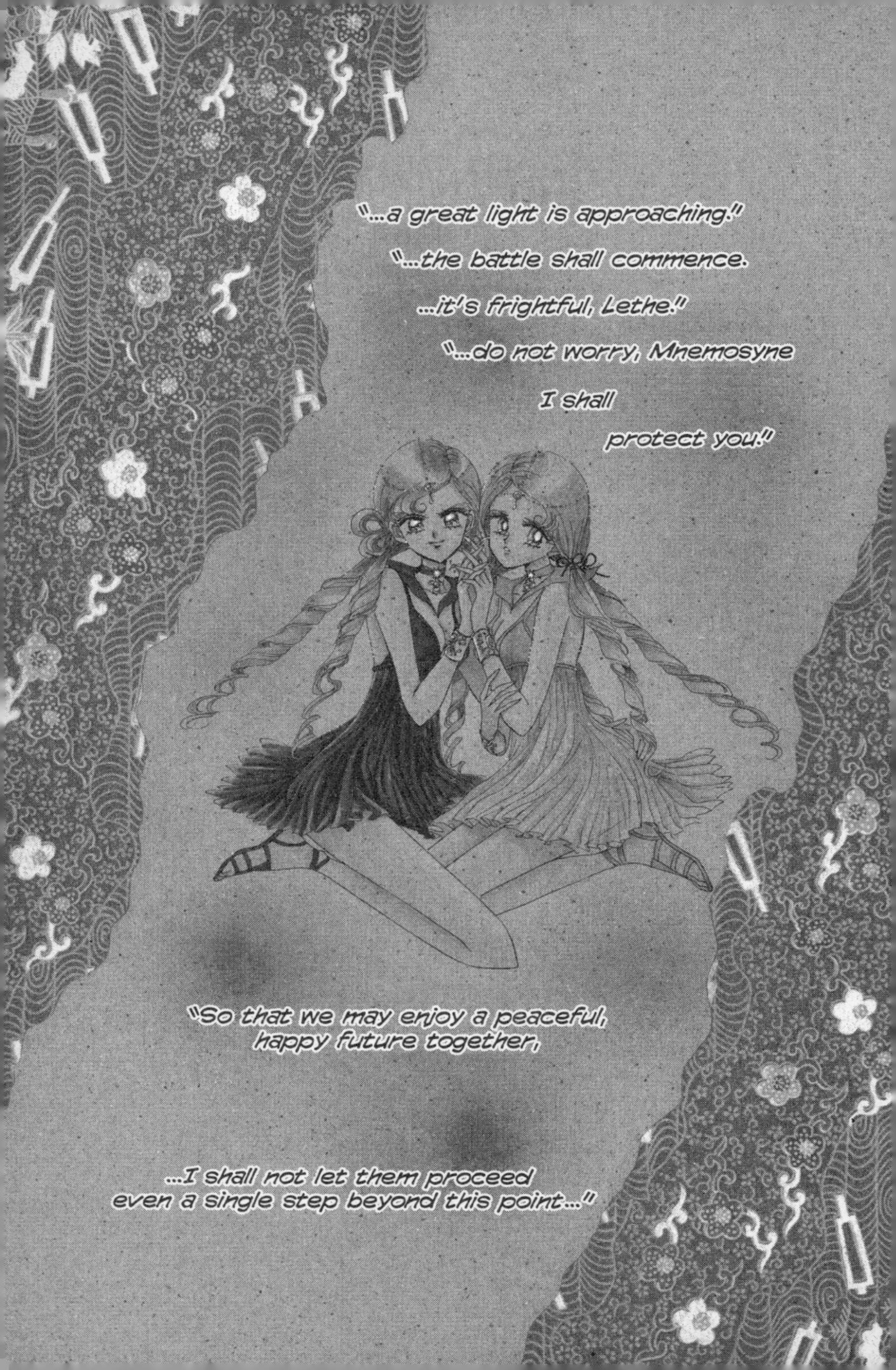
"...a great light is approaching."
"...the battle shall commence.
...it's frightful, Lethe."
"...do not worry, Mnemosyne
I shall
protect you."
"So that we may enjoy a peaceful, happy future together,
...I shall not let them proceed even a single step beyond this point..."

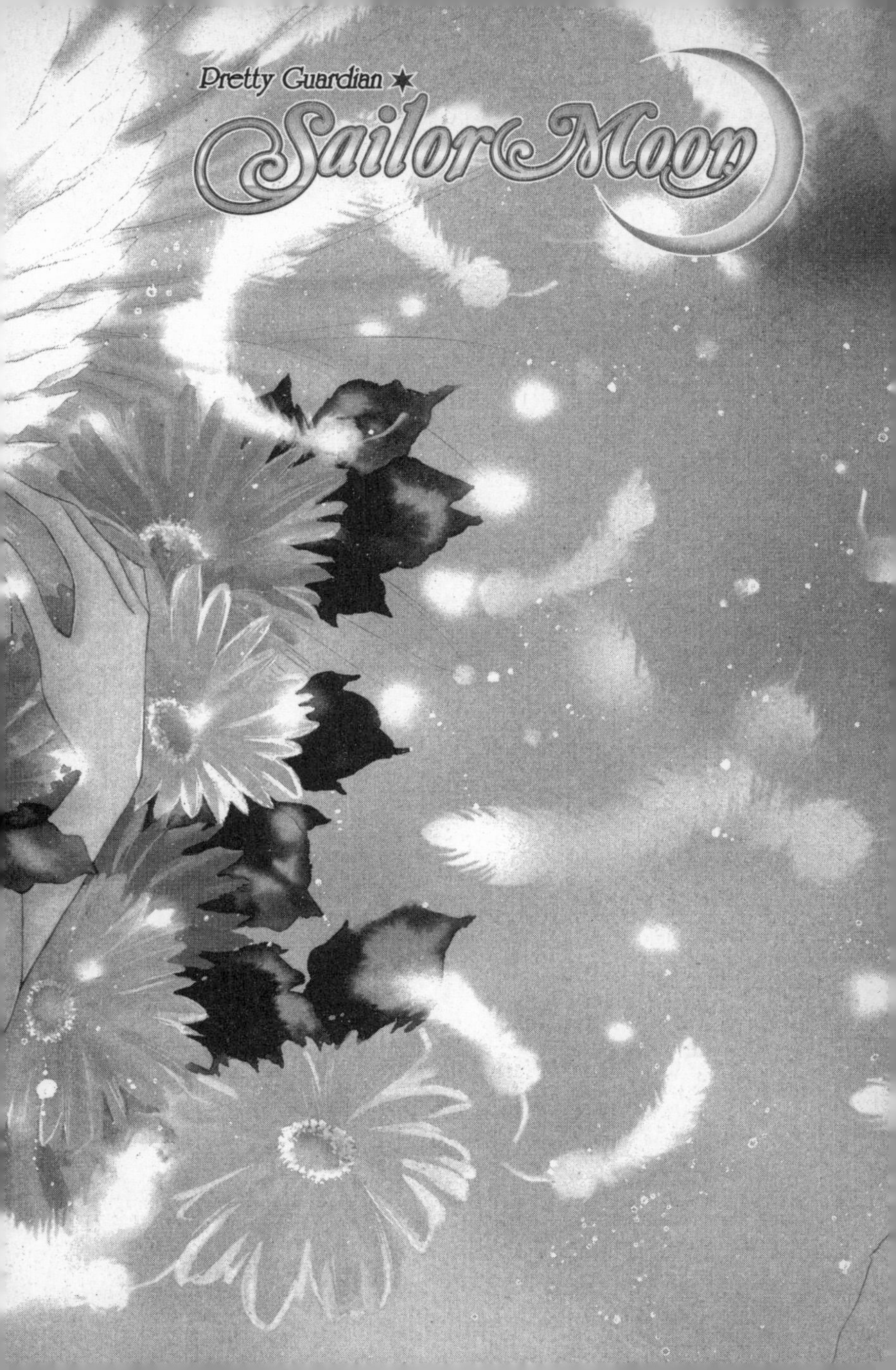
Pretty Guardian
Sailor Moon

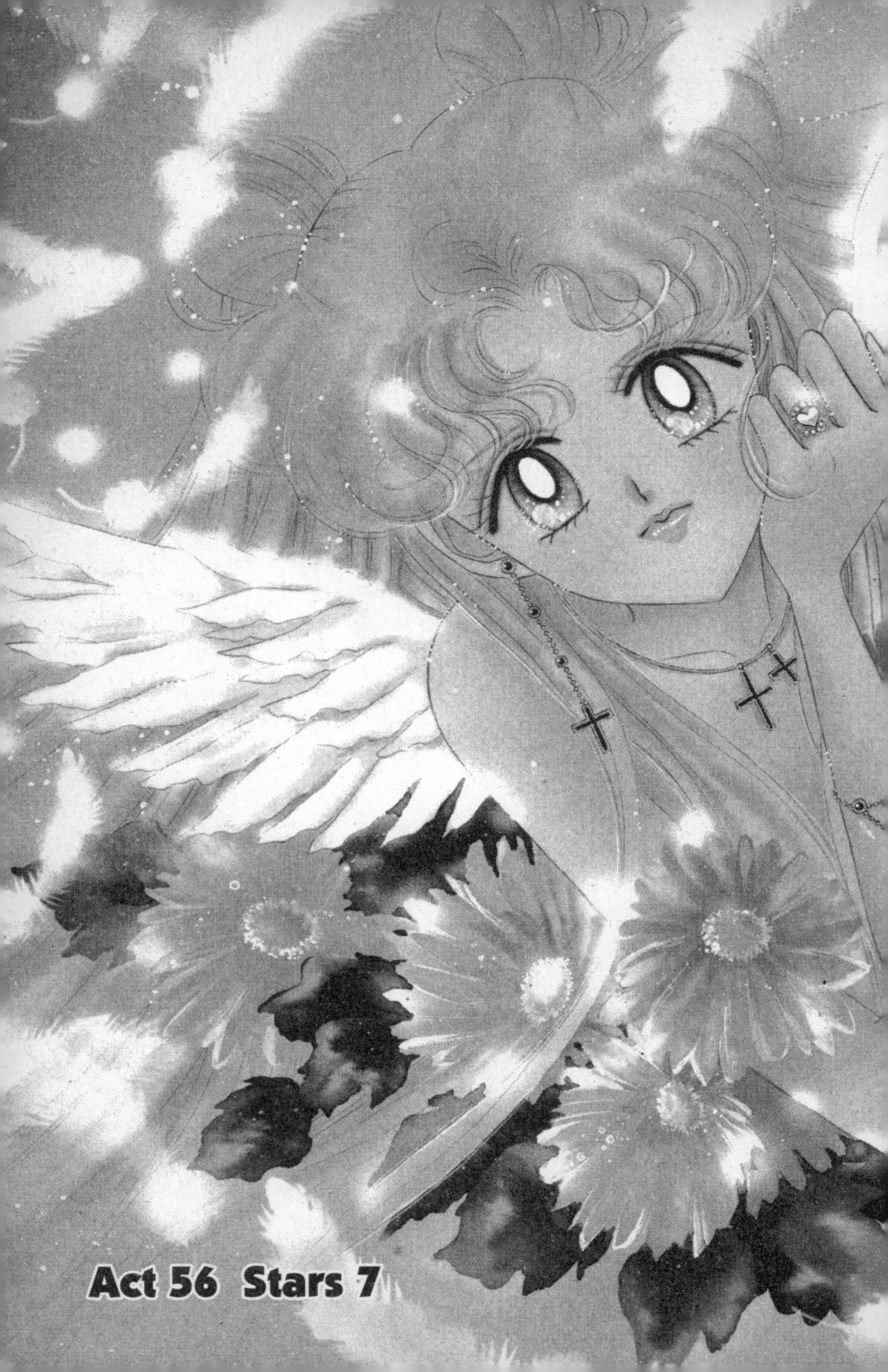
Act 56 Stars 7

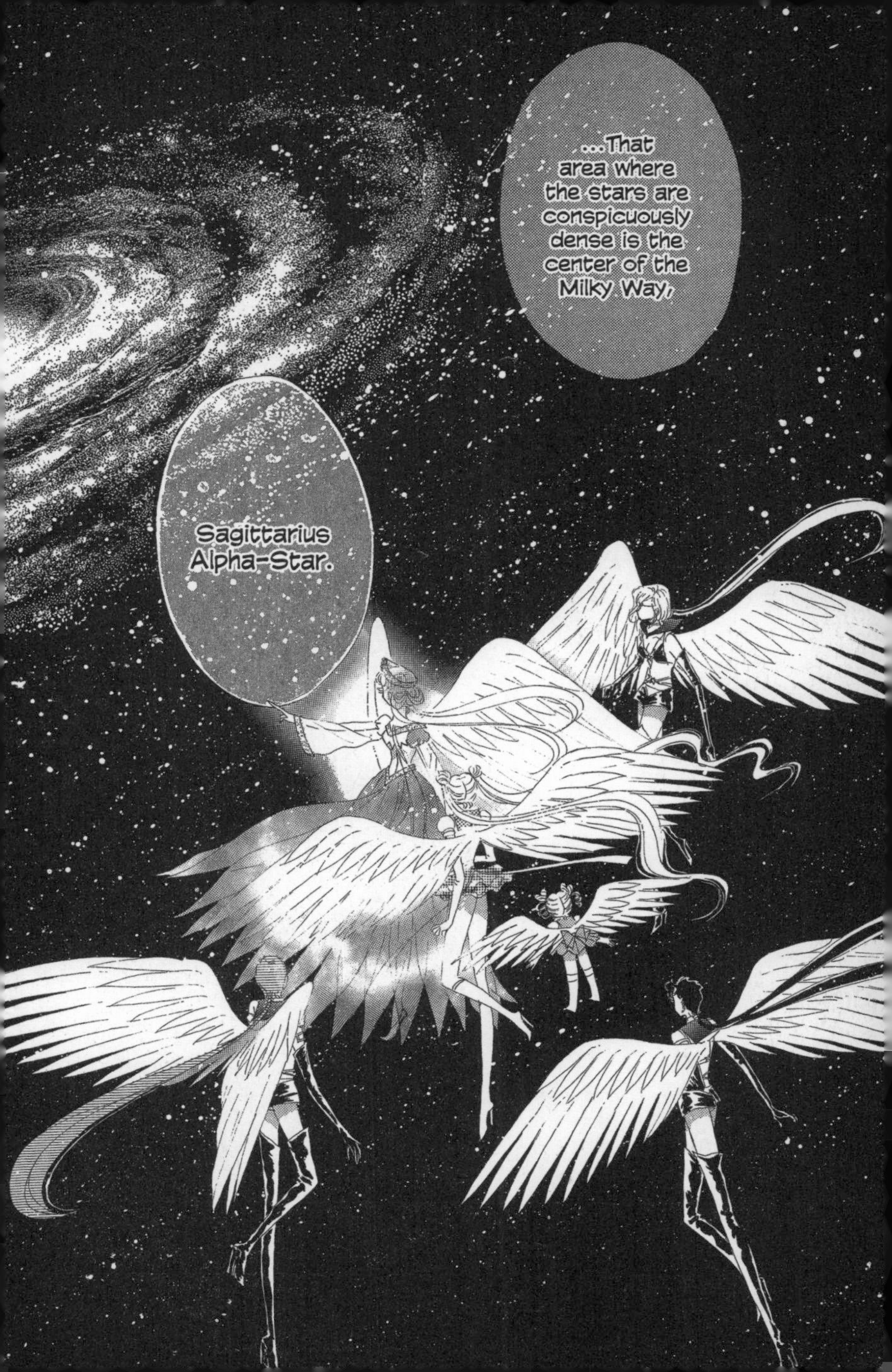
...That area where the stars are conspicuously dense is the center of the Milky Way,
Sagittarius Alpha-Star.

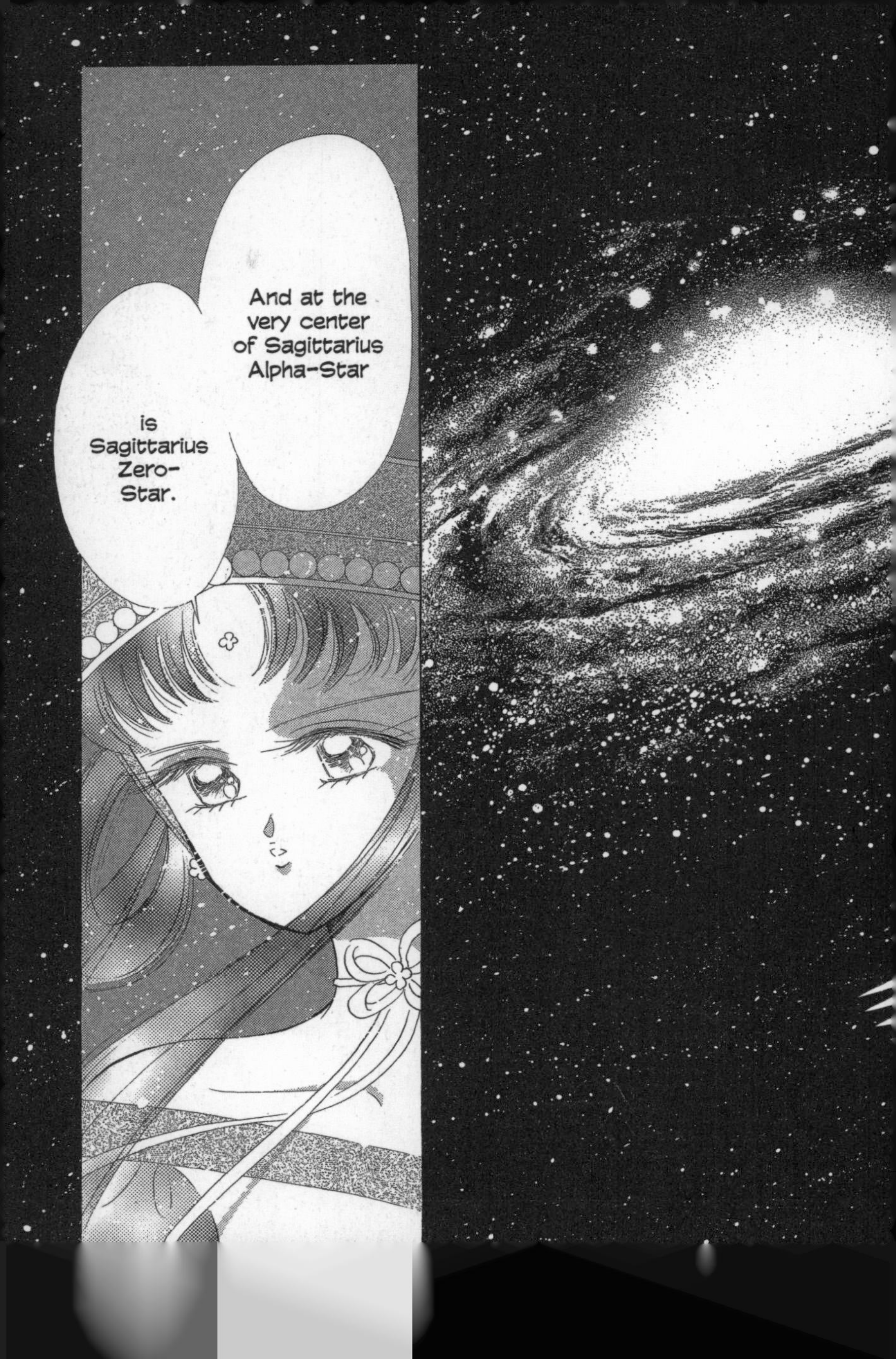
And at the very center of Sagittarius Alpha-Star
is Sagittarius Zero-Star.

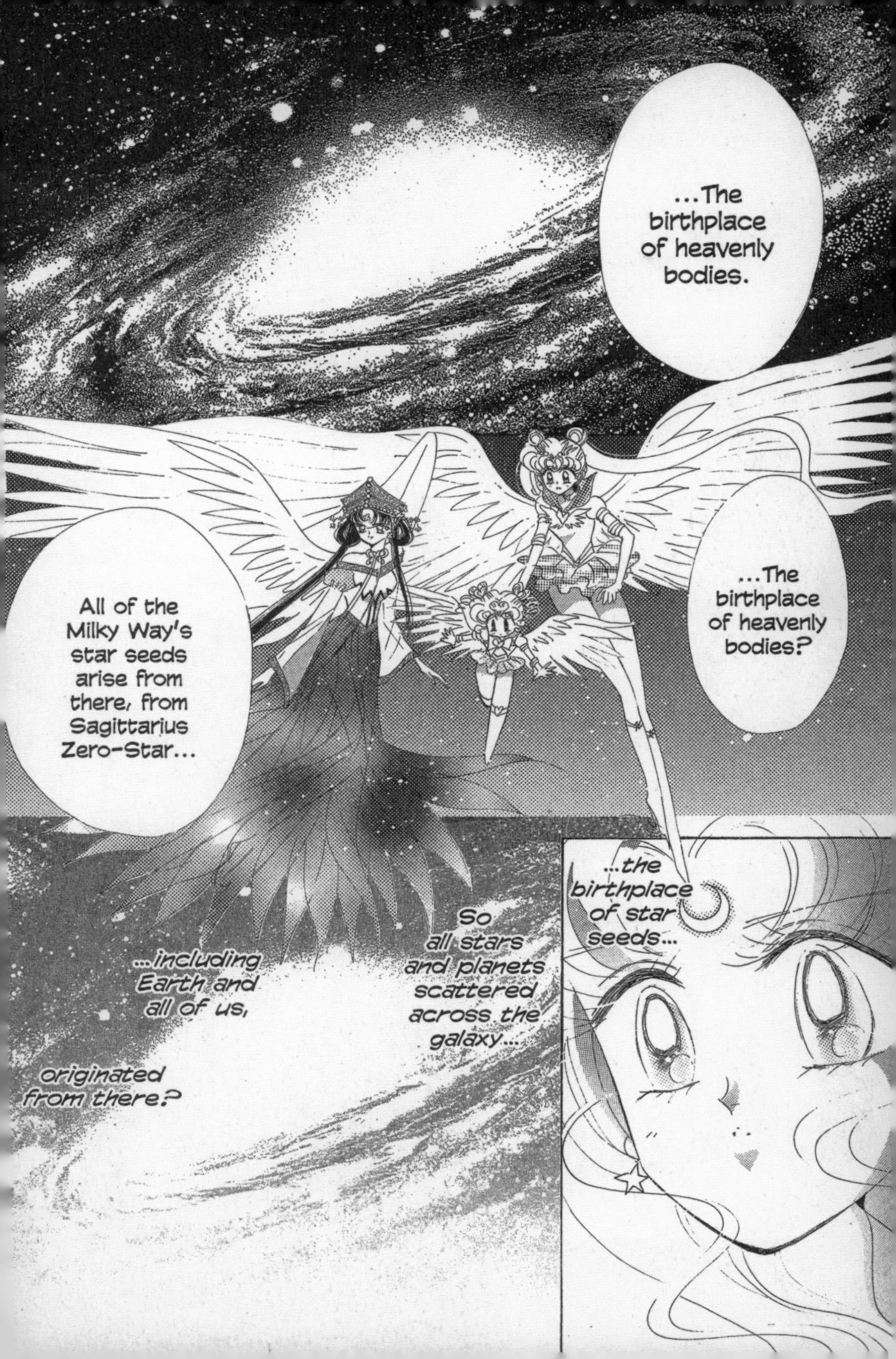
...The birthplace of heavenly bodies.
...The birthplace of heavenly bodies?
All of the Milky Way's star seeds arise from there, from Sagittarius Zero-Star...
...the birthplace of star seeds...
So all stars and planets scattered across the galaxy...
...including Earth and all of us,
originated from there?

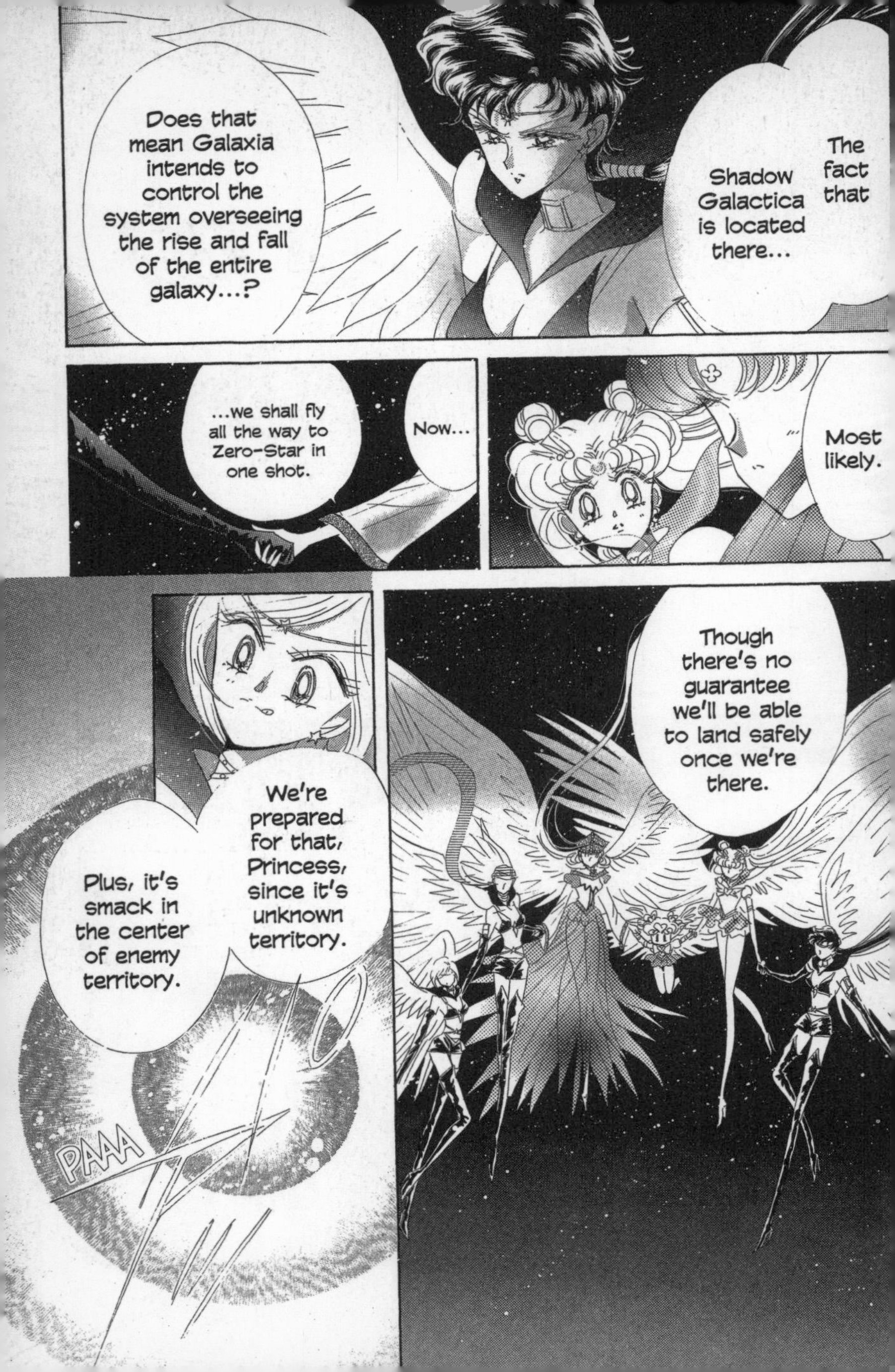

The fact that Shadow Galactica is located there...
Does that mean Galaxia intends to control the system overseeing the rise and fall of the entire galaxy...?
Most likely.
Now...
...we shall fly all the way to Zero-Star in one shot.
Though there's no guarantee we'll be able to land safely once we're there.
We're prepared for that, Princess, since it's unknown territory.
Plus, it's smack in the center of enemy territory.
PAAA

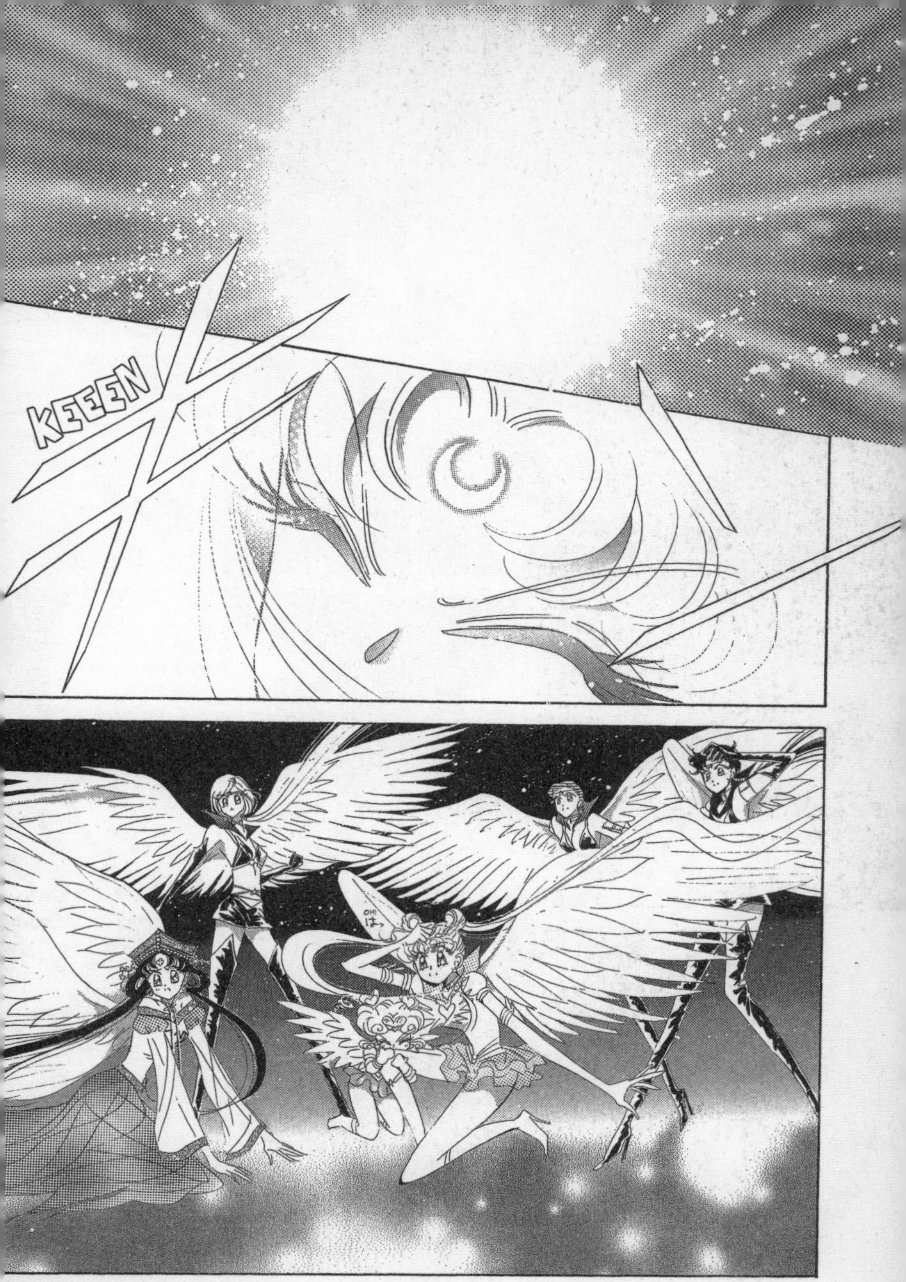
KEEEN
OH!
はっ

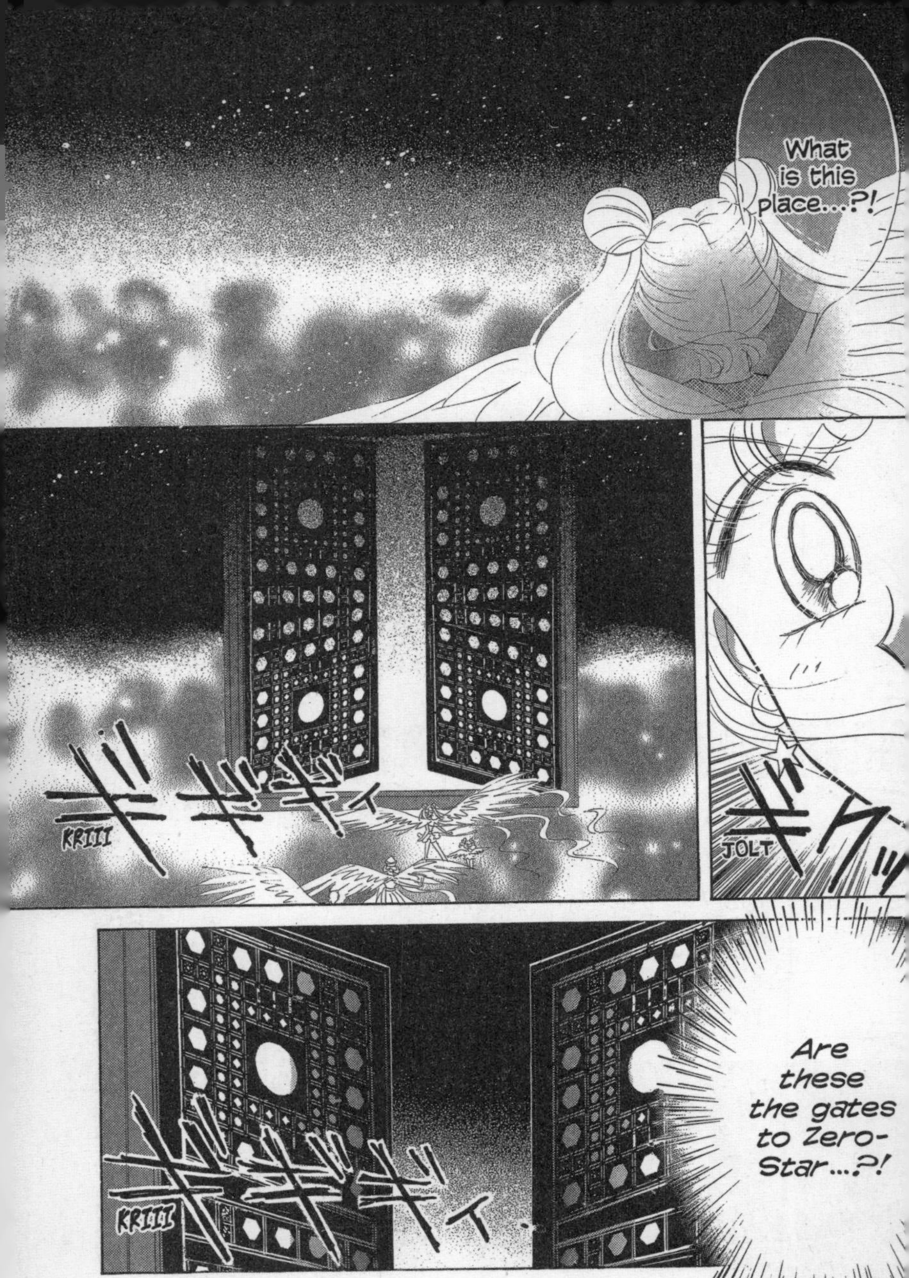
What is this place...?!
JOLT
KRIII
Are these the gates to Zero-Star...?!
KRIII

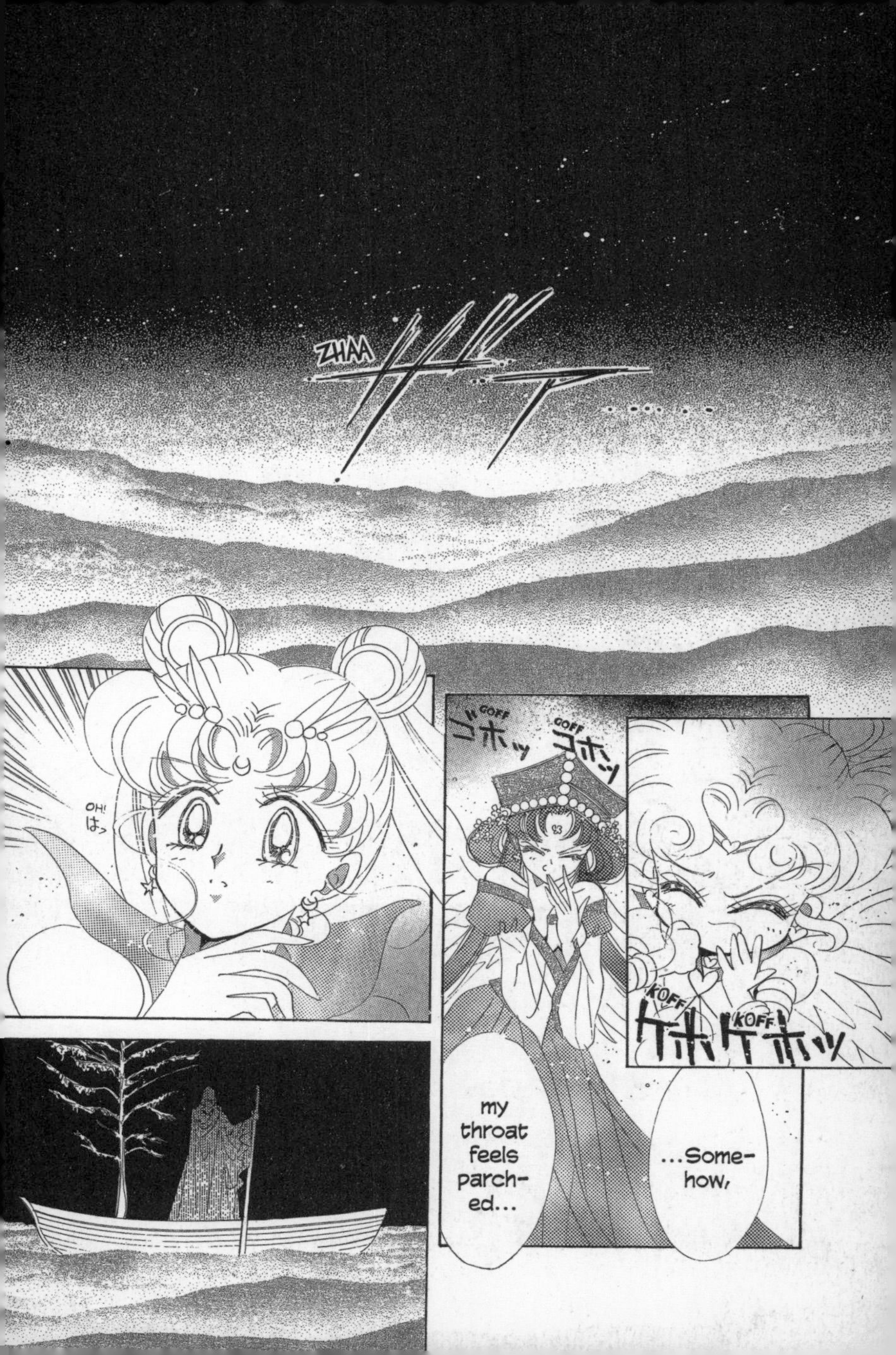
ZHAA
. . . . . .
KOFF
ケホケホッ
KOFF
GOFF
コホッ
GOFF
ゴホッ
...Some-how,
my throat feels parch-ed...
OH!
はっ

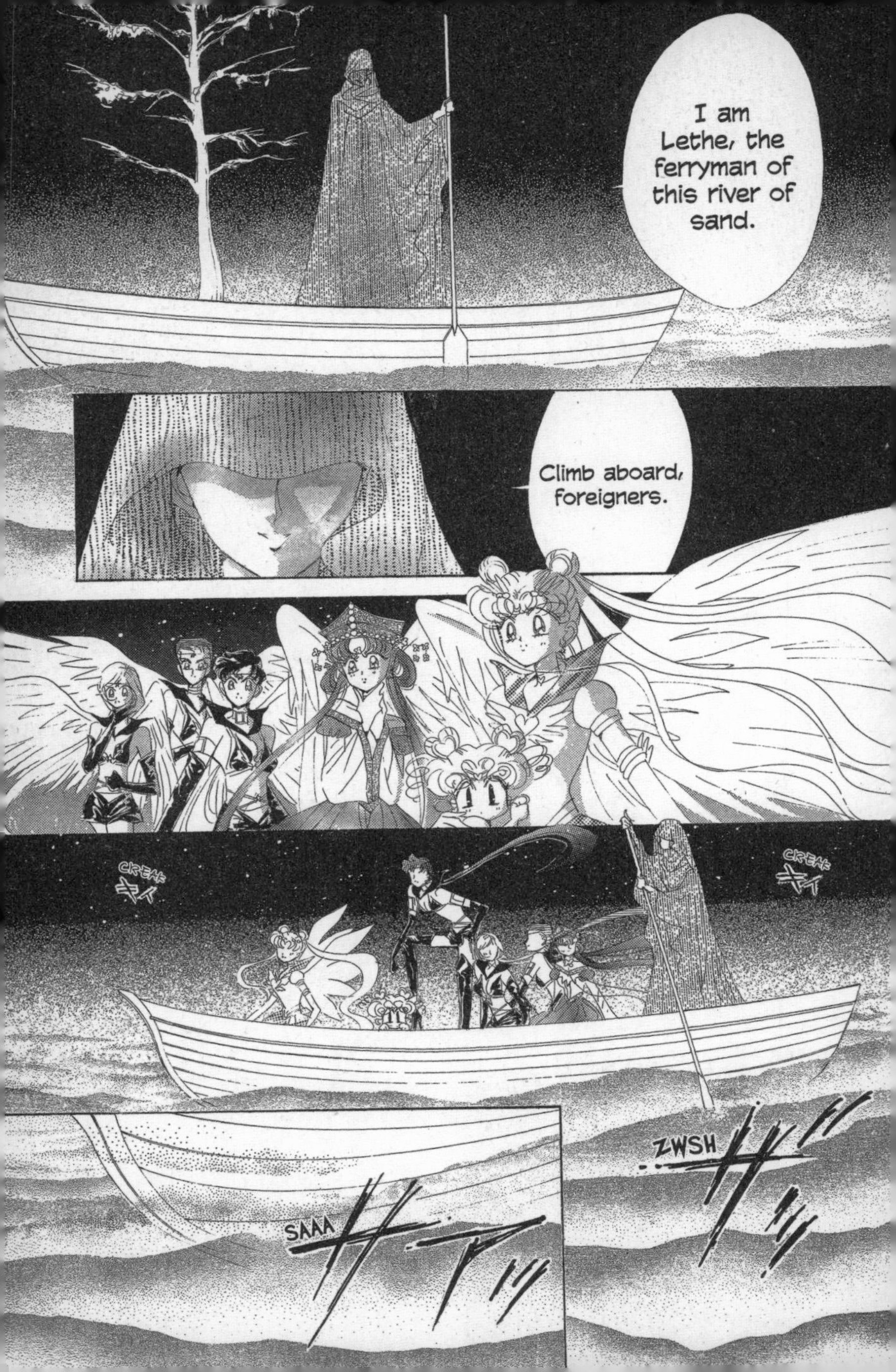
I am Lethe, the ferryman of this river of sand.
Climb aboard, foreigners.
CREAK
キイ
CREAK
キイ
ZWSH
SAAA

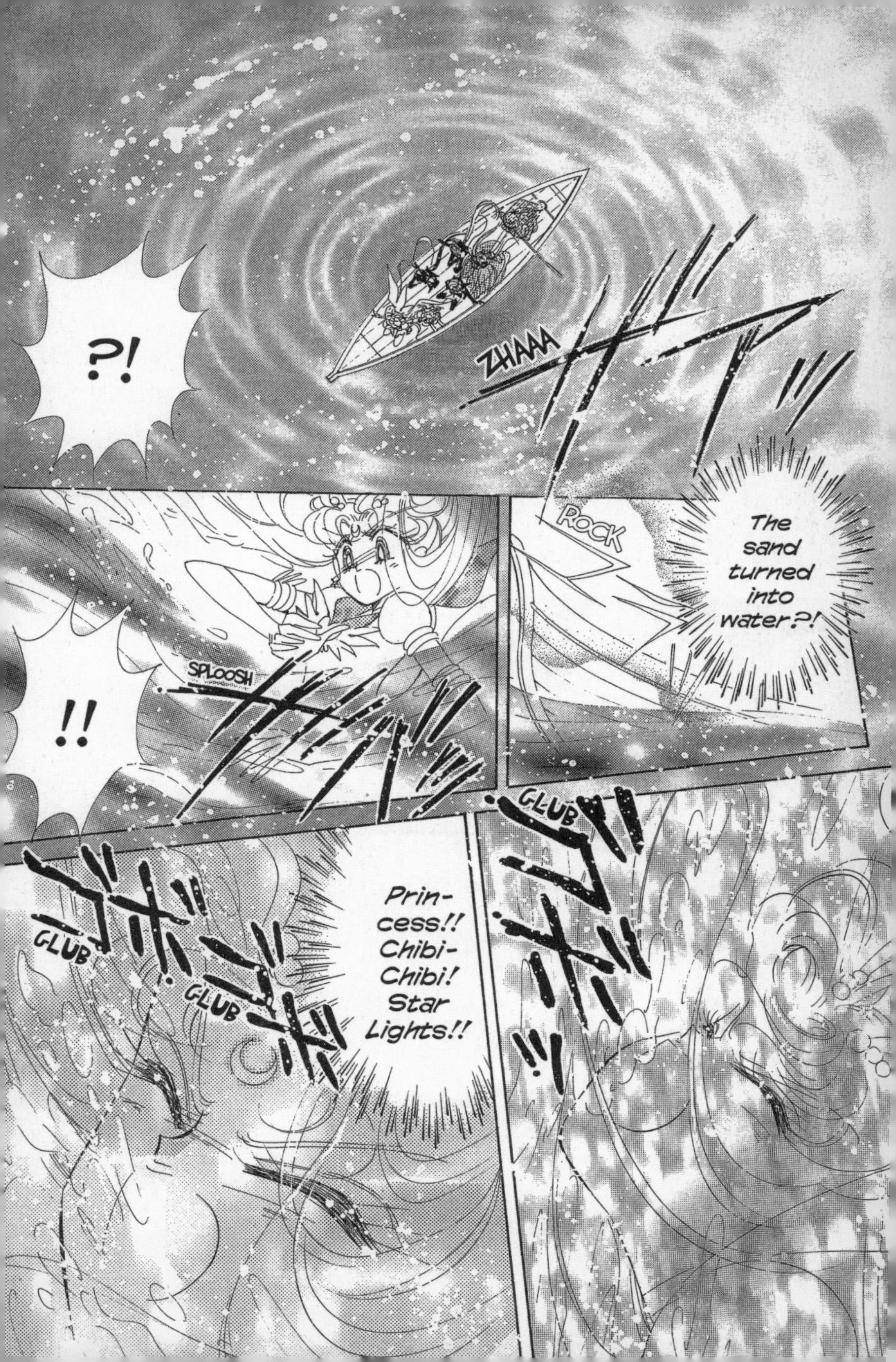
ZHAAA
?!
ROCK
The sand turned into water?!
SPLOOSH
!!
GLUB
Prin-cess!! Chibi-Chibi! Star Lights!!
GLUB
GLUB

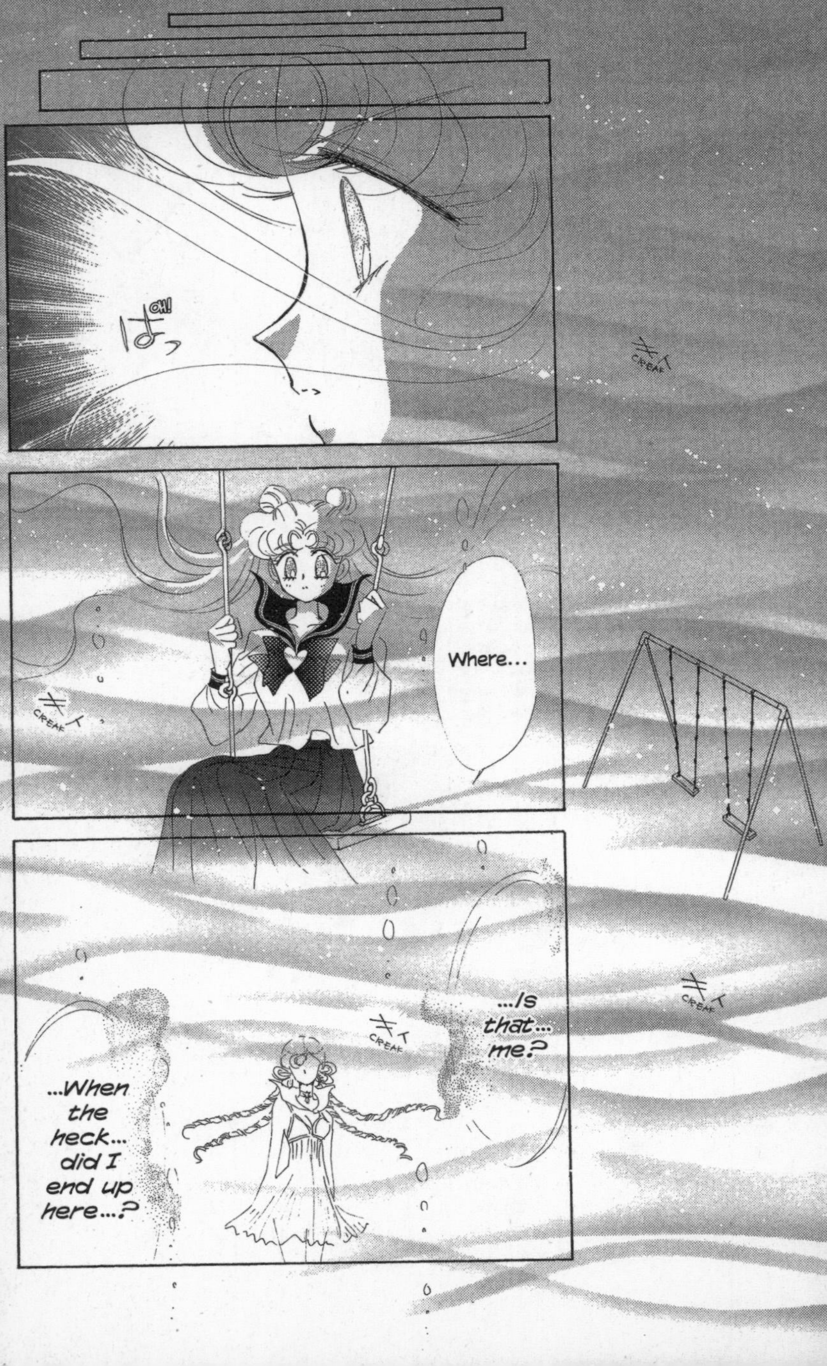

OH!
CREAK
Where...
CREAK
CREAK
...Is that... me?
...When the heck... did I end up here...?

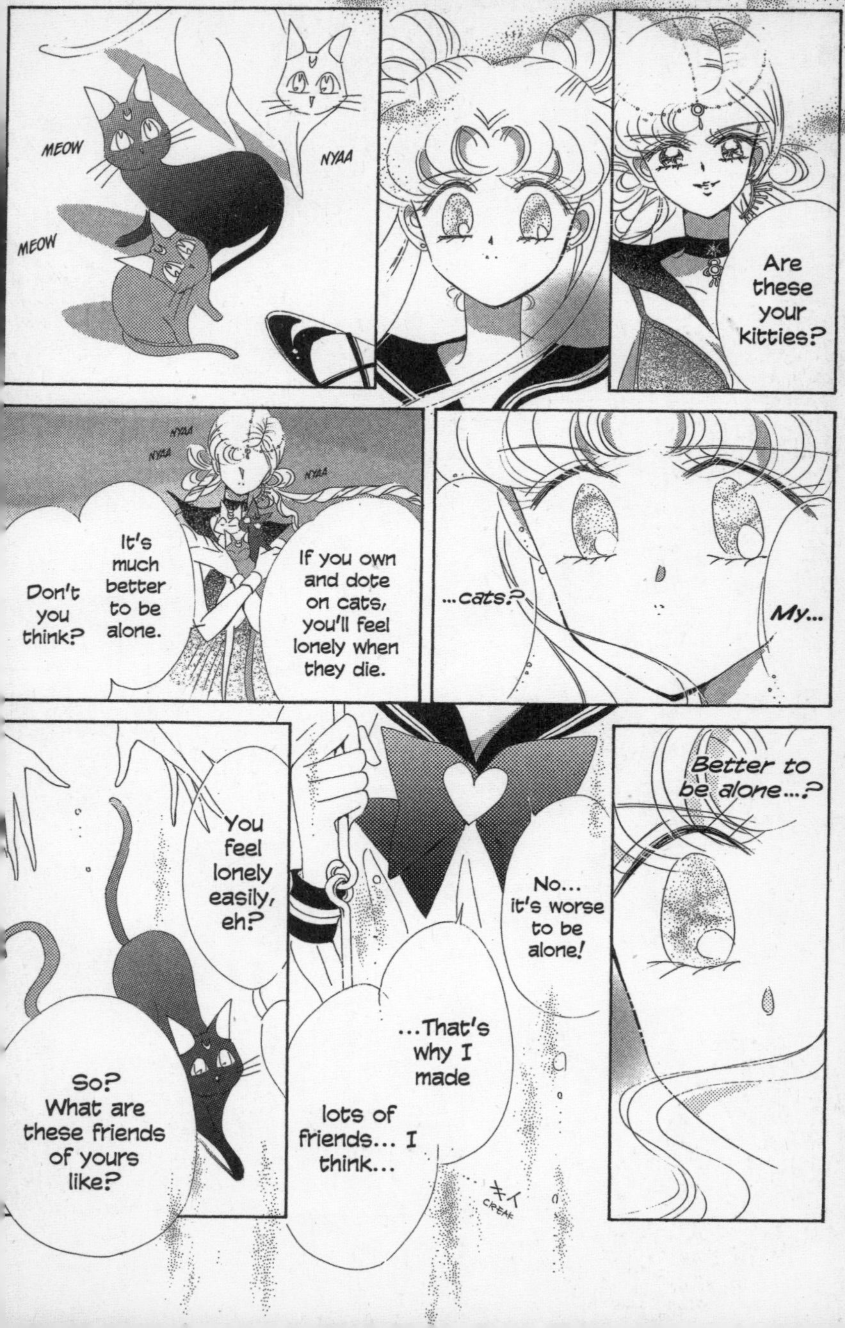

Are these your kitties?
NYAA
MEOW
MEOW
My...
...cats?
NYAA
NYAA
NYAA
If you own and dote on cats, you'll feel lonely when they die.
It's much better to be alone.
Don't you think?
Better to be alone...?
No... it's worse to be alone!
You feel lonely easily, eh?
...That's why I made
lots of friends... I think...
キイ CREAK
So? What are these friends of yours like?

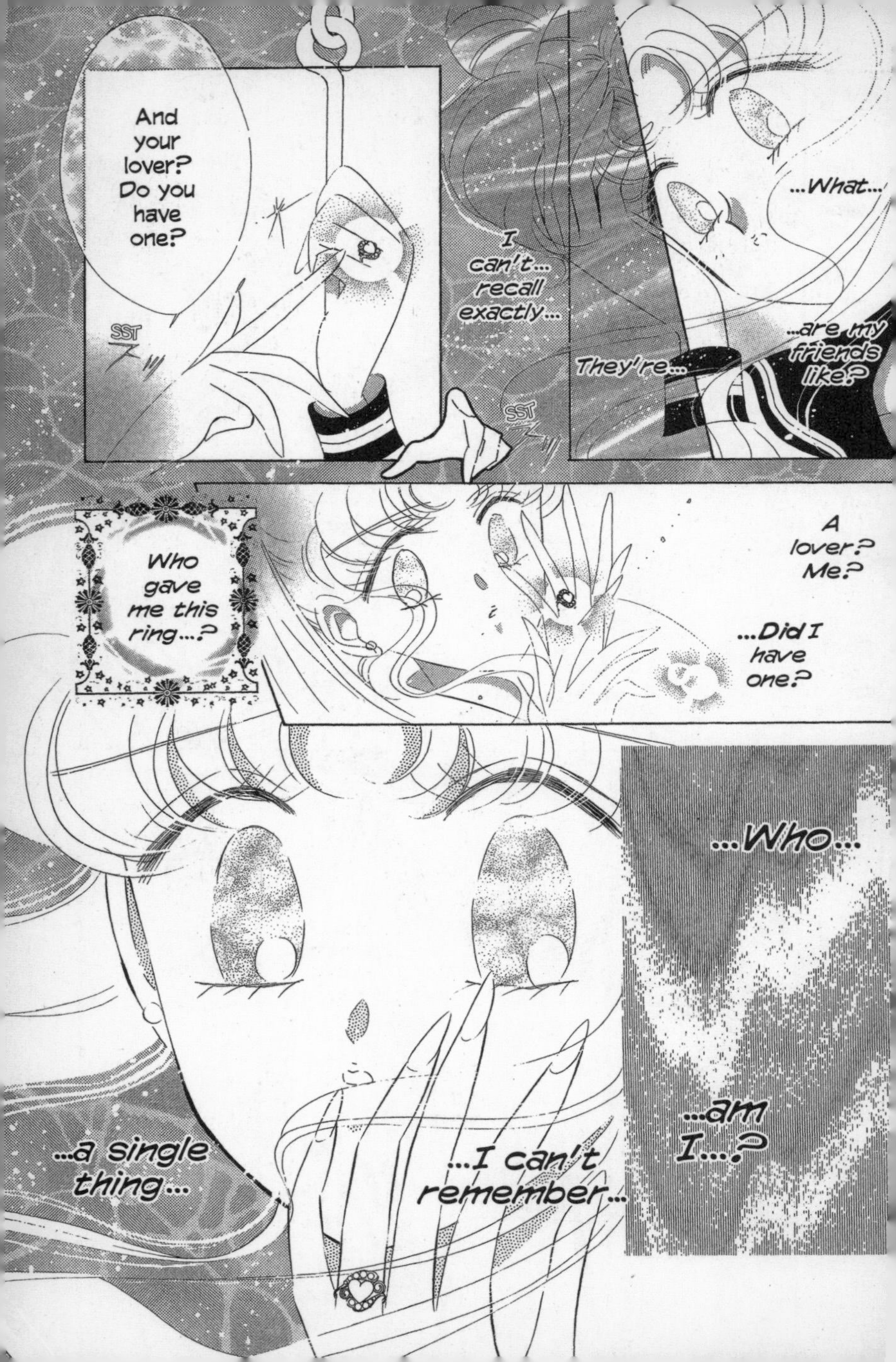
...What...
...are my friends like?
They're...
I can't... recall exactly...
And your lover? Do you have one?
SST
SST
A lover? Me?
...Did I have one?
Who gave me this ring...?
...Who...
...am I...?
...I can't remember...
...a single thing...

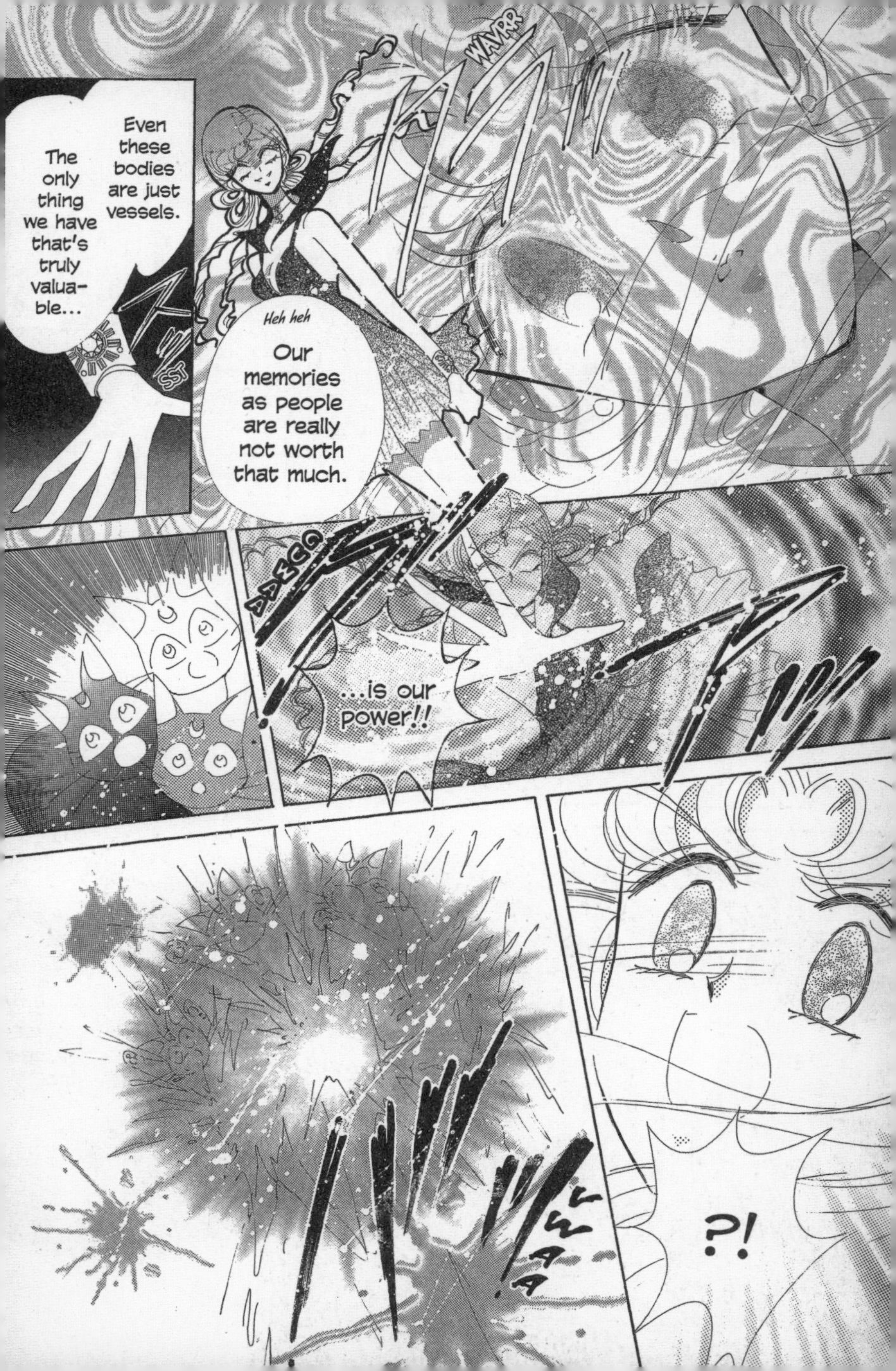
WAVRR
Heh heh
Our memories as people are really not worth that much.
Even these bodies are just vessels.
The only thing we have that's truly valua-ble...
SST
AAWGG
...is our power!!
?!
UWAAA

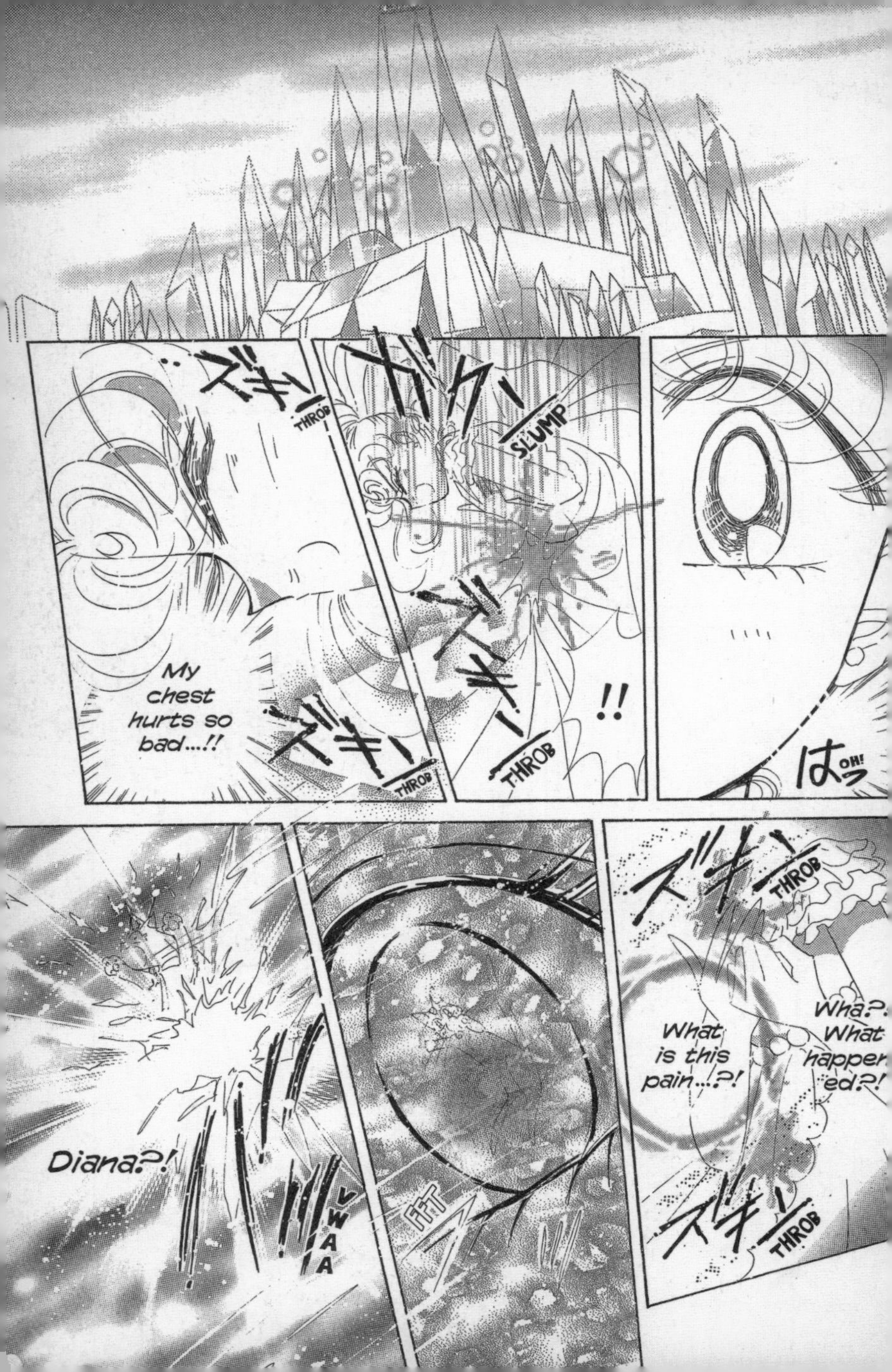
OH!
SLUMP
THROB
!!
THROB
My chest hurts so bad...!!
THROB
THROB
Wha?.. What happen ed?!
What is this pain...?!
THROB
FZT
VWAA
Diana?!

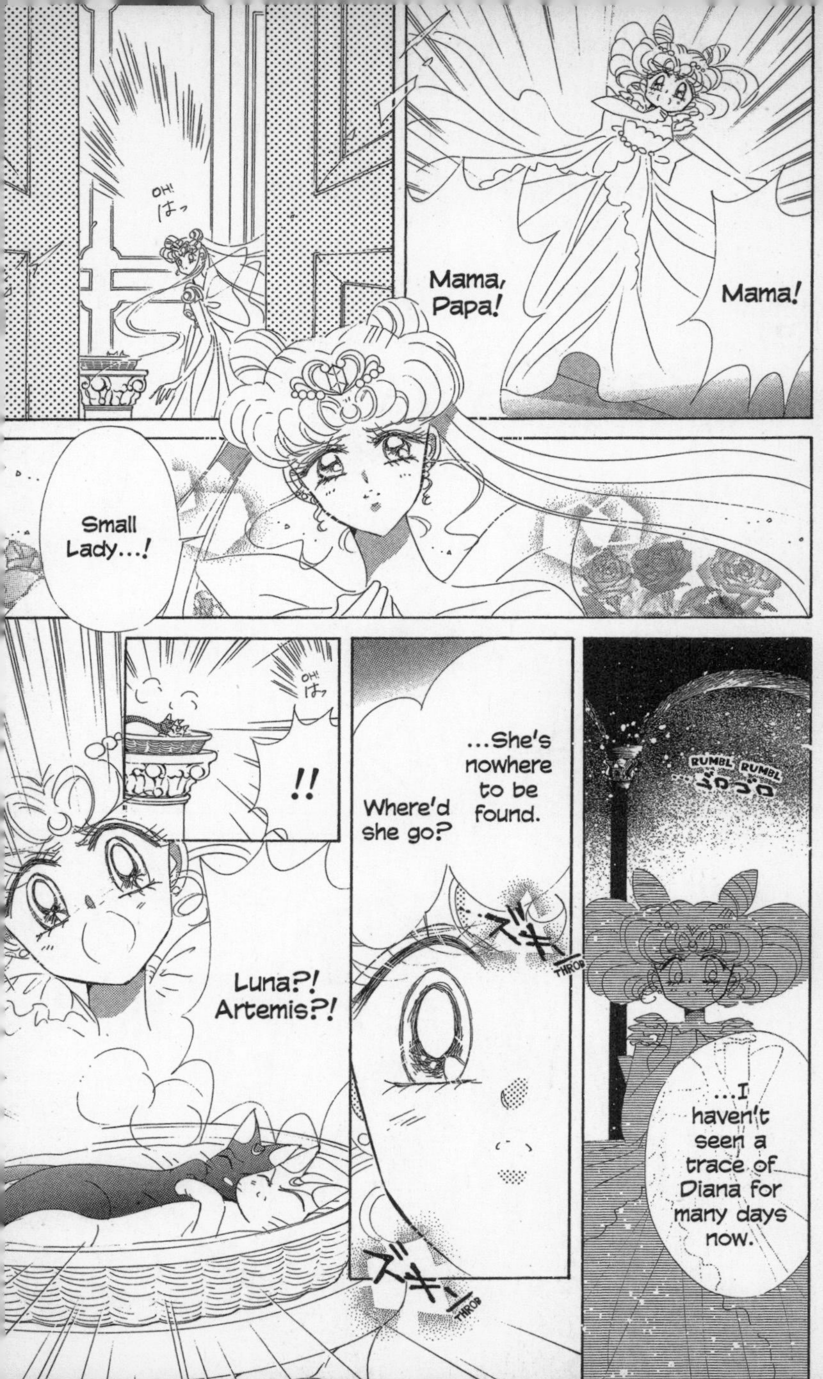
Mama!
Mama, Papa!
OH!
はっ
Small Lady...!
RUMBL RUMBL
ゴロゴロ
...I haven't seen a trace of Diana for many days now.
...She's nowhere to be found.
Where'd she go?
ズキ
THROB
ズキ
THROB
OH!
はっ
!!
Luna?! Artemis?!

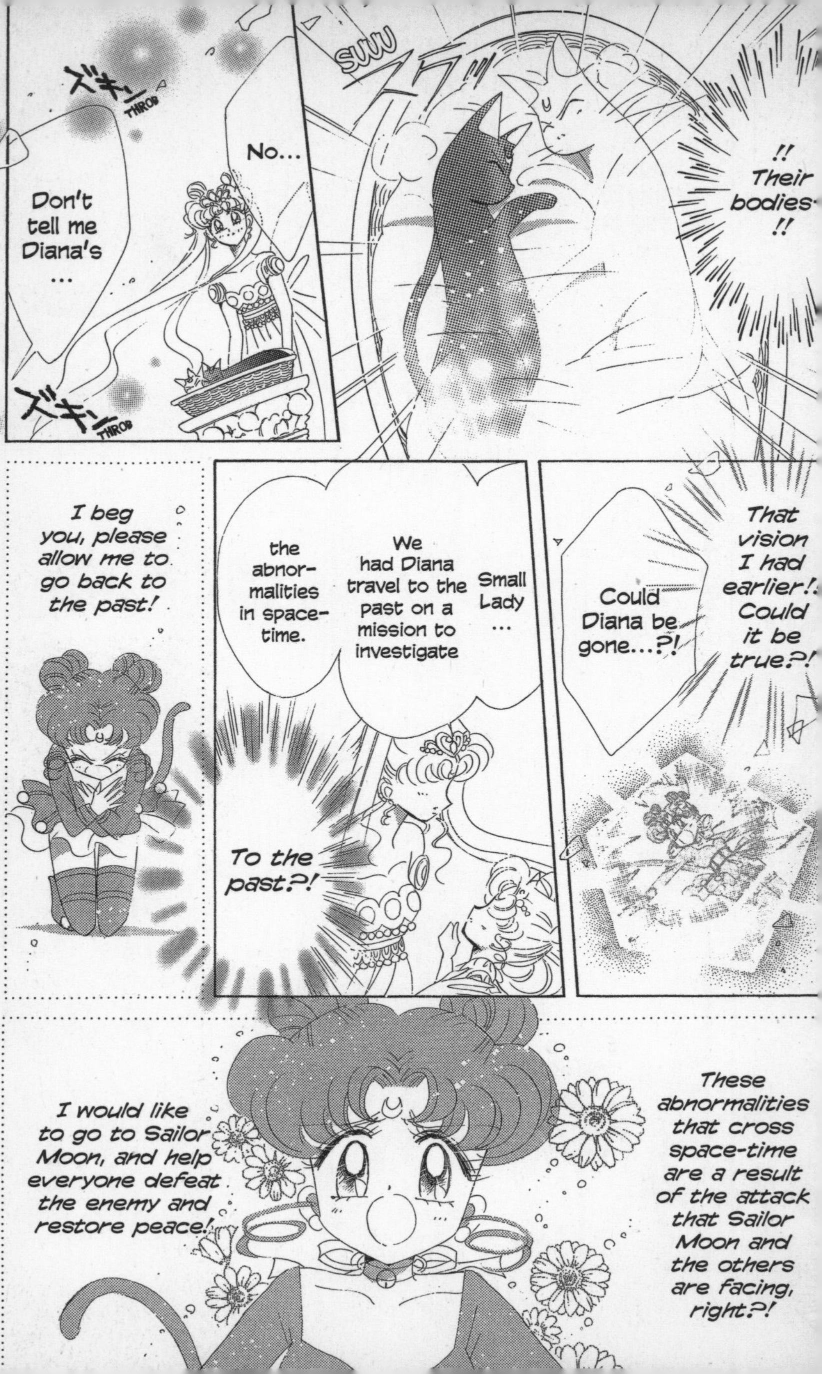
SUUU
!! Their bodies !!
No...
Don't tell me Diana's ...
THROB
THROB
That vision I had earlier!! Could it be true?!
Could Diana be gone...?!
Small Lady ...
We had Diana travel to the past on a mission to investigate the abnormalities in space-time.
To the past?!
I beg you, please allow me to go back to the past!
These abnormalities that cross space-time are a result of the attack that Sailor Moon and the others are facing, right?!
I would like to go to Sailor Moon, and help everyone defeat the enemy and restore peace!

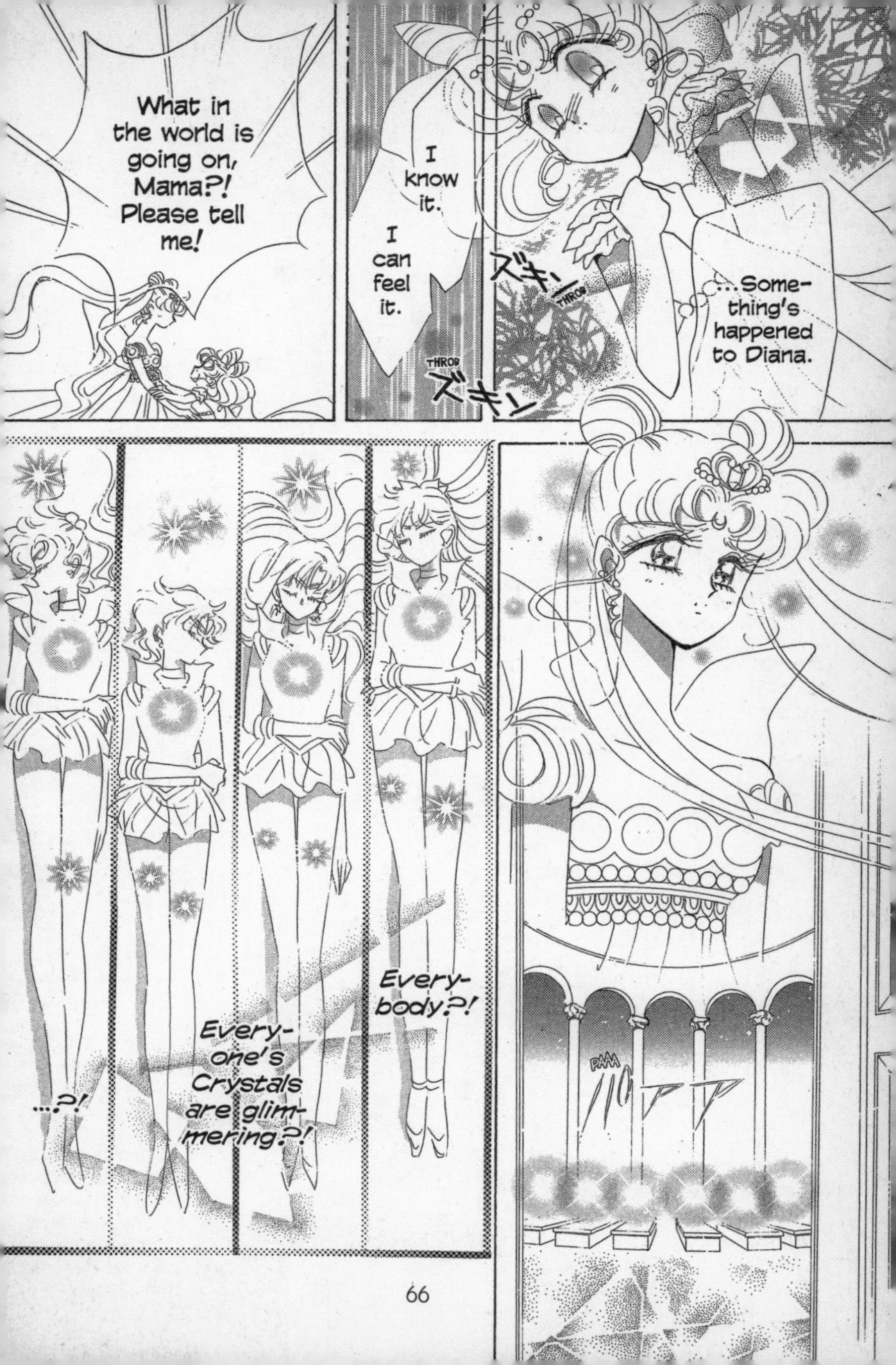
ズキン
THROB
...Some-thing's happened to Diana.
I know it.
I can feel it.
THROB
ズキン
What in the world is going on, Mama?! Please tell me!
PAAA
パァァ
Every-body?!
Every-one's Crystals are glim-mering?!
...?!

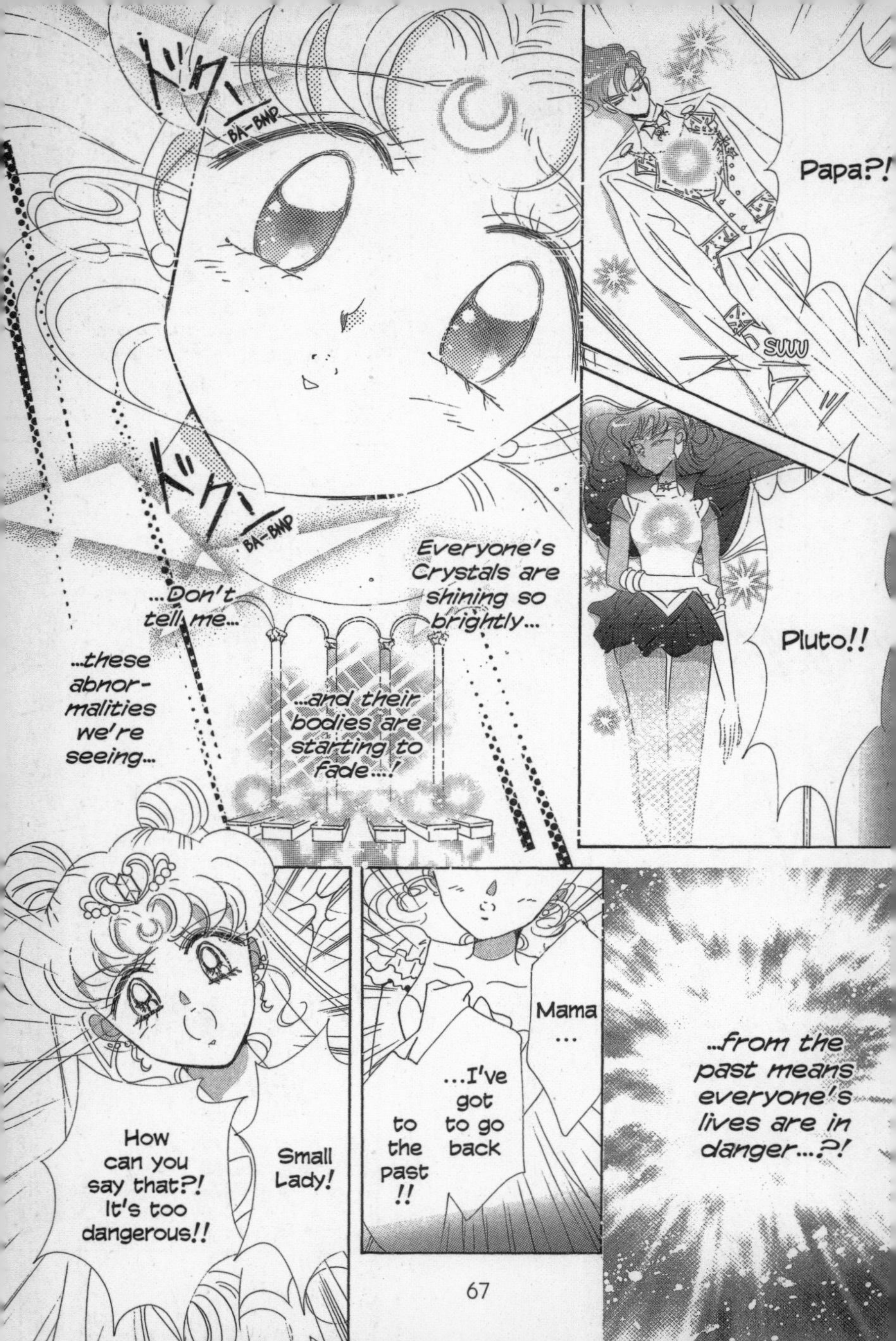
Papa?!
SUUU
Pluto!!
BA-BMP
BA-BMP
Everyone's Crystals are shining so brightly...
...and their bodies are starting to fade....!
...Don't tell me...
...these abnormalities we're seeing...
...from the past means everyone's lives are in danger...?!
Mama...
...I've got to go back to the past!!
Small Lady!
How can you say that?! It's too dangerous!!

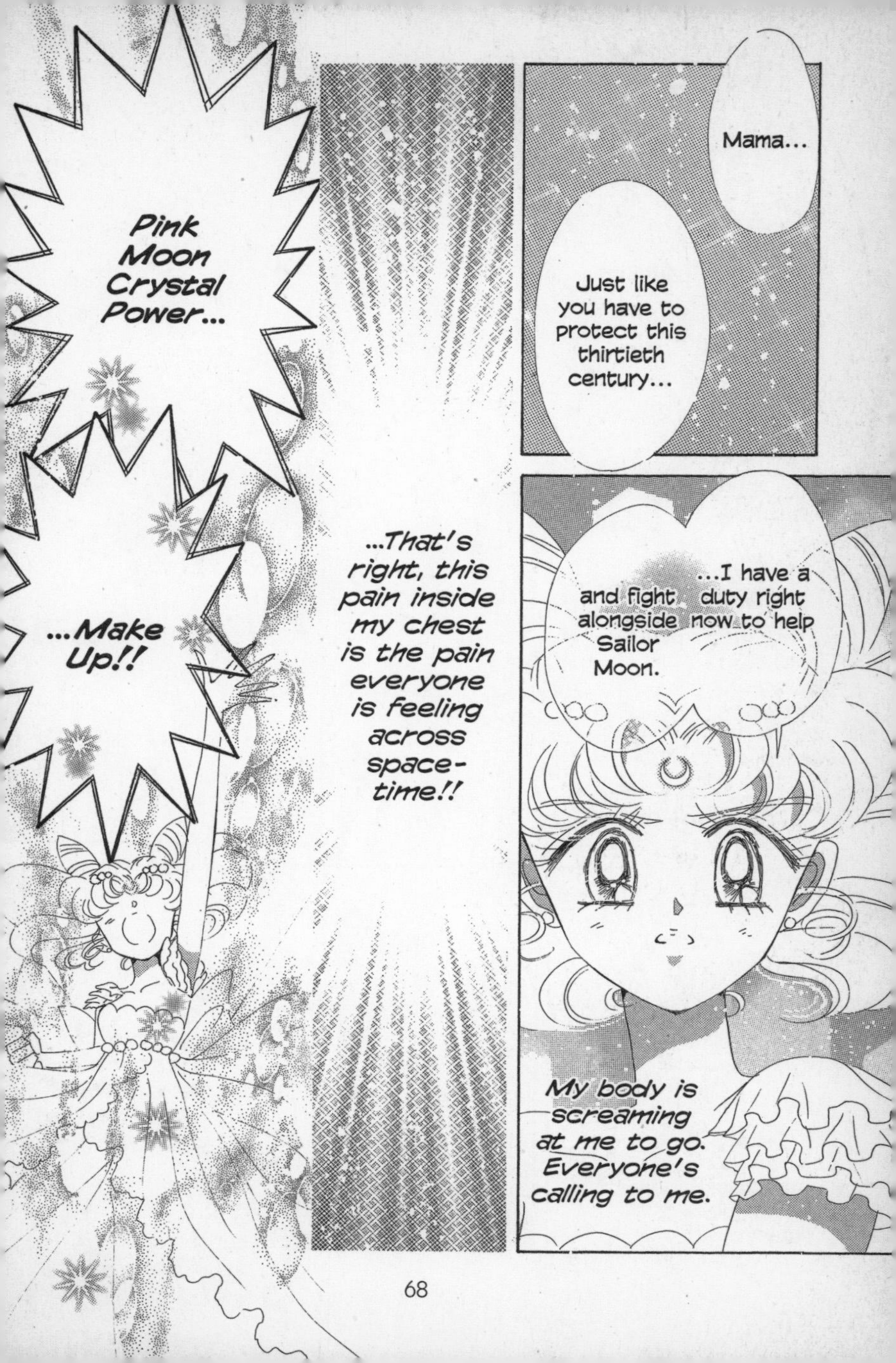
Mama...
Just like you have to protect this thirtieth century...
...I have a duty right now to help and fight alongside Sailor Moon.
My body is screaming at me to go. Everyone's calling to me.
...That's right, this pain inside my chest is the pain everyone is feeling across space-time!!
Pink Moon Crystal Power...
...Make Up!!

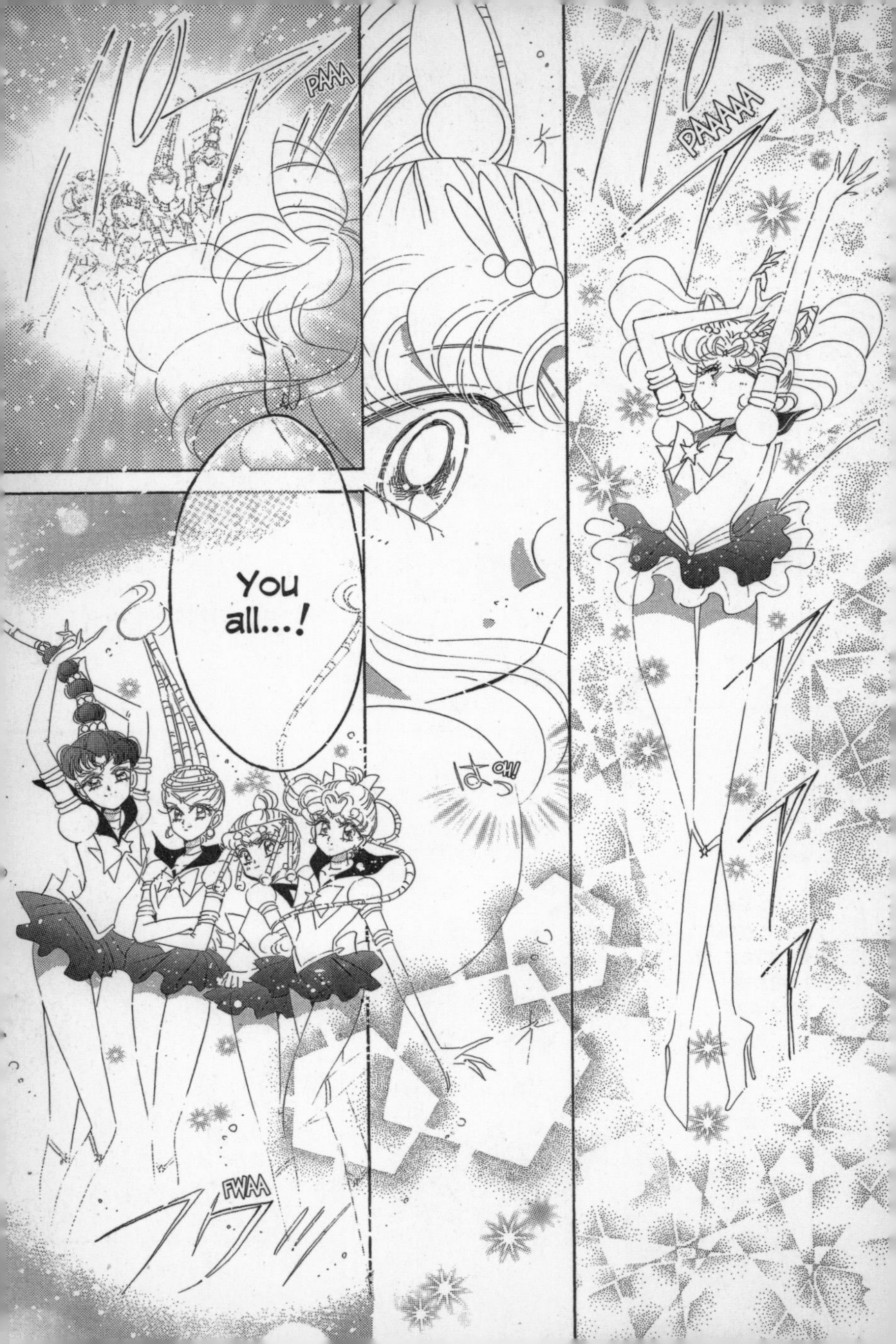
PAAAAA
OH!
You all...!
PAAA
FWAA

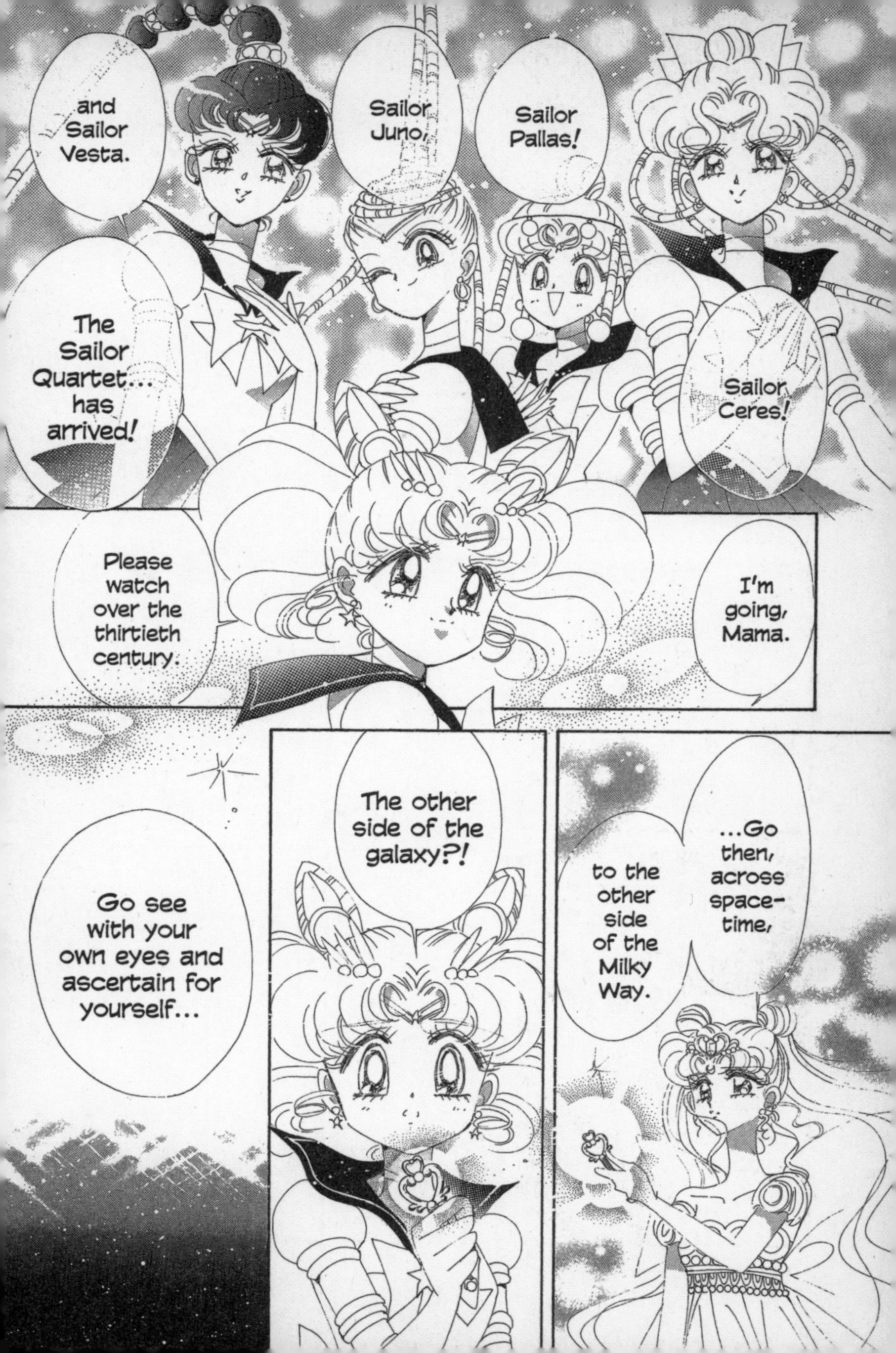
Sailor Ceres!
Sailor Pallas!
Sailor Juno,
and Sailor Vesta.
The Sailor Quartet... has arrived!
I'm going, Mama.
Please watch over the thirtieth century.
...Go then, across space-time,
to the other side of the Milky Way.
The other side of the galaxy?!
Go see with your own eyes and ascertain for yourself...

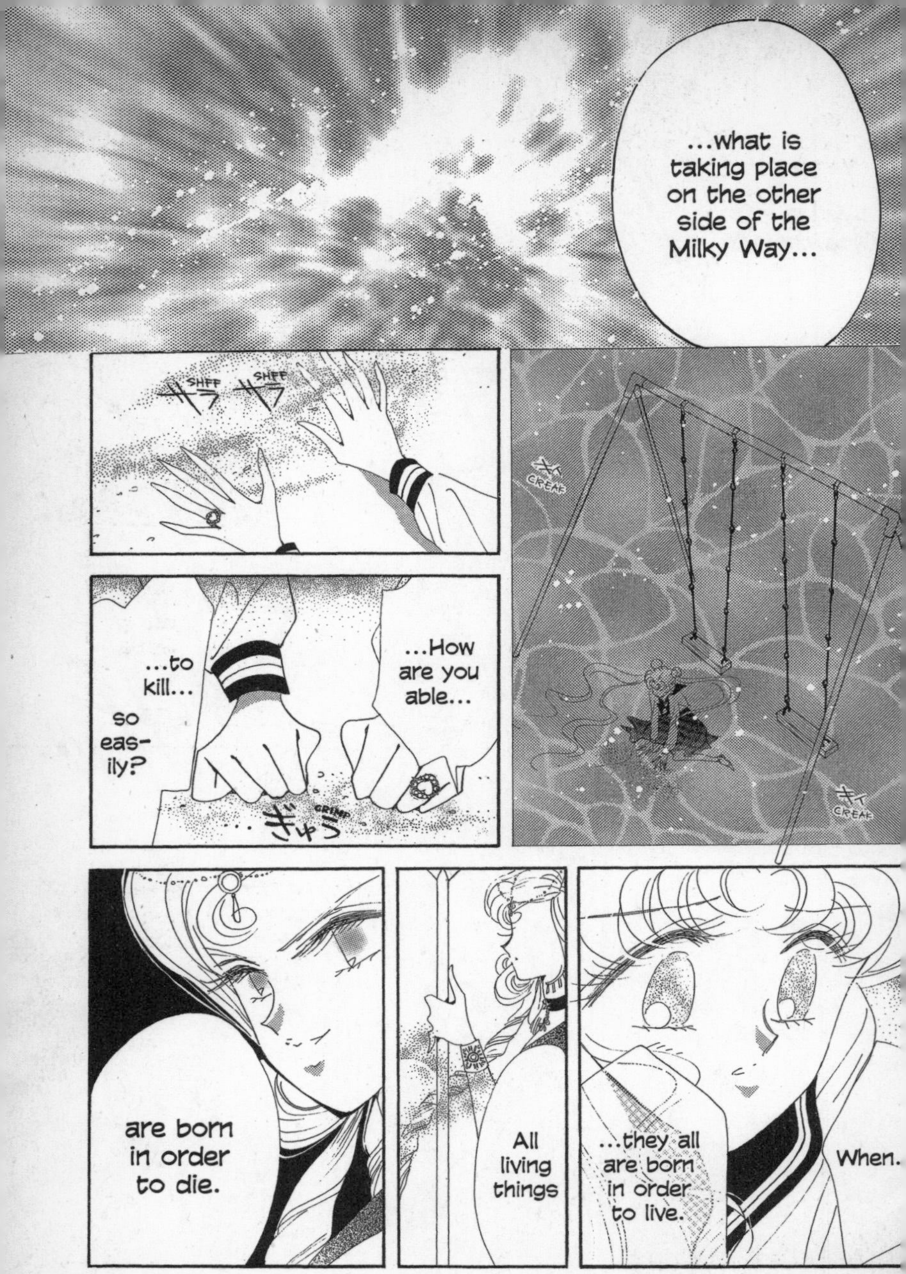
...what is taking place on the other side of the Milky Way...
CREAK
CREAK
SHFF SHFF
...How are you able...
...to kill...
so eas-ily?
CRIMP
When.
...they all are born in order to live.
All living things
are born in order to die.

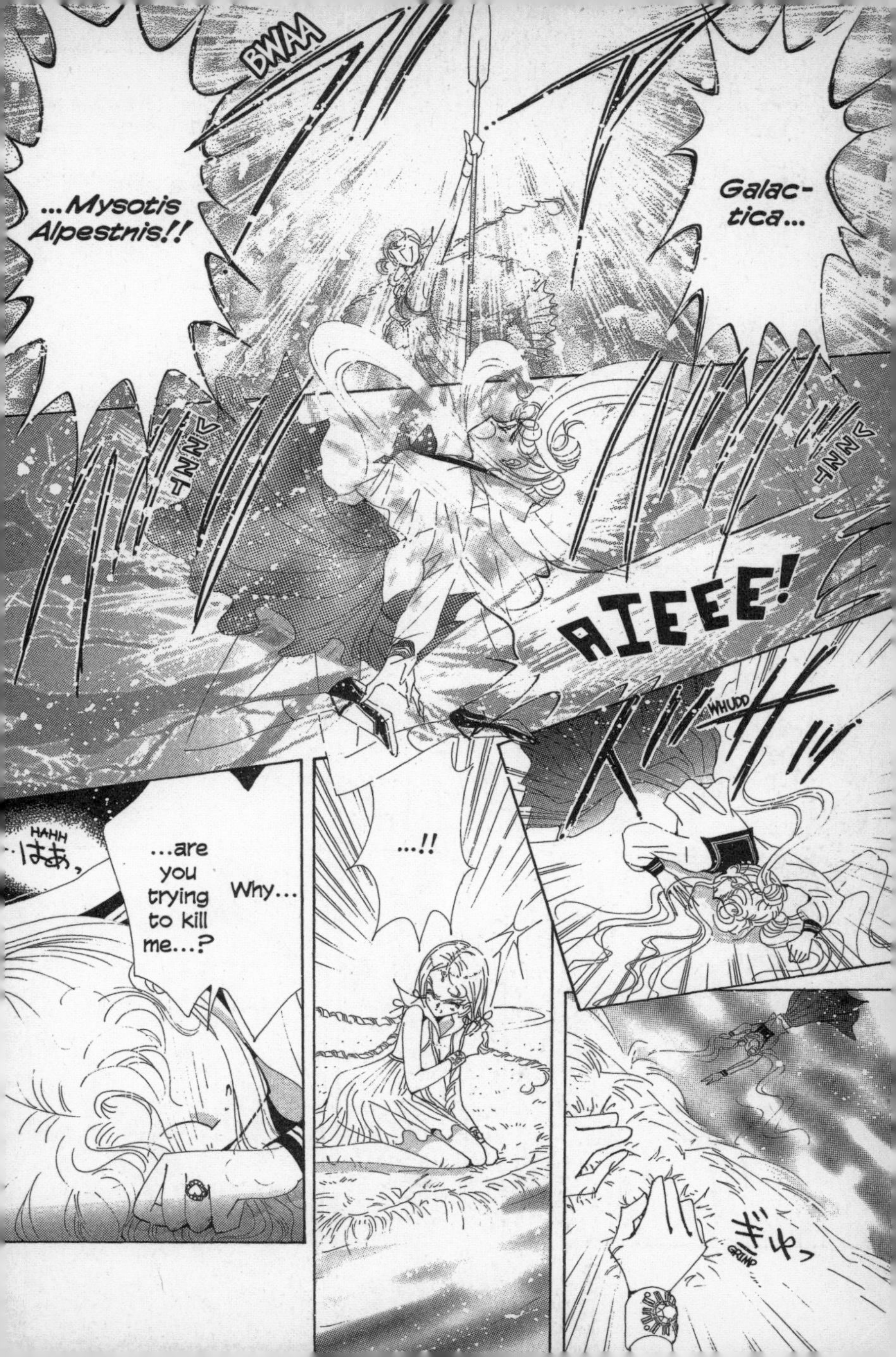

Galac-tica...
BWAA
...Mysotis Alpestnis!!
VNNT
VNNT
AIEEE!
WHUDD
ぎゅっ
GRIMP
...!!
Why...
...are you trying to kill me...?
はあ、
HAHH

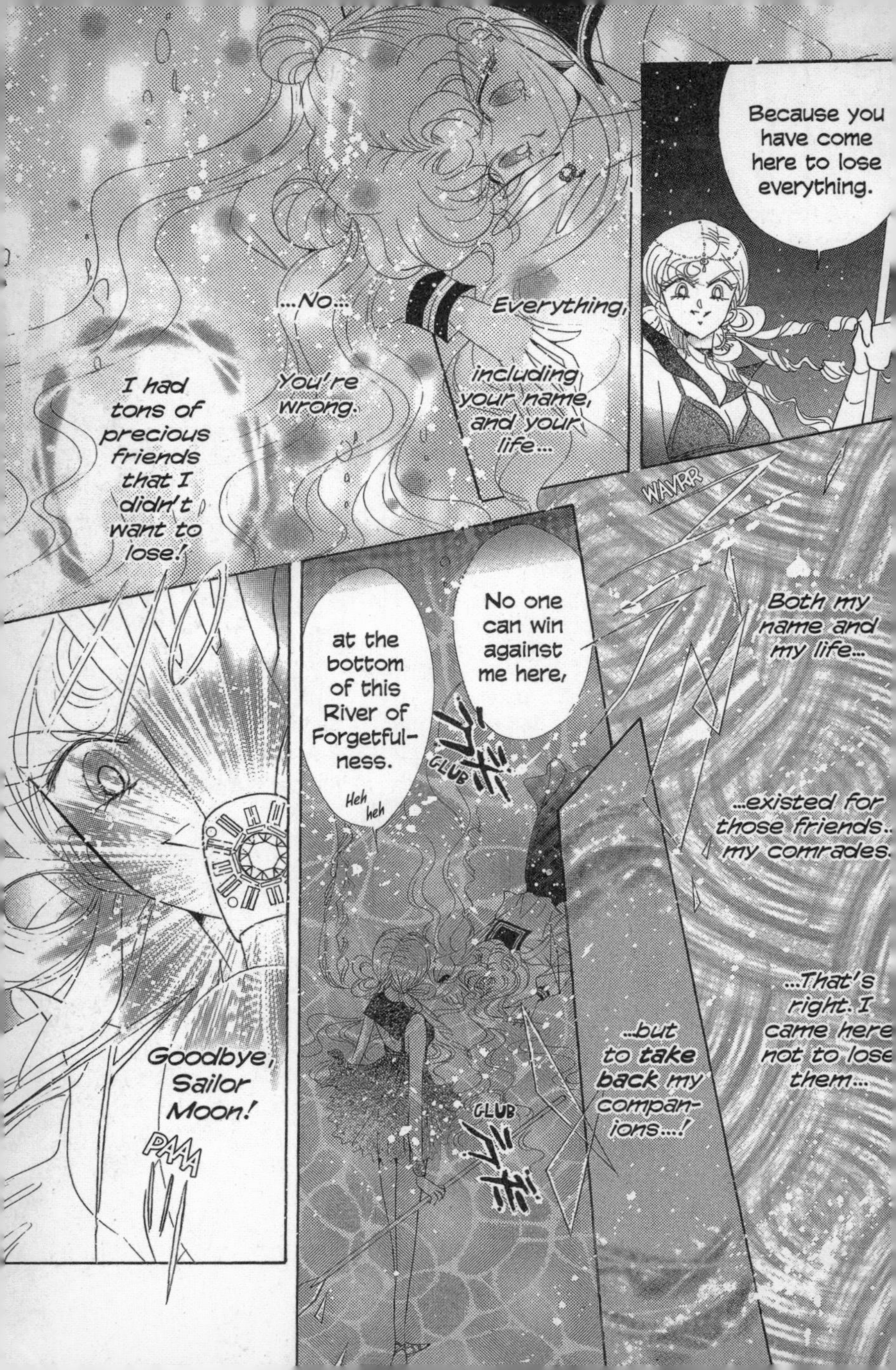
Because you have come here to lose everything.
Everything,
including your name, and your life...
...No...
You're wrong.
I had tons of precious friends that I didn't want to lose!
WAVRR
Both my name and my life...
...existed for those friends... my comrades.
...That's right. I came here not to lose them...
...but to take back my companions...!
No one can win against me here,
at the bottom of this River of Forgetfulness.
Heh heh
GLUB
GLUB
Goodbye, Sailor Moon!
PAAA

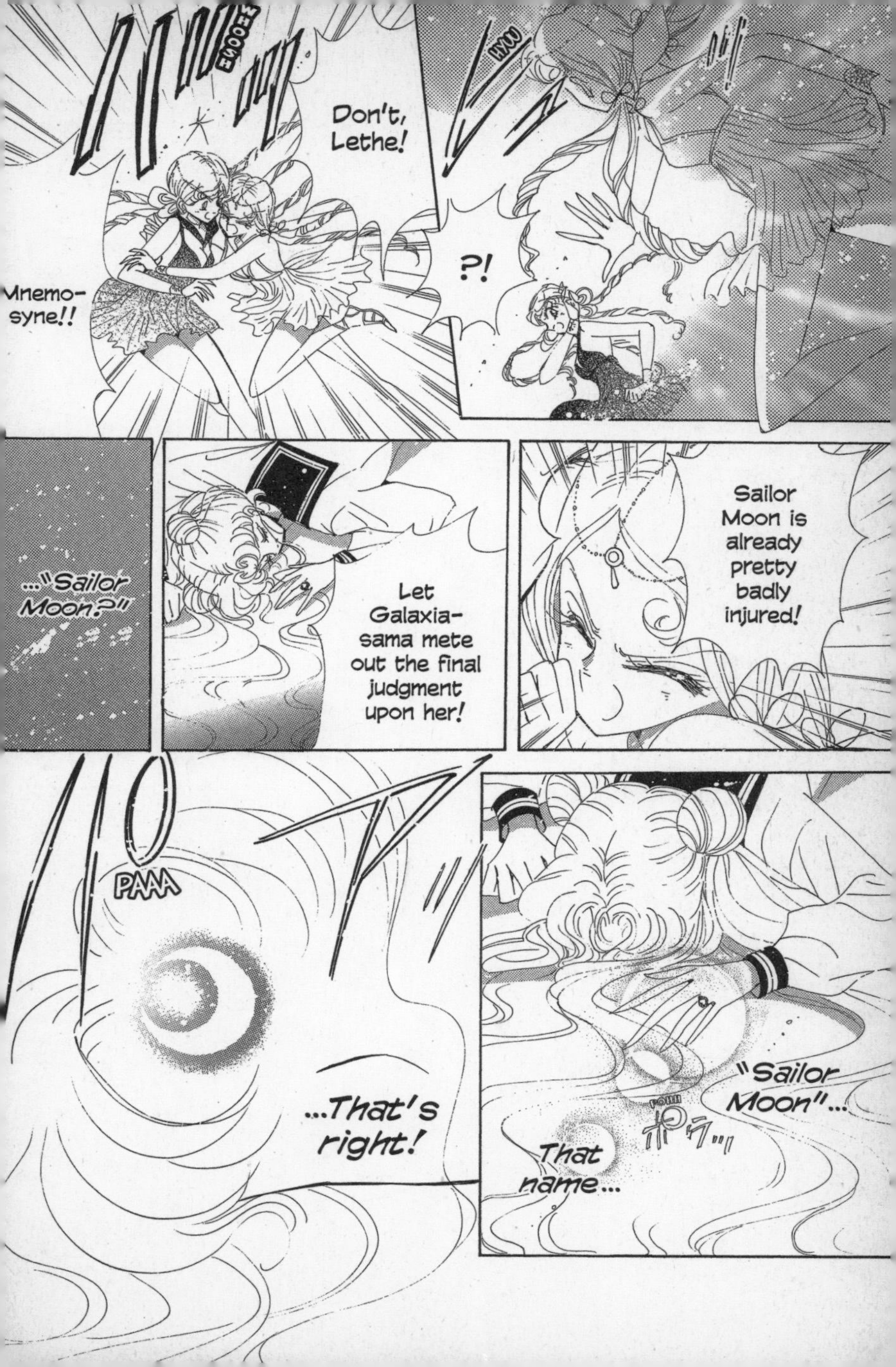
HYUU
?!
WHOOSH
Don't, Lethe!
Mnemo-syne!!
Sailor Moon is already pretty badly injured!
Let Galaxia-sama mete out the final judgment upon her!
..."Sailor Moon?"
"Sailor Moon"...
POHH
That name...
PAAA
...That's right!

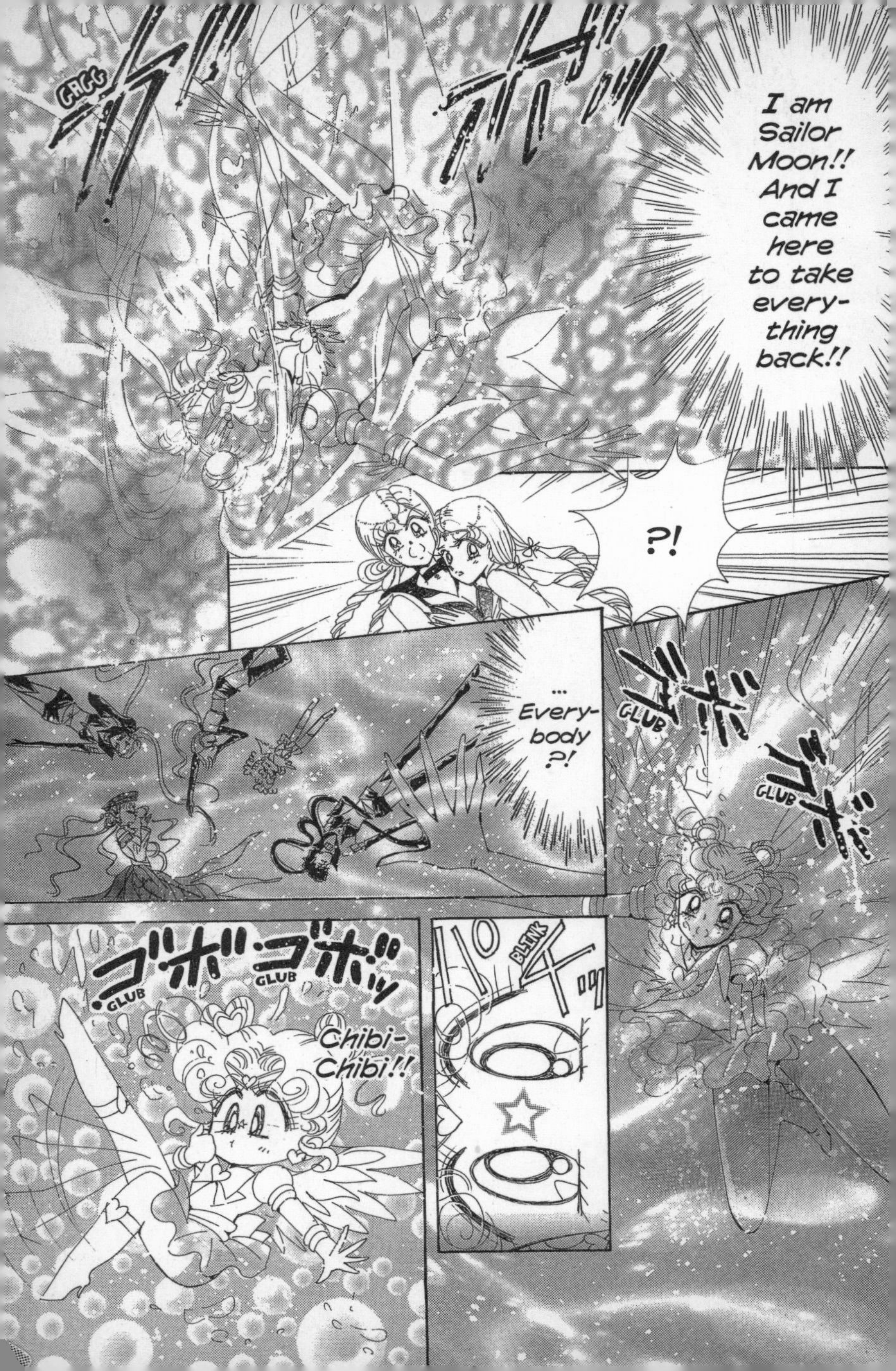

I am Sailor Moon!! And I came here to take every-thing back!!
CRGG
?!
GLUB
GLUB
... Every-body ?!
BLINK
GLUB
GLUB
Chibi-Chibi!!

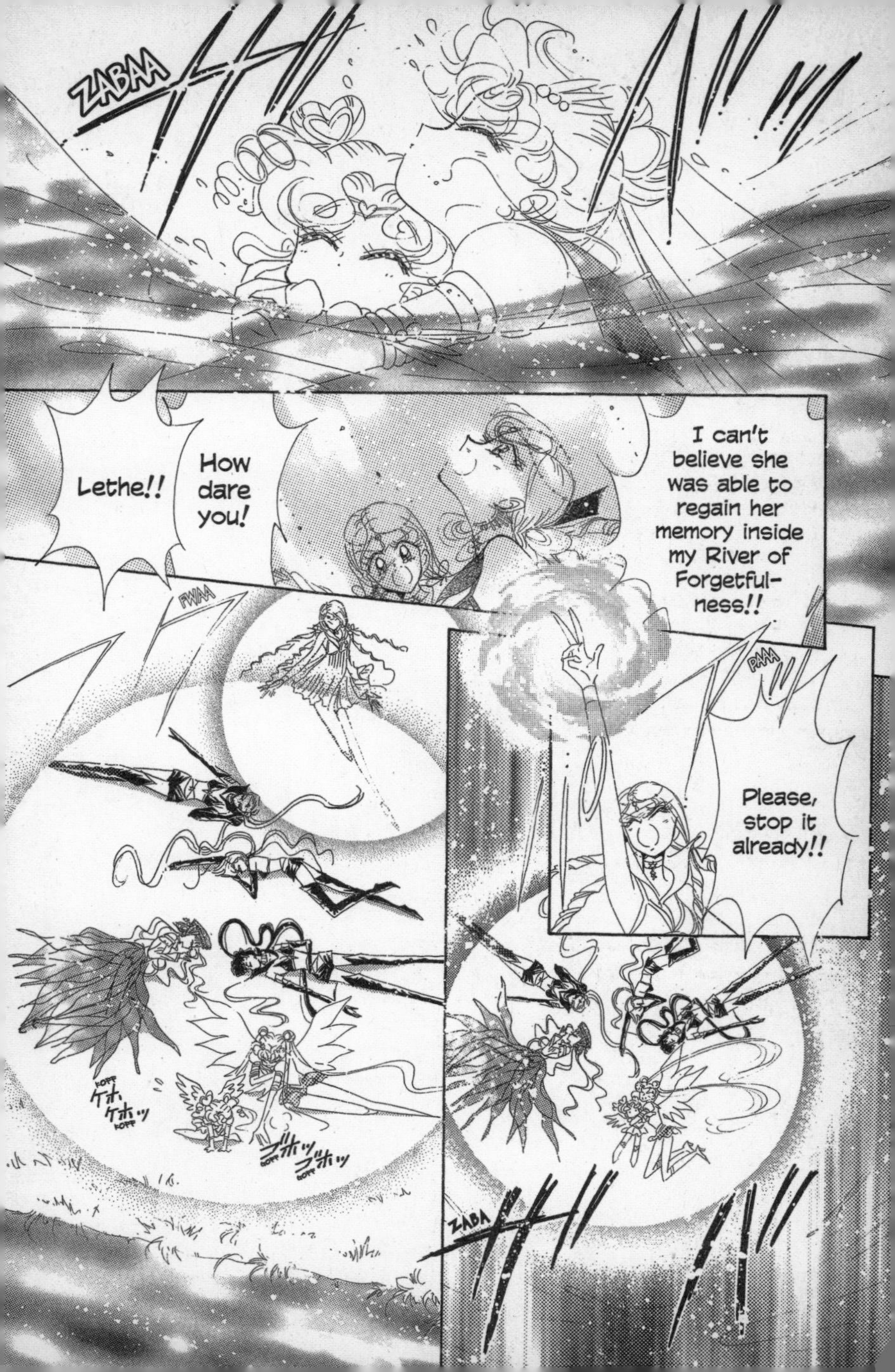
ZABAA
I can't believe she was able to regain her memory inside my River of Forgetfulness!!
How dare you!
Lethe!!
PAAA
Please, stop it already!!
ZABA
FWAA
ケホ ケホッ
KOFF KOFF
ゴホッ ゴホッ
GOFF GOFF

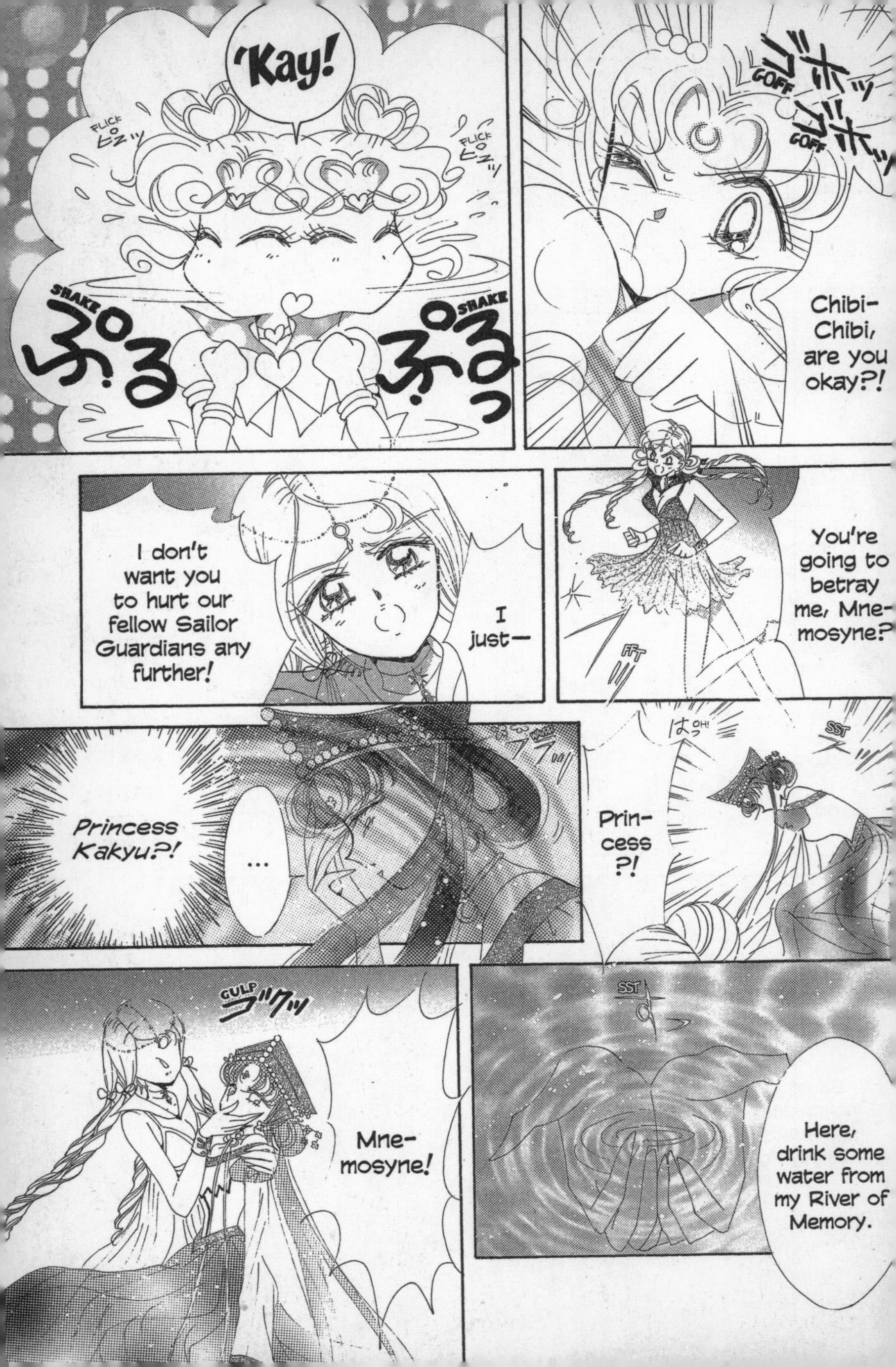
GOFF ゴホッ
GOFF ゴホッ
Chibi-Chibi, are you okay?!
'Kay!
FLICK ピクッ
FLICK ピクッ
SHAKE ぷる
SHAKE ぷるっ
You're going to betray me, Mne-mosyne?
FFT
I just—
I don't want you to hurt our fellow Sailor Guardians any further!
SST
はっ OH!
Prin-cess?!
WAVER フラッ
...
Princess Kakyu?!
SST
Here, drink some water from my River of Memory.
Mne-mosyne!
GULP ゴクッ

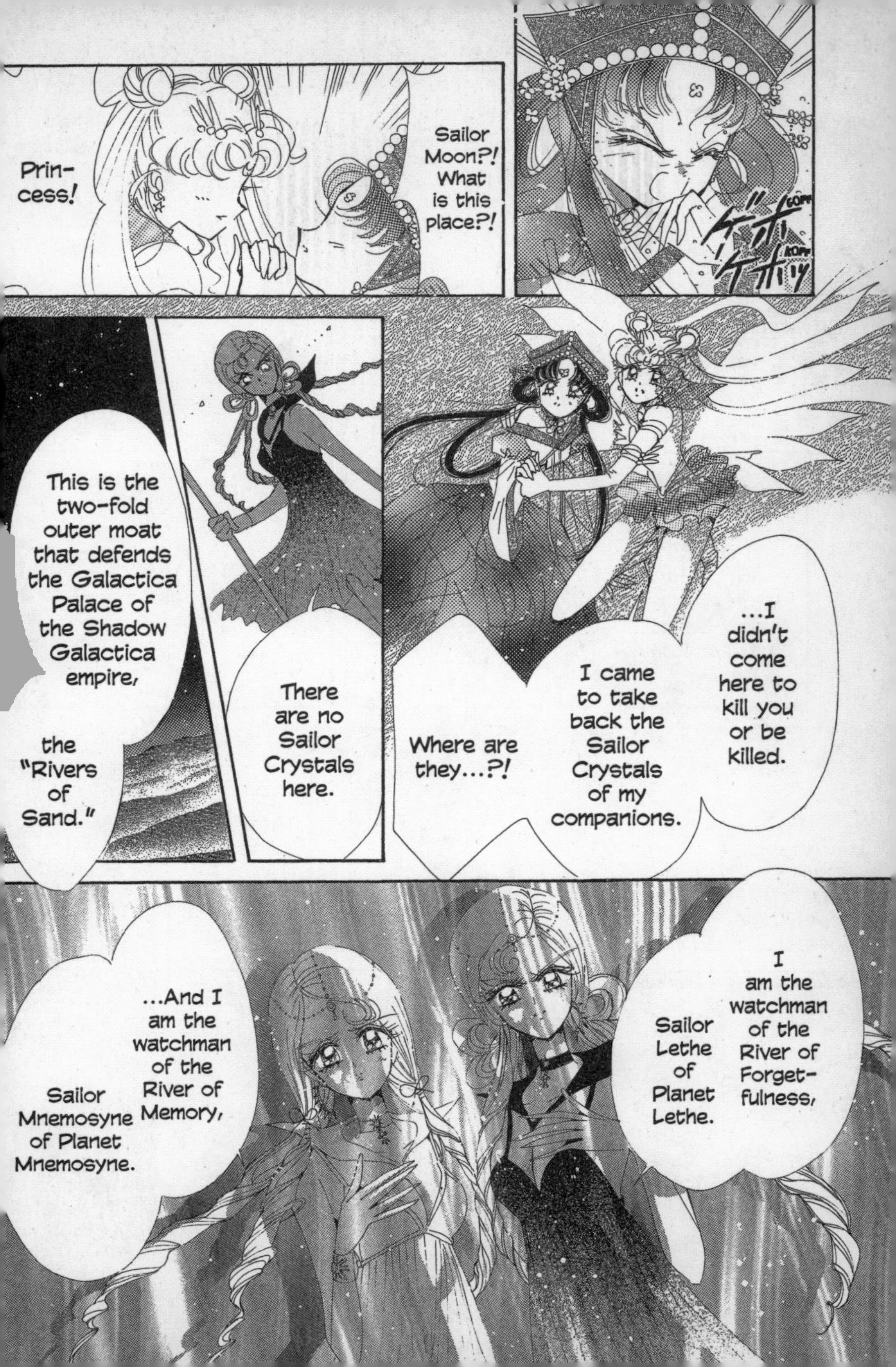
ゲホ KOFF
ゲホッ KOFF
Sailor Moon?! What is this place?!
Prin-cess!
...I didn't come here to kill you or be killed.
I came to take back the Sailor Crystals of my companions.
Where are they...?!
There are no Sailor Crystals here.
This is the two-fold outer moat that defends the Galactica Palace of the Shadow Galactica empire,
the "Rivers of Sand."
I am the watchman of the River of Forget-fulness,
Sailor Lethe of Planet Lethe.
...And I am the watchman of the River of Memory,
Sailor Mnemosyne of Planet Mnemosyne.

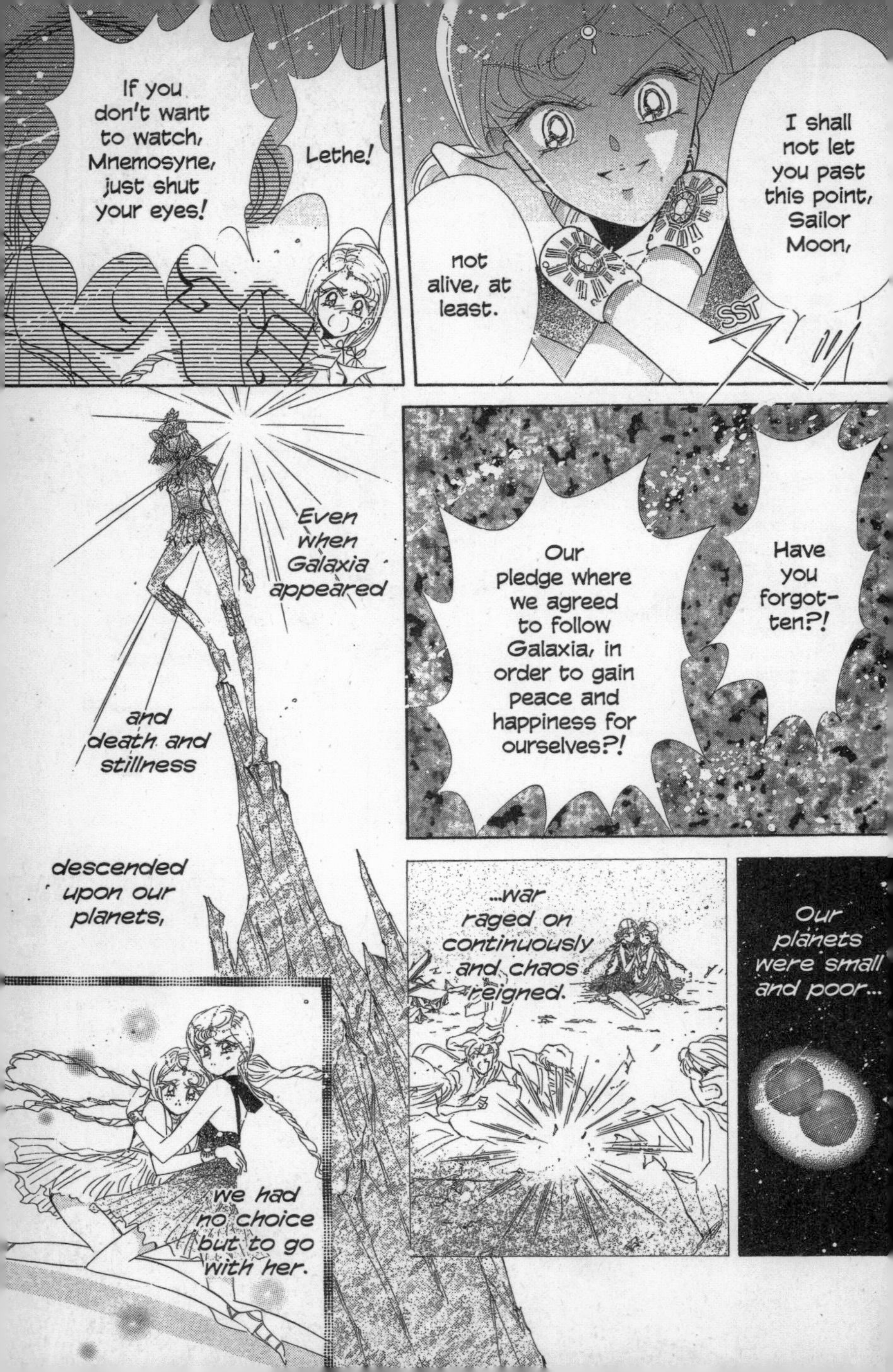
I shall not let you past this point, Sailor Moon,
not alive, at least.
SST
If you don't want to watch, Mnemosyne, just shut your eyes!
Lethe!
Have you forgot-ten?!
Our pledge where we agreed to follow Galaxia, in order to gain peace and happiness for ourselves?!
Our planets were small and poor...
...war raged on continuously and chaos reigned.
Even when Galaxia appeared
and death and stillness
descended upon our planets,
we had no choice but to go with her.

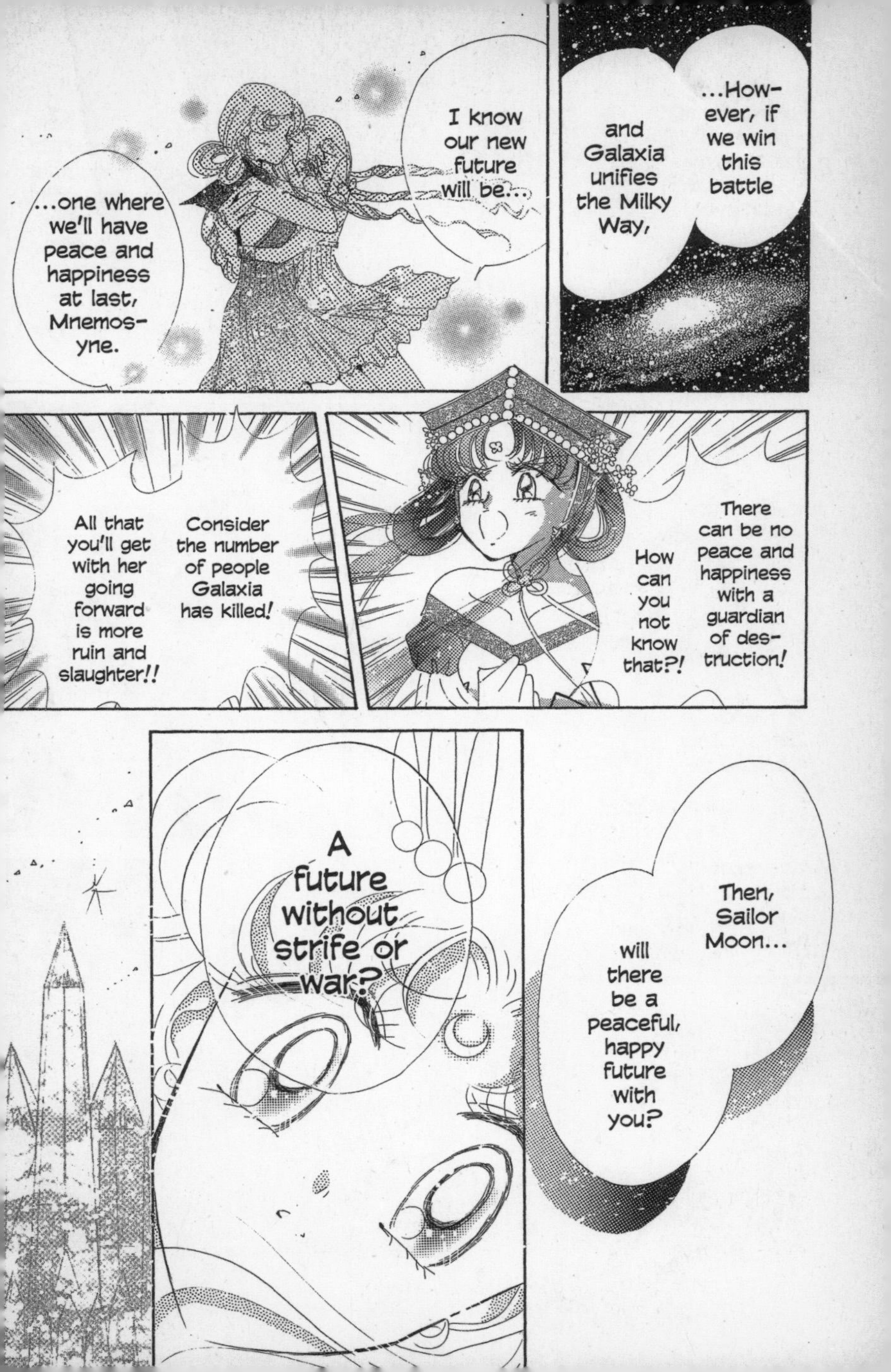
...However, if we win this battle
and Galaxia unifies the Milky Way,
I know our new future will be...
...one where we'll have peace and happiness at last, Mnemosyne.
There can be no peace and happiness with a guardian of destruction!
How can you not know that?!
Consider the number of people Galaxia has killed!
All that you'll get with her going forward is more ruin and slaughter!!
Then, Sailor Moon...
will there be a peaceful, happy future with you?
A future without strife or war?

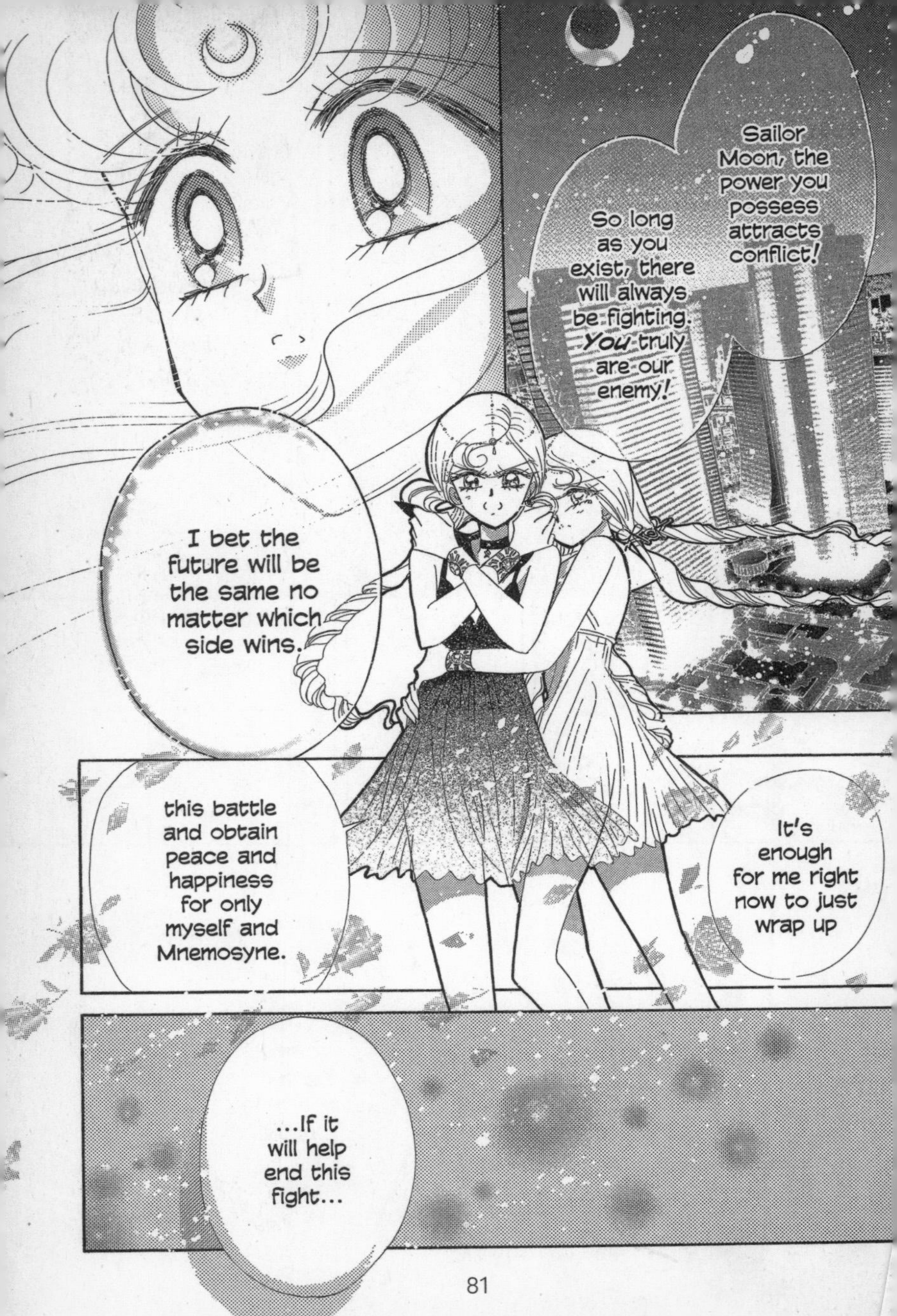
Sailor Moon, the power you possess attracts conflict!
So long as you exist, there will always be fighting. You truly are our enemy!
I bet the future will be the same no matter which side wins.
It's enough for me right now to just wrap up
this battle and obtain peace and happiness for only myself and Mnemosyne.
...If it will help end this fight...

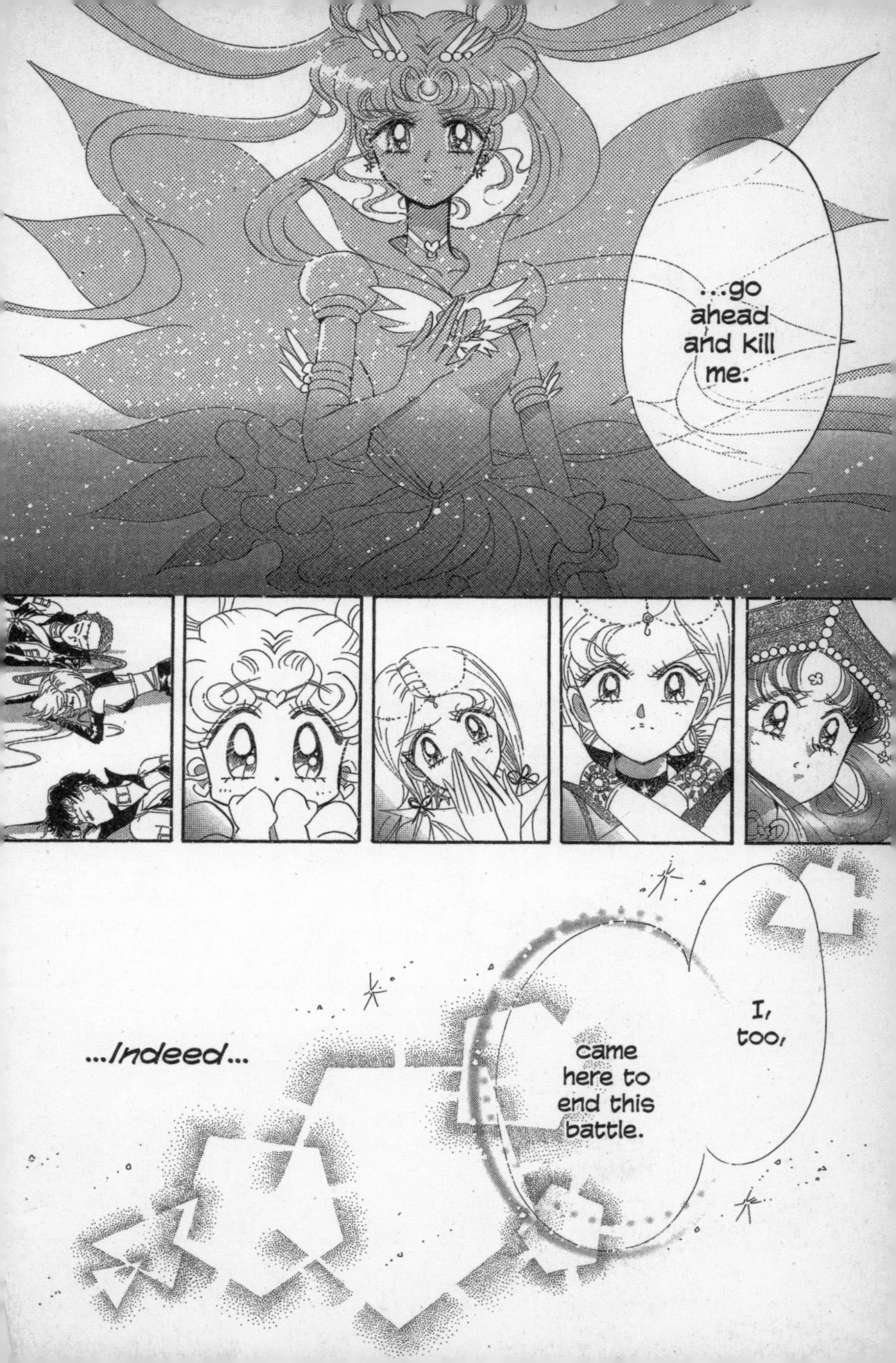
...go ahead and kill me.
I, too, came here to end this battle.
...Indeed...

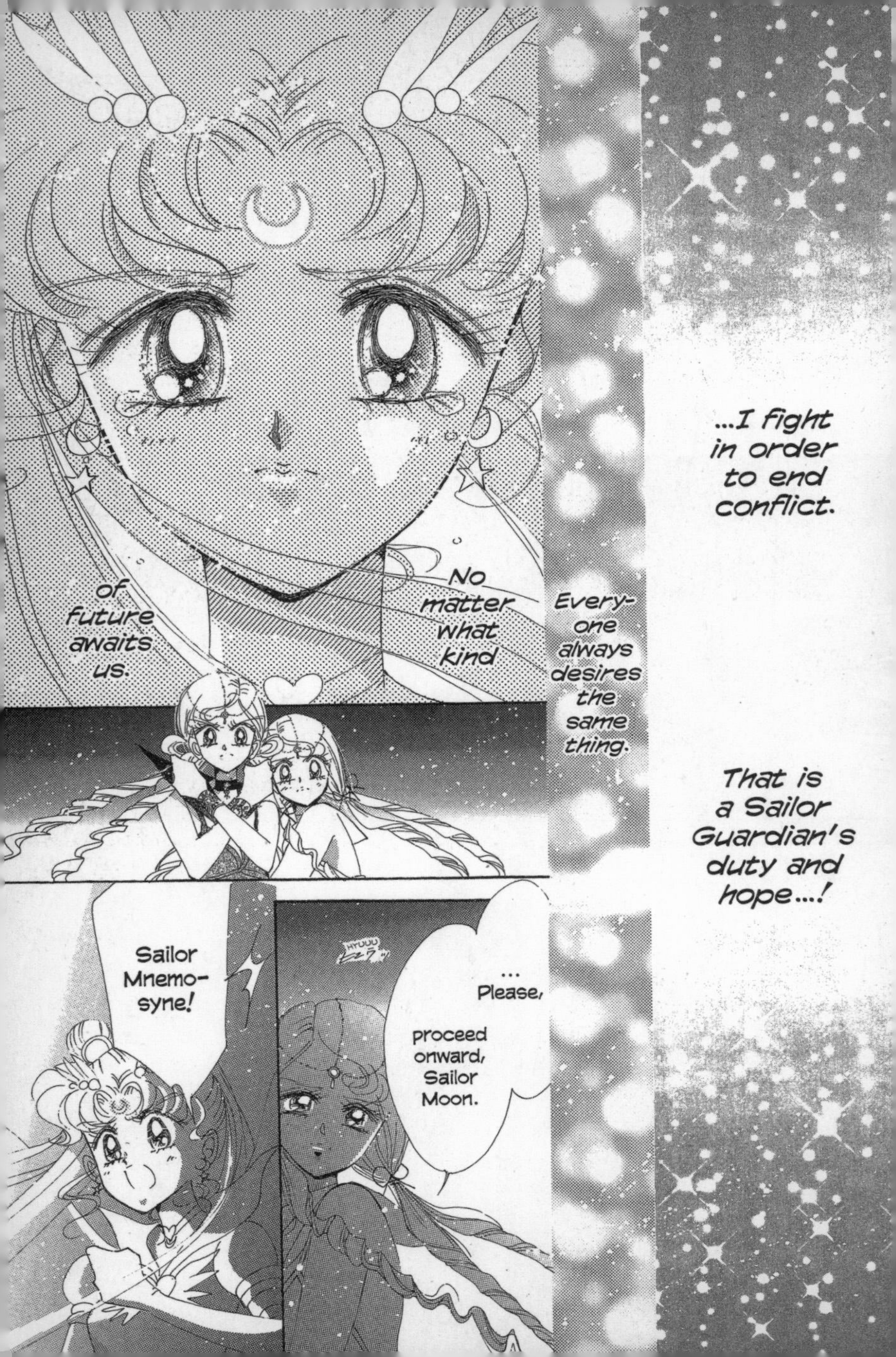
No matter what kind
of future awaits us.
Every-one always desires the same thing.
...I fight in order to end conflict.
That is a Sailor Guardian's duty and hope...!
HYUUU
... Please,
proceed onward, Sailor Moon.
Sailor Mnemo-syne!

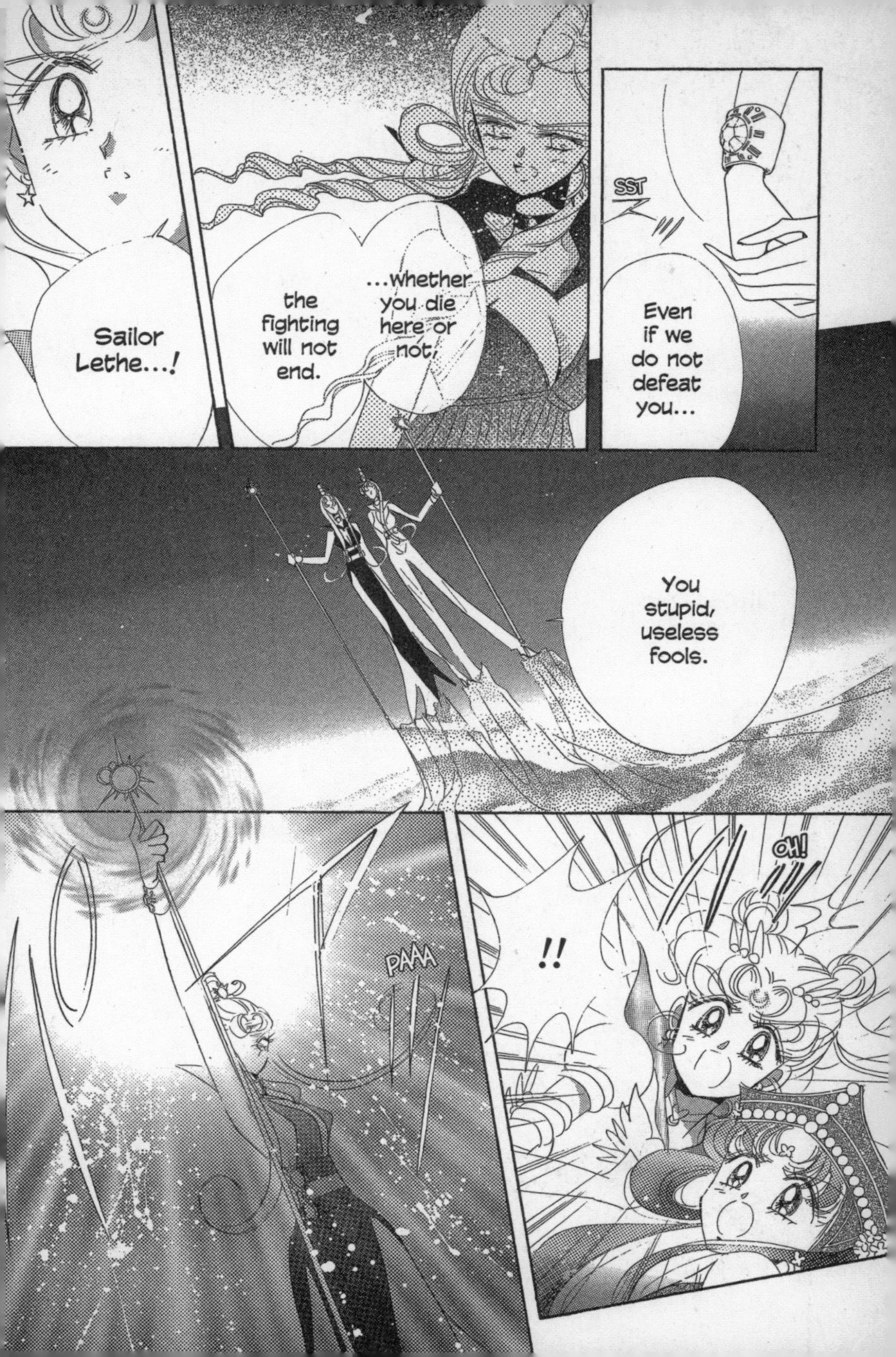
SST
Even if we do not defeat you...
...whether you die here or not,
the fighting will not end.
Sailor Lethe...!
You stupid, useless fools.
OH!
!!
PAAA

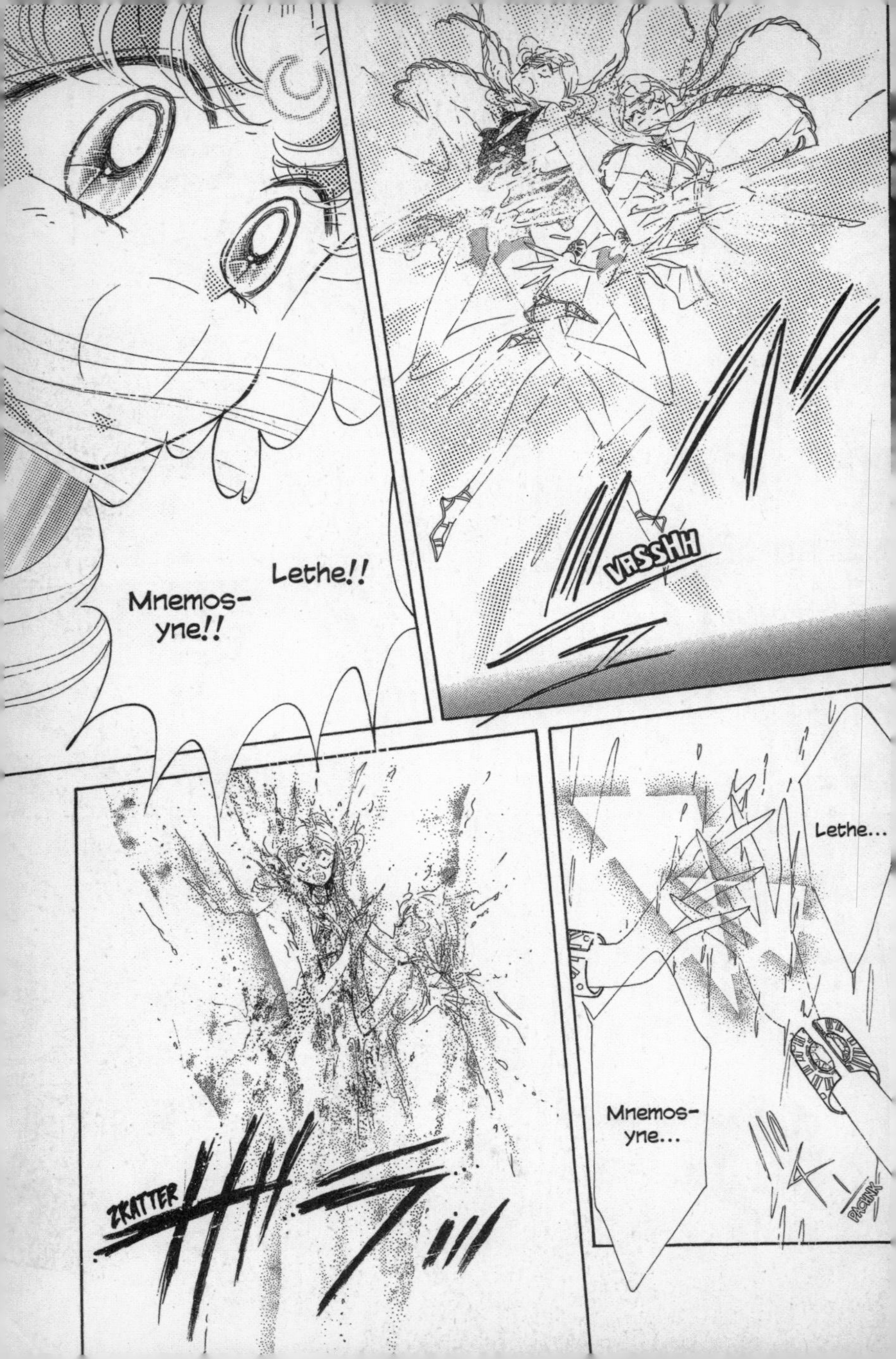
VASSHH
Lethe!!
Mnemosyne!!
Lethe...
Mnemosyne...
PACHNK
ZRATTER

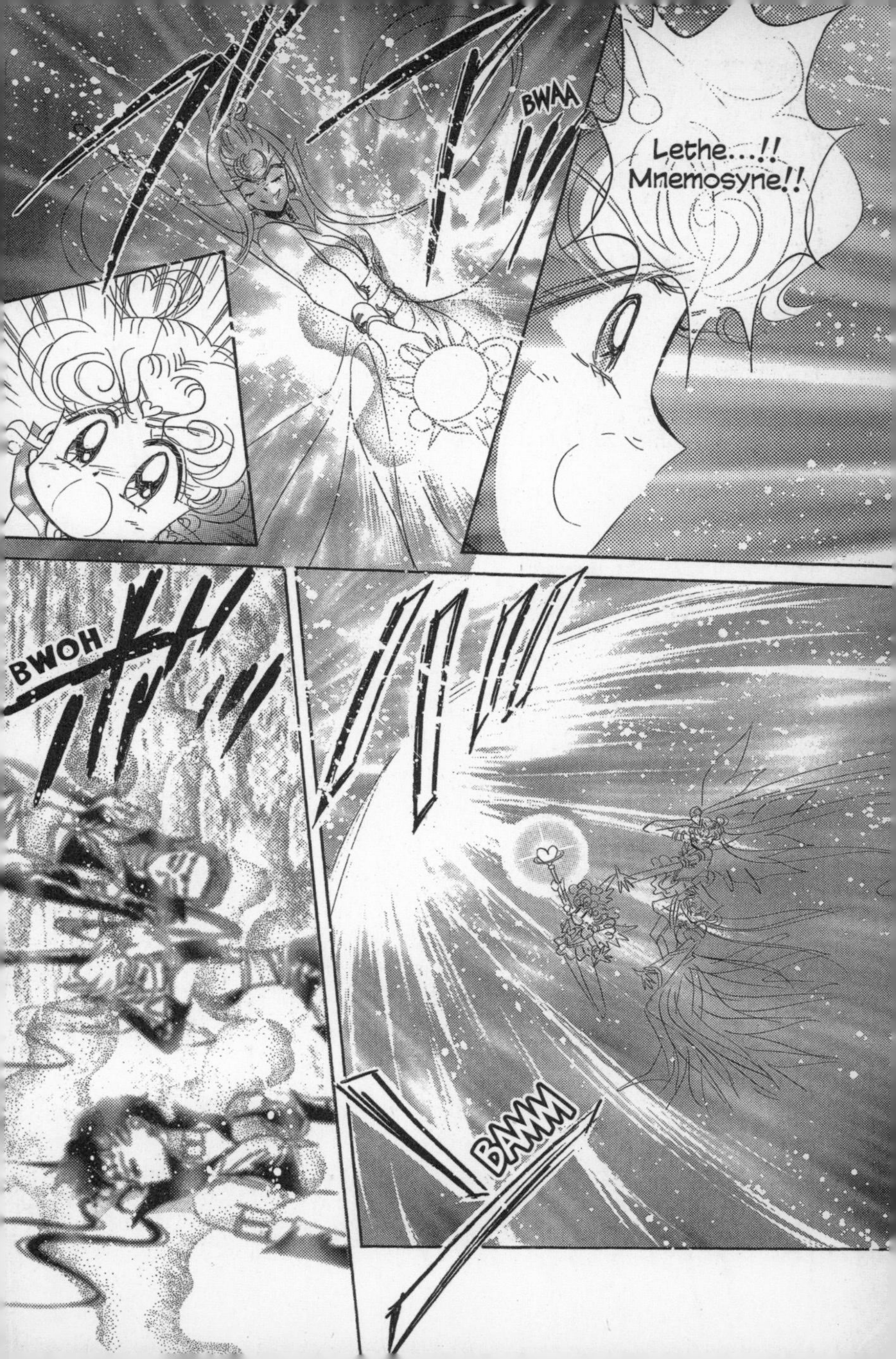
Lethe...!! Mnemosyne!!
BWAA
BAMM
BWOH

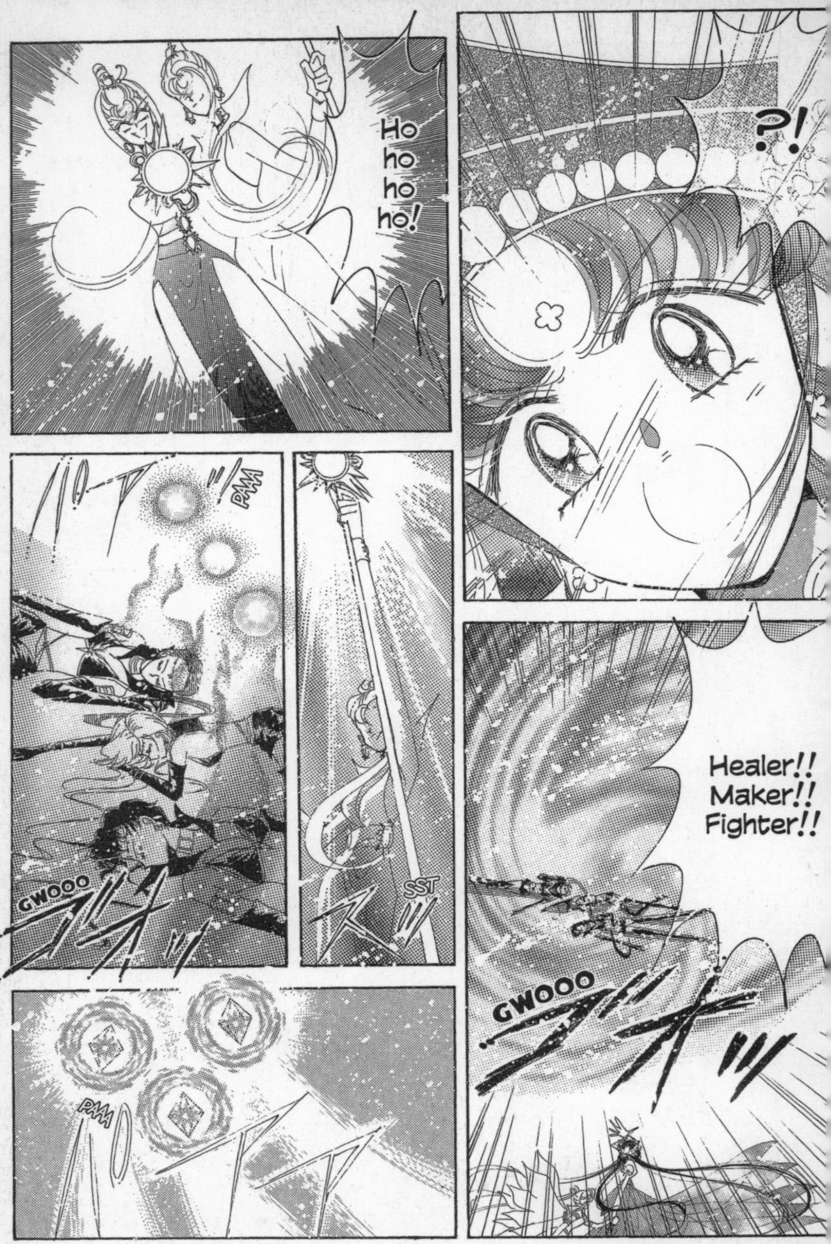
?!
Ho ho ho ho!
SST
PAAA
GWOOO
Healer!! Maker!! Fighter!!
GWOOO
PAAA

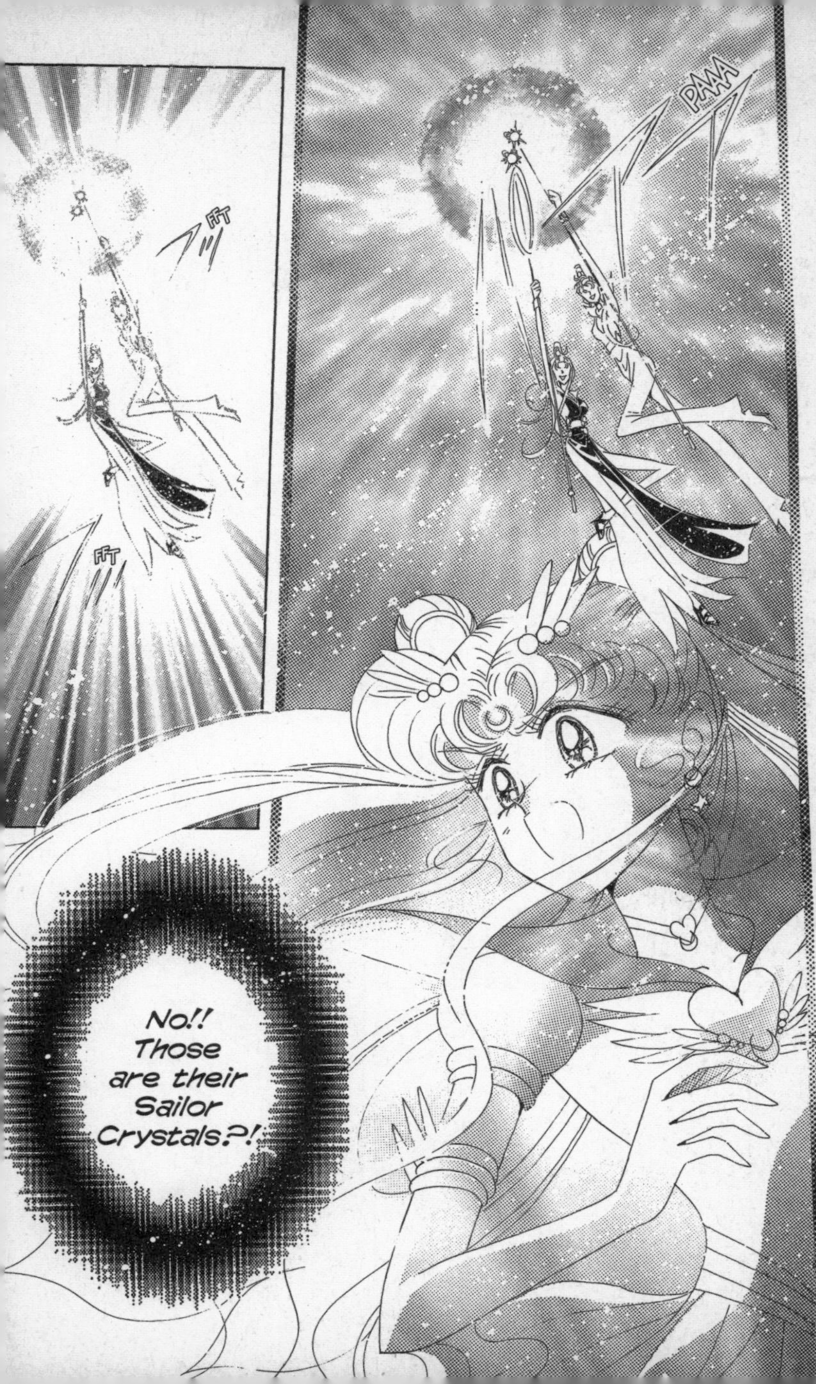
PAAA
FFT
FFT
No!! Those are their Sailor Crystals?!

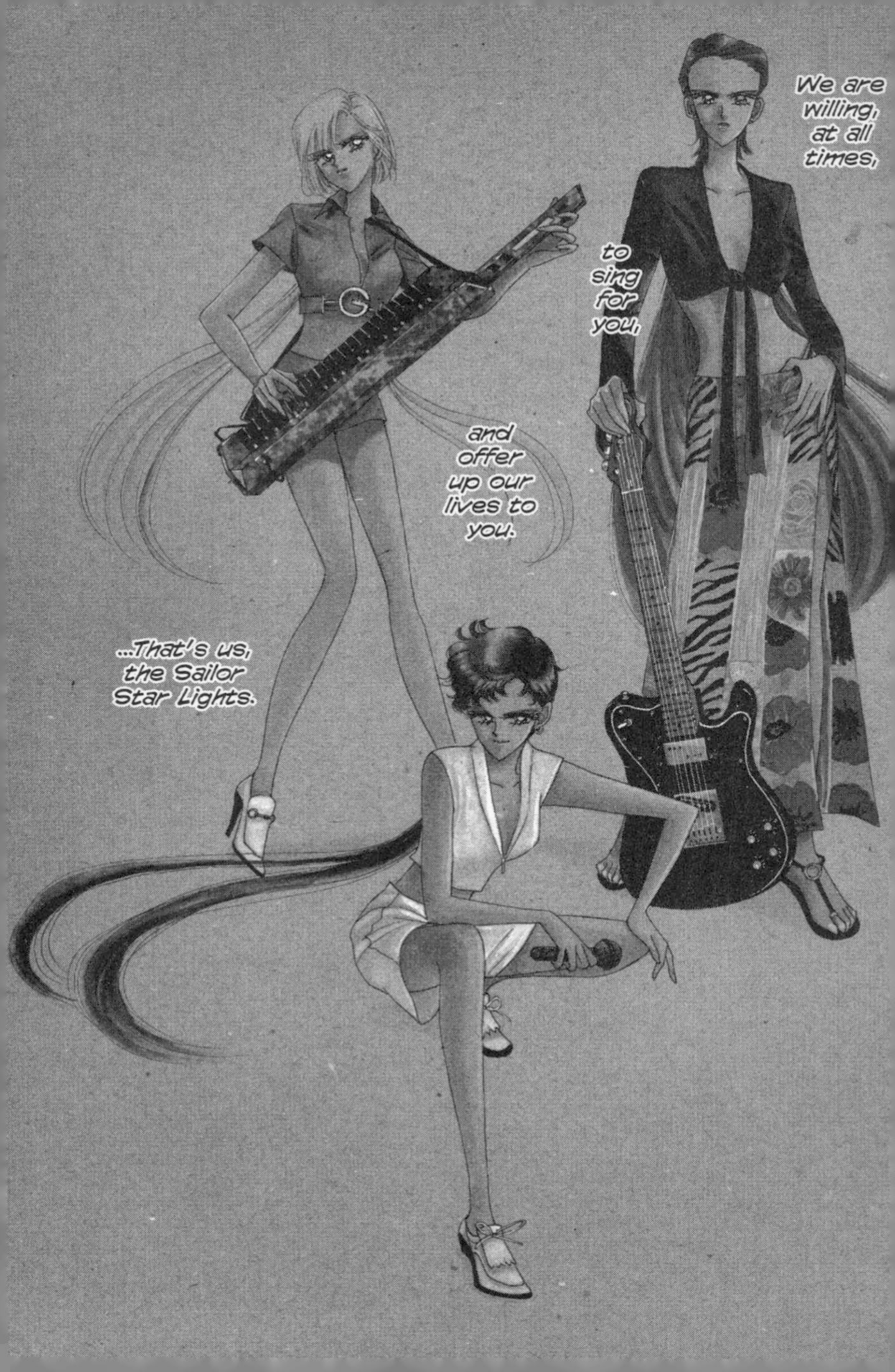
We are willing, at all times,
to sing for you,
and offer up our lives to you.
...That's us, the Sailor Star Lights.

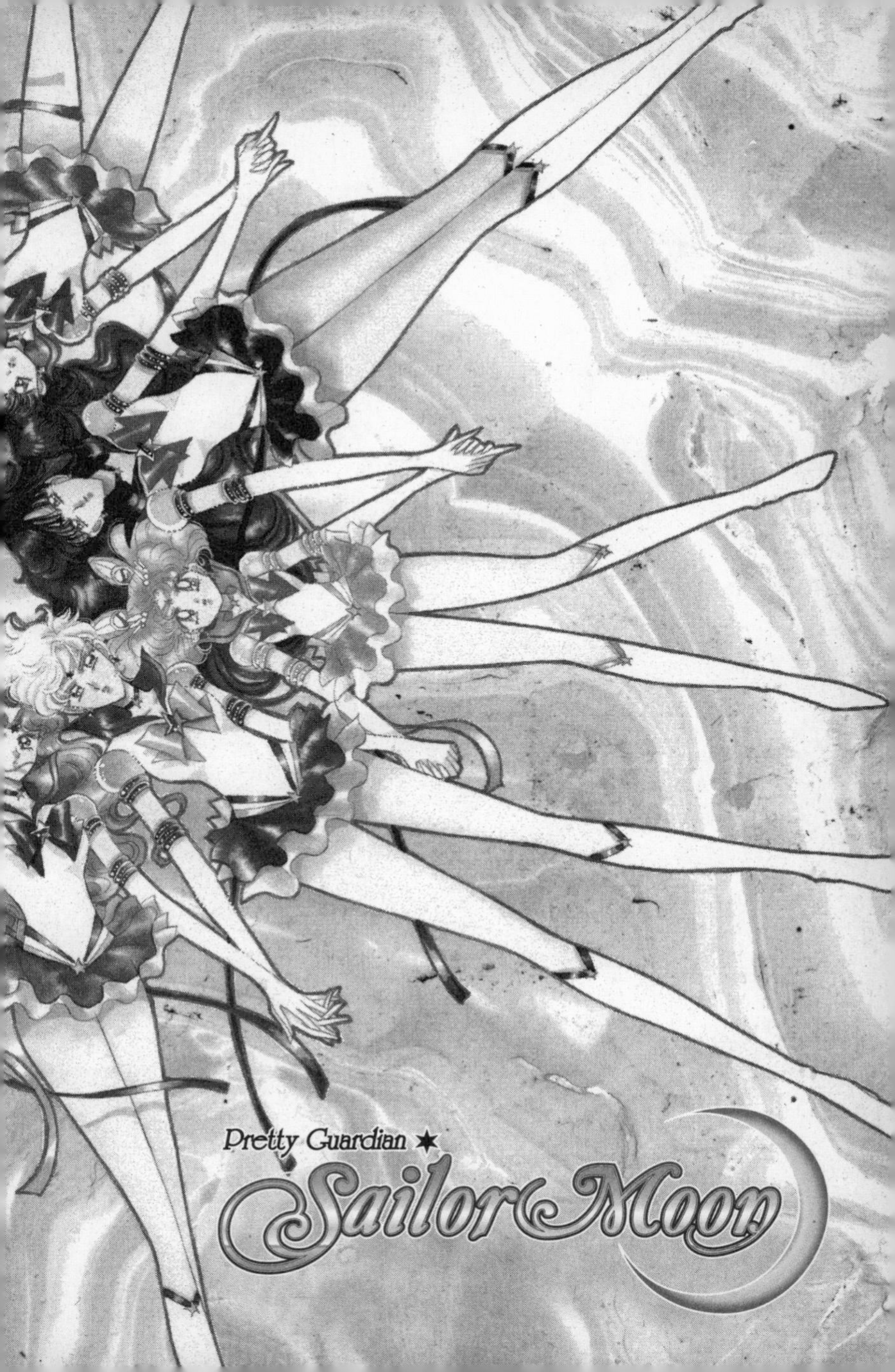
Pretty Guardian ★
Sailor Moon

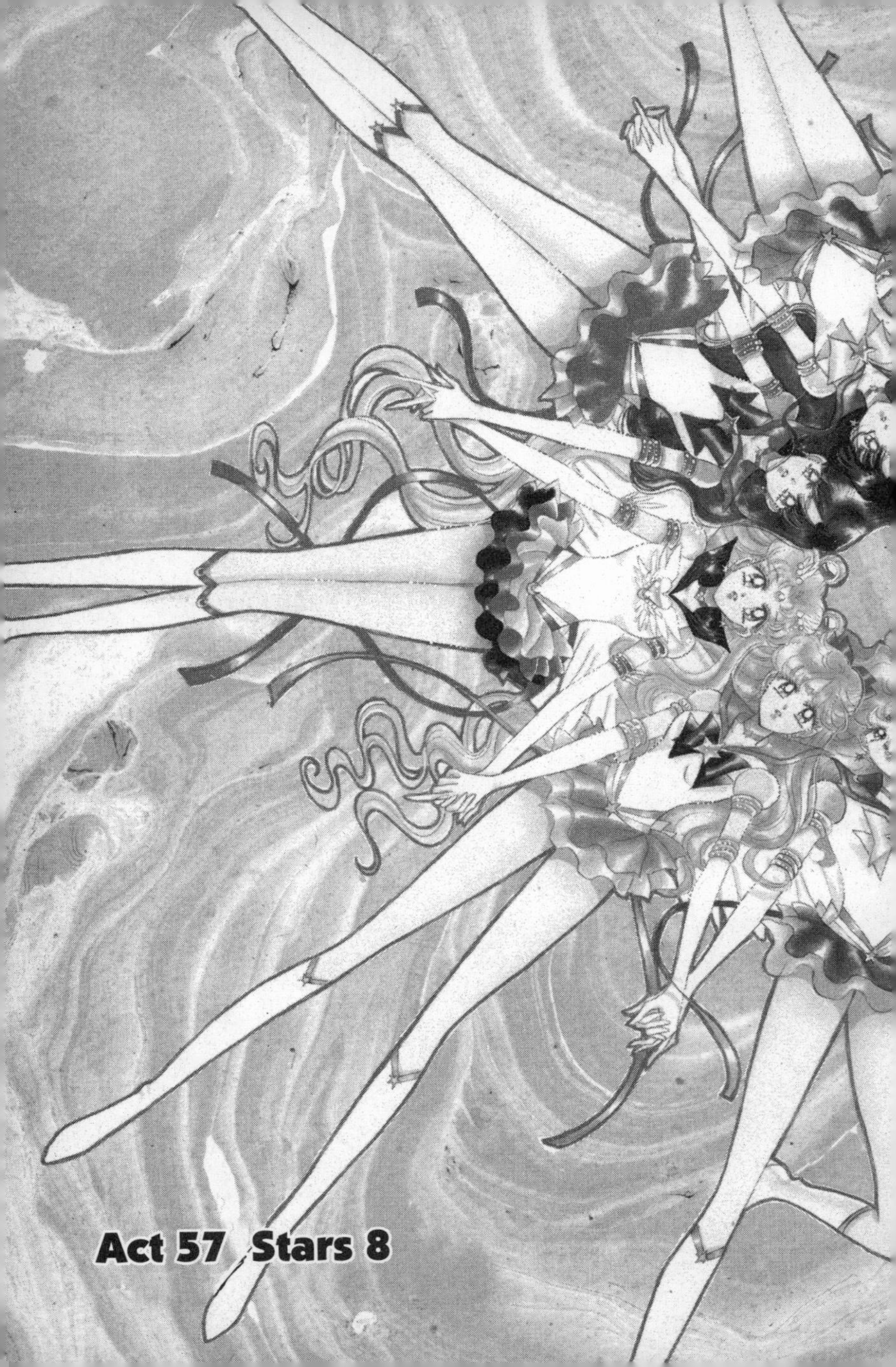

Act 57 Stars 8

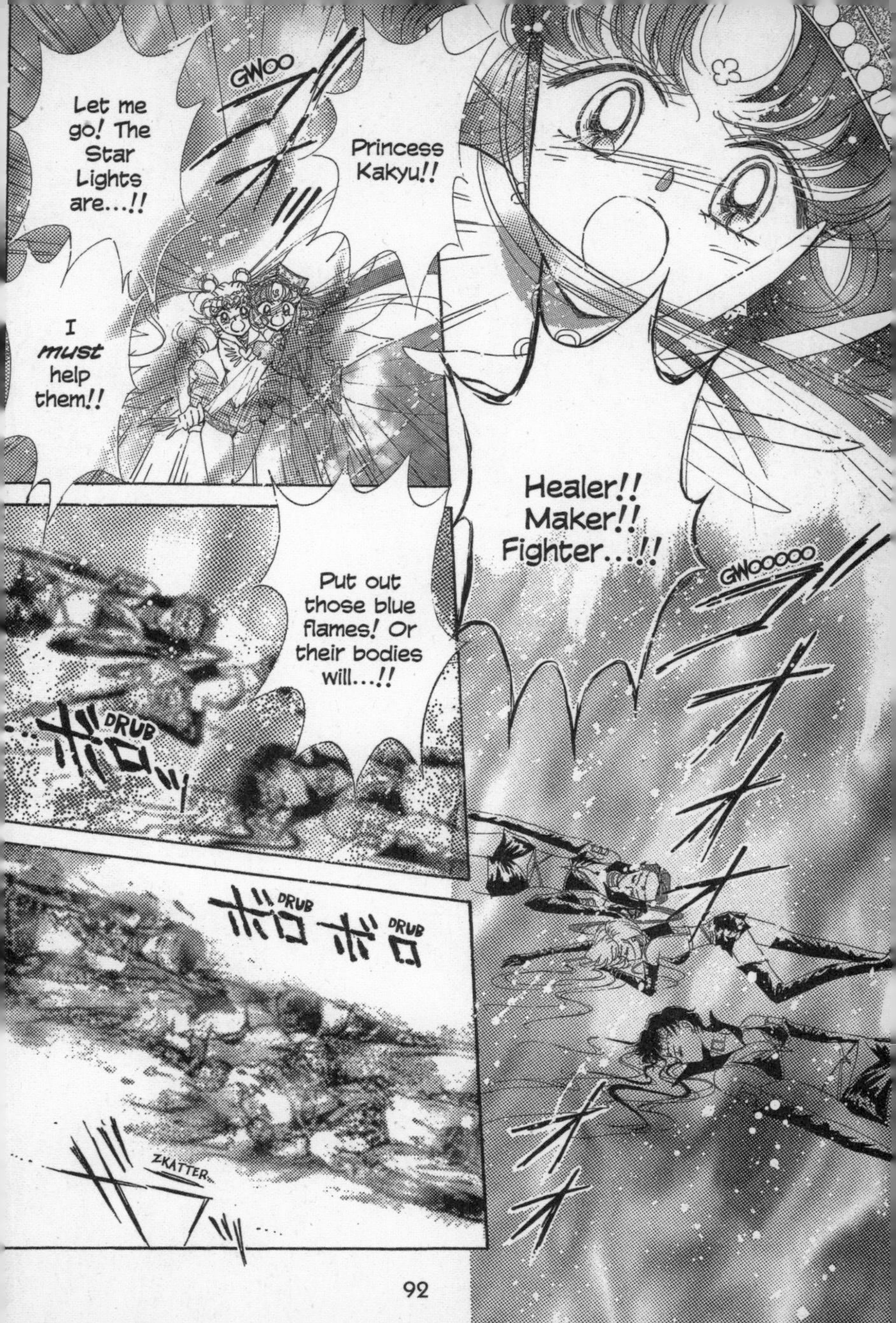

Princess Kakyu!!
GWOO
Let me go! The Star Lights are...!!
I *must* help them!!
Healer!! Maker!! Fighter...!!
GWOOOOO
Put out those blue flames! Or their bodies will...!!
DRUB
DRUB
DRUB
ZKATTER

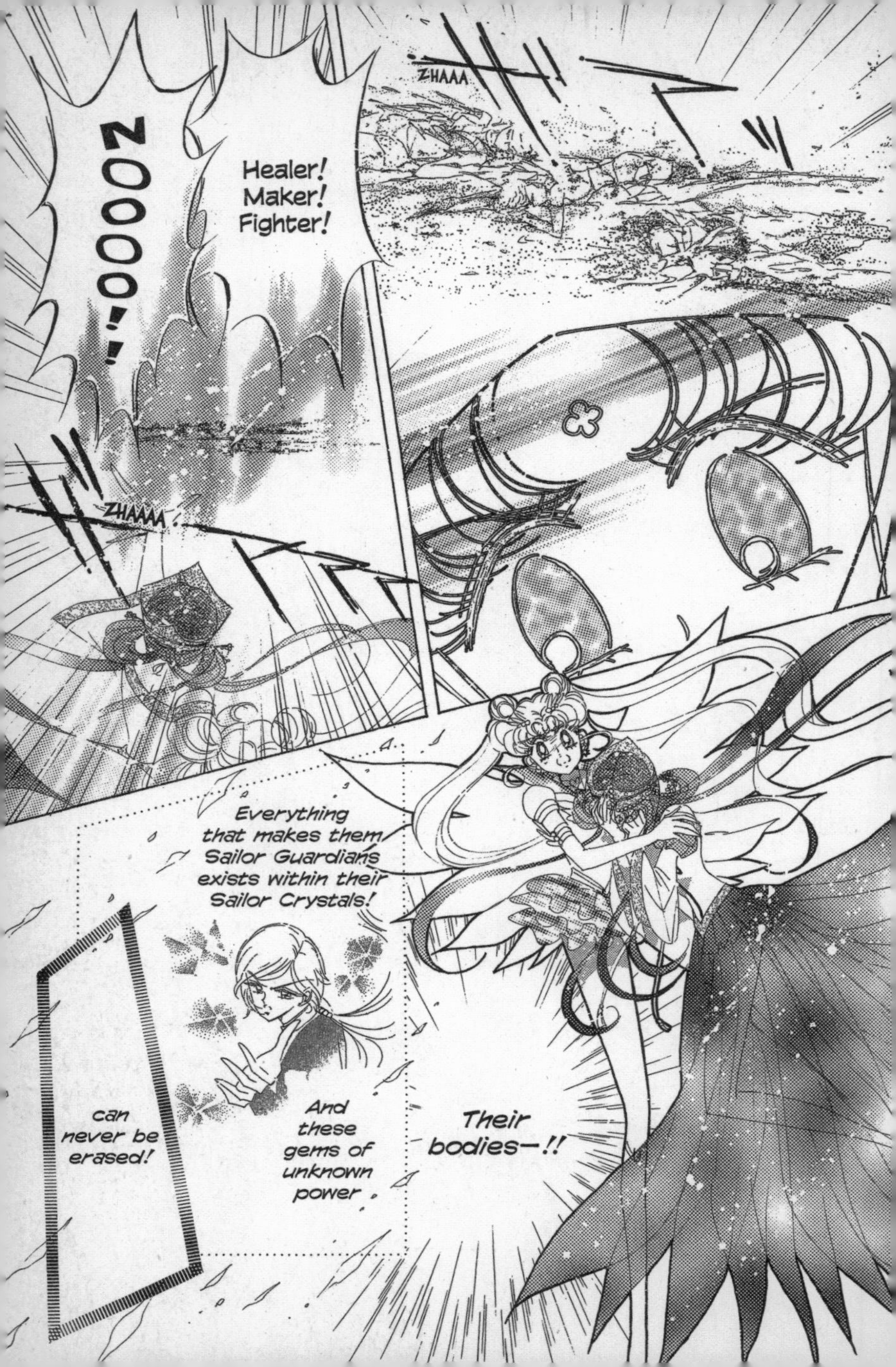
ZHAAA
Healer! Maker! Fighter!
NOOOO!!
ZHAAAA
Their bodies—!!
Everything that makes them Sailor Guardians exists within their Sailor Crystals!
And these gems of unknown power
can never be erased!

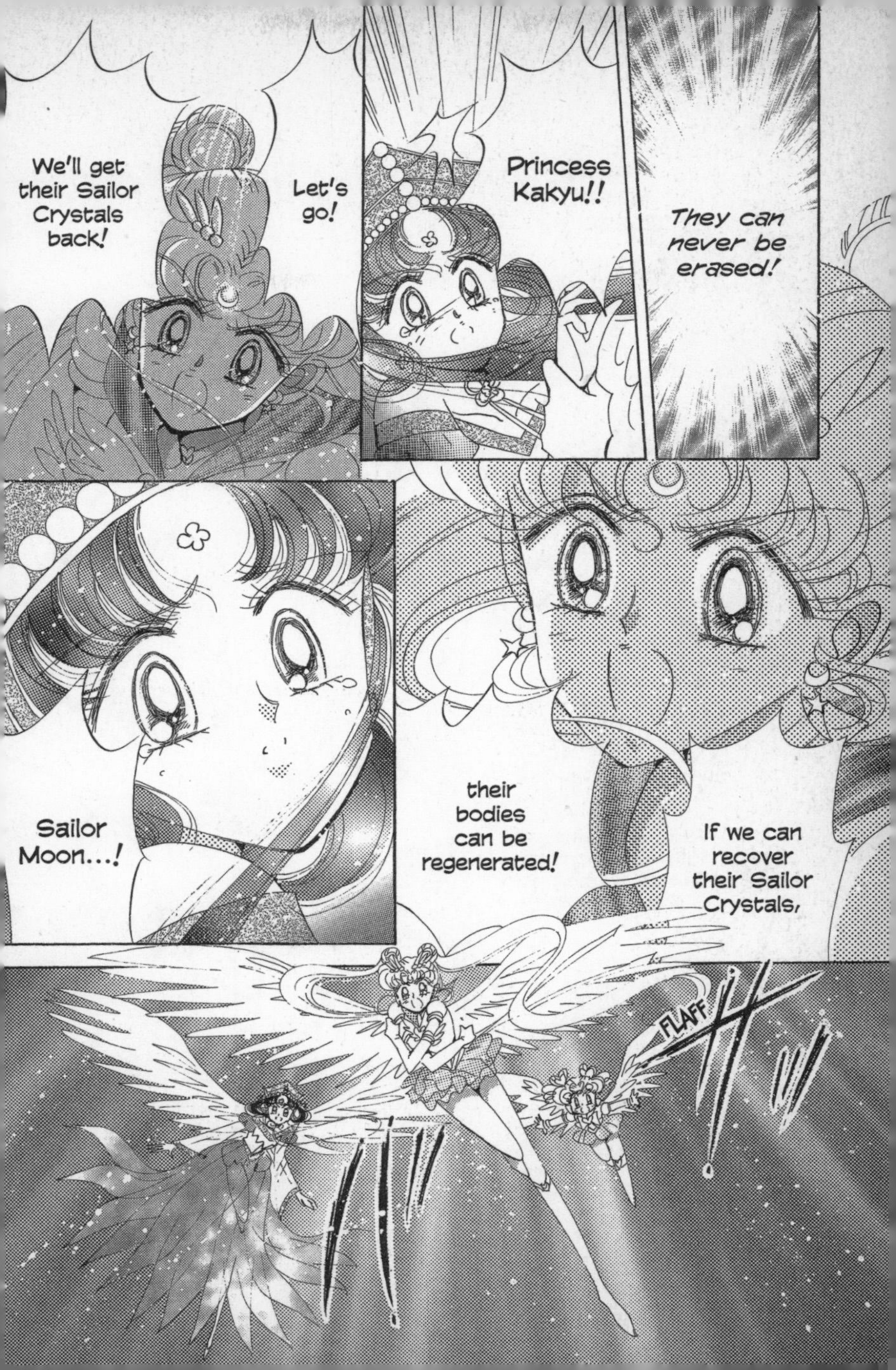
They can never be erased!
Princess Kakyu!!
Let's go!
We'll get their Sailor Crystals back!
If we can recover their Sailor Crystals,
their bodies can be regenerated!
Sailor Moon...!
FLAFF

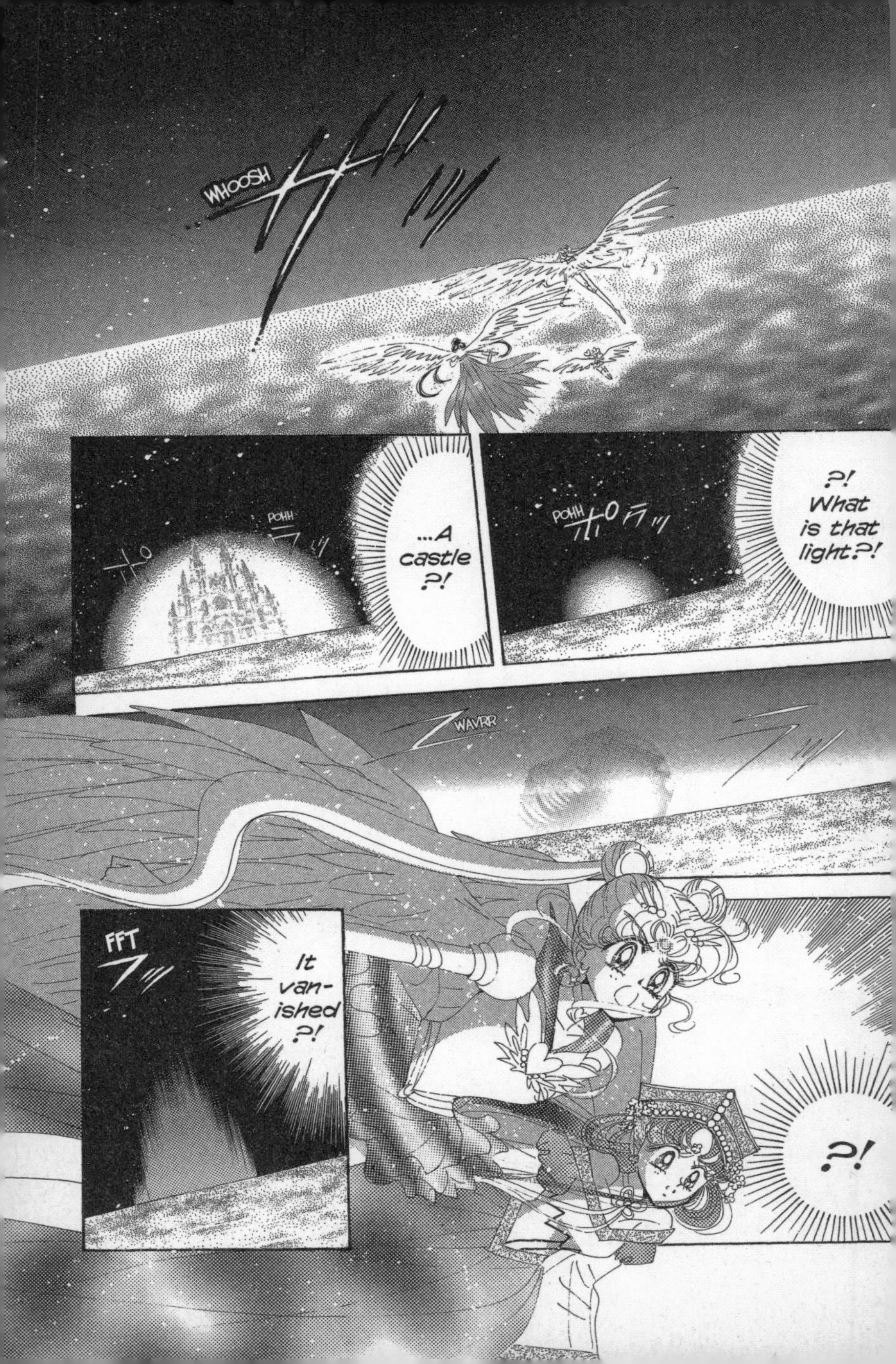
WHOOSH
POHH
?! What is that light?!
POHH
...A castle ?!
WAVRR
?!
FFT
It vanished ?!

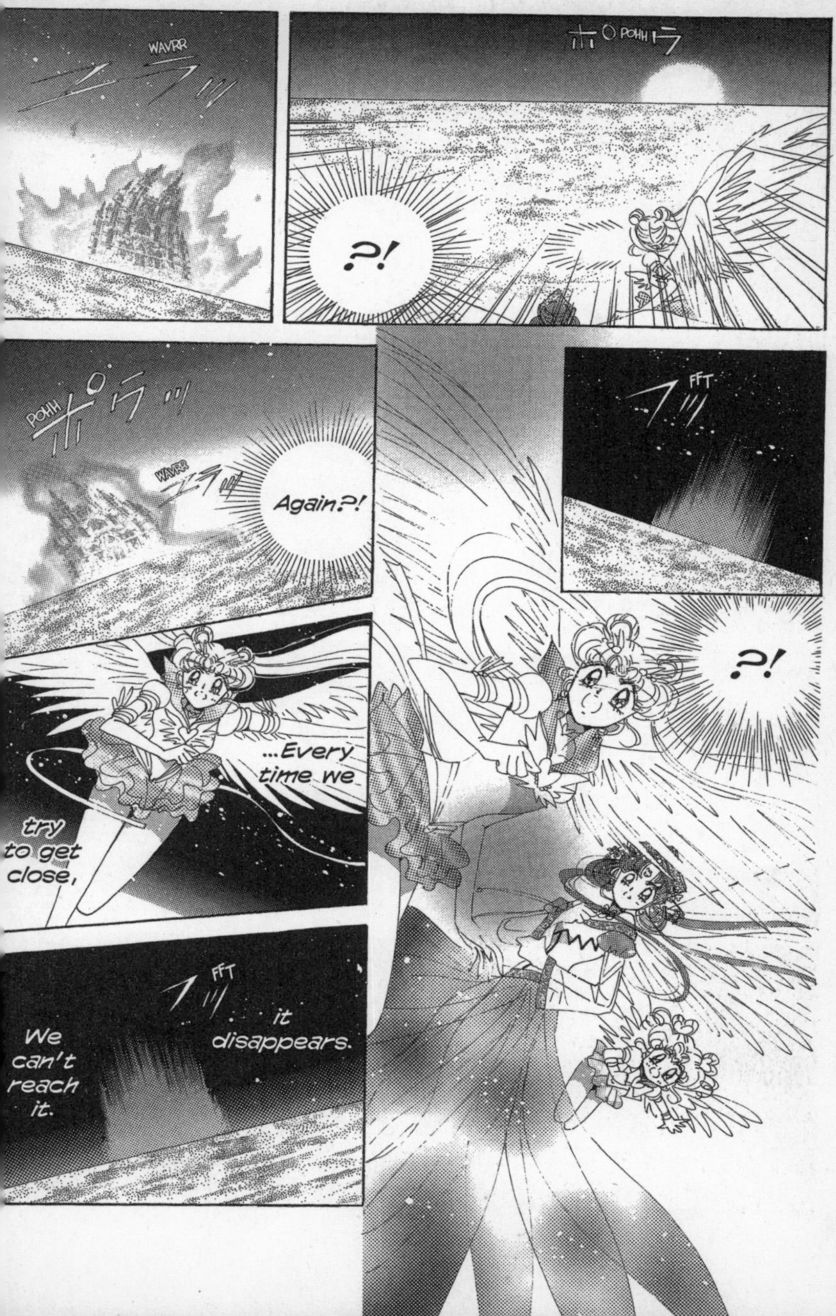
POHH
?!
WAVRR
FFT
?!
POHH
WAVRR
Again?!
...Every time we
try to get close,
FFT
it disappears.
We can't reach it.

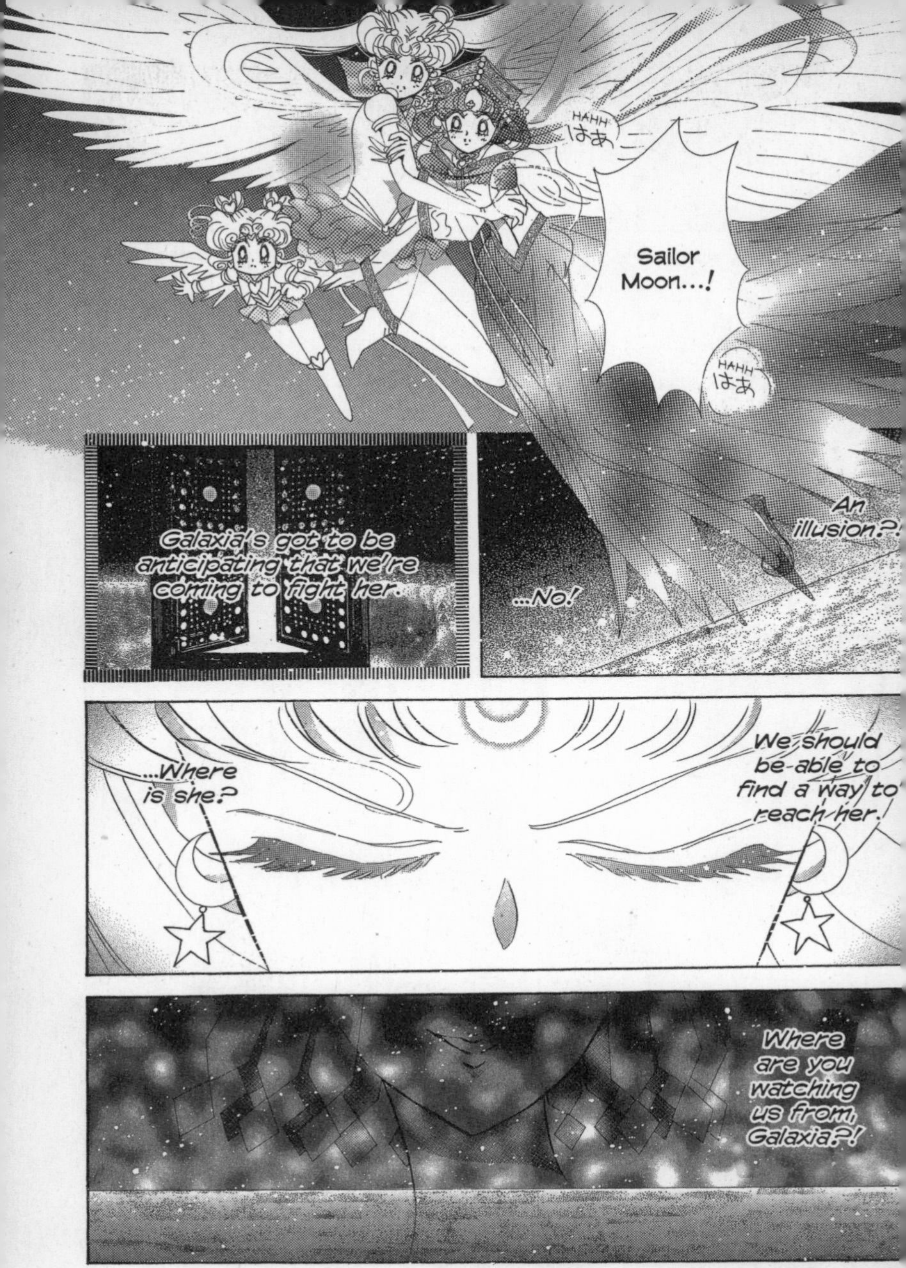
HAHH はあ
Sailor Moon...!
HAHH はあ
An illusion?!
...No!
Galaxia's got to be anticipating that we're coming to fight her.
We should be able to find a way to reach her.
...Where is she?
Where are you watching us from, Galaxia?!

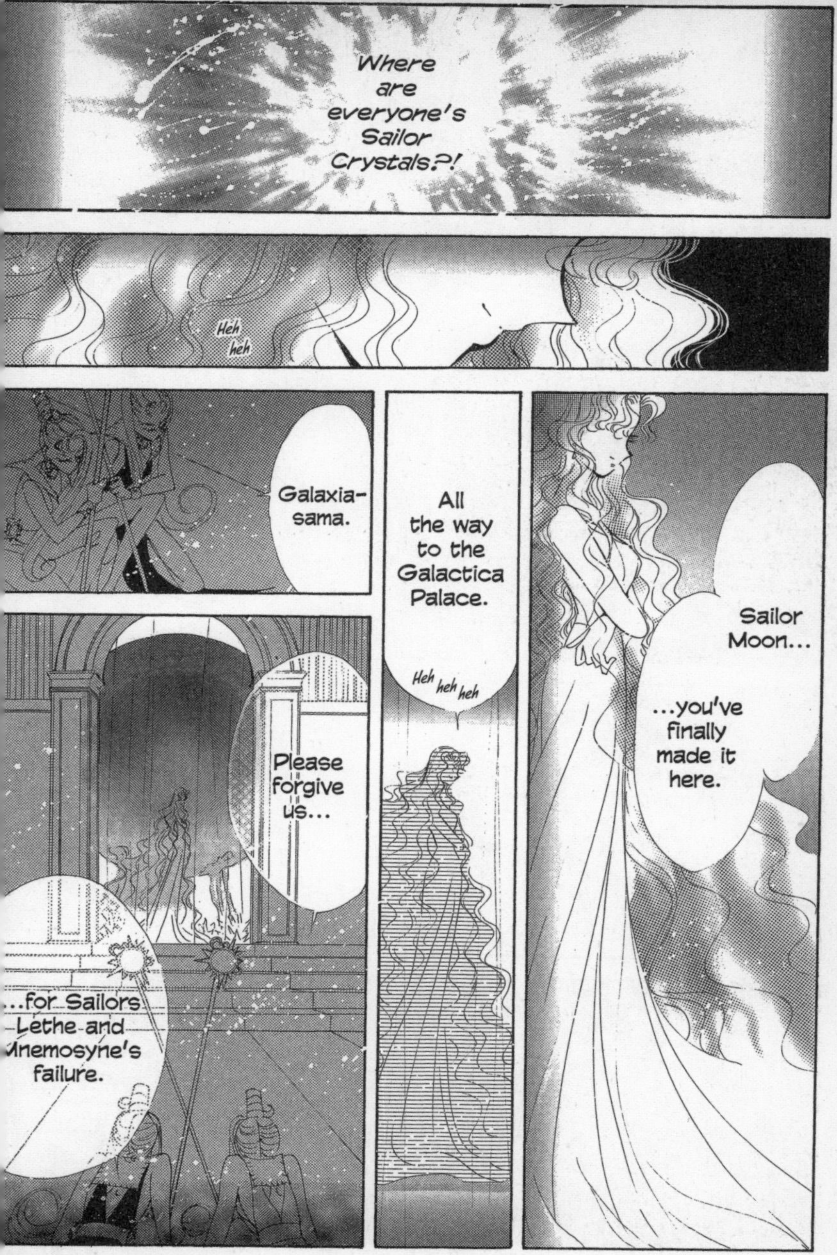
Where are everyone's Sailor Crystals?!
Heh heh
Sailor Moon...
...you've finally made it here.
All the way to the Galactica Palace.
Heh heh heh
Galaxia-sama.
Please forgive us...
...for Sailors Lethe and Mnemosyne's failure.

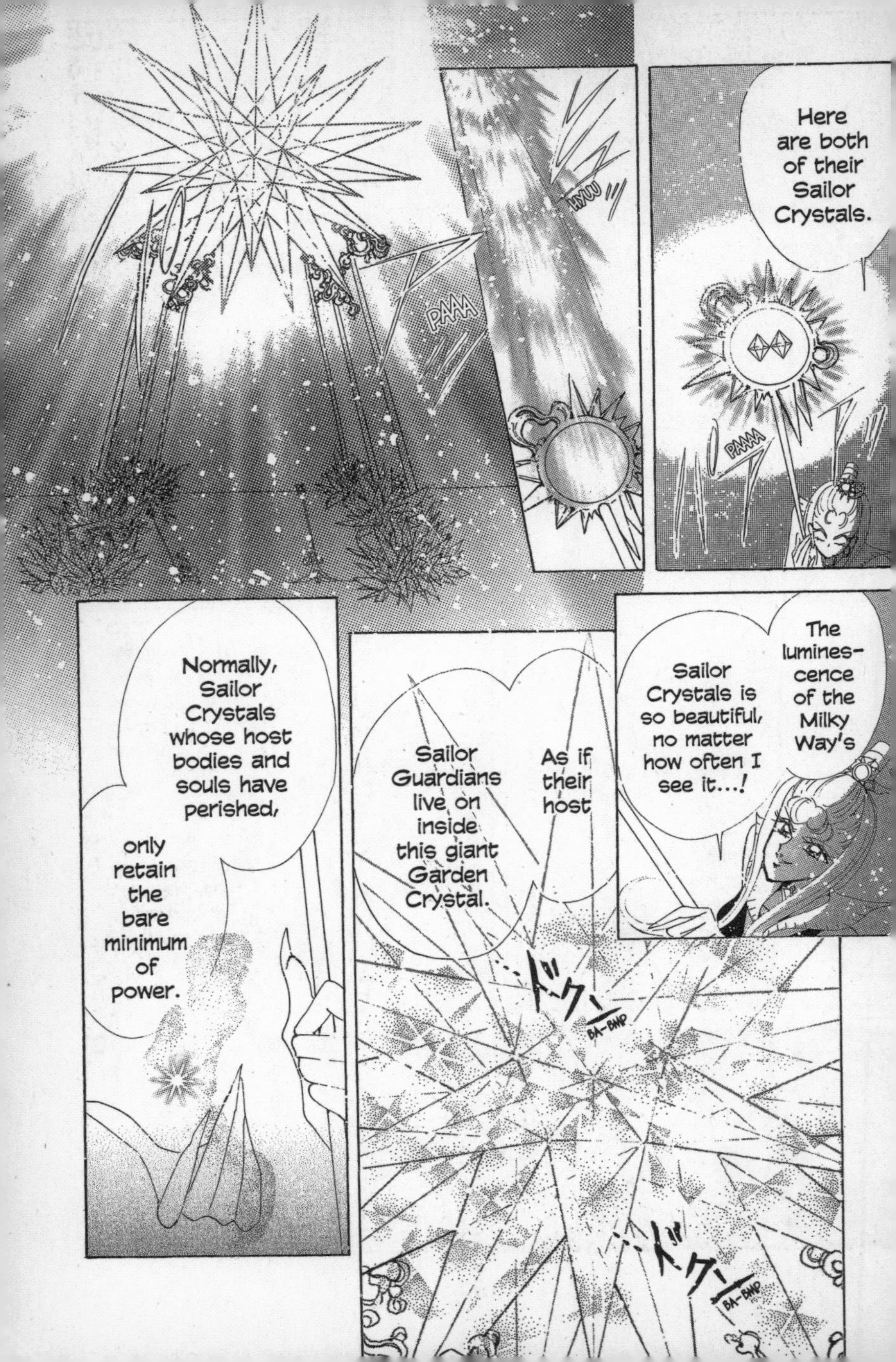

Here are both of their Sailor Crystals.
PAAAA
HYUU
PAAA
The luminescence of the Milky Way's Sailor Crystals is so beautiful, no matter how often I see it...!
As if their host Sailor Guardians live on inside this giant Garden Crystal.
BA-BMP
BA-BMP
Normally, Sailor Crystals whose host bodies and souls have perished,
only retain the bare minimum of power.

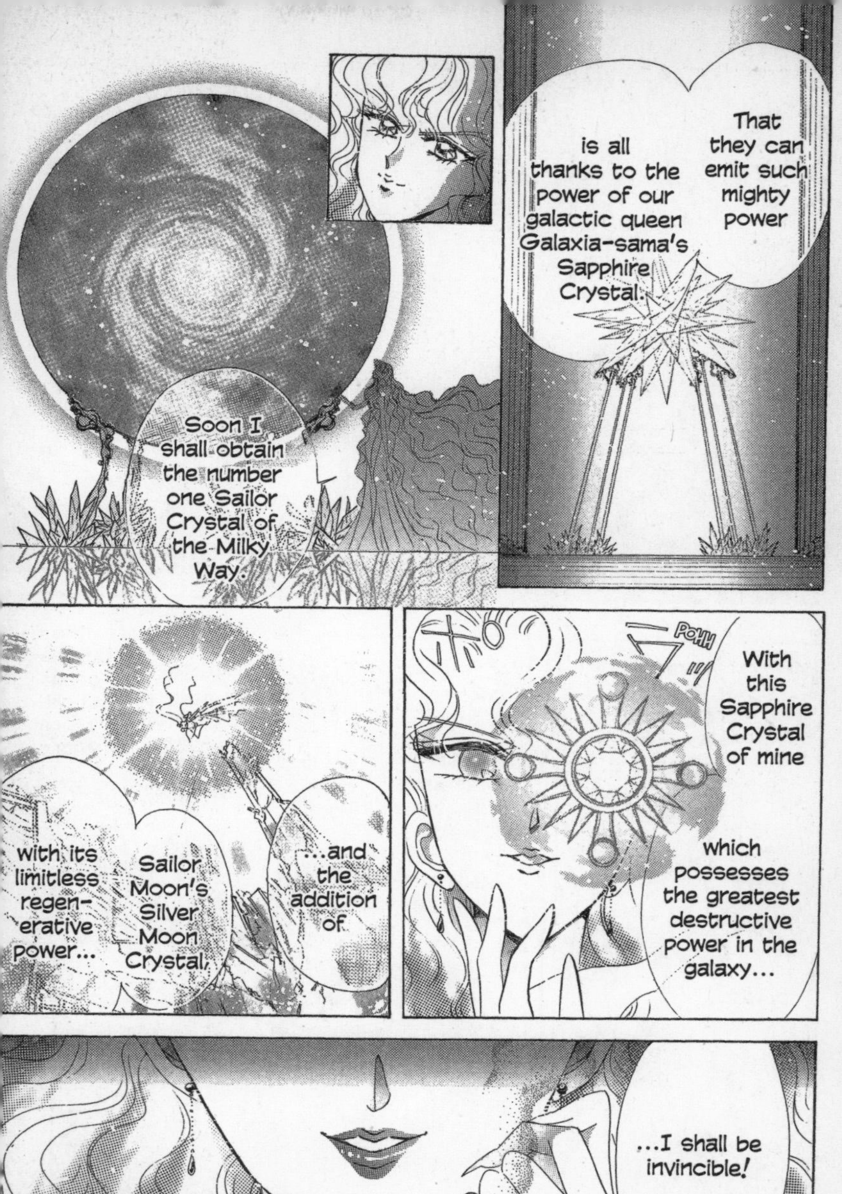
That they can emit such mighty power
is all thanks to the power of our galactic queen Galaxia-sama's Sapphire Crystal.
Soon I shall obtain the number one Sailor Crystal of the Milky Way.
POHH
With this Sapphire Crystal of mine
which possesses the greatest destructive power in the galaxy...
...and the addition of
Sailor Moon's Silver Moon Crystal,
with its limitless regen-erative power...
...I shall be invincible!

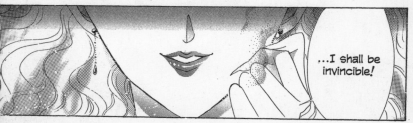

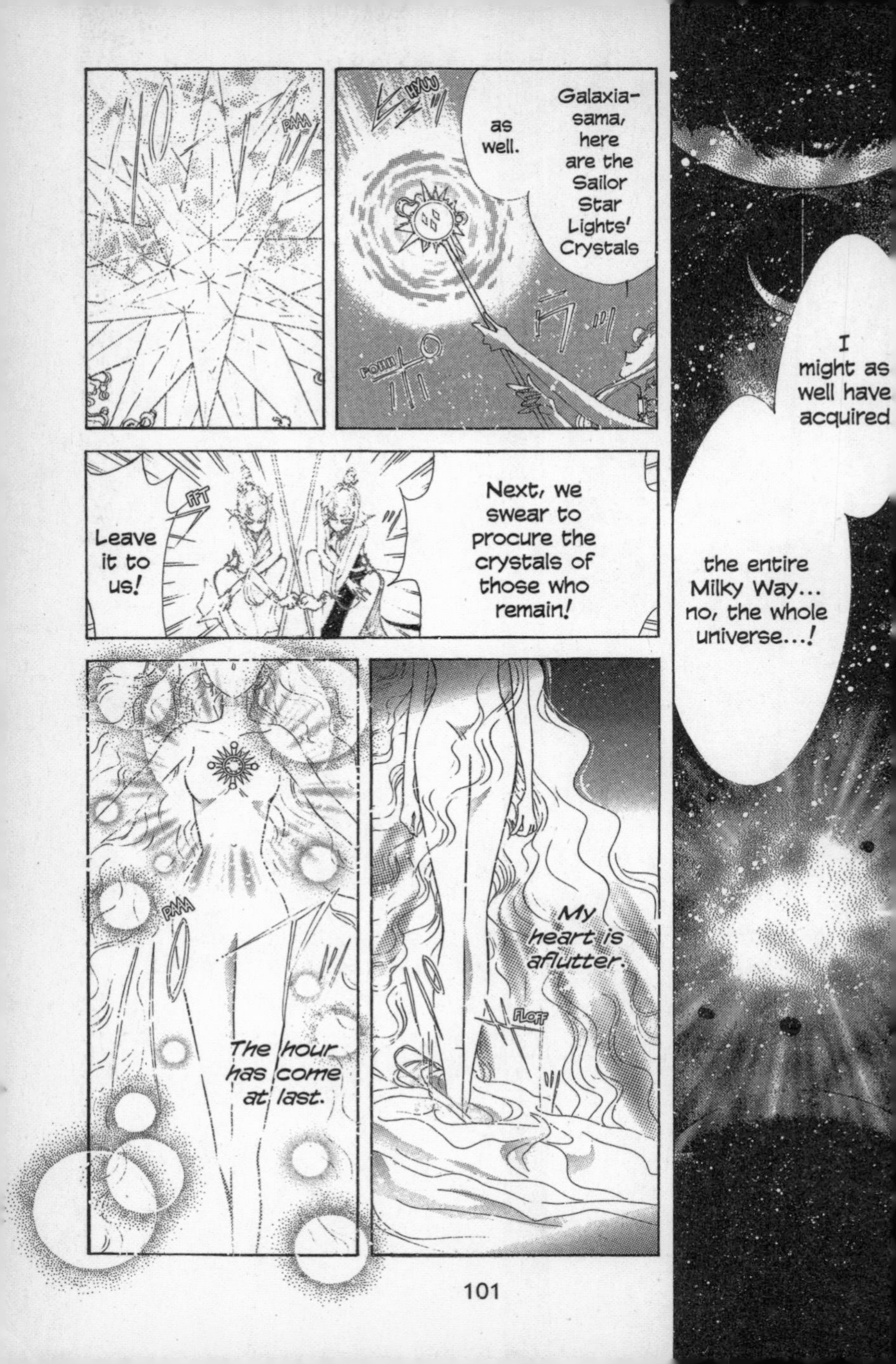
I might as well have acquired
the entire Milky Way… no, the whole universe…!
HYUU
Galaxia-sama, here are the Sailor Star Lights' Crystals
as well.
POHH
PAAA
Next, we swear to procure the crystals of those who remain!
FFT
Leave it to us!
My heart is aflutter.
FLOFF
PAAA
The hour has come at last.

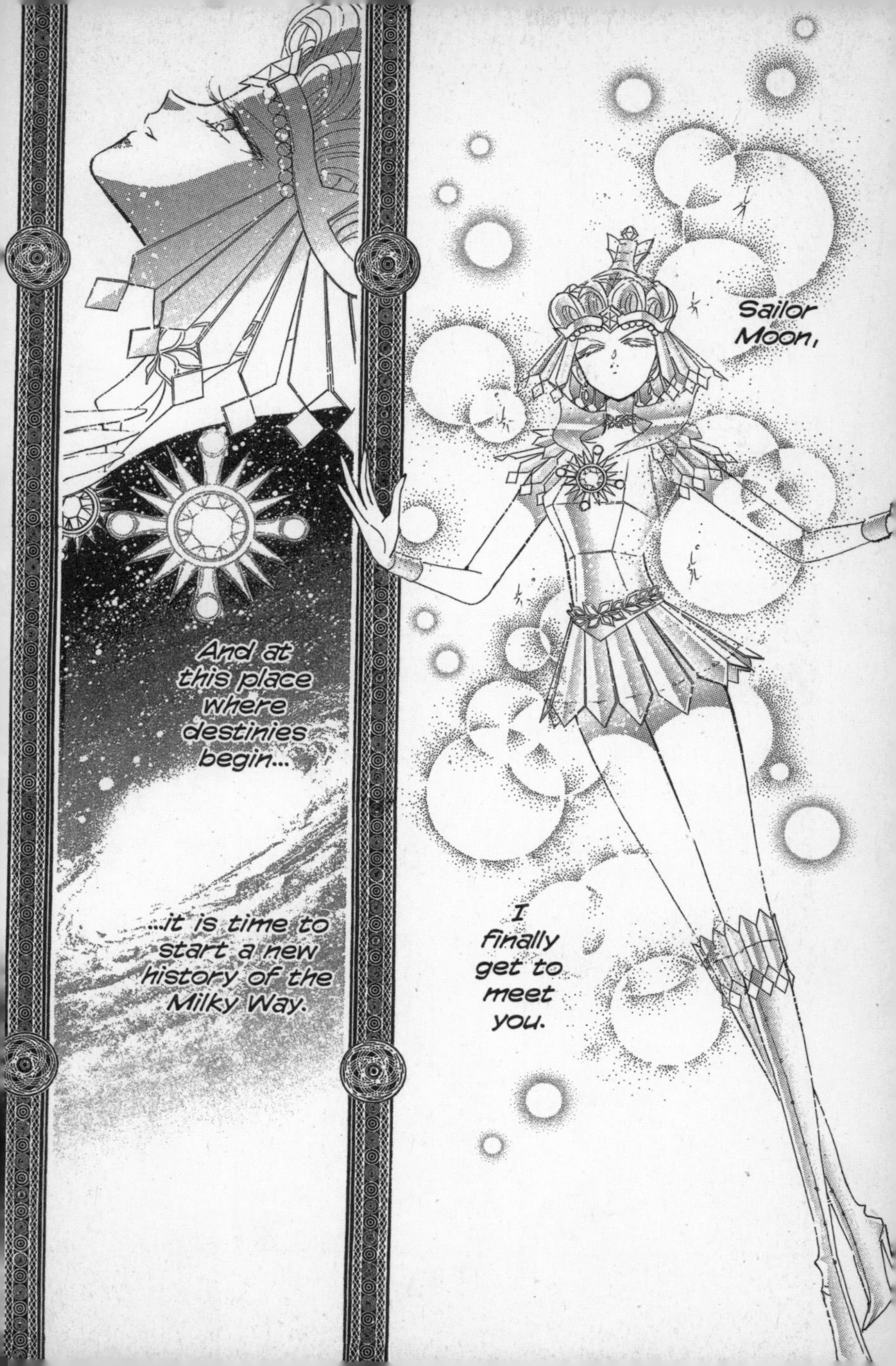
Sailor Moon,
I finally get to meet you.
And at this place where destinies begin...
...it is time to start a new history of the Milky Way.

The much anticipated moment

has arrived at last.

Chaos-sama.

The time has finally come, eh.

Ahhh...

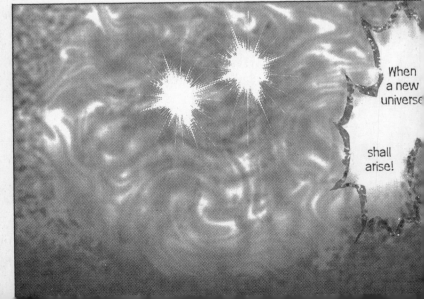

When a new universe

shall arise!

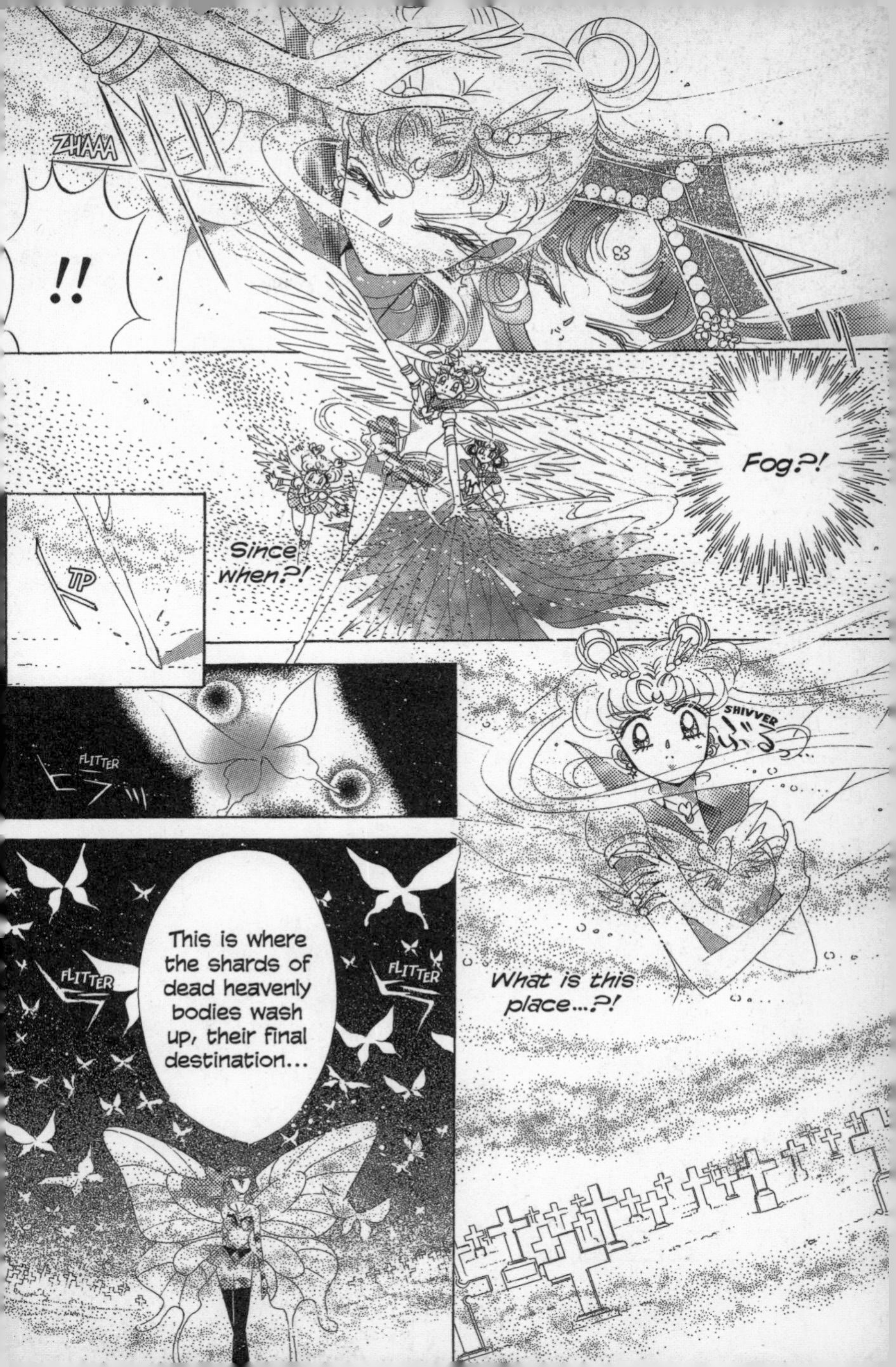
ZHAAA
!!
Fog?!
Since when?!
TP
SHIVVER
What is this place...?!
FLITTER
This is where the shards of dead heavenly bodies wash up, their final destination...
FLITTER
FLITTER

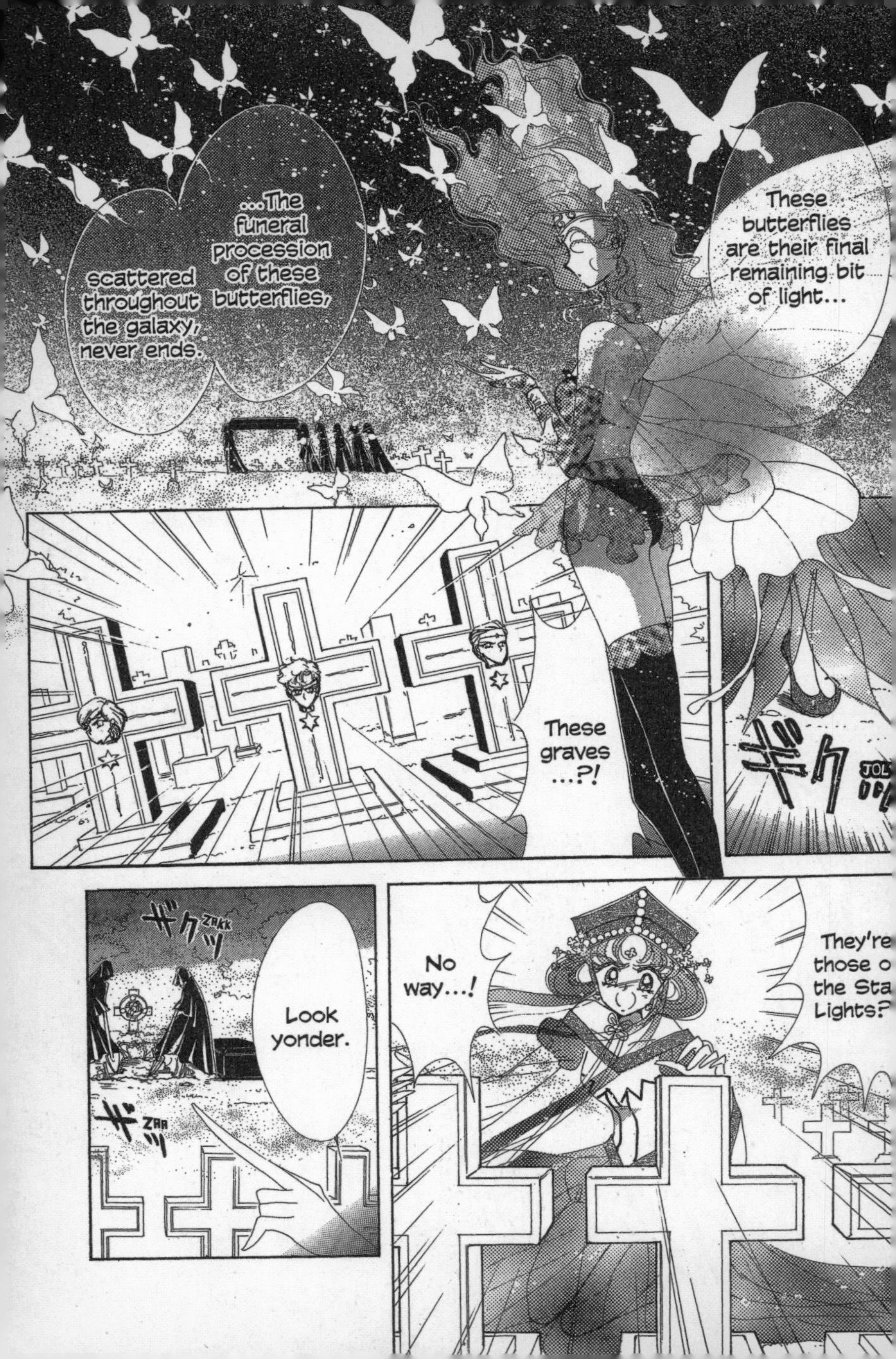

These butterflies are their final remaining bit of light...
...The funeral procession of these butterflies,
scattered throughout the galaxy, never ends.
JOL
These graves ...?!
They're those o the Sta Lights?
No way...!
ZAKK
Look yonder.
ZAA

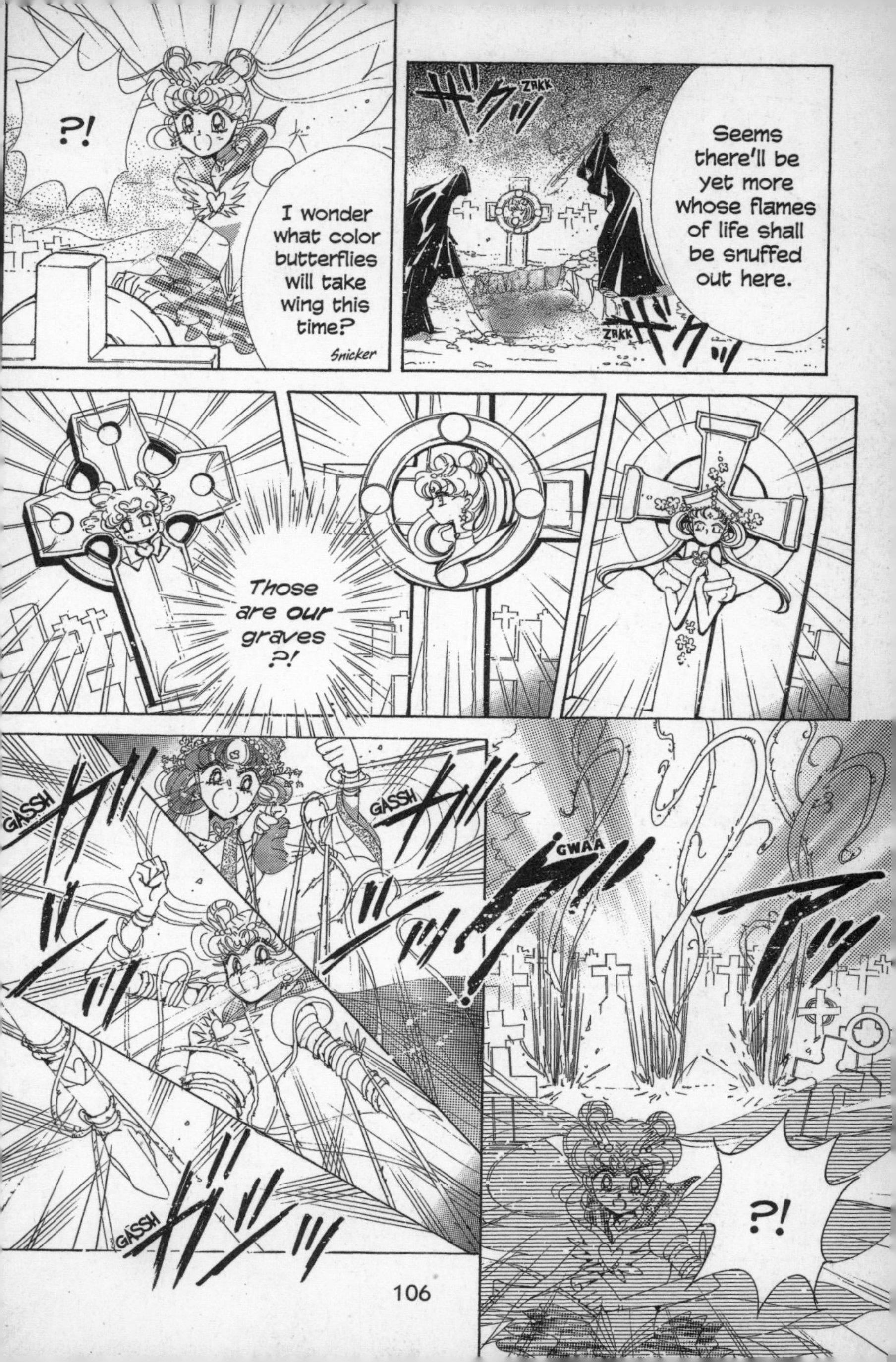
ZAKK
Seems there'll be yet more whose flames of life shall be snuffed out here.
ZAKK
?!
I wonder what color butterflies will take wing this time?
Snicker
Those are our graves ?!
GWAA
?!
GASSH
GASSH
GASSH

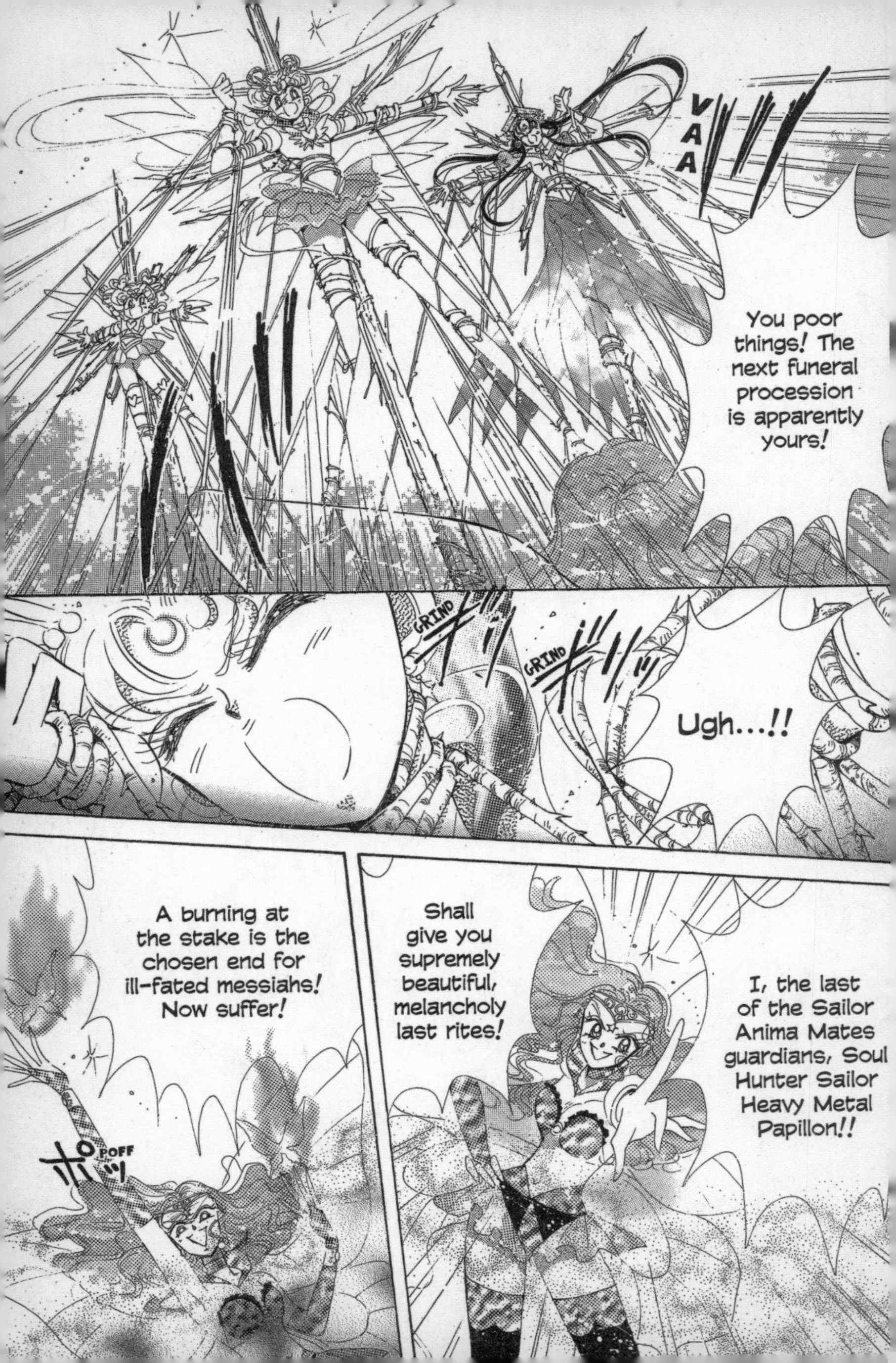
VAA
You poor things! The next funeral procession is apparently yours!
Ugh...!!
GRIND
GRIND
I, the last of the Sailor Anima Mates guardians, Soul Hunter Sailor Heavy Metal Papillon!!
Shall give you supremely beautiful, melancholy last rites!
A burning at the stake is the chosen end for ill-fated messiahs! Now suffer!
POFF

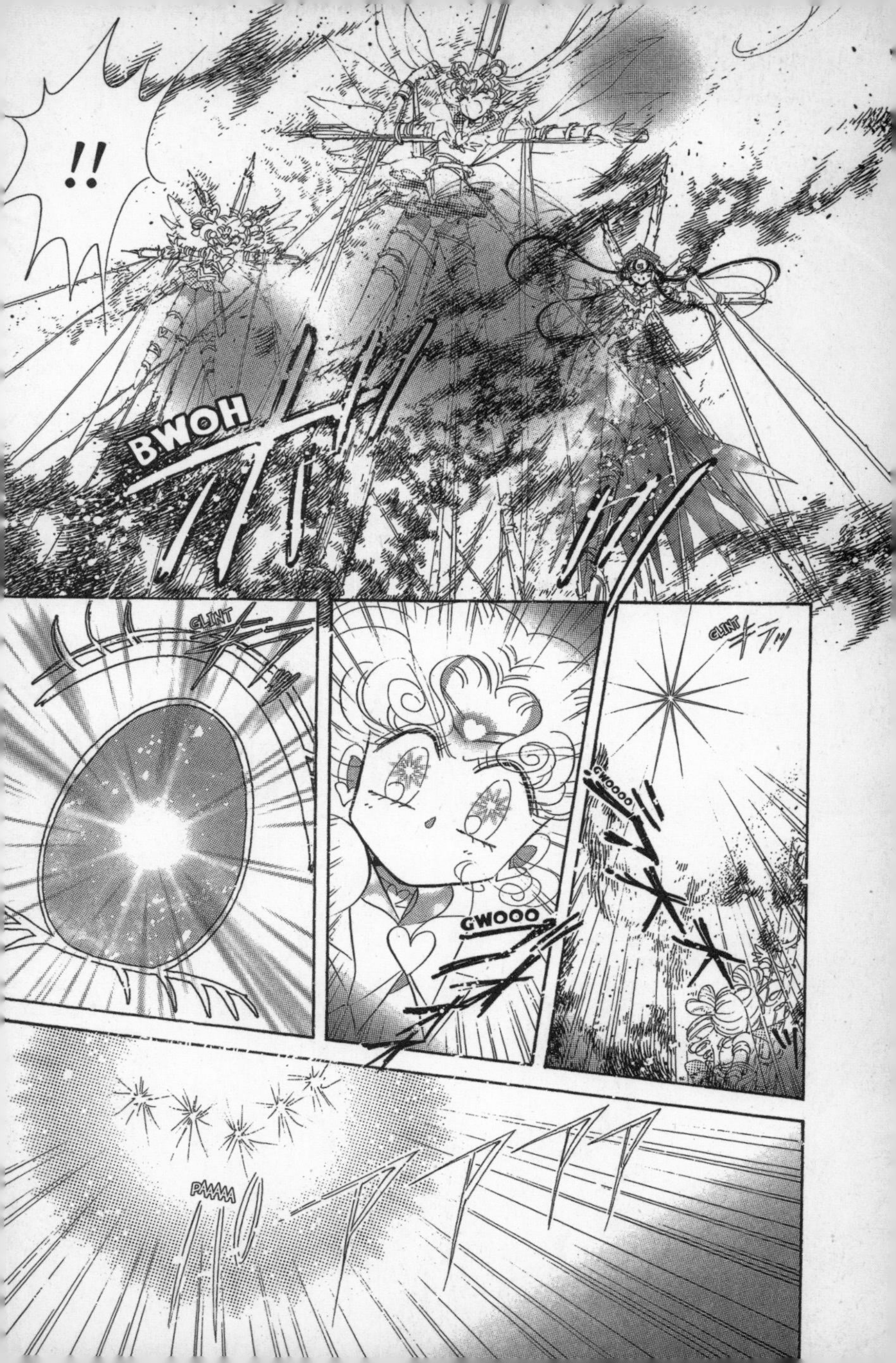

!!
BWOH
GLINT
GWOOOO
GWOOO
GLINT
PAAAA

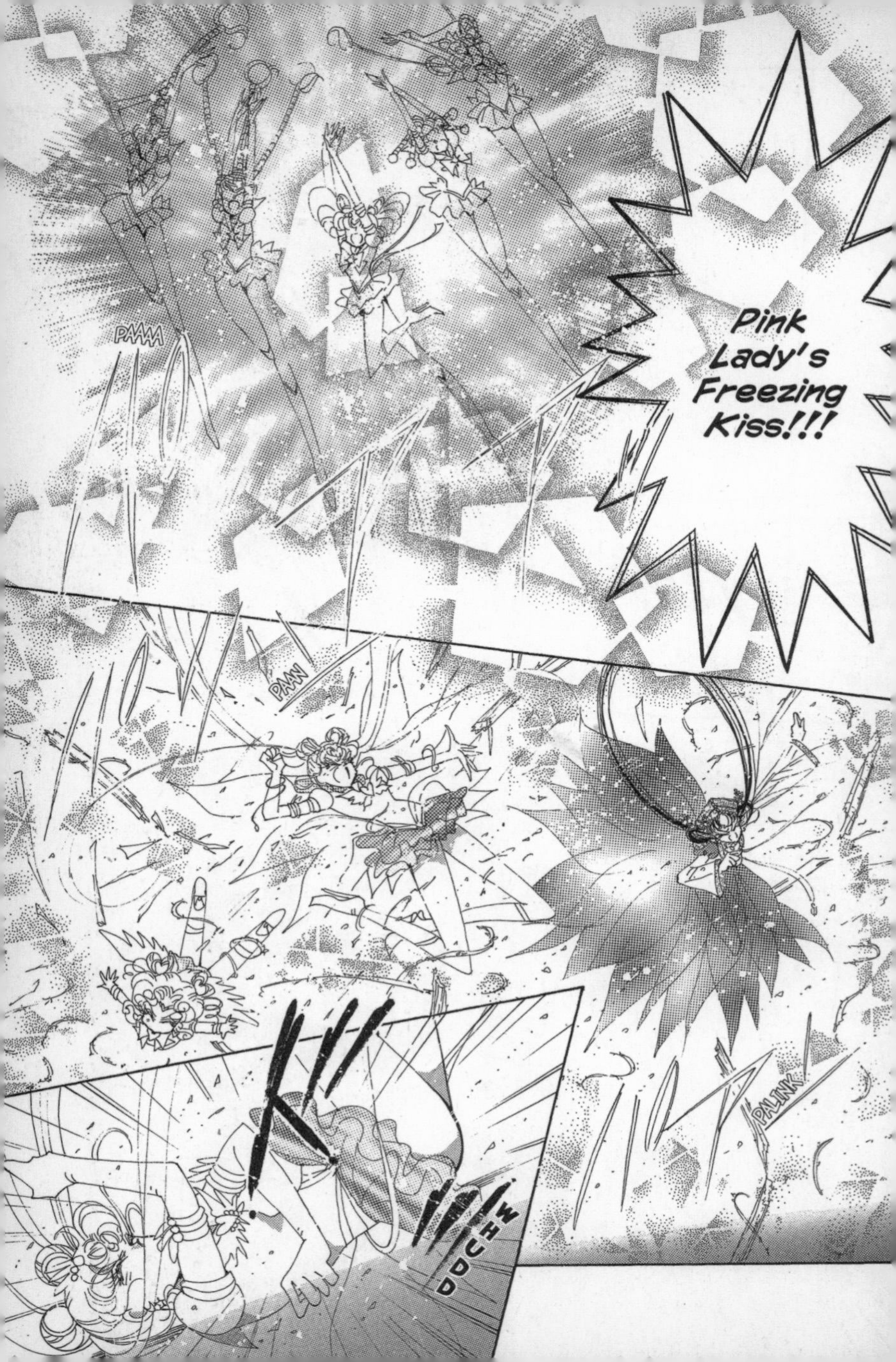
Pink Lady's Freezing Kiss!!!
PAAAA
PAAN
PALINK
WHUDD

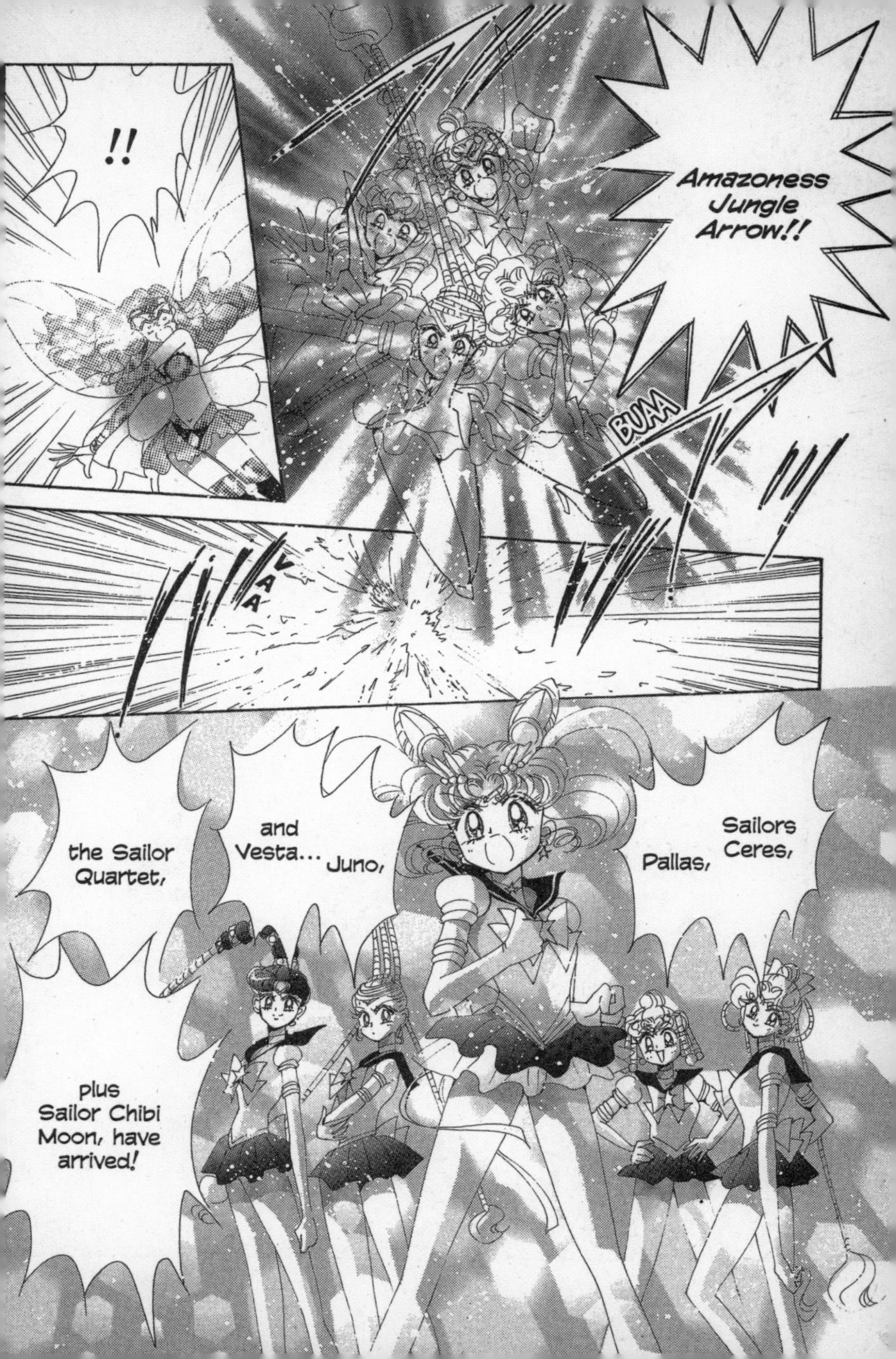
Amazoness Jungle Arrow!!
BUAA
!!
VAA
Sailors Ceres,
Pallas,
Juno,
and Vesta...
the Sailor Quartet,
plus Sailor Chibi Moon, have arrived!

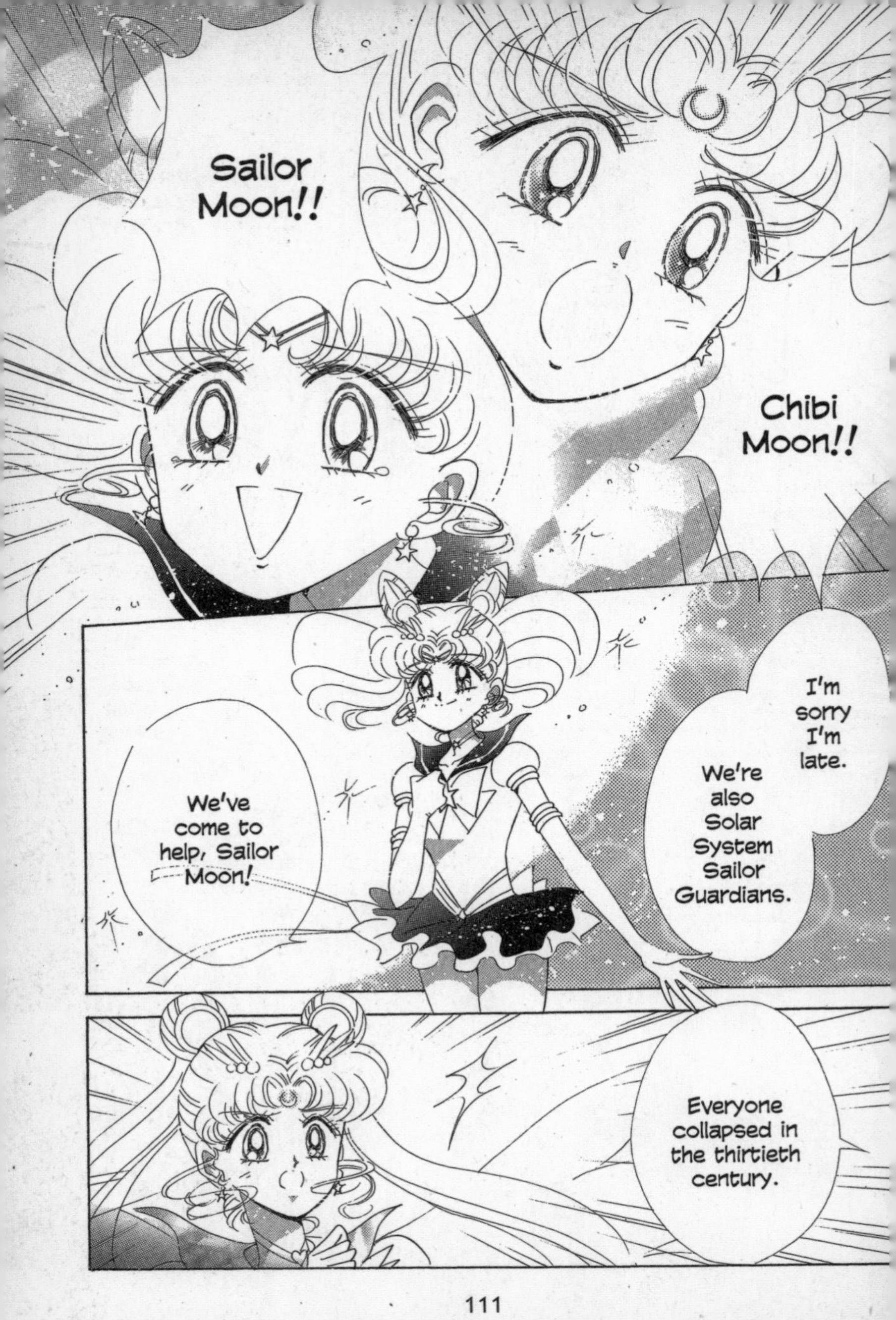
Chibi Moon!!
Sailor Moon!!
I'm sorry I'm late.
We're also Solar System Sailor Guardians.
We've come to help, Sailor Moon!
Everyone collapsed in the thirtieth century.

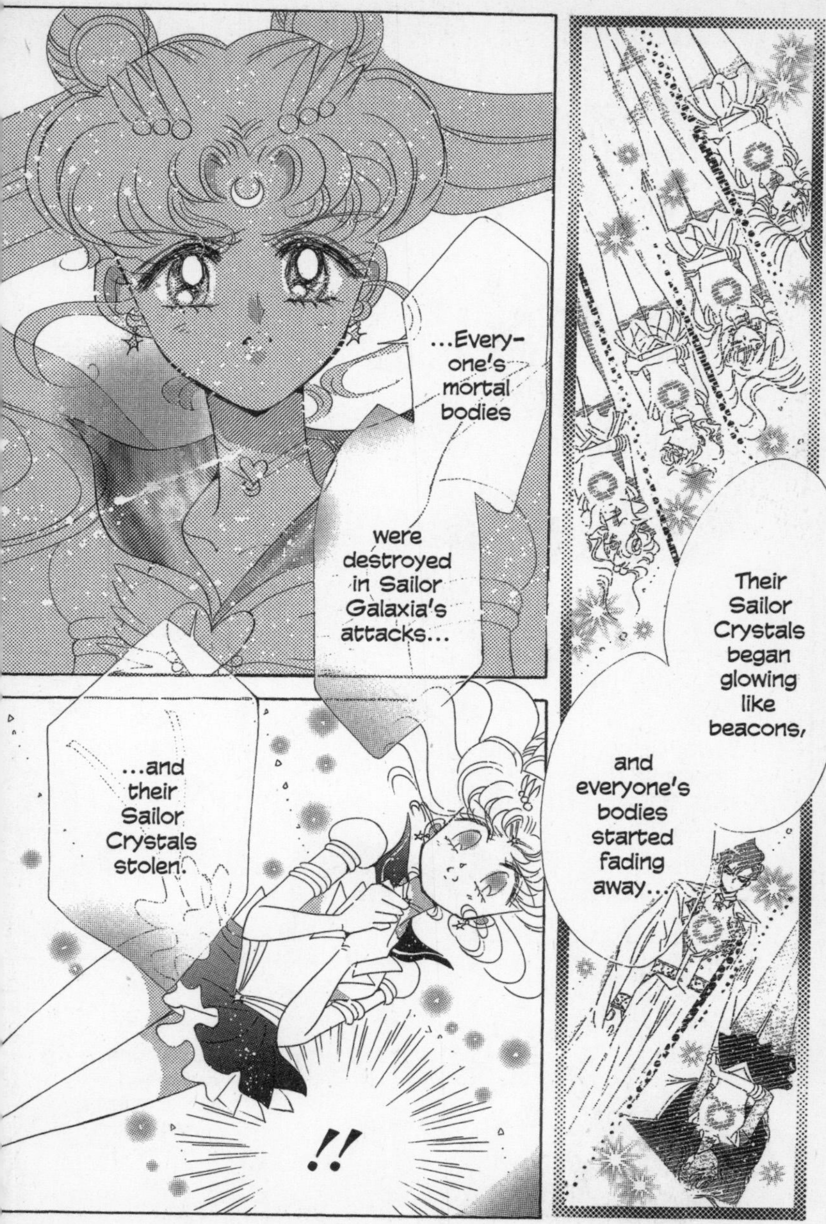
Their Sailor Crystals began glowing like beacons,
and everyone's bodies started fading away...
...Every-one's mortal bodies
were destroyed in Sailor Galaxia's attacks...
...and their Sailor Crystals stolen.
!!

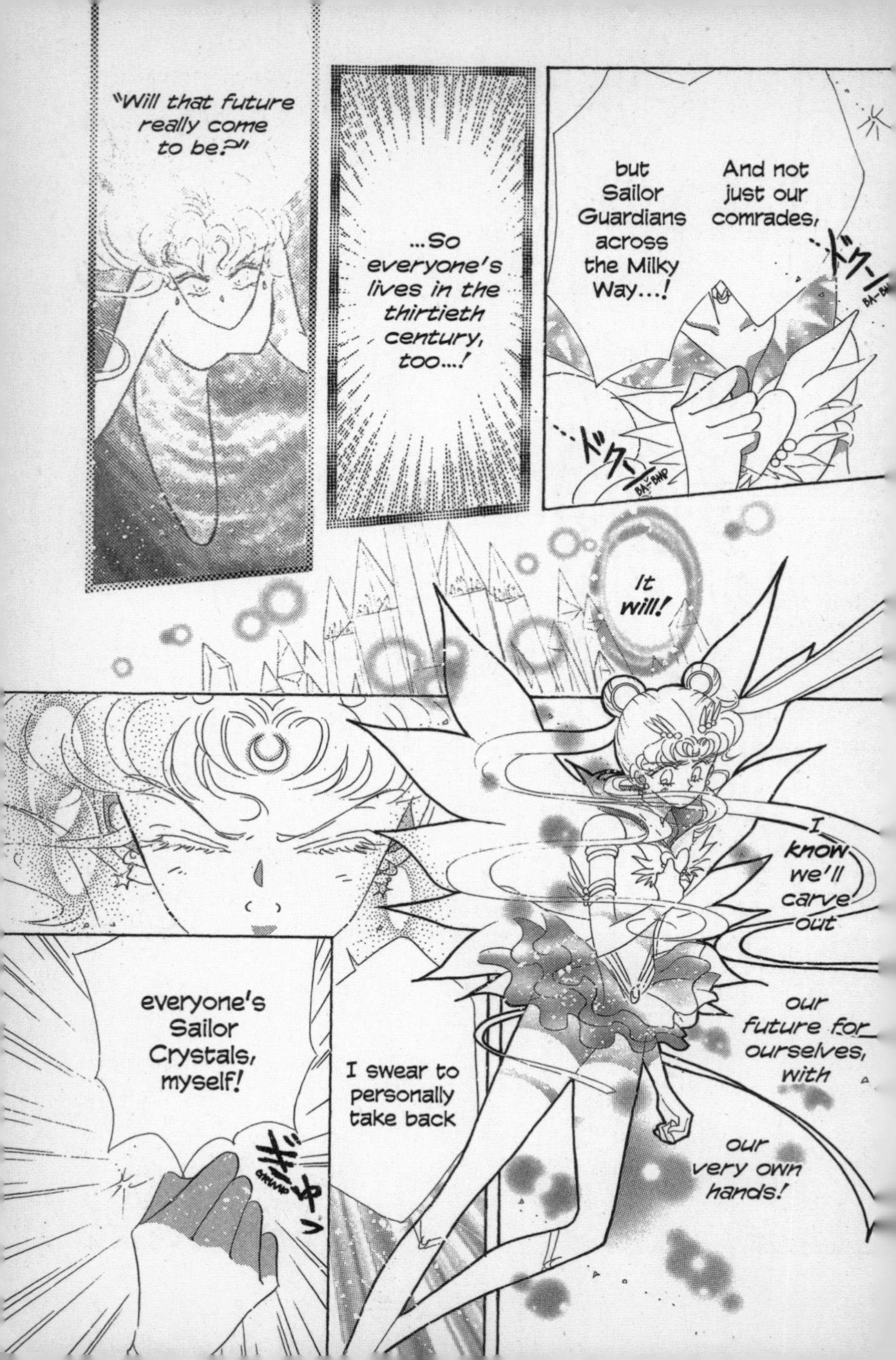
And not just our comrades,
but Sailor Guardians across the Milky Way...!
BA-BUMP
BA-BMP
...So everyone's lives in the thirtieth century, too...!
"Will that future really come to be?"
It will!
I know we'll carve out
our future for ourselves, with
our very own hands!
I swear to personally take back
everyone's Sailor Crystals, myself!

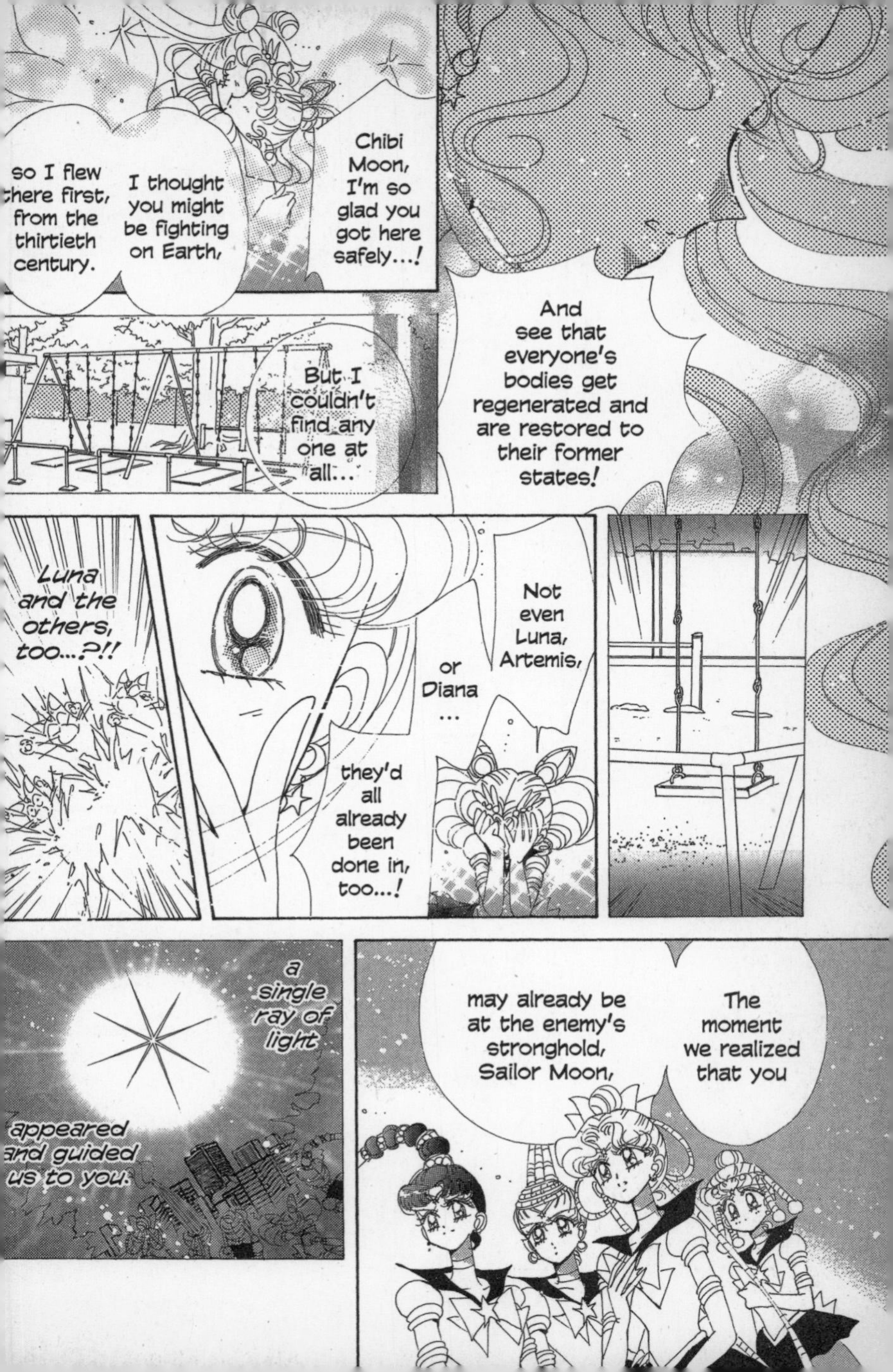

And see that everyone's bodies get regenerated and are restored to their former states!
Chibi Moon, I'm so glad you got here safely...!
I thought you might be fighting on Earth,
so I flew there first, from the thirtieth century.
But I couldn't find any one at all...
Not even Luna, Artemis,
or Diana ...
they'd all already been done in, too...!
Luna and the others, too...?!!
The moment we realized that you
may already be at the enemy's stronghold, Sailor Moon,
a single ray of light
appeared and guided us to you.

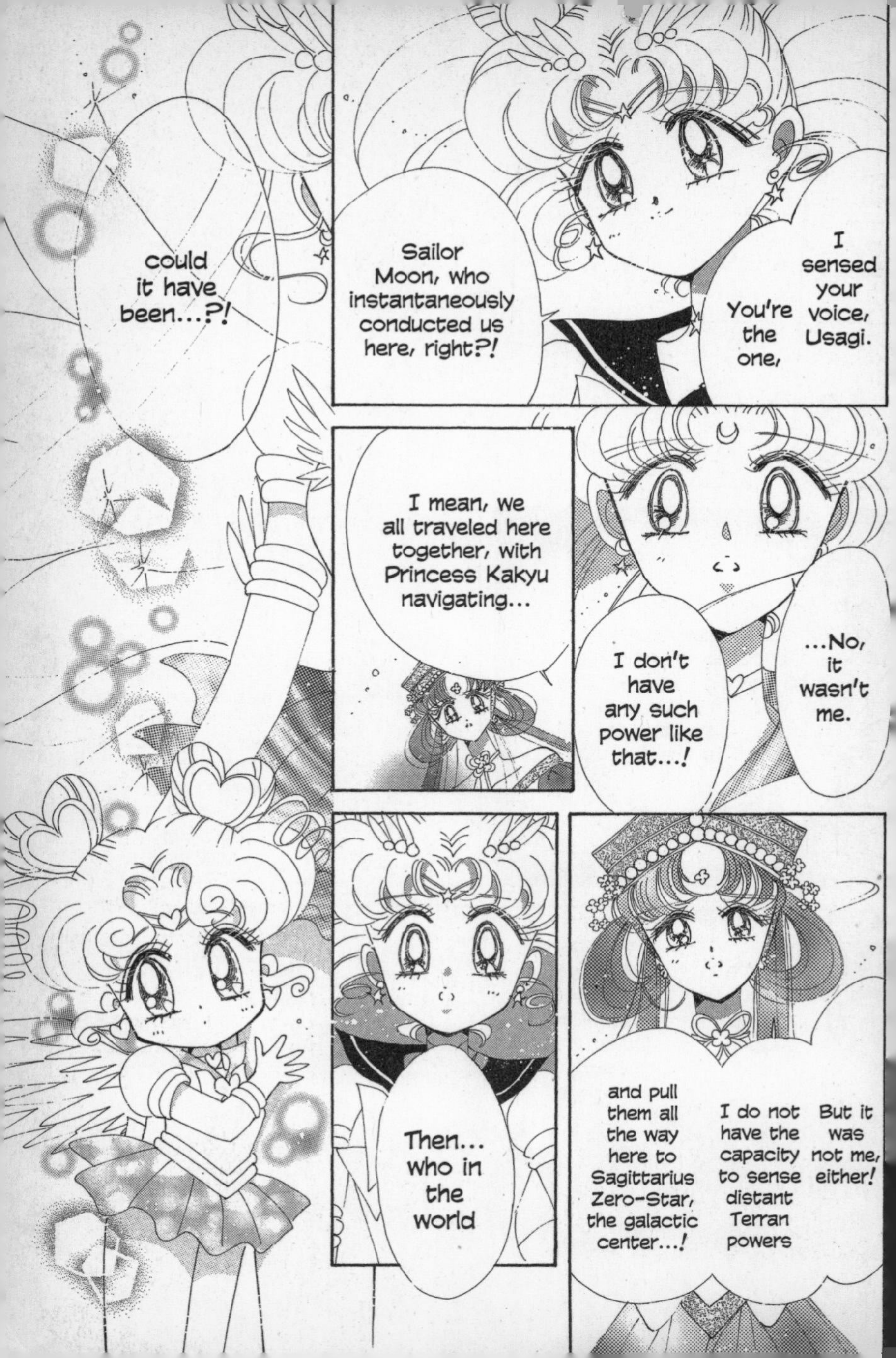

I sensed your voice, Usagi.
You're the one,
Sailor Moon, who instantaneously conducted us here, right?!
...No, it wasn't me.
I don't have any such power like that...!
I mean, we all traveled here together, with Princess Kakyu navigating...
But it was not me, either!
I do not have the capacity to sense distant Terran powers
and pull them all the way here to Sagittarius Zero-Star, the galactic center...!
Then... who in the world
could it have been...?!

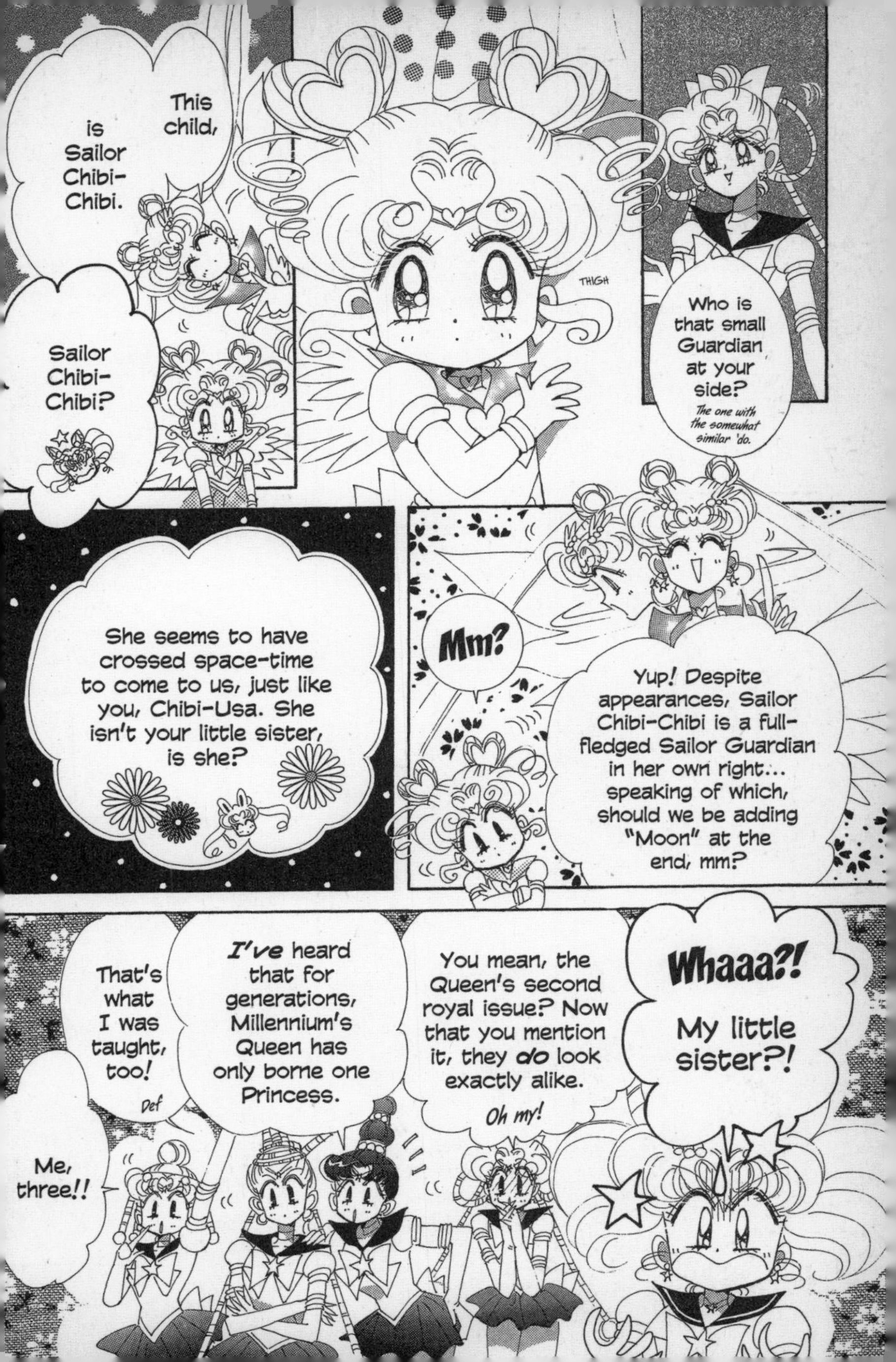
Who is that small Guardian at your side?
The one with the somewhat similar 'do.
THIGH
This child, is Sailor Chibi-Chibi.
Sailor Chibi-Chibi?
Yup! Despite appearances, Sailor Chibi-Chibi is a full-fledged Sailor Guardian in her own right... speaking of which, should we be adding "Moon" at the end, mm?
Mm?
She seems to have crossed space-time to come to us, just like you, Chibi-Usa. She isn't your little sister, is she?
Whaaa?!
My little sister?!
You mean, the Queen's second royal issue? Now that you mention it, they *do* look exactly alike.
Oh my!
I've heard that for generations, Millennium's Queen has only borne one Princess.
That's what I was taught, too!
Def
Me, three!!

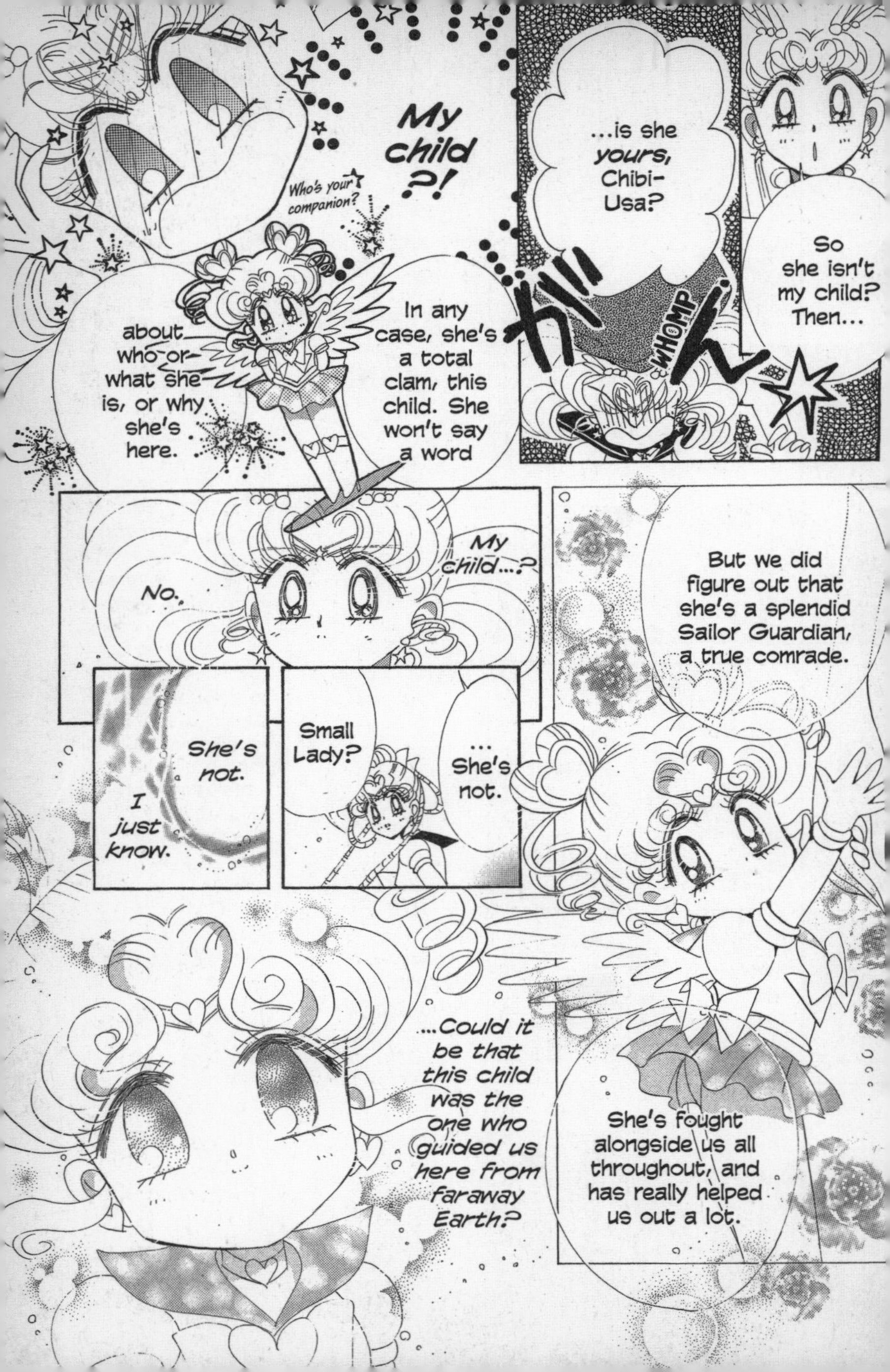
So she isn't my child? Then...
...is she yours, Chibi-Usa?
WHOMP
My child?!
Who's your companion?
In any case, she's a total clam, this child. She won't say a word
about who or what she is, or why she's here.
But we did figure out that she's a splendid Sailor Guardian, a true comrade.
She's fought alongside us all throughout, and has really helped us out a lot.
My child...?
No.
... She's not.
Small Lady?
She's not.
I just know.
...Could it be that this child was the one who guided us here from faraway Earth?

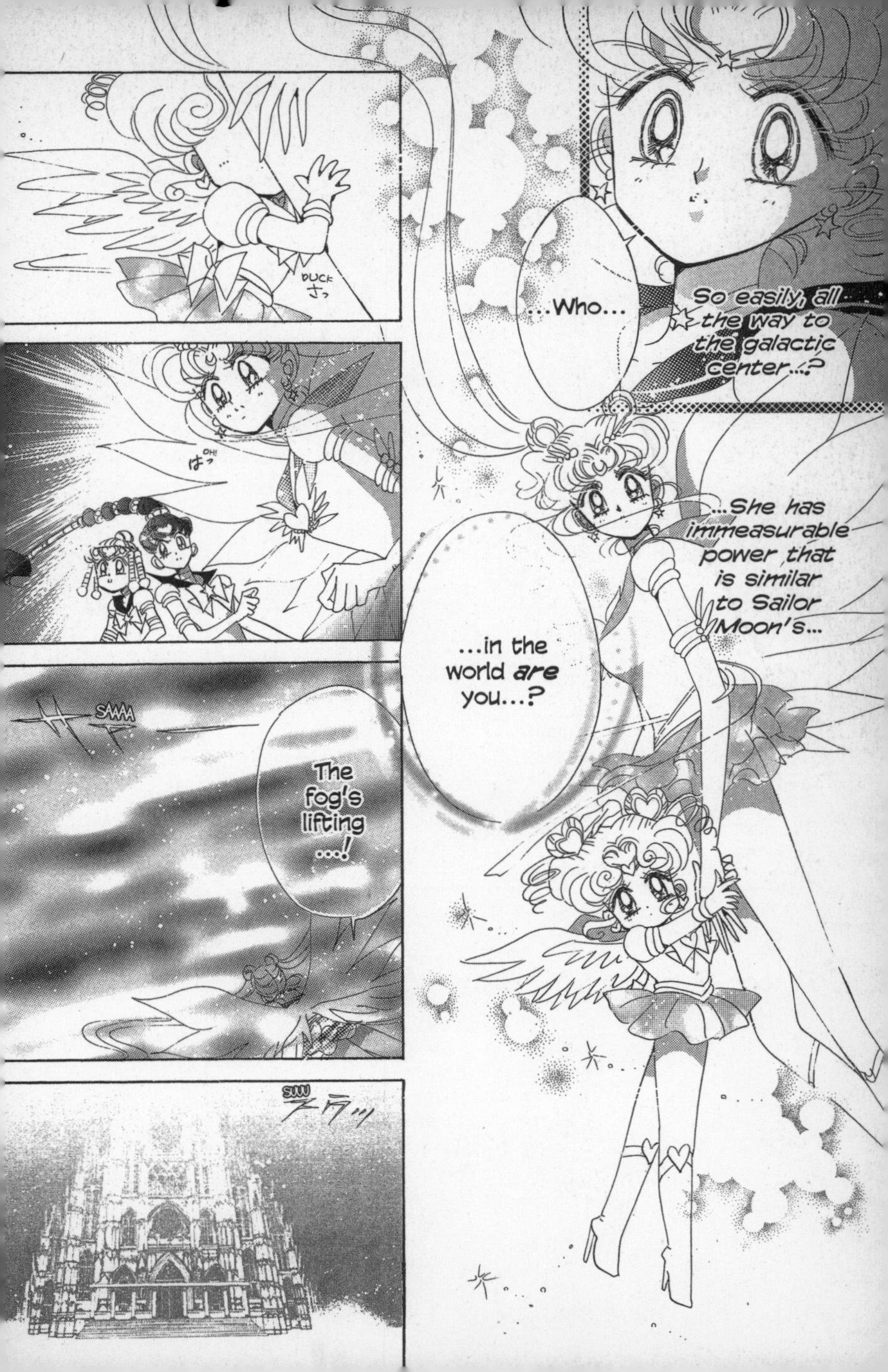
So easily, all the way to the galactic center...?
...Who...
...She has immeasurable power that is similar to Sailor Moon's...
...in the world *are* you...?
DUCK
さっ
OH!
はっ
SAAAA
The fog's lifting ...!
SUUU

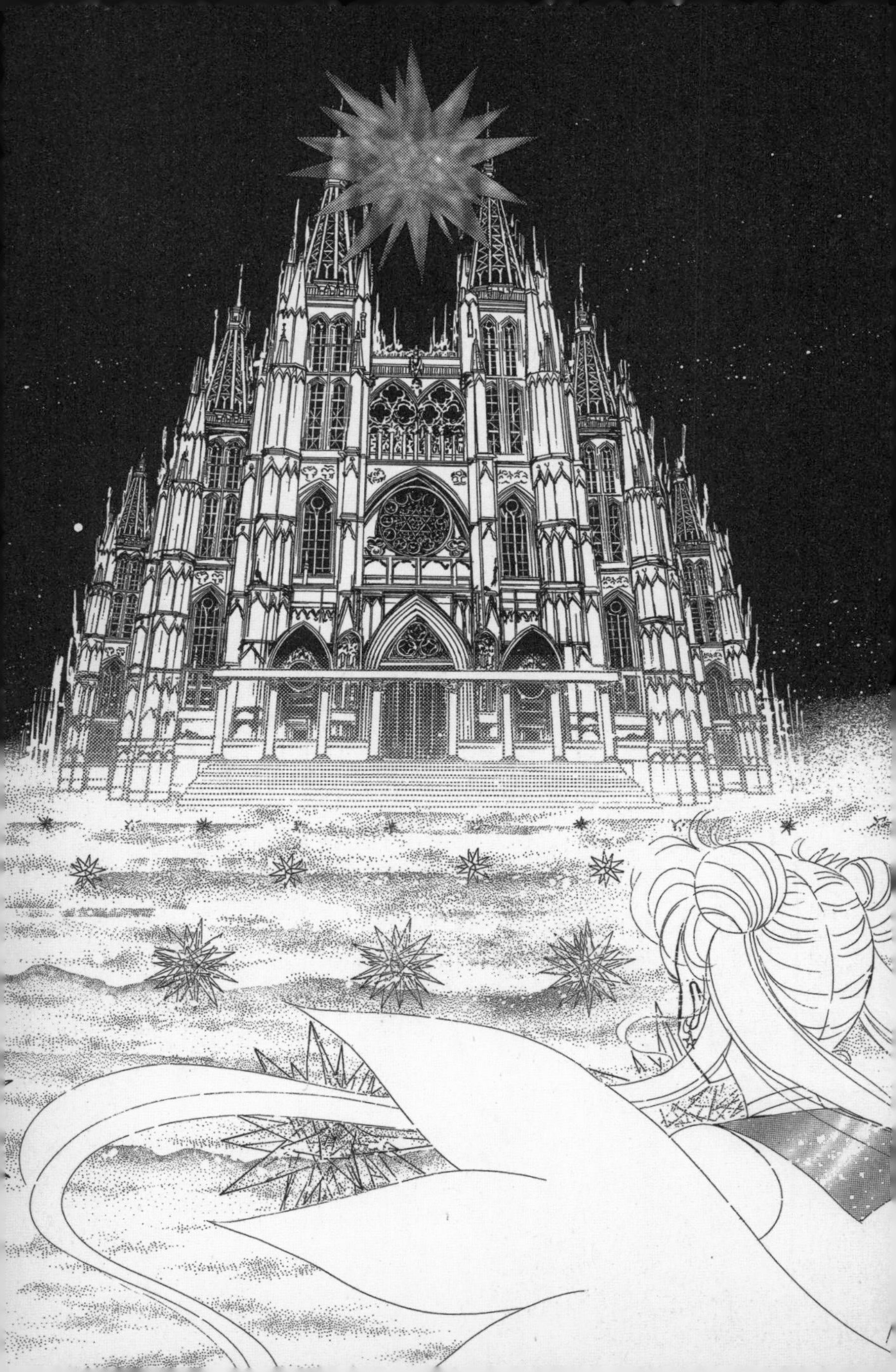

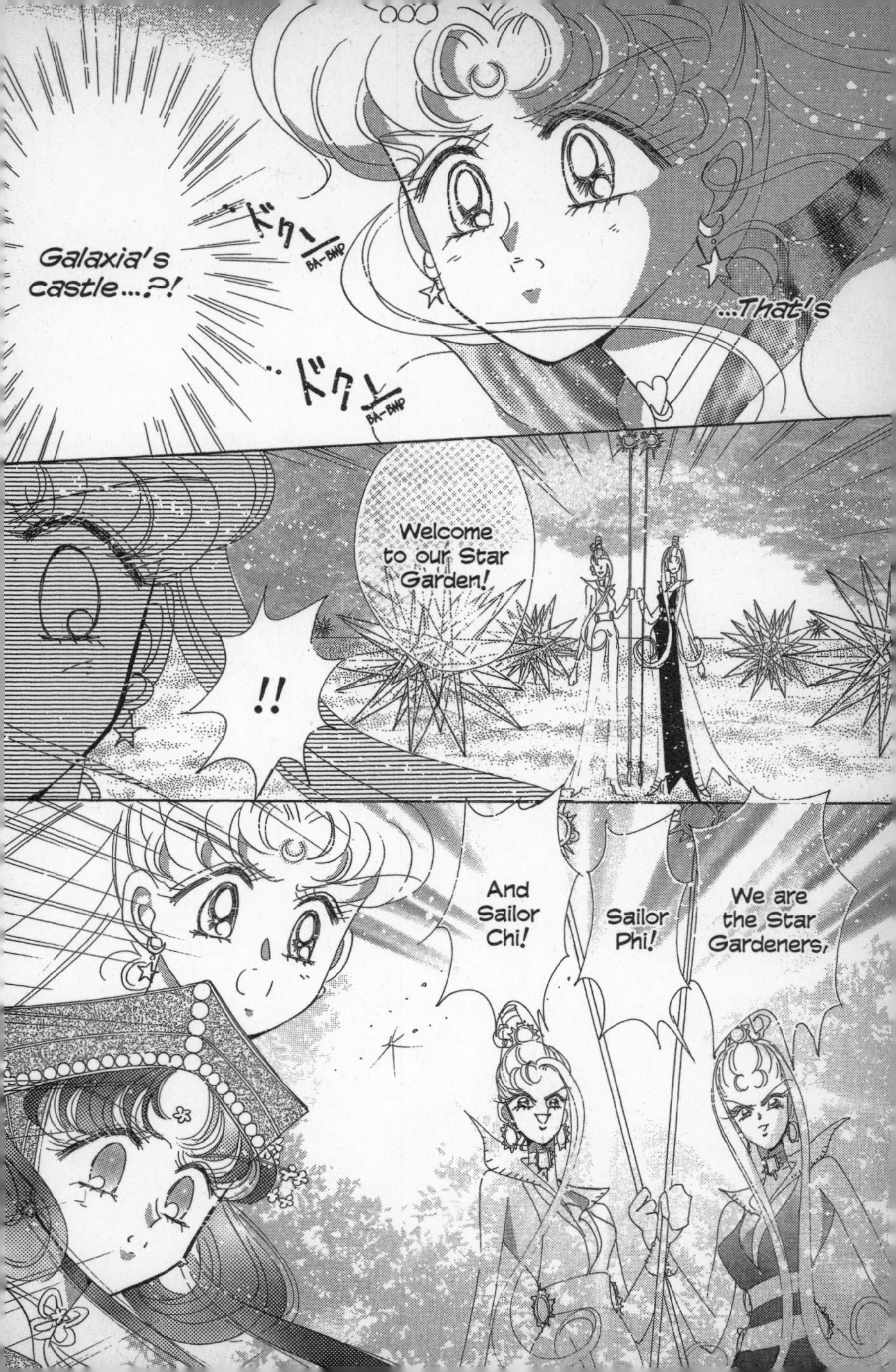
...That's
Galaxia's castle...?!
ドクン
BA-BMP
ドクン
BA-BMP
Welcome to our Star Garden!
!!
We are the Star Gardeners,
Sailor Phi!
And Sailor Chi!

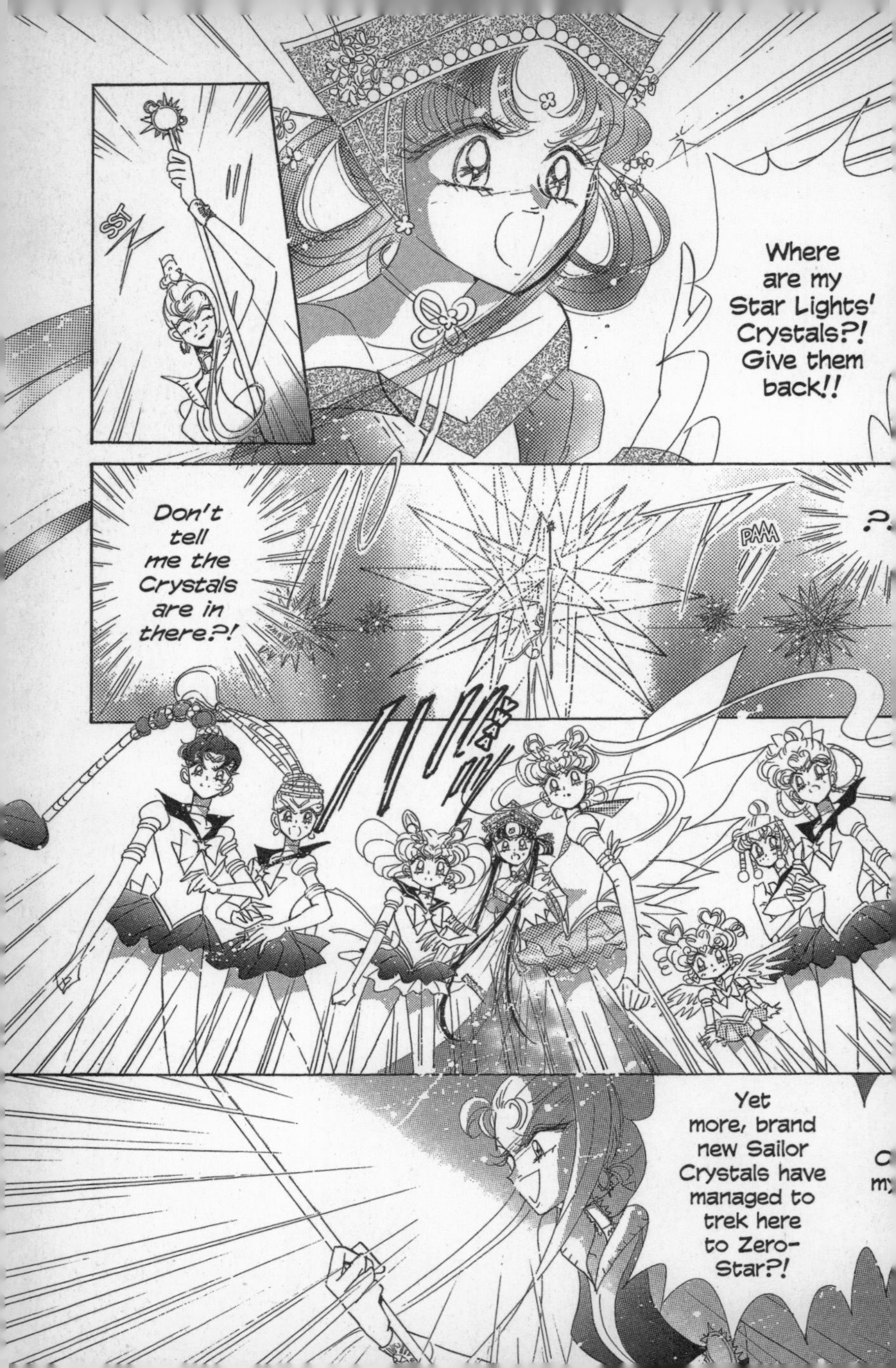
Where are my Star Lights' Crystals?! Give them back!!
SST
?!
PAAA
Don't tell me the Crystals are in there?!
VWAA
Yet more, brand new Sailor Crystals have managed to trek here to Zero-Star?!

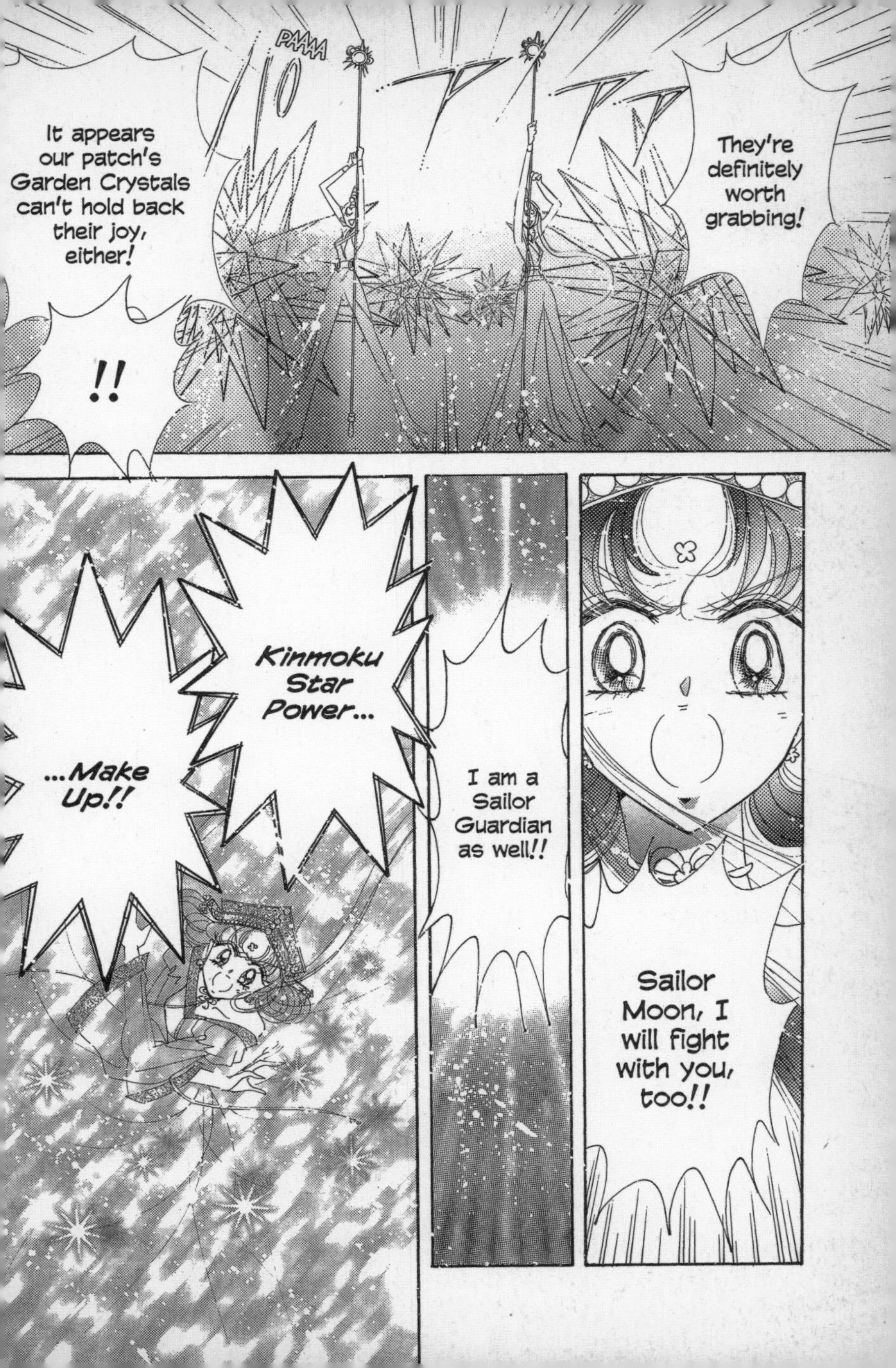

They're definitely worth grabbing!
PAAAA
It appears our patch's Garden Crystals can't hold back their joy, either!
!!
Sailor Moon, I will fight with you, too!!
I am a Sailor Guardian as well!!
Kinmoku Star Power...
...Make Up!!

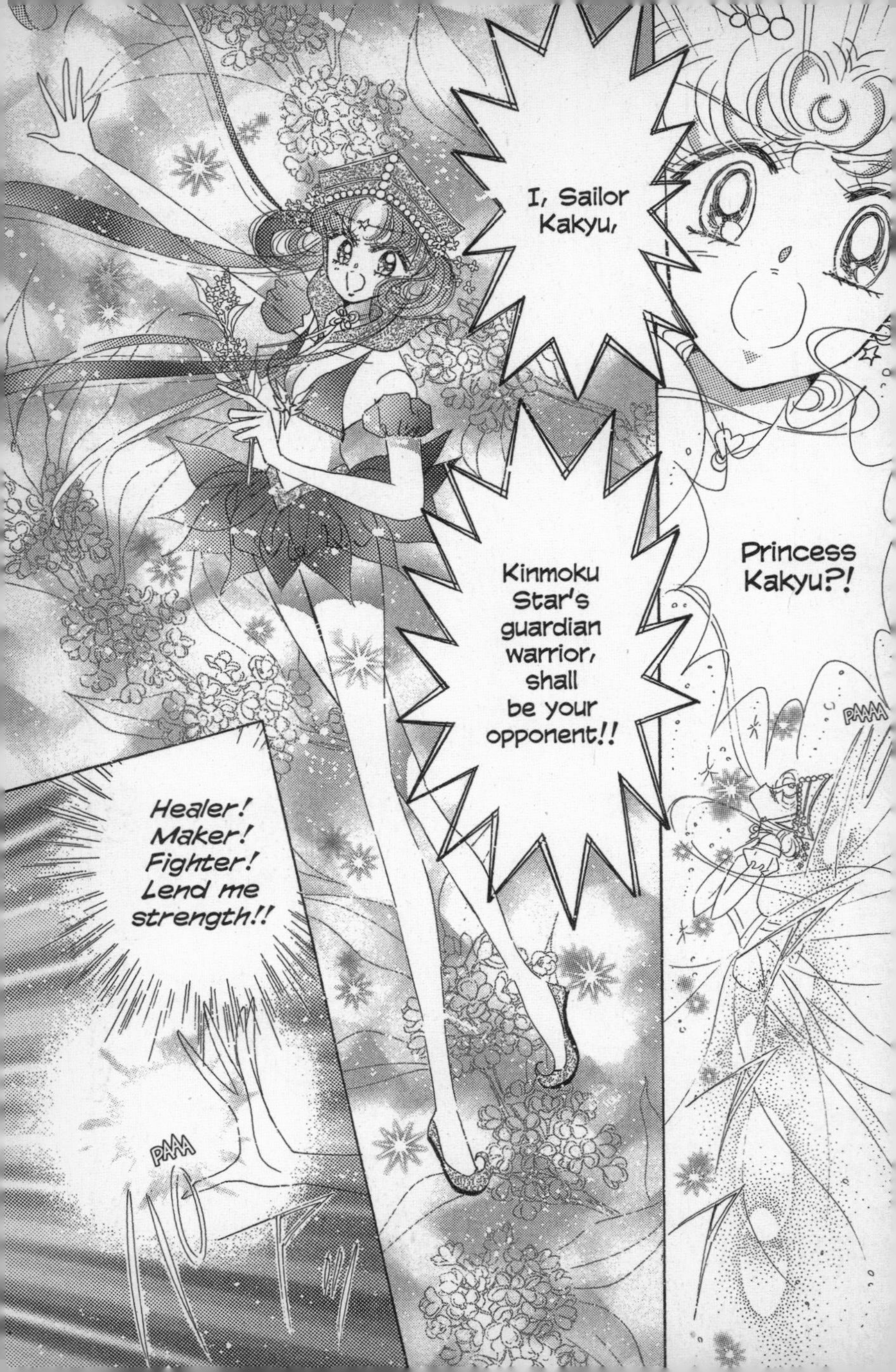
Princess Kakyu?!
PAAAA
I, Sailor Kakyu,
Kinmoku Star's guardian warrior, shall be your opponent!!
Healer! Maker! Fighter! Lend me strength!!
PAAA

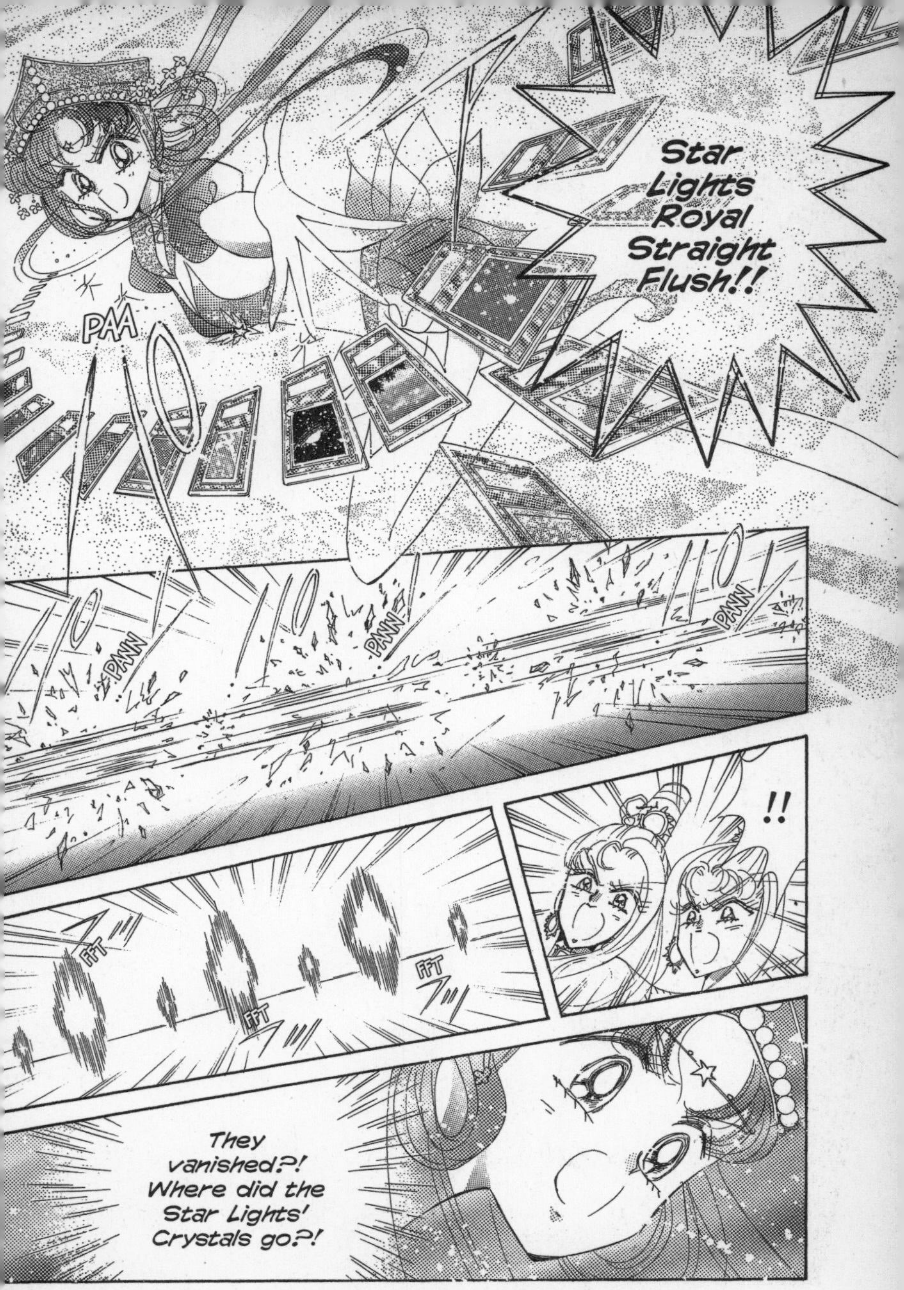
Star Lights Royal Straight Flush!!
PAA
PANN
PANN
PANN
PANN
!!
FFT
FFT
FFT
They vanished?! Where did the Star Lights' Crystals go?!

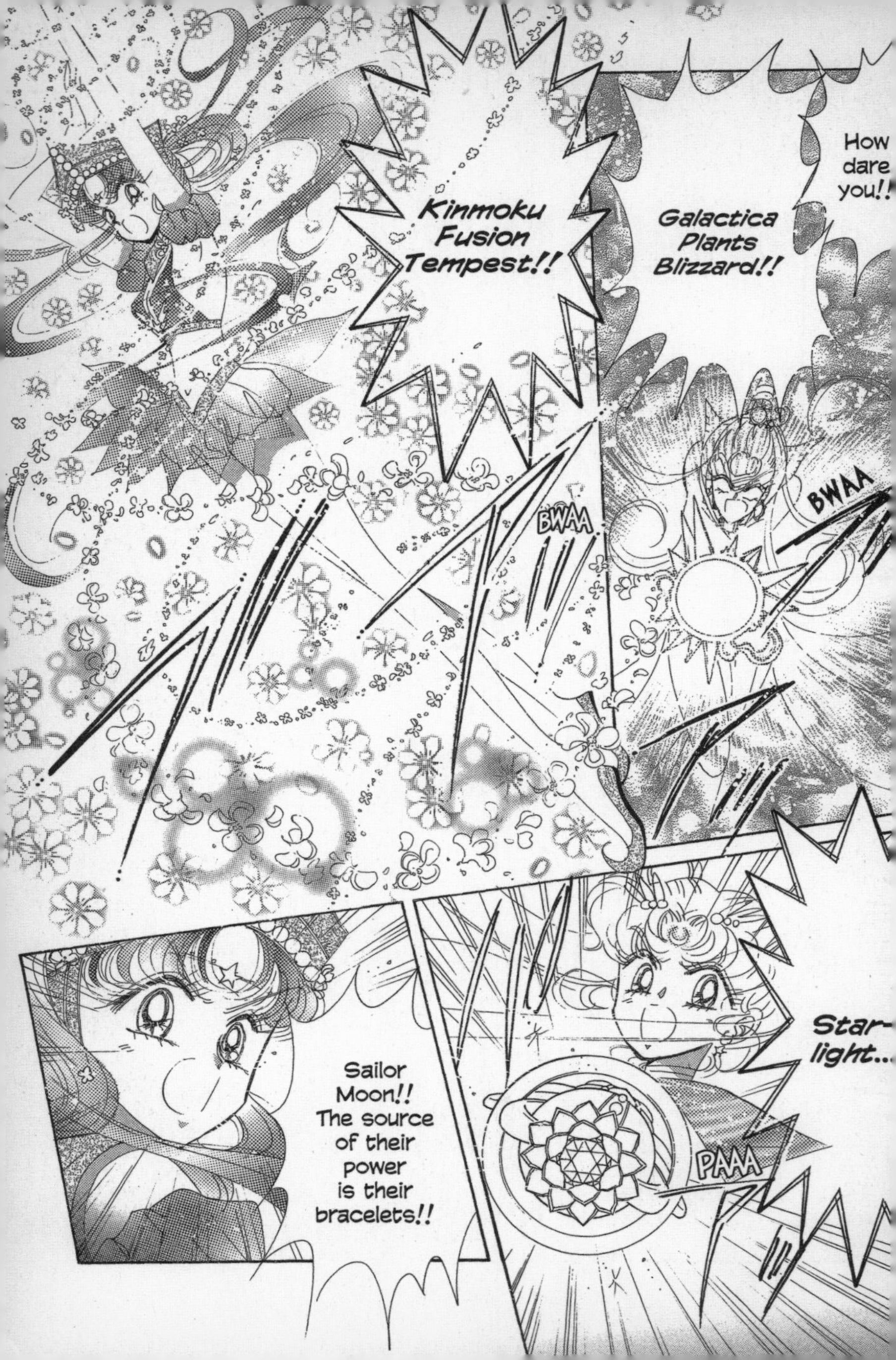
How dare you!!
Galactica Plants Blizzard!!
BWAA
Kinmoku Fusion Tempest!!
BWAA
Star-light...
PAAA
Sailor Moon!! The source of their power is their bracelets!!

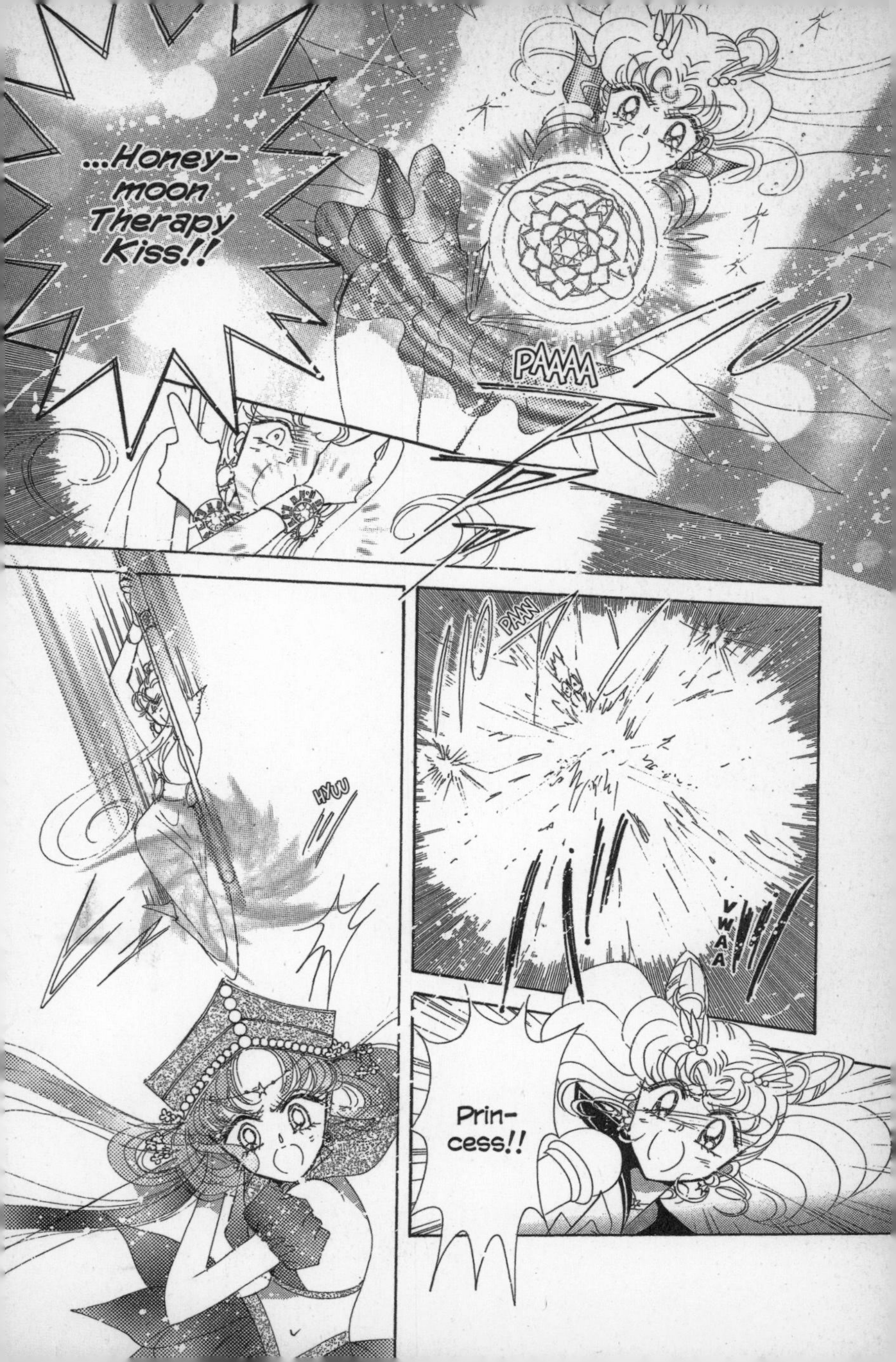
...Honey-moon Therapy Kiss!!
PAAAA
PAAN
VWAA
Prin-cess!!
HYUU

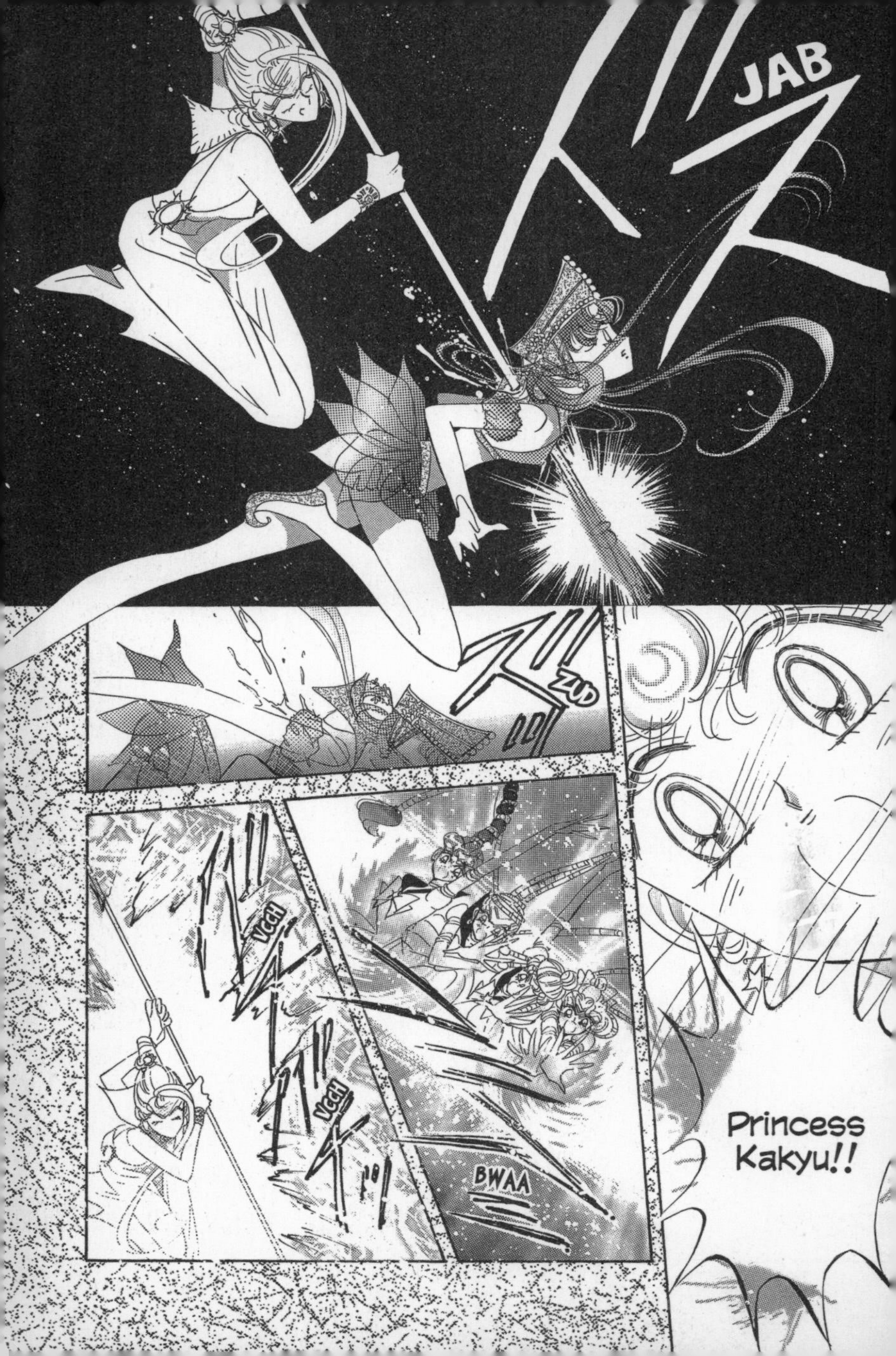
JAB
Princess Kakyu!!
ZUD
BWAA
VCCH
VCCH

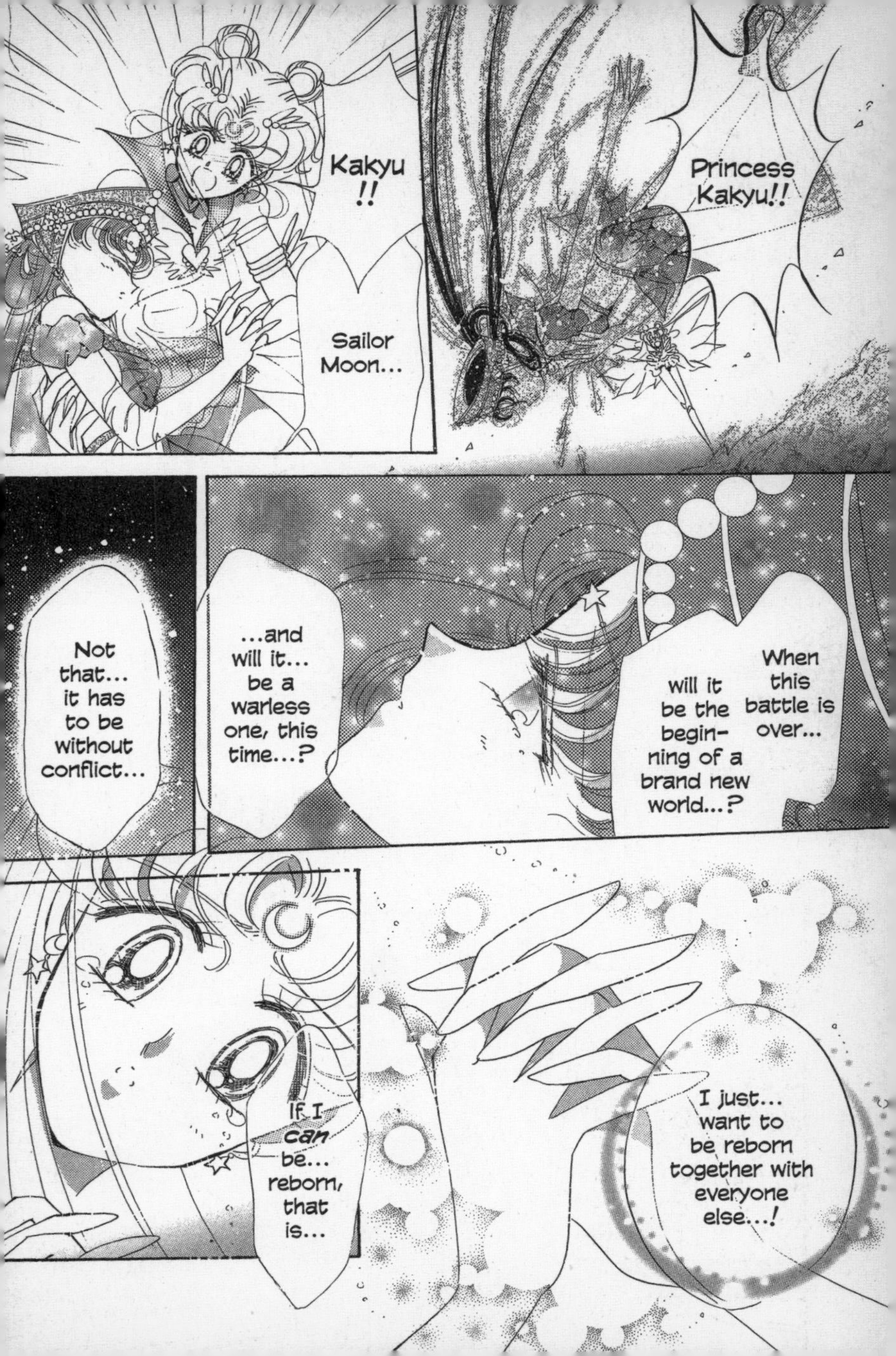

Princess Kakyu!!
Kakyu !!
Sailor Moon...
When this battle is over...
will it be the begin-ning of a brand new world...?
...and will it... be a warless one, this time...?
Not that... it has to be without conflict...
I just... want to be reborn together with everyone else...!
If I *can* be... reborn, that is...

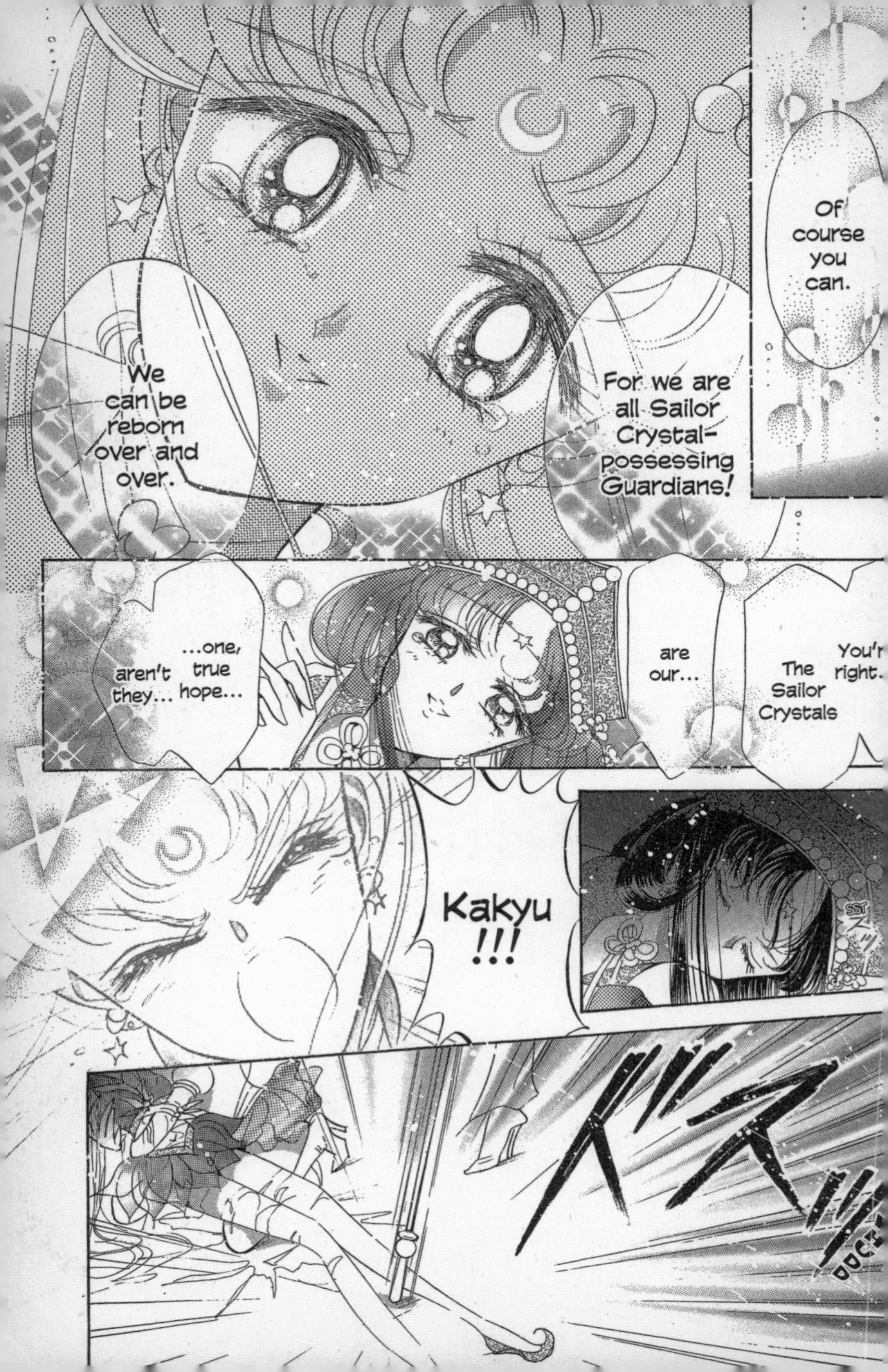

Of course you can.
For we are all Sailor Crystal-possessing Guardians!
We can be reborn over and over.
You'r right...
The Sailor Crystals
are our...
...one, true hope...
aren't they...
SST
Kakyu !!!

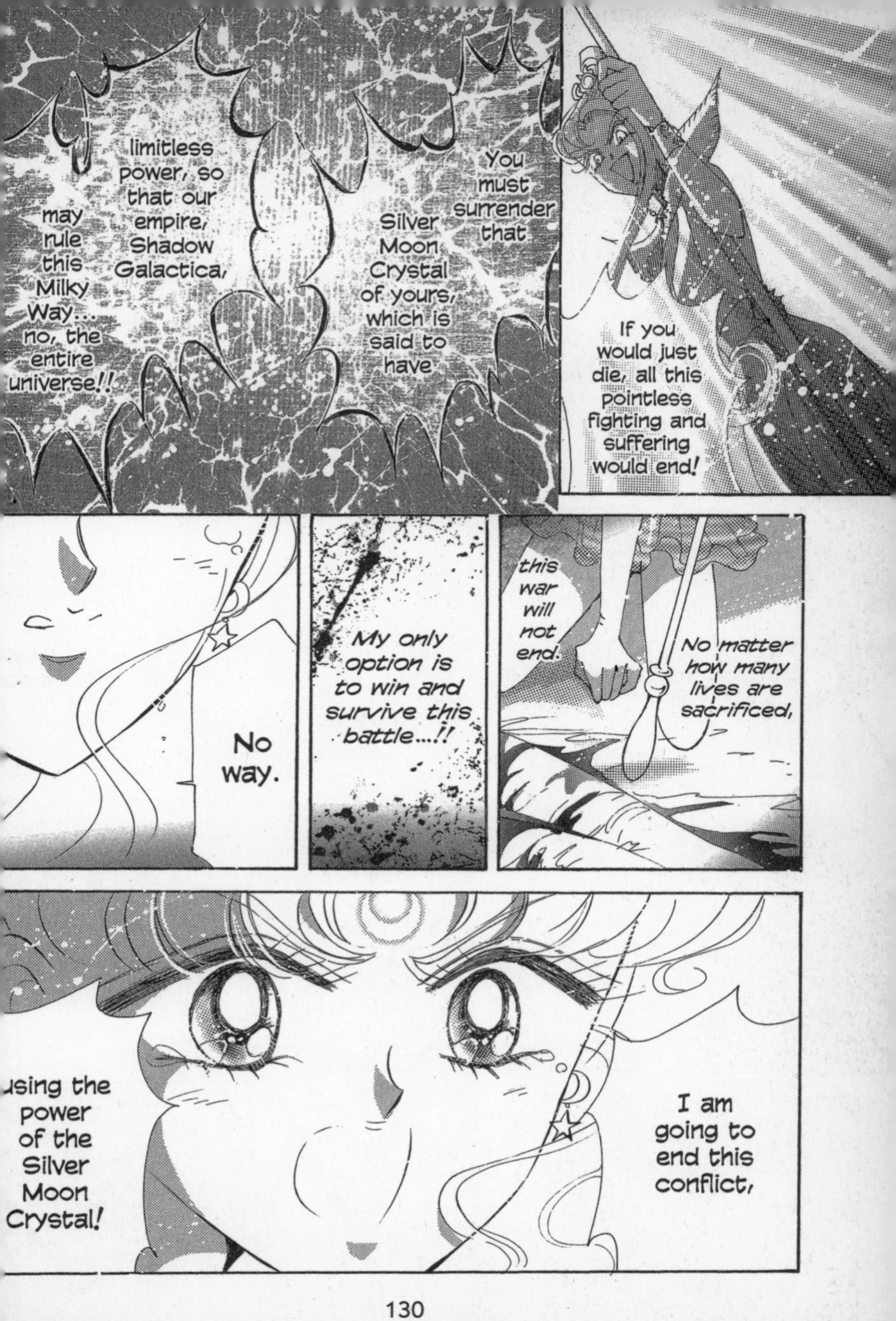
If you would just die, all this pointless fighting and suffering would end!
You must surrender that
Silver Moon Crystal of yours, which is said to have
limitless power, so that our empire, Shadow Galactica,
may rule this Milky Way... no, the entire universe!!
No matter how many lives are sacrificed,
this war will not end.
My only option is to win and survive this battle...!!
No way.
I am going to end this conflict,
using the power of the Silver Moon Crystal!

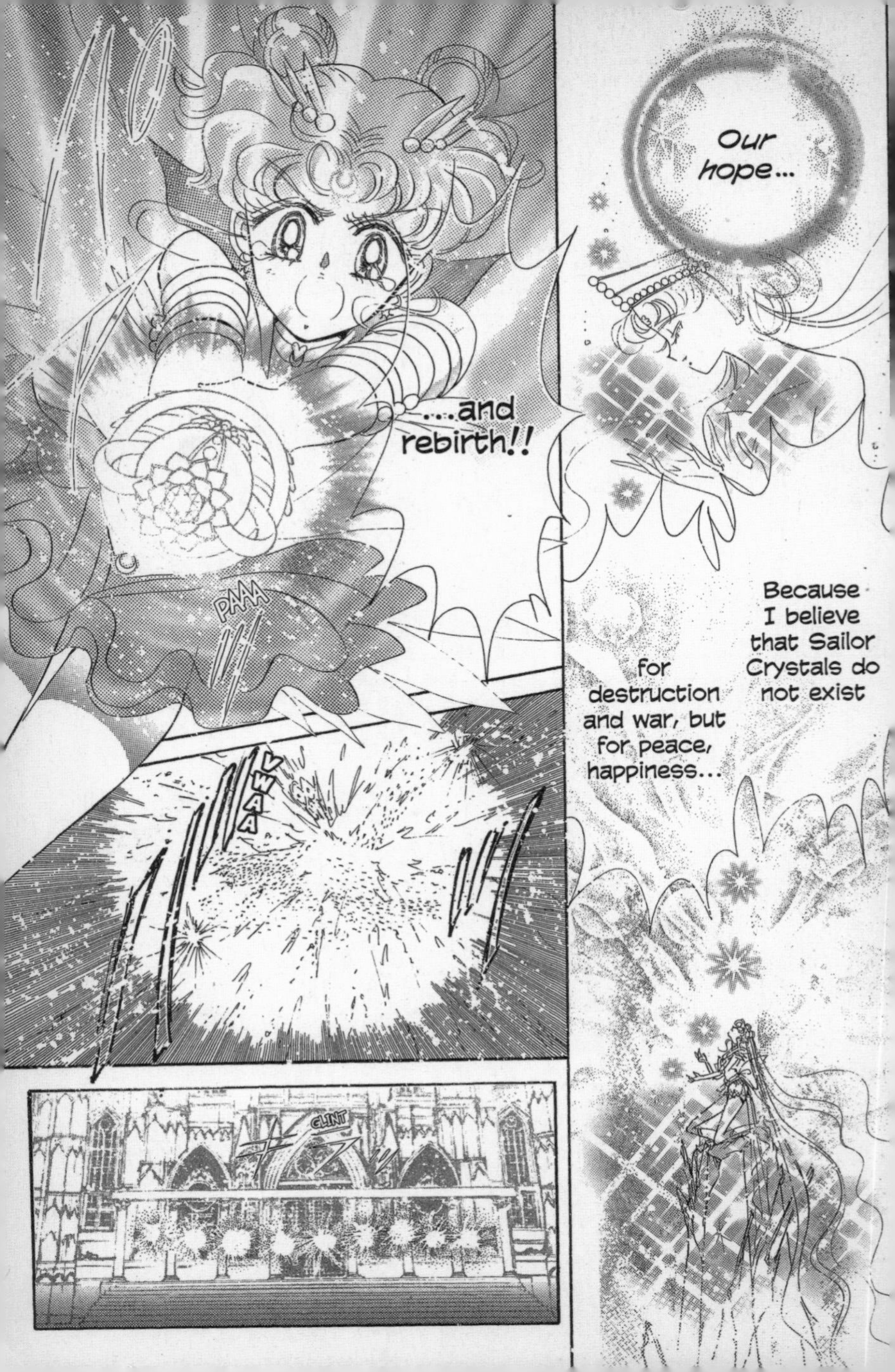
Our hope...
Because I believe that Sailor Crystals do not exist
for destruction and war, but for peace, happiness...
...and rebirth!!
PAAA
VWAAA
CLINT

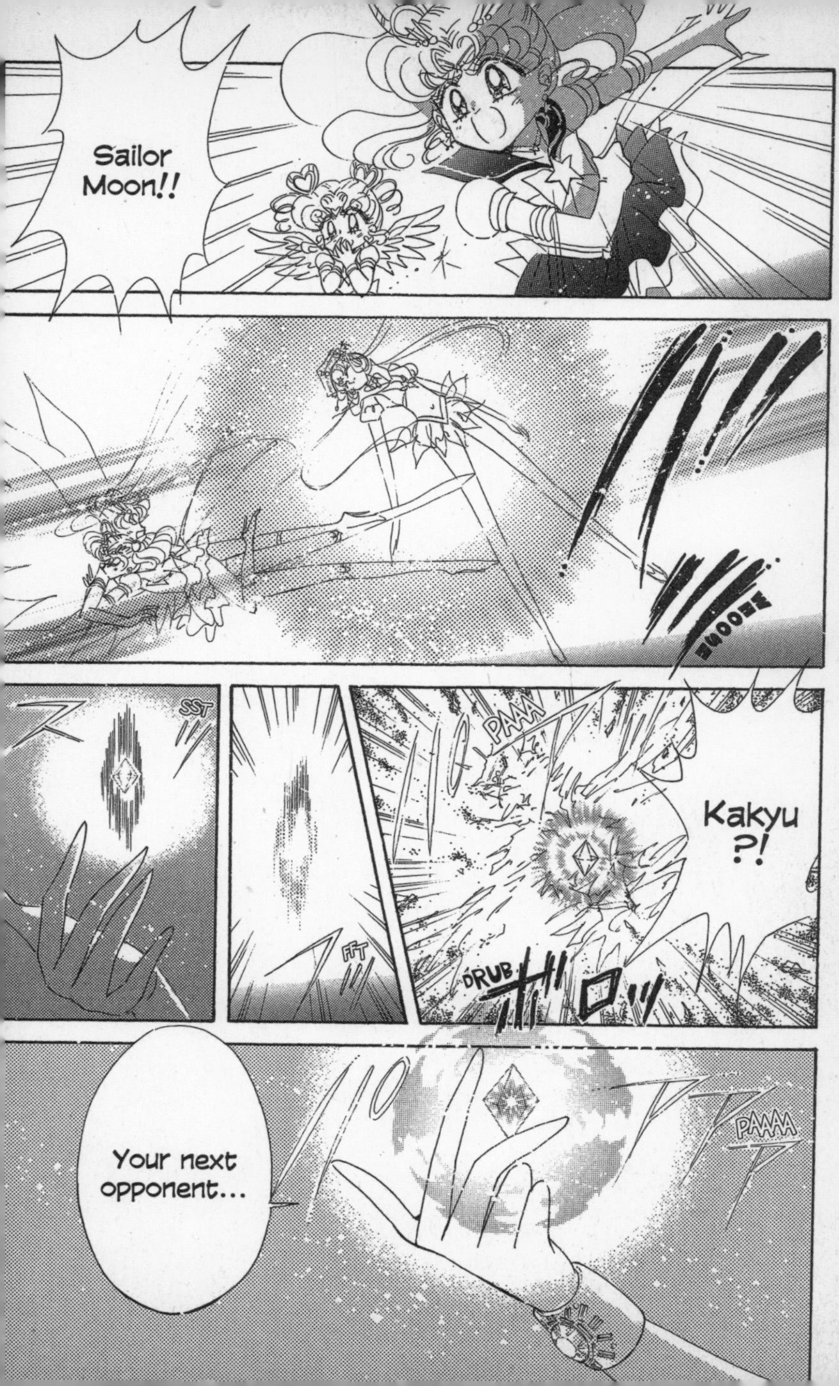
Sailor Moon!!
WHOOSH
Kakyu ?!
PAAA
DRUB
FFT
SST
PAAAA
Your next opponent...

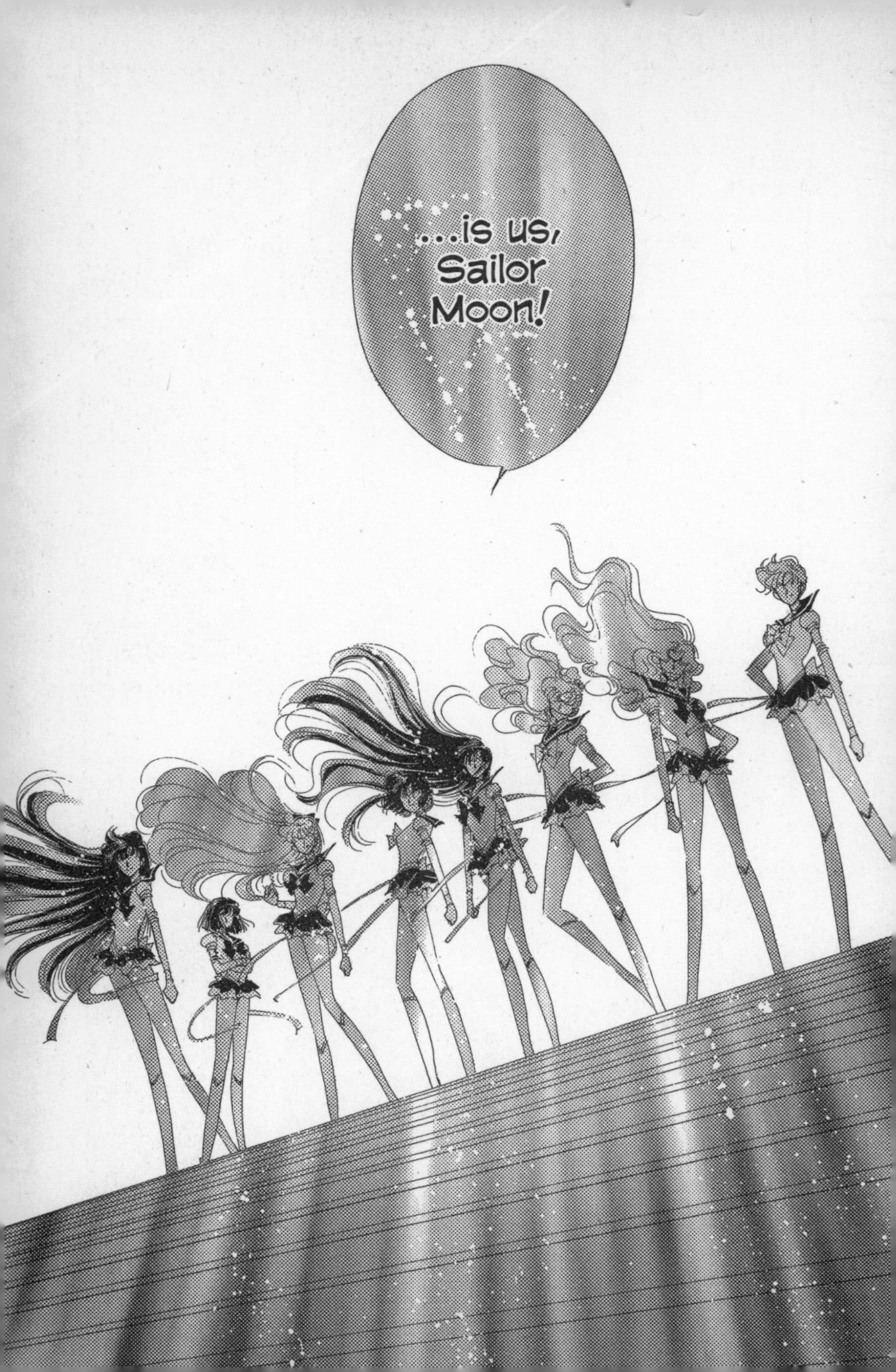
...is us, Sailor Moon!

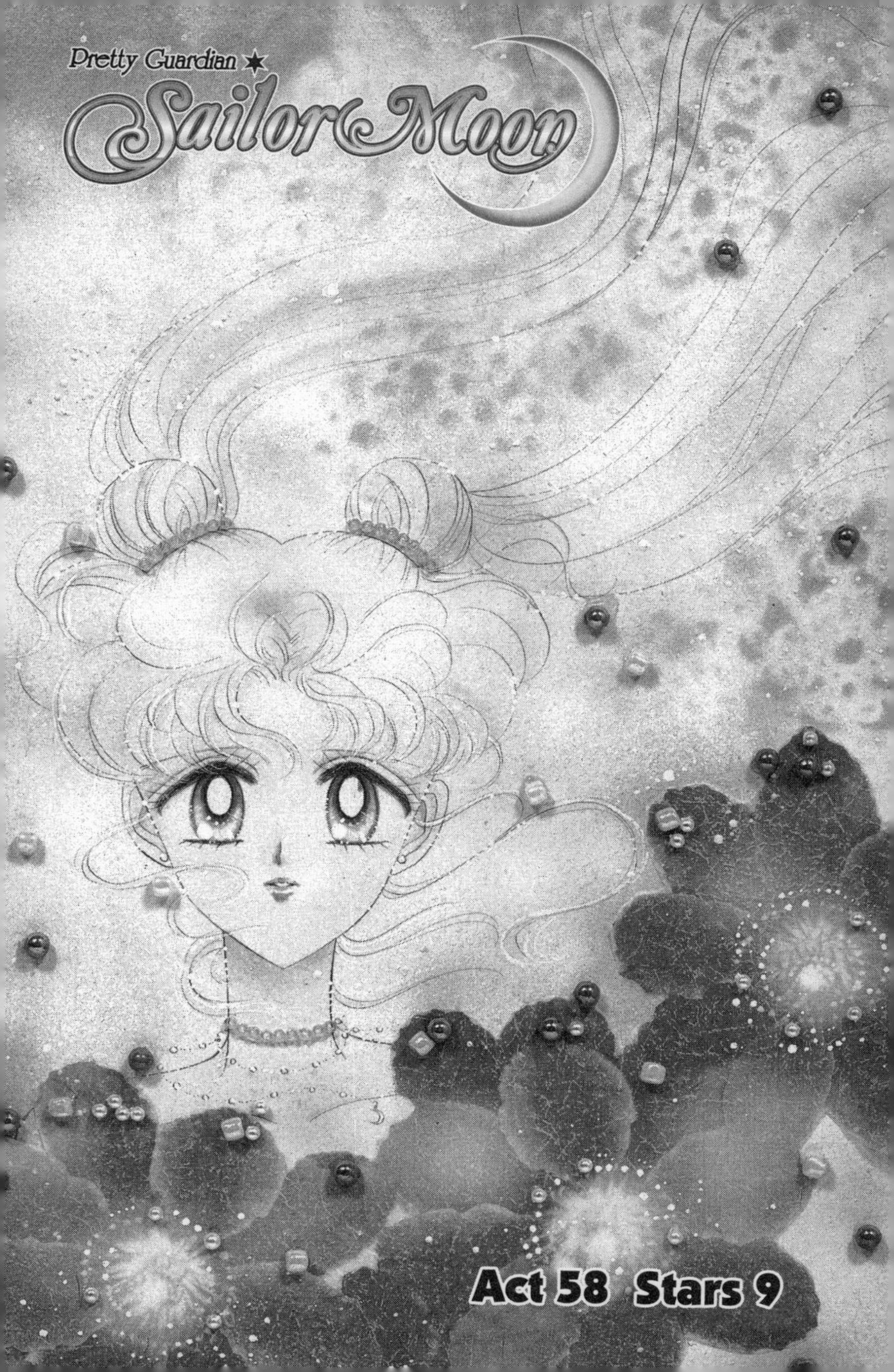
Pretty Guardian
Sailor Moon
Act 58 Stars 9

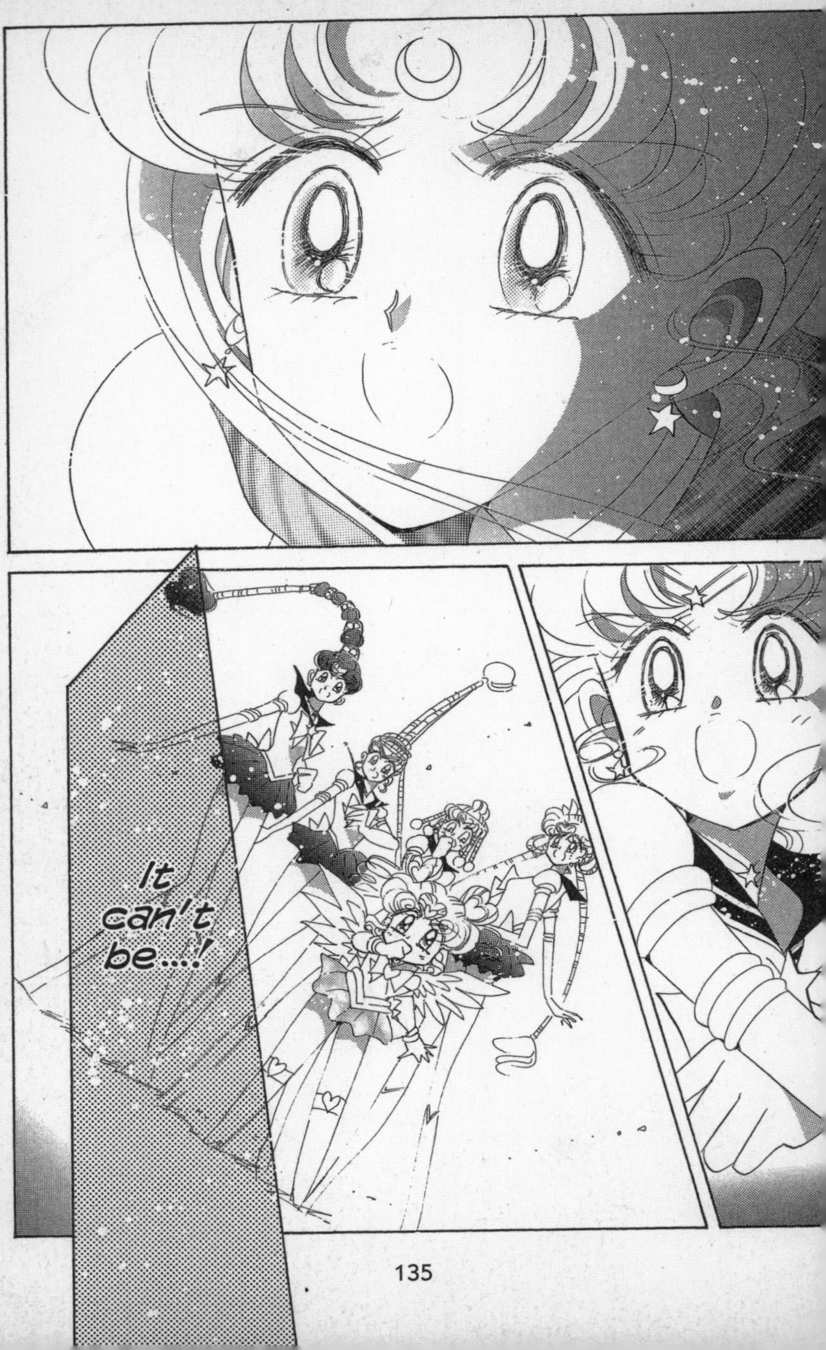
It can't be...!

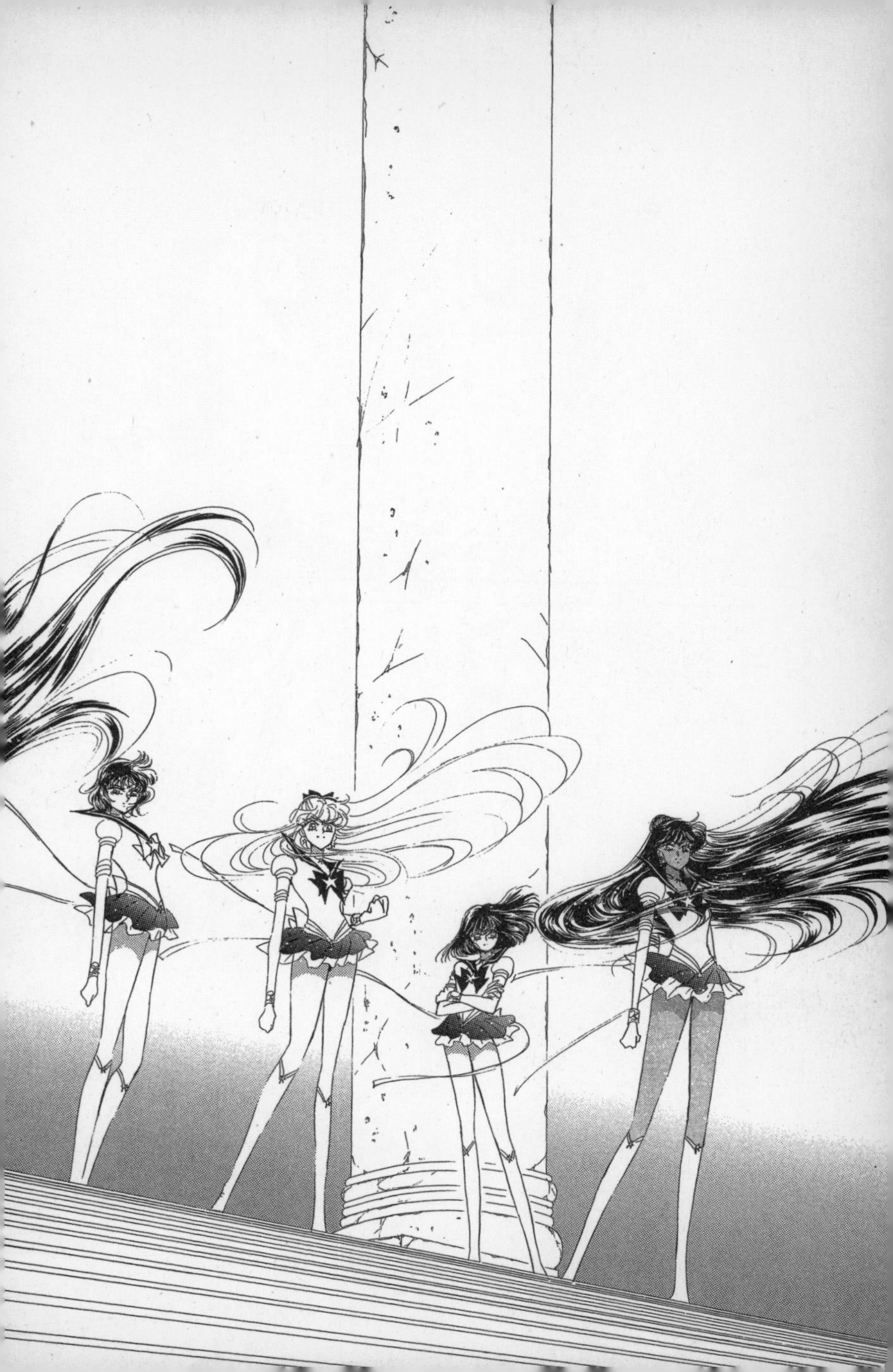

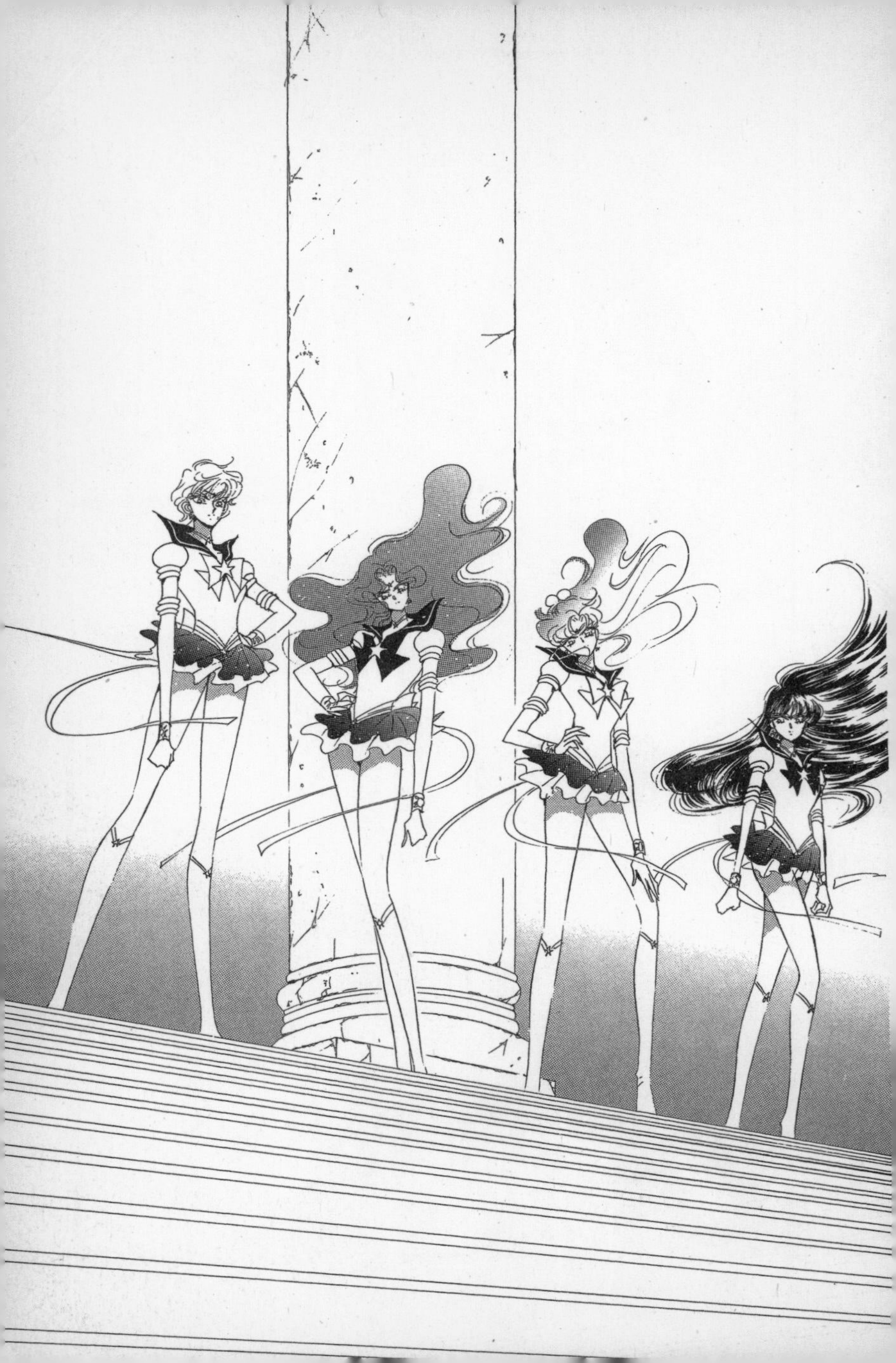

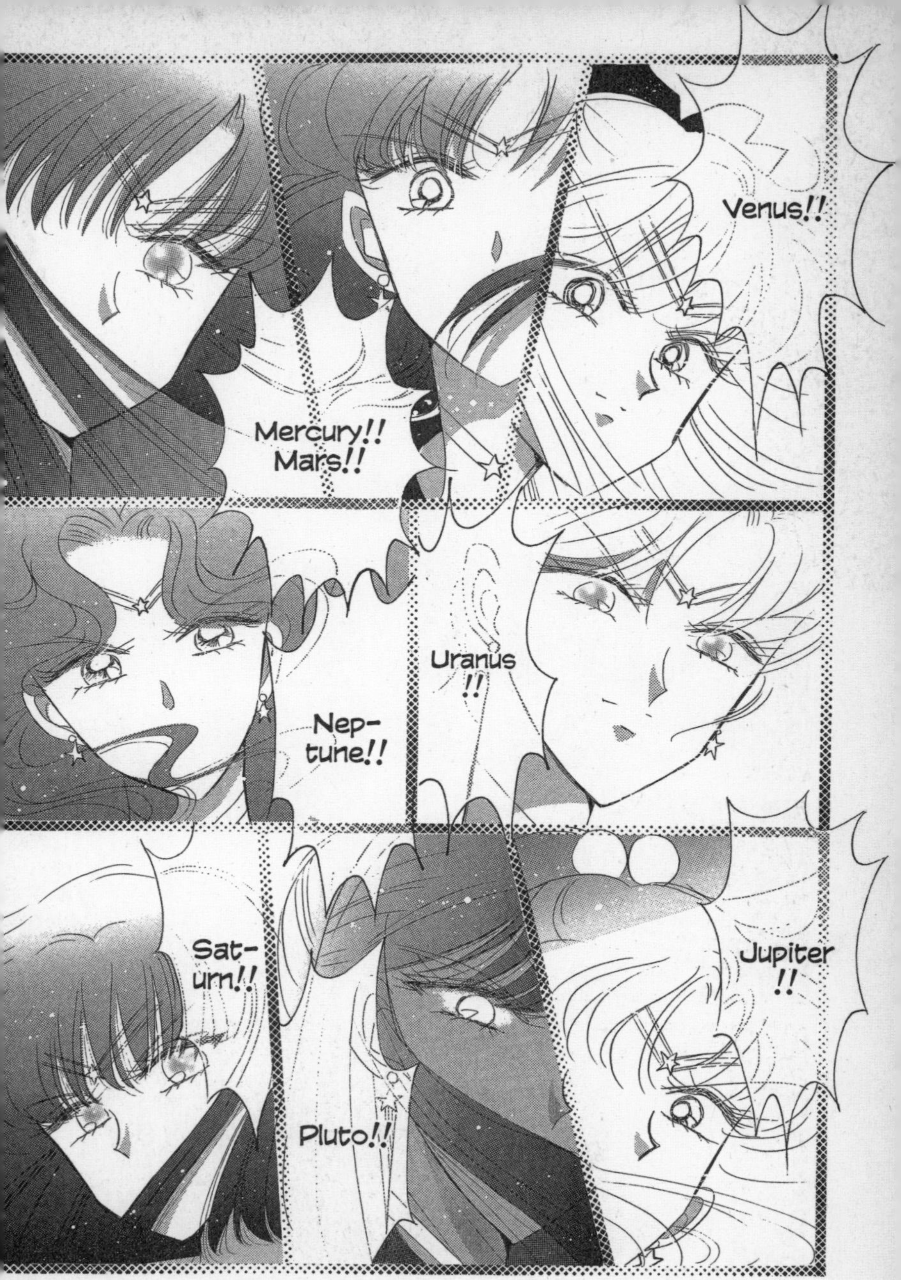
Venus!!
Mercury!!
Mars!!
Uranus!!
Nep-tune!!
Jupiter!!
Pluto!!
Sat-urn!!

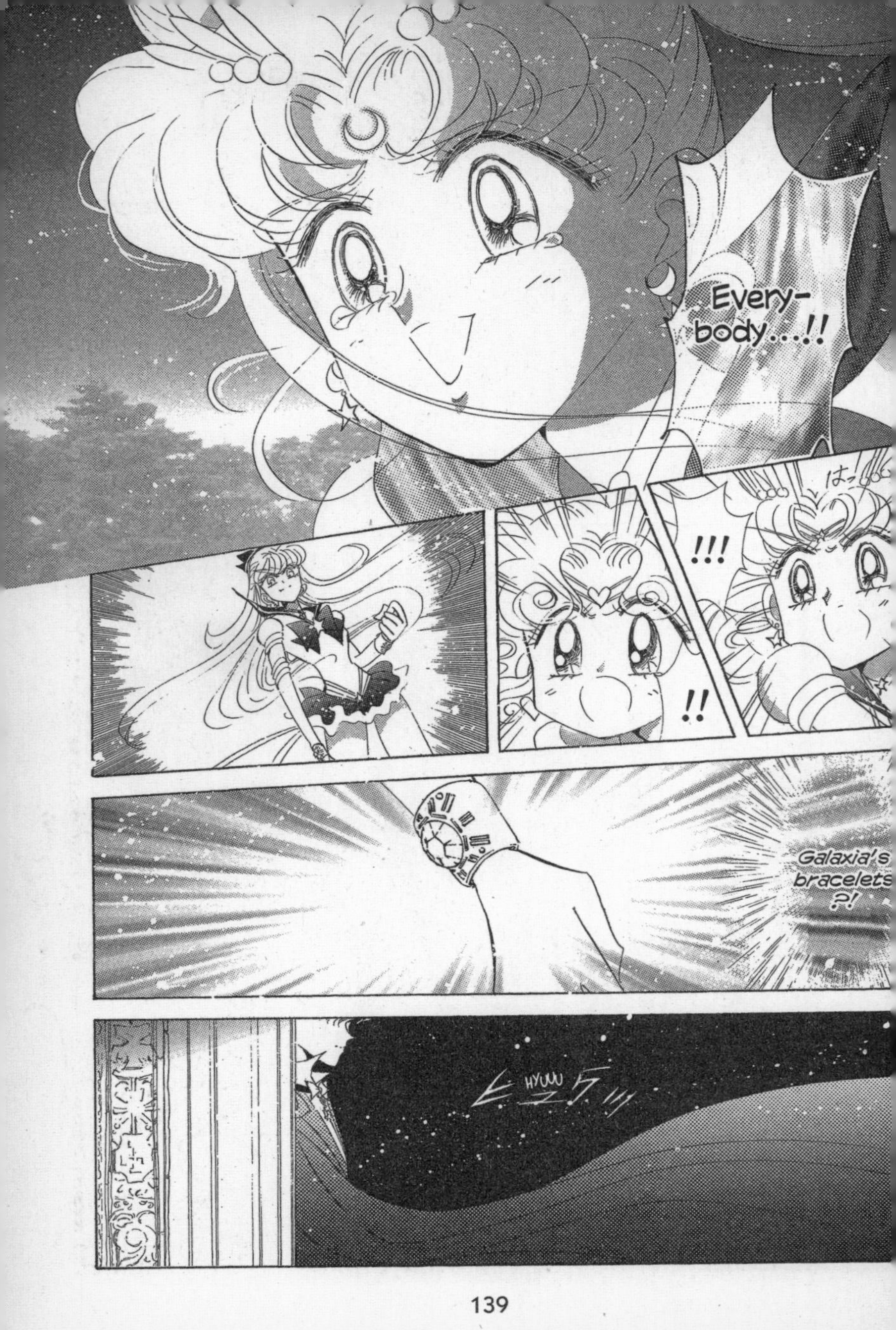
Every-body...!!
はっ!
!!!
!!
Galaxia's bracelets ?!
HYUUU

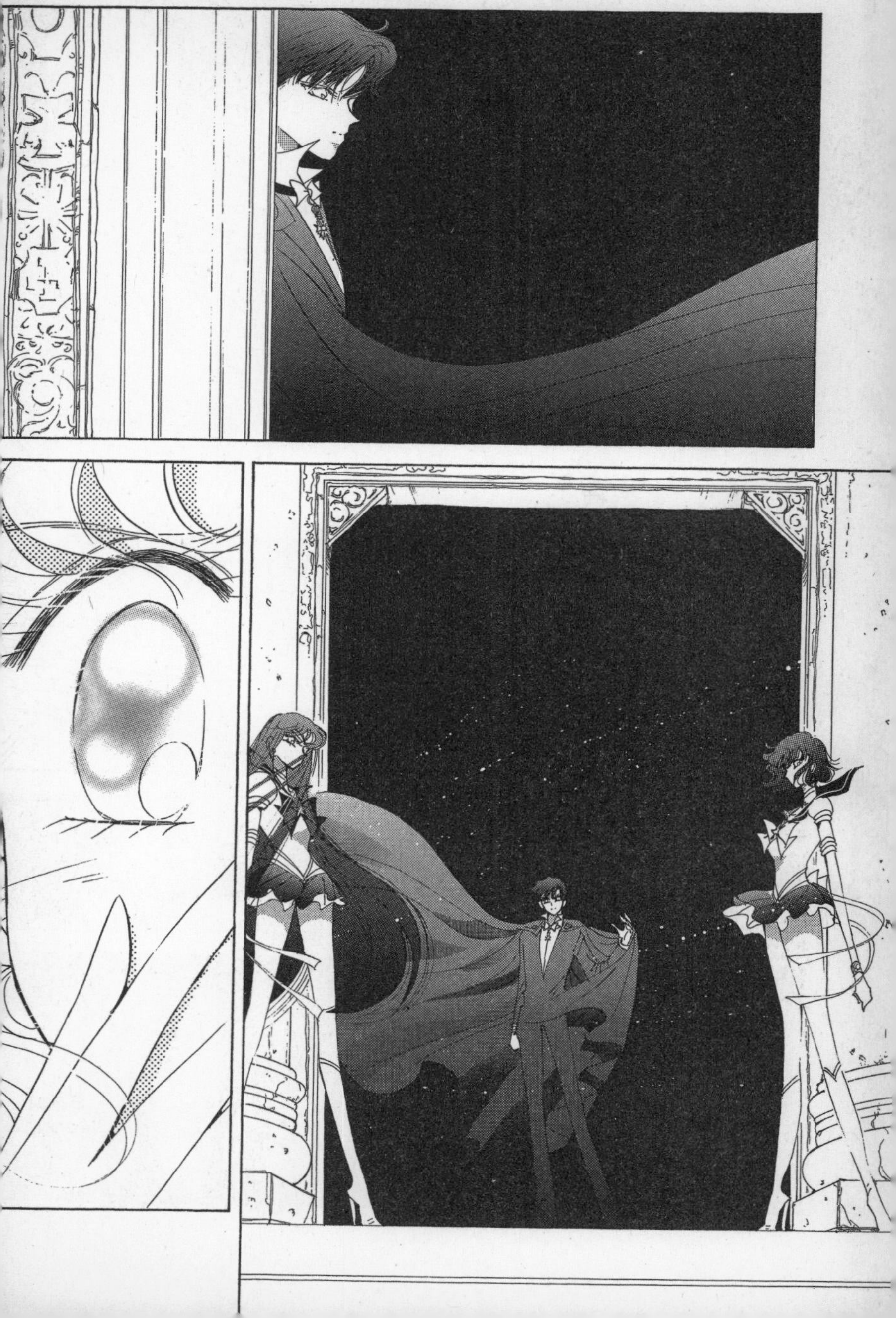

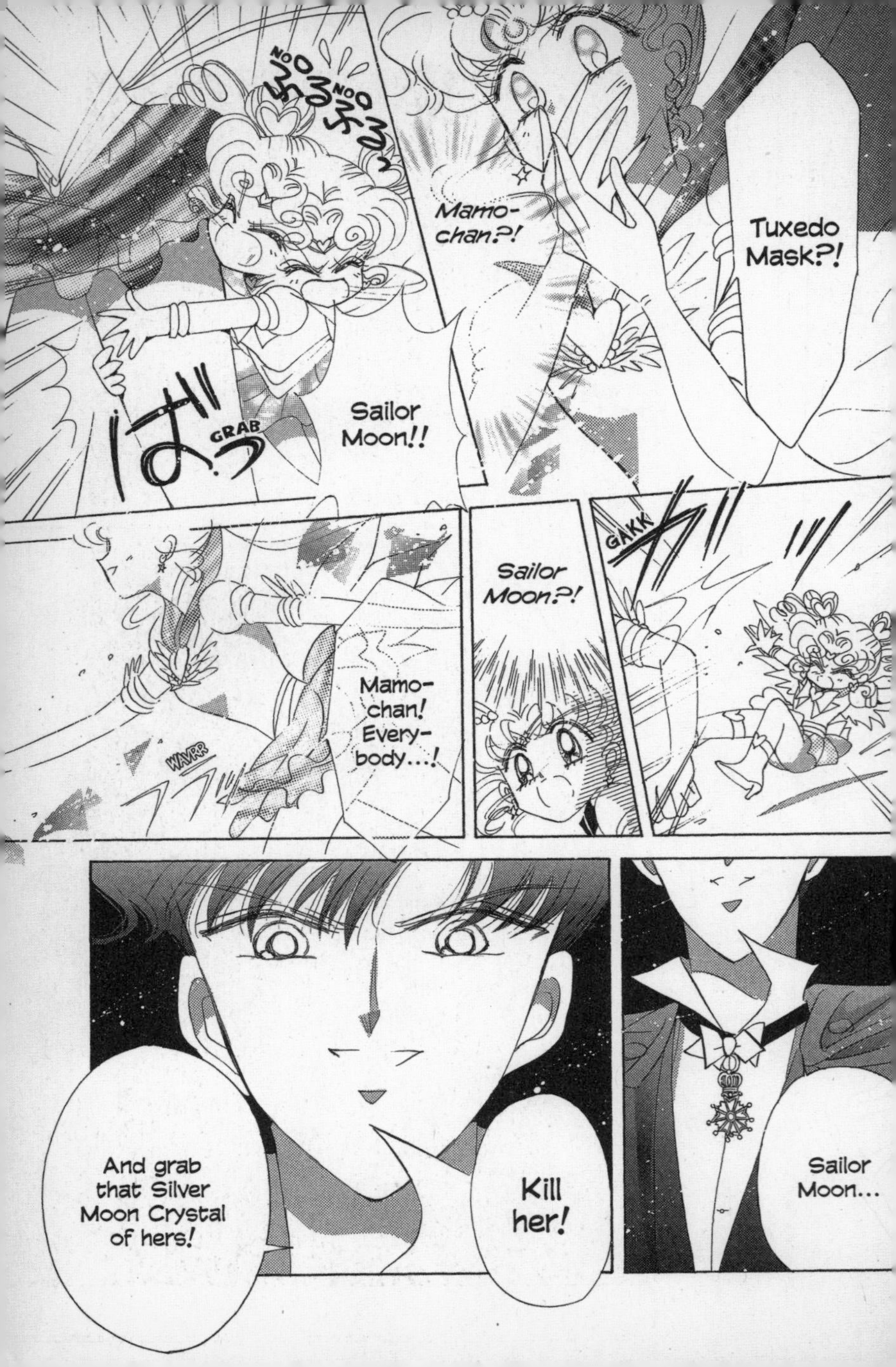
Tuxedo Mask?!
Mamo-chan?!
NOO NOO
ふるふる
Sailor Moon!!
ばっ
GRAB
GAKK
Sailor Moon?!
Mamo-chan! Everybody...!
WAVRR
Sailor Moon...
Kill her!
And grab that Silver Moon Crystal of hers!

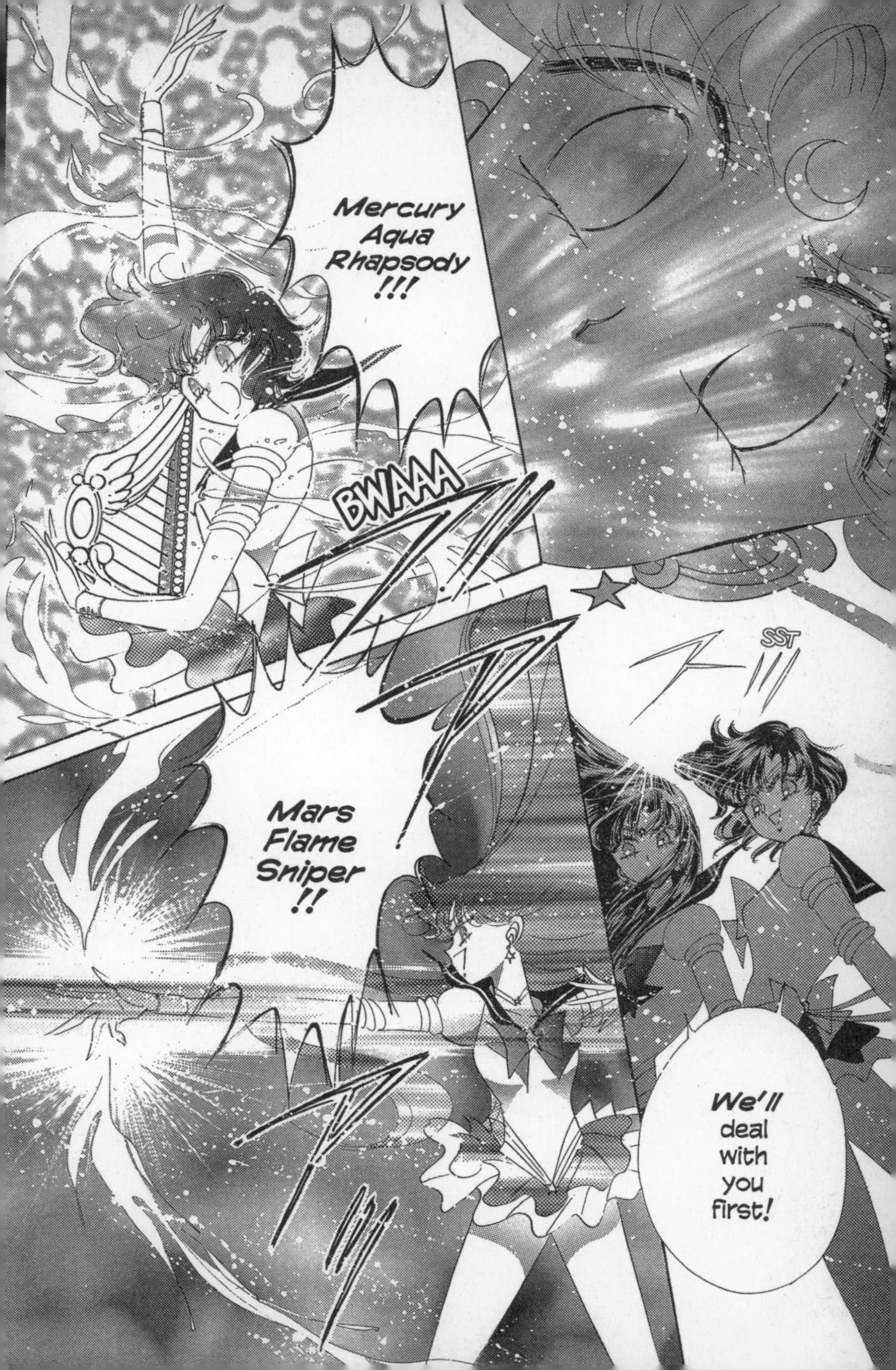
Mercury Aqua Rhapsody !!!
BWAAA
SST
We'll deal with you first!
Mars Flame Sniper !!

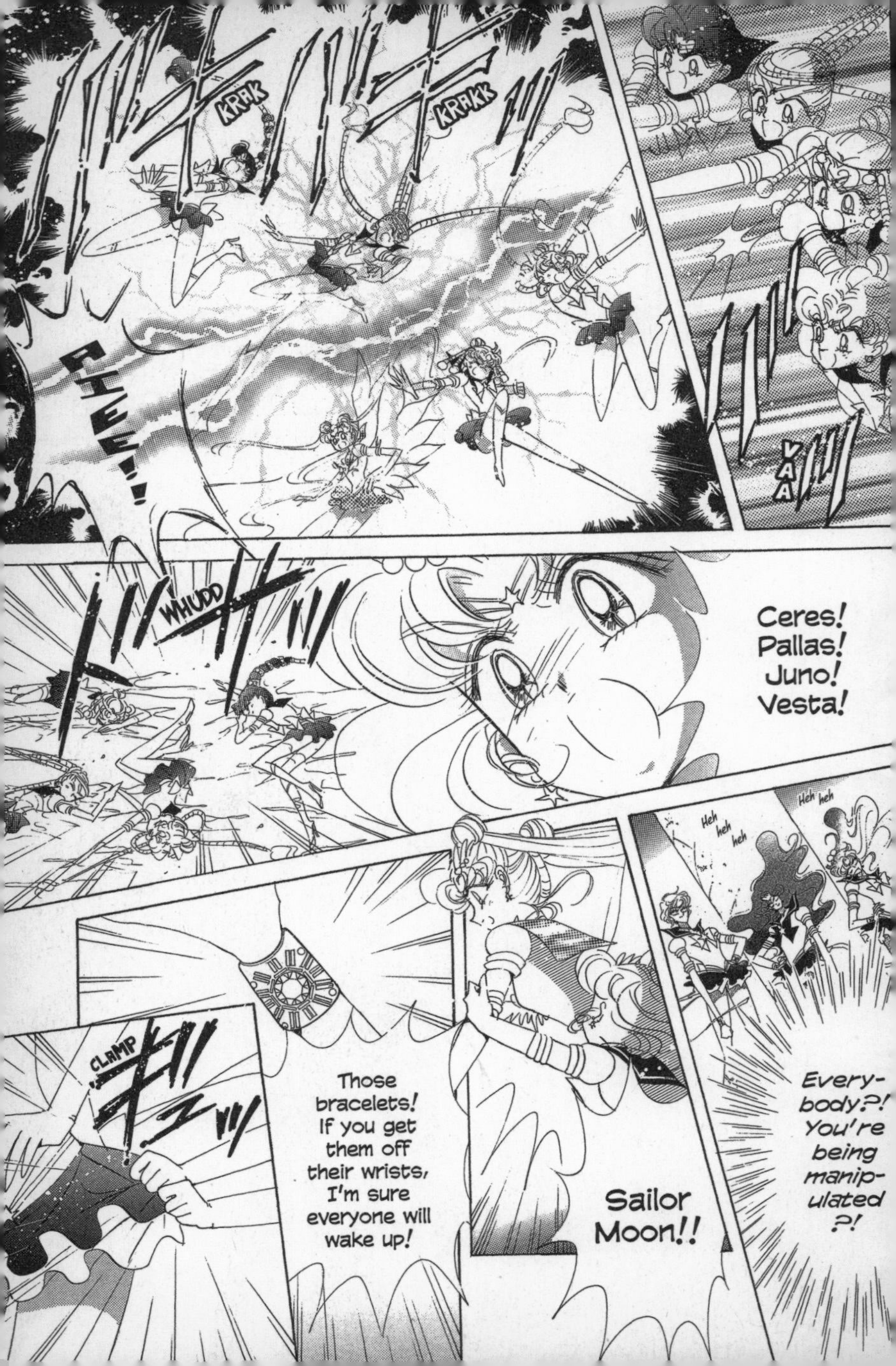
VAA
KRAKK
KRAK
PIEE!!
Ceres! Pallas! Juno! Vesta!
WHUDD
Heh heh
Heh heh heh
Every-body?! You're being manip-ulated?!
Sailor Moon!!
Those bracelets! If you get them off their wrists, I'm sure everyone will wake up!
CLAMP

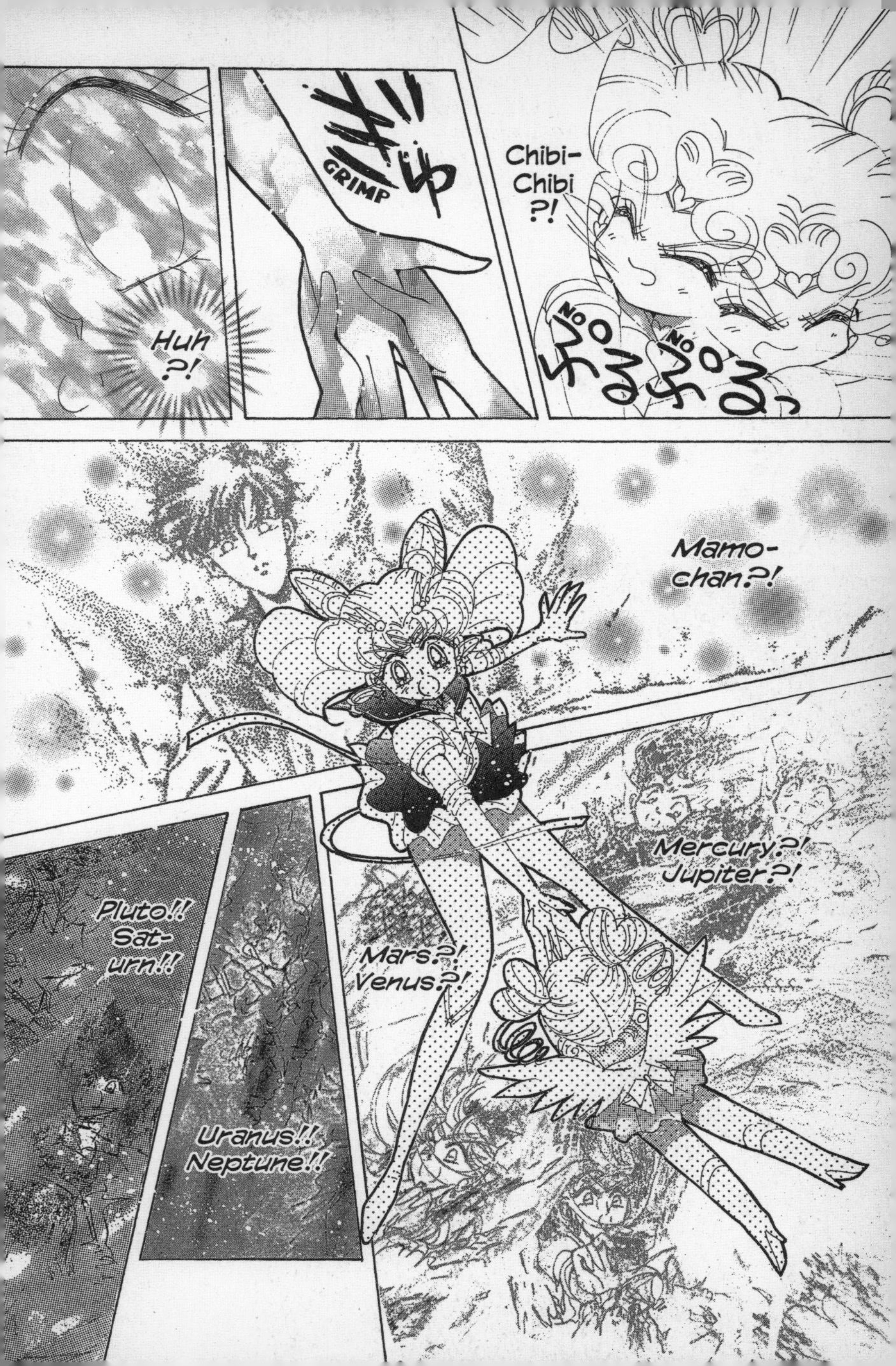
Chibi-
Chibi
?!
NO NO
ふるふるっ
GRIMP
ぎゅ
Huh
?!
Mamo-
chan?!
Mercury?!
Jupiter?!
Mars?!
Venus?!
Uranus!!
Neptune!!
Pluto!!
Sat-
urn!!

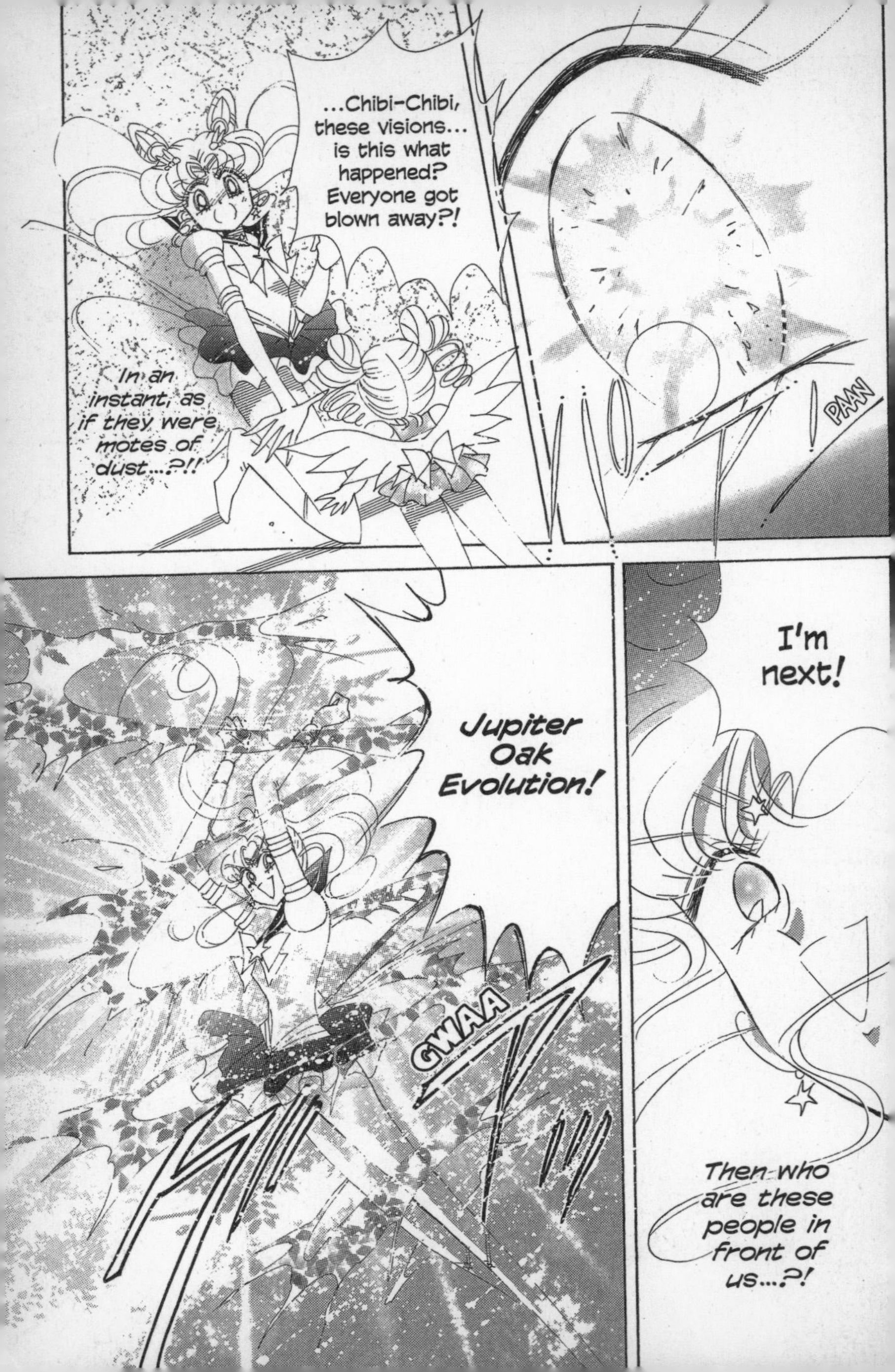
PAAN
...Chibi-Chibi, these visions... is this what happened? Everyone got blown away?!
In an instant, as if they were motes of dust...?!!
I'm next!
Then who are these people in front of us...?!
Jupiter Oak Evolution!
GWAA

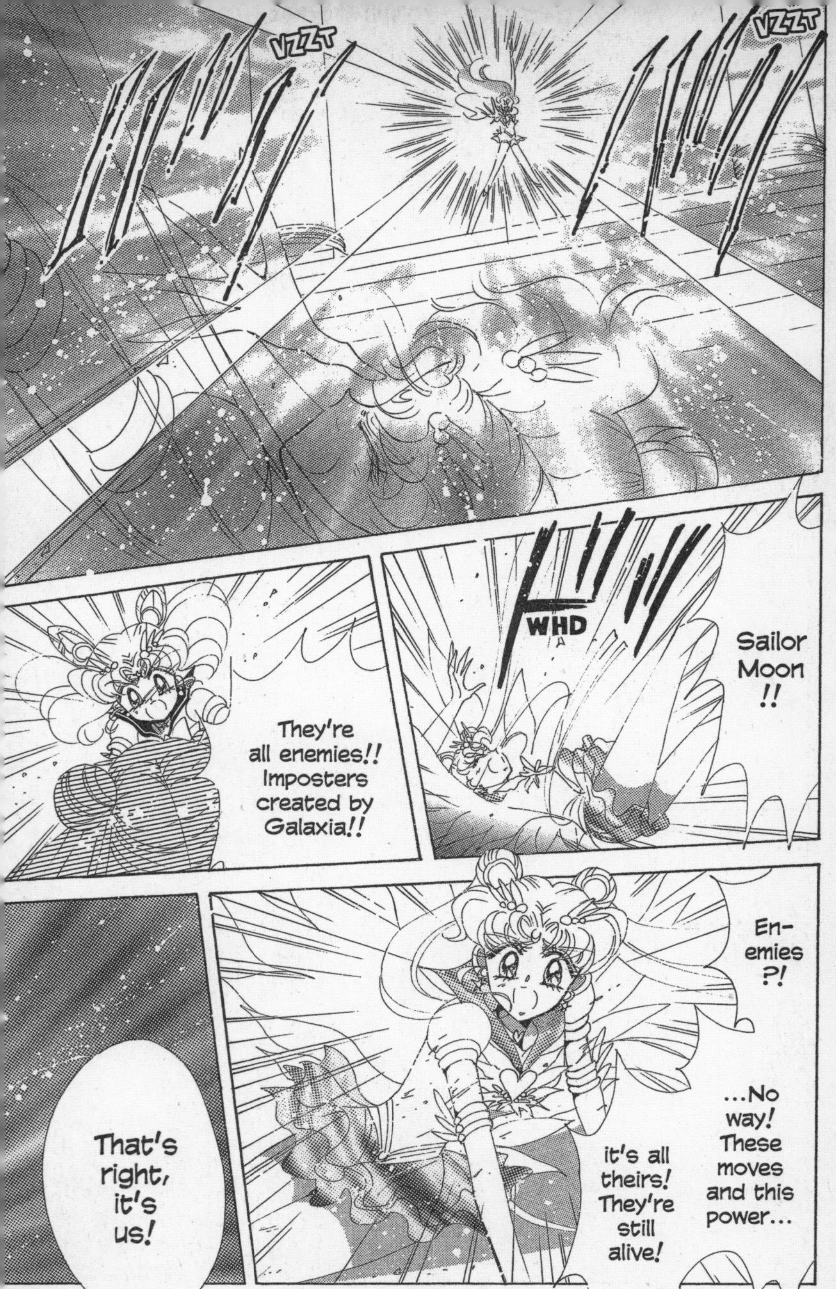
VZZT
VZZT
WHD
Sailor Moon !!
They're all enemies!! Imposters created by Galaxia!!
En-emies ?!
...No way! These moves and this power...
it's all theirs! They're still alive!
That's right, it's us!

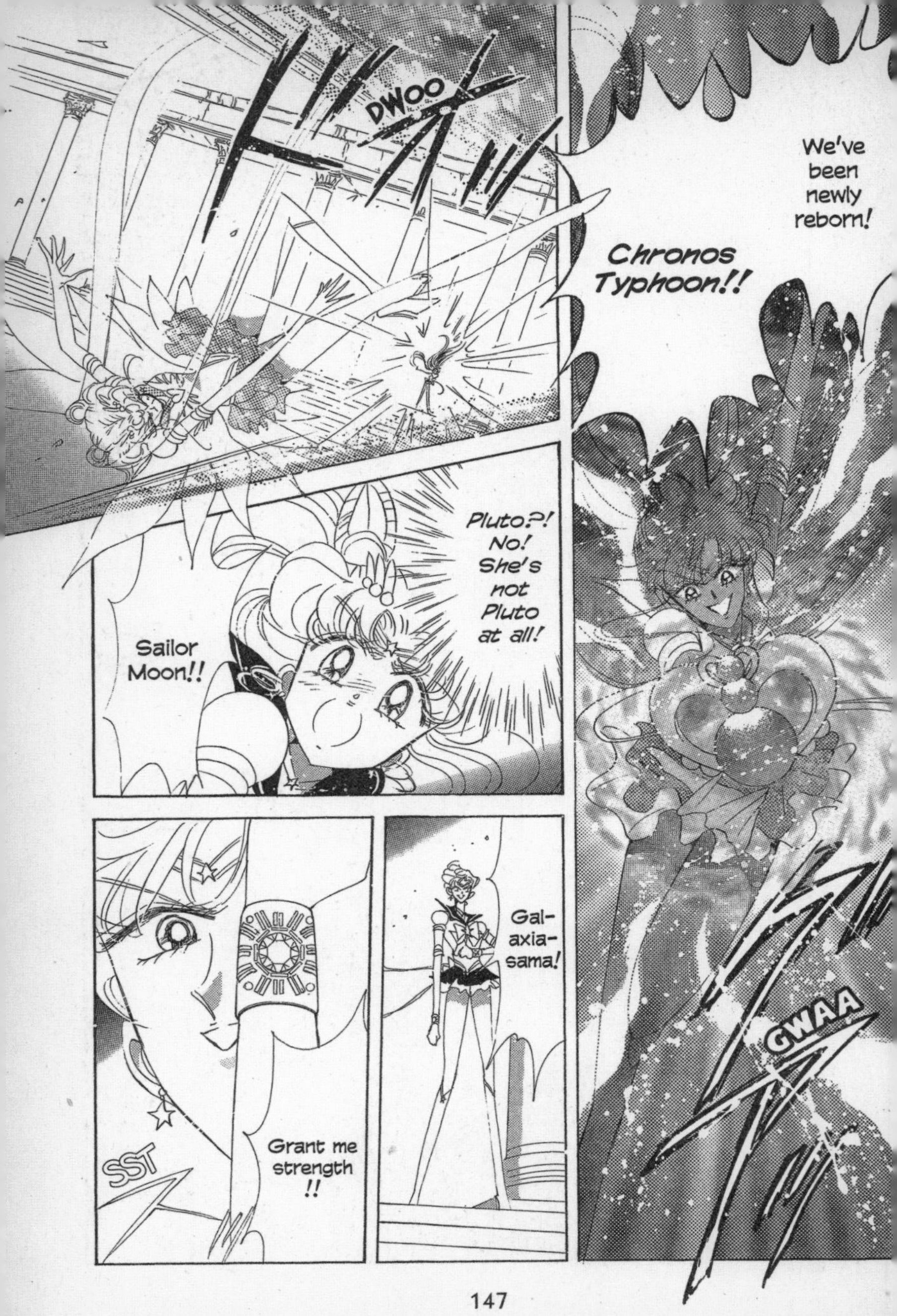

We've been newly reborn!
Chronos Typhoon!!
GWAA
DWOO
Pluto?! No! She's not Pluto at all!
Sailor Moon!!
Gal-axia-sama!
Grant me strength !!
SST

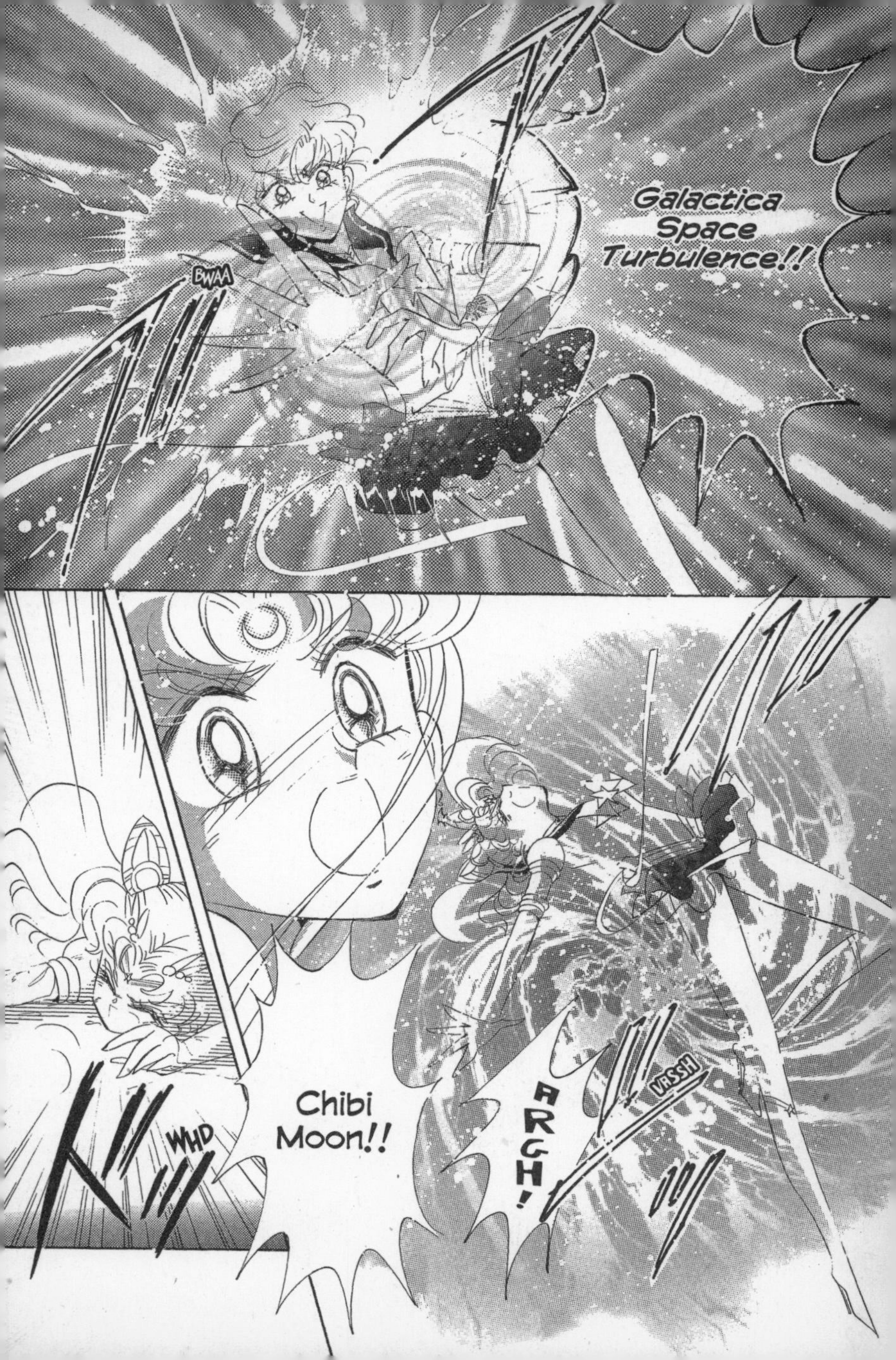
Galactica Space Turbulence!!
BWAA
VASSH
ARGH!
Chibi Moon!!
WHD

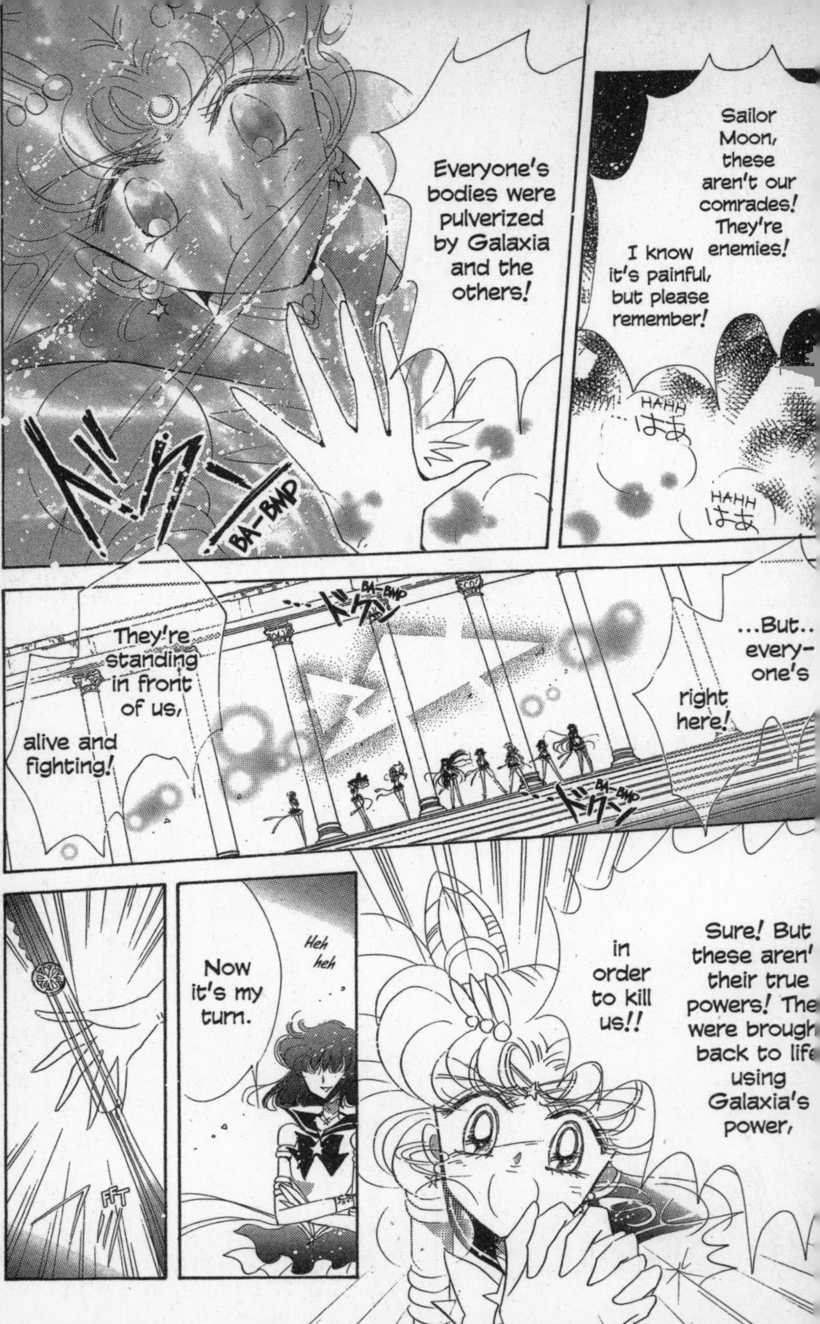
Sailor Moon, these aren't our comrades! They're enemies!
I know it's painful, but please remember!
HAHH はあ
HAHH はあ
Everyone's bodies were pulverized by Galaxia and the others!
BA-BMP
...But... every-one's
right here!
They're standing in front of us,
alive and fighting!
BA-BMP
BA-BMP
Sure! But these aren' their true powers! The were brough back to lif using Galaxia's power,
in order to kill us!!
Heh heh
Now it's my turn.
FFT

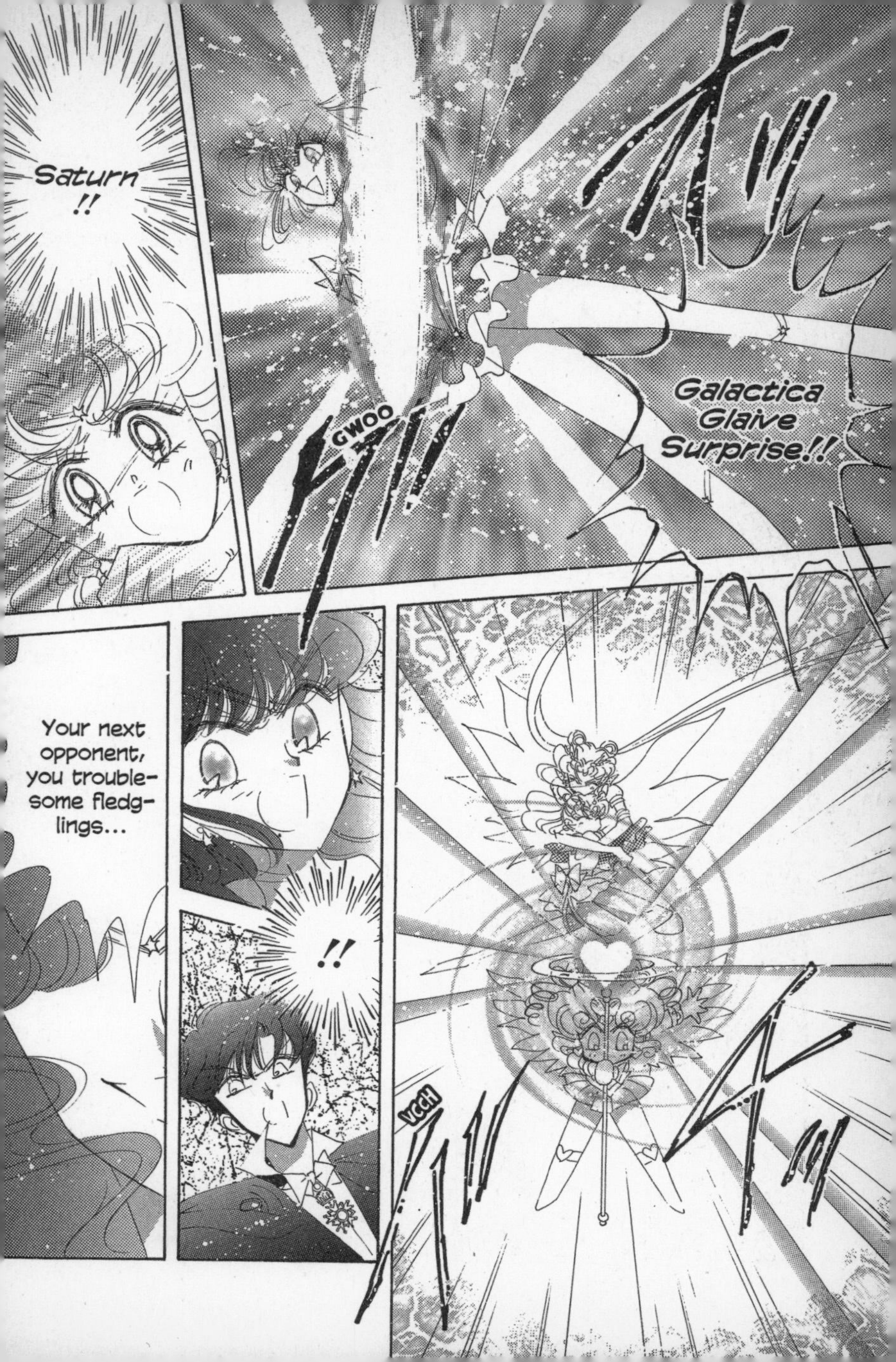
Galactica Glaive Surprise!!
GWOO
Saturn !!
VCCH
!!
Your next opponent, you trouble-some fledg-lings...

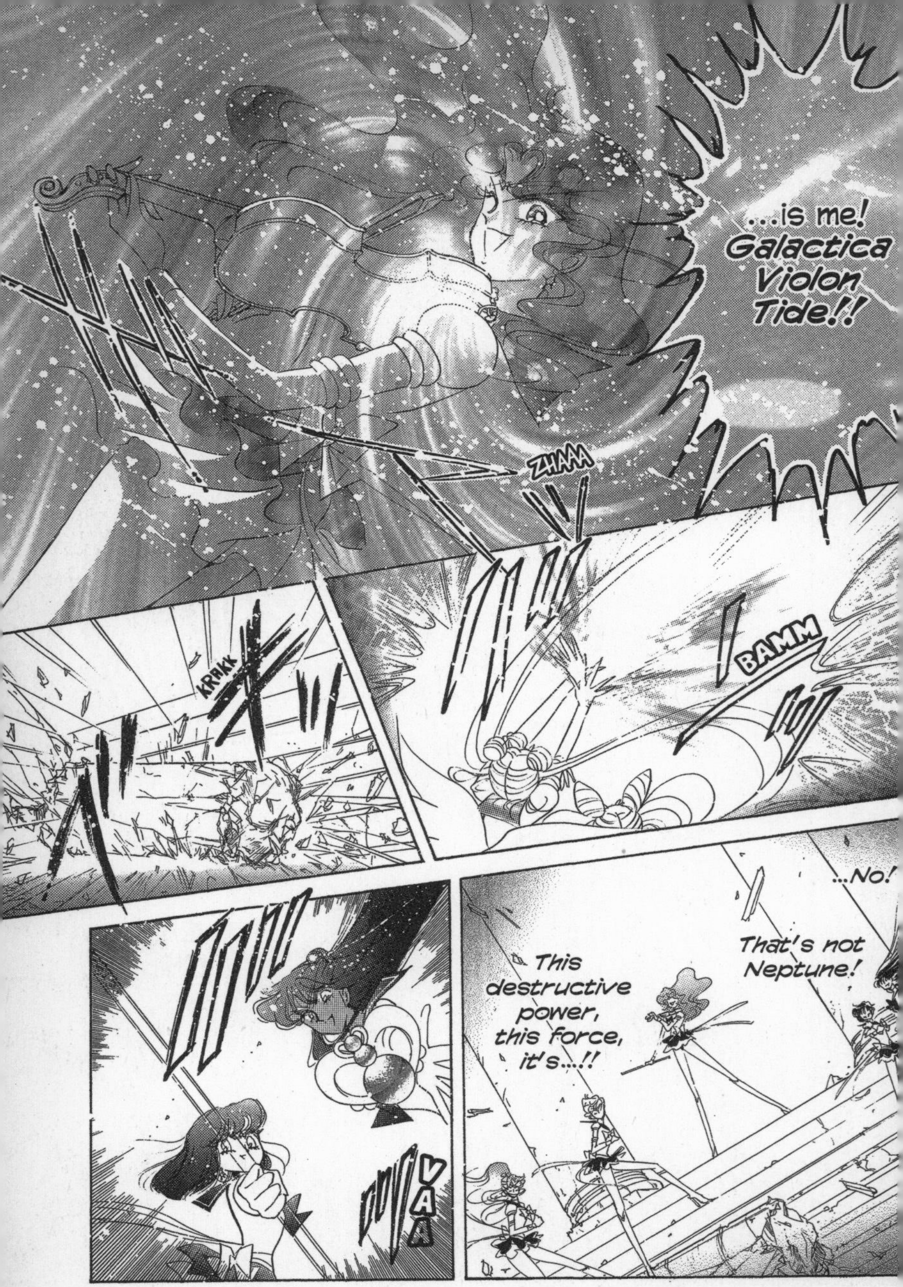
...is me! Galactica Violon Tide!!
ZHAAA
BAMM
KRAKK
...No!
That's not Neptune!
This destructive power, this force, it's...!!
VAA

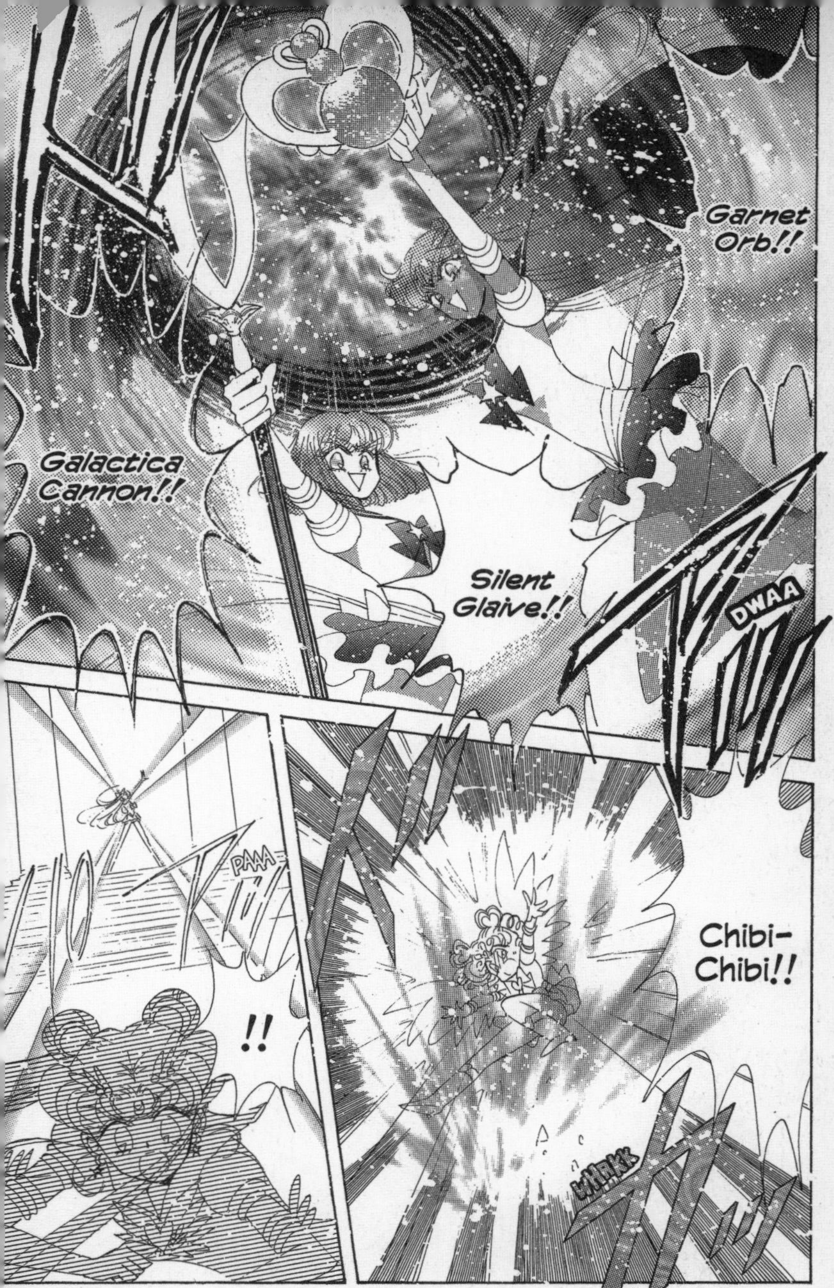
Garnet Orb!!
Galactica Cannon!!
Silent Glaive!!
DWAA
Chibi-Chibi!!
WHAKK
PAAA
!!

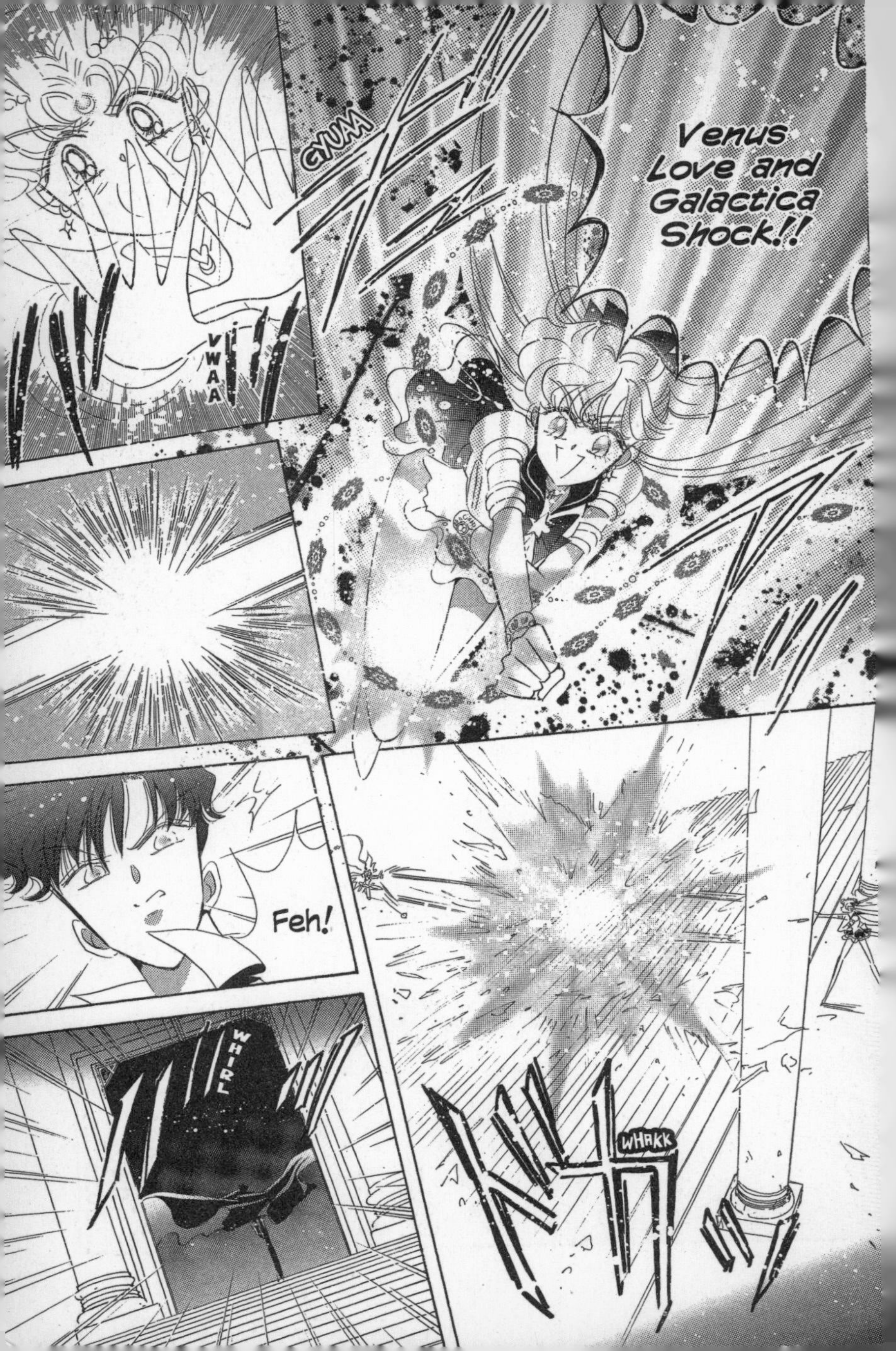
Venus Love and Galactica Shock!!
GYUAA
VWAA
WHAKK
Feh!
WHIRL

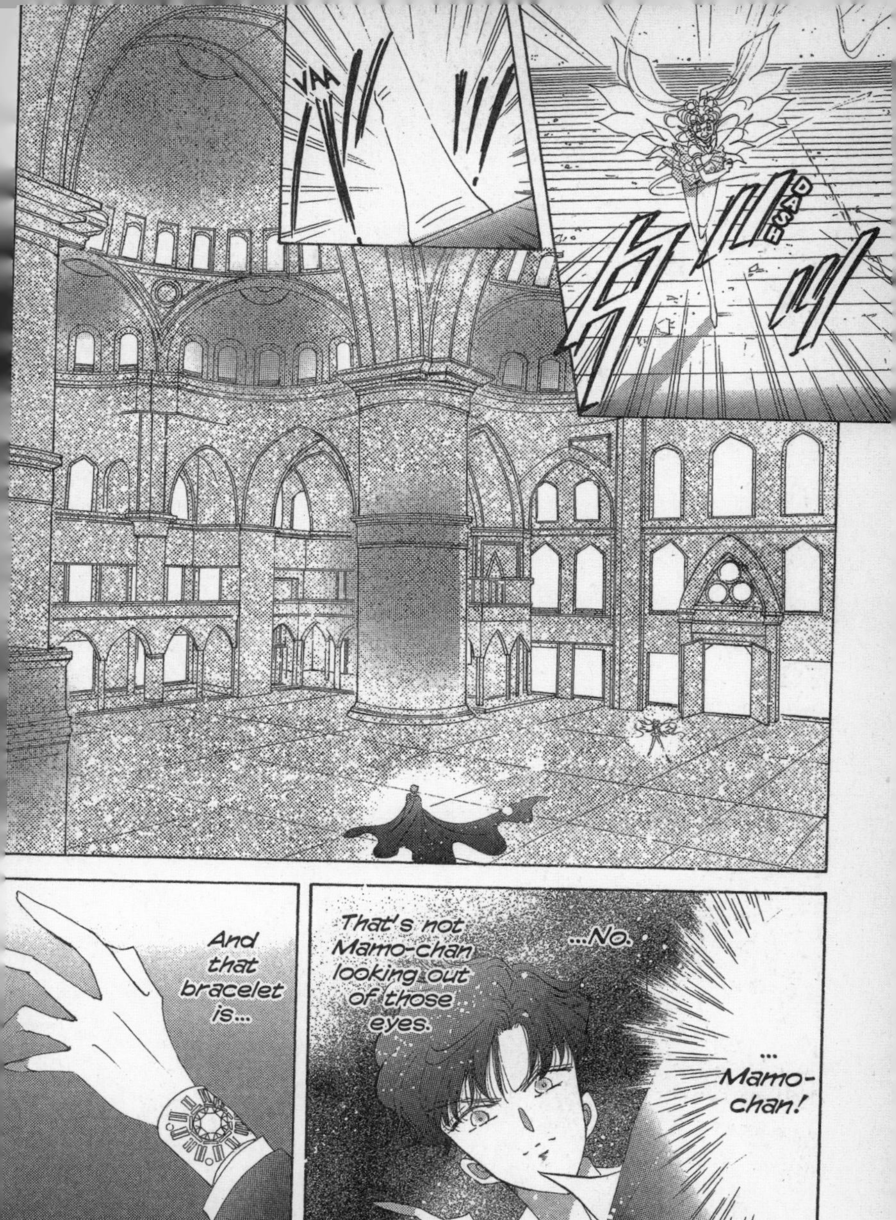
DASH
VAA
...Mamo-chan!
...No.
That's not Mamo-chan looking out of those eyes.
And that bracelet is...

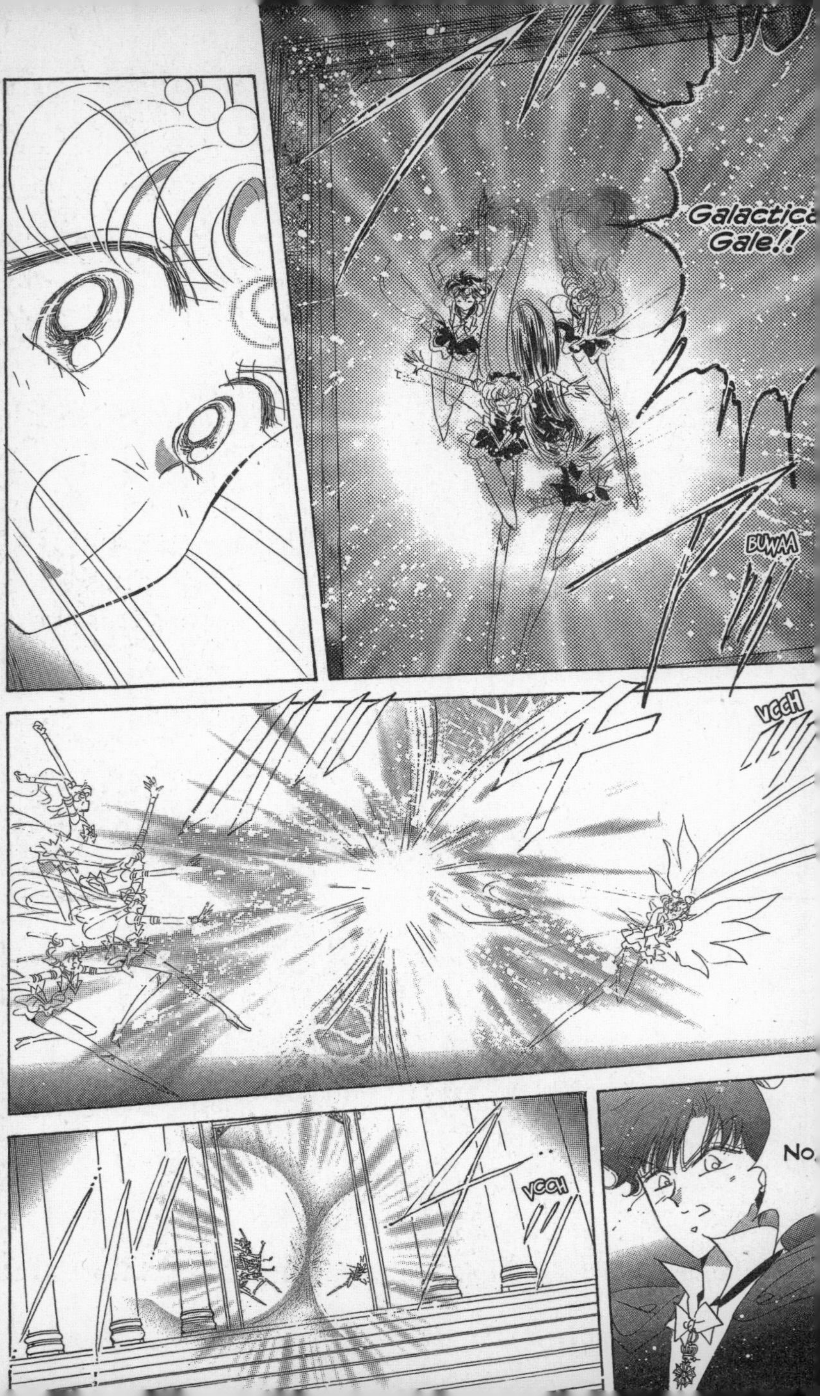
Galactica Gale!!
BUWAA
VCCH
No...
VCCH

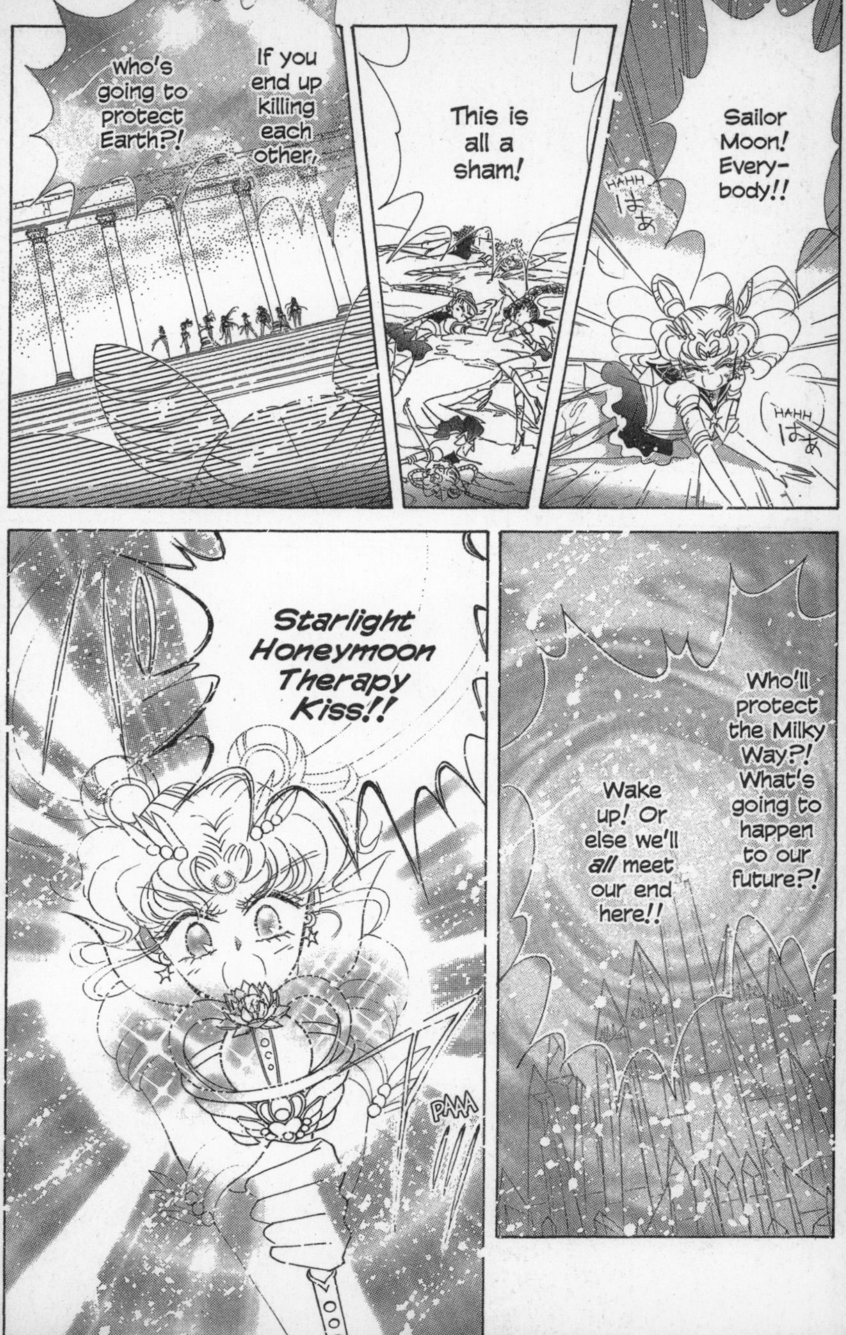
Sailor Moon! Every-body!!
HAHH はあ
HAHH はあ
This is all a sham!
If you end up killing each other,
who's going to protect Earth?!
Who'll protect the Milky Way?! What's going to happen to our future?!
Wake up! Or else we'll *all* meet our end here!!
Starlight Honeymoon Therapy Kiss!!
PAAA

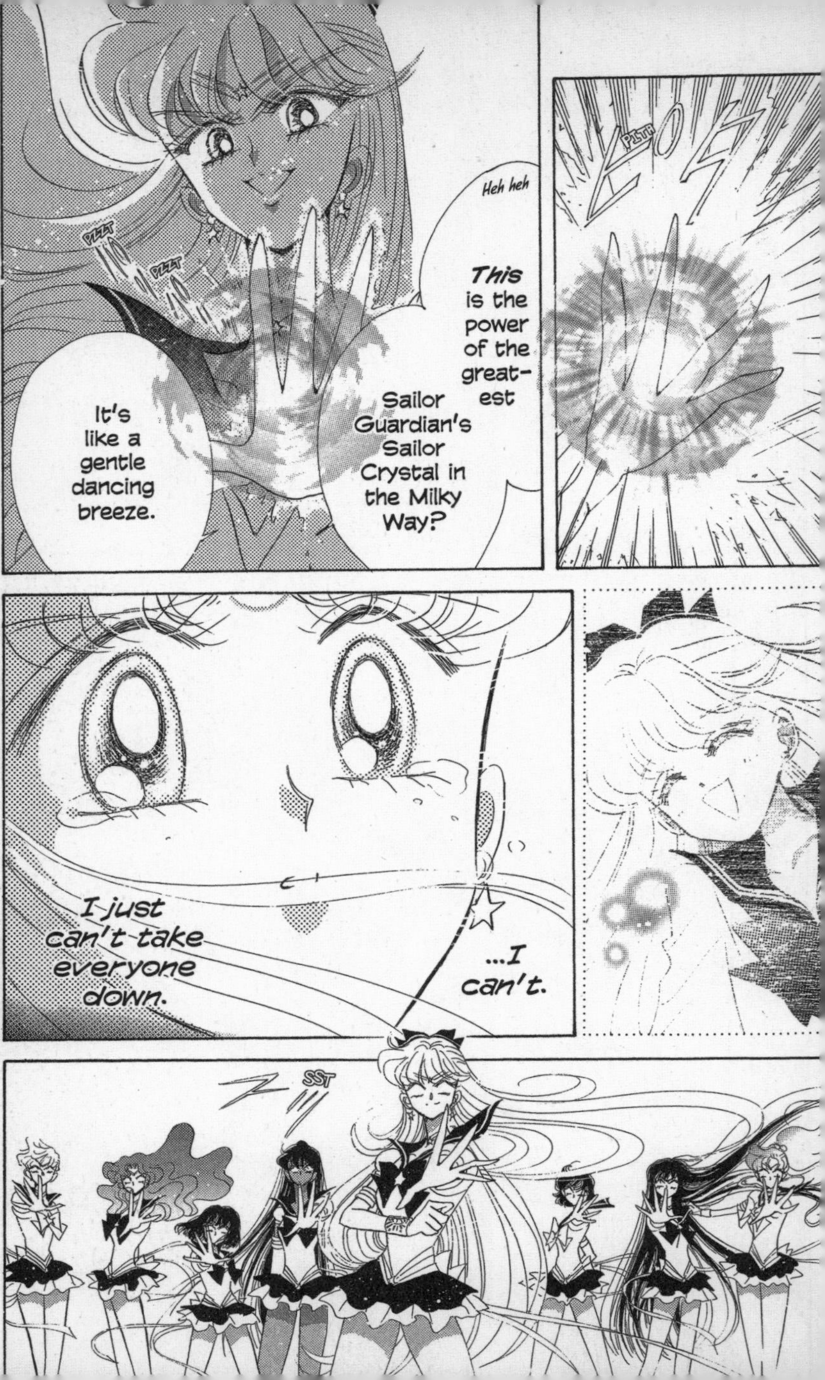
PITA
Heh heh
This is the power of the greatest Sailor Guardian's Sailor Crystal in the Milky Way?
It's like a gentle dancing breeze.
PIZZT
PIZZT
...I can't.
I just can't take everyone down.
SST

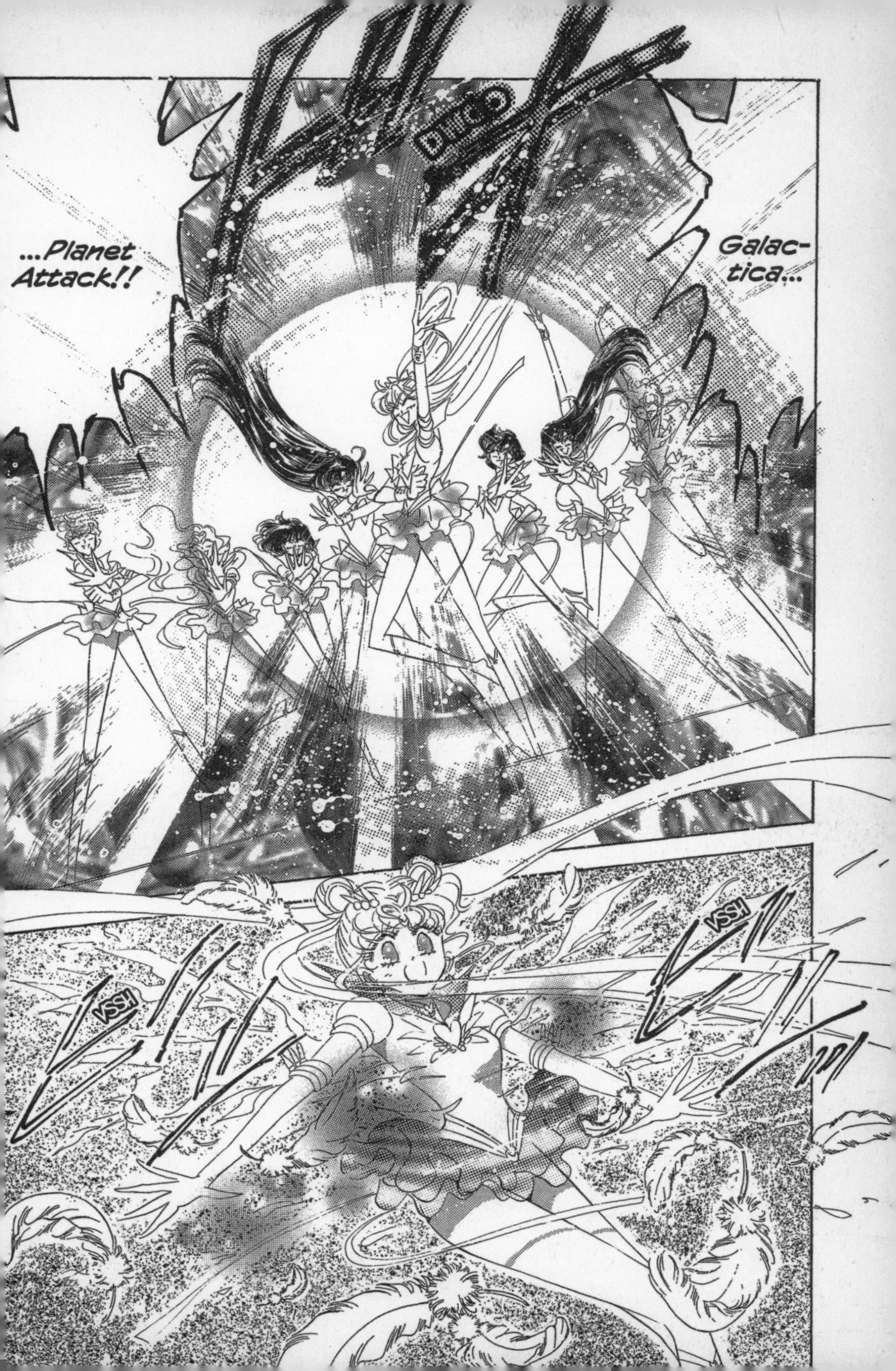
Galac-
tica...
...Planet
Attack!!
VSSH
VSSH

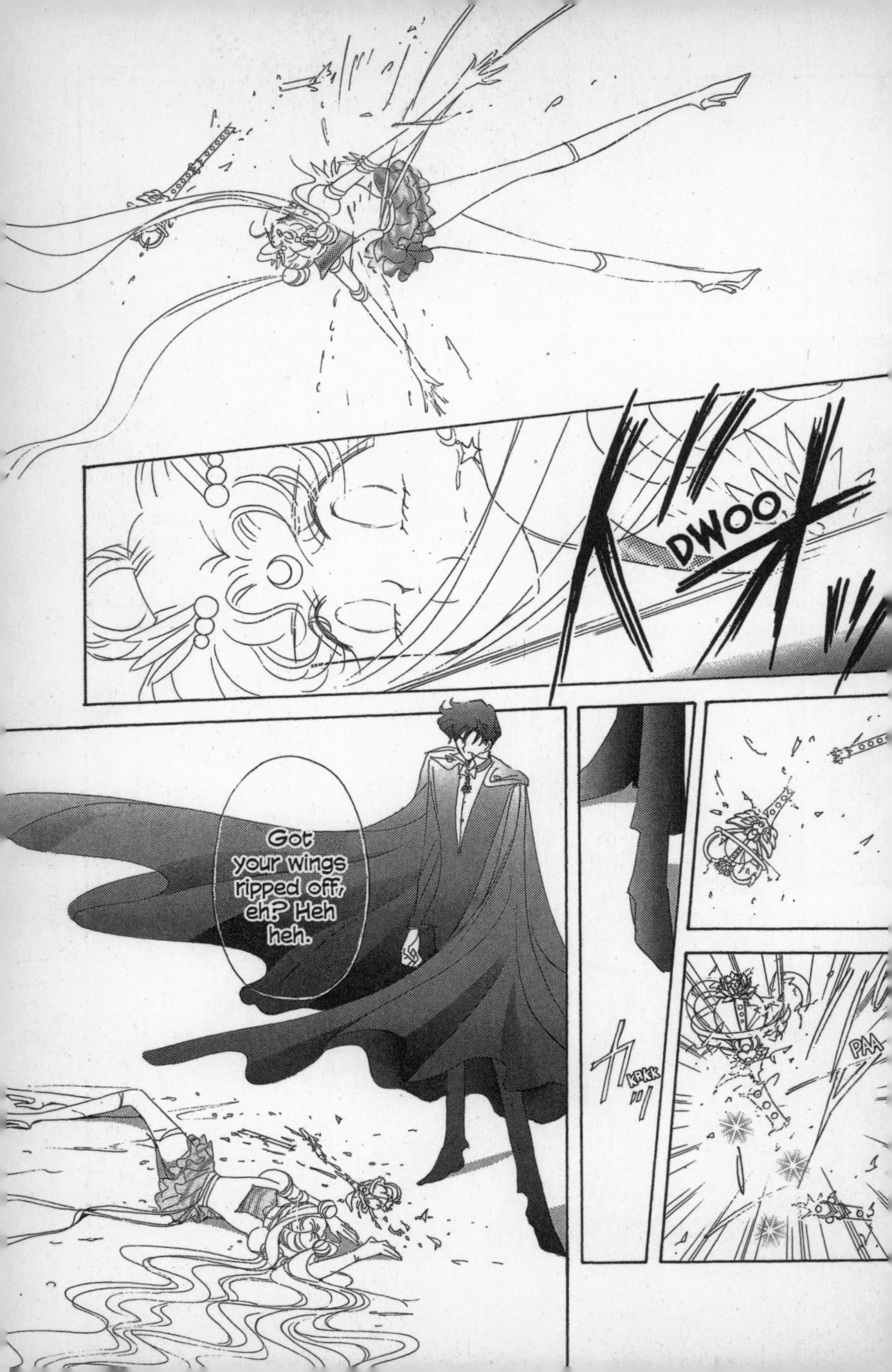
DWOO
PAA
KAKK
Got your wings ripped off, eh? Heh heh.

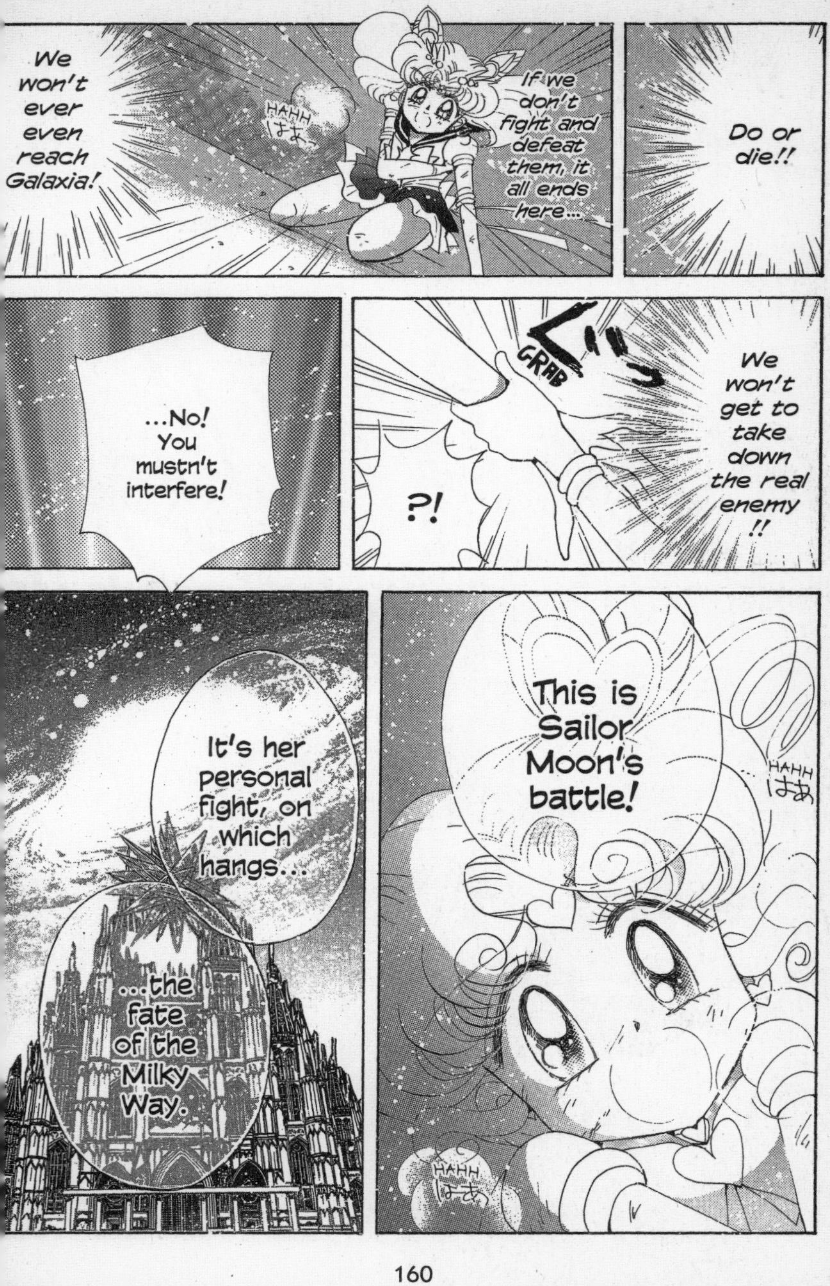
Do or die!!
If we don't fight and defeat them, it all ends here...
HAHH はあ
We won't ever even reach Galaxia!
GRAB
We won't get to take down the real enemy!!
?!
...No! You mustn't interfere!
This is Sailor Moon's battle!
HAHH はあ
HAHH はあ
It's her personal fight, on which hangs...
...the fate of the Milky Way.

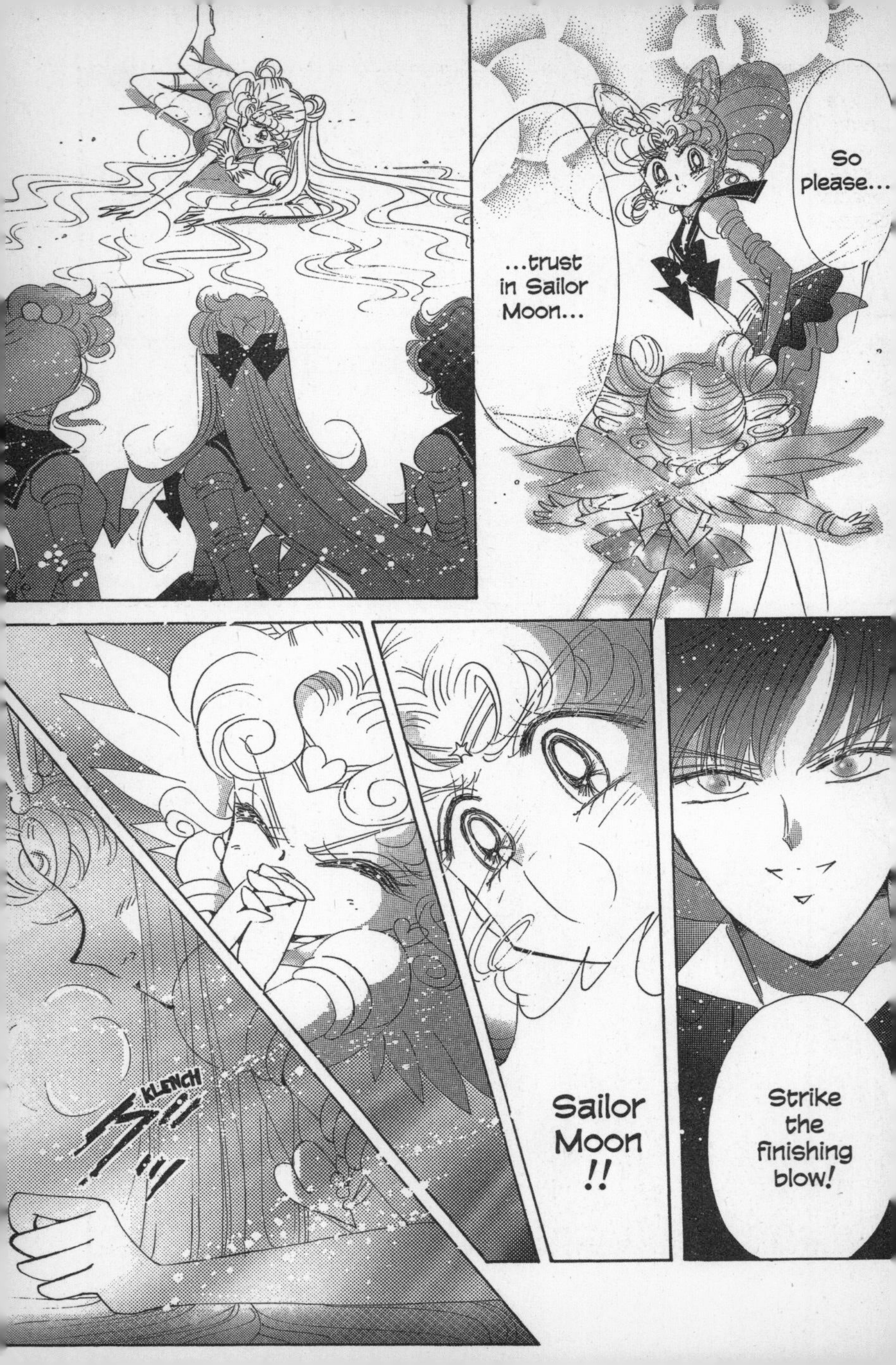
So please...
...trust in Sailor Moon...
Strike the finishing blow!
Sailor Moon!!
KLENCH

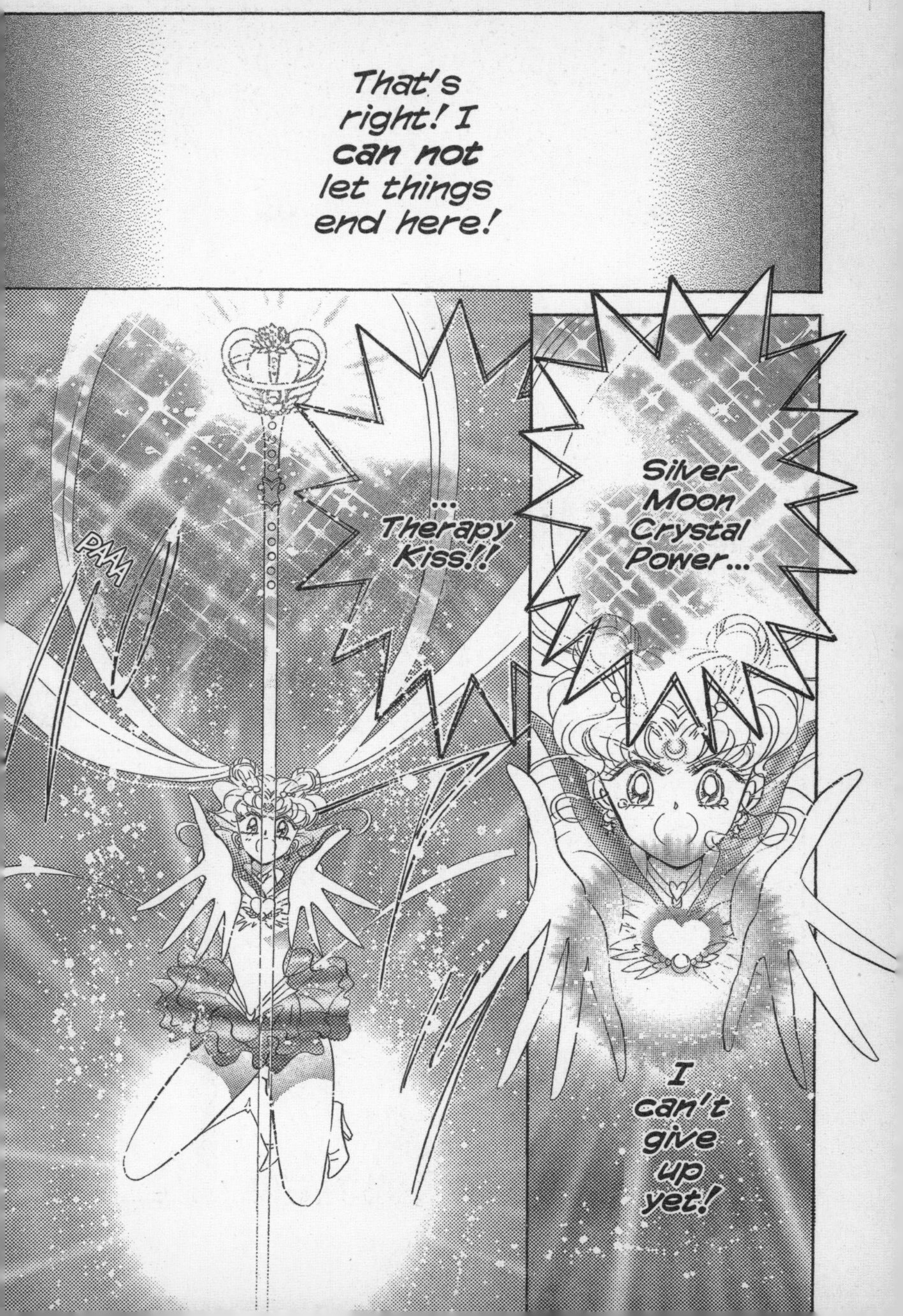

That's right! I can not let things end here!
Silver Moon Crystal Power...
I can't give up yet!
...Therapy Kiss!!
PAAA

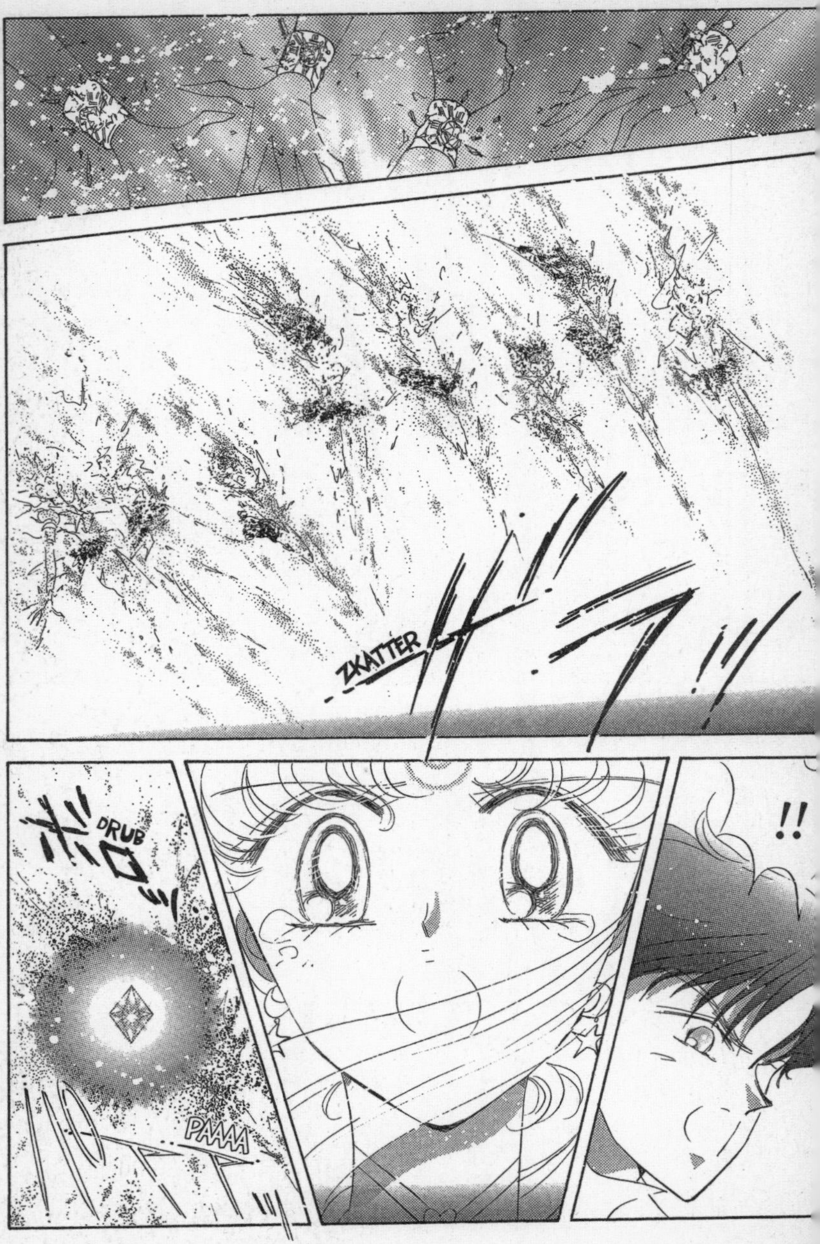
ZKATTER
!!
DRUB
PAAAA

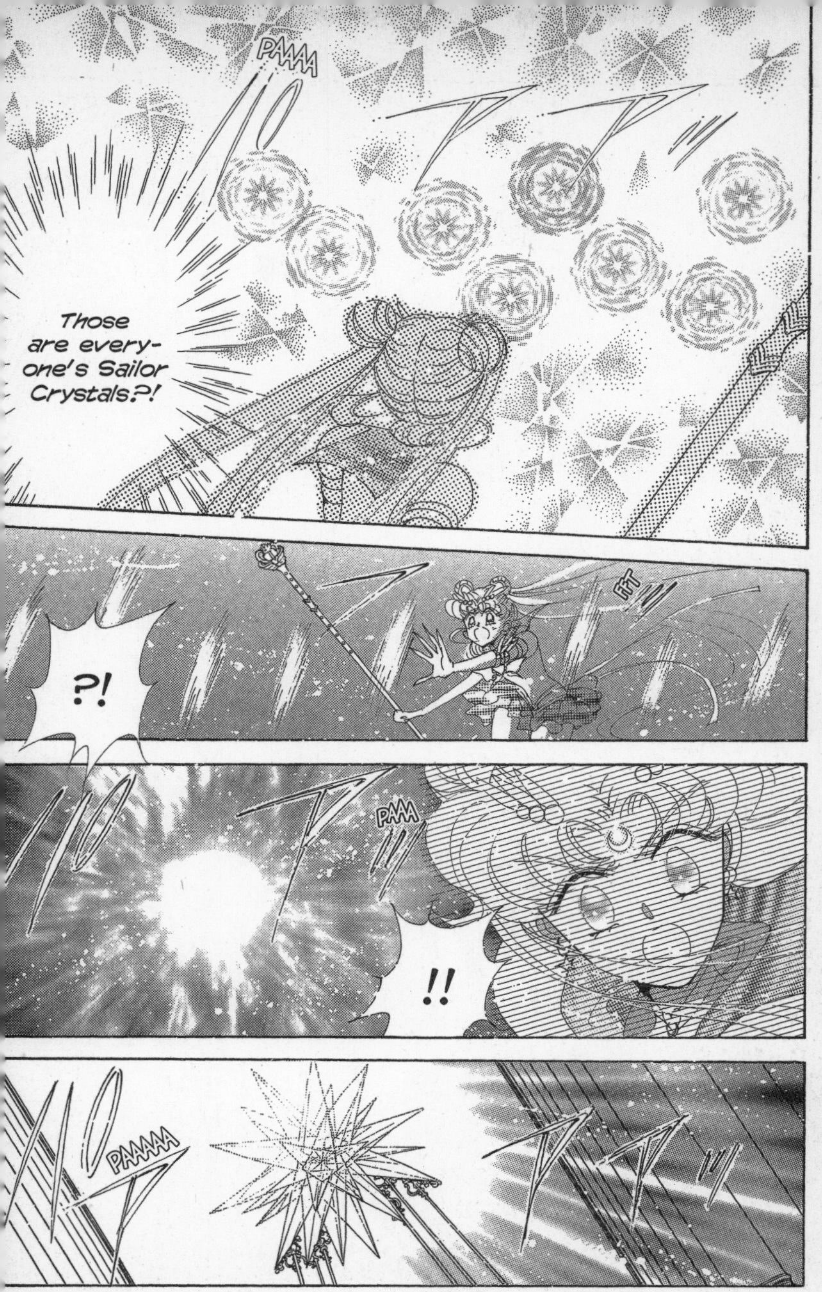
PAAAA
Those are every-one's Sailor Crystals?!
FT
?!
PAAA
!!
PAAAAA

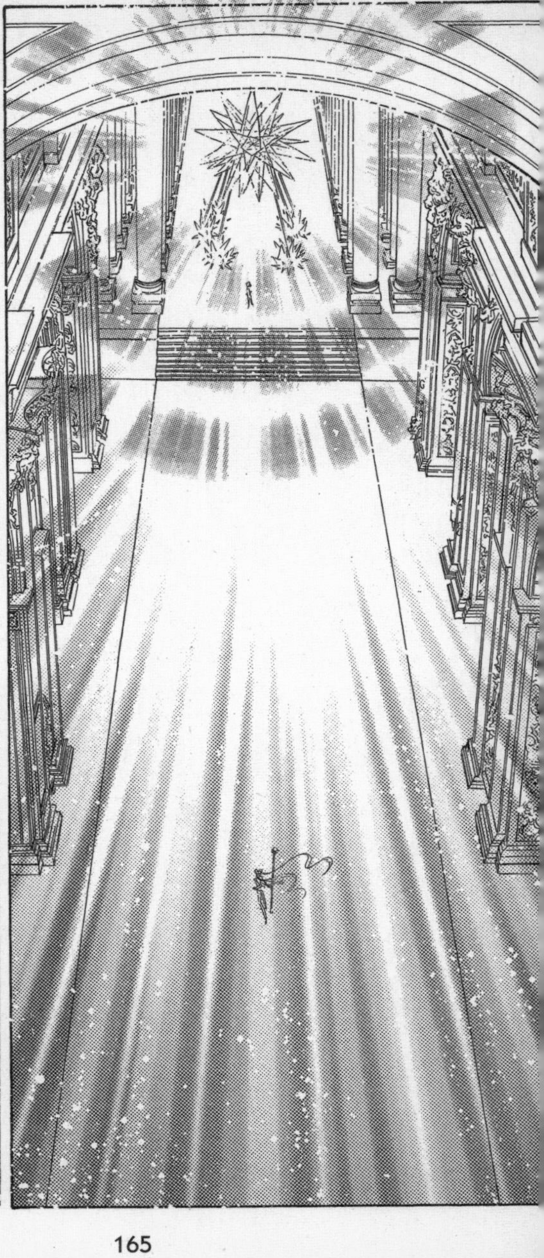
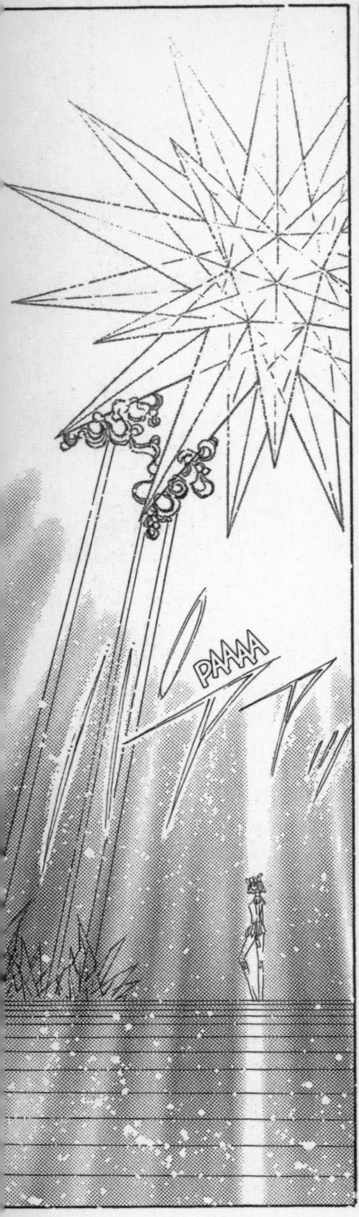
PAAAA

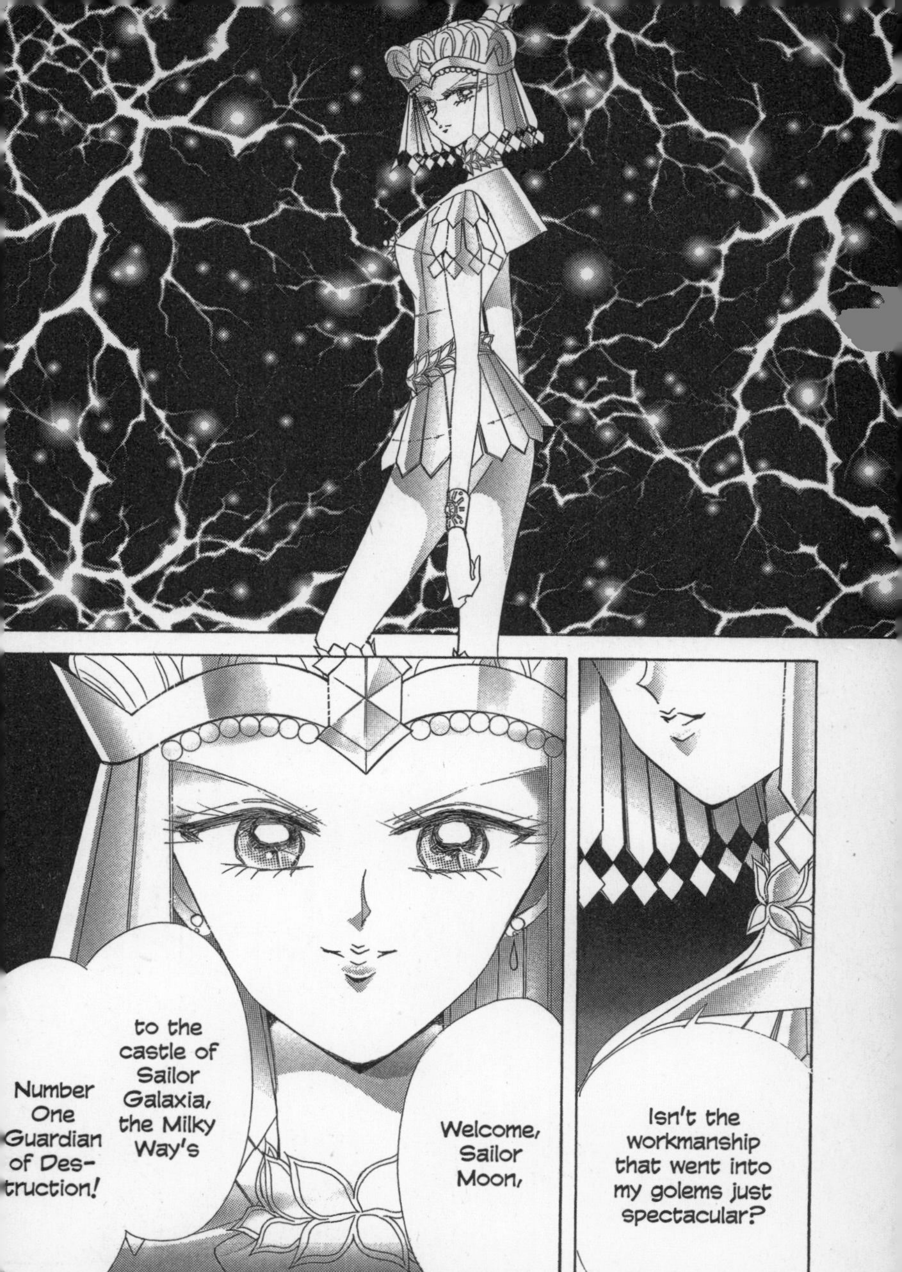
Isn't the workmanship that went into my golems just spectacular?
Welcome, Sailor Moon,
to the castle of Sailor Galaxia, the Milky Way's
Number One Guardian of Destruction!

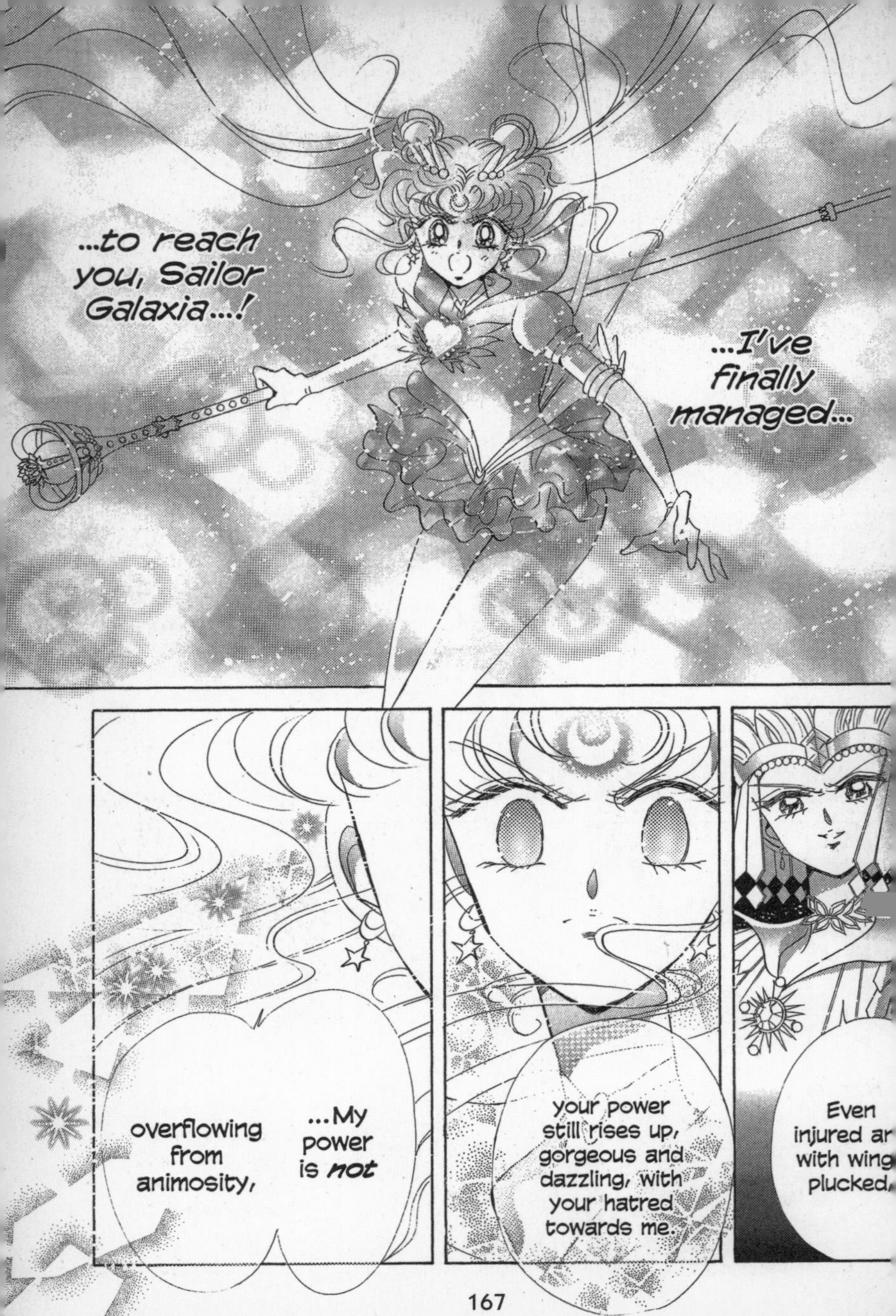

...I've finally managed...
...to reach you, Sailor Galaxia...!
Even injured ar with wing plucked,
your power still rises up, gorgeous and dazzling, with your hatred towards me.
...My power is *not*
overflowing from animosity,

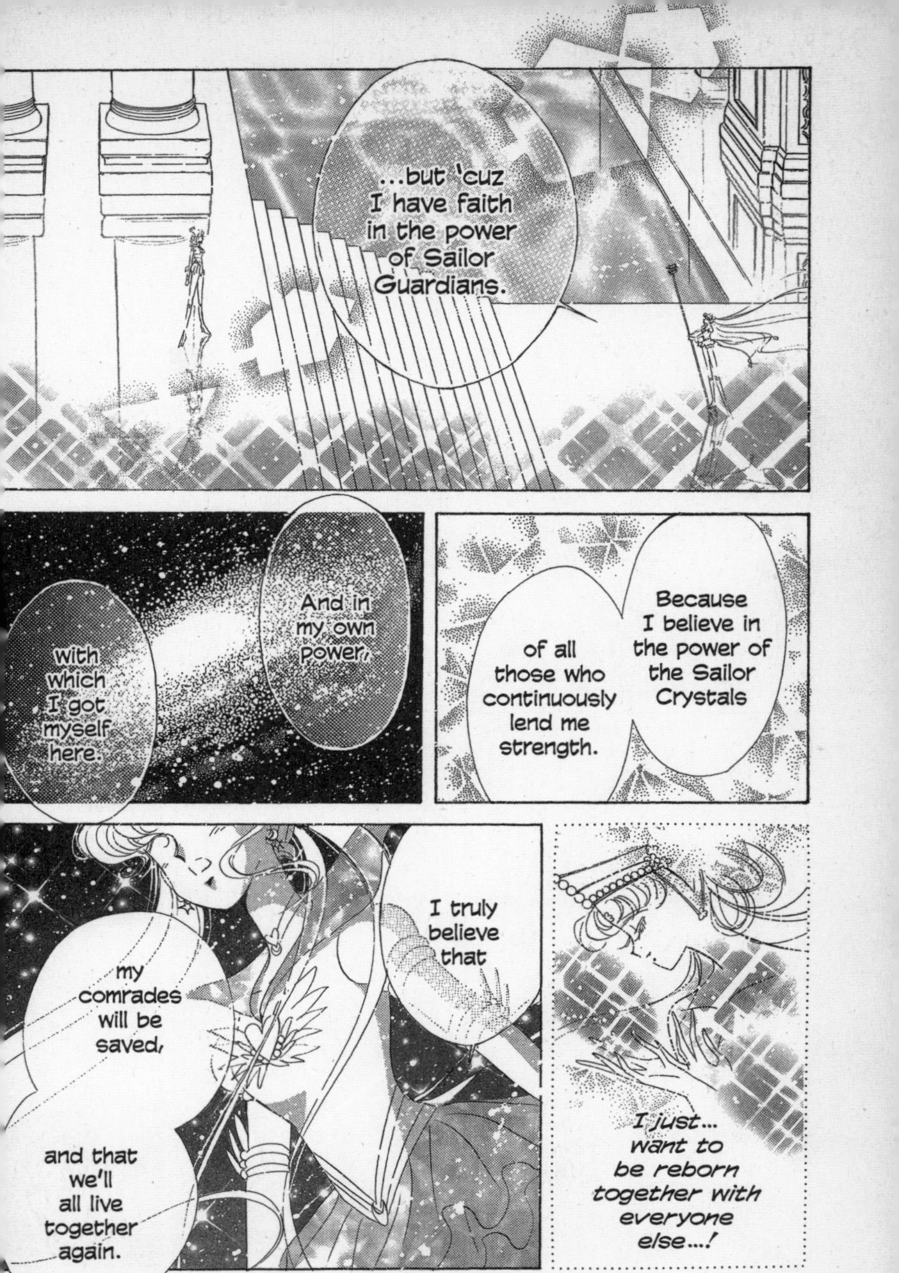
...but 'cuz I have faith in the power of Sailor Guardians.
Because I believe in the power of the Sailor Crystals
of all those who continuously lend me strength.
And in my own power,
with which I got myself here.
I just... want to be reborn together with everyone else...!
I truly believe that
my comrades will be saved,
and that we'll all live together again.

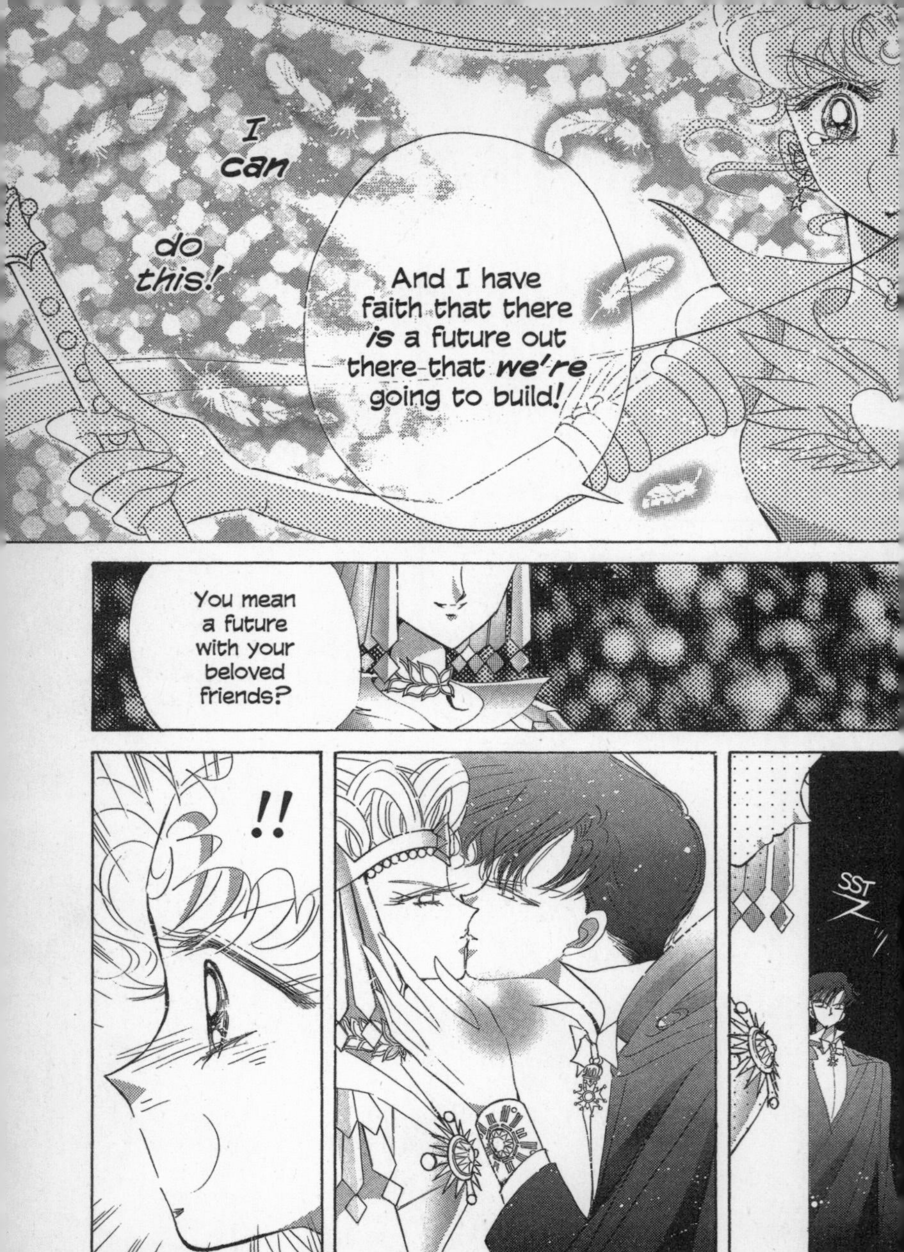

I can do this!
And I have faith that there *is* a future out there that *we're* going to build!
You mean a future with your beloved friends?
SST
!!

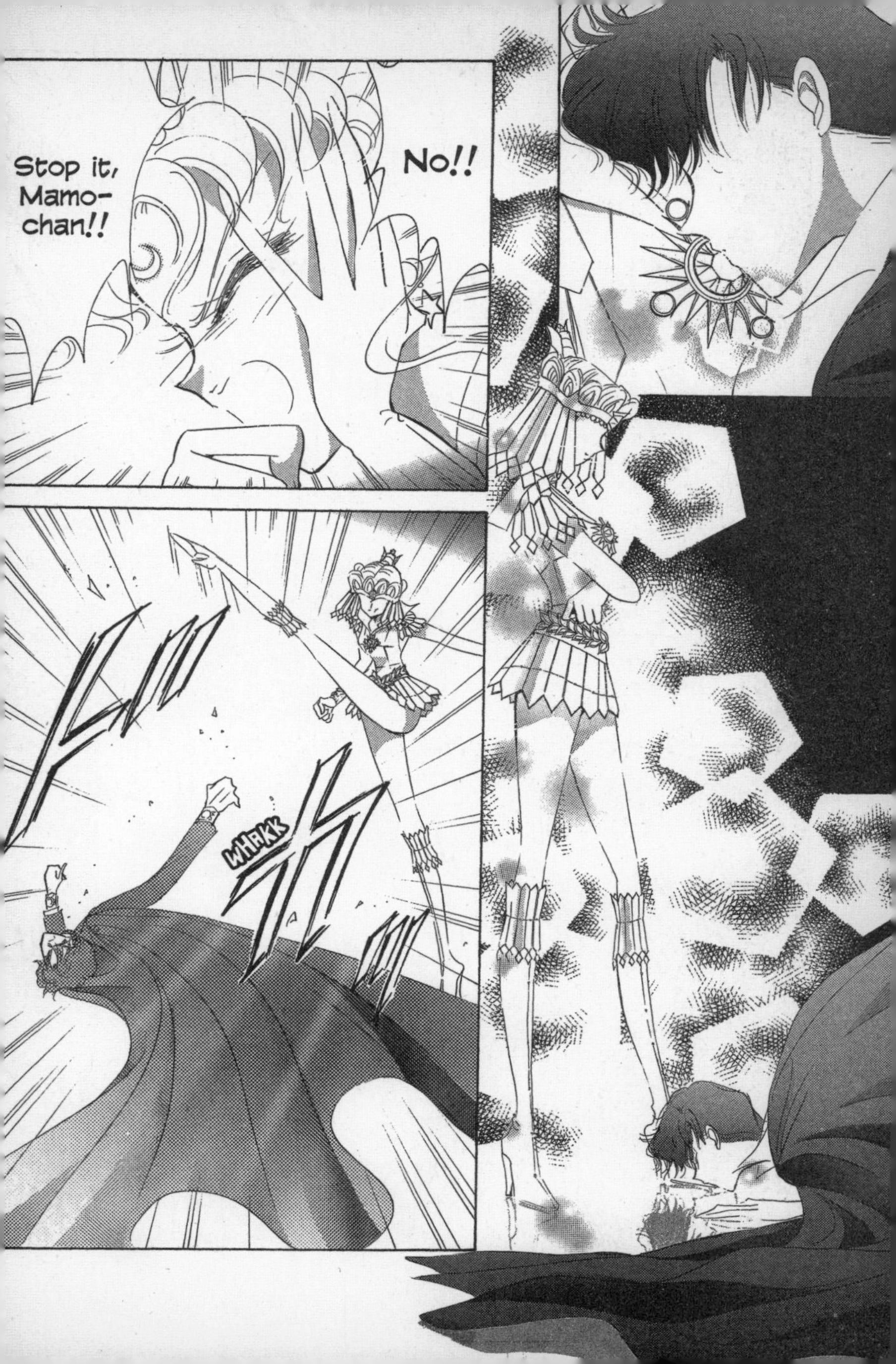
No!!
Stop it, Mamo-chan!!
WHAKK

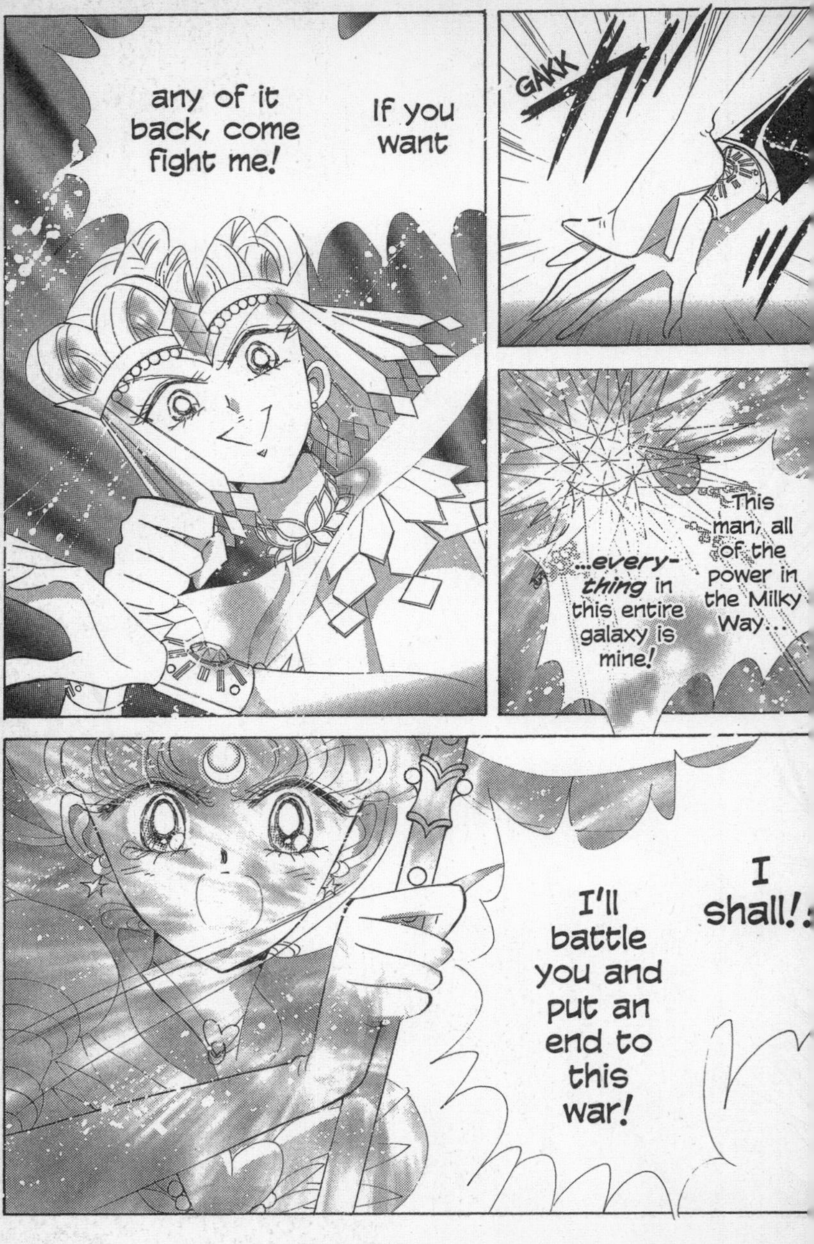
GAKK
This man, all of the power in the Milky Way...
...everything in this entire galaxy is mine!
If you want
any of it back, come fight me!
I shall!
I'll battle you and put an end to this war!

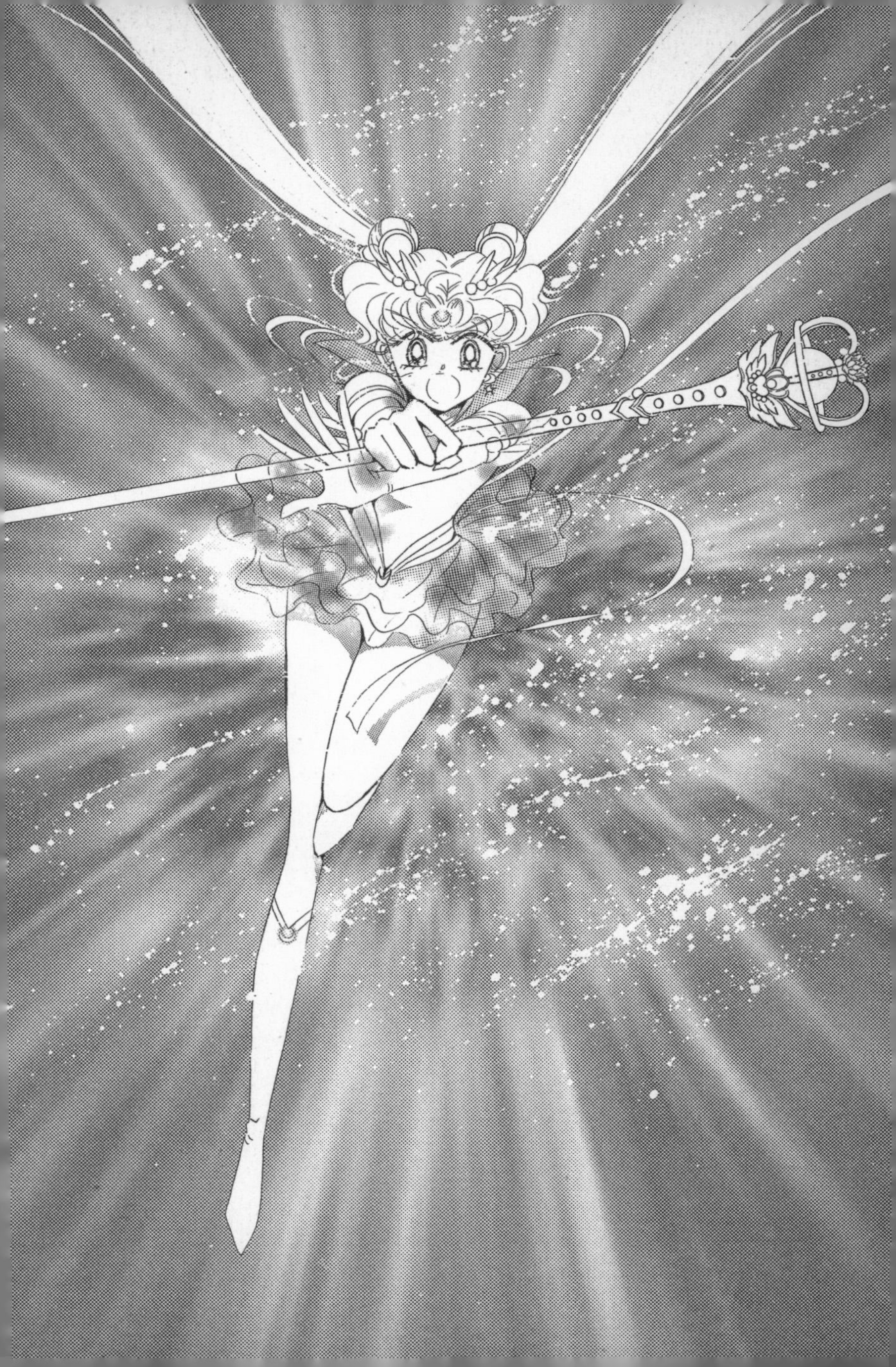

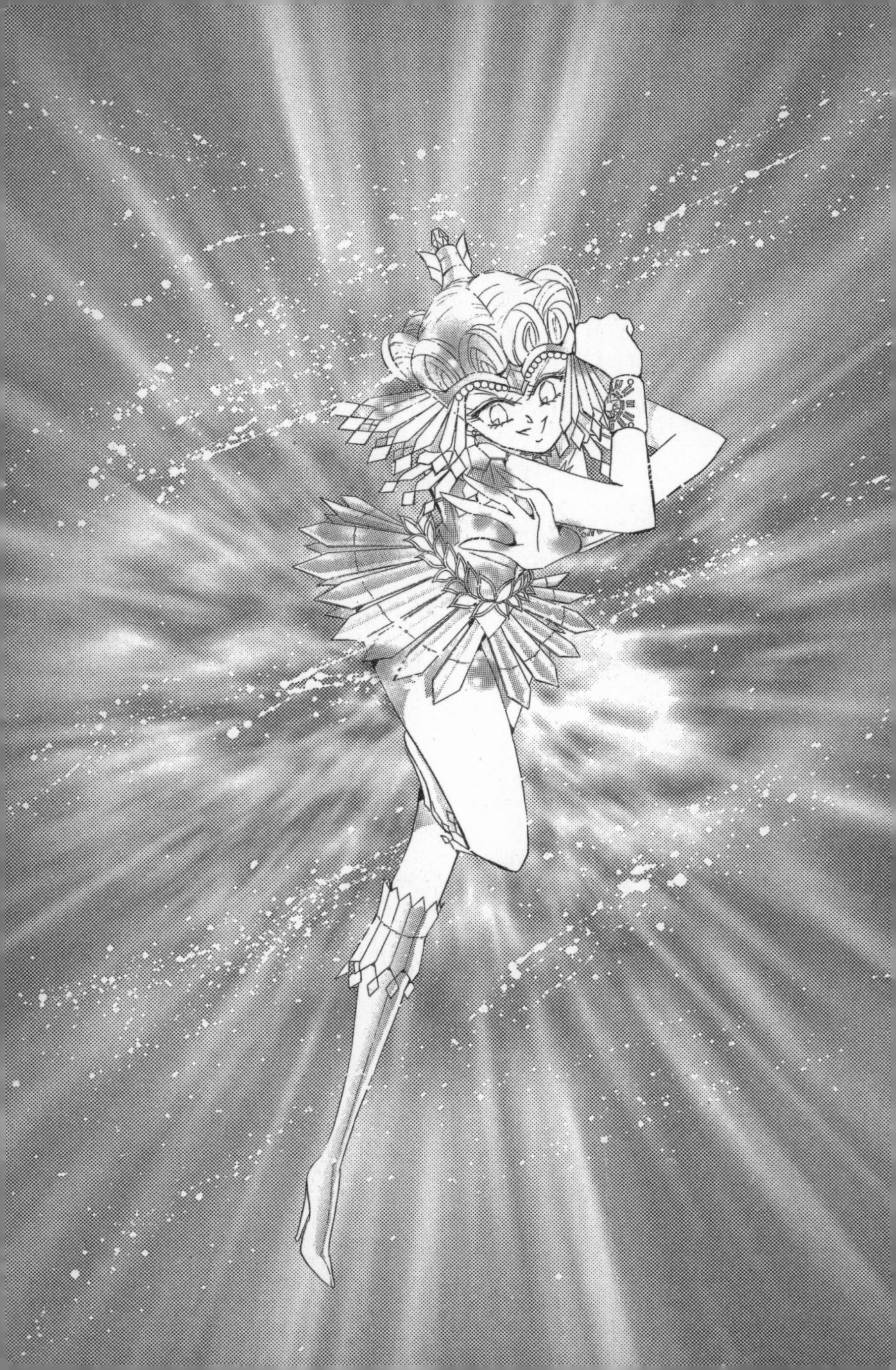

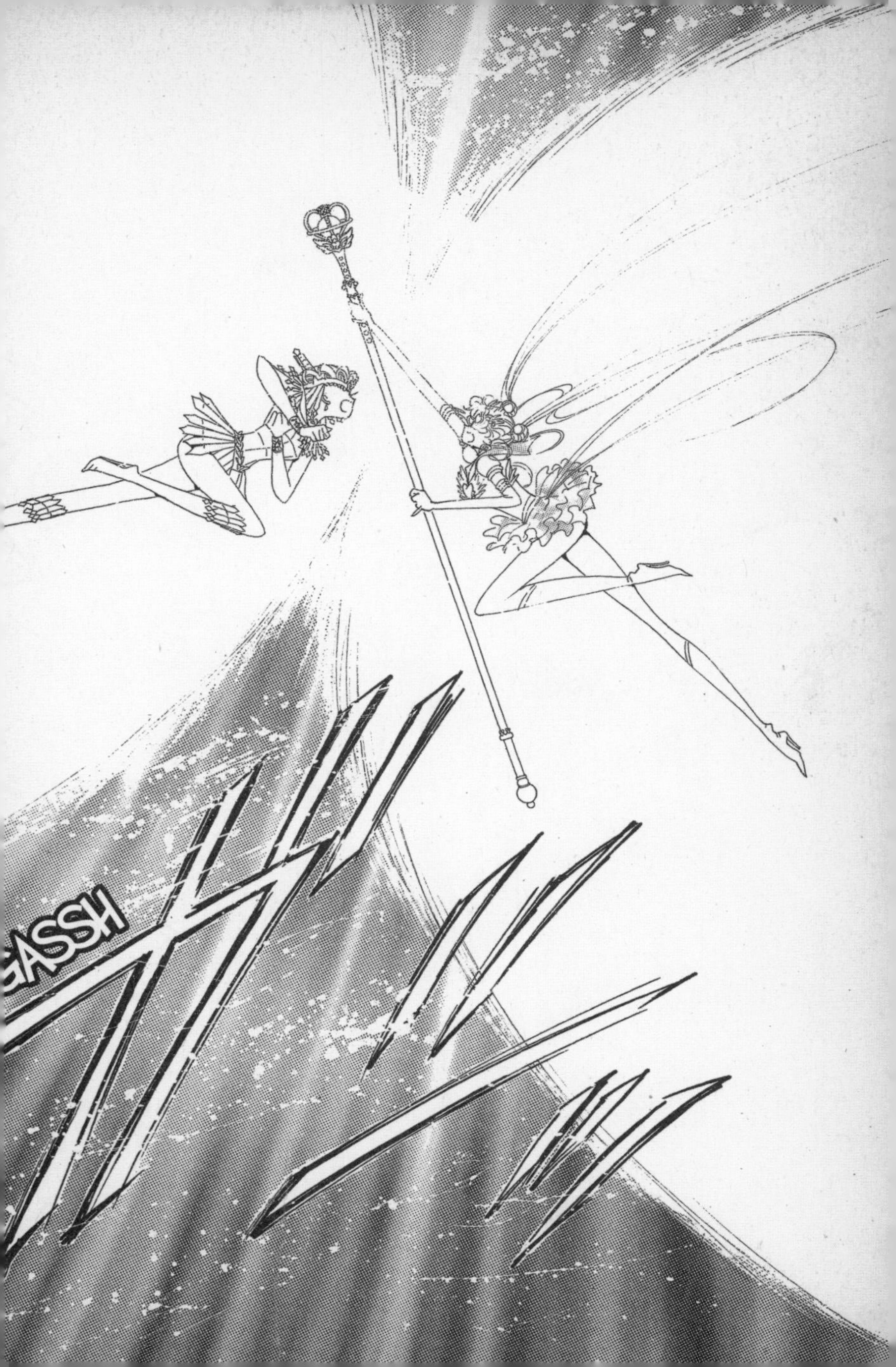
GASSH

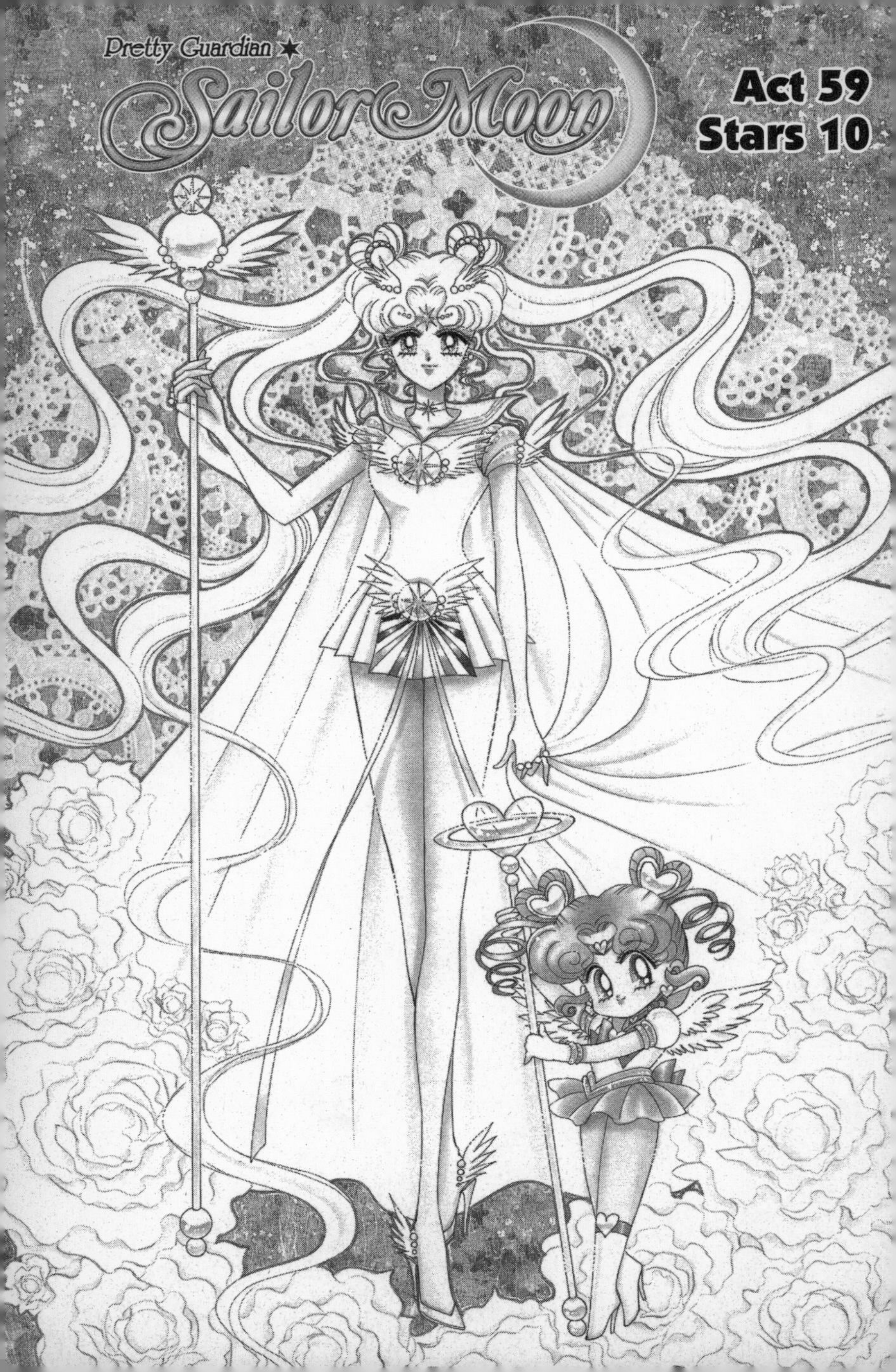
Pretty Guardian ★
Sailor Moon
Act 59
Stars 10

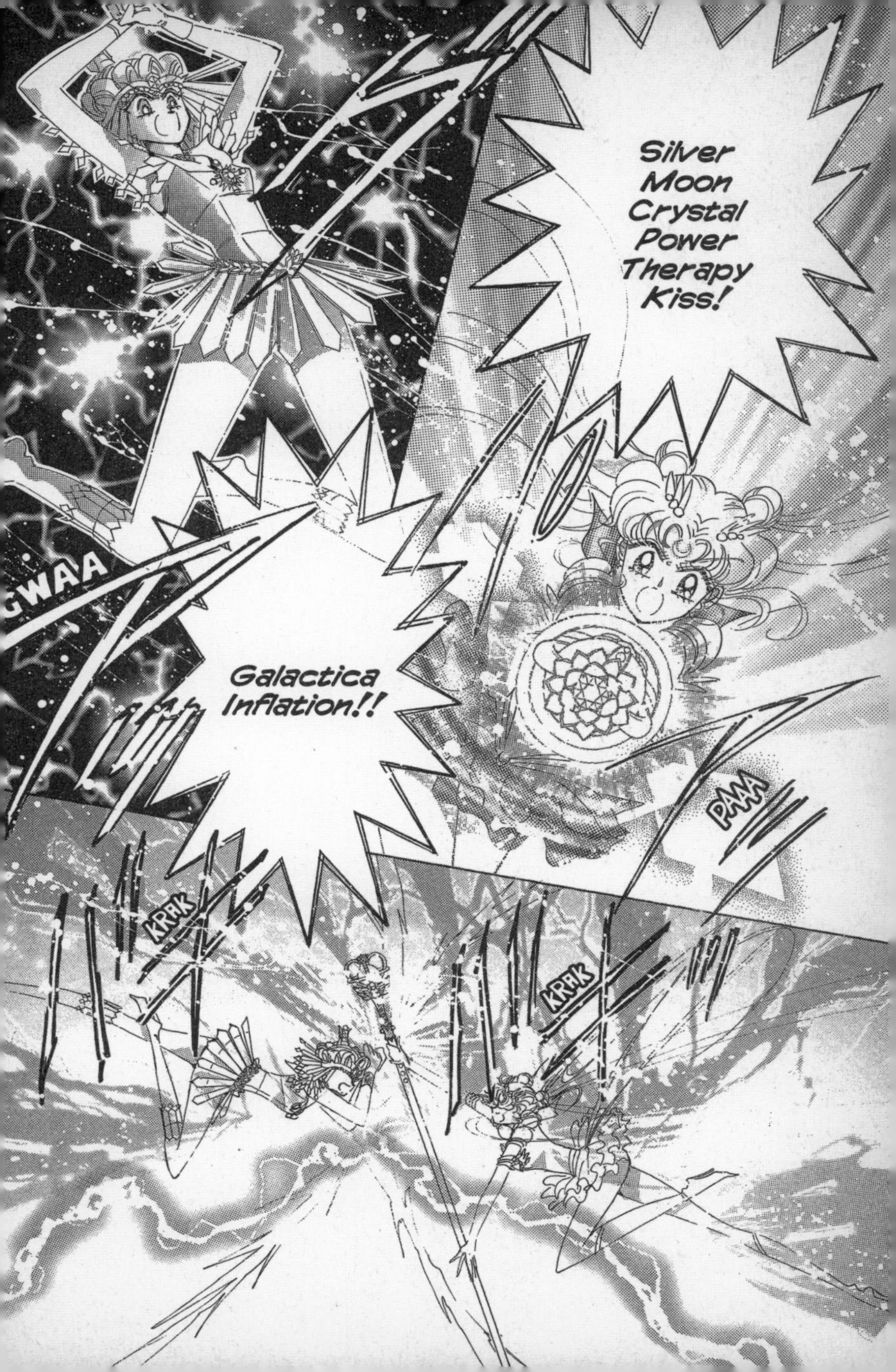
Silver Moon Crystal Power Therapy Kiss!
PAAA
GWAA
Galactica Inflation!!
KRAK
KRAK

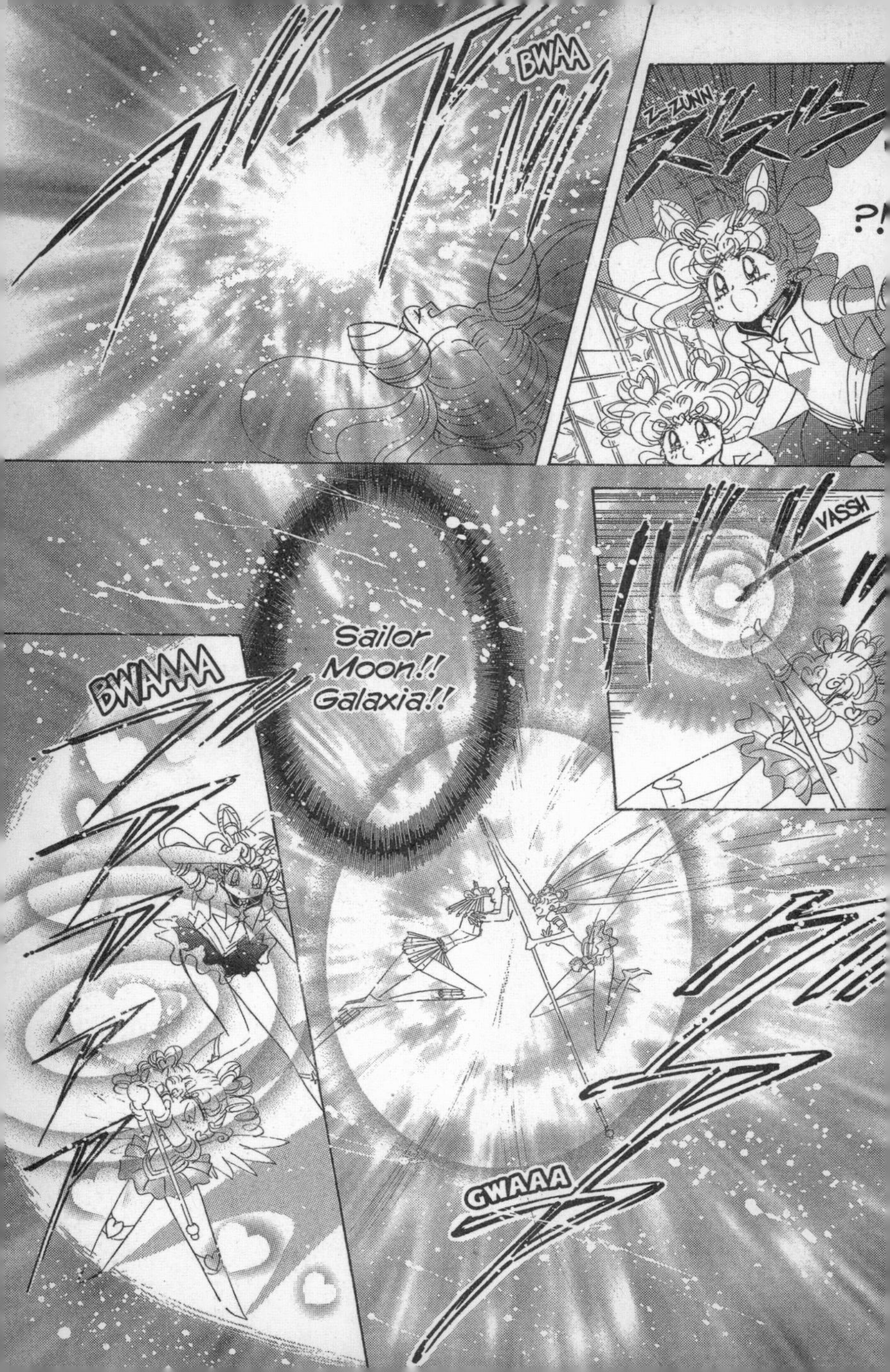
Z-ZUNN
?!
BWAA
VASSH
Sailor Moon!! Galaxia!!
GWAAA
BWAAAA

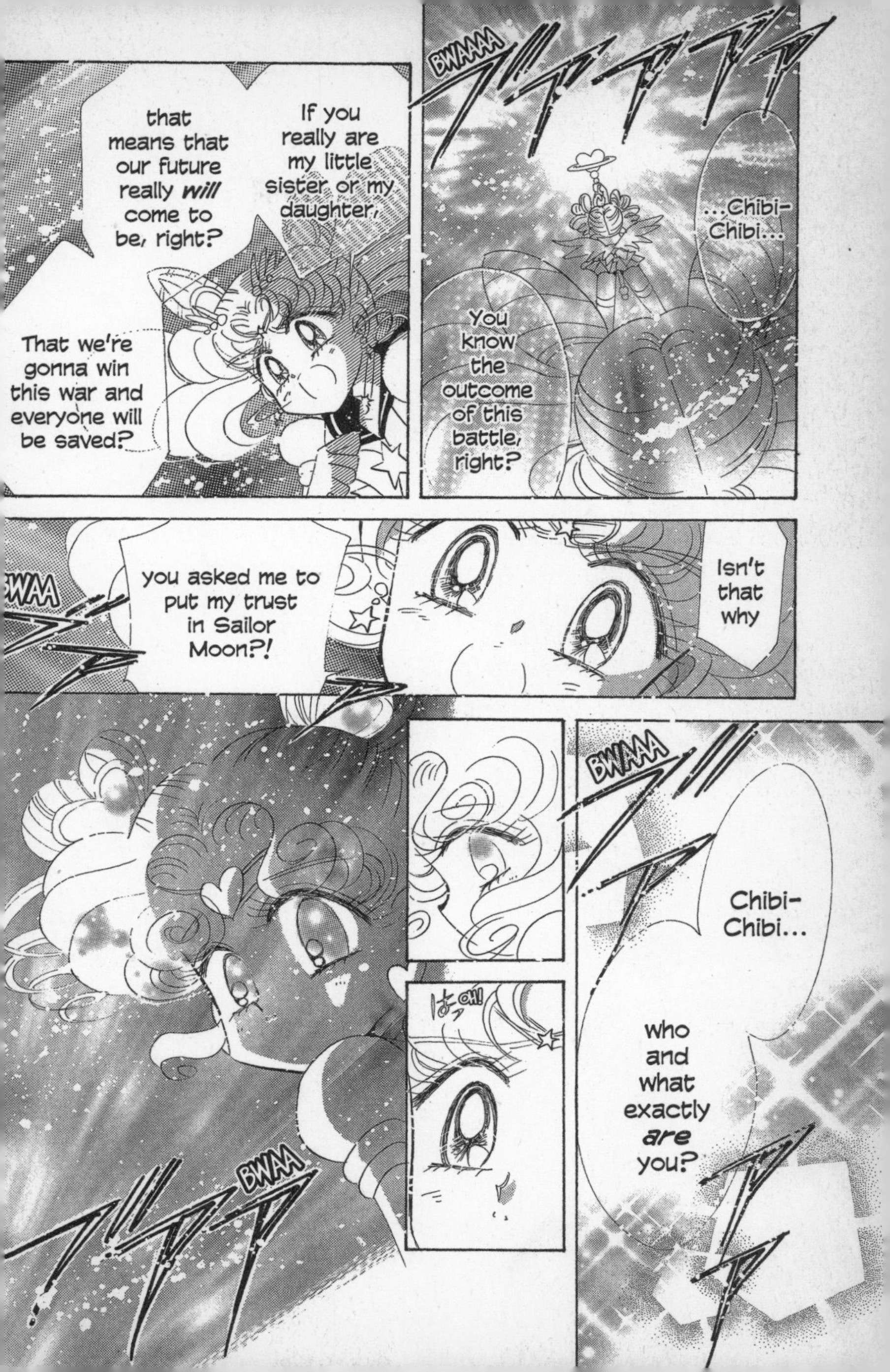
BWAAAA
...Chibi-Chibi...
You know the outcome of this battle, right?
If you really are my little sister or my daughter,
that means that our future really *will* come to be, right?
That we're gonna win this war and everyone will be saved?
BWAA
Isn't that why
you asked me to put my trust in Sailor Moon?!
BWAAA
Chibi-Chibi...
who and what exactly *are* you?
はっ OH!
BWAA

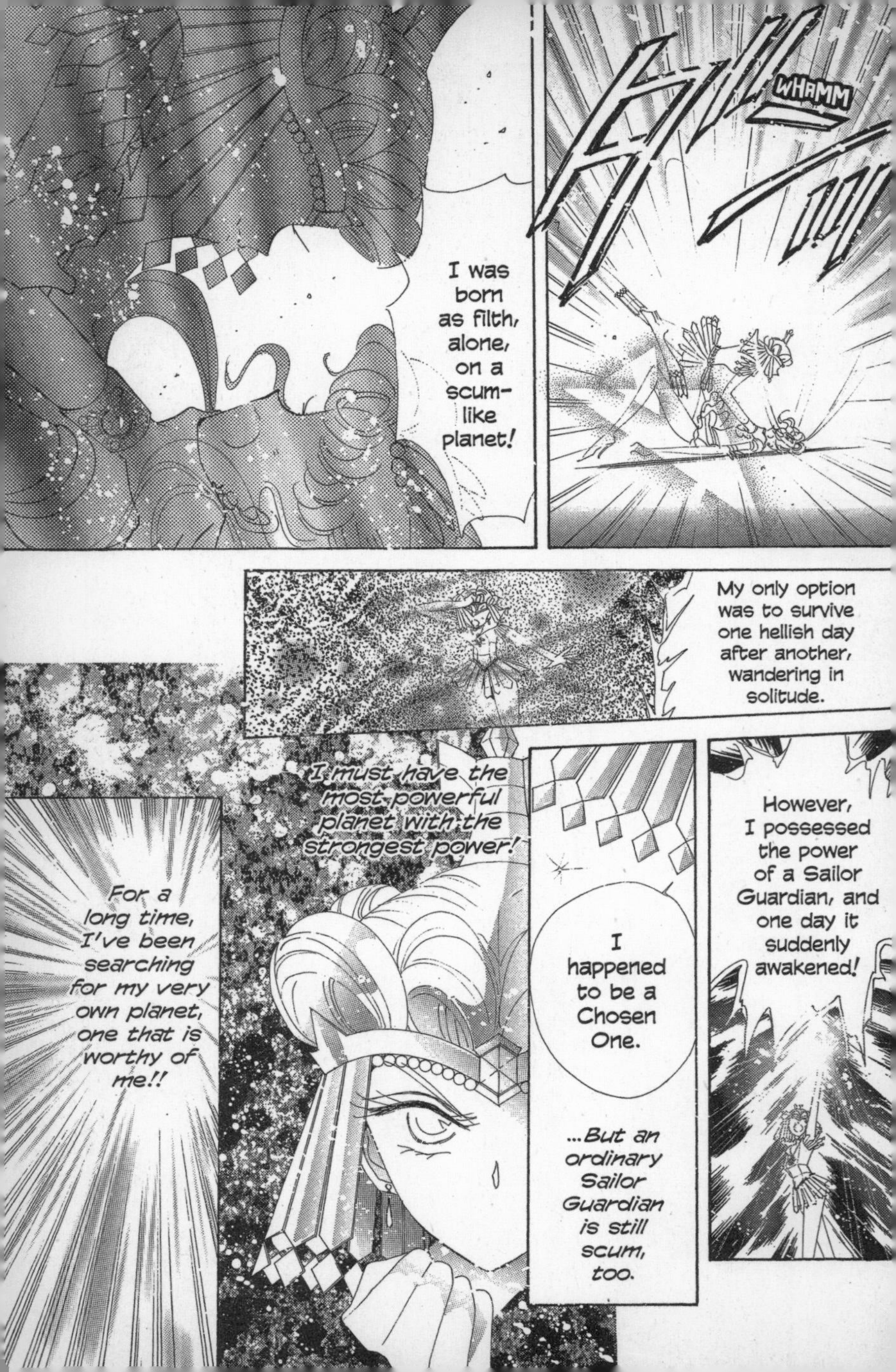
WHAMM
I was born as filth, alone, on a scum-like planet!
My only option was to survive one hellish day after another, wandering in solitude.
However, I possessed the power of a Sailor Guardian, and one day it suddenly awakened!
I happened to be a Chosen One.
...But an ordinary Sailor Guardian is still scum, too.
I must have the most powerful planet with the strongest power!
For a long time, I've been searching for my very own planet, one that is worthy of me!!

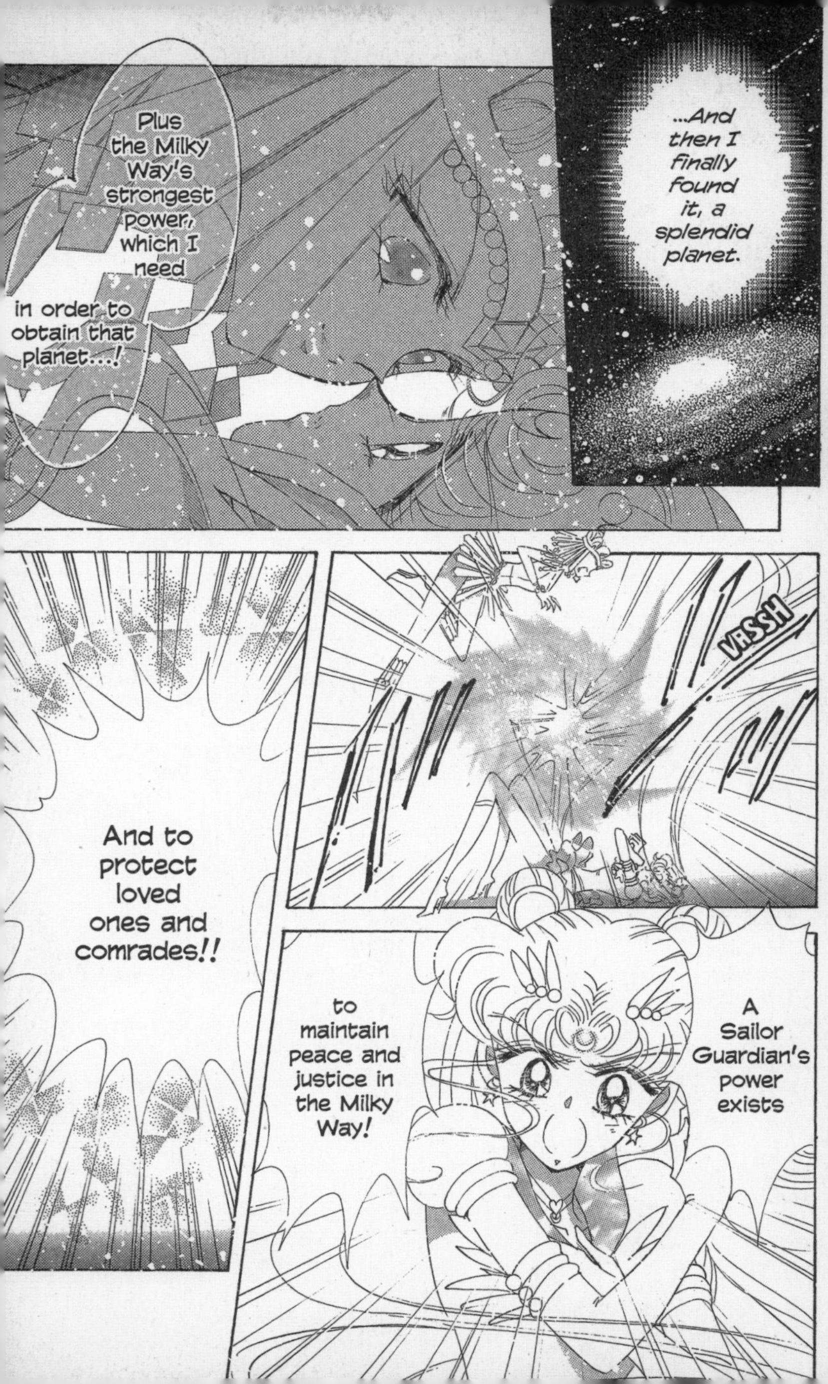
...And then I finally found it, a splendid planet.
Plus the Milky Way's strongest power, which I need
in order to obtain that planet...!
VASSH
A Sailor Guardian's power exists
to maintain peace and justice in the Milky Way!
And to protect loved ones and comrades!!

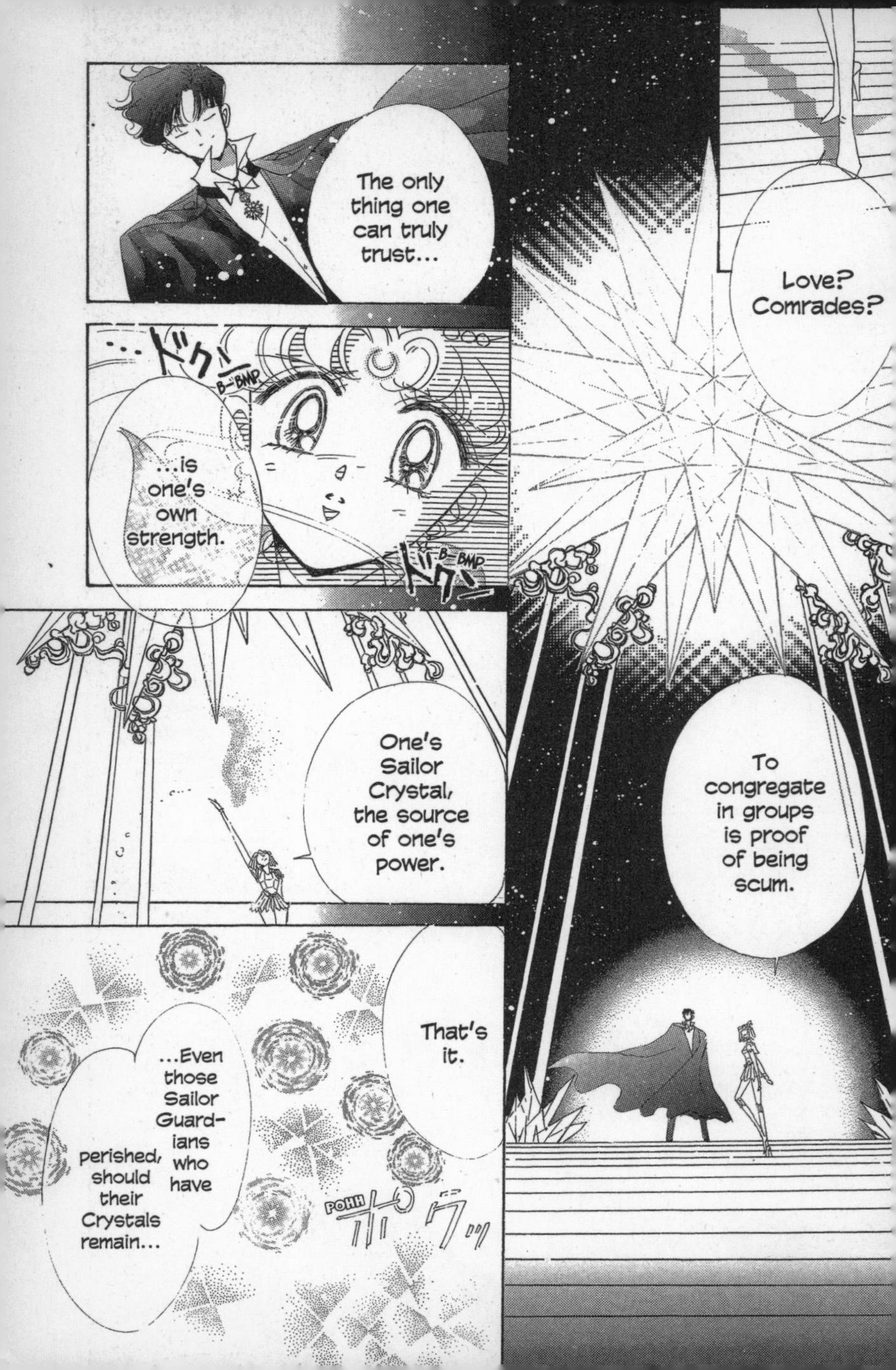
Love? Comrades?
To congregate in groups is proof of being scum.
The only thing one can truly trust...
B-BMP
...is one's own strength.
B-BMP
One's Sailor Crystal, the source of one's power.
That's it.
...Even those Sailor Guardians who have perished, should their Crystals remain...
POHH

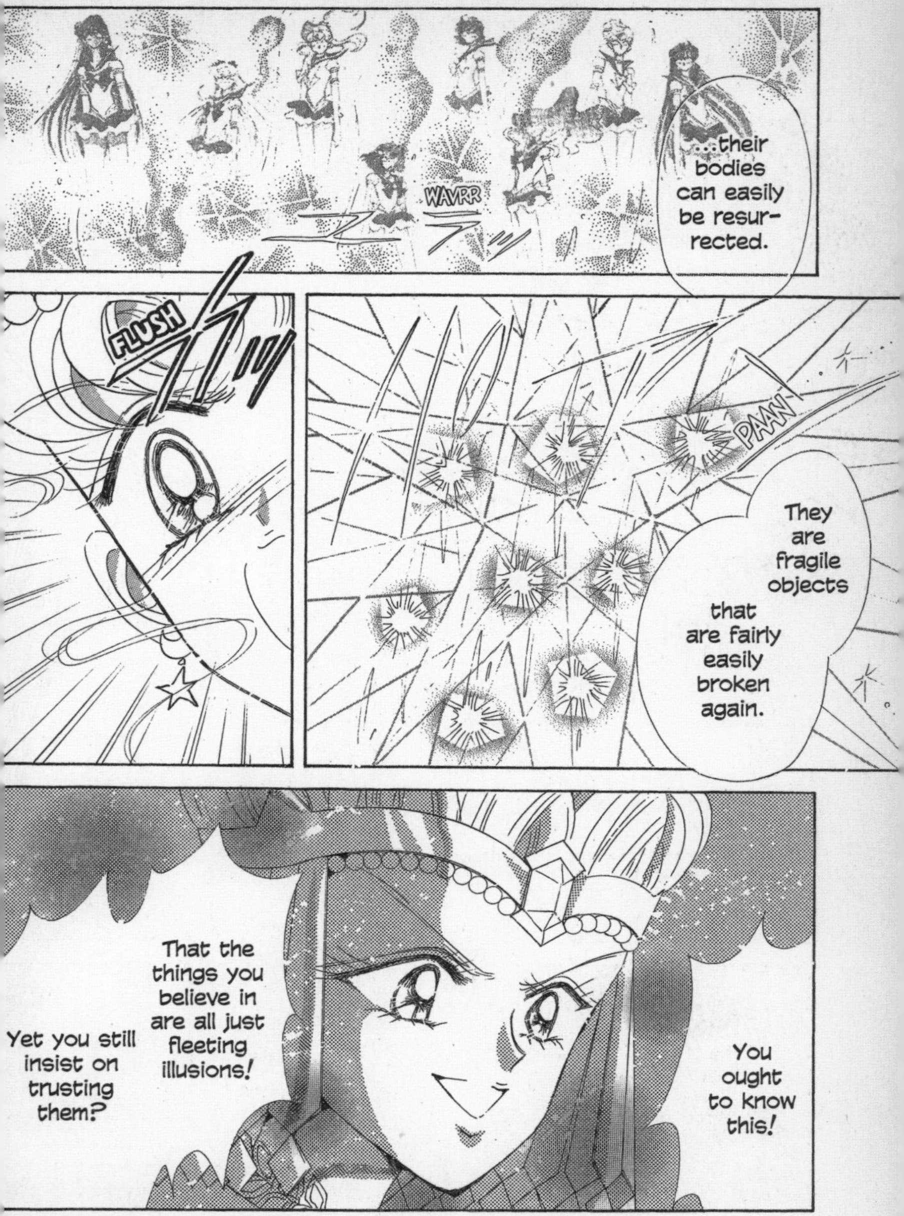
...their bodies can easily be resur-rected.
WAVRR
PAAN
They are fragile objects
that are fairly easily broken again.
FLUSH
You ought to know this!
That the things you believe in are all just fleeting illusions!
Yet you still insist on trusting them?

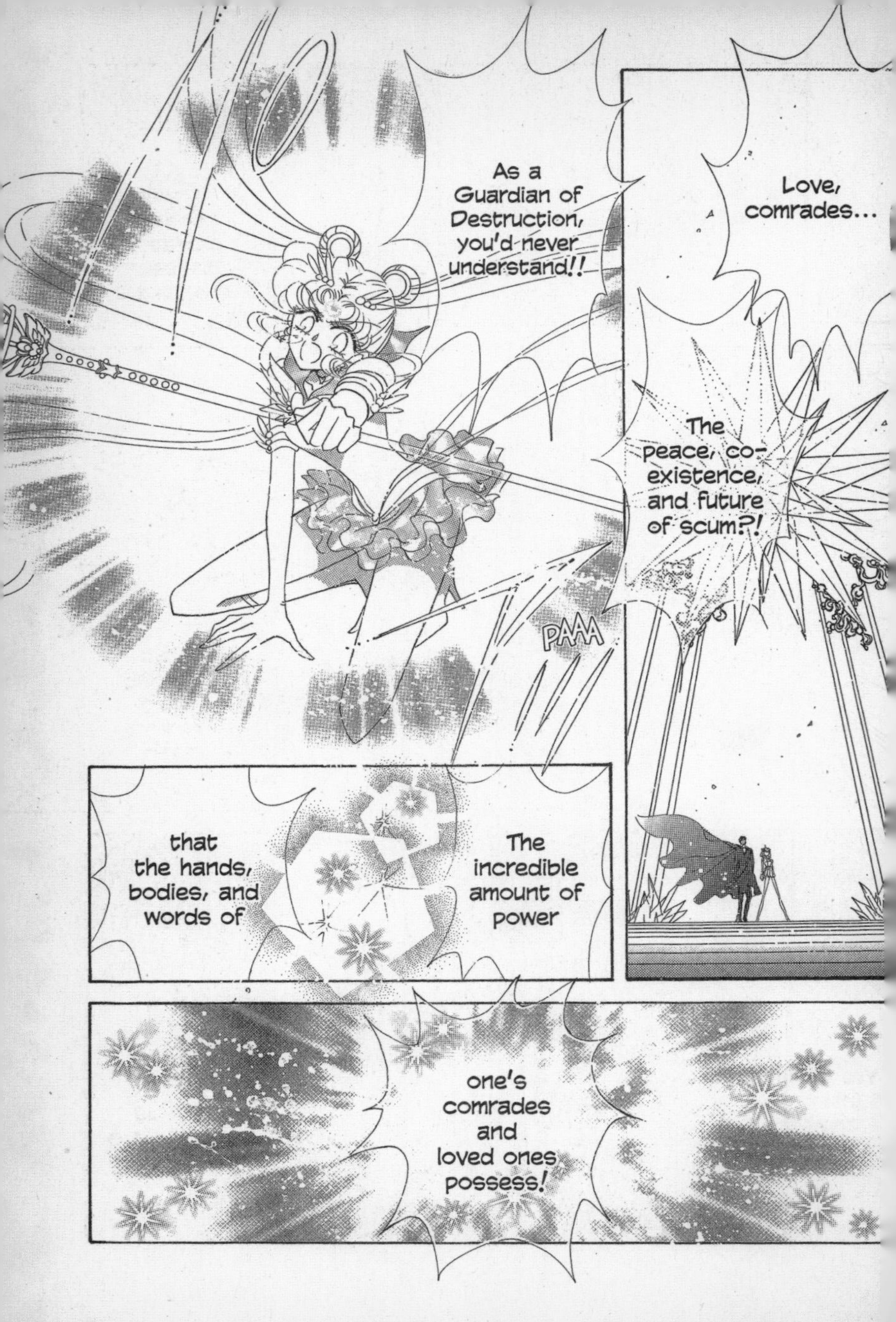
Love, comrades...
The peace, co-existence, and future of scum?!
As a Guardian of Destruction, you'd never understand!!
PAAA
The incredible amount of power
that the hands, bodies, and words of
one's comrades and loved ones possess!

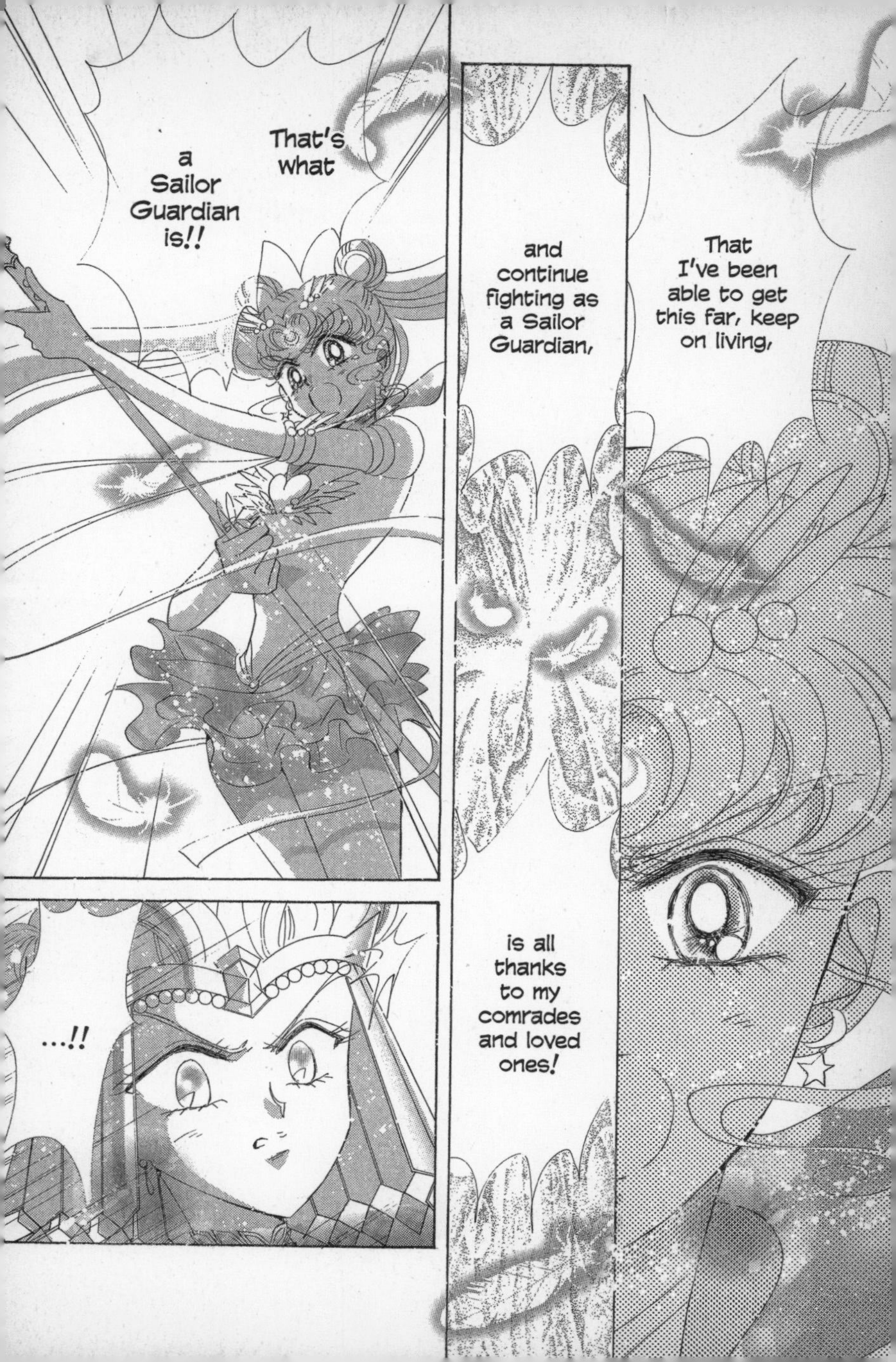
That I've been able to get this far, keep on living,
and continue fighting as a Sailor Guardian,
is all thanks to my comrades and loved ones!
That's what
a Sailor Guardian is!!
...!!

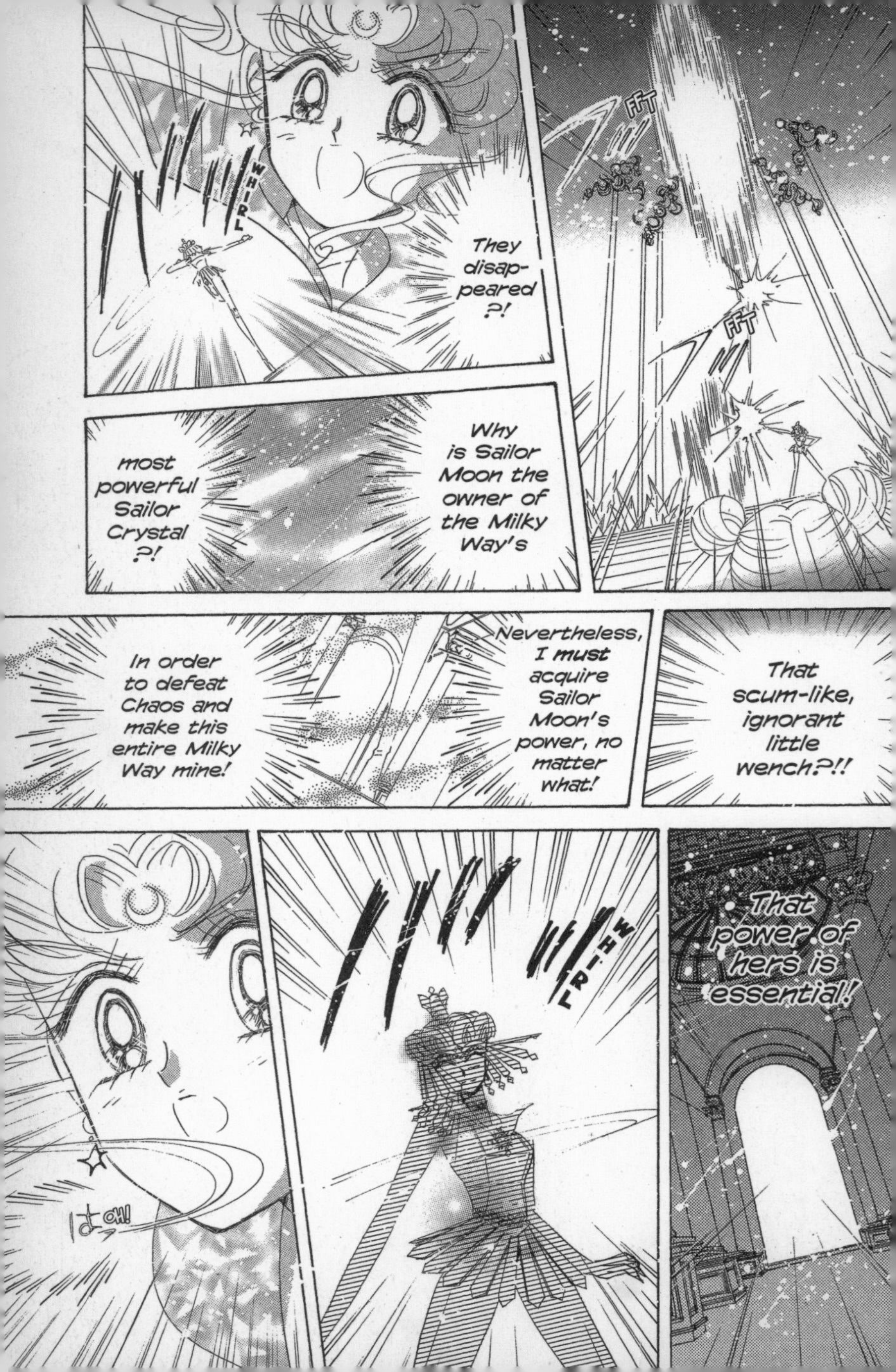
FFT
FFT
They disappeared?!
WHIRL
Why is Sailor Moon the owner of the Milky Way's
most powerful Sailor Crystal?!
That scum-like, ignorant little wench?!!
Nevertheless, I must acquire Sailor Moon's power, no matter what!
In order to defeat Chaos and make this entire Milky Way mine!
That power of hers is essential!
WHIRL
OH!

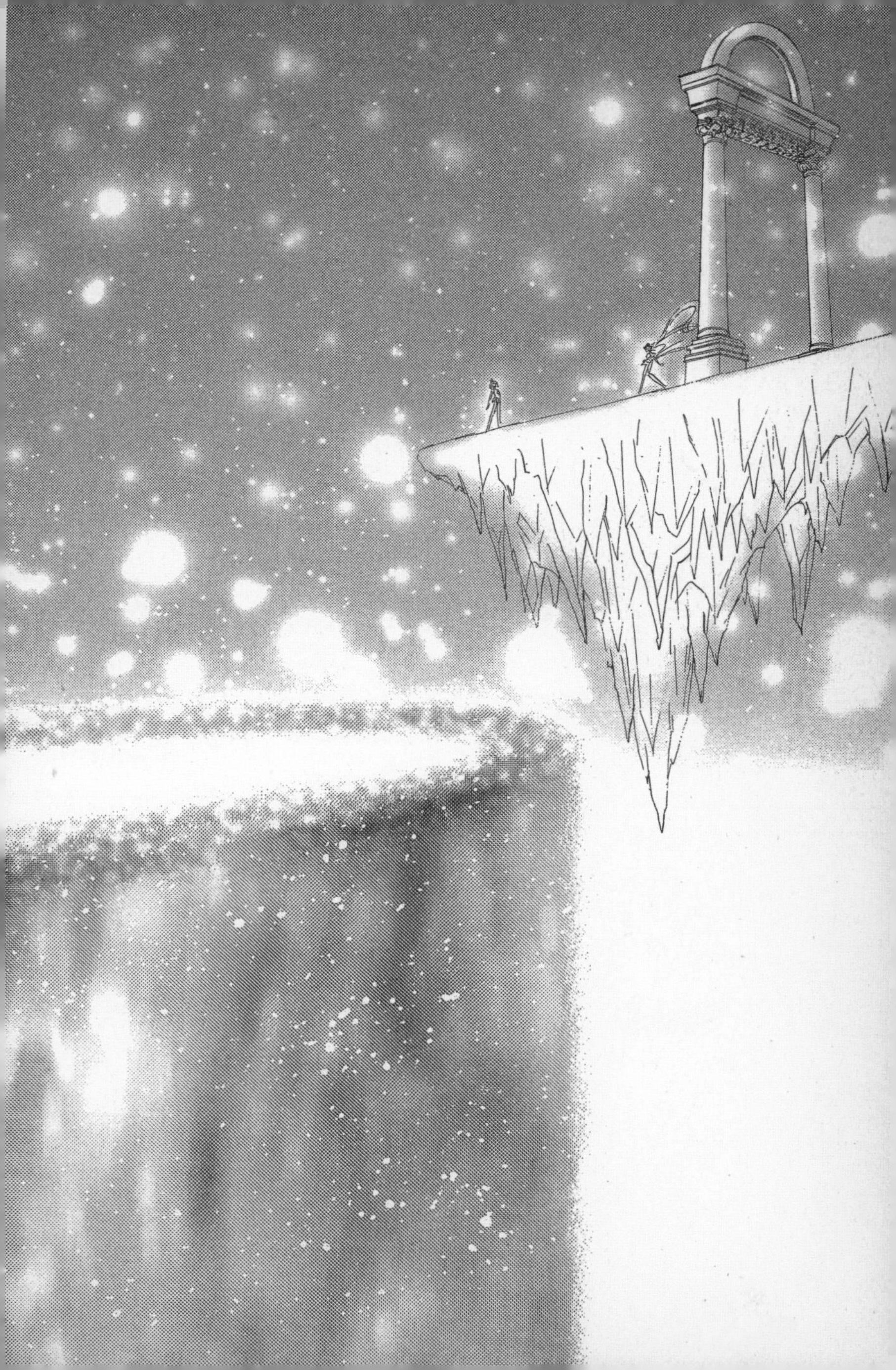

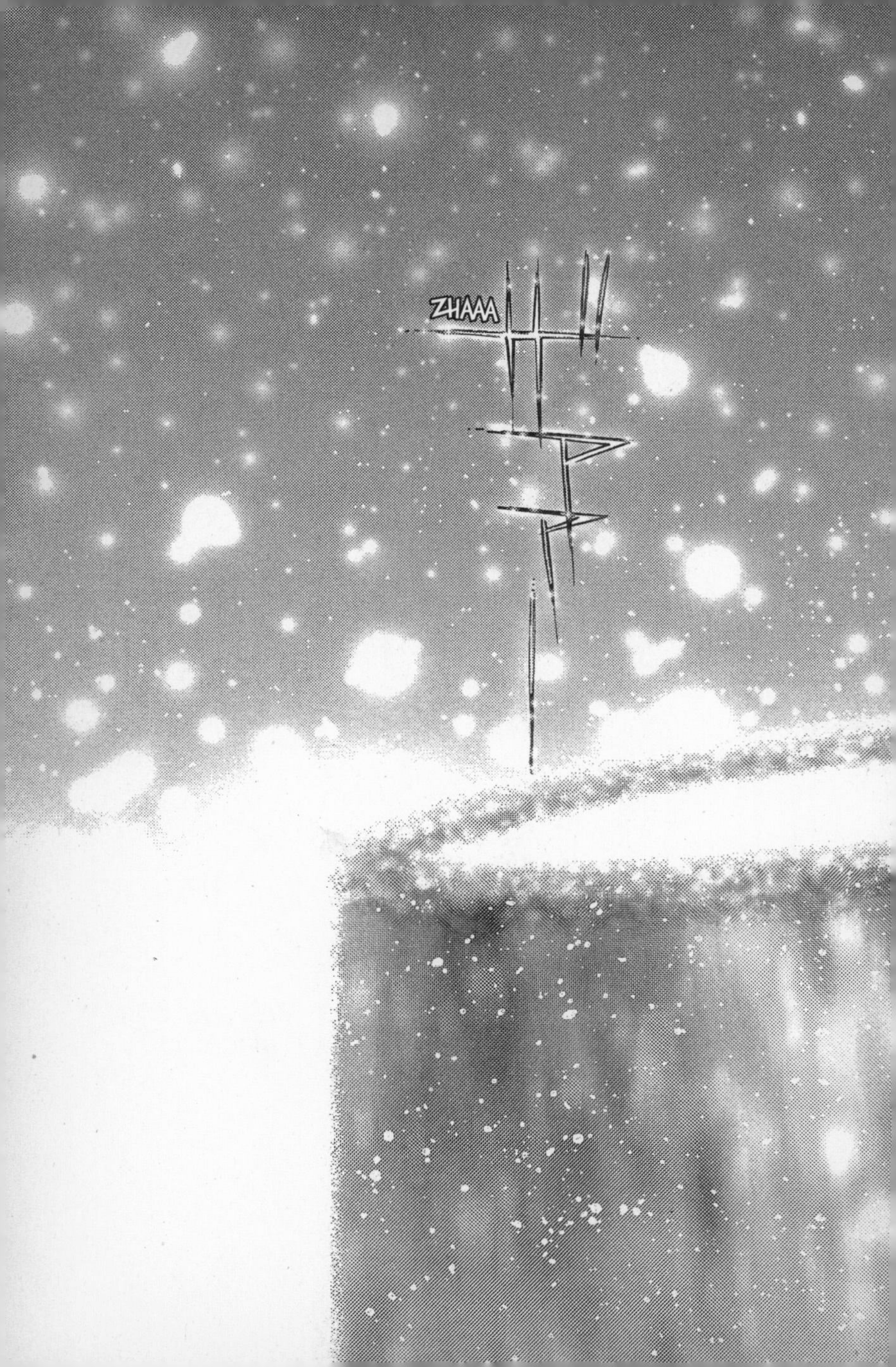
ZHAAA

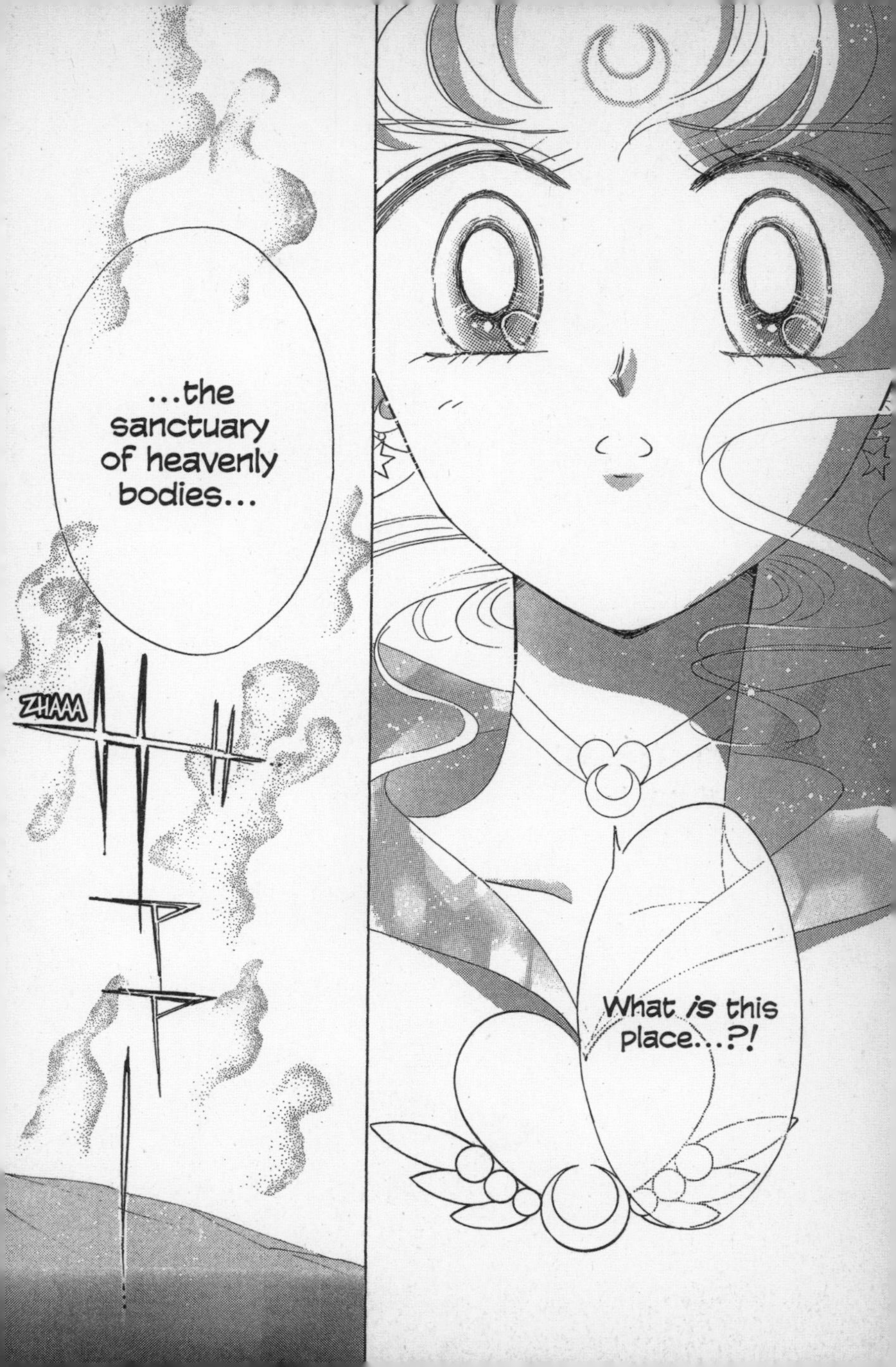
What *is* this place...?!
...the sanctuary of heavenly bodies...
ZHAAA

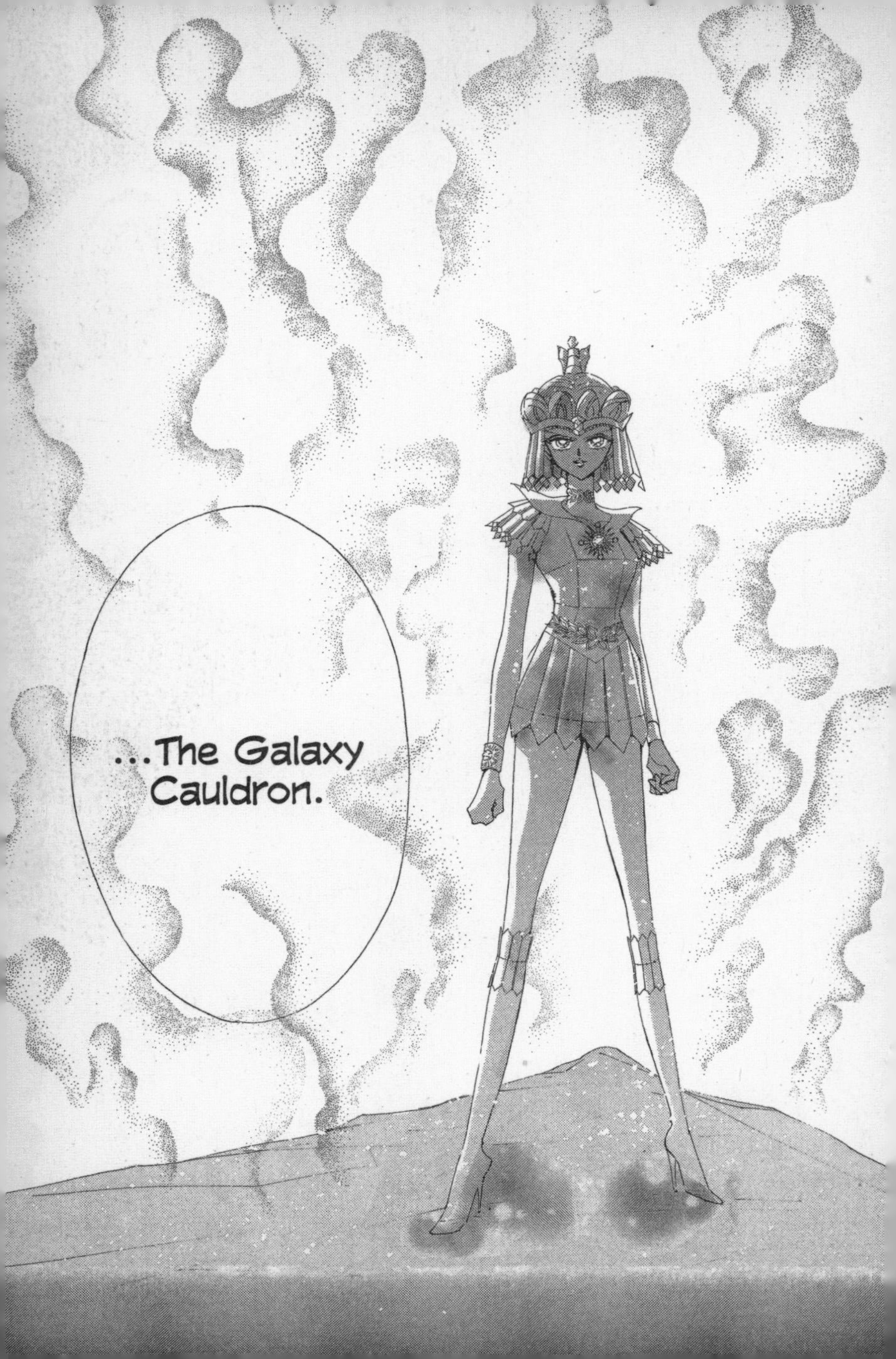
...The Galaxy Cauldron.

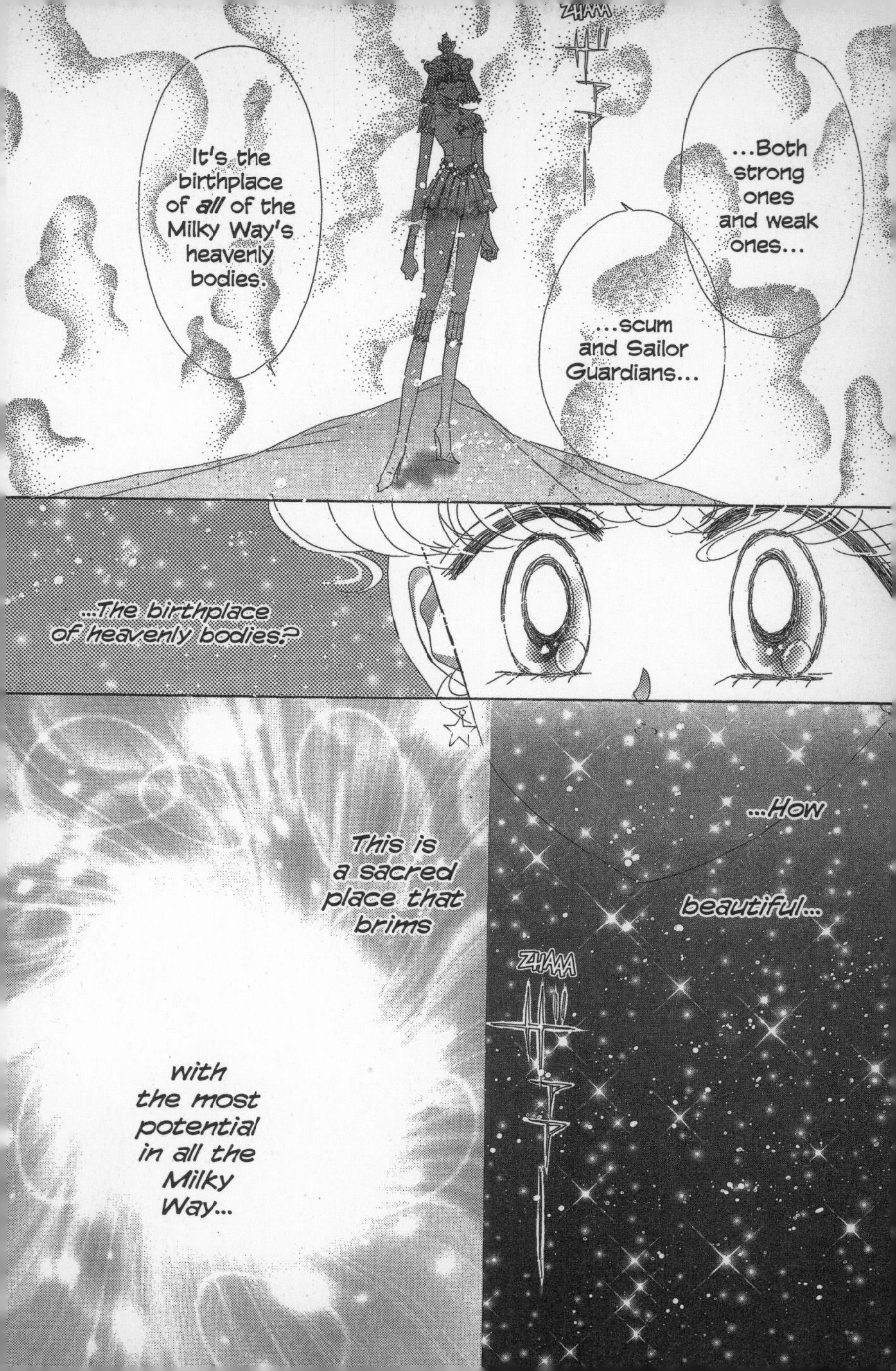
ZHAAA
...Both strong ones and weak ones...
...scum and Sailor Guardians...
It's the birthplace of *all* of the Milky Way's heavenly bodies.
...The birthplace of heavenly bodies?
...How beautiful...
ZHAAA
This is a sacred place that brims
with the most potential in all the Milky Way...

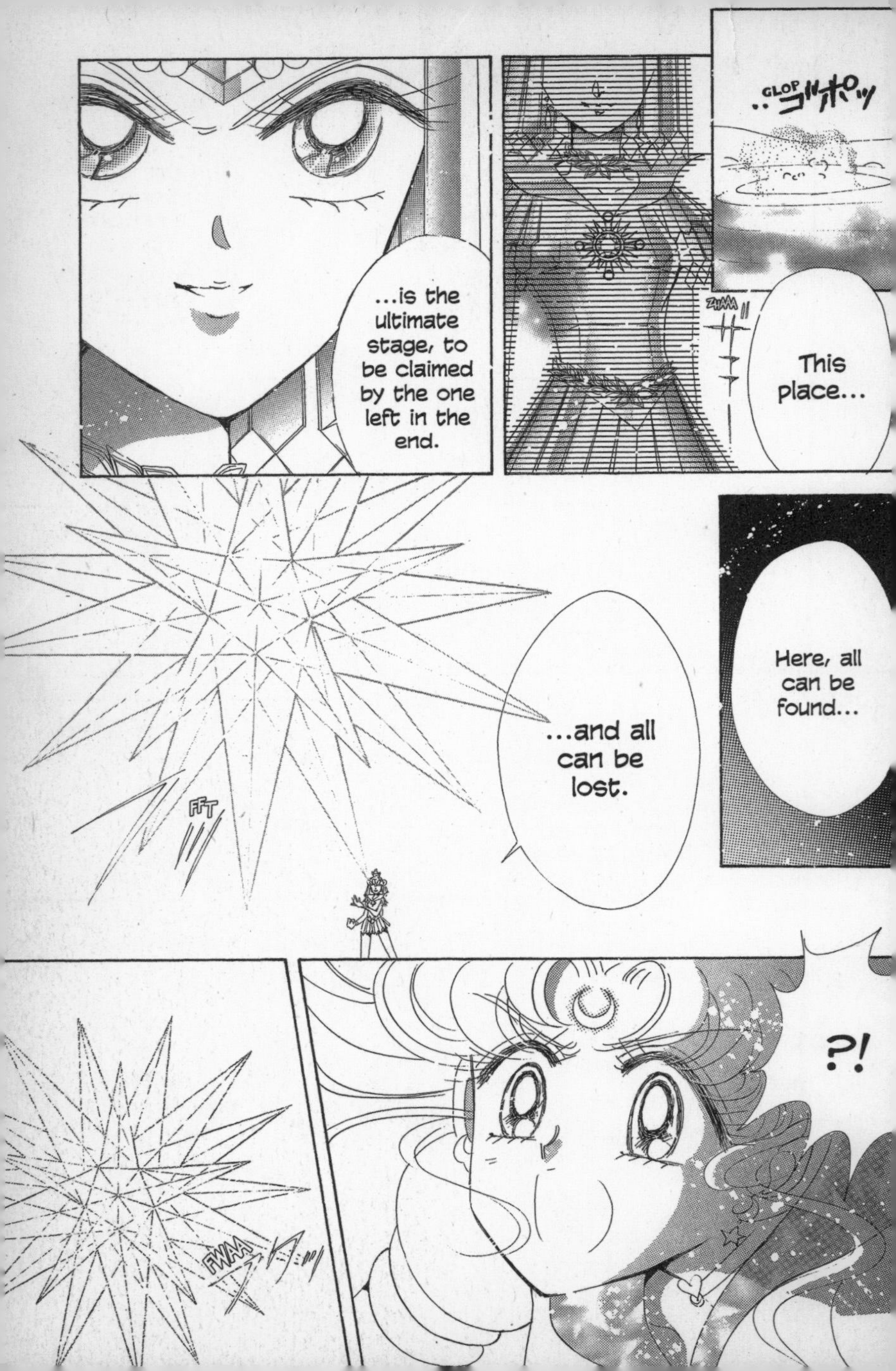
..GLOP ゴポッ
This place...
ZWAA
...is the ultimate stage, to be claimed by the one left in the end.
Here, all can be found...
...and all can be lost.
FFT
?!
FWAA

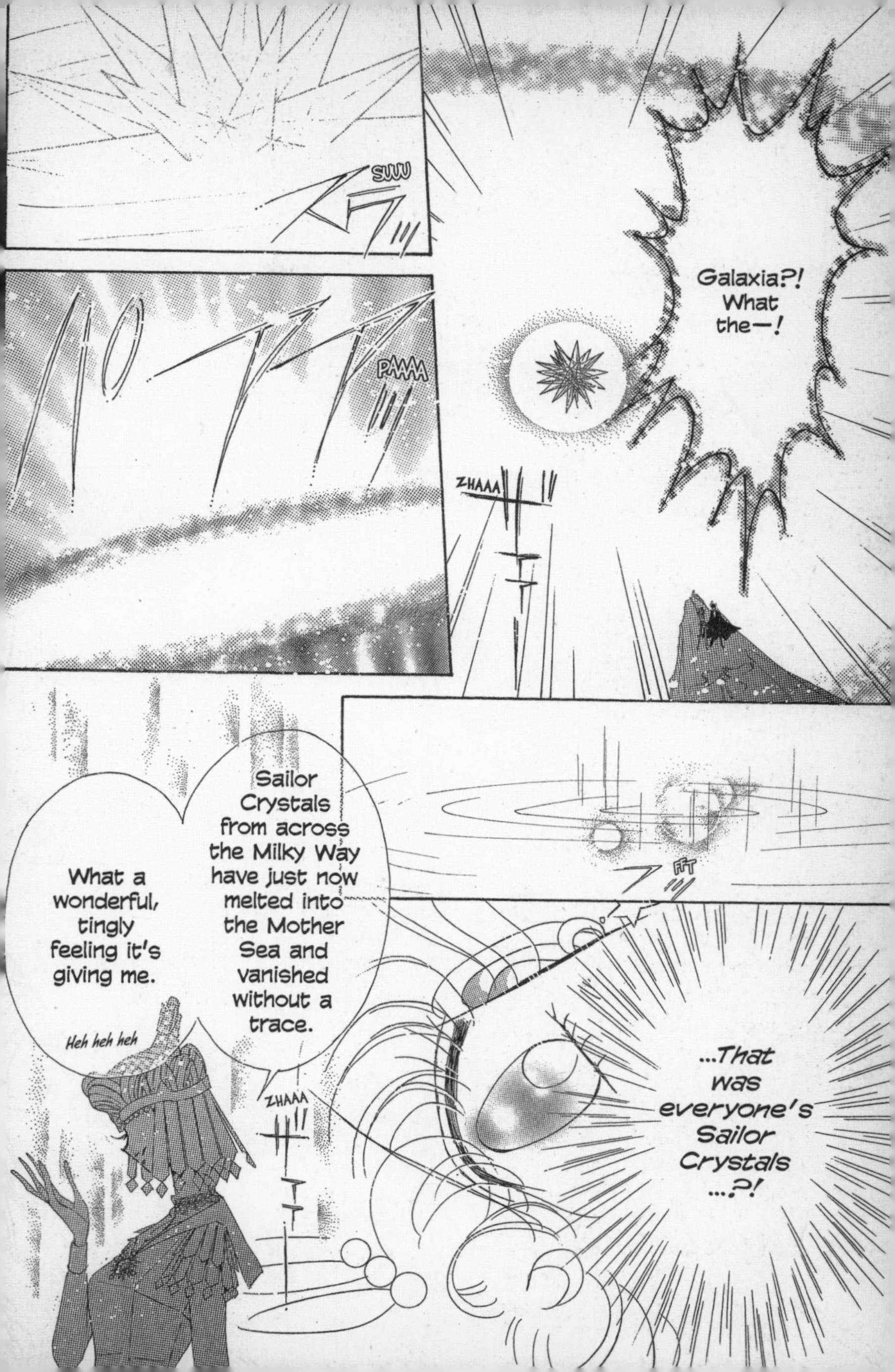
Galaxia?! What the—!
ZHAAA
SUUU
PAAAA
FFT
...That was everyone's Sailor Crystals ...?!
Sailor Crystals from across the Milky Way have just now melted into the Mother Sea and vanished without a trace.
What a wonderful, tingly feeling it's giving me.
Heh heh heh
ZHAAA

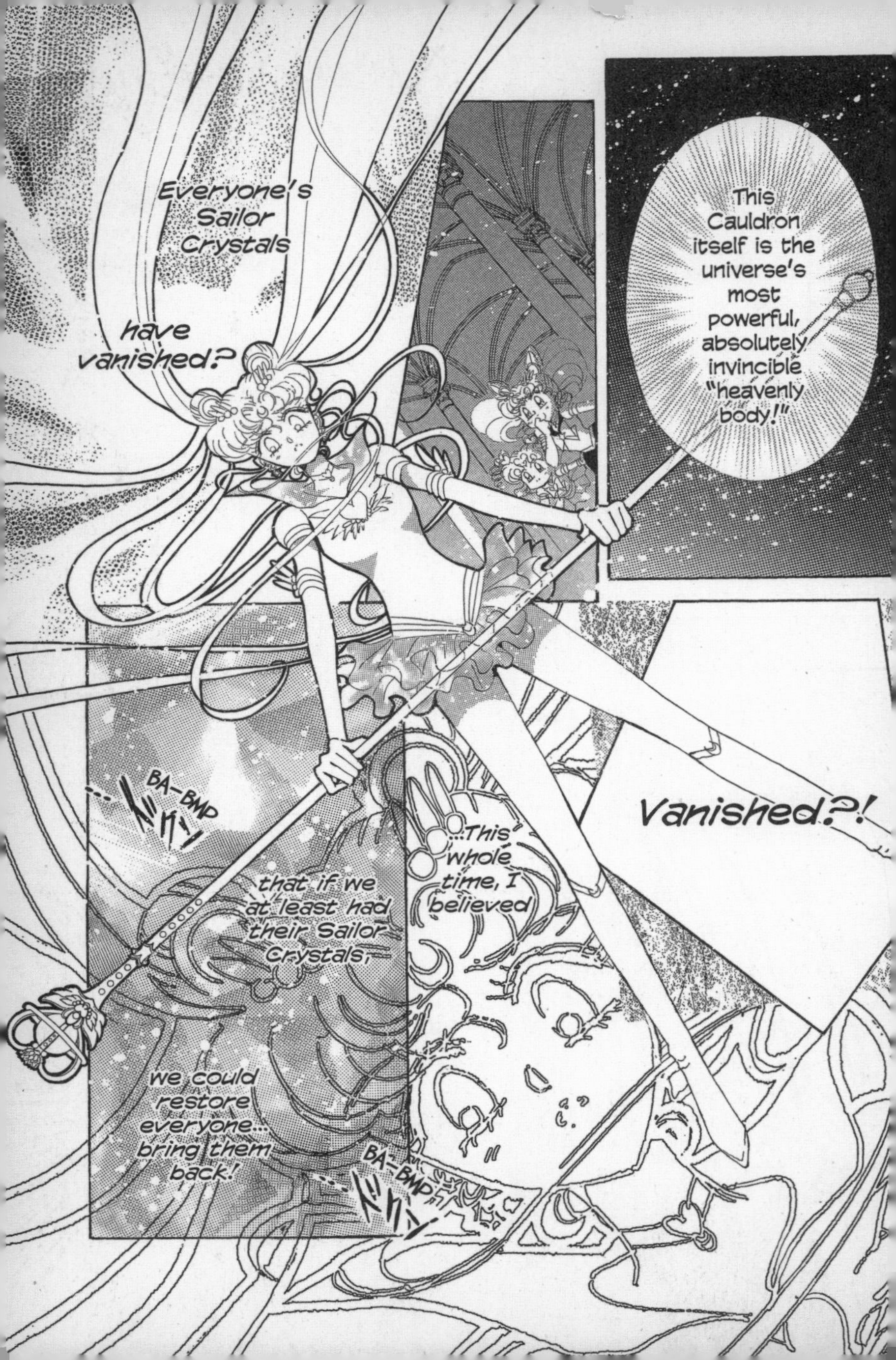

This Cauldron itself is the universe's most powerful, absolutely invincible "heavenly body!"
Everyone's Sailor Crystals
have vanished?
Vanished?!
...This whole time, I believed
that if we at least had their Sailor Crystals,
BA-BMP
we could restore everyone... bring them back!
BA-BMP

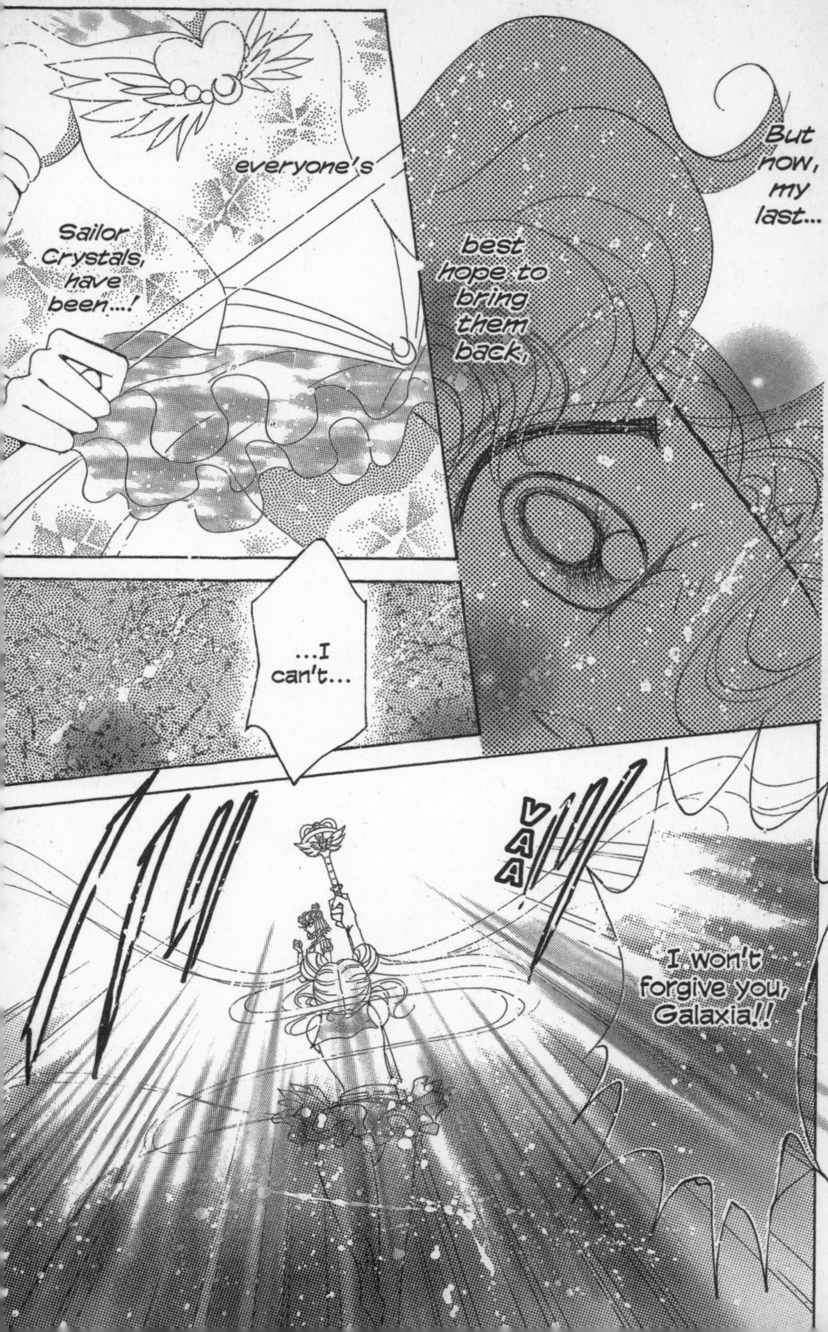
But now, my last...
best hope to bring them back,
everyone's
Sailor Crystals, have been...!
...I can't...
VAAA
I won't forgive you, Galaxia!!

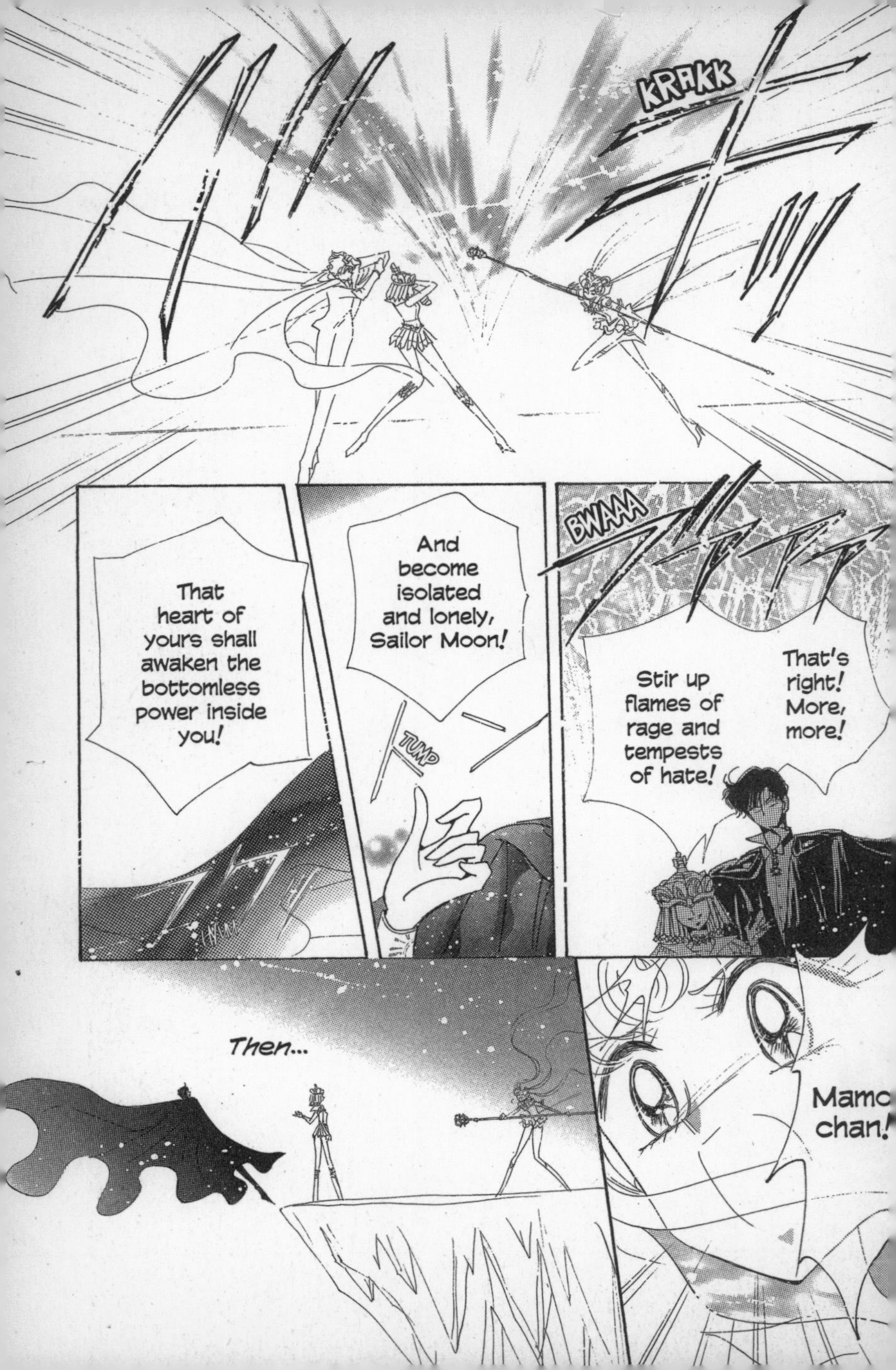
KRAKK
BWAAA
That's right! More, more!
Stir up flames of rage and tempests of hate!
TUMP
And become isolated and lonely, Sailor Moon!
That heart of yours shall awaken the bottomless power inside you!
Mamo chan!
Then...

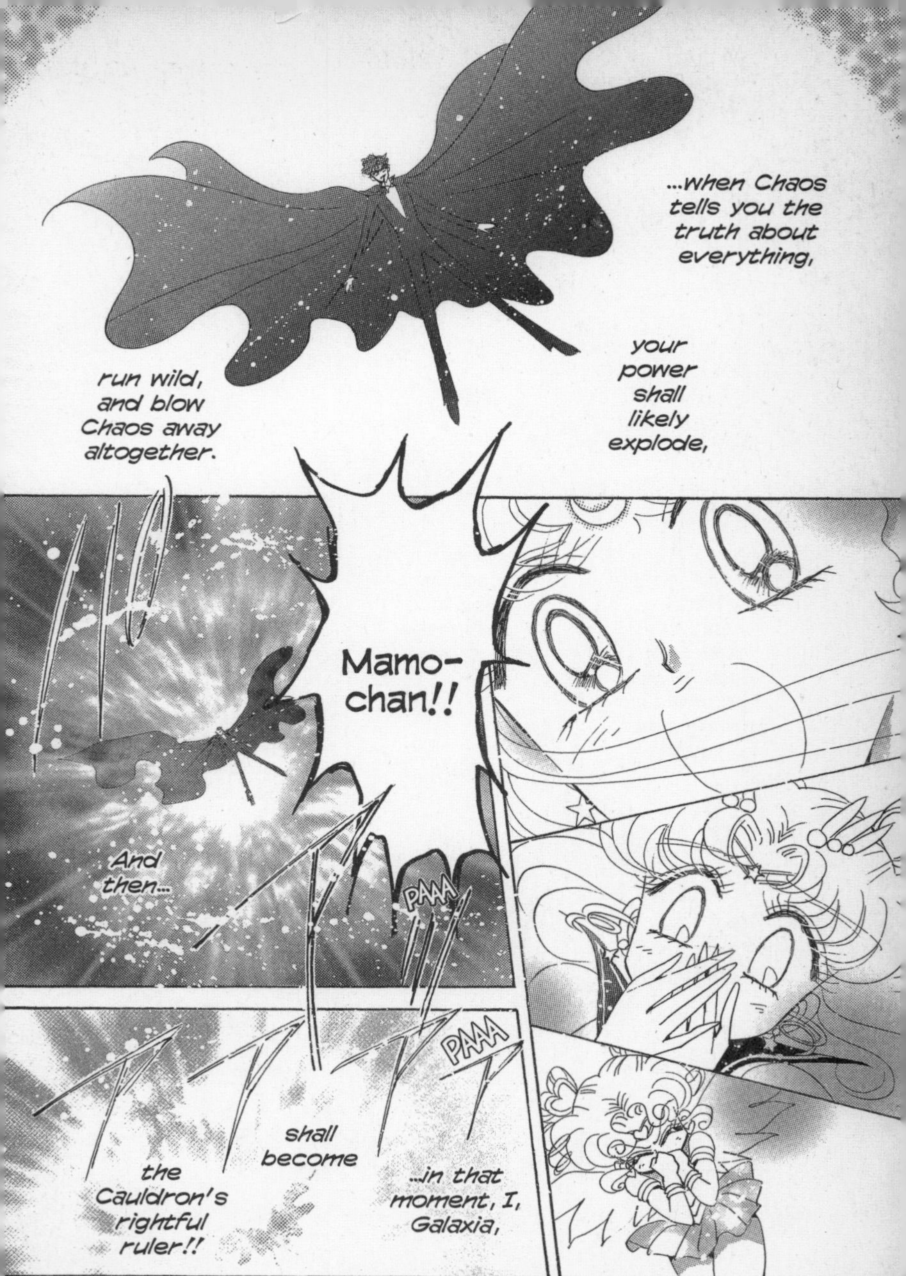
...when Chaos tells you the truth about everything,
your power shall likely explode,
run wild, and blow Chaos away altogether.
Mamo-chan!!
And then...
PAAA
...in that moment, I, Galaxia,
shall become
the Cauldron's rightful ruler!!
PAAA

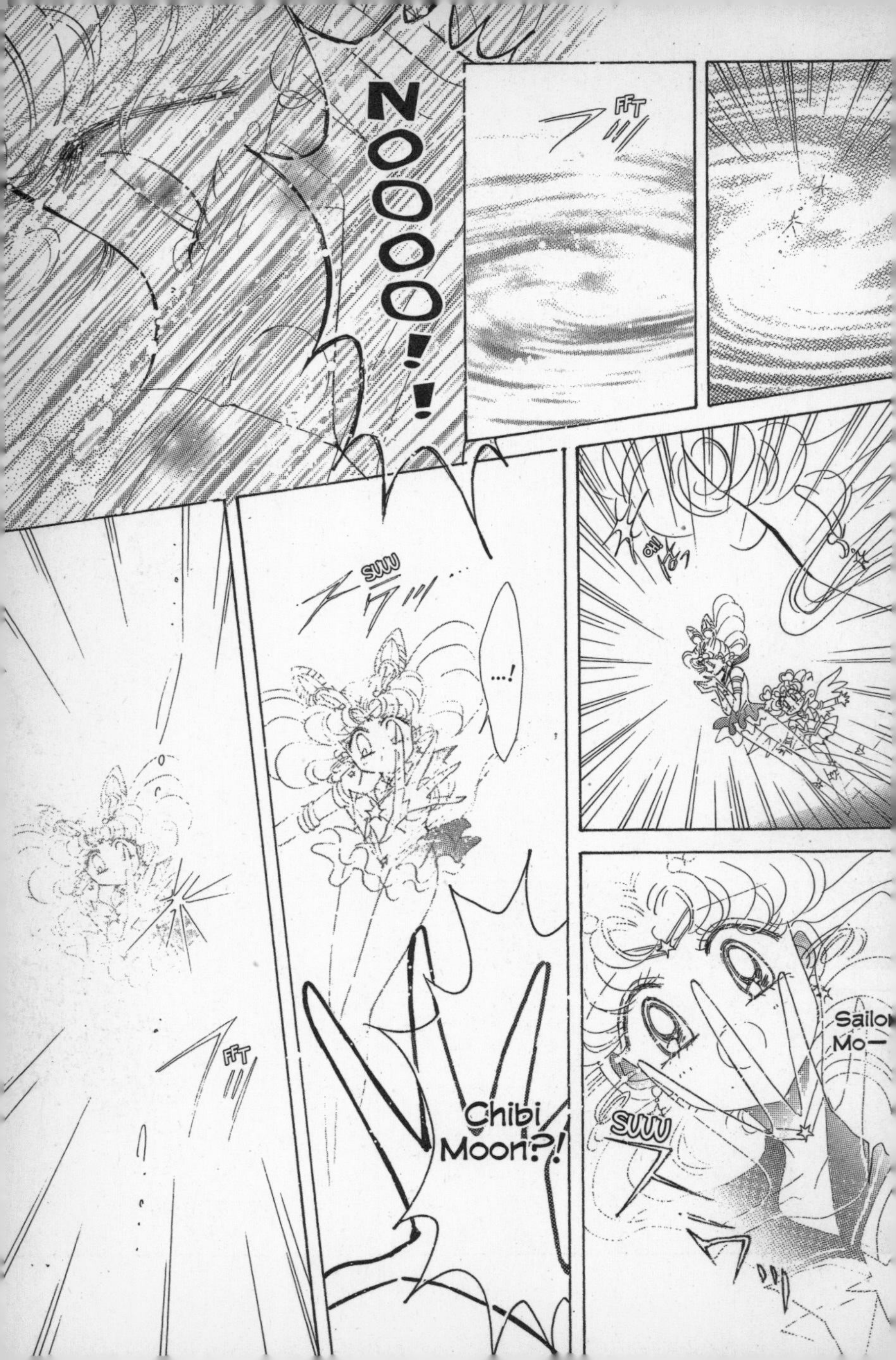
FFT
NOOOO!!
OH!
Sailor Mo—
SUUU
SUUU
...!
Chibi Moon?!
FFT

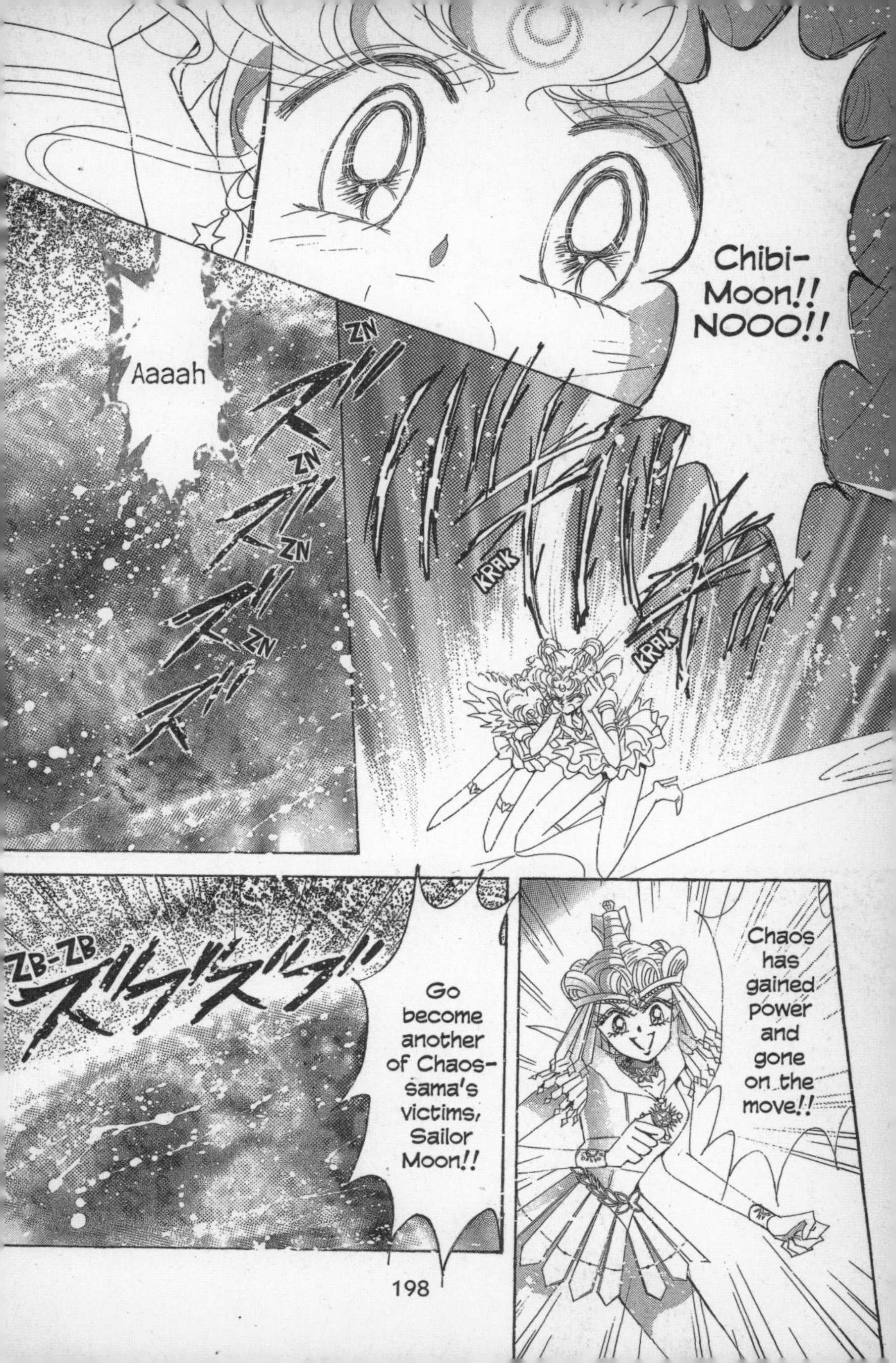
Chibi-Moon!! NOOO!!
ZN
KRAK
KRAK
Aaaah
ZN
ZN
ZN
Chaos has gained power and gone on the move!!
Go become another of Chaos-sama's victims, Sailor Moon!!
ZB-ZB

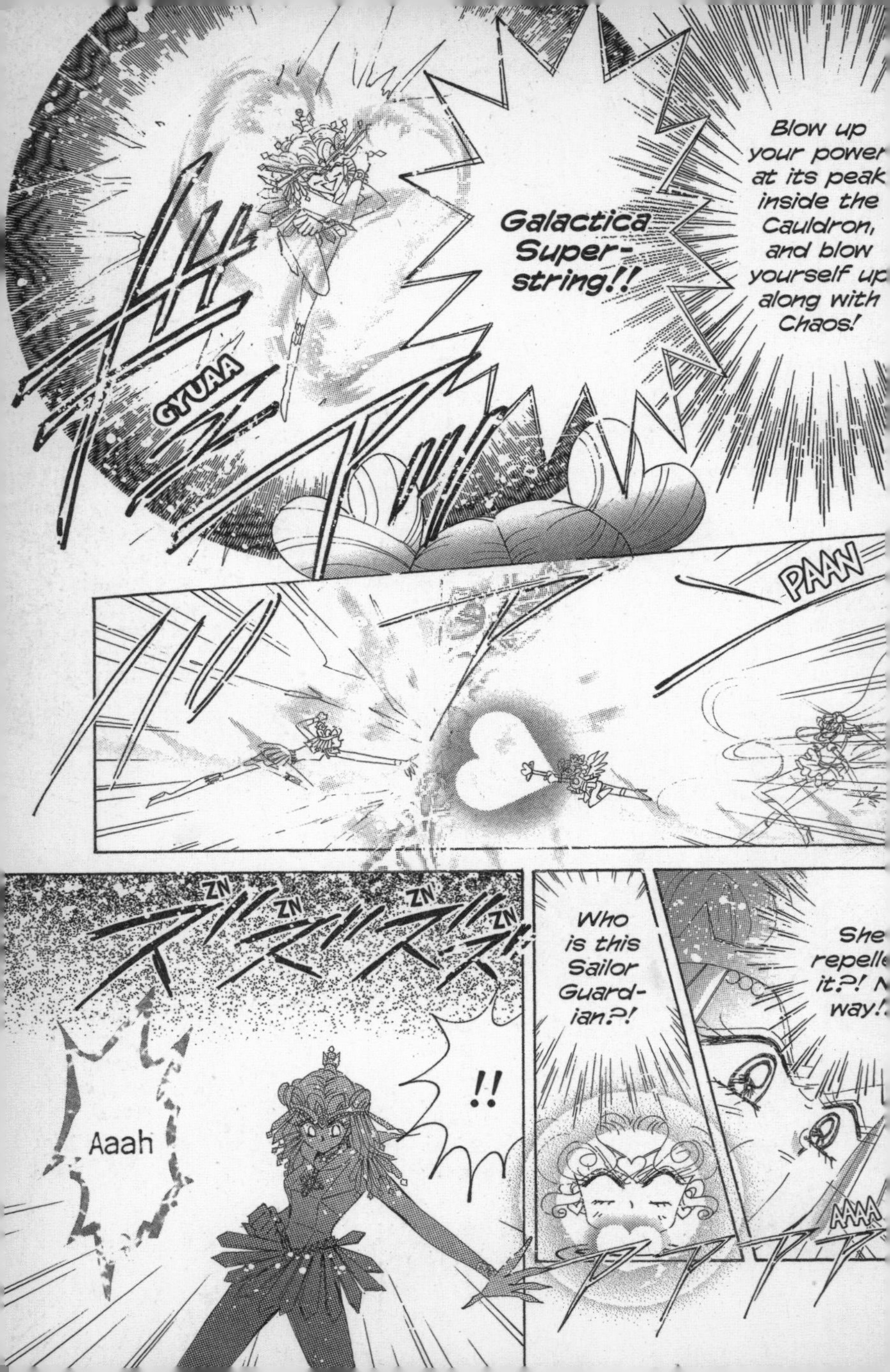

Blow up your powe at its peak inside the Cauldron, and blow yourself u along with Chaos!
Galactica Super-string!!
GYUAA
PAAN
She repelle it?! N way!
AAAA
Who is this Sailor Guard-ian?!
ZN
ZN
ZN
ZN
!!
Aaah

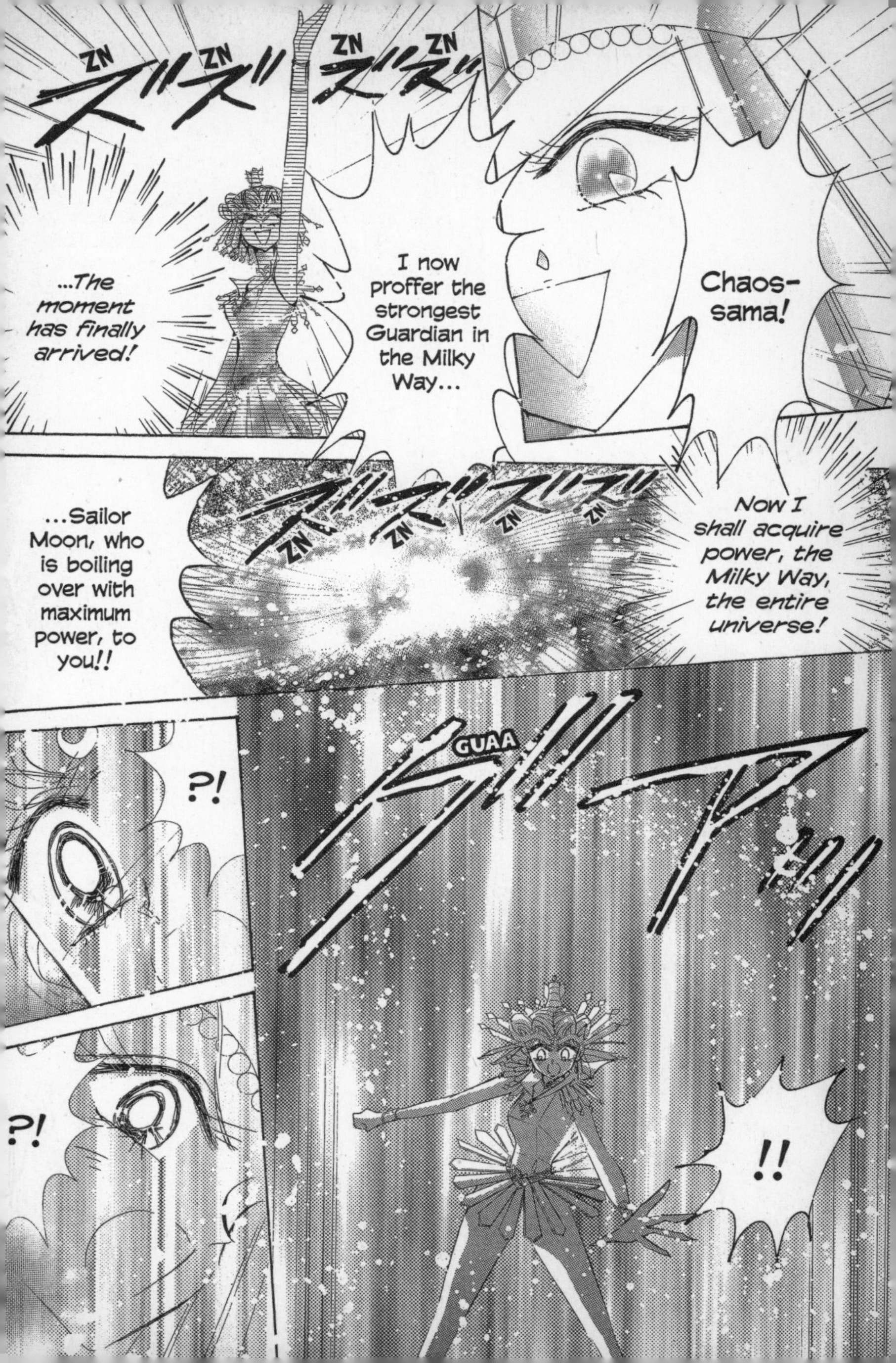

ZN ZN ZN ZN
Chaos-sama!
I now proffer the strongest Guardian in the Milky Way...
...The moment has finally arrived!
Now I shall acquire power, the Milky Way, the entire universe!
ZN ZN ZN ZN
...Sailor Moon, who is boiling over with maximum power, to you!!
GUAA
!!
?!
?!

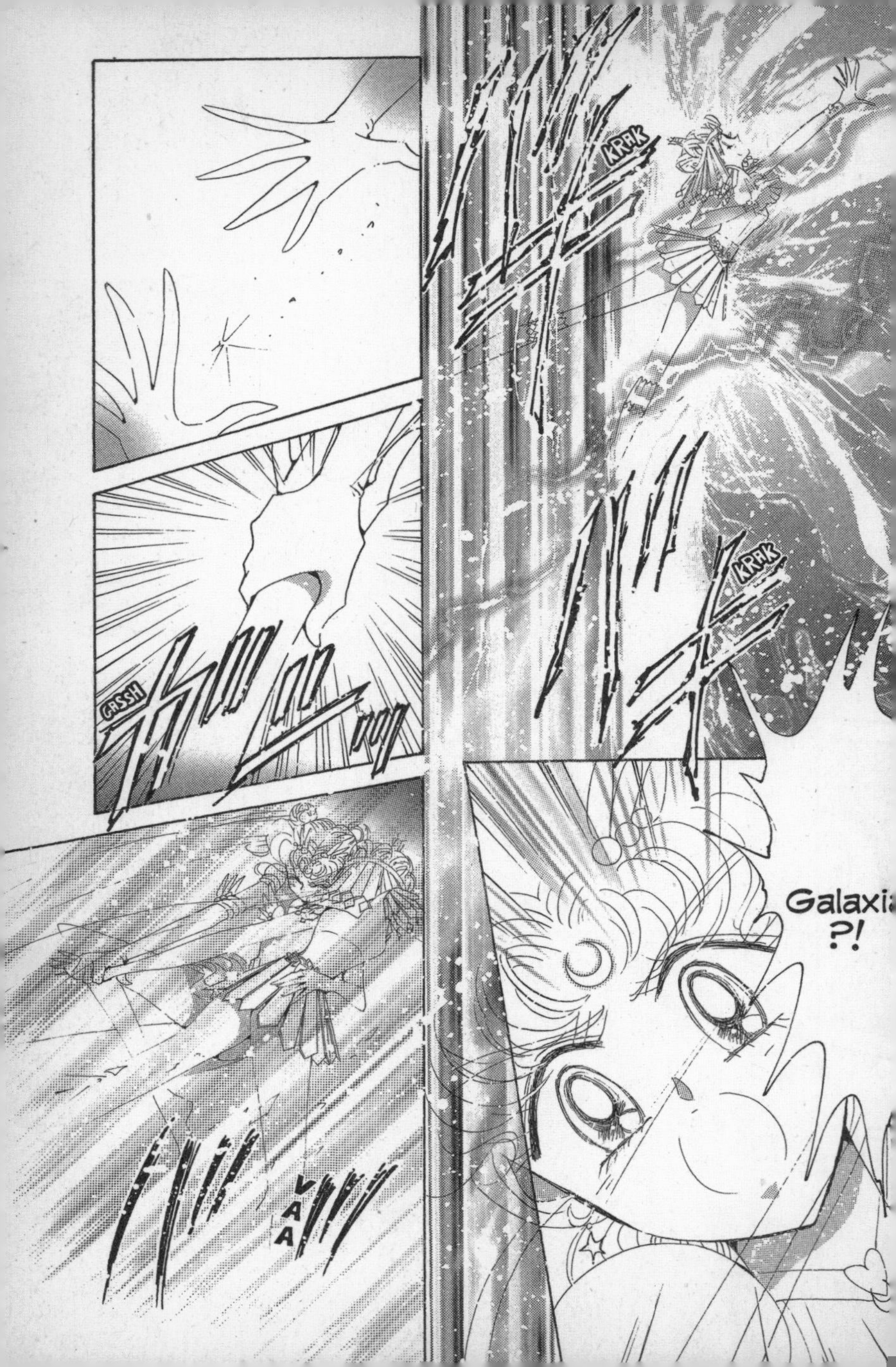
KRAK
KRAK
Galaxia
?!
GASSH
VAA

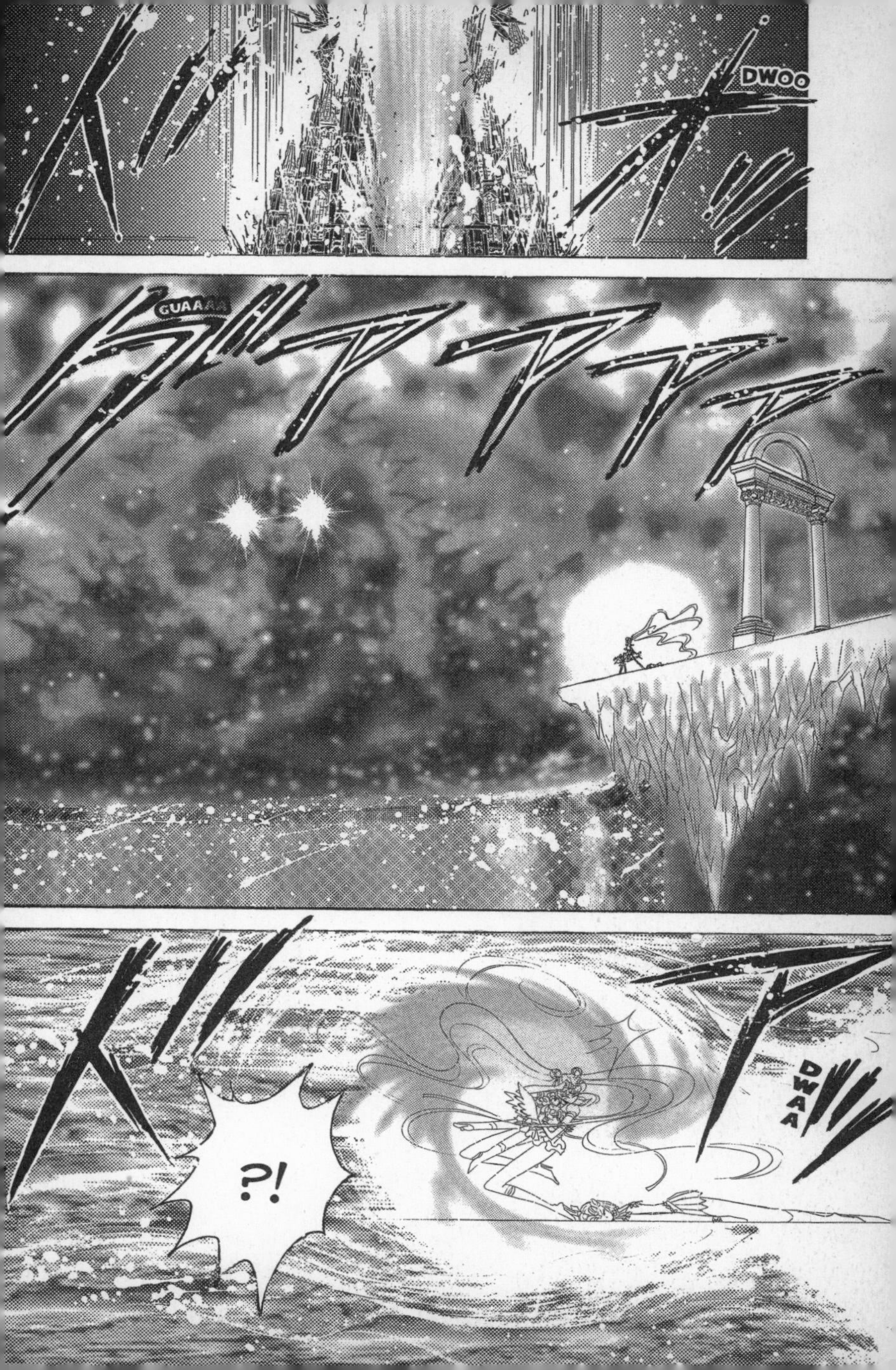
DWOO
GUAAAA
DWAA
?!

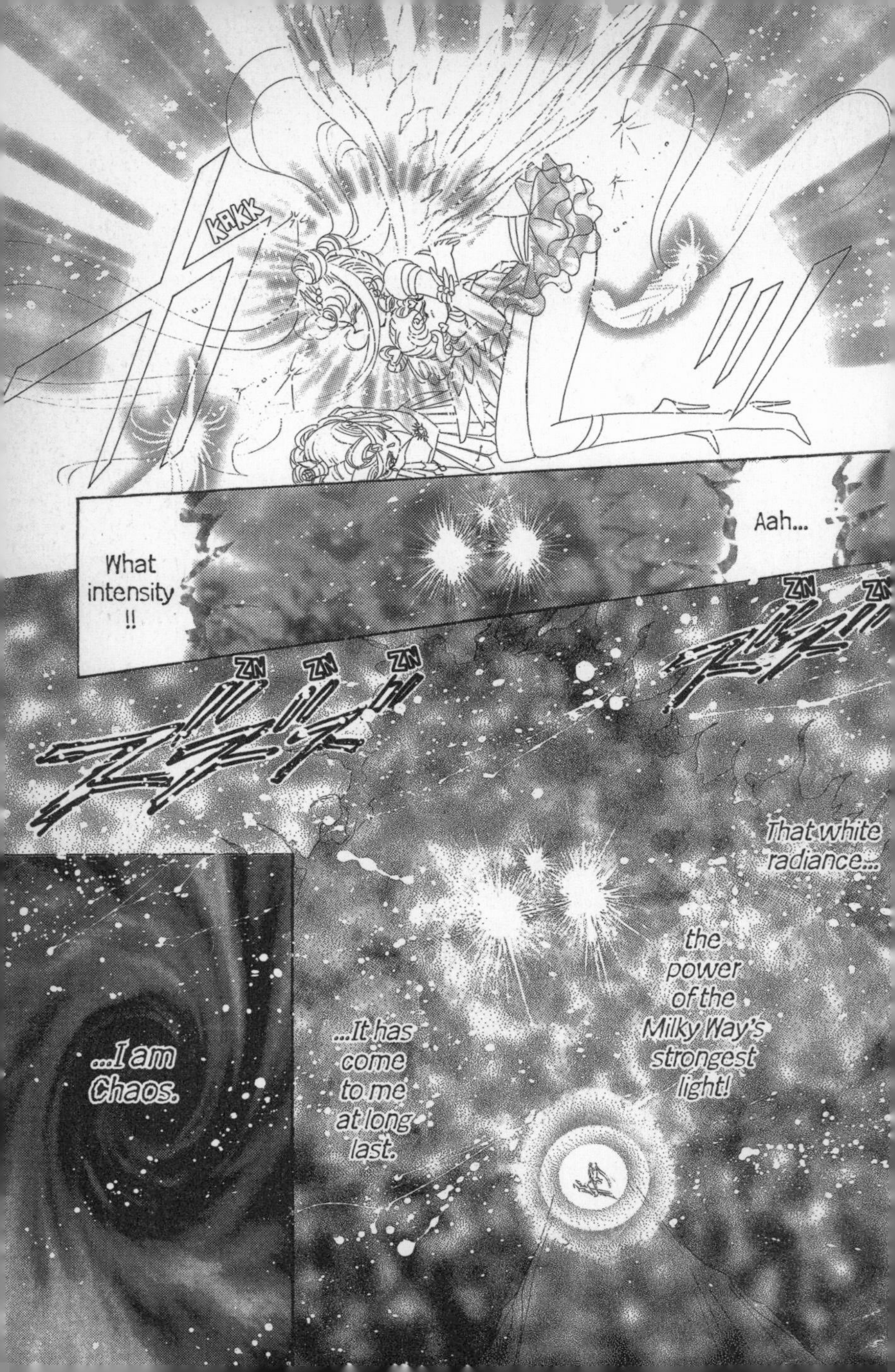
KAKK
Aah...
What intensity !!
ZN ZN
ZN ZN ZN
That white radiance...
the power of the Milky Way's strongest light!
...It has come to me at long last.
...I am Chaos.

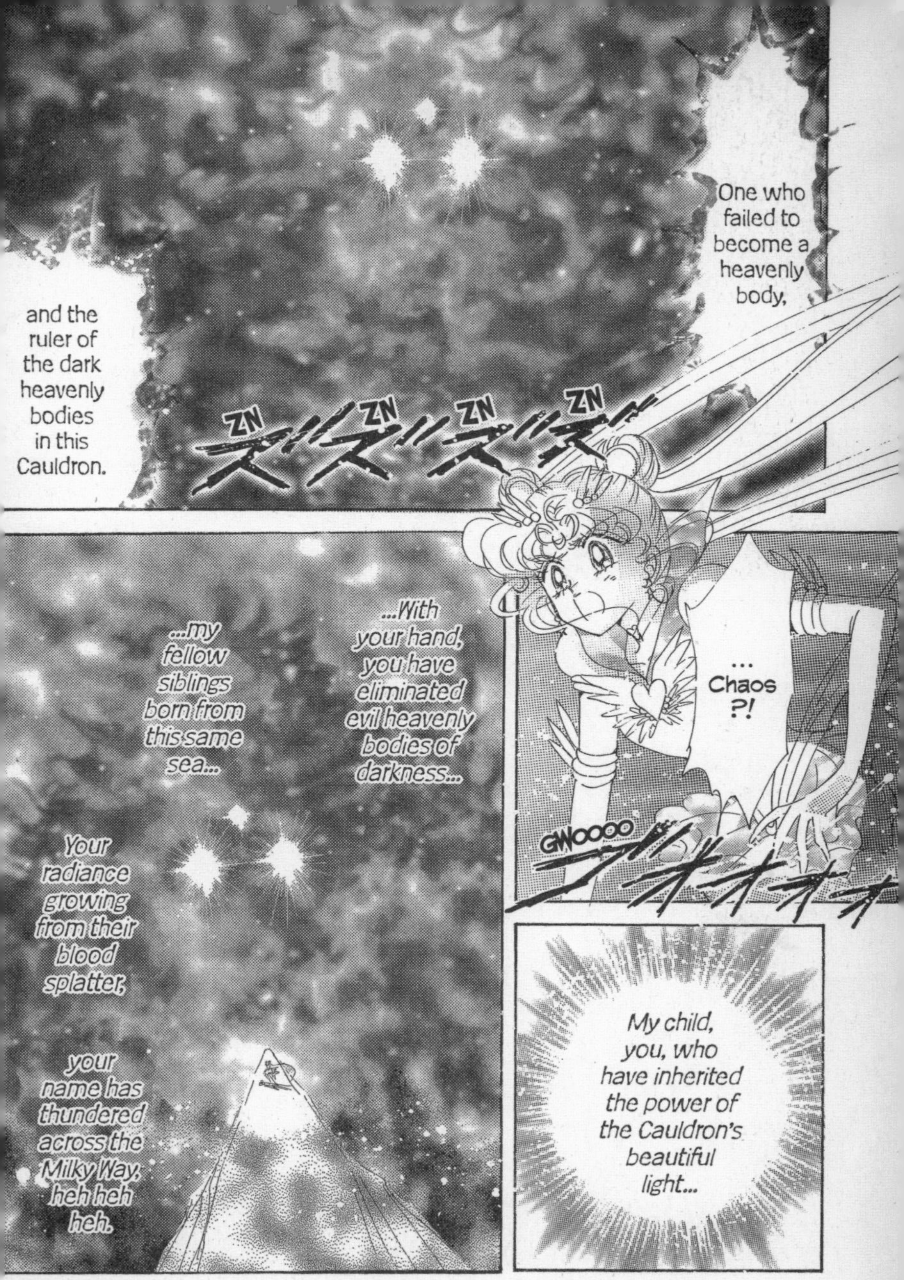
One who failed to become a heavenly body,
and the ruler of the dark heavenly bodies in this Cauldron.
ZN ZN ZN ZN
... Chaos ?!
GWOOOO
My child, you, who have inherited the power of the Cauldron's beautiful light...
...With your hand, you have eliminated evil heavenly bodies of darkness...
...my fellow siblings born from this same sea...
Your radiance growing from their blood splatter,
your name has thundered across the Milky Way, heh heh heh.

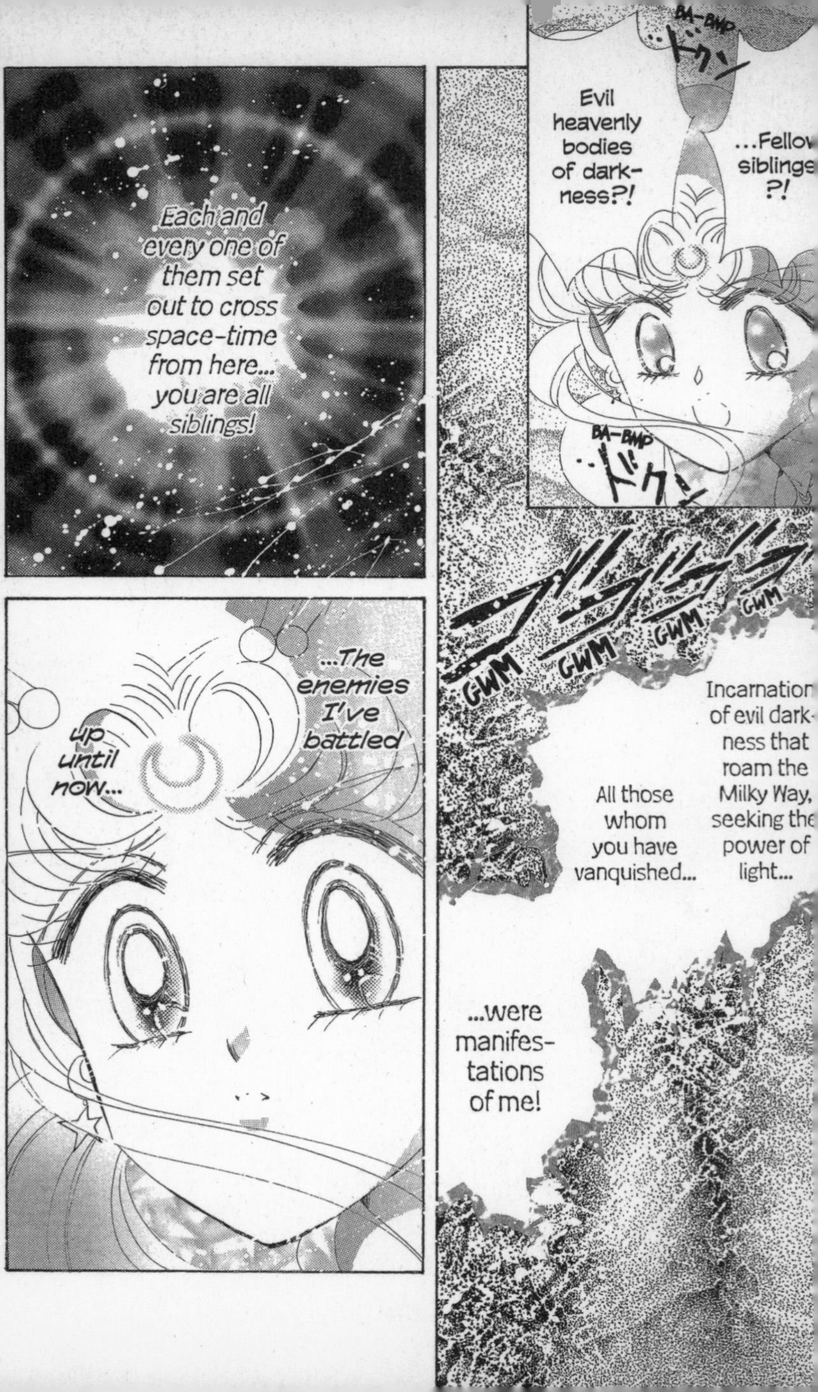
BA-BMP
ドクン
...Fellow siblings?!
Evil heavenly bodies of darkness?!
BA-BMP
ドクン
GWM
GWM
GWM
GWM
Incarnation of evil darkness that roam the Milky Way, seeking the power of light...
All those whom you have vanquished...
...were manifestations of me!
Each and every one of them set out to cross space-time from here... you are all siblings!
...The enemies I've battled
up until now...

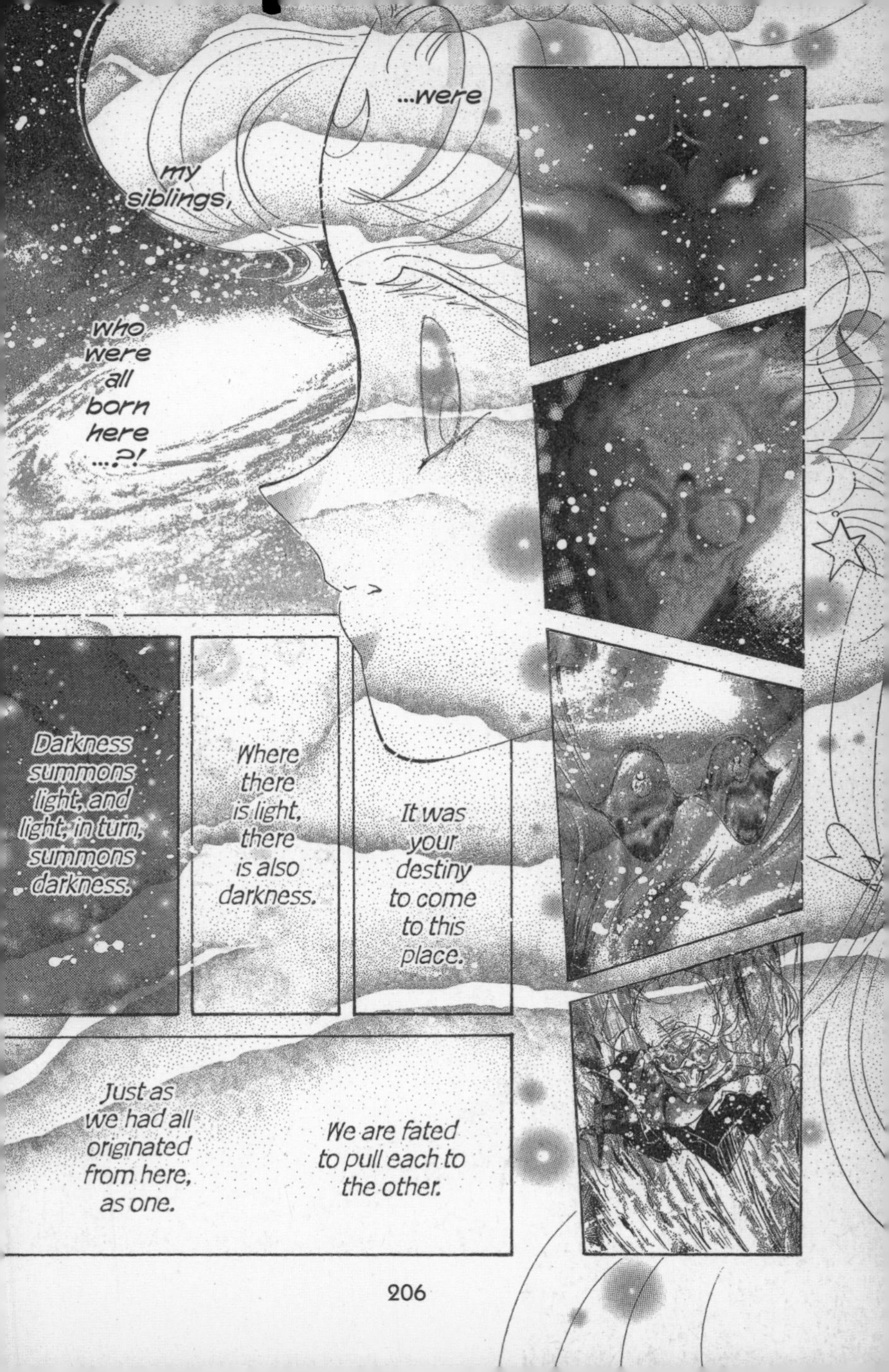
...were
my siblings,
who were all born here ...?!
It was your destiny to come to this place.
Where there is light, there is also darkness.
Darkness summons light, and light, in turn, summons darkness.
We are fated to pull each to the other.
Just as we had all originated from here, as one.

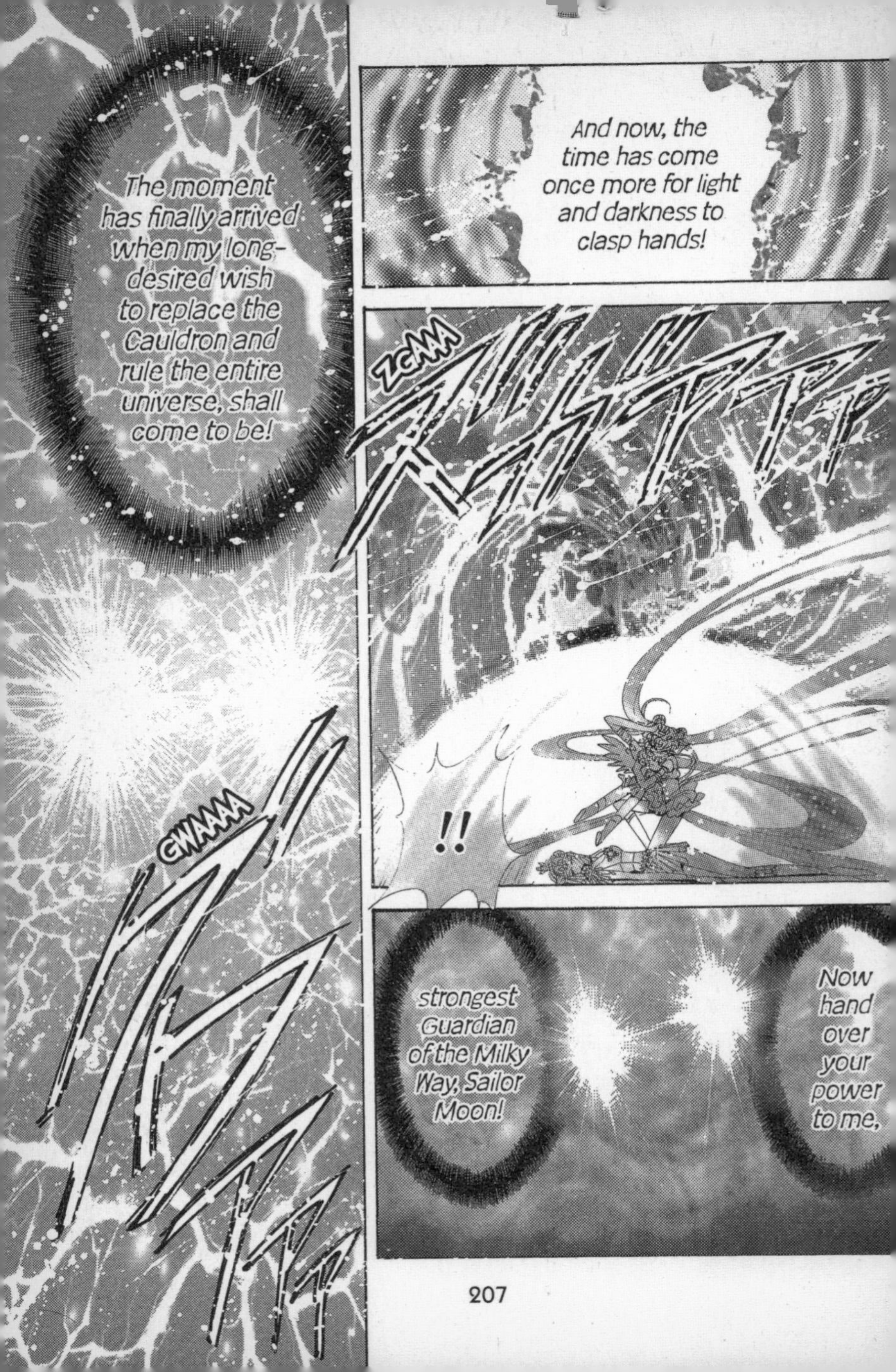

And now, the time has come once more for light and darkness to clasp hands!
ZCAAA
!!
Now hand over your power to me,
strongest Guardian of the Milky Way, Sailor Moon!
The moment has finally arrived when my long-desired wish to replace the Cauldron and rule the entire universe, shall come to be!
GWAAAA

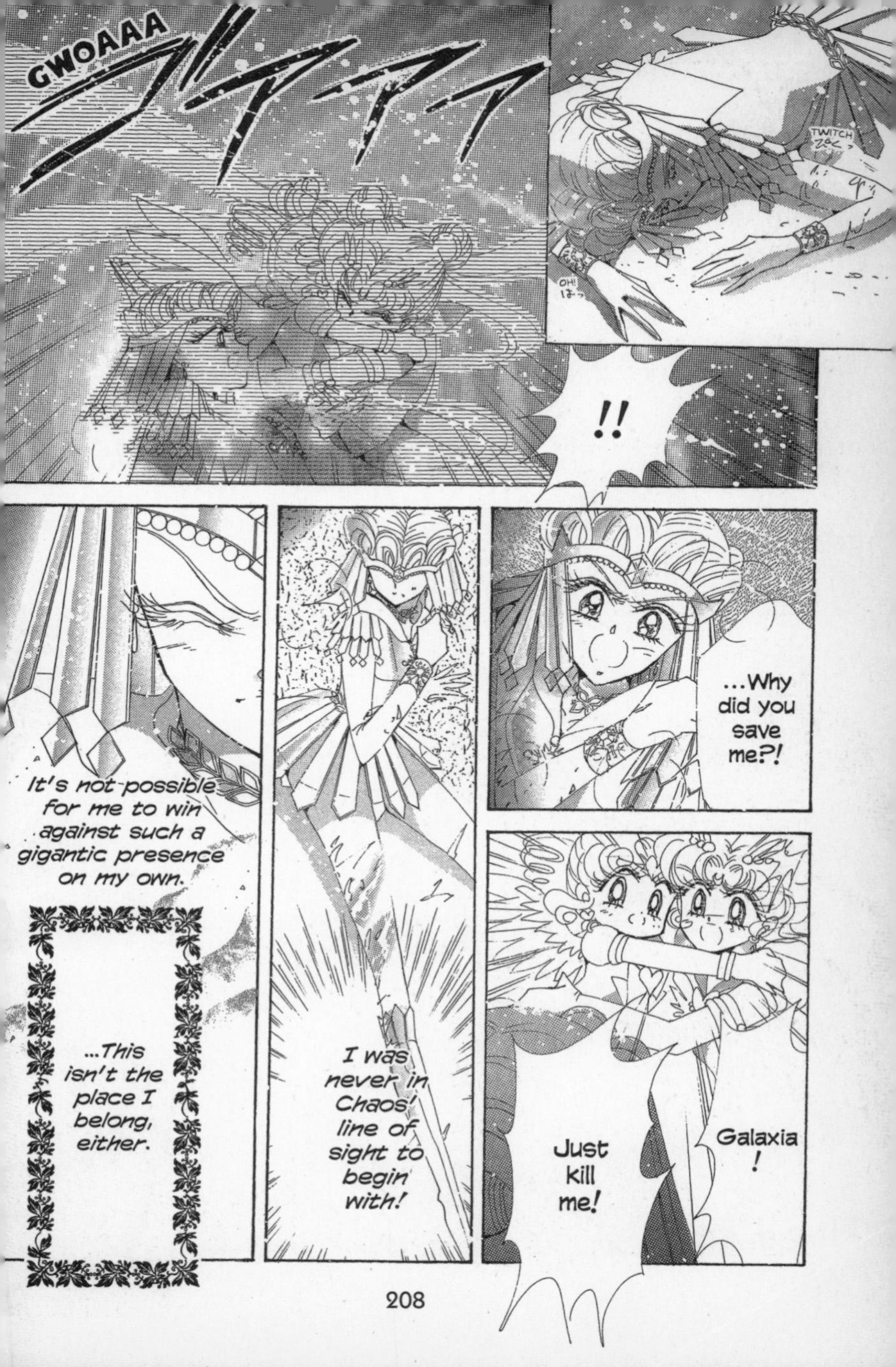
TWITCH
OH!
GWOAAA
!!
...Why did you save me?!
Galaxia!
Just kill me!
I was never in Chaos' line of sight to begin with!
It's not possible for me to win against such a gigantic presence on my own.
...This isn't the place I belong, either.

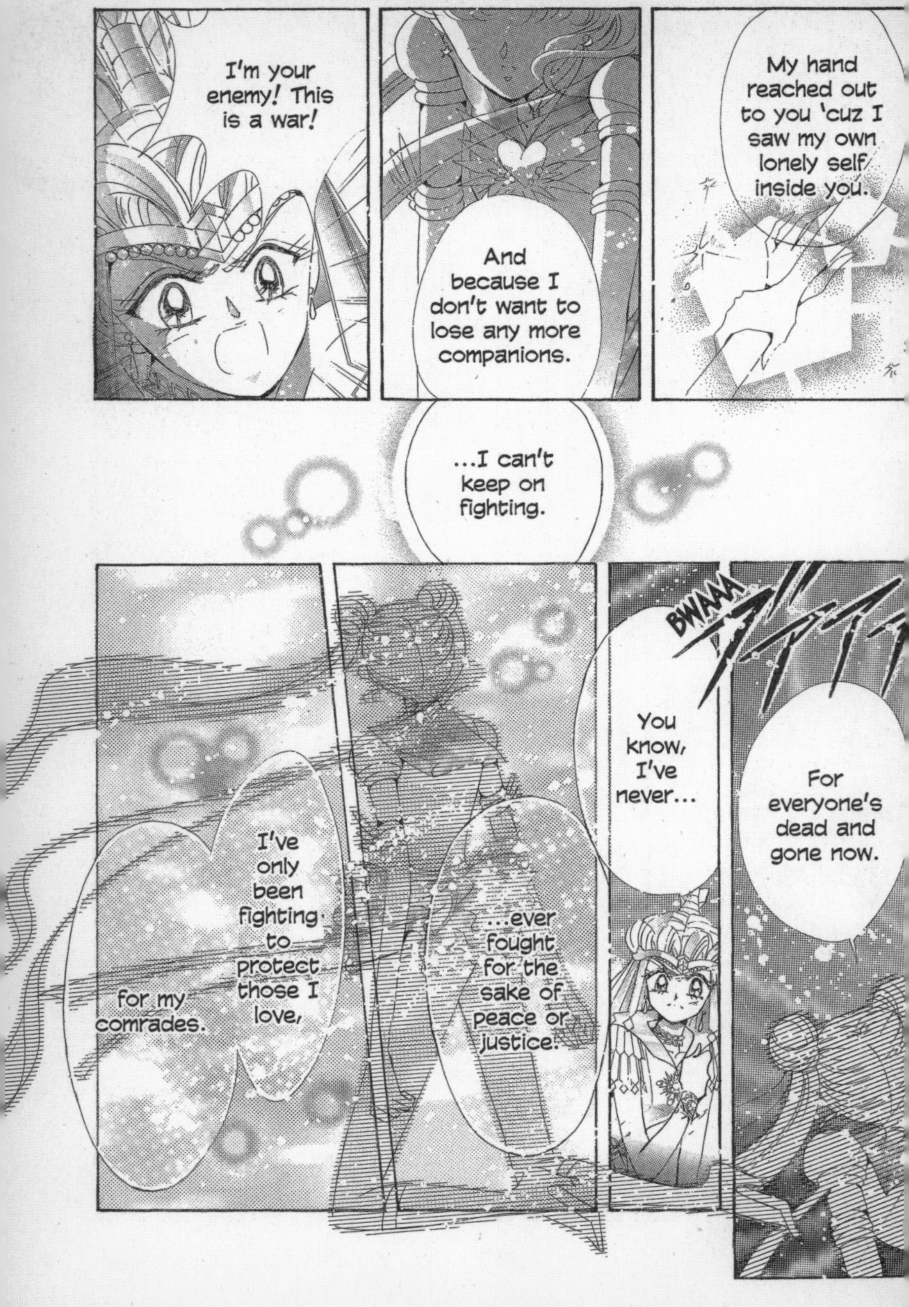
My hand reached out to you 'cuz I saw my own lonely self inside you.
And because I don't want to lose any more companions.
I'm your enemy! This is a war!
...I can't keep on fighting.
For everyone's dead and gone now.
BWAAA
You know, I've never...
...ever fought for the sake of peace or justice.
I've only been fighting to protect those I love,
for my comrades.

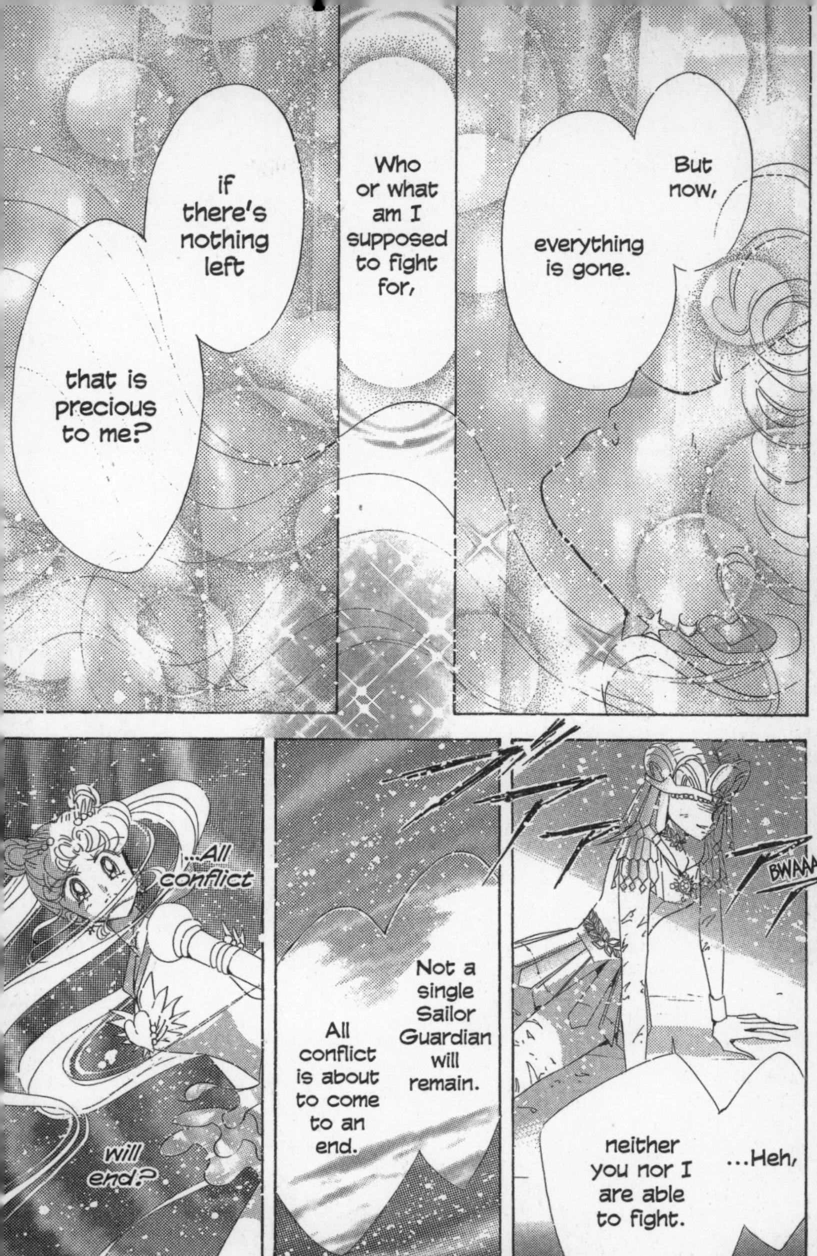
But now,
everything is gone.
Who or what am I supposed to fight for,
if there's nothing left
that is precious to me?
BWAAAA
...Heh,
neither you nor I are able to fight.
Not a single Sailor Guardian will remain.
All conflict is about to come to an end.
...All conflict
will end?

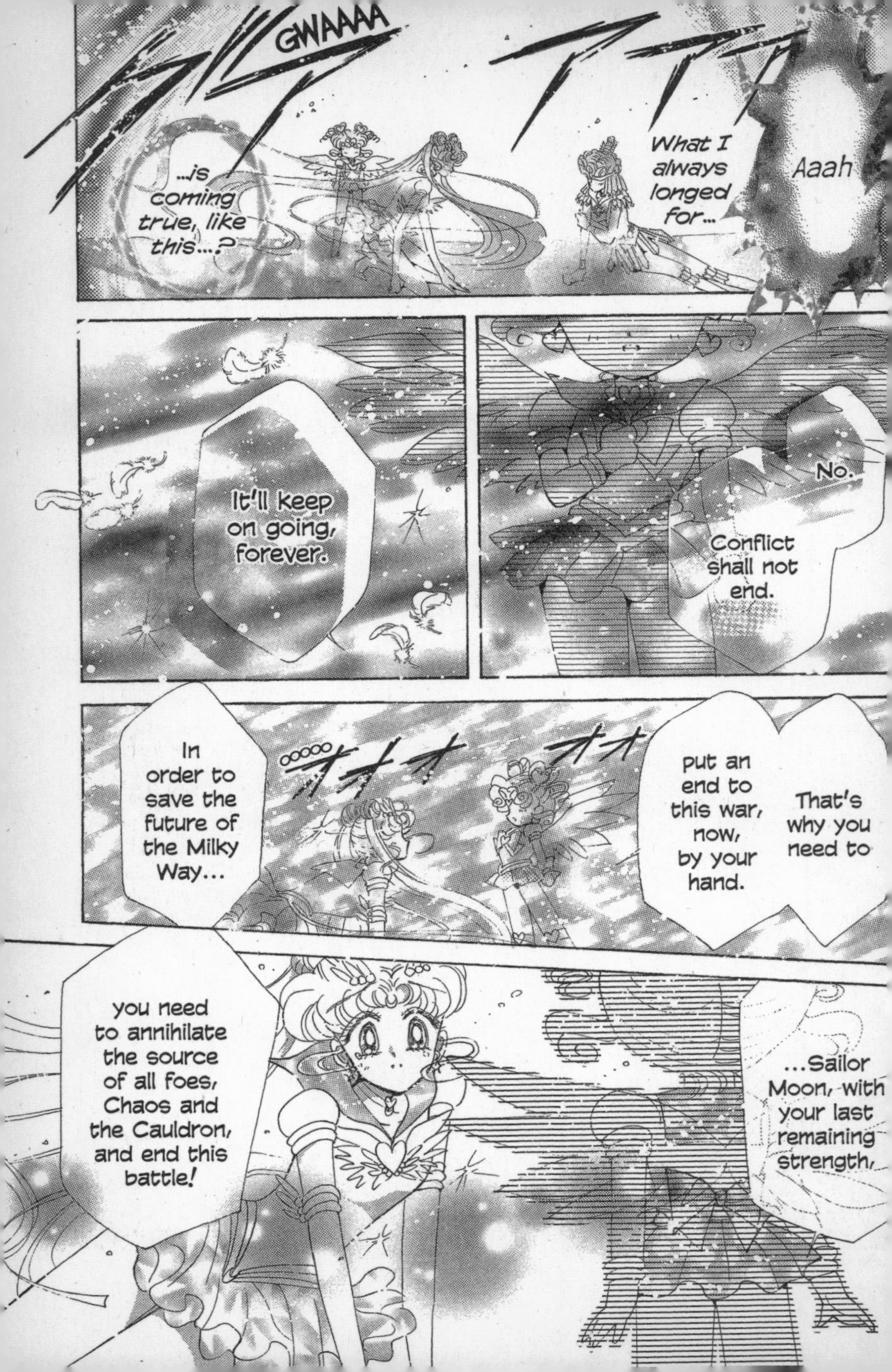
GWAAAA
Aaah
What I always longed for...
...is coming true, like this...?
No.
Conflict shall not end.
It'll keep on going, forever.
That's why you need to
put an end to this war, now, by your hand.
OOOOO
In order to save the future of the Milky Way...
...Sailor Moon, with your last remaining strength,
you need to annihilate the source of all foes, Chaos and the Cauldron, and end this battle!

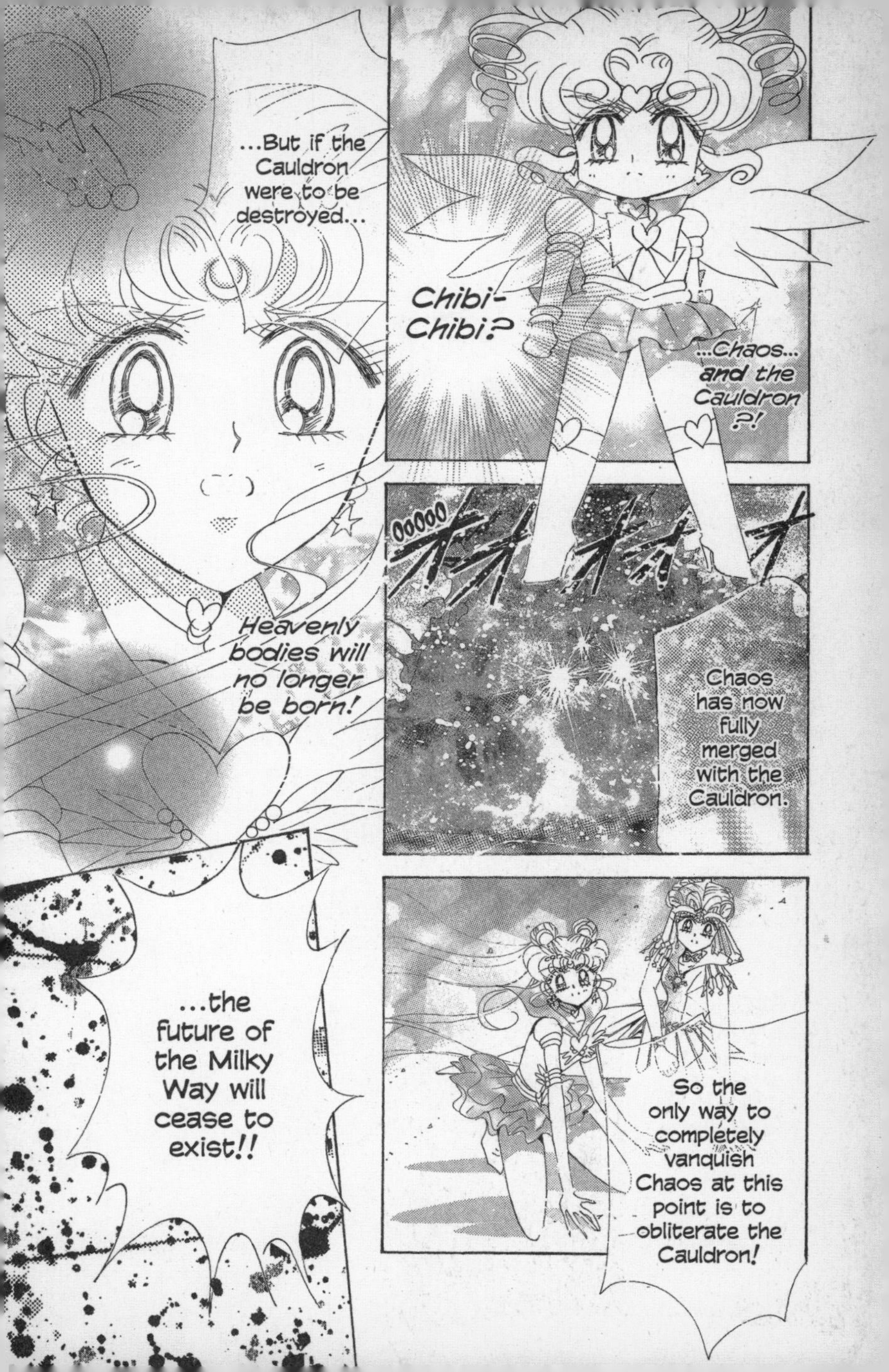
Chibi-Chibi?
...Chaos... and the Cauldron ?!
OOOOO
Chaos has now fully merged with the Cauldron.
So the only way to completely vanquish Chaos at this point is to obliterate the Cauldron!
...But if the Cauldron were to be destroyed...
Heavenly bodies will no longer be born!
...the future of the Milky Way will cease to exist!!

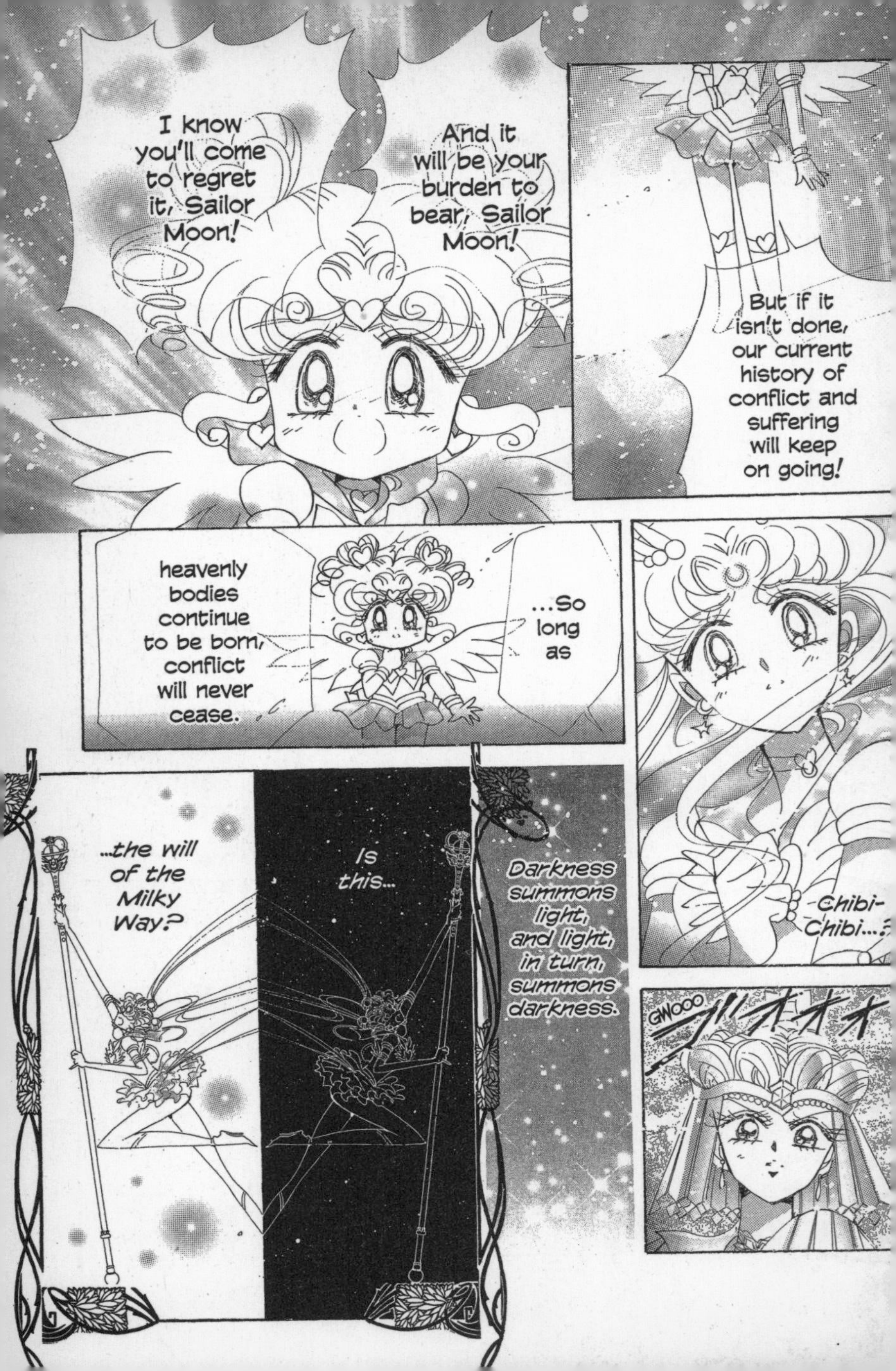
But if it isn't done, our current history of conflict and suffering will keep on going!
And it will be your burden to bear, Sailor Moon!
I know you'll come to regret it, Sailor Moon!
...So long as
heavenly bodies continue to be born, conflict will never cease.
Chibi-Chibi...?
GWOOO
Darkness summons light, and light, in turn, summons darkness.
Is this...
...the will of the Milky Way?

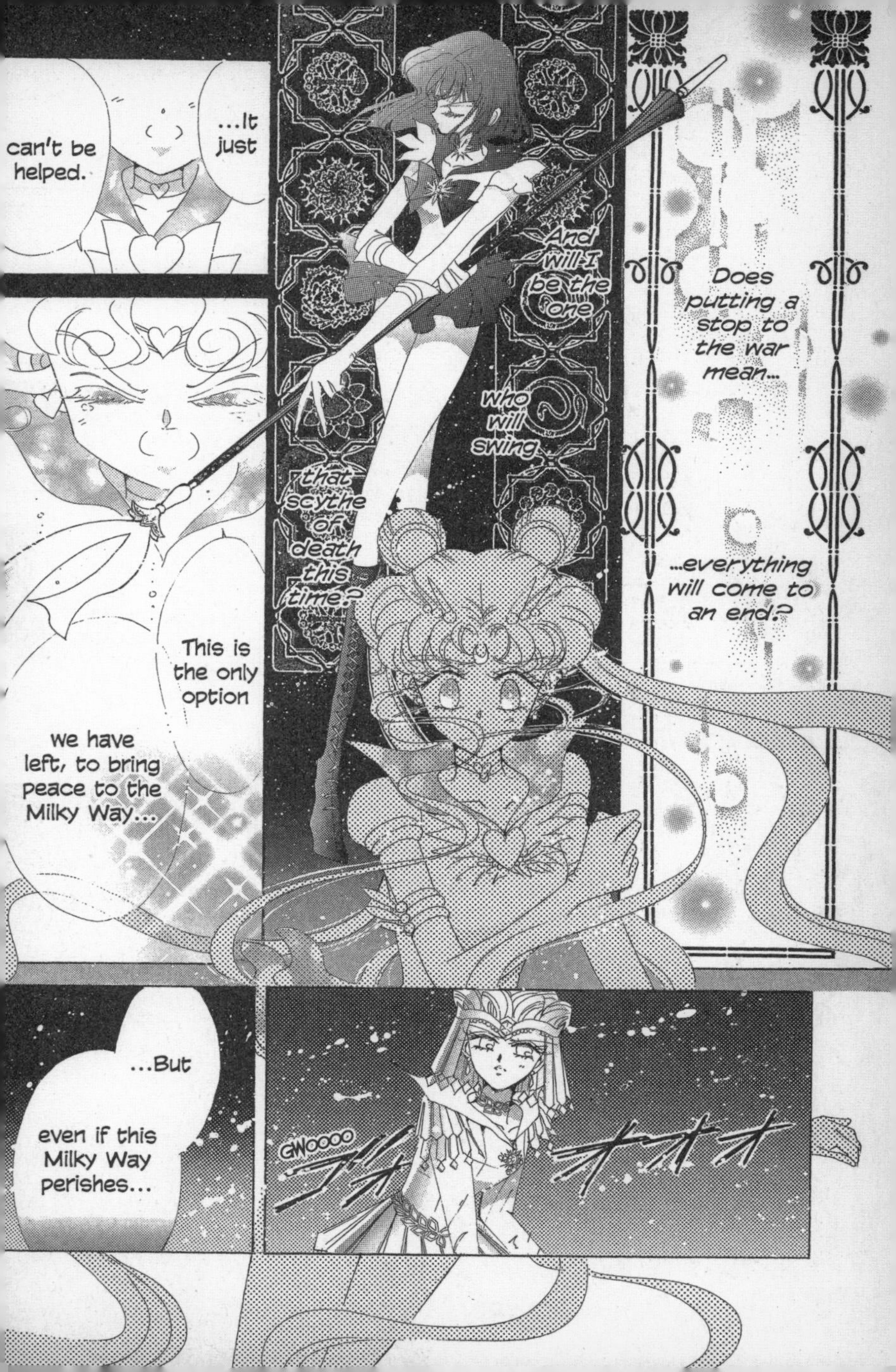

Does putting a stop to the war mean...
...everything will come to an end?
And will I be the one
who will swing
that scythe of death this time?
...It just
can't be helped.
This is the only option
we have left, to bring peace to the Milky Way...
GWOOOO
...But
even if this Milky Way perishes...

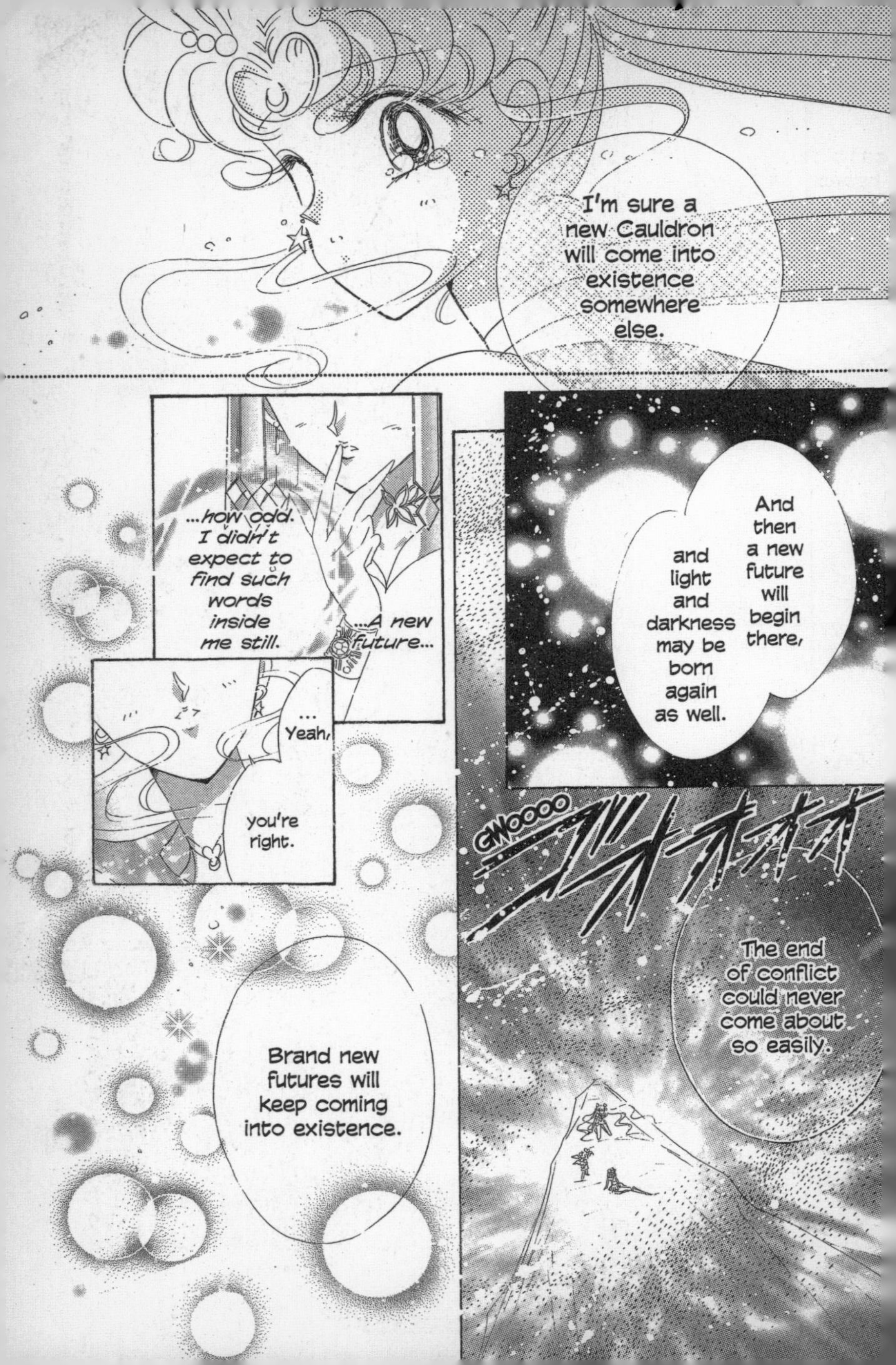
I'm sure a new Cauldron will come into existence somewhere else.
And then a new future will begin there,
and light and darkness may be born again as well.
...A new future...
...how odd. I didn't expect to find such words inside me still.
... Yeah,
you're right.
GWOOOO
The end of conflict could never come about so easily.
Brand new futures will keep coming into existence.

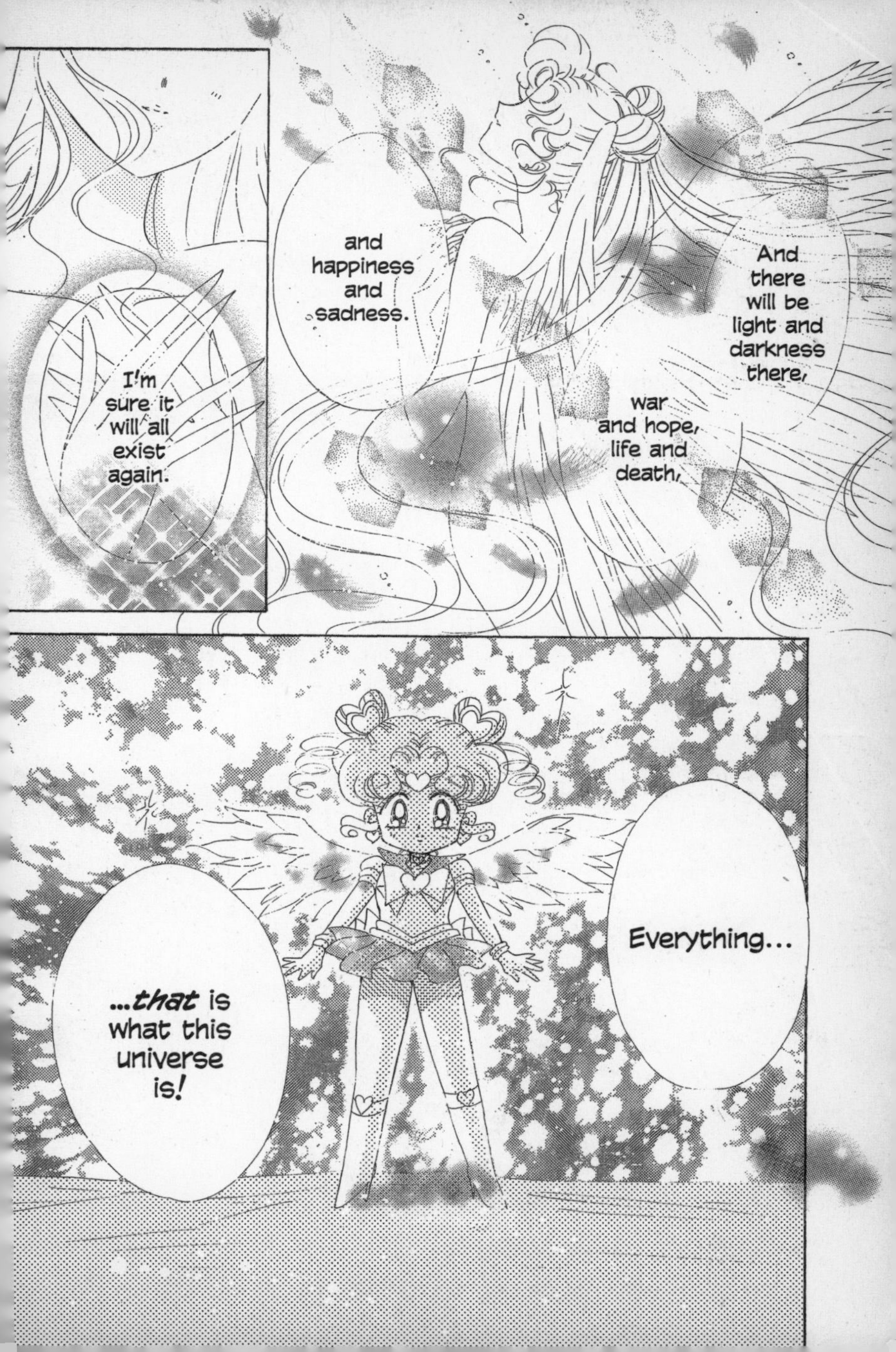
And there will be light and darkness there,
war and hope, life and death,
and happiness and sadness.
I'm sure it will all exist again.
Everything...
...*that* is what this universe is!

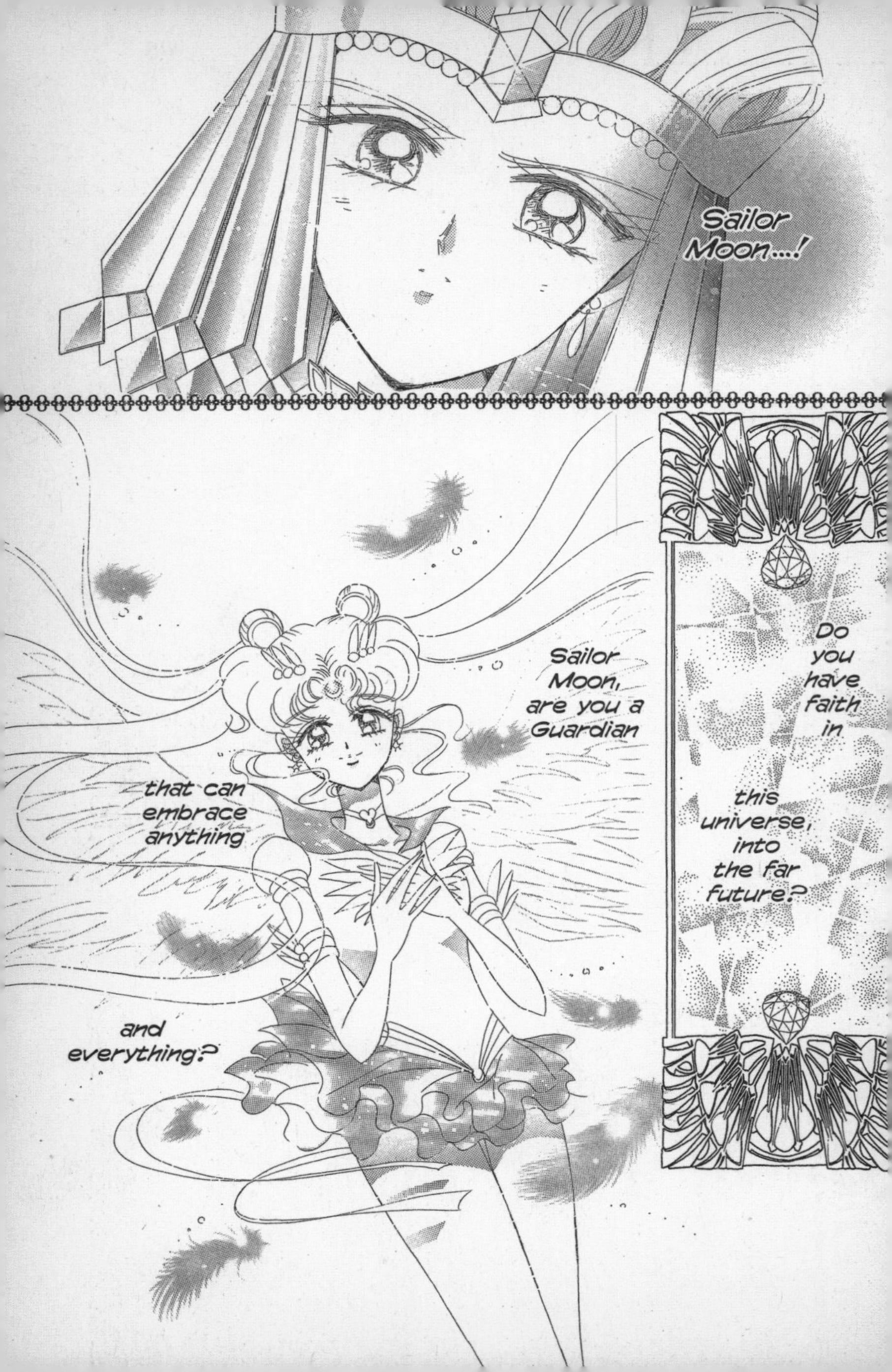
Sailor Moon...!
Do you have faith in
this universe, into the far future?
Sailor Moon, are you a Guardian
that can embrace anything
and everything?

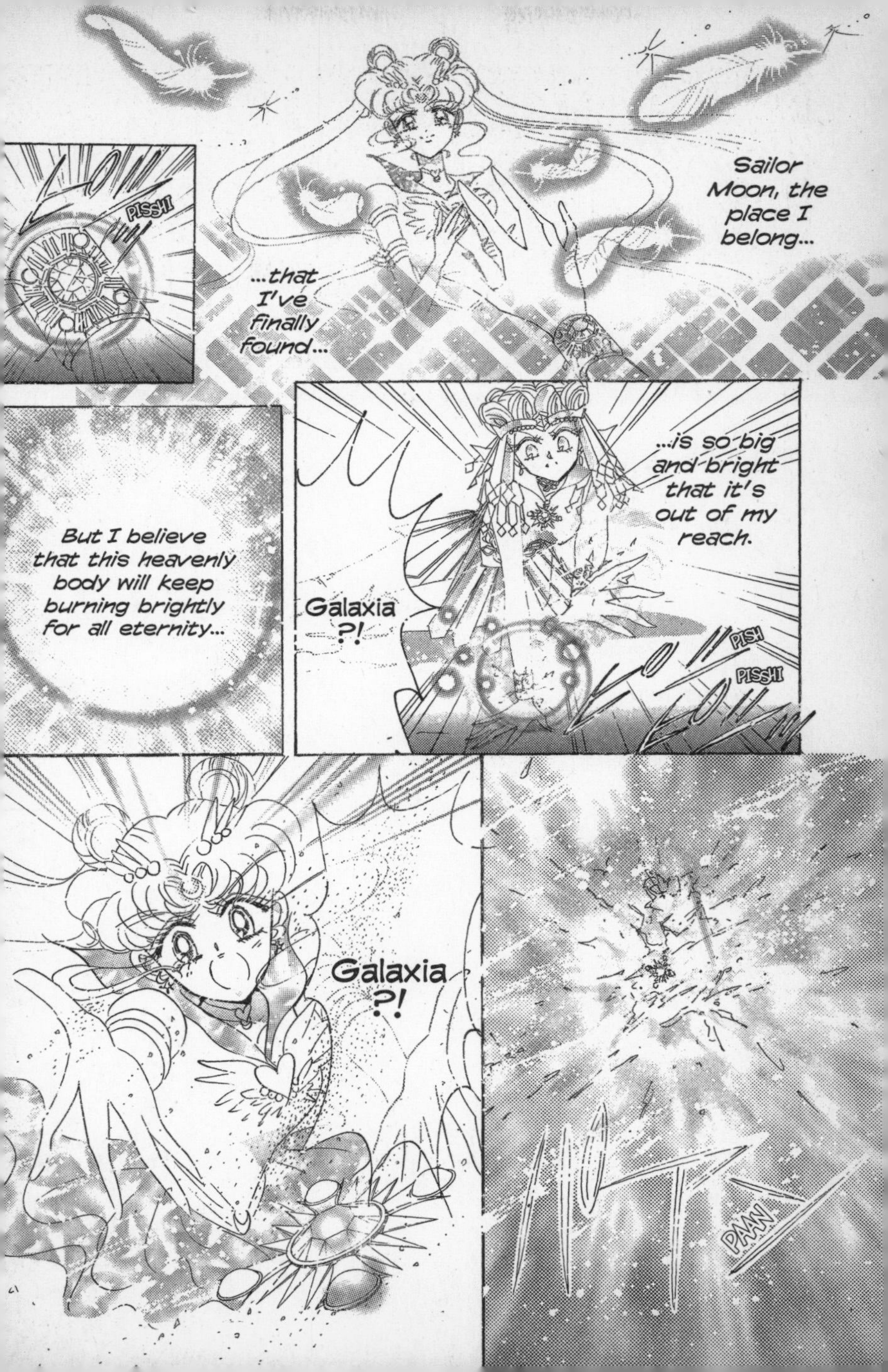
Sailor Moon, the place I belong...
...that I've finally found...
PISSHI
...is so big and bright that it's out of my reach.
Galaxia ?!
PISH
PISSHI
But I believe that this heavenly body will keep burning brightly for all eternity...
PAAN
Galaxia ?!

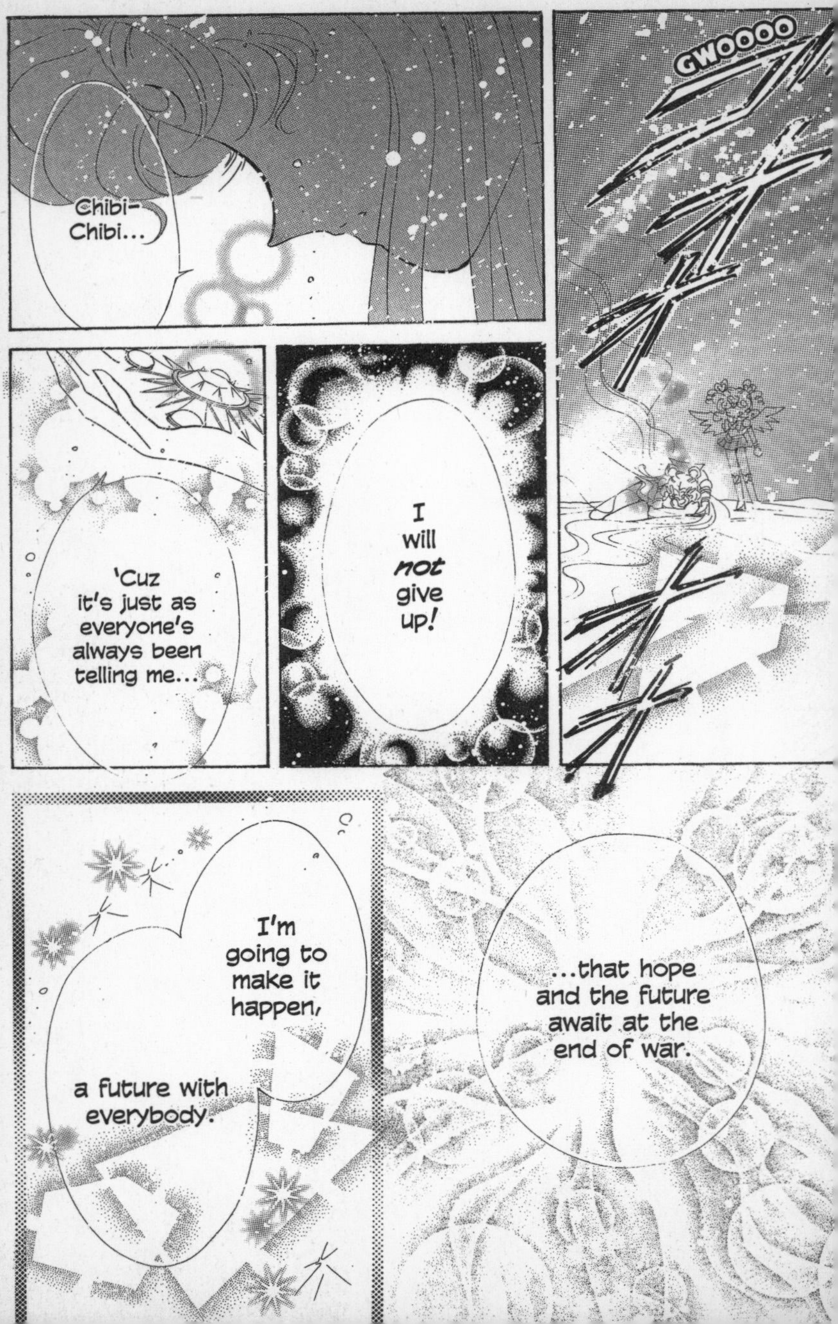
GWOOOO
Chibi-Chibi...
I will *not* give up!
'Cuz it's just as everyone's always been telling me...
...that hope and the future await at the end of war.
I'm going to make it happen,
a future with everybody.

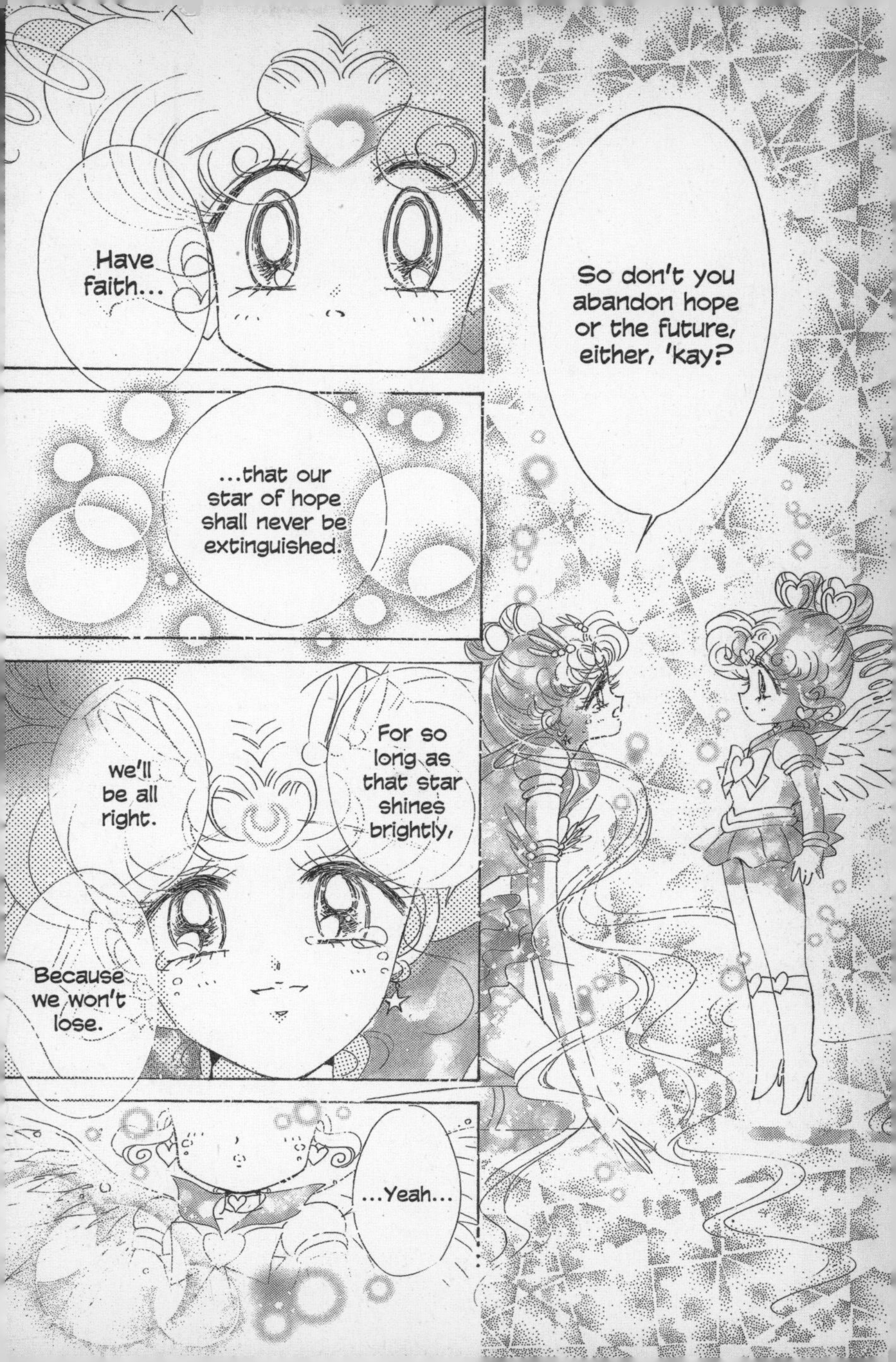
So don't you abandon hope or the future, either, 'kay?
Have faith...
...that our star of hope shall never be extinguished.
For so long as that star shines brightly,
we'll be all right.
Because we won't lose.
...Yeah...

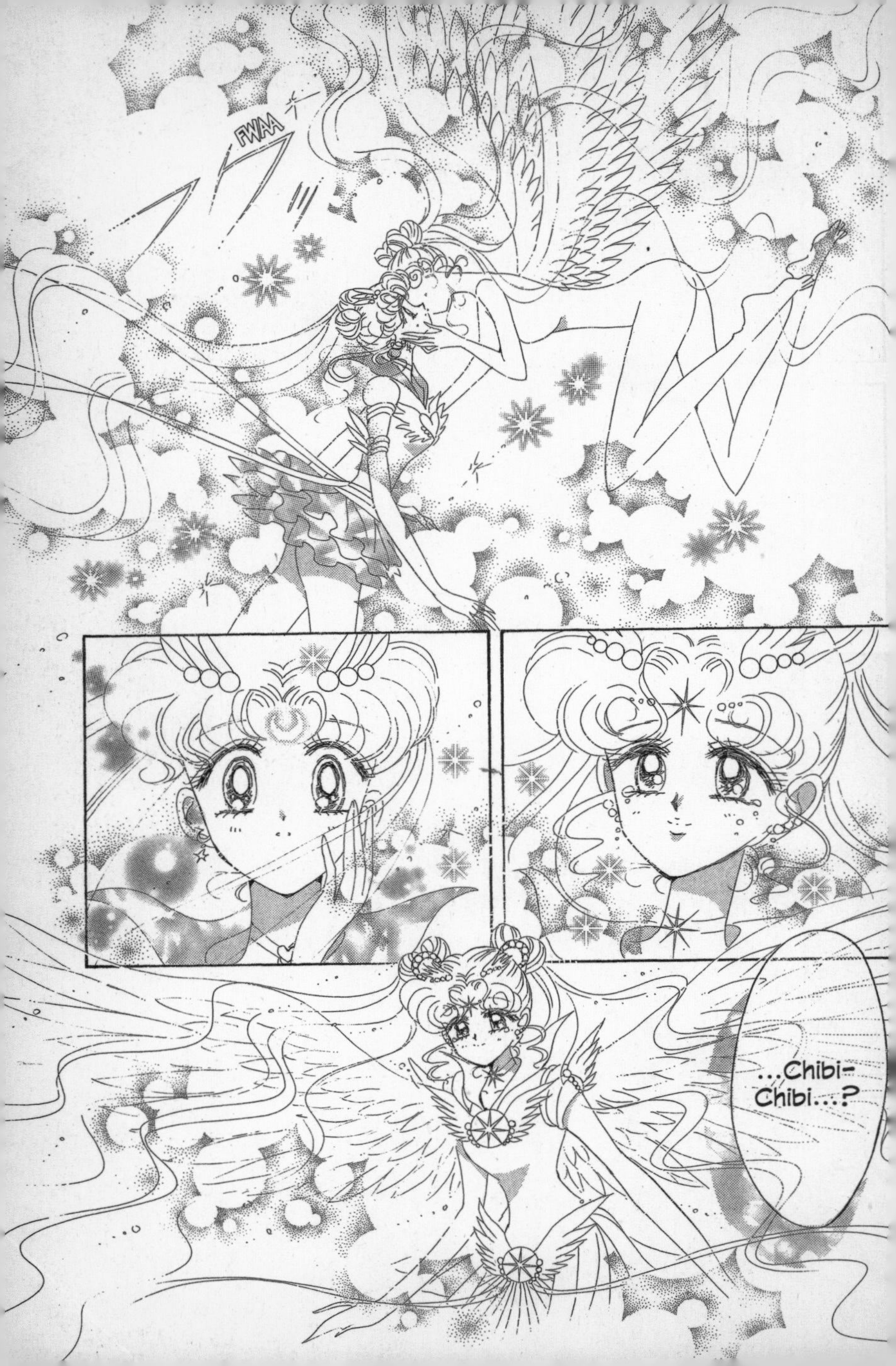
FWAA
...Chibi-Chibi...?

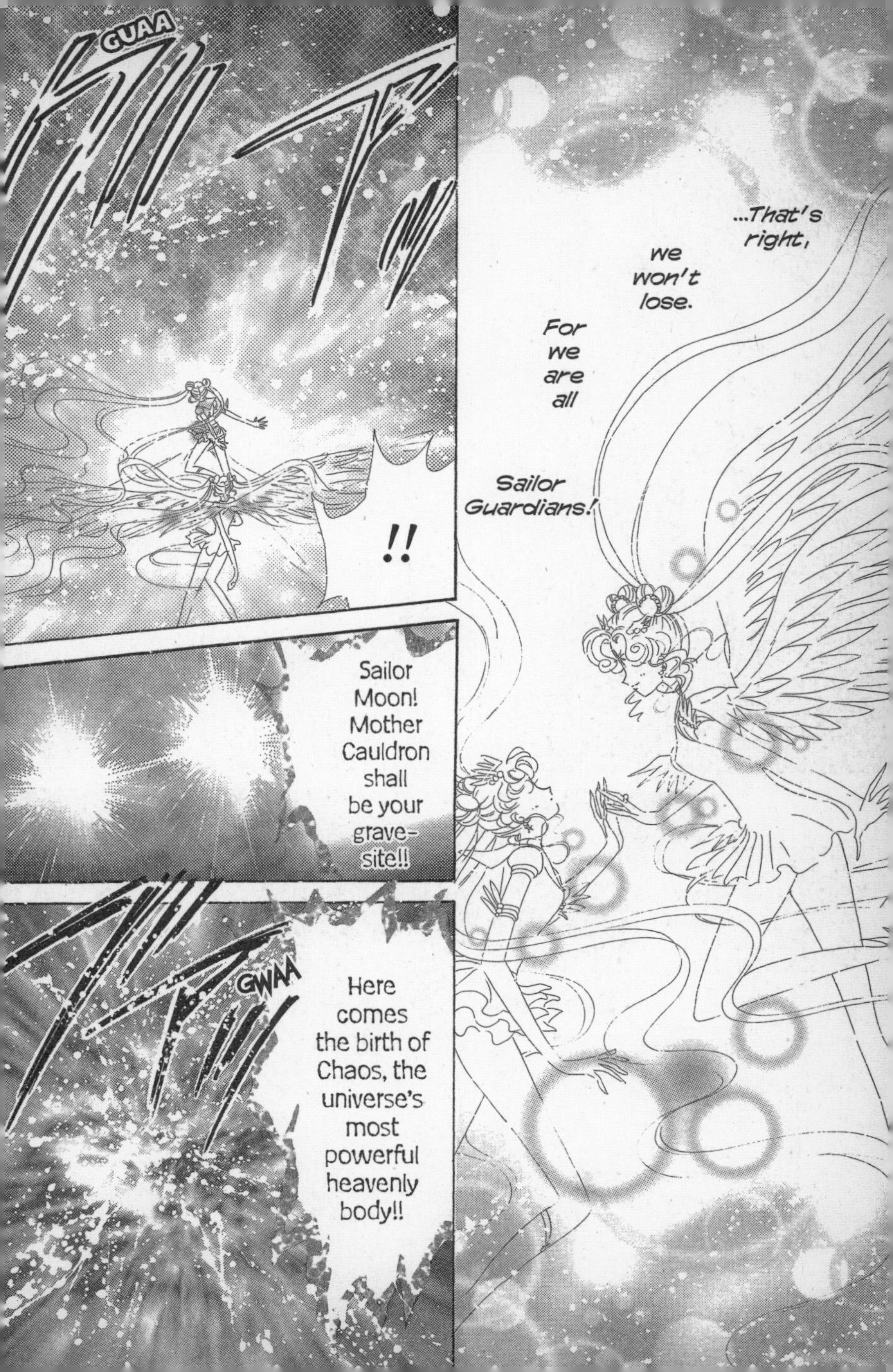
...That's right,
we won't lose.
For we are all
Sailor Guardians!
GUAA
!!
Sailor Moon! Mother Cauldron shall be your grave-site!!
GWAA
Here comes the birth of Chaos, the universe's most powerful heavenly body!!

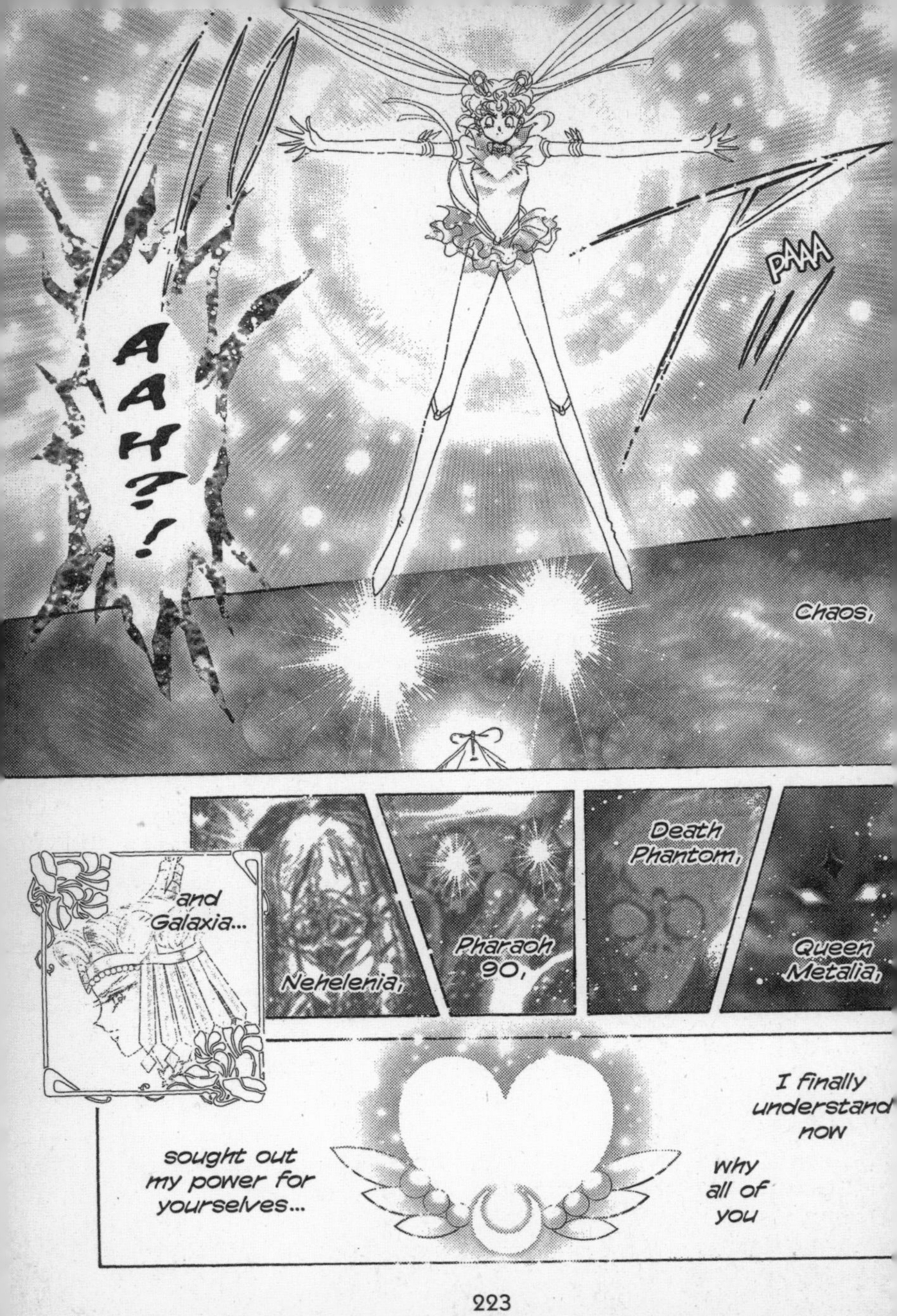
PAAA
AAH?!
Chaos,
Queen Metalia,
Death Phantom,
Pharaoh 90,
Nehelenia,
and Galaxia...
I finally understand now
why all of you
sought out my power for yourselves...

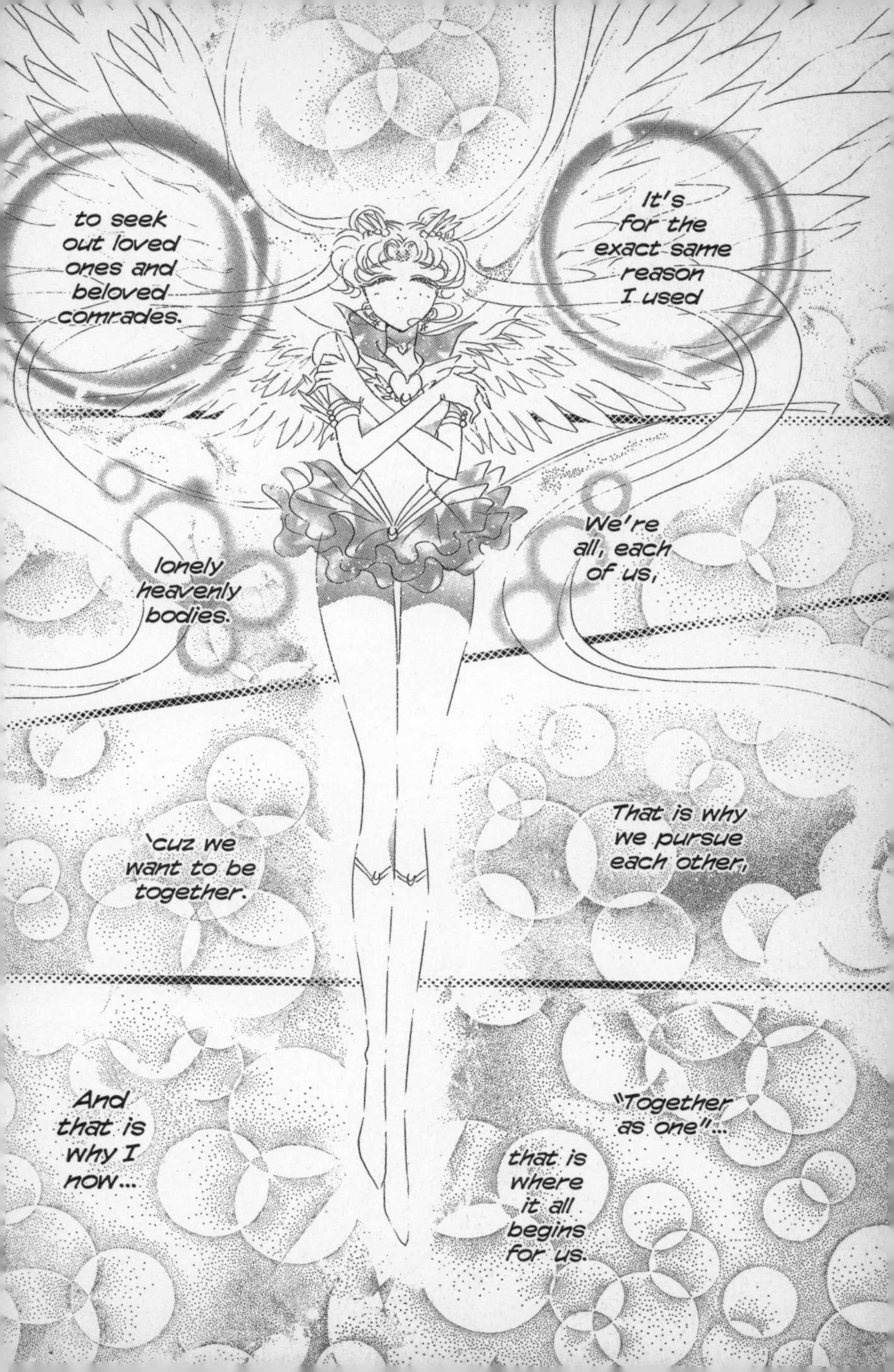
It's for the exact same reason I used
to seek out loved ones and beloved comrades.
We're all, each of us,
lonely heavenly bodies.
That is why we pursue each other,
'cuz we want to be together.
"Together as one"...
that is where it all begins for us.
And that is why I now...

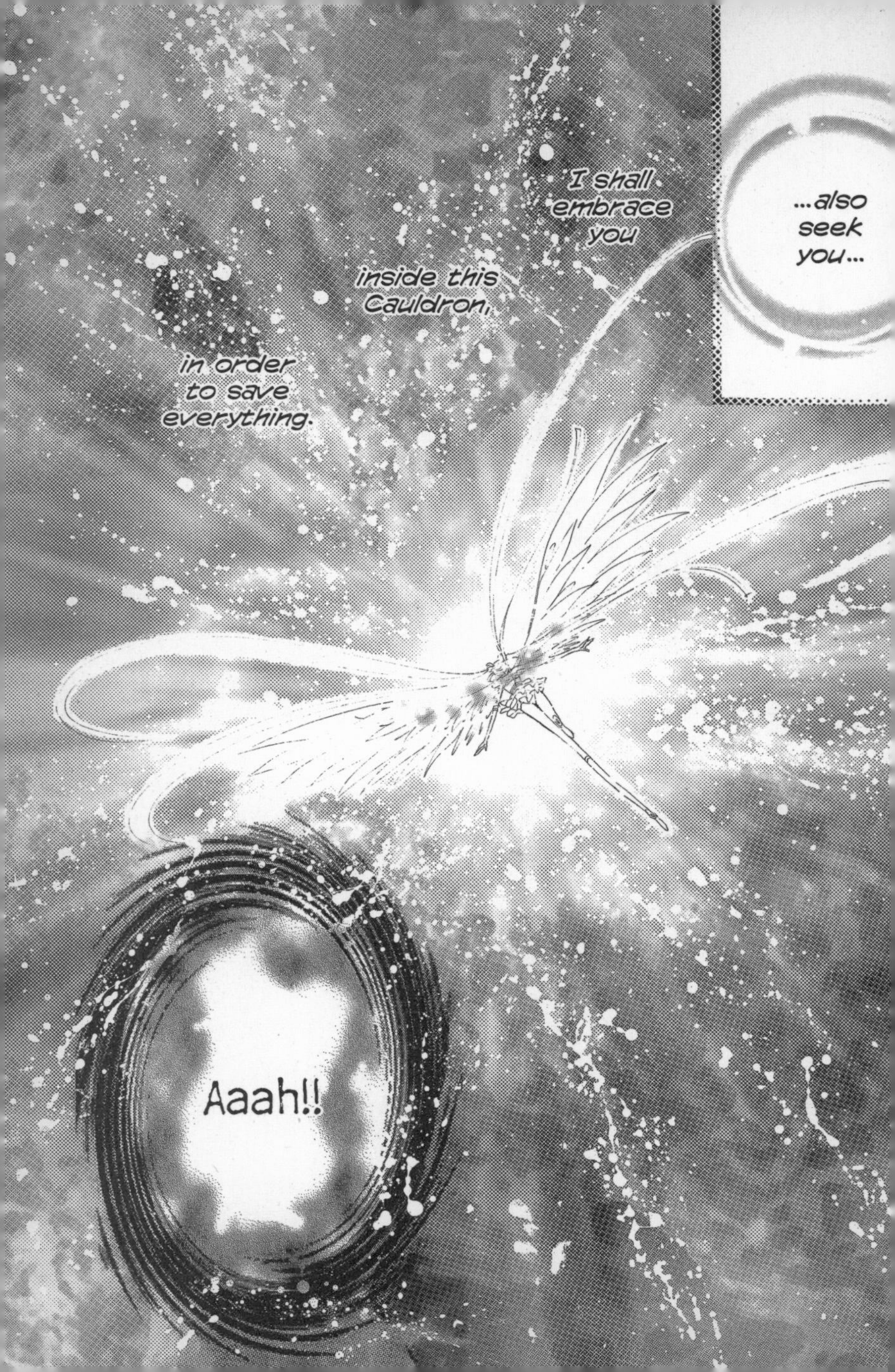
...also seek you...
I shall embrace you
inside this Cauldron,
in order to save everything.
Aaah!!

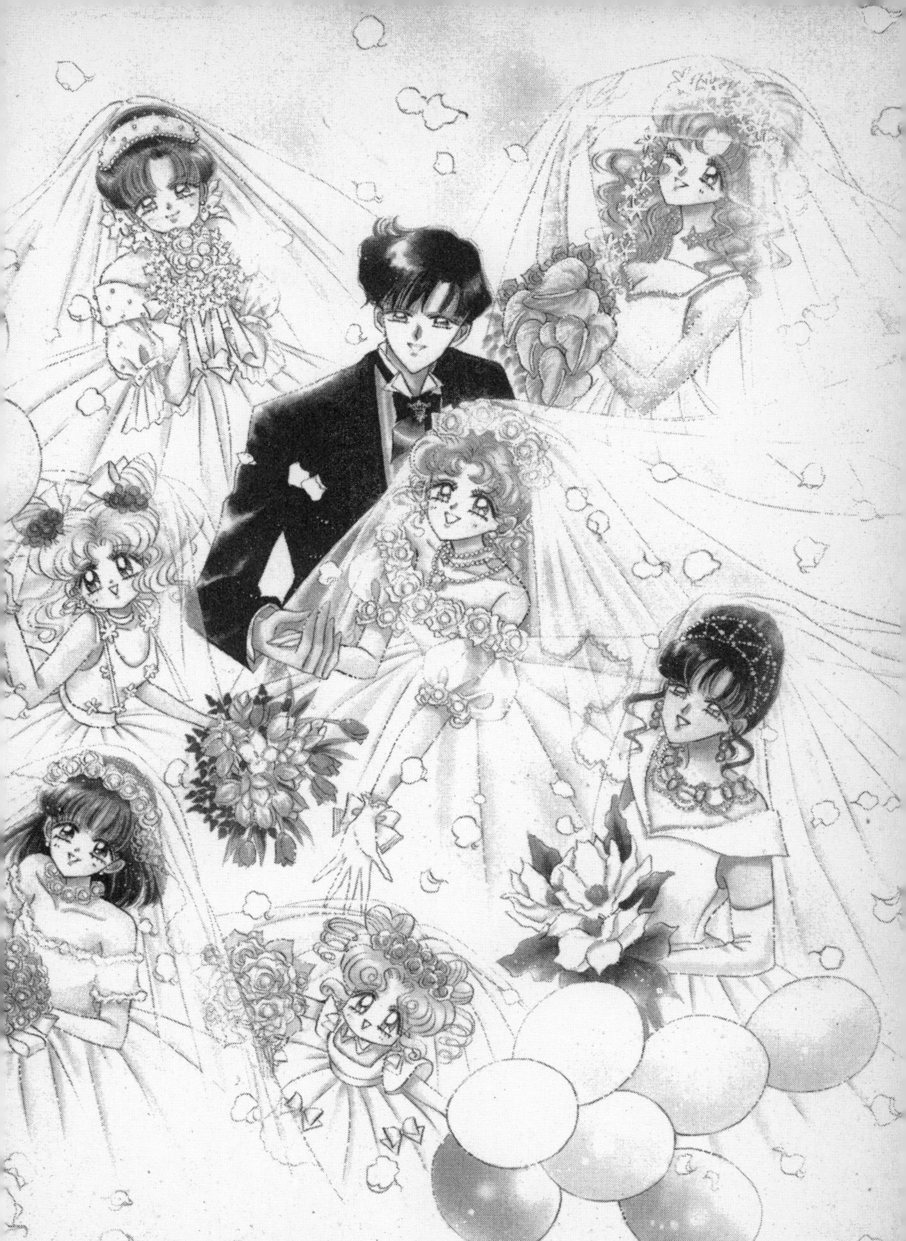

Act 60 Stars 11

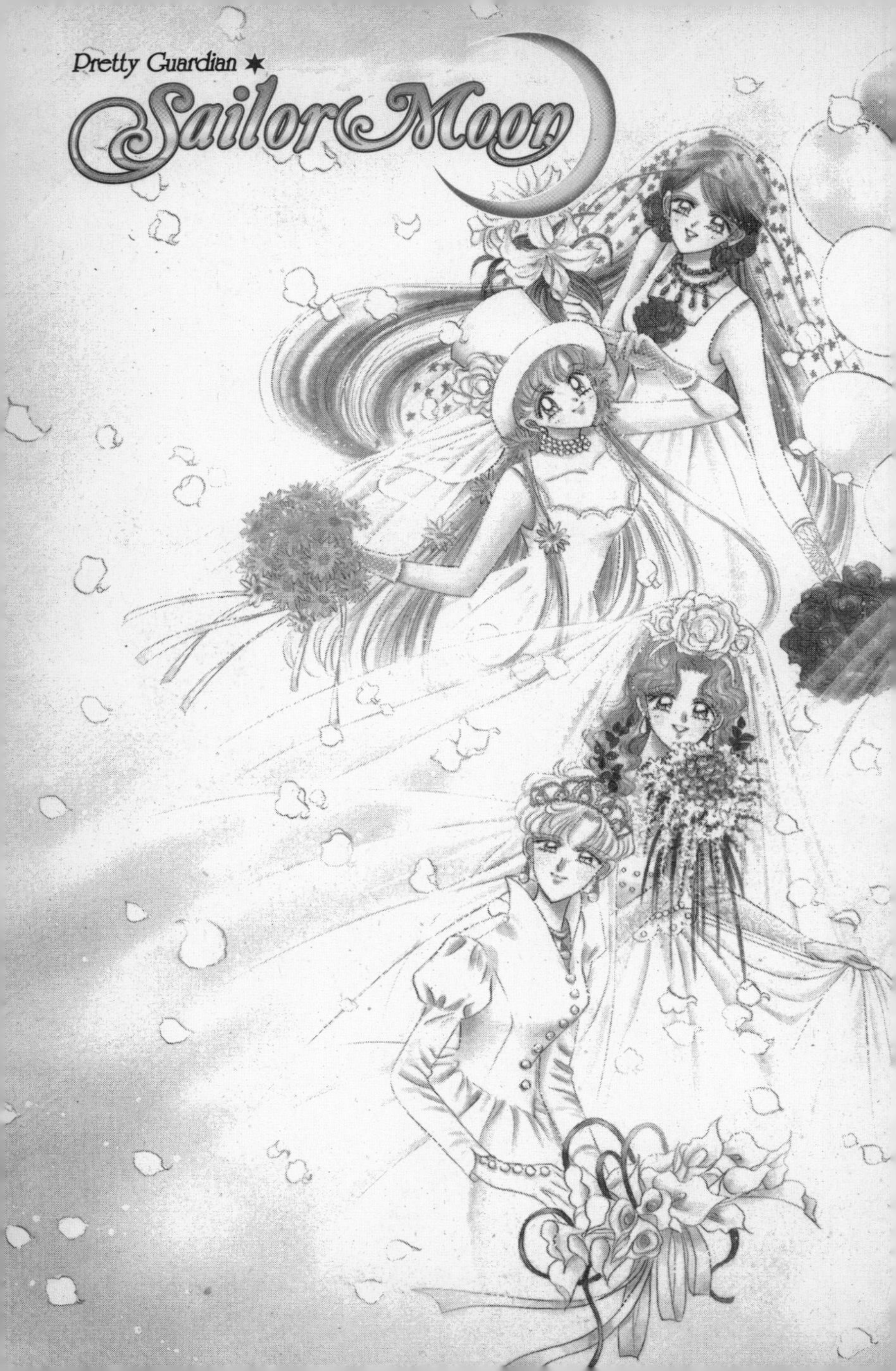
Pretty Guardian ★
Sailor Moon

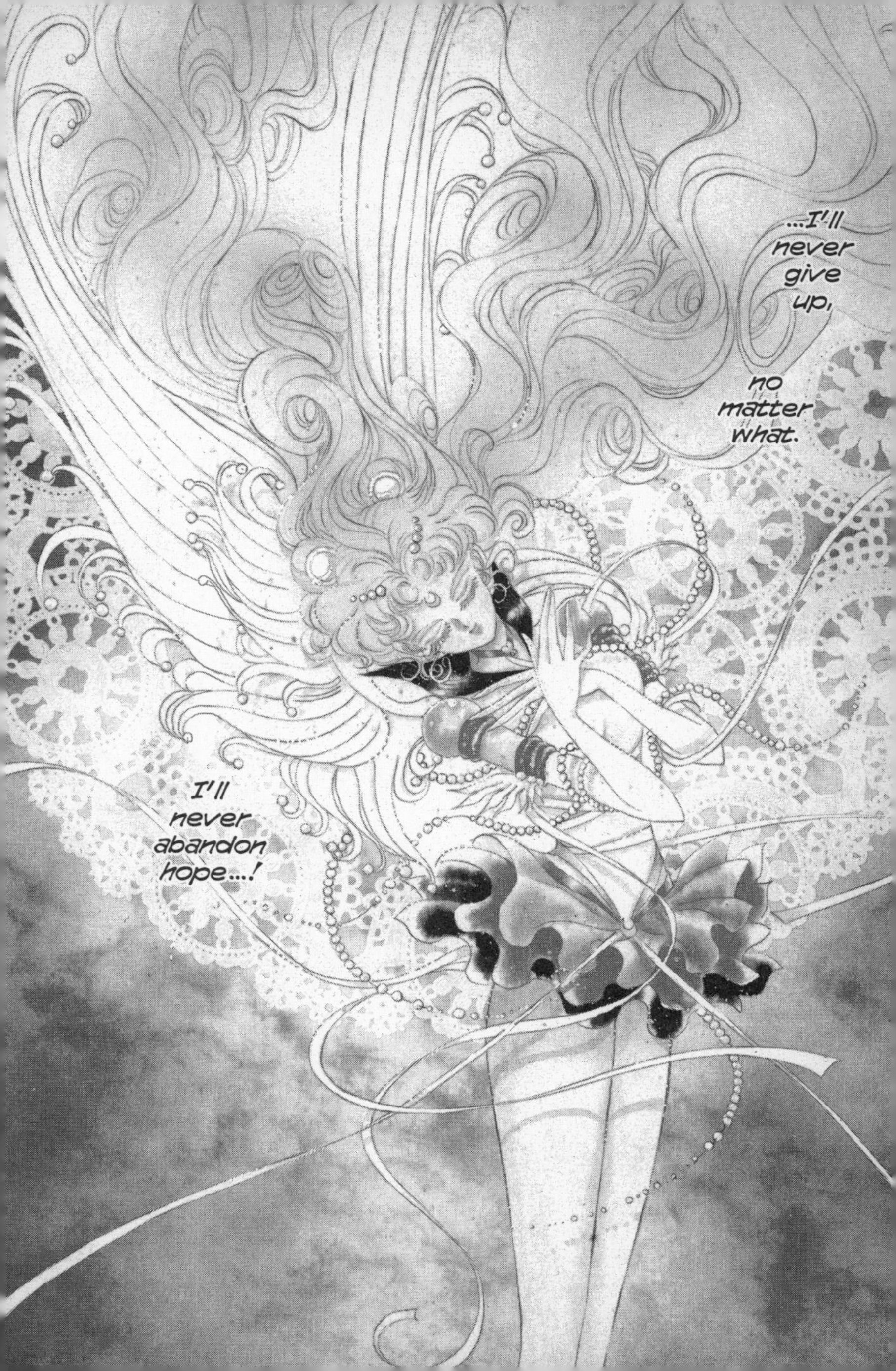
...I'll never give up,
no matter what.
I'll never abandon hope...!

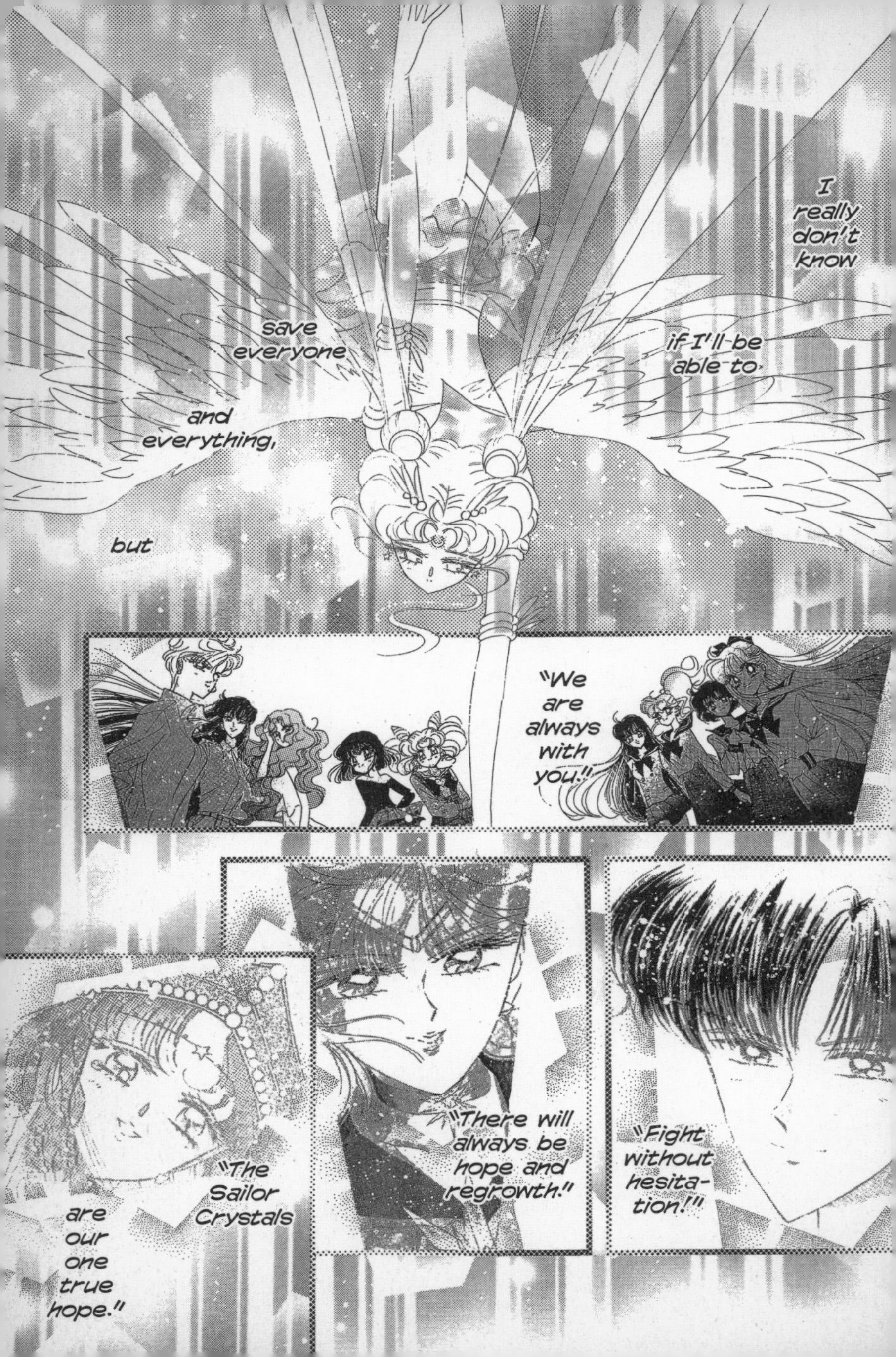
I really don't know
if I'll be able to
save everyone
and everything,
but
"We are always with you!!"
"Fight without hesita-tion!!"
"There will always be hope and regrowth!"
"The Sailor Crystals
are our one true hope."

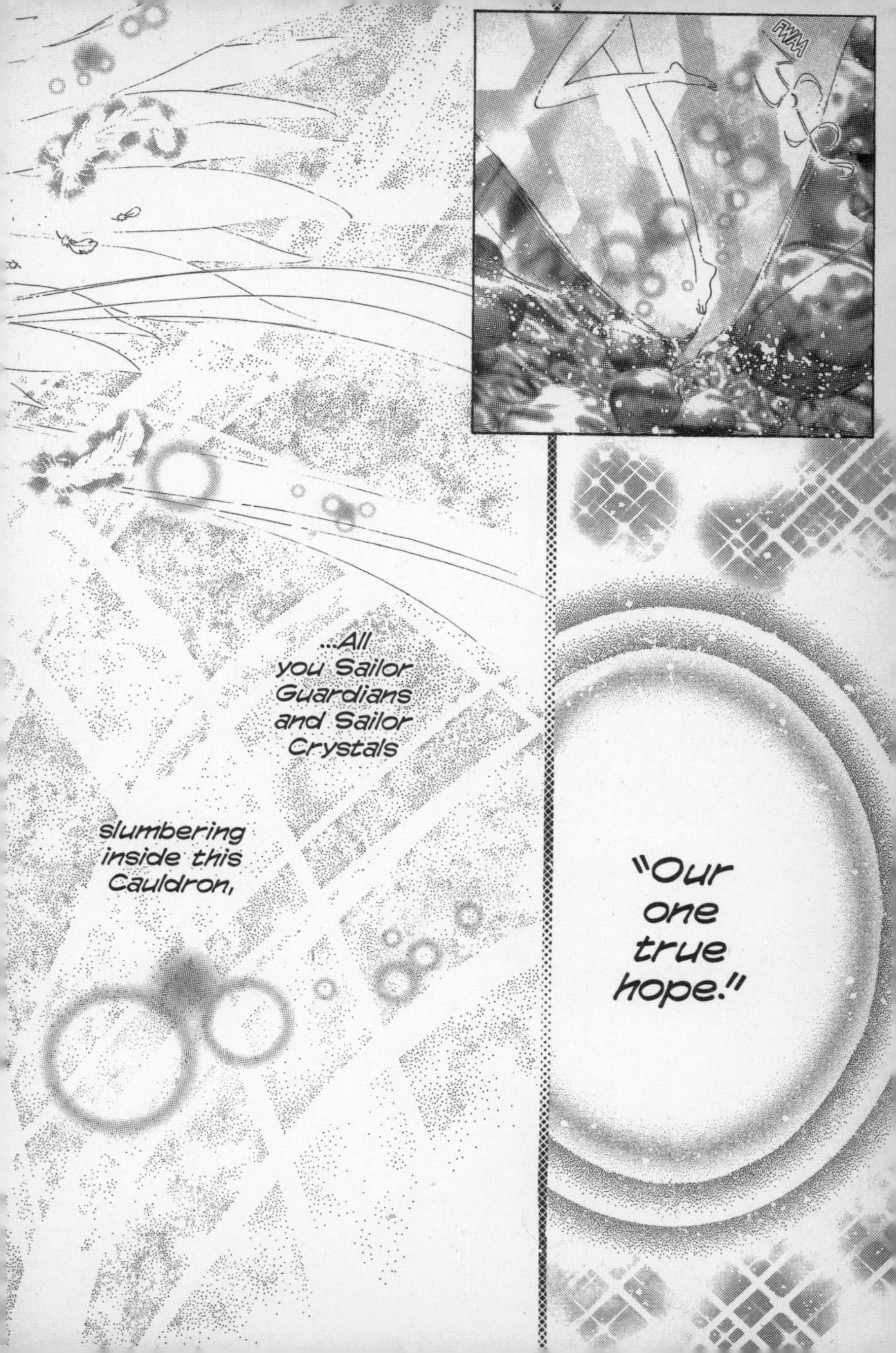
FWAA
"Our one true hope."
...All you Sailor Guardians and Sailor Crystals
slumbering inside this Cauldron,

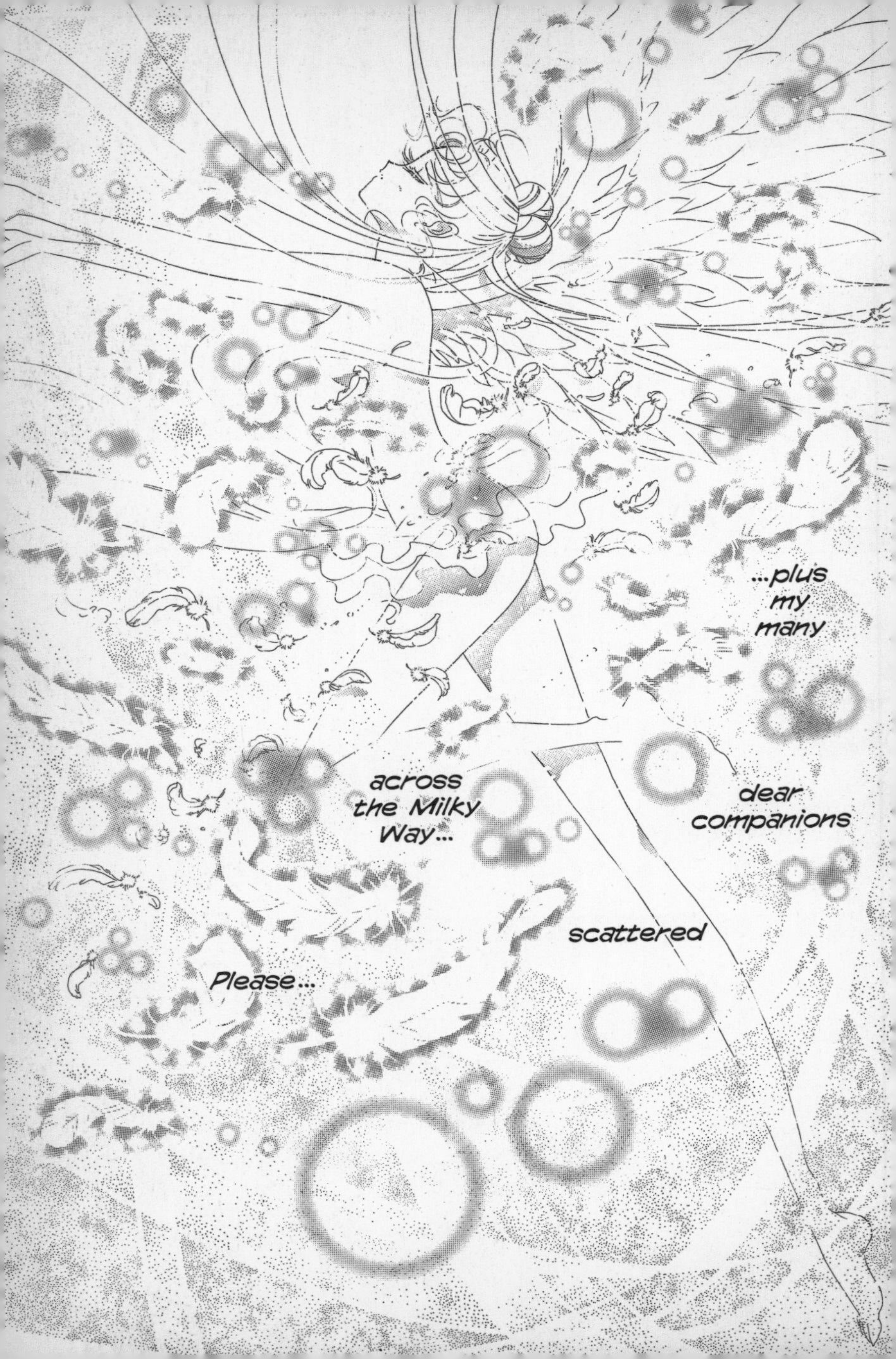
...plus my many
dear companions
scattered
across the Milky Way...
Please...

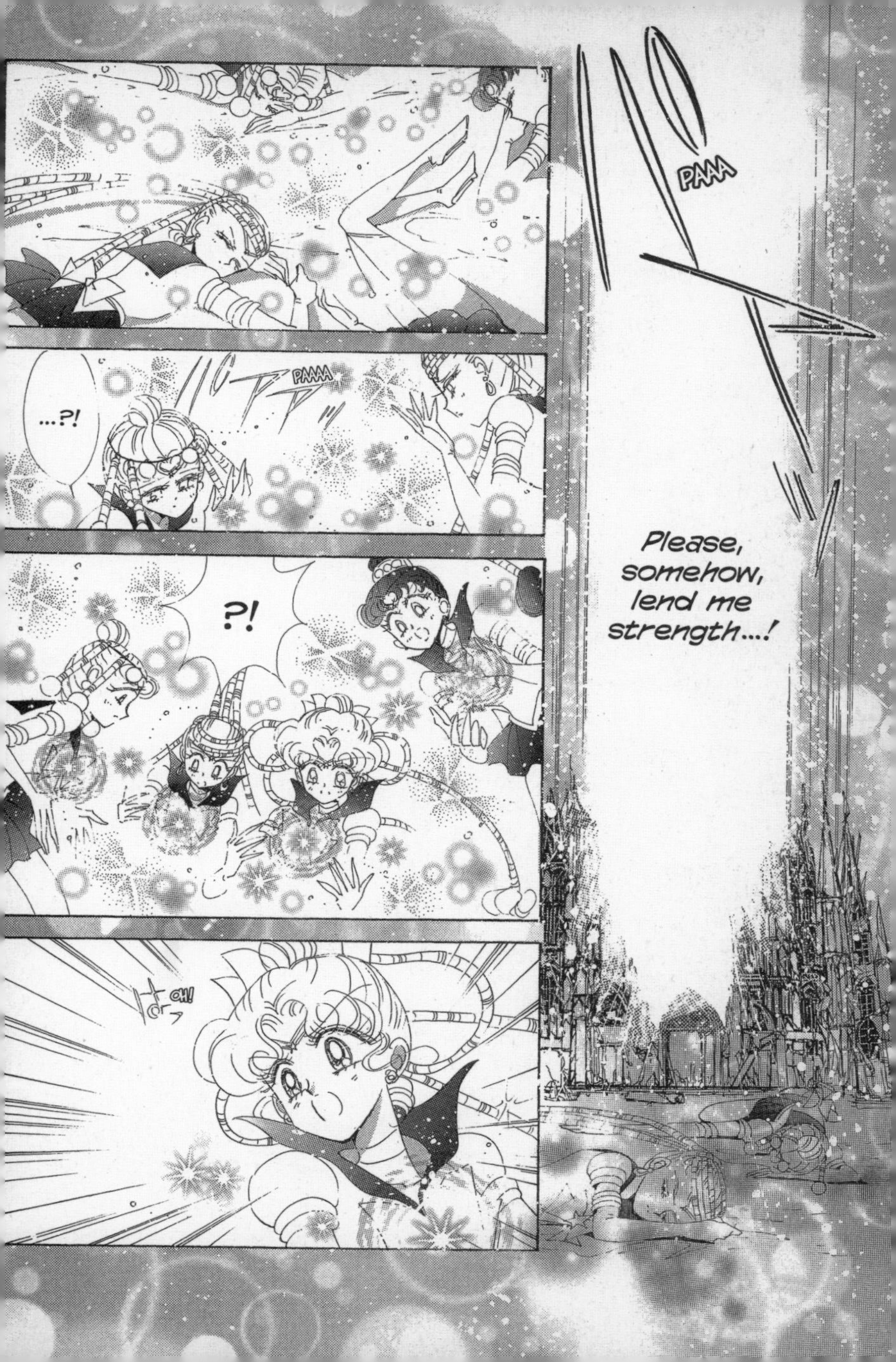
PAAA
Please, somehow, lend me strength...!
PAAAA
...?!
?!
OH!

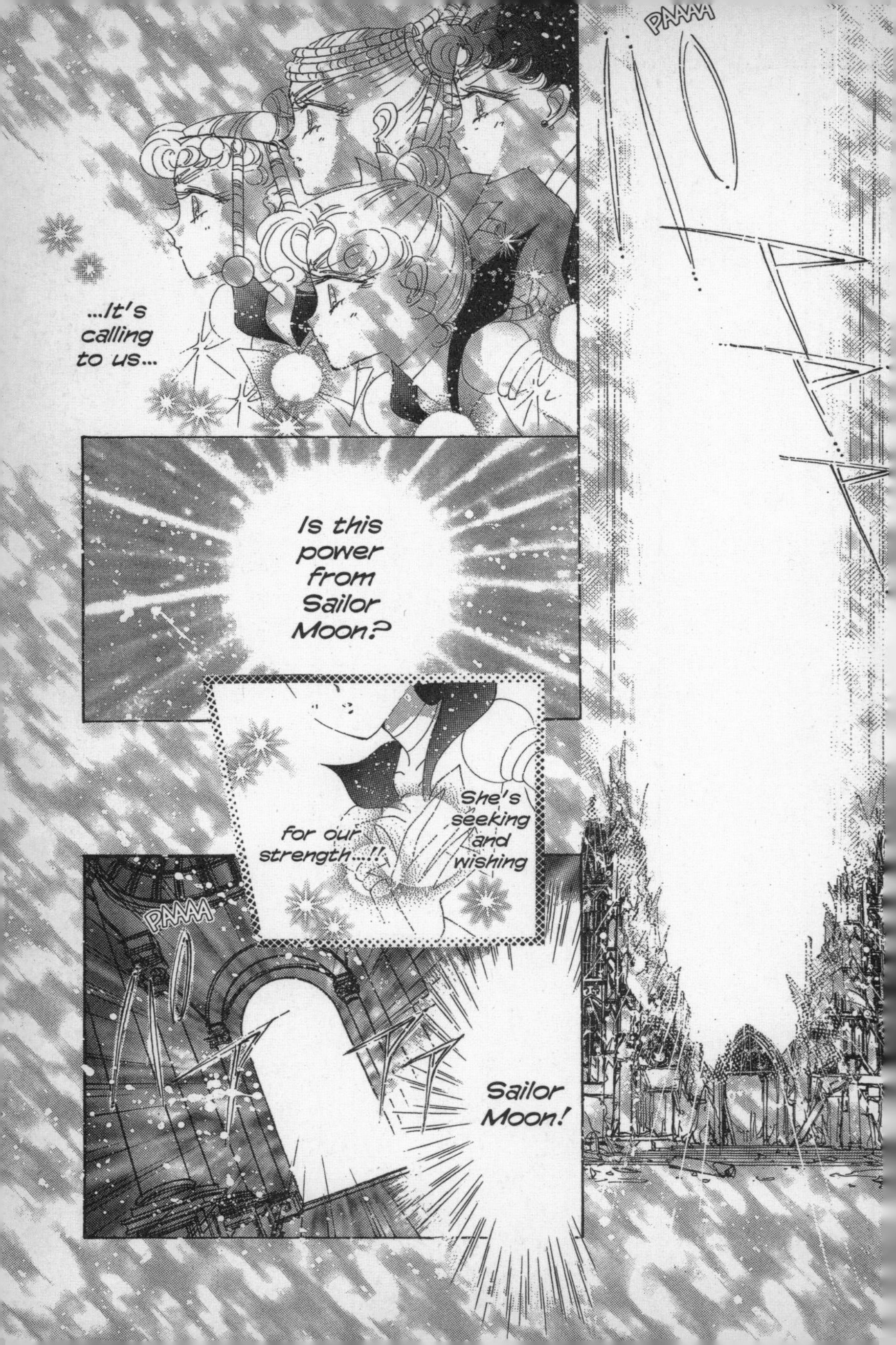
PAAAA
...It's calling to us...
Is this power from Sailor Moon?
She's seeking and wishing
for our strength...!!
PAAAA
Sailor Moon!

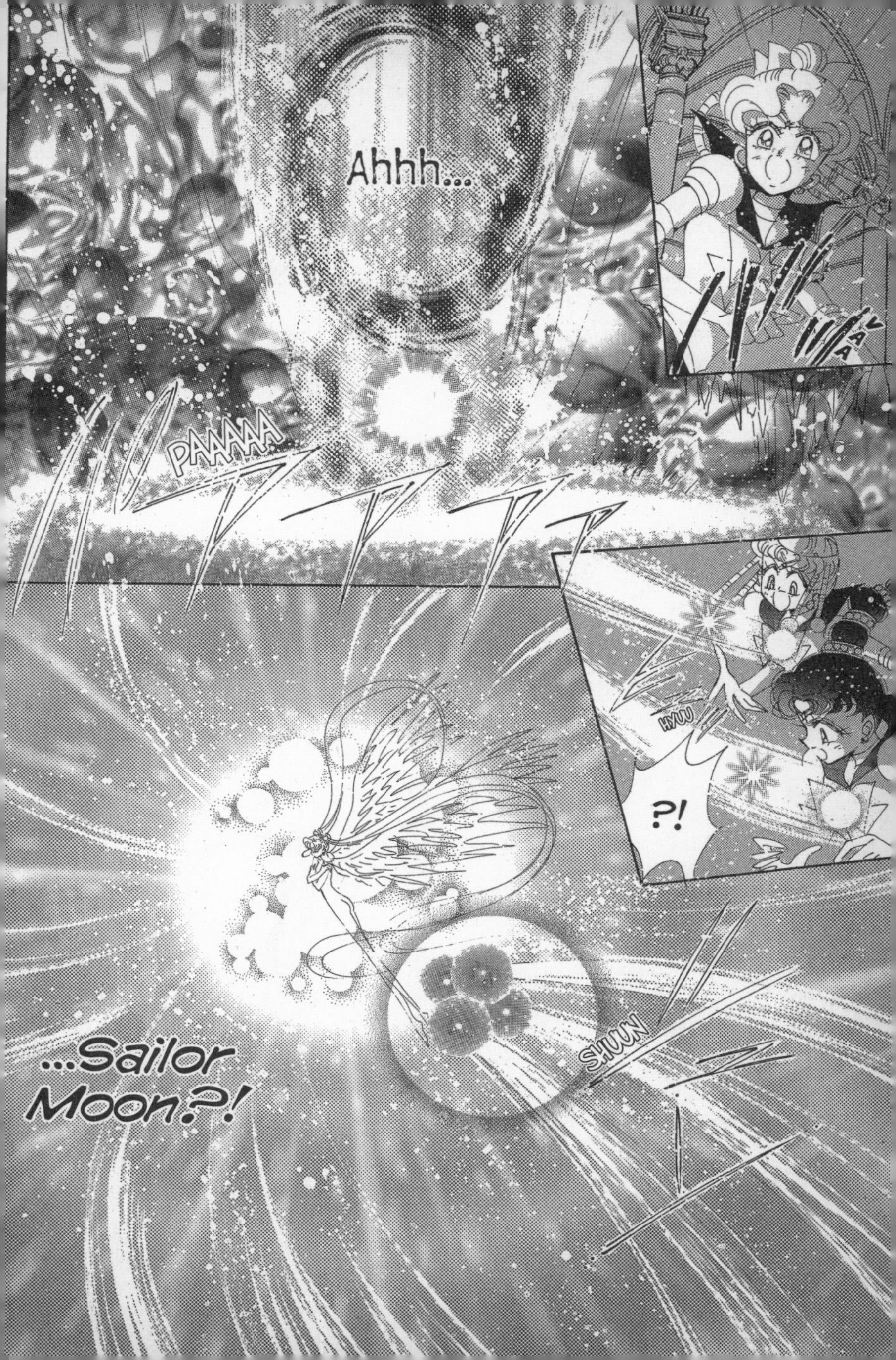

VAA
Ahhh...
PAAAAA
?!
HYUU
...Sailor Moon?!
SHUUN

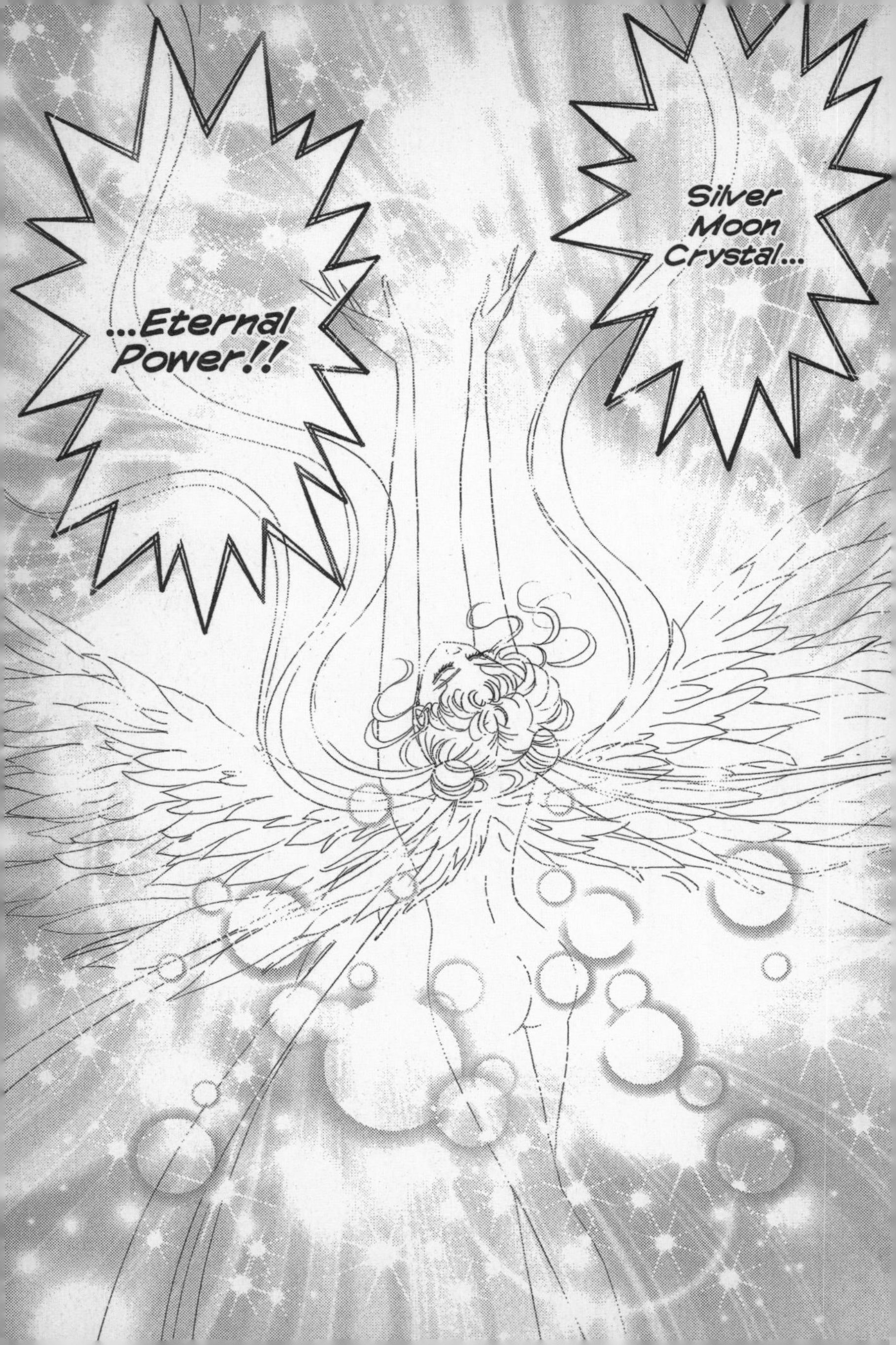
Silver Moon Crystal...
...Eternal Power!!

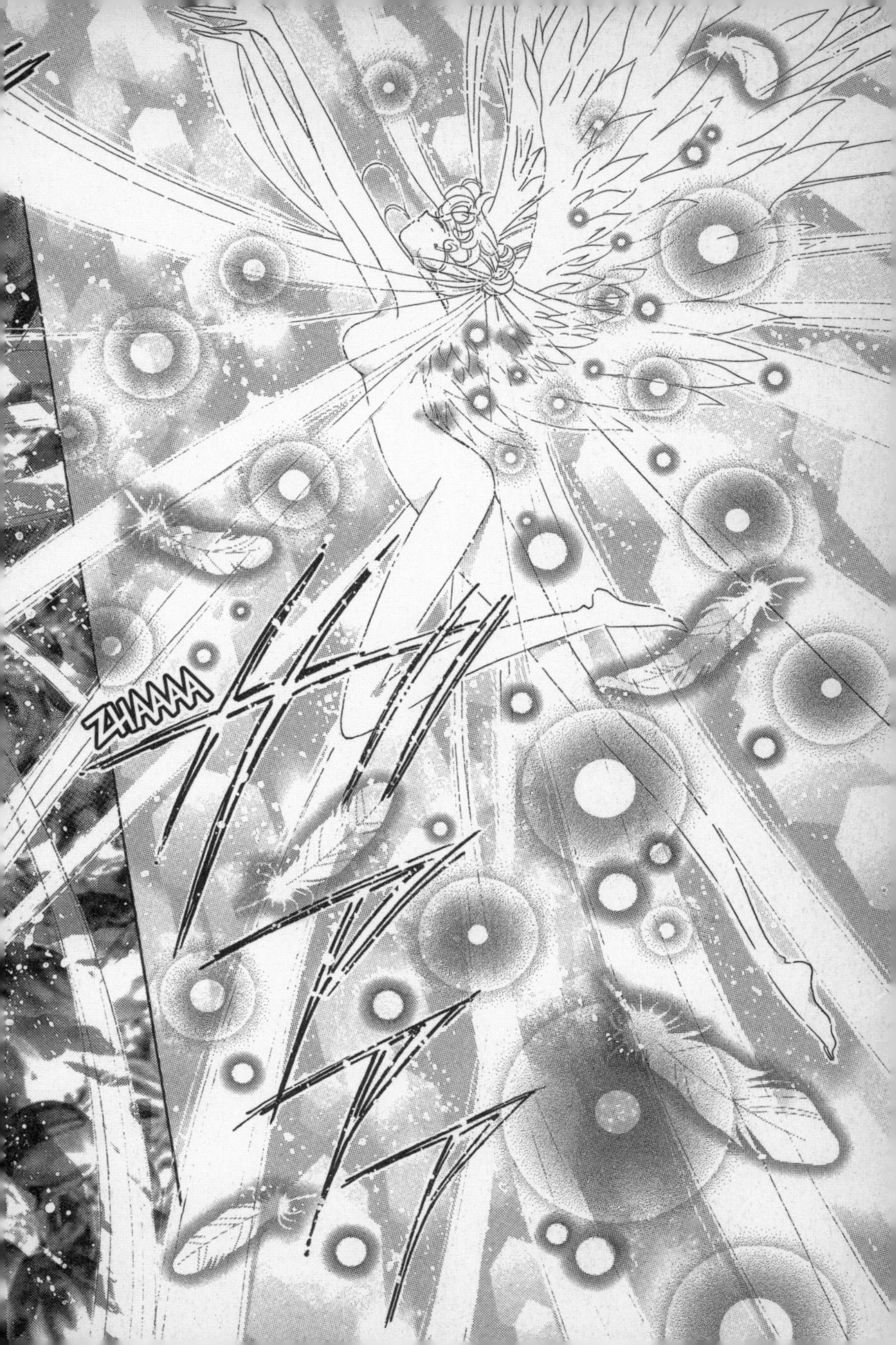
ZHAAAA

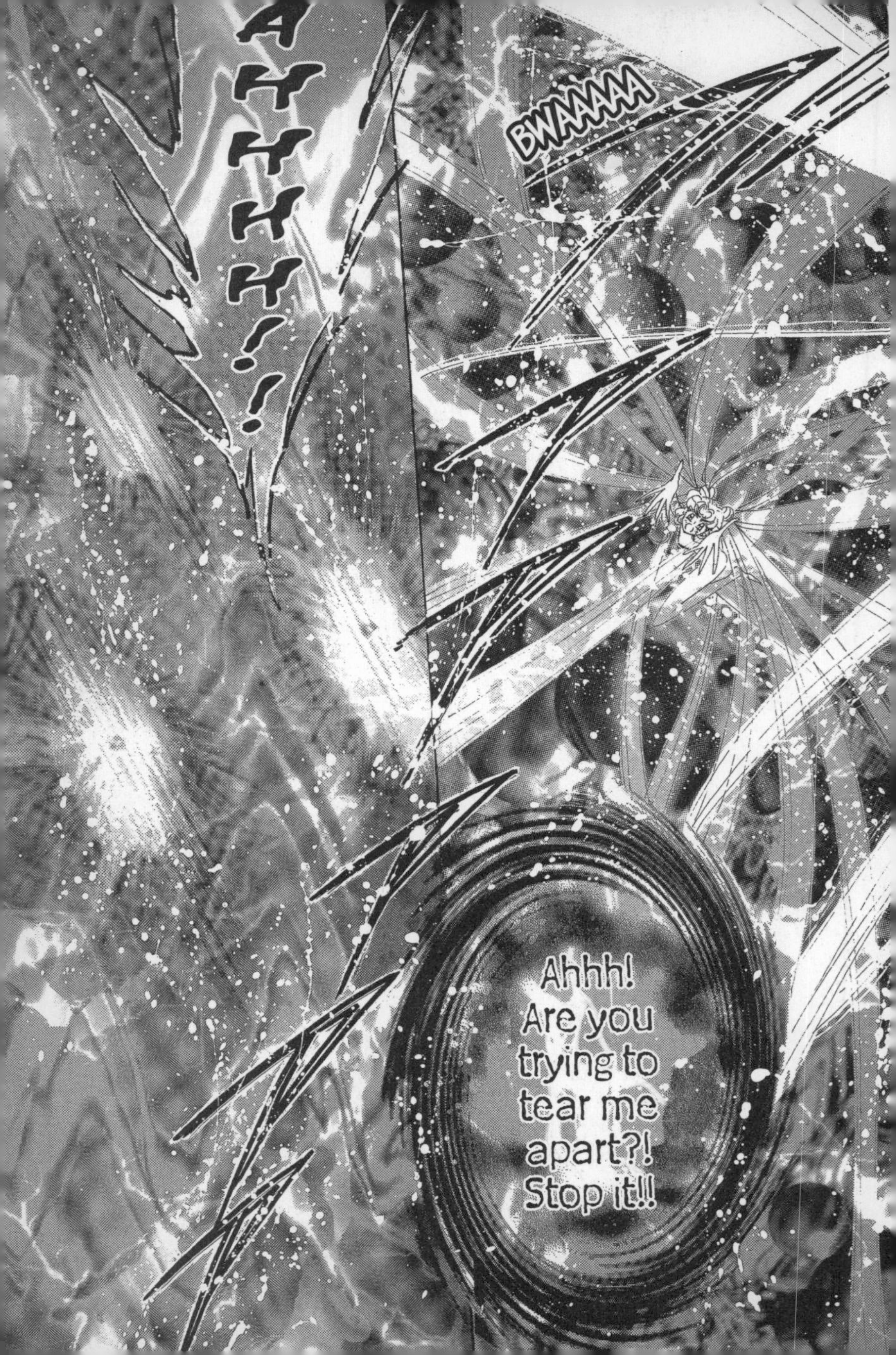
BWAAAAA
AHHHH!!
Ahhh! Are you trying to tear me apart?! Stop it!!

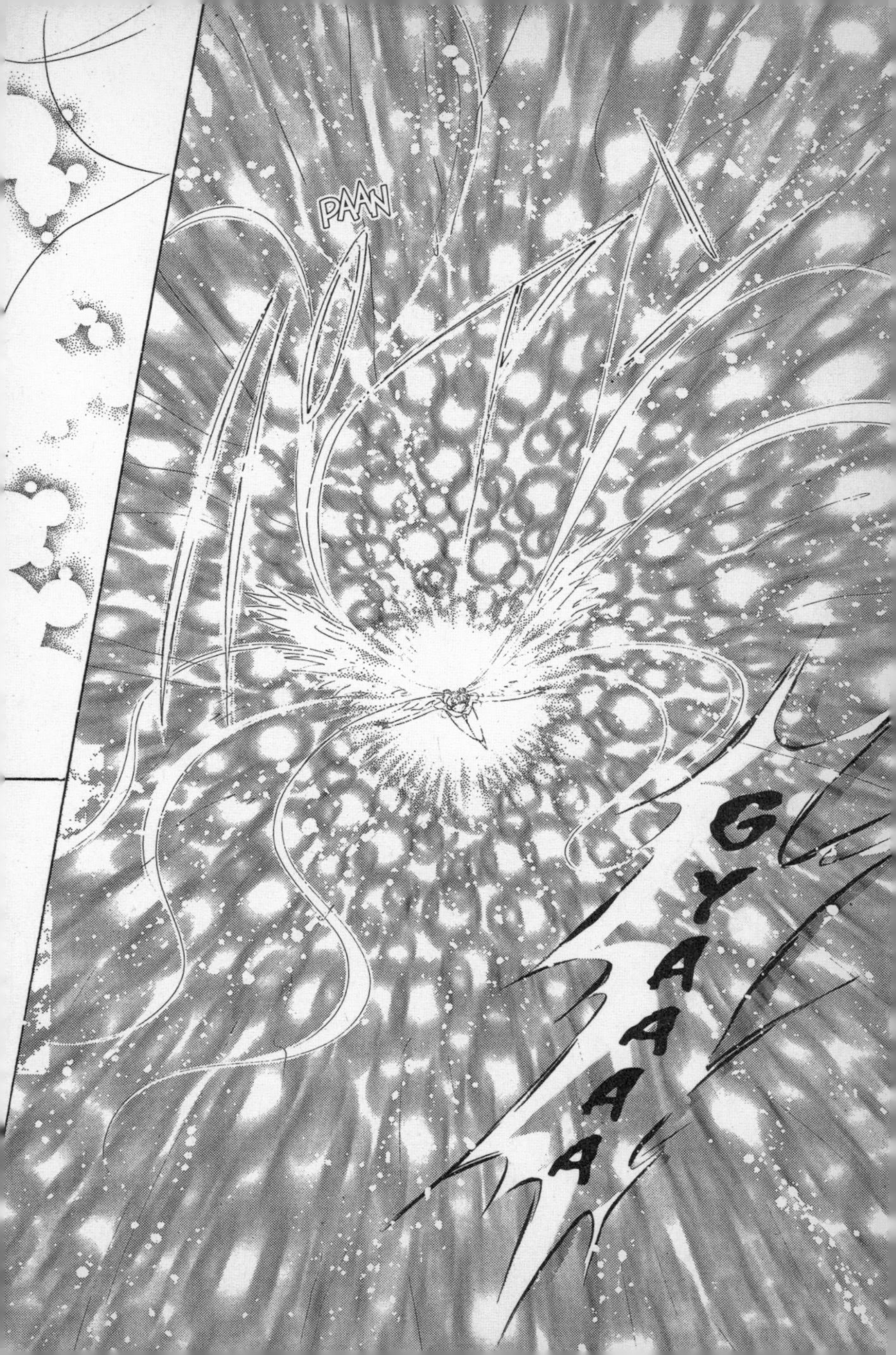
PAAN
GYAAAAA

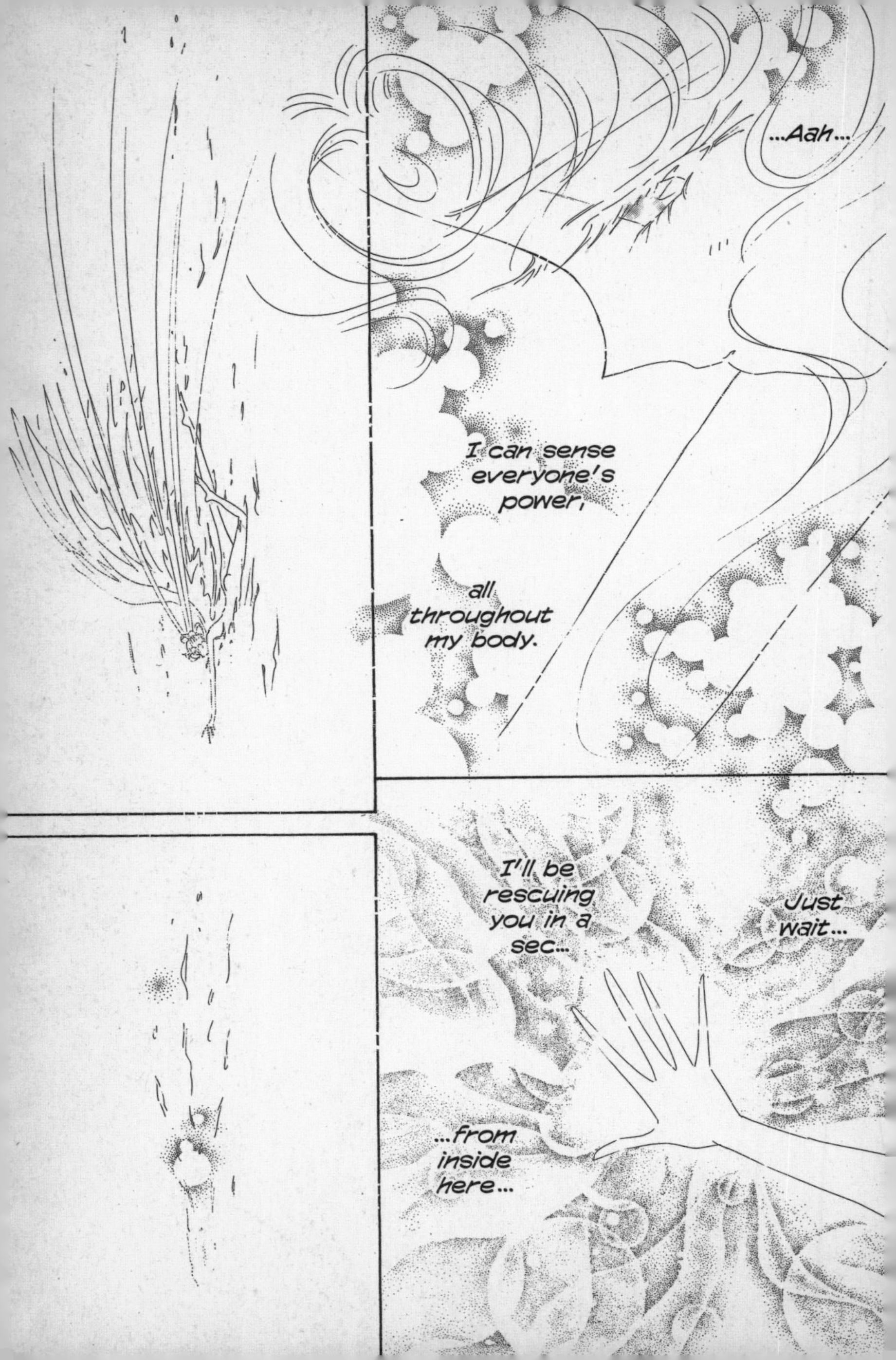
...Aah...
I can sense everyone's power,
all throughout my body.
Just wait...
I'll be rescuing you in a sec...
...from inside here...

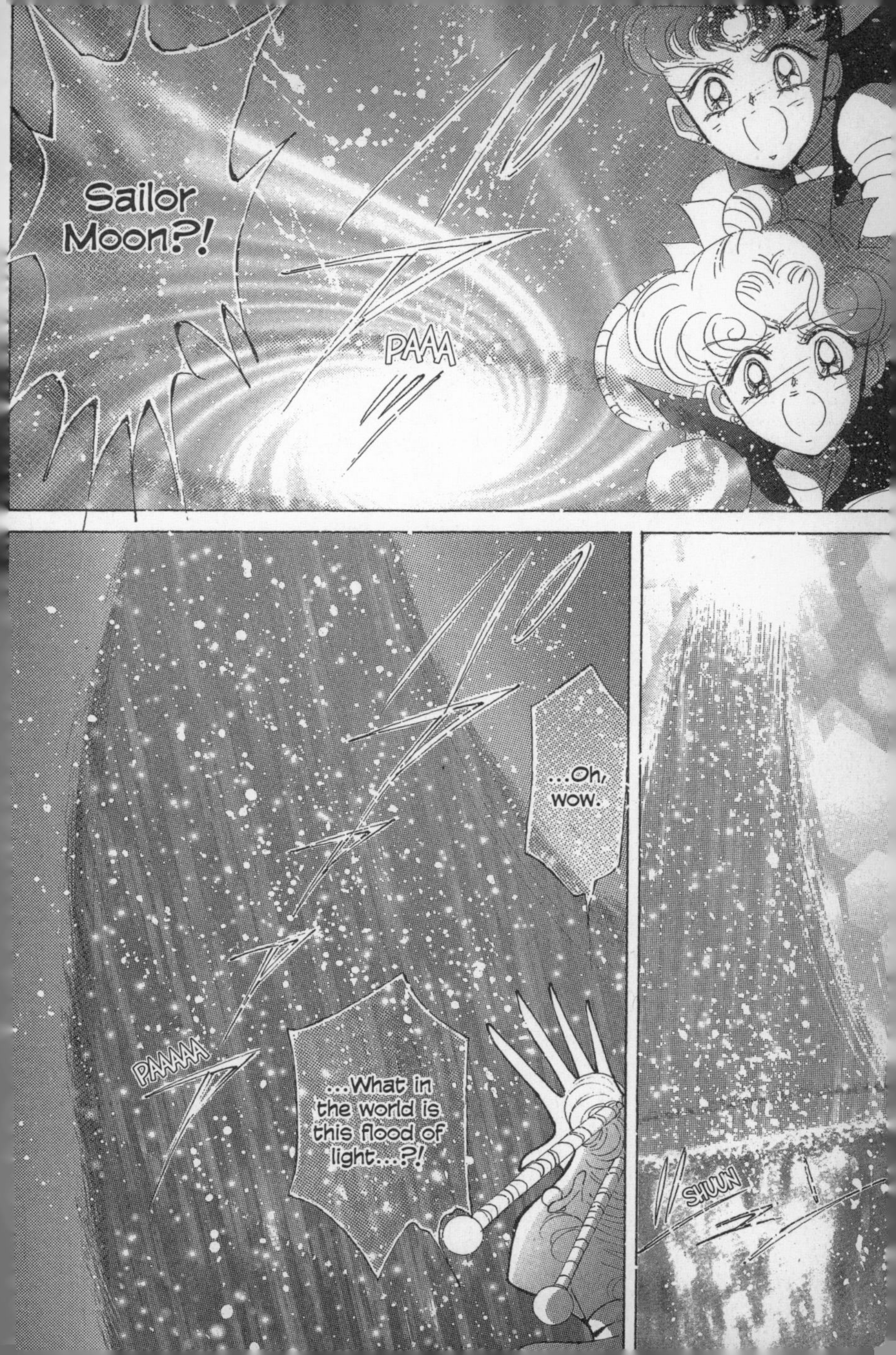
Sailor Moon?!
PAAA
SHUUN
...Oh, wow.
PAAAAA
...What in the world is this flood of light...?!

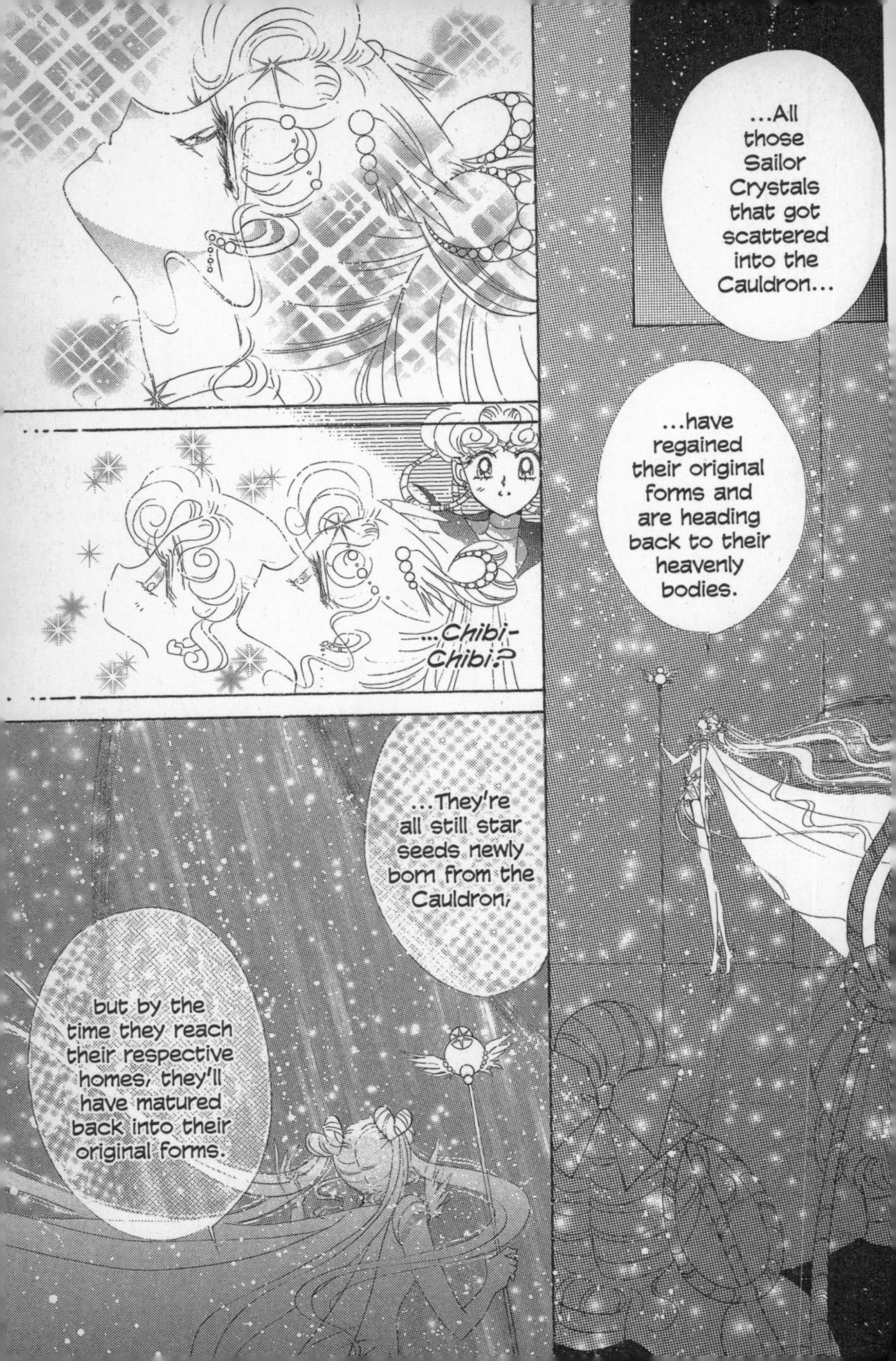
...All those Sailor Crystals that got scattered into the Cauldron...
...have regained their original forms and are heading back to their heavenly bodies.
...Chibi-Chibi?
...They're all still star seeds newly born from the Cauldron,
but by the time they reach their respective homes, they'll have matured back into their original forms.

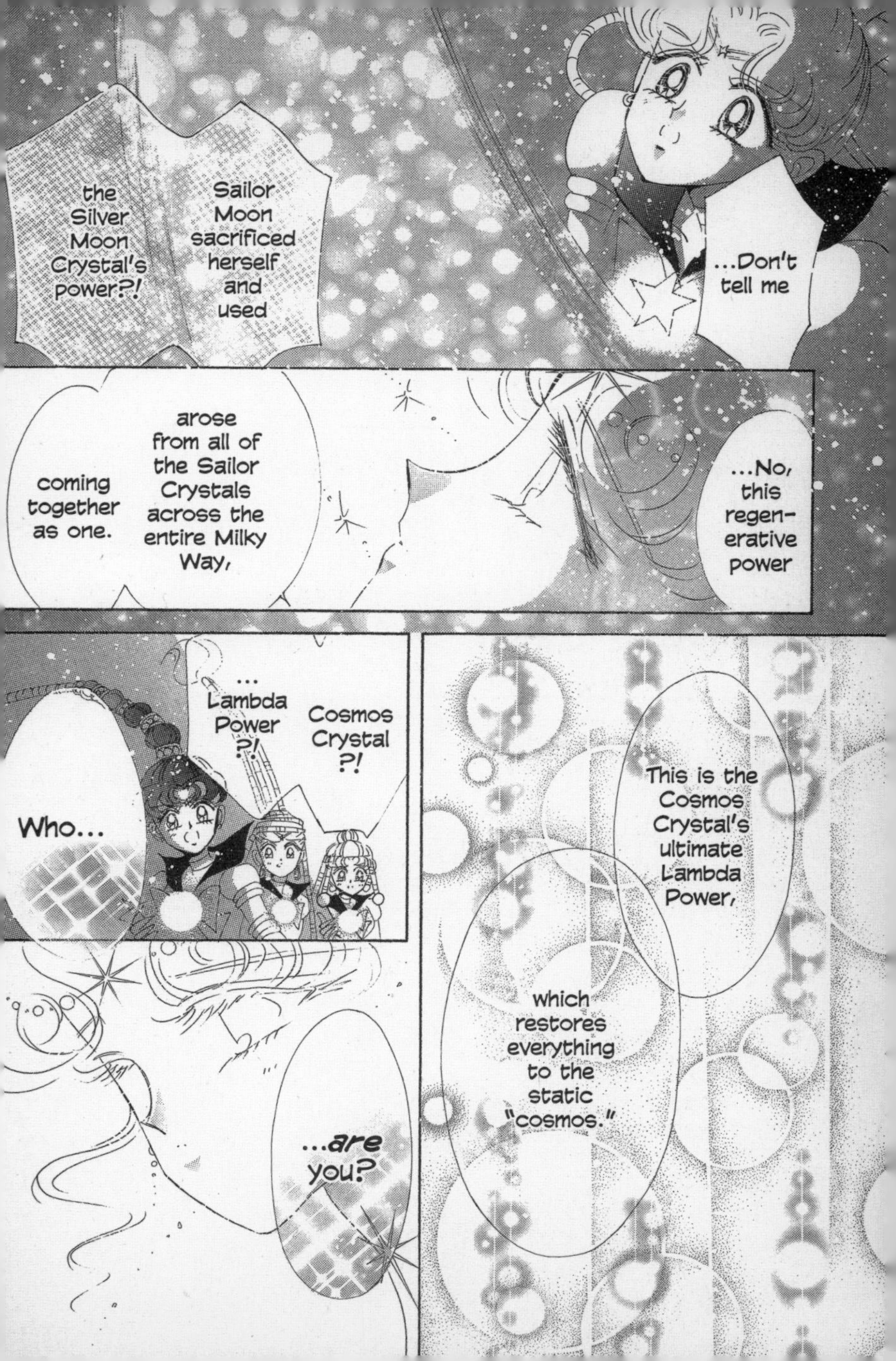
...Don't tell me
Sailor Moon sacrificed herself and used
the Silver Moon Crystal's power?!
...No, this regen-erative power
arose from all of the Sailor Crystals across the entire Milky Way,
coming together as one.
This is the Cosmos Crystal's ultimate Lambda Power,
which restores everything to the static "cosmos."
Cosmos Crystal ?!
... Lambda Power ?!
Who...
...are you?

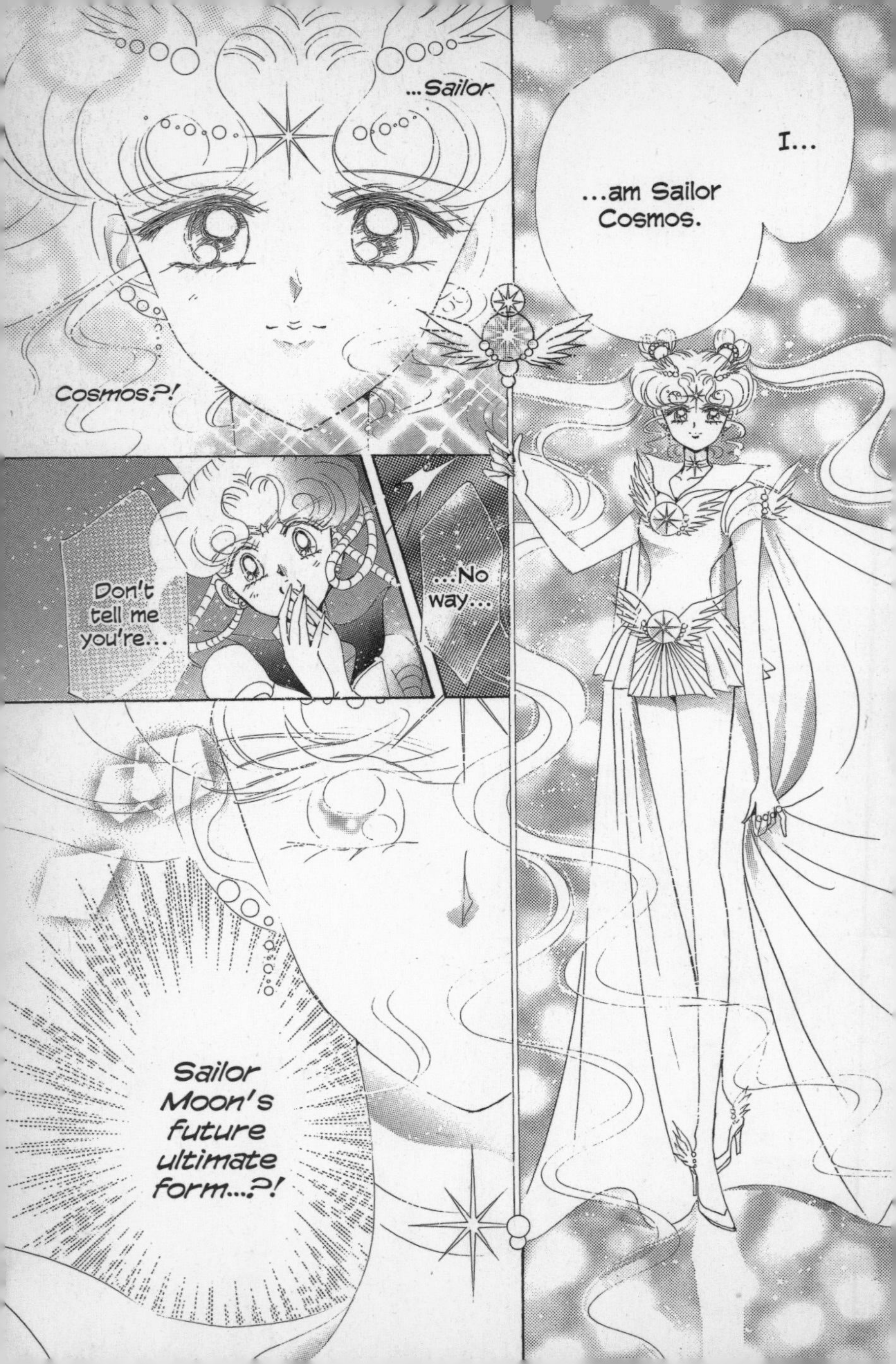
I...
...am Sailor Cosmos.
...Sailor
Cosmos?!
...No way...
Don't tell me you're...
Sailor Moon's future ultimate form...?!

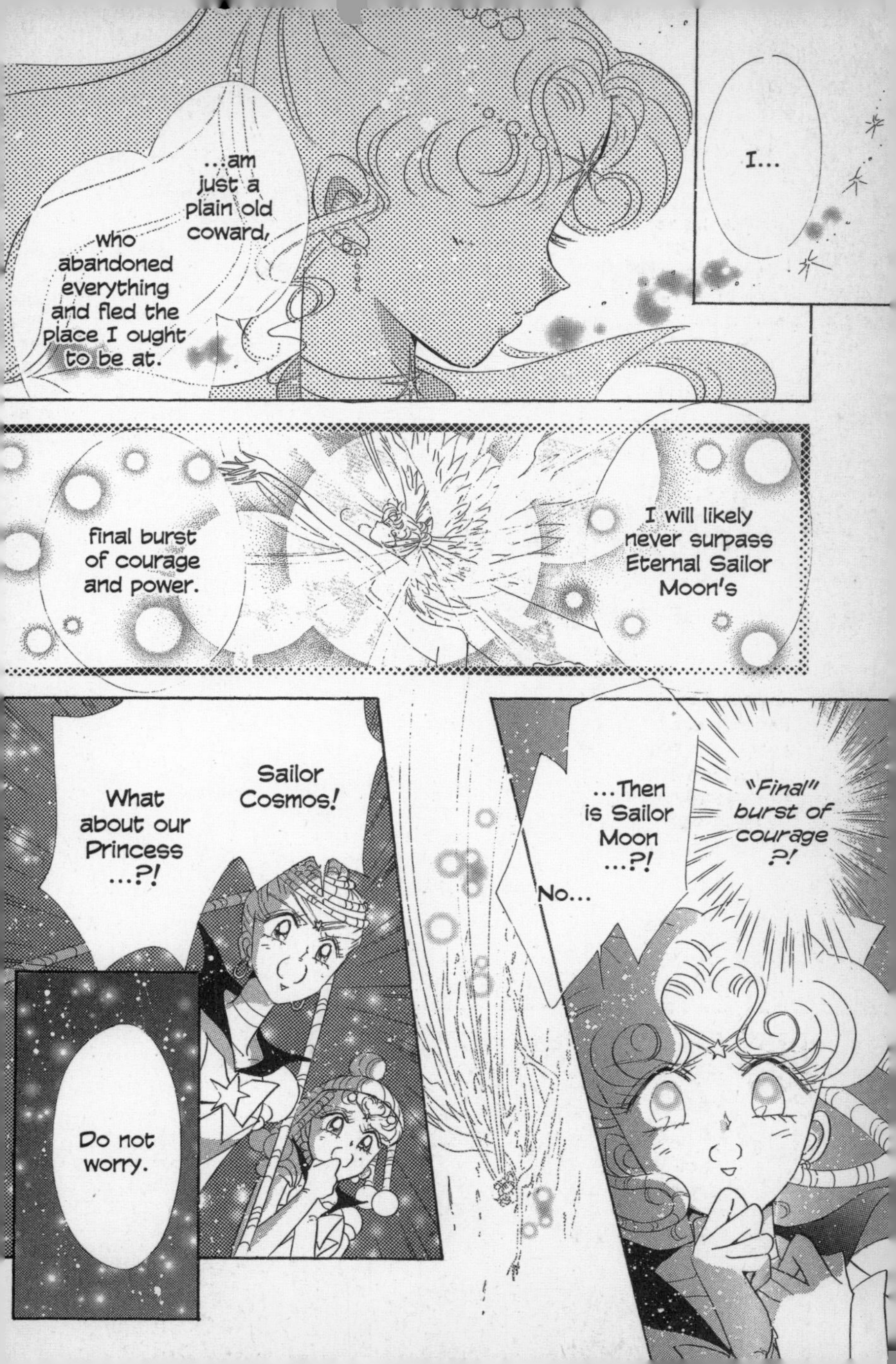
I...
...am just a plain old coward,
who abandoned everything and fled the place I ought to be at.
I will likely never surpass Eternal Sailor Moon's
final burst of courage and power.
"Final" burst of courage ?!
...Then is Sailor Moon ...?!
No...
Sailor Cosmos!
What about our Princess ...?!
Do not worry.

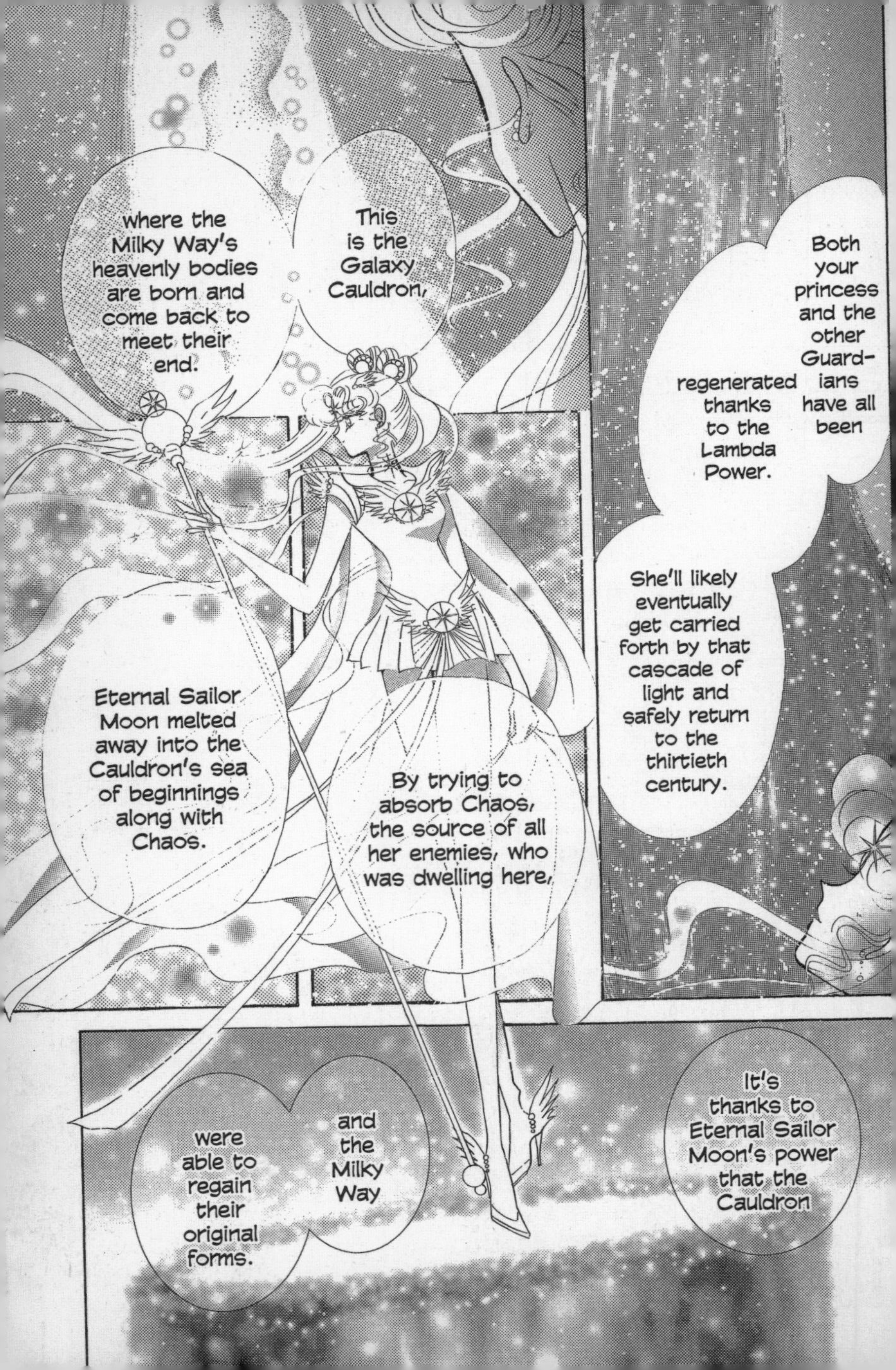
Both your princess and the other Guardians have all been regenerated thanks to the Lambda Power.
She'll likely eventually get carried forth by that cascade of light and safely return to the thirtieth century.
This is the Galaxy Cauldron,
where the Milky Way's heavenly bodies are born and come back to meet their end.
By trying to absorb Chaos, the source of all her enemies, who was dwelling here,
Eternal Sailor Moon melted away into the Cauldron's sea of beginnings along with Chaos.
It's thanks to Eternal Sailor Moon's power that the Cauldron
and the Milky Way
were able to regain their original forms.

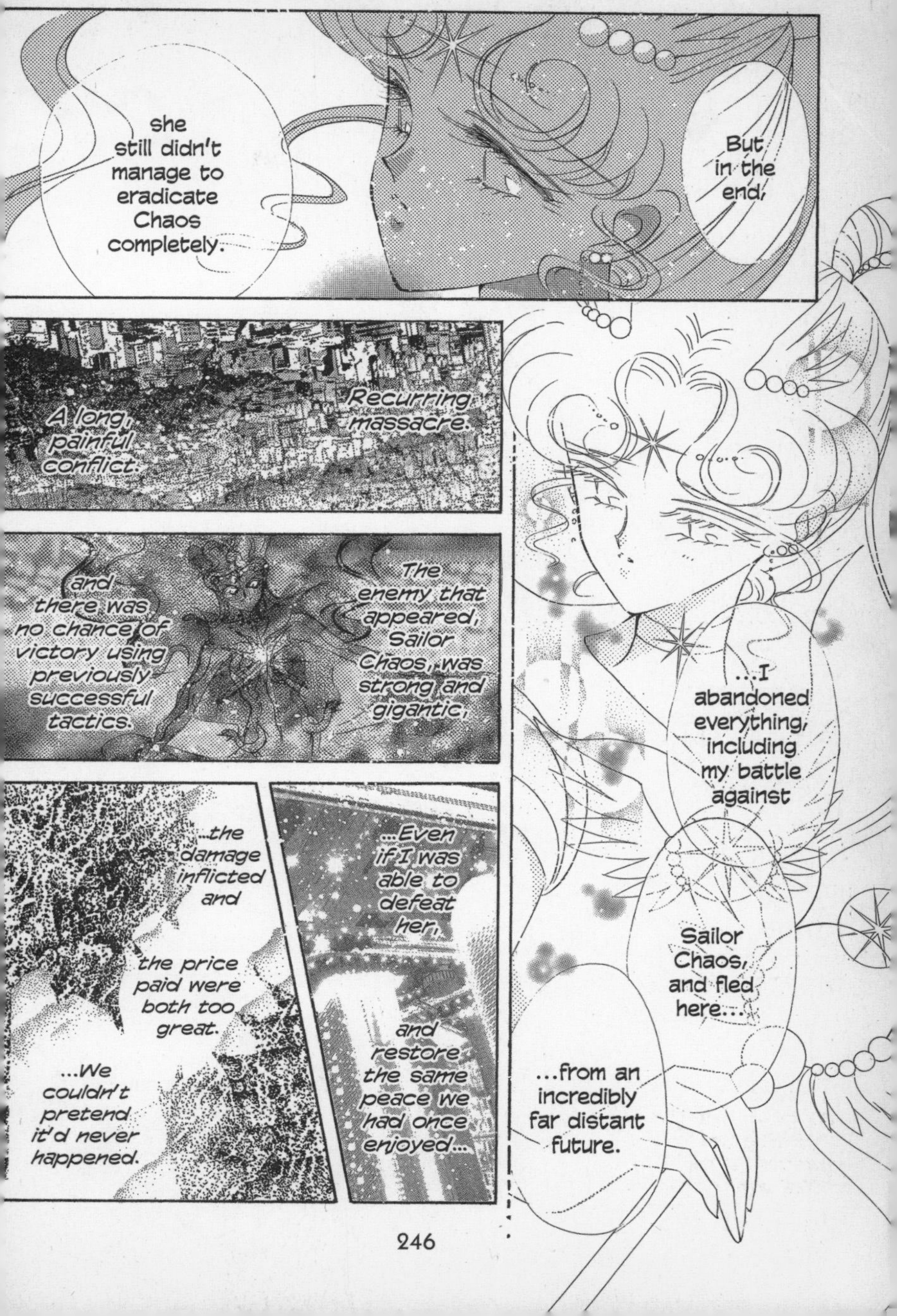
But in the end,
she still didn't manage to eradicate Chaos completely.
...I abandoned everything, including my battle against
Sailor Chaos, and fled here...
...from an incredibly far distant future.
Recurring massacre.
A long, painful conflict.
The enemy that appeared, Sailor Chaos, was strong and gigantic,
and there was no chance of victory using previously successful tactics.
...Even if I was able to defeat her,
and restore the same peace we had once enjoyed...
...the damage inflicted and
the price paid were both too great.
...We couldn't pretend it'd never happened.

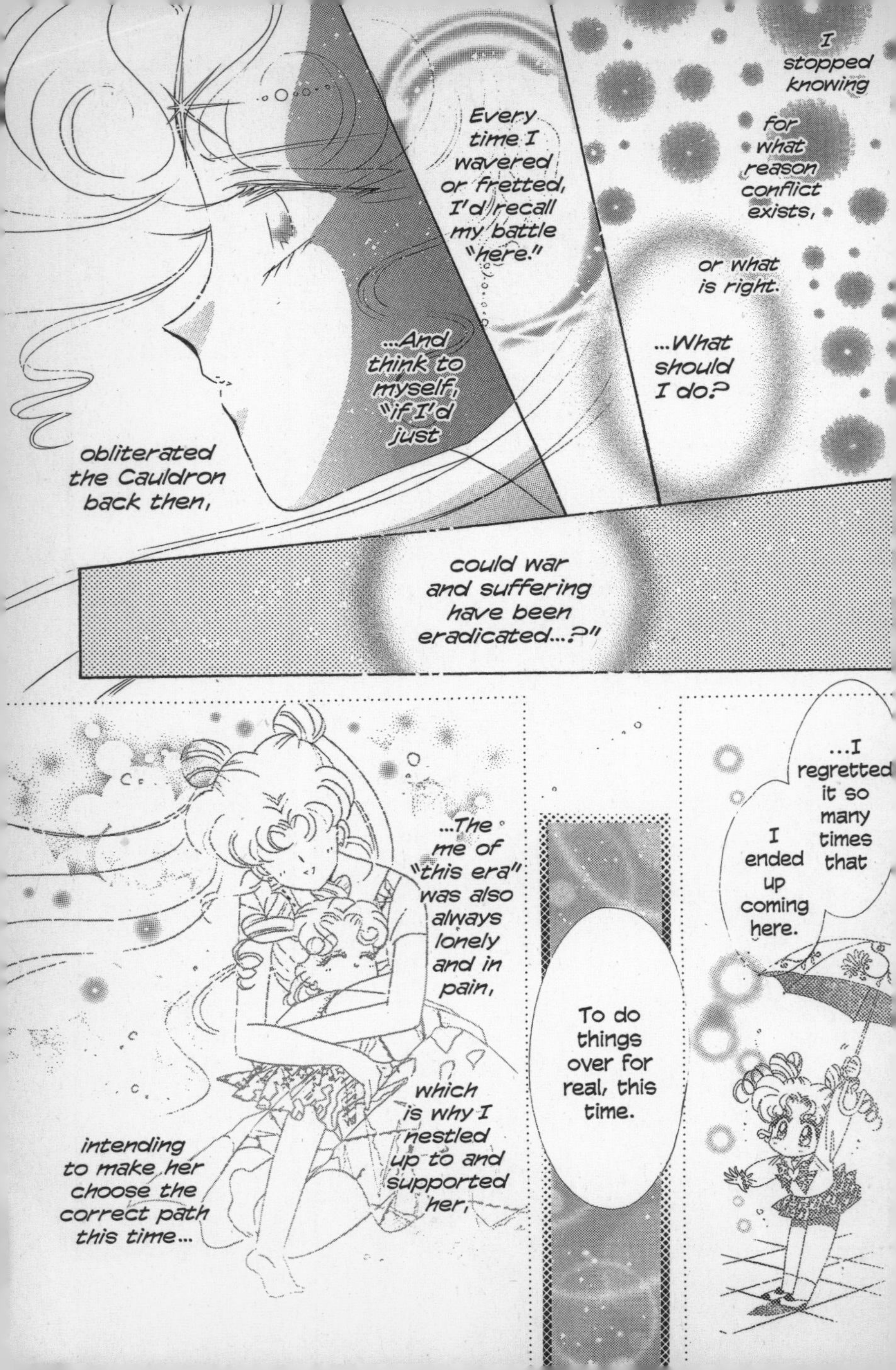
I stopped knowing
for what reason conflict exists,
or what is right.
...What should I do?
Every time I wavered or fretted, I'd recall my battle "here."
...And think to myself, "if I'd just
obliterated the Cauldron back then,
could war and suffering have been eradicated...?"
...I regretted it so many times that
I ended up coming here.
To do things over for real, this time.
...The me of "this era" was also always lonely and in pain,
which is why I nestled up to and supported her,
intending to make her choose the correct path this time...

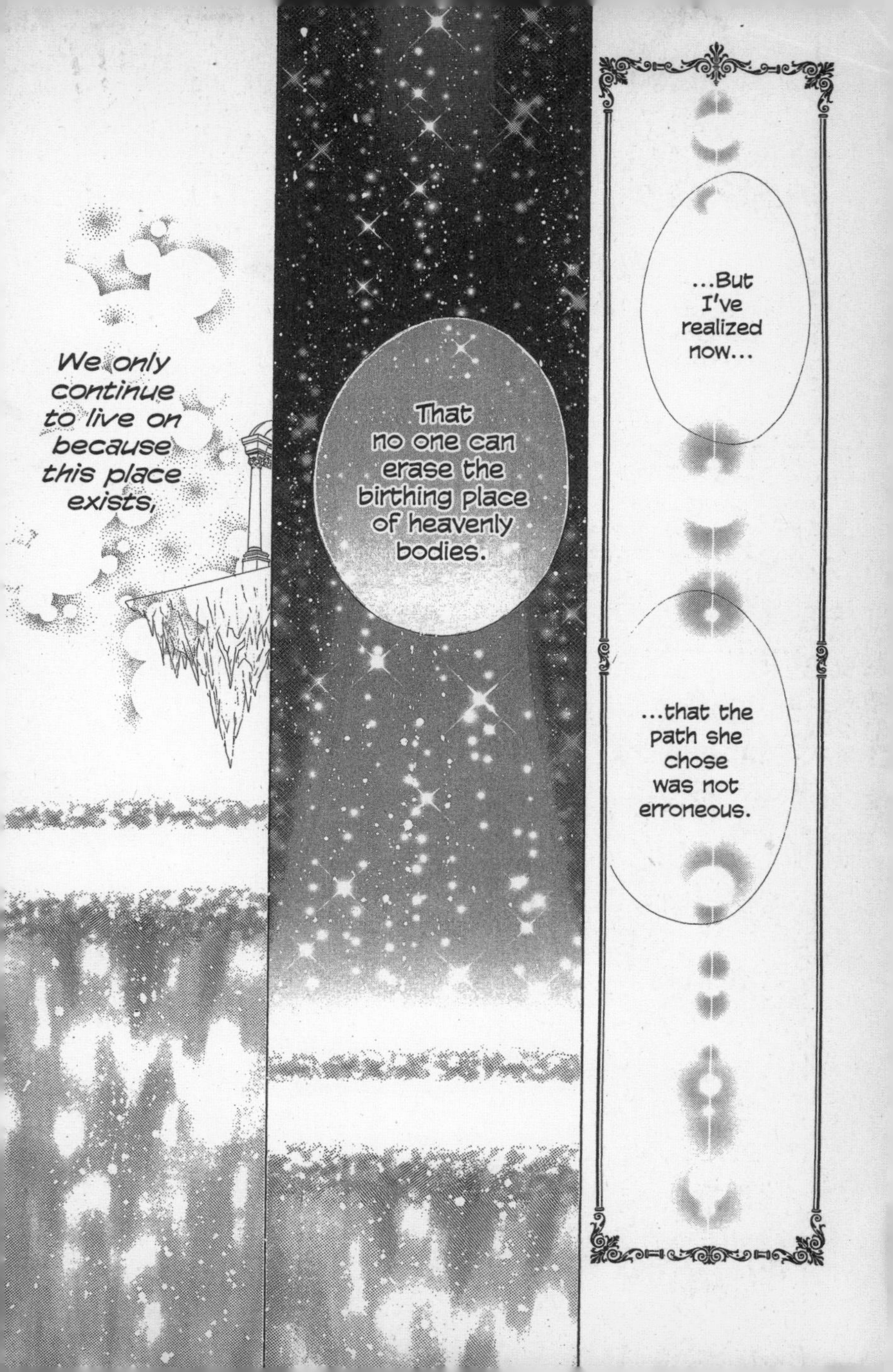
...But I've realized now...
...that the path she chose was not erroneous.
That no one can erase the birthing place of heavenly bodies.
We only continue to live on because this place exists,

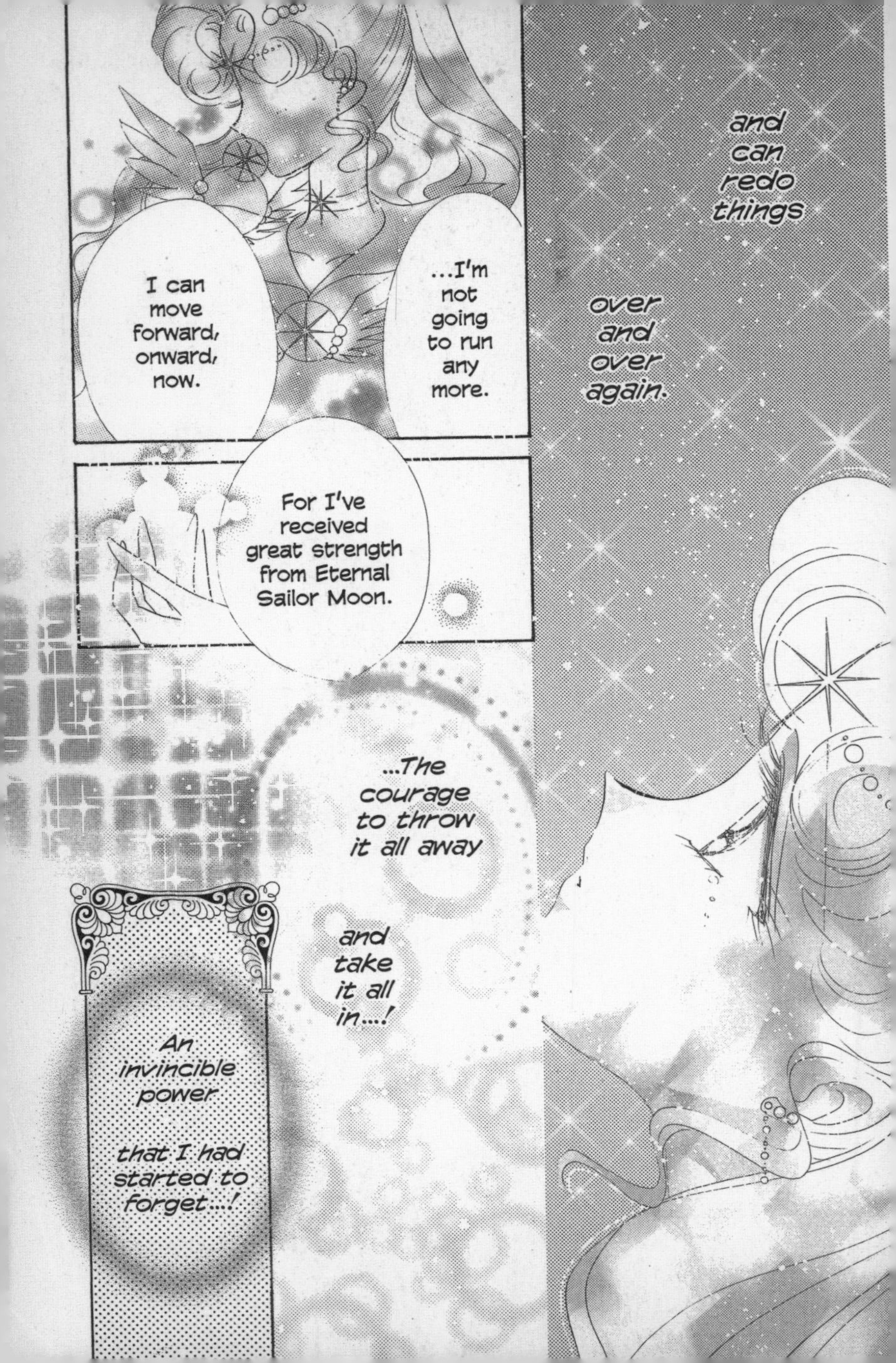
and can redo things
over and over again.
...I'm not going to run any more.
I can move forward, onward, now.
For I've received great strength from Eternal Sailor Moon.
...The courage to throw it all away
and take it all in...!
An invincible power that I had started to forget...!

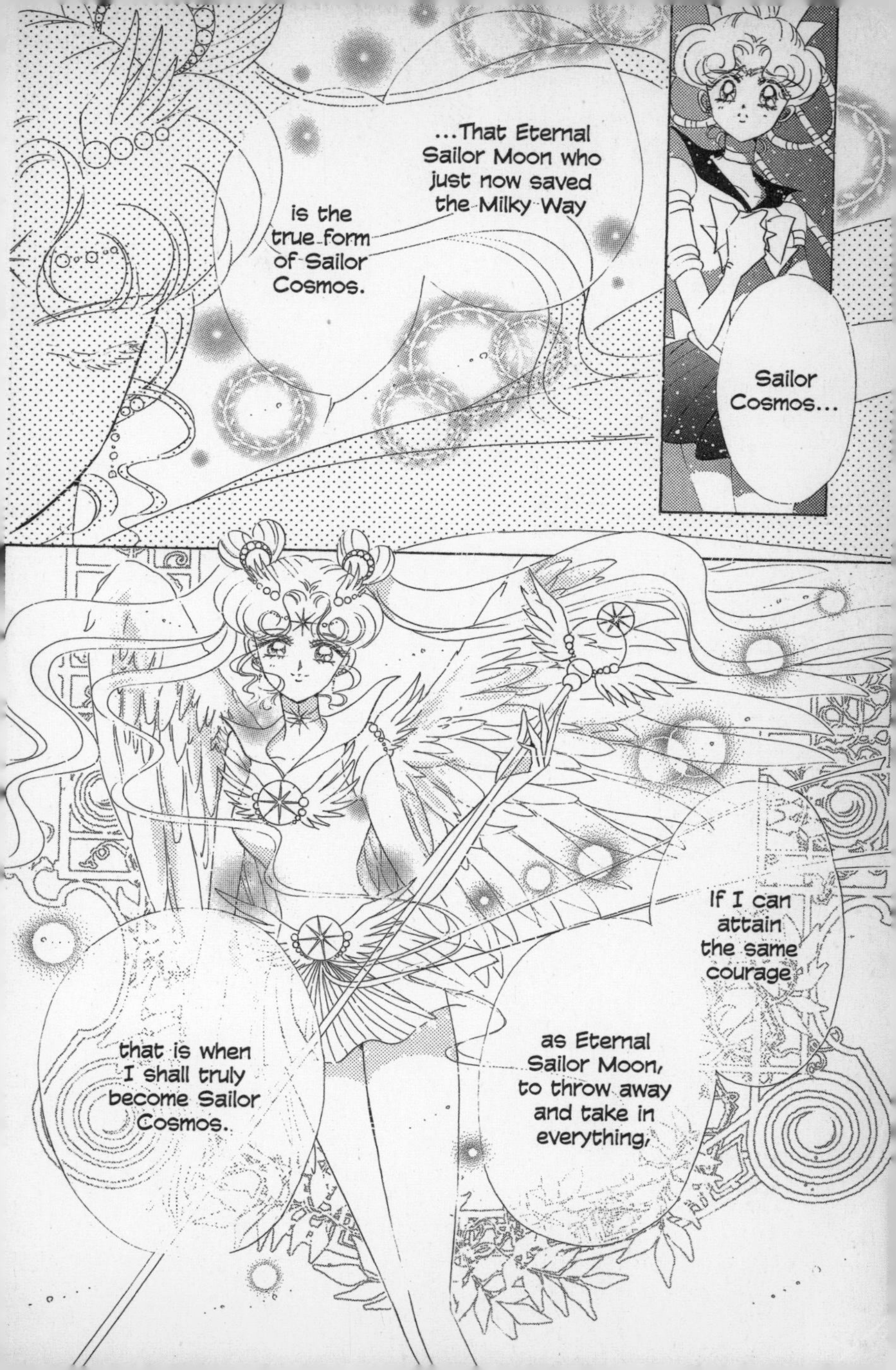
Sailor Cosmos...
...That Eternal Sailor Moon who just now saved the Milky Way
is the true form of Sailor Cosmos.
If I can attain the same courage
as Eternal Sailor Moon, to throw away and take in everything,
that is when I shall truly become Sailor Cosmos.

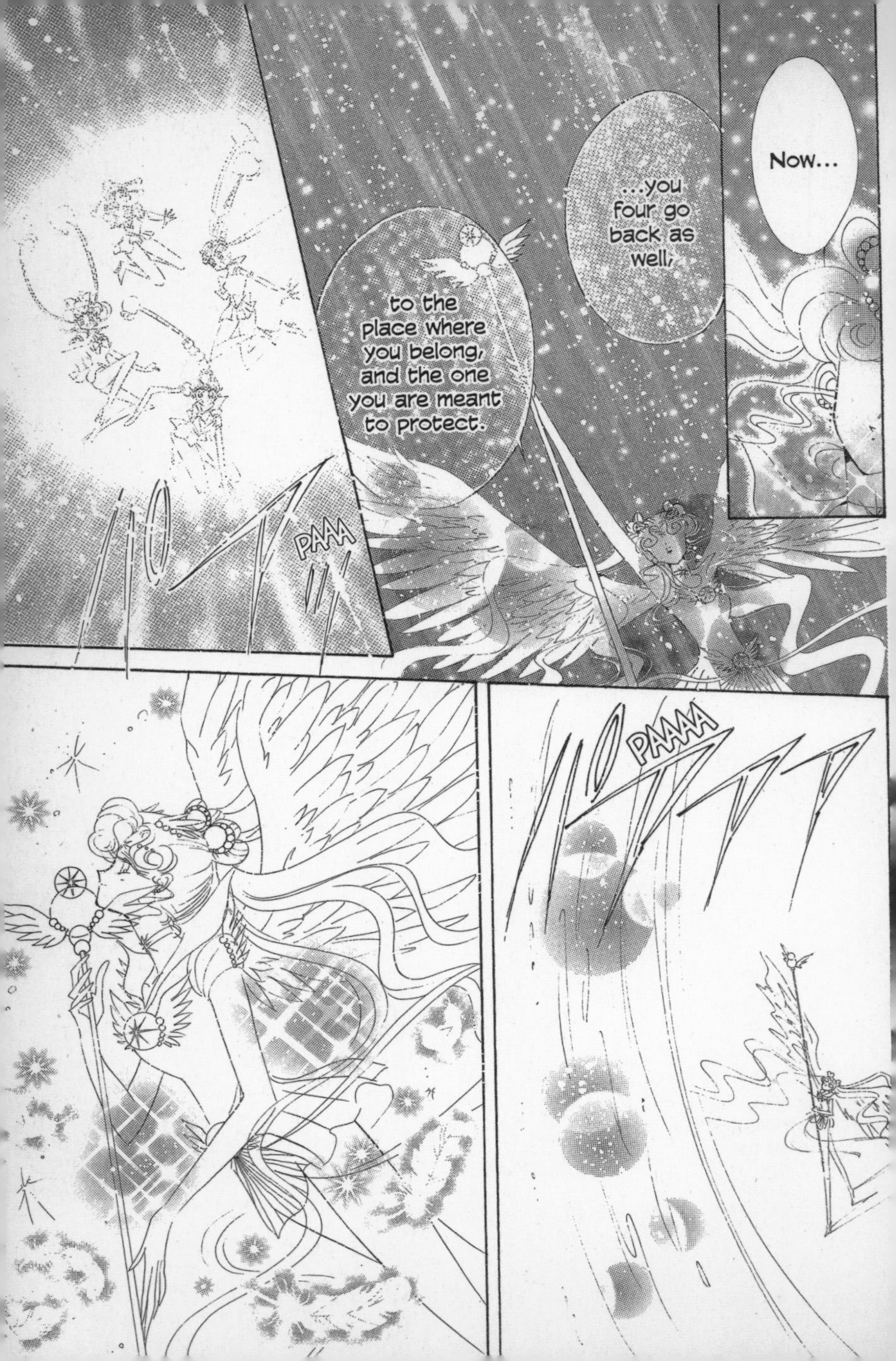
Now...
...you four go back as well,
to the place where you belong, and the one you are meant to protect.
PAAA
PAAAA

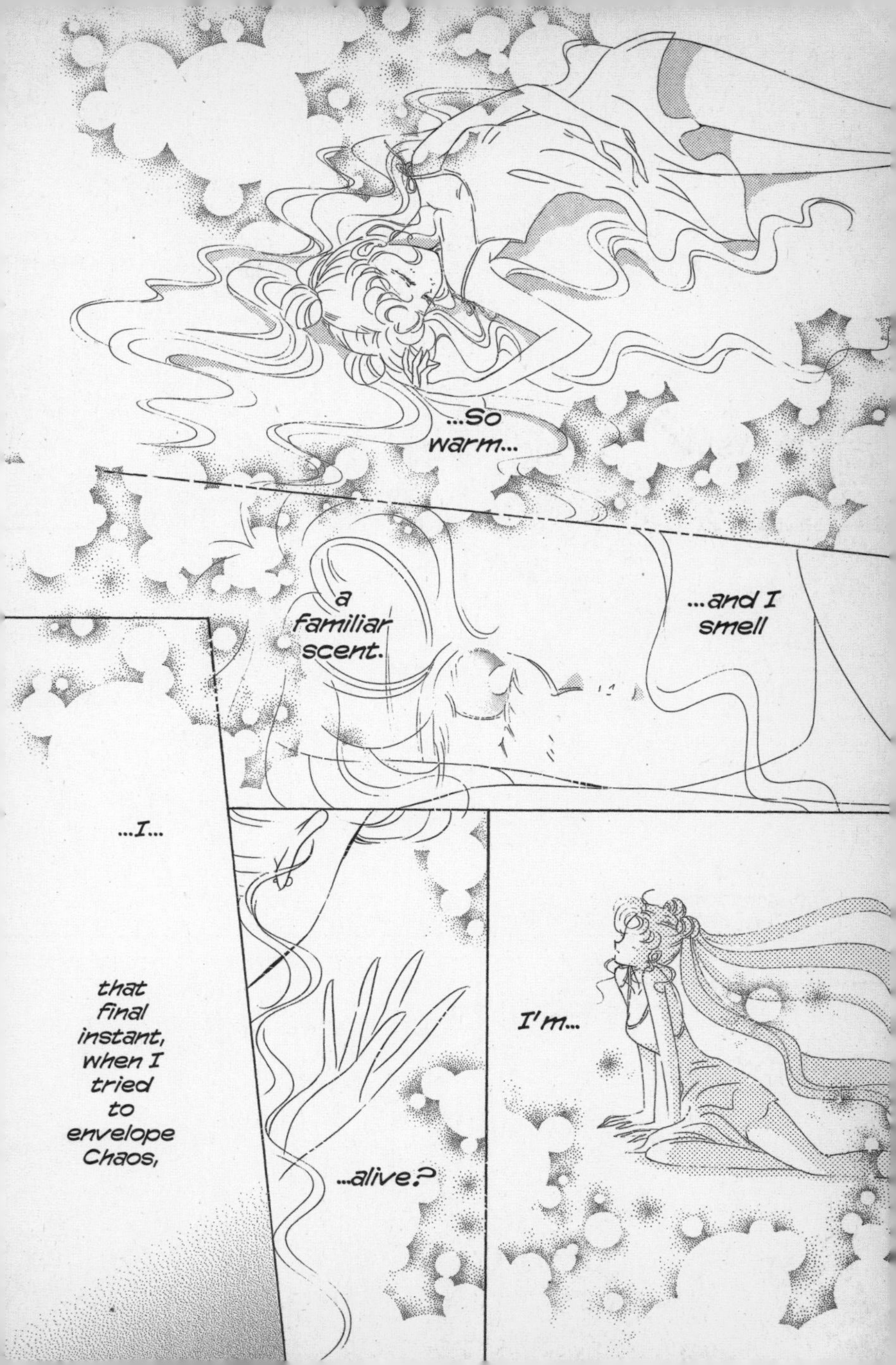
...So warm...
...and I smell
a familiar scent.
I'm...
...alive?
...I...
that final instant, when I tried to envelope Chaos,

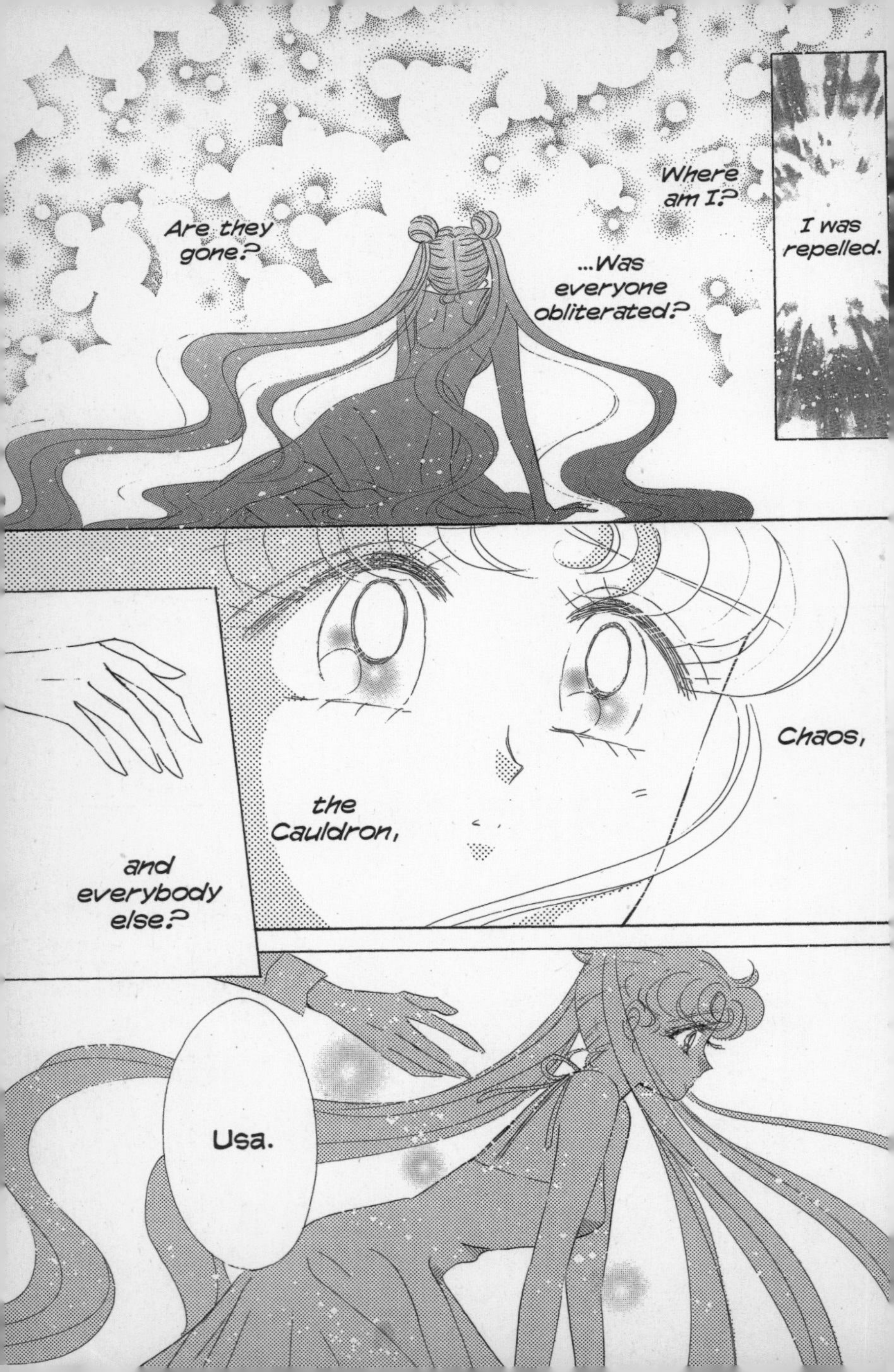
I was repelled.
Where am I?
...Was everyone obliterated?
Are they gone?
Chaos,
the Cauldron,
and everybody else?
Usa.

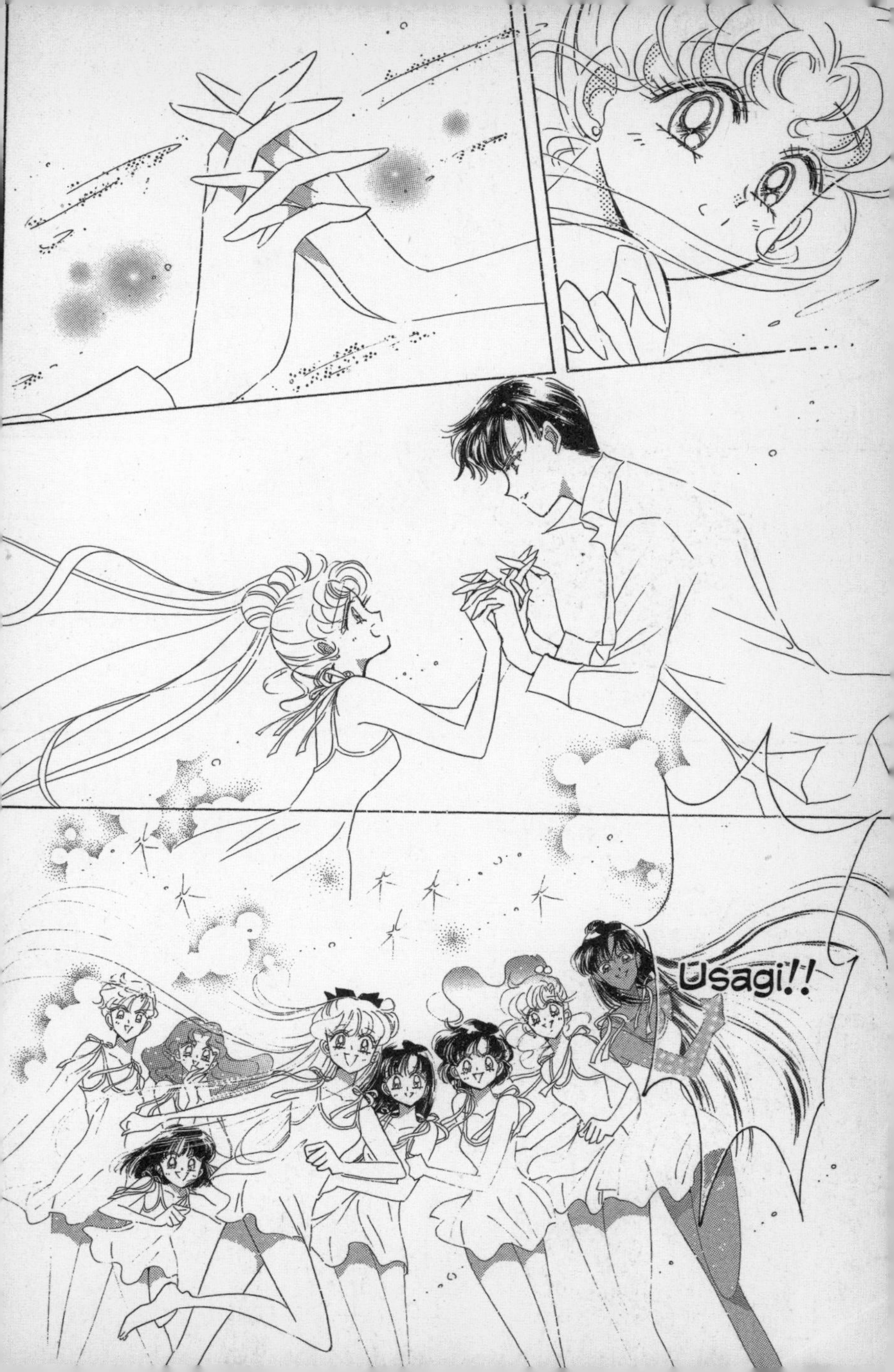
Usagi!!

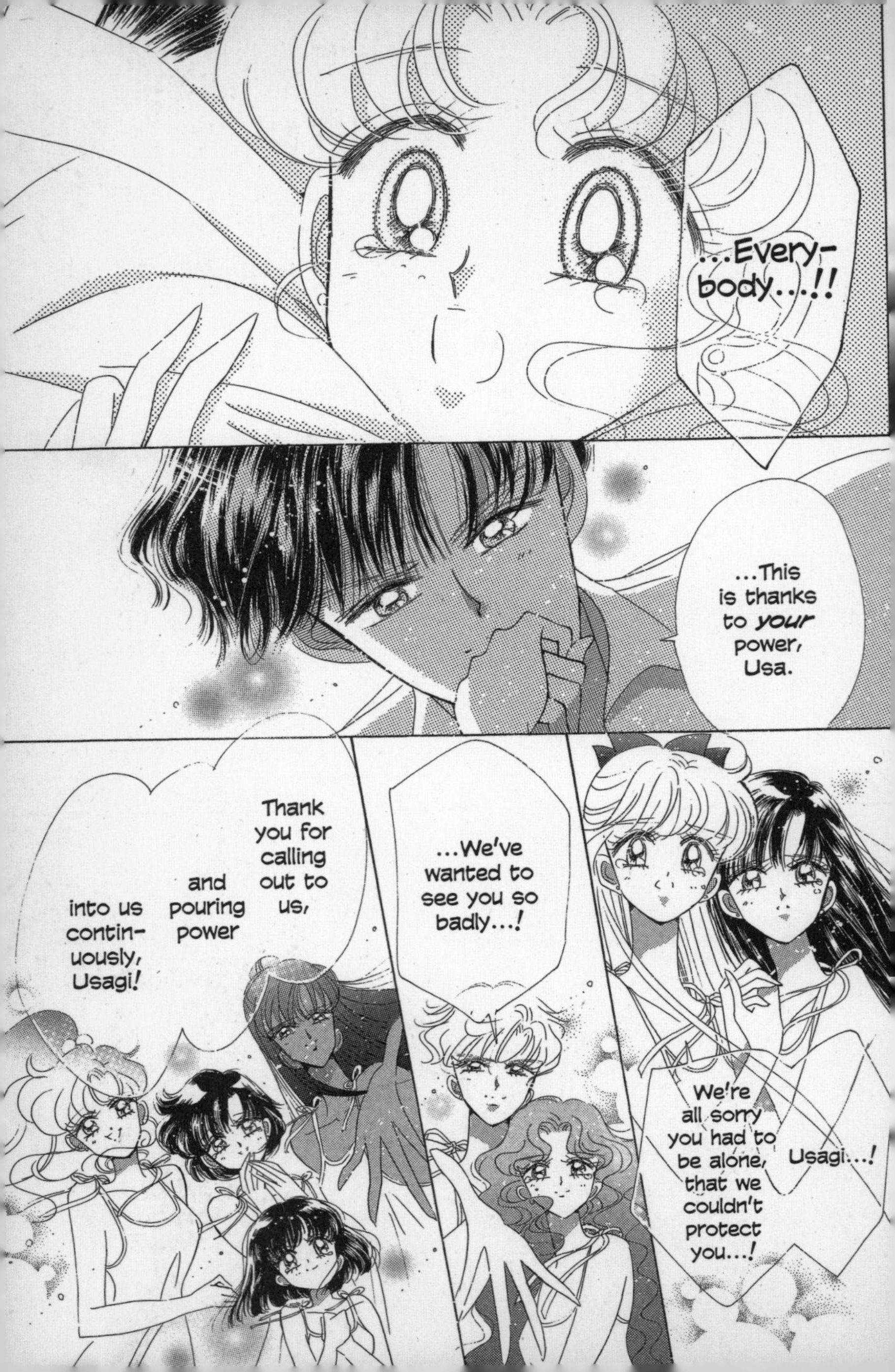
...Every-body...!!
...This is thanks to *your* power, Usa.
Usagi...!
We're all sorry you had to be alone, that we couldn't protect you...!
...We've wanted to see you so badly...!
Thank you for calling out to us, and pouring power into us continuously, Usagi!

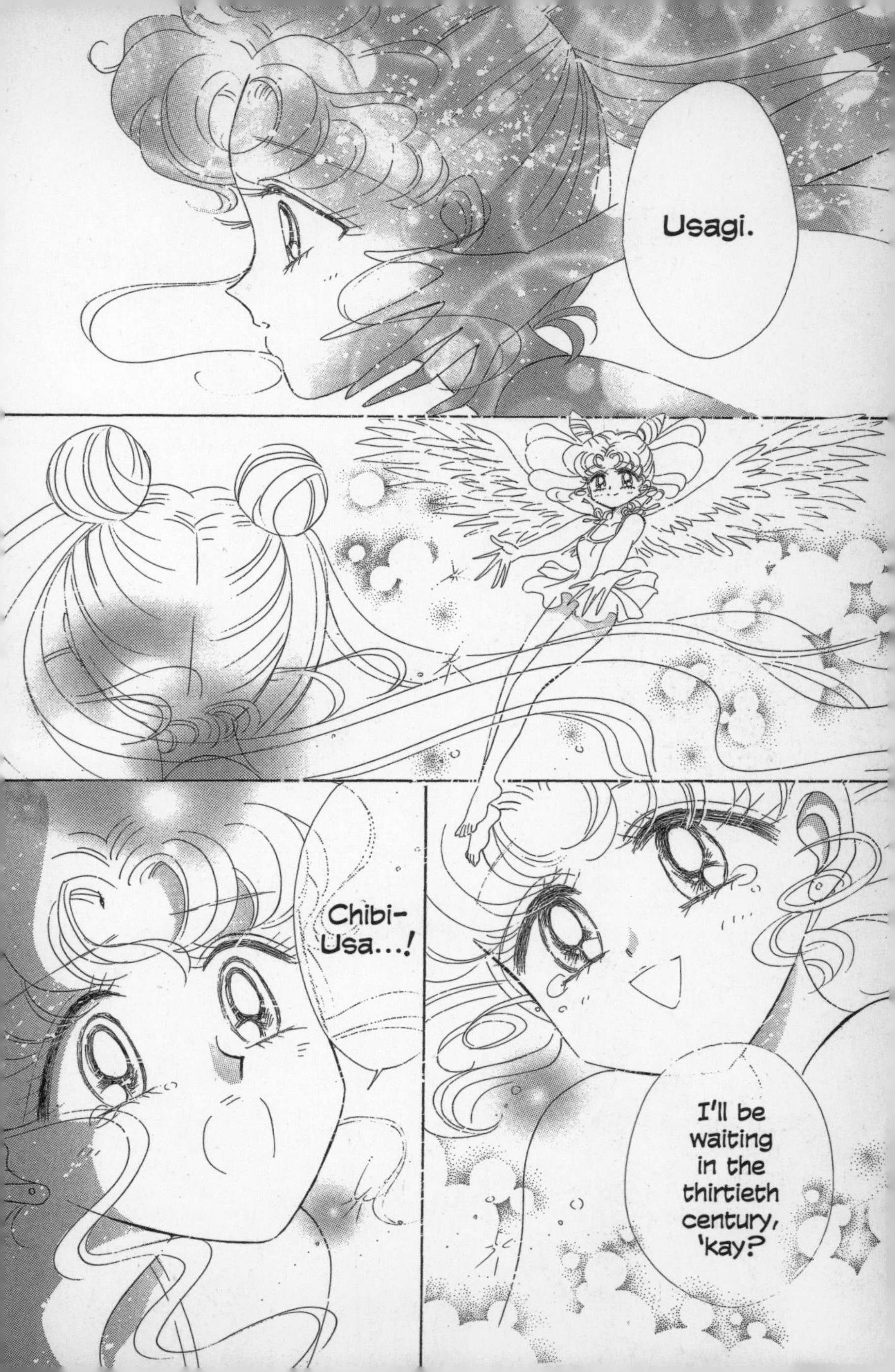
Usagi.
I'll be waiting in the thirtieth century, 'kay?
Chibi-Usa...!

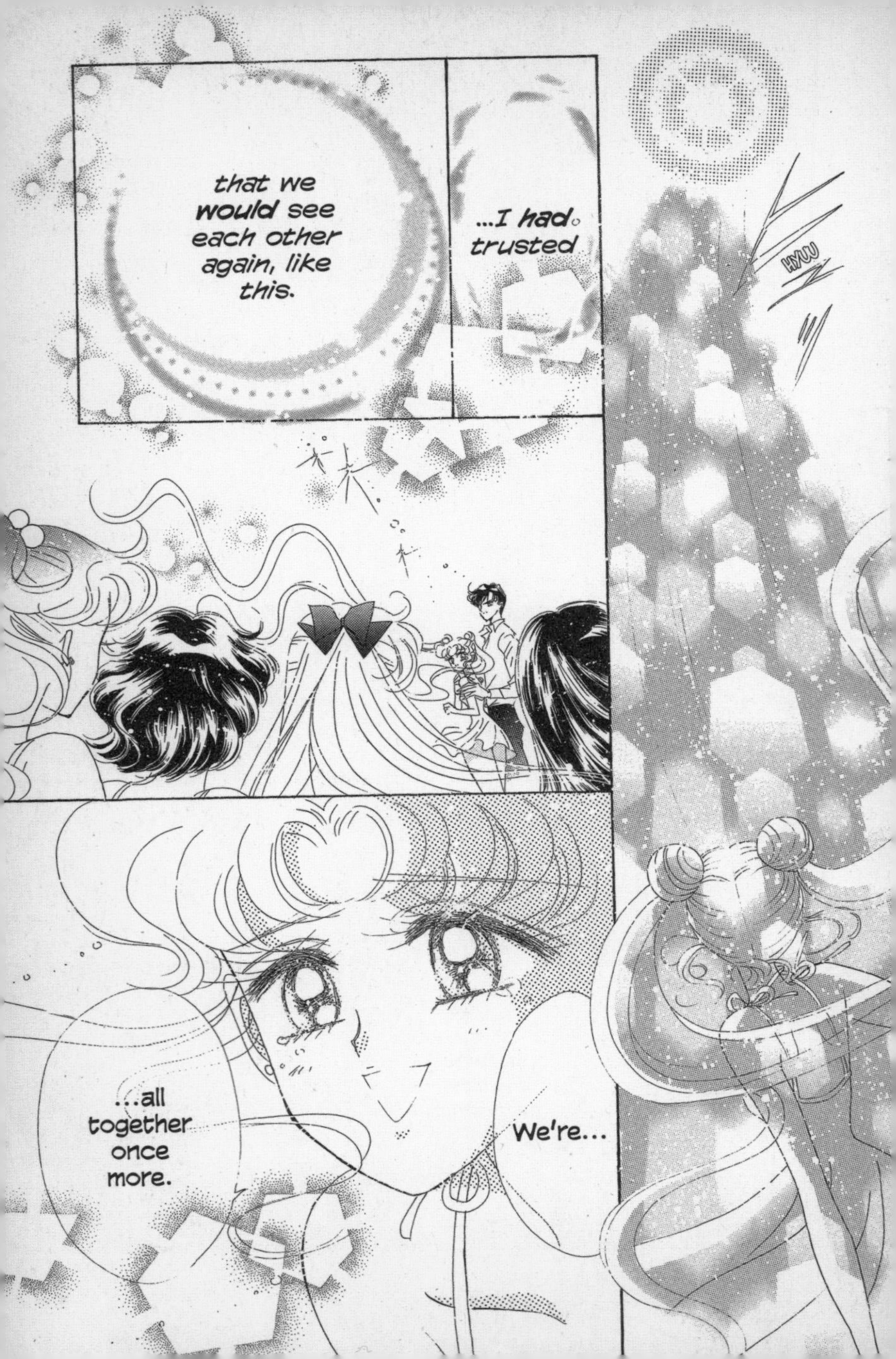
HYUU
...I had trusted
that we would see each other again, like this.
We're...
...all together once more.

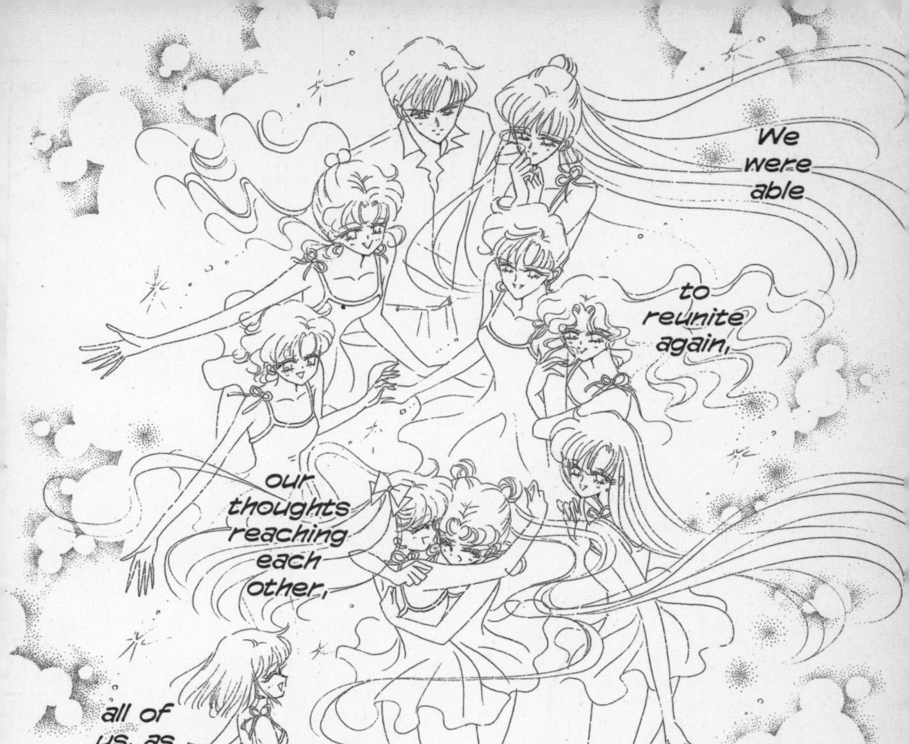
We were able
to reunite again,
our thoughts reaching each other,
all of us, as one.

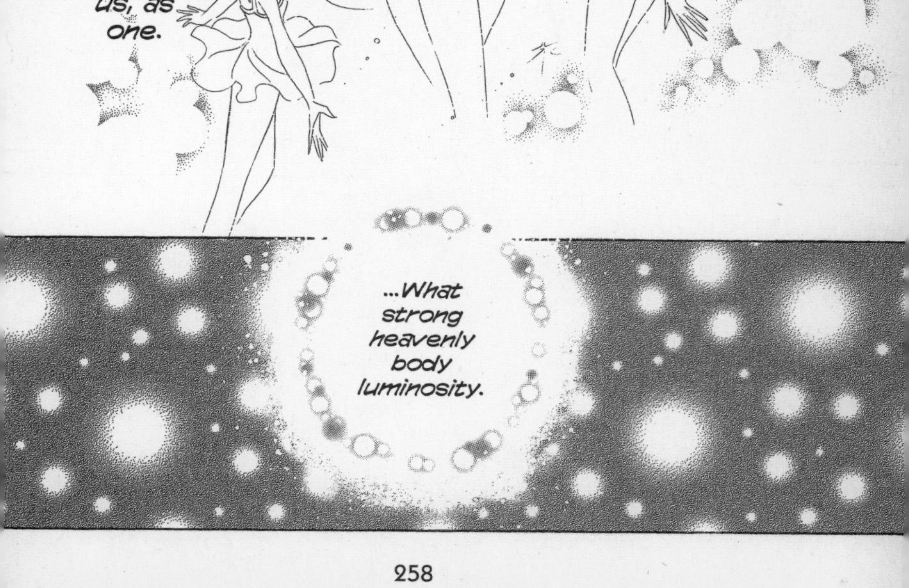
...What strong heavenly body luminosity.

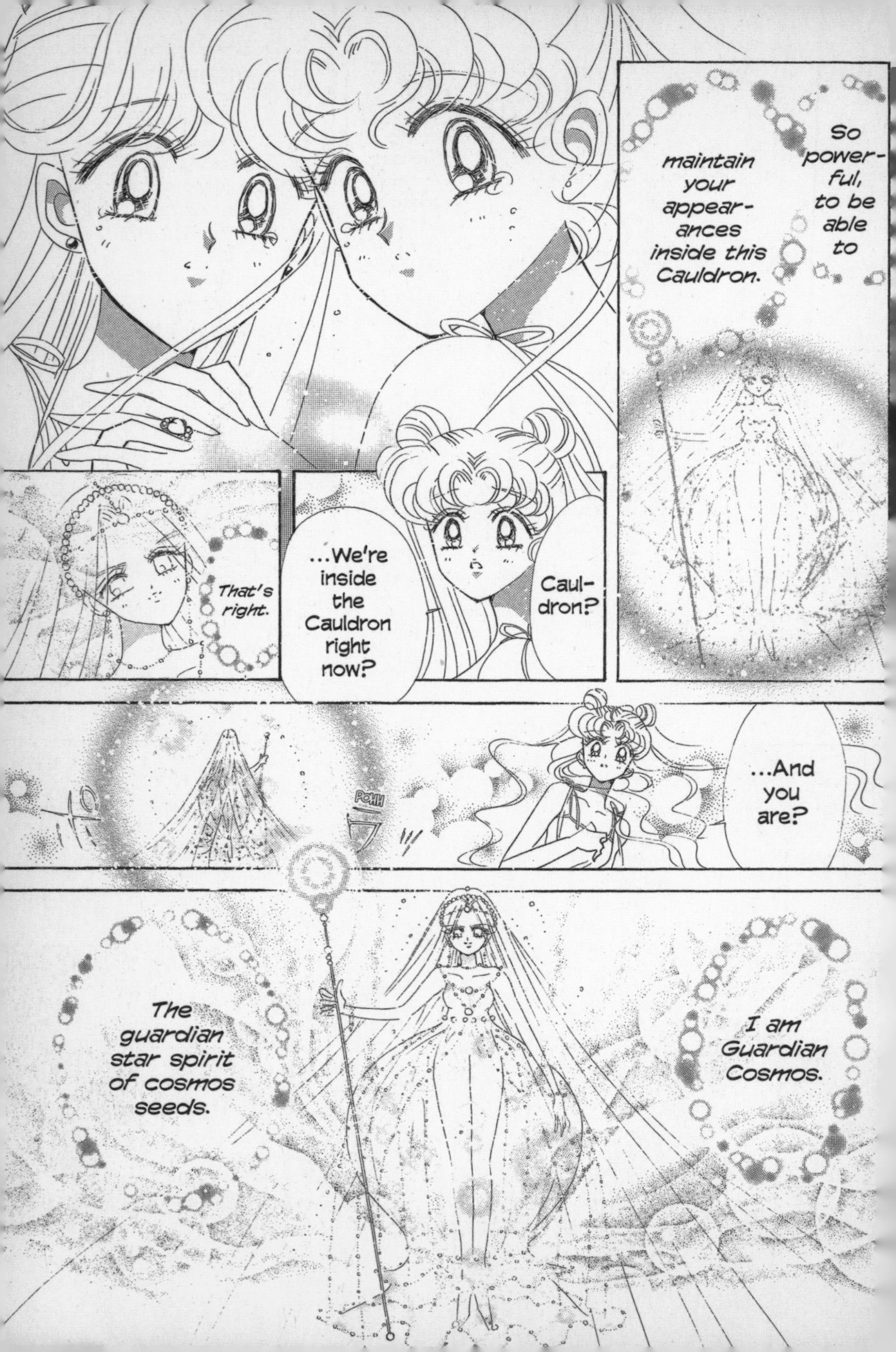
So powerful, to be able to maintain your appearances inside this Cauldron.
Cauldron?
...We're inside the Cauldron right now?
That's right.
...And you are?
POHH
I am Guardian Cosmos.
The guardian star spirit of cosmos seeds.

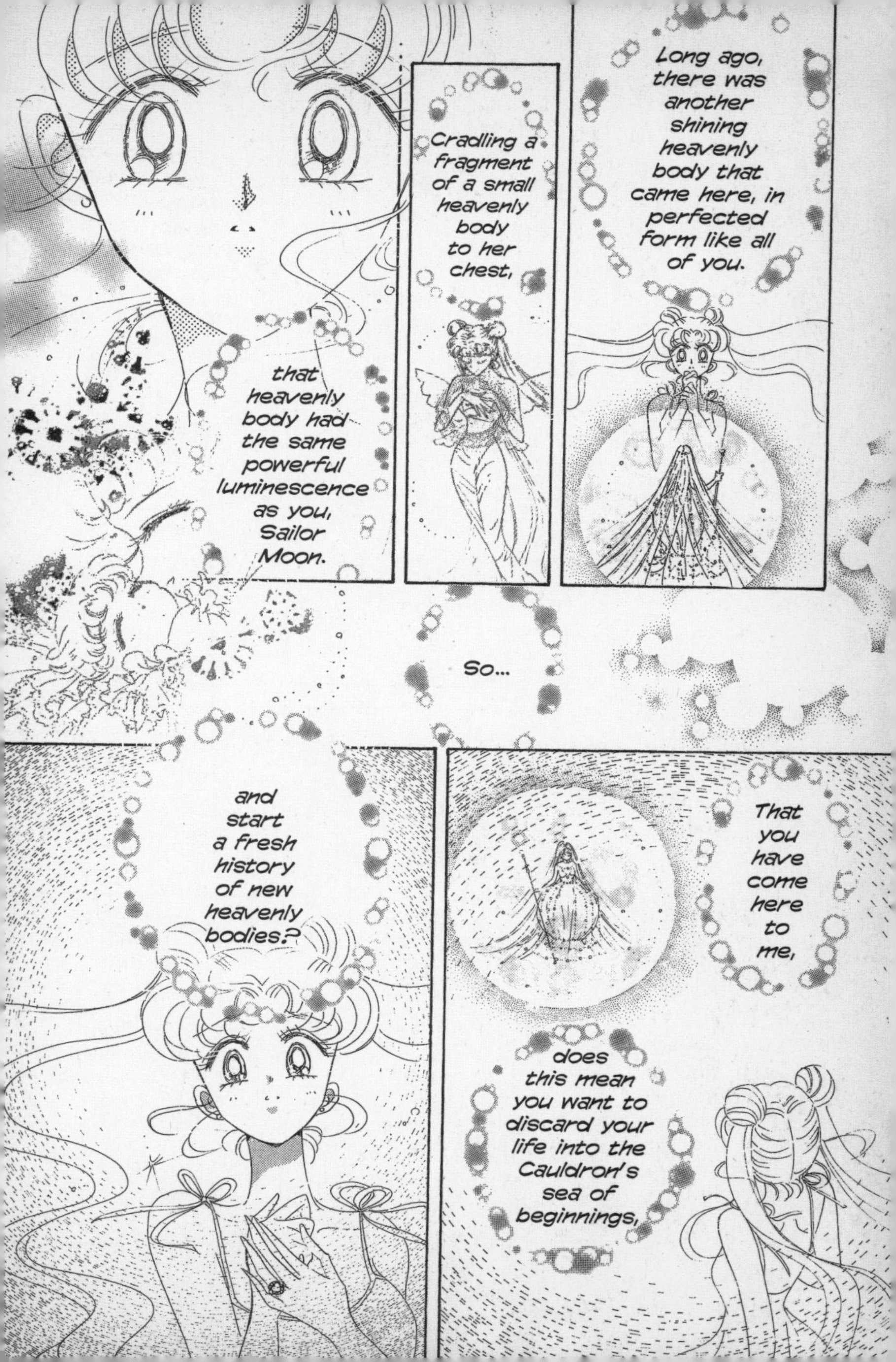
Long ago, there was another shining heavenly body that came here, in perfected form like all of you.
Cradling a fragment of a small heavenly body to her chest,
that heavenly body had the same powerful luminescence as you, Sailor Moon.
So...
That you have come here to me,
does this mean you want to discard your life into the Cauldron's sea of beginnings,
and start a fresh history of new heavenly bodies?

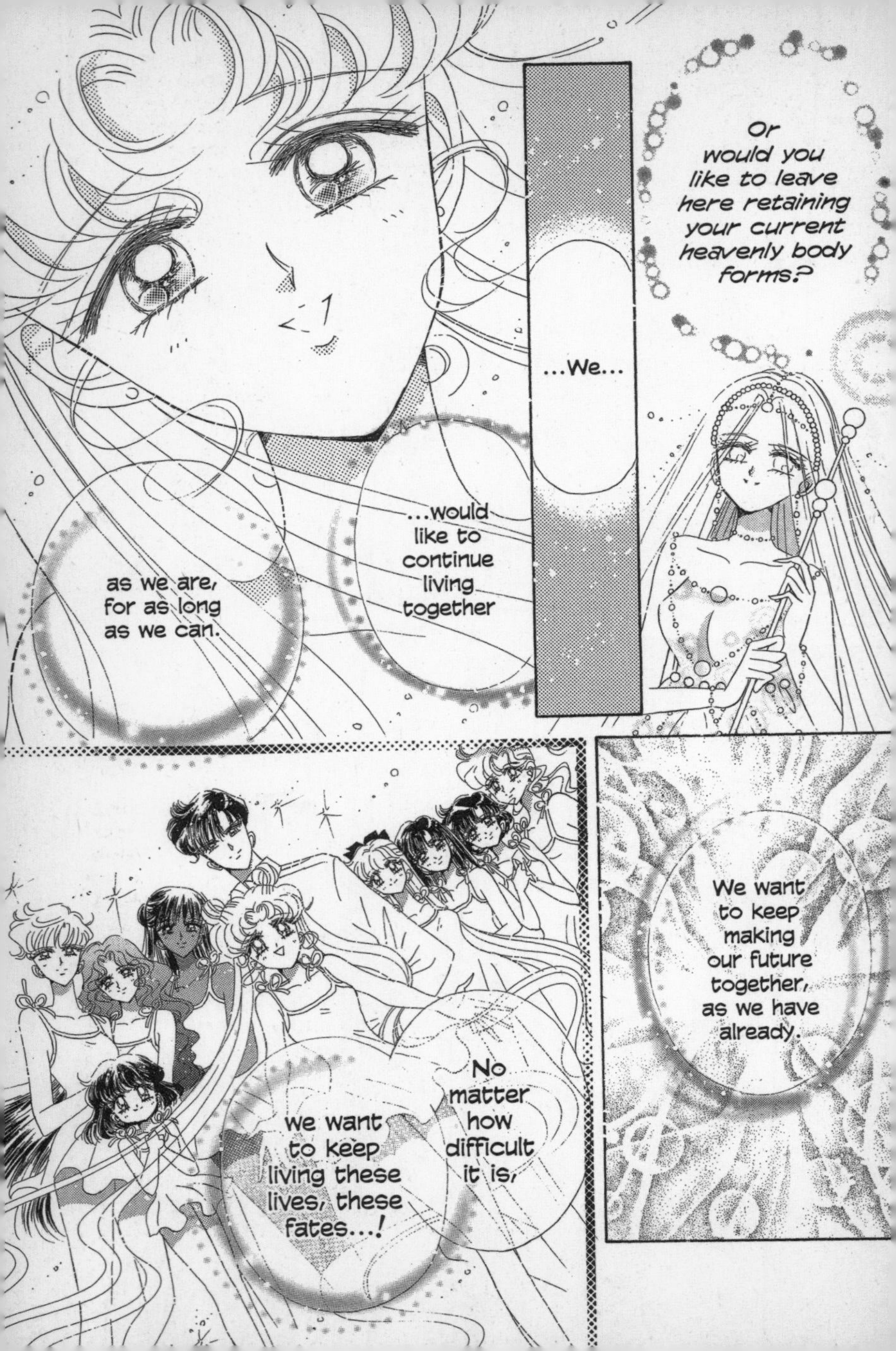
Or would you like to leave here retaining your current heavenly body forms?
...We...
...would like to continue living together
as we are, for as long as we can.
We want to keep making our future together, as we have already.
No matter how difficult it is,
we want to keep living these lives, these fates...!

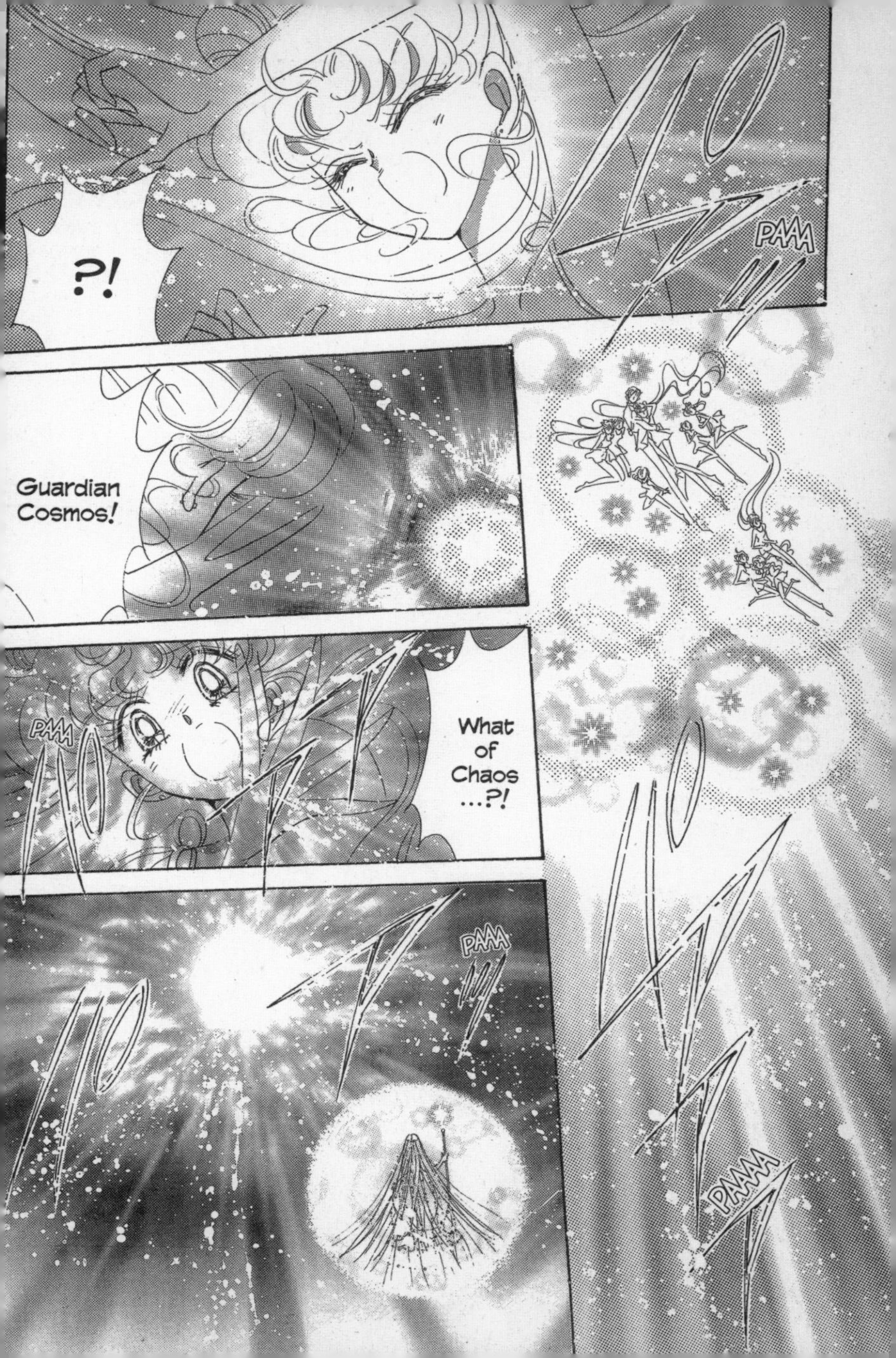
PAAA
?!
PAAAA
Guardian Cosmos!
What of Chaos ...?!
PAAA
PAAA

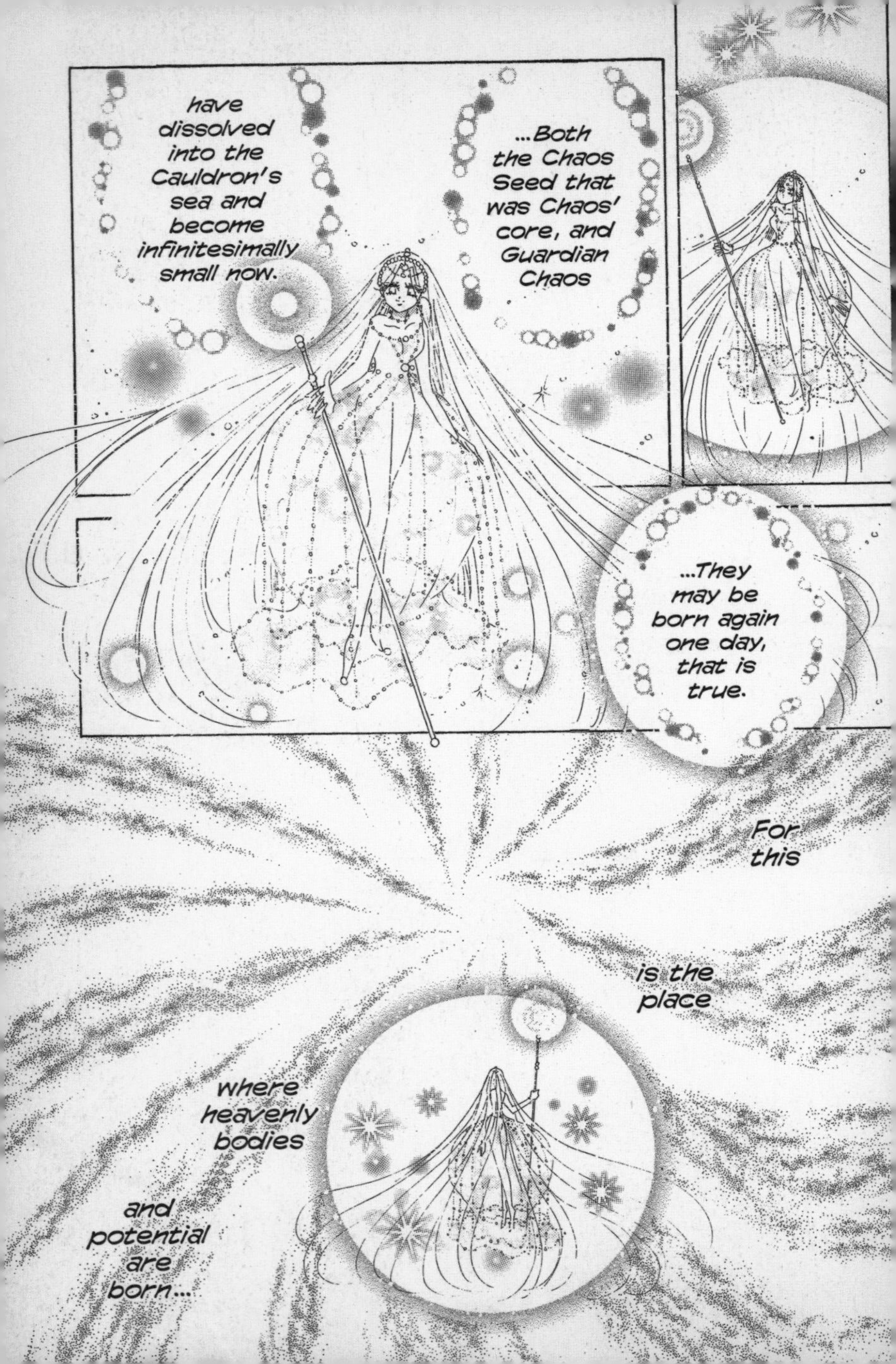
...Both the Chaos Seed that was Chaos' core, and Guardian Chaos
have dissolved into the Cauldron's sea and become infinitesimally small now.
...They may be born again one day, that is true.
For this
is the place
where heavenly bodies
and potential are born...

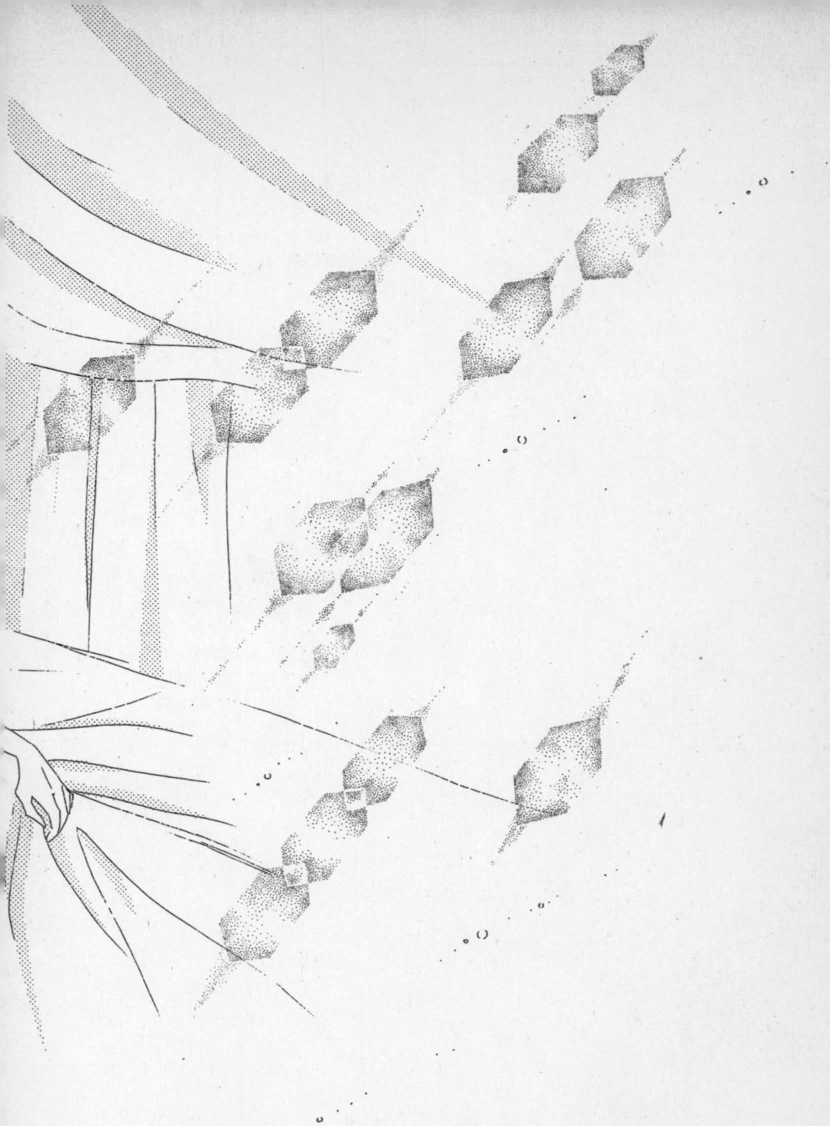

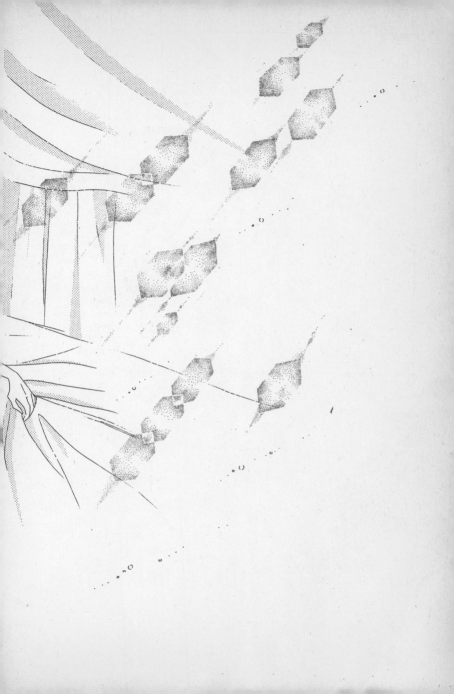

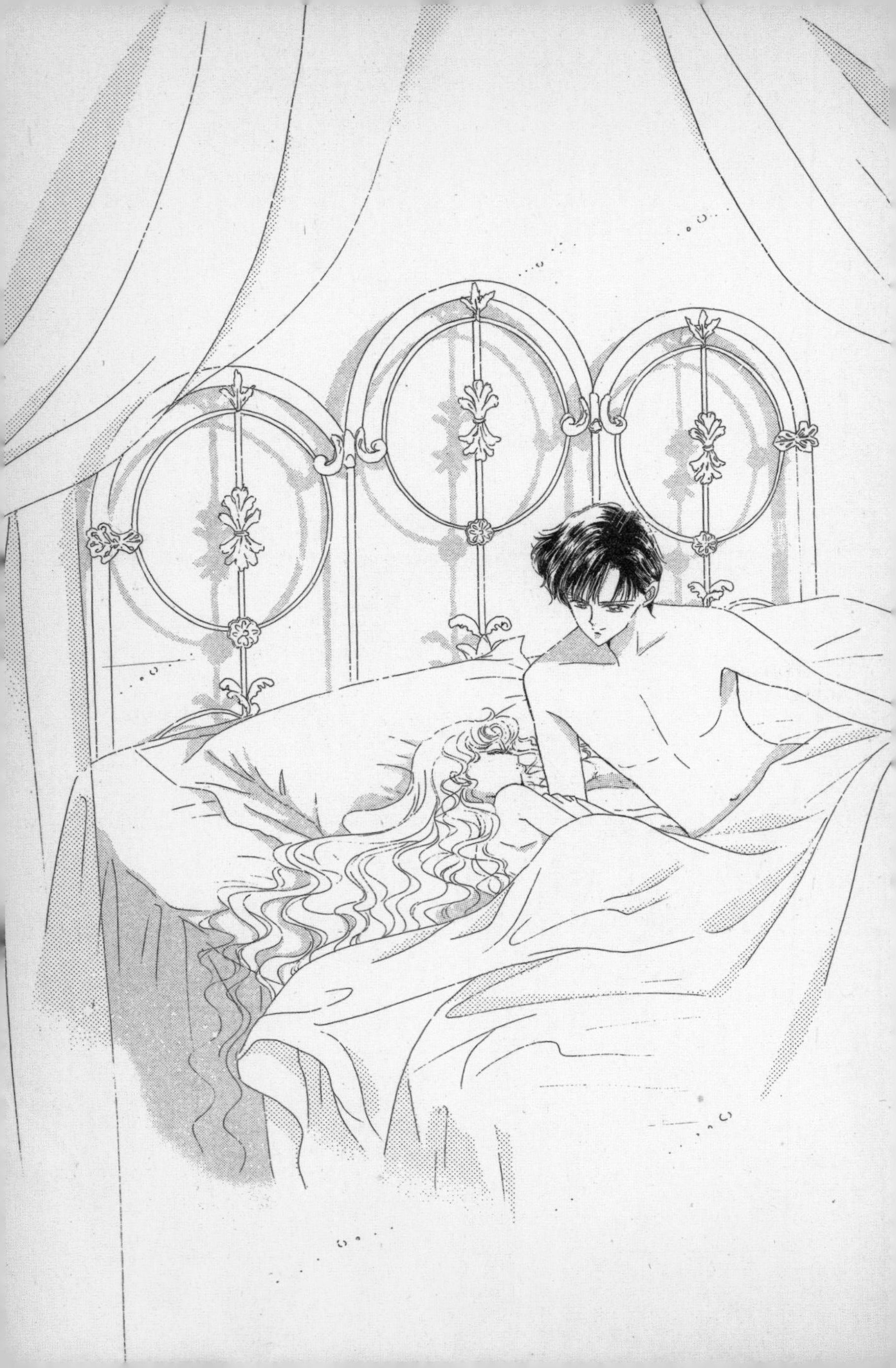

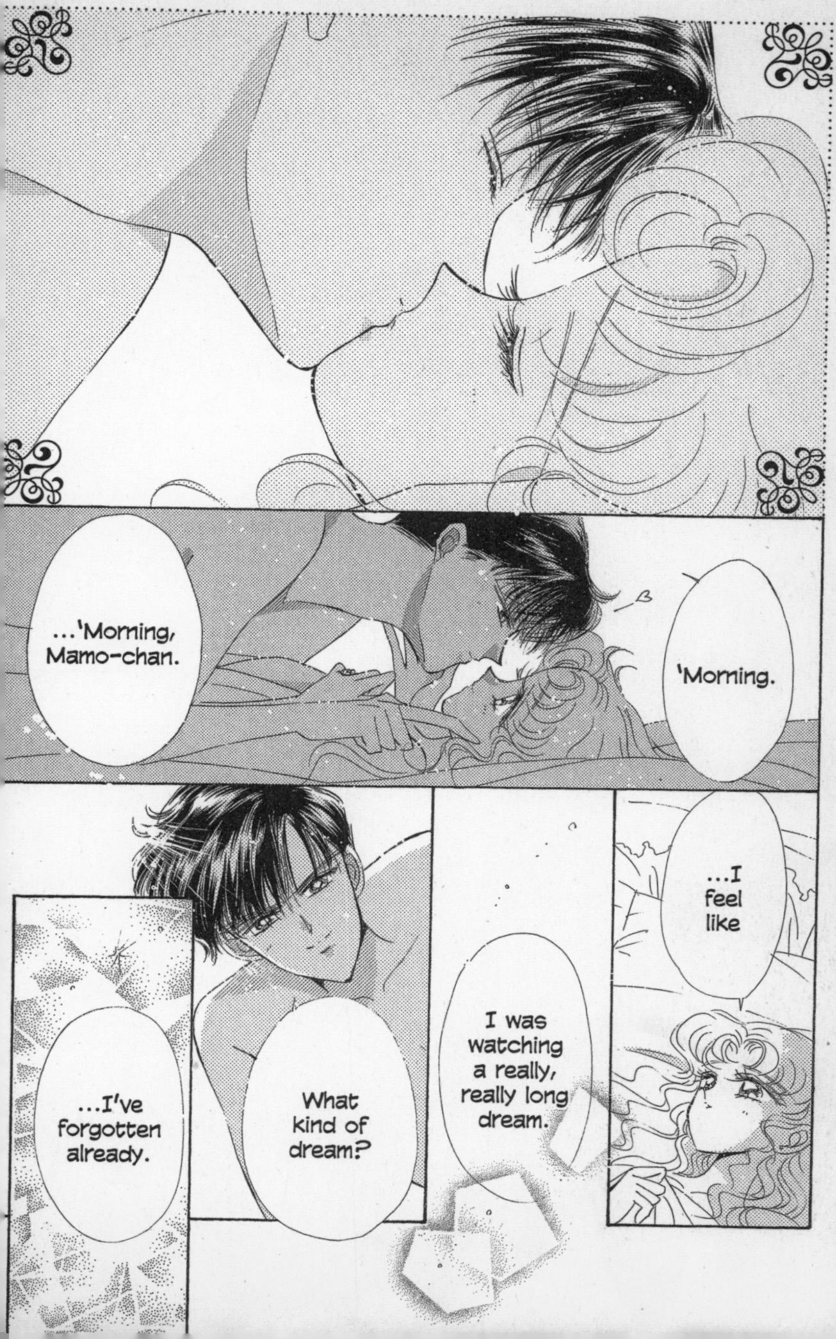
'Morning.
...'Morning, Mamo-chan.
...I feel like
I was watching a really, really long dream.
What kind of dream?
...I've forgotten already.

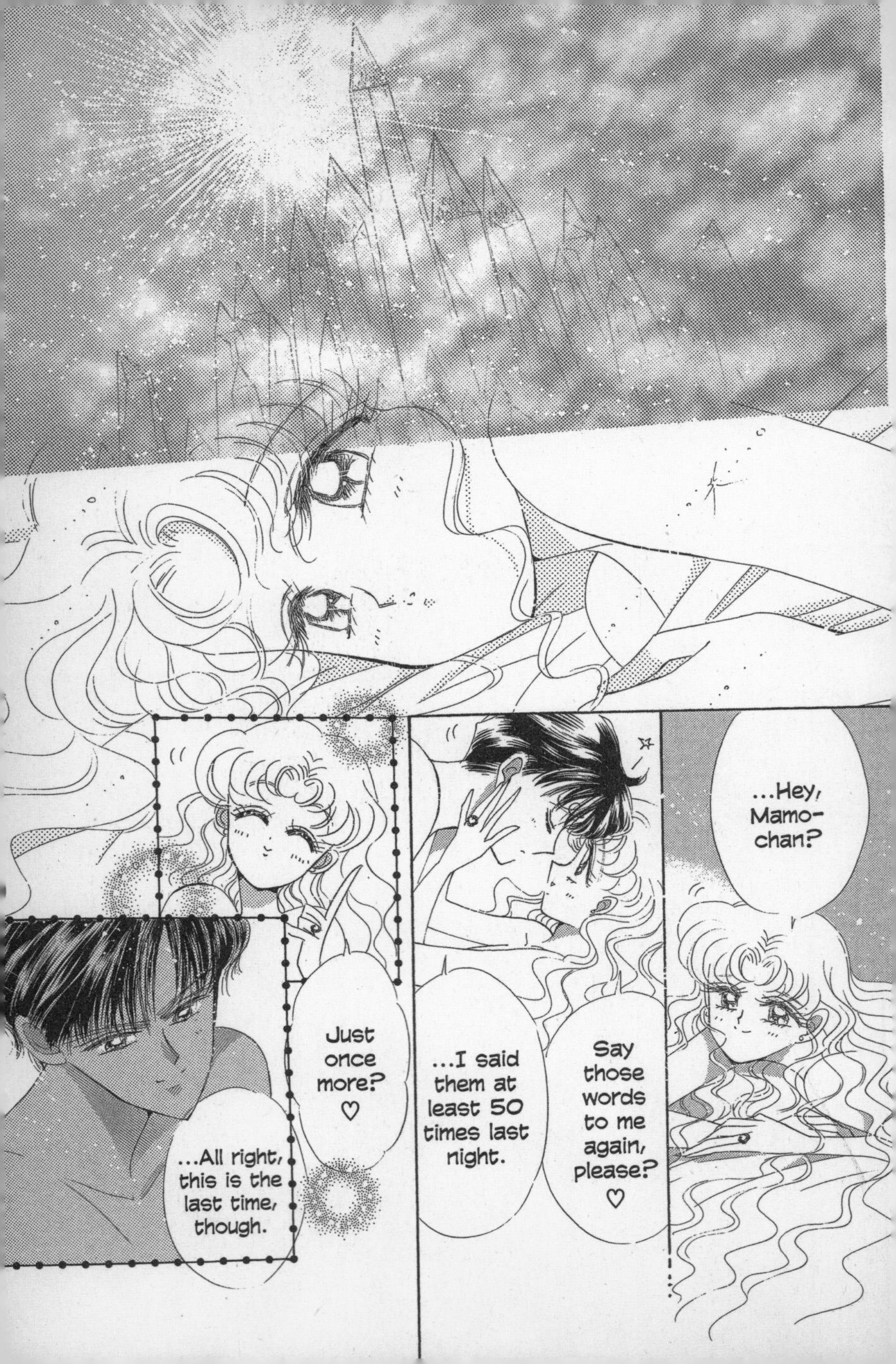
...Hey, Mamo-chan?
Say those words to me again, please? ♡
...I said them at least 50 times last night.
Just once more? ♡
...All right, this is the last time, though.

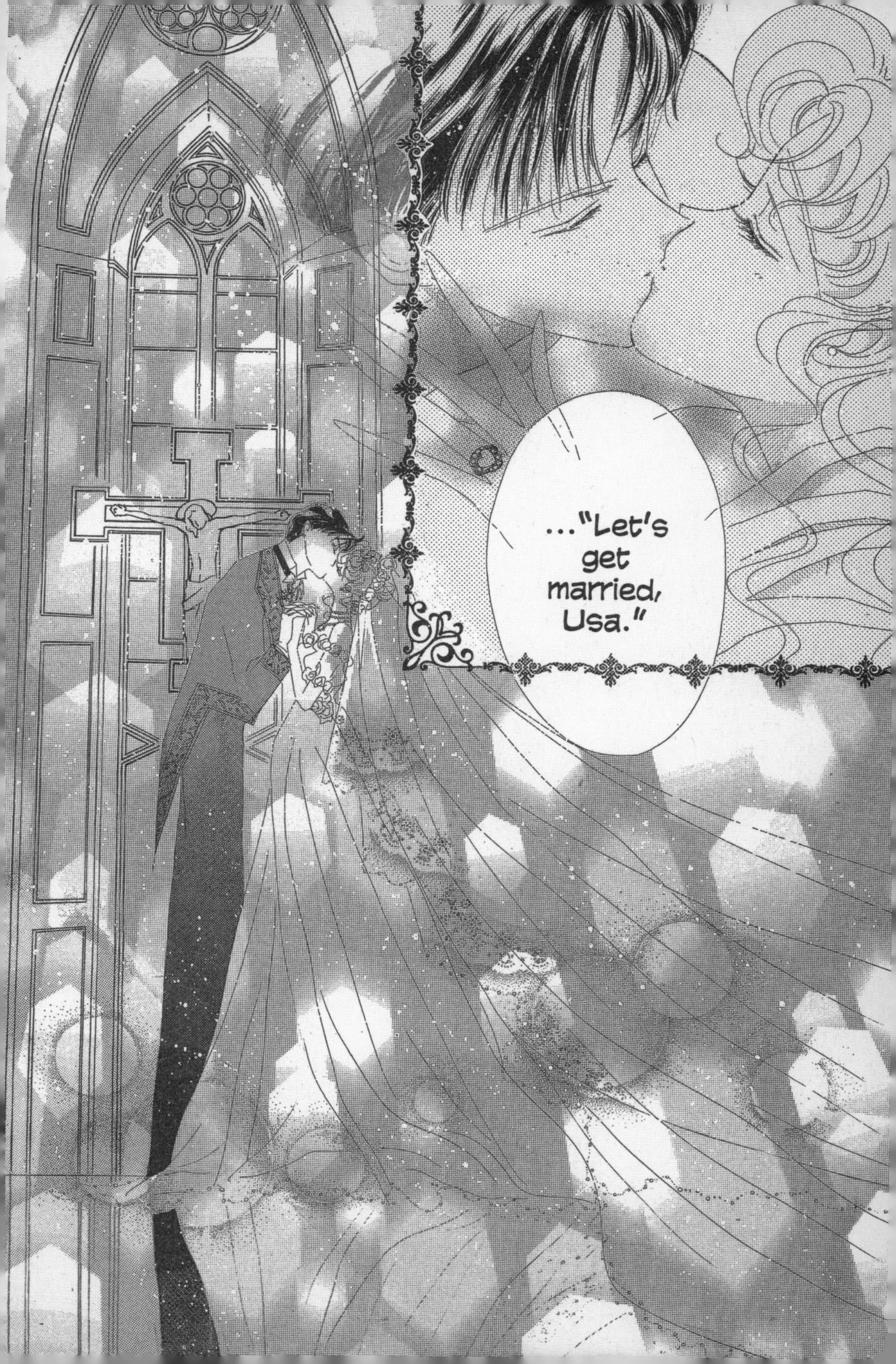
..."Let's get married, Usa."

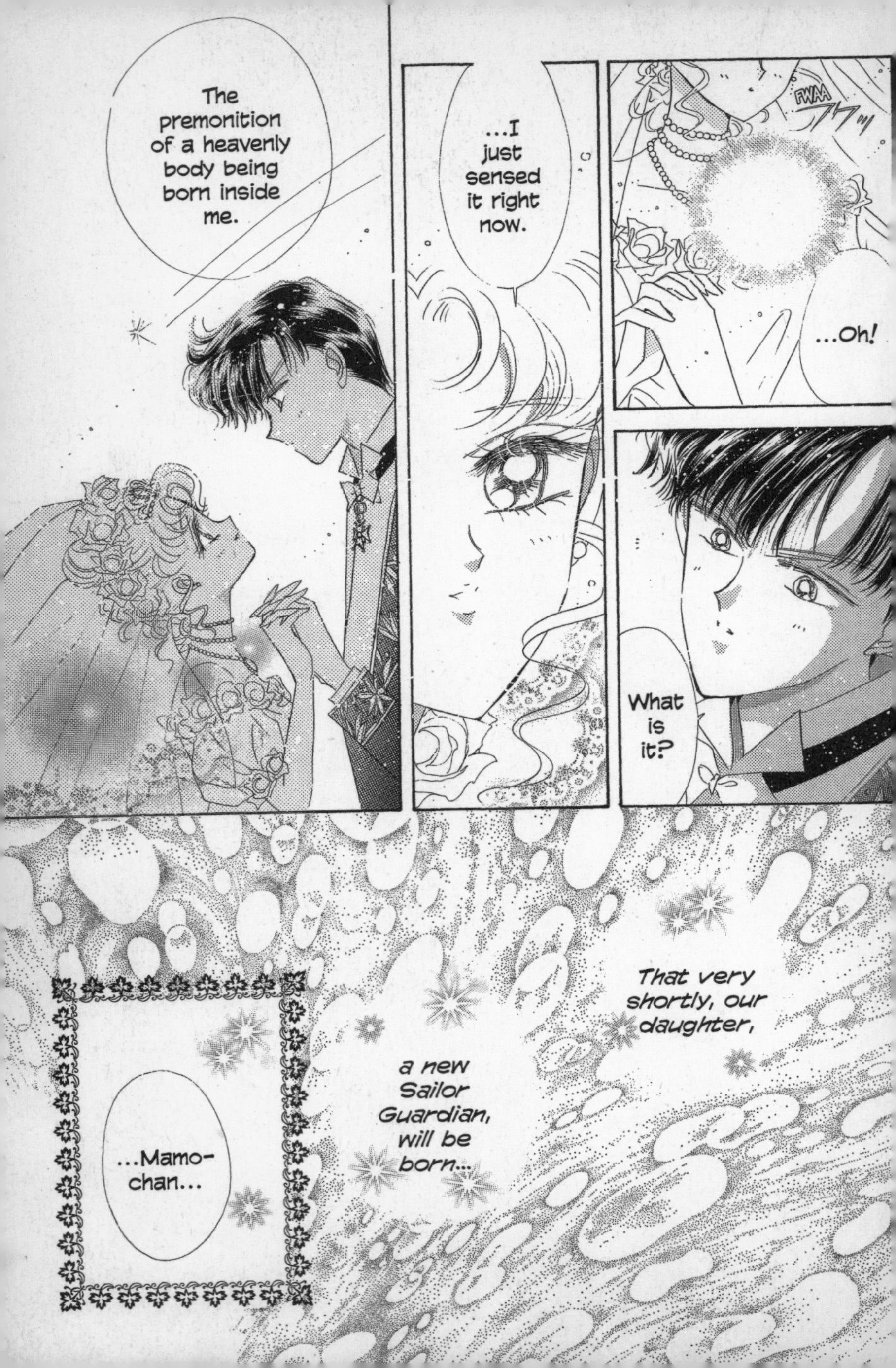
FWAA
...Oh!
What is it?
...I just sensed it right now.
The premonition of a heavenly body being born inside me.
That very shortly, our daughter,
a new Sailor Guardian, will be born...
...Mamo-chan...

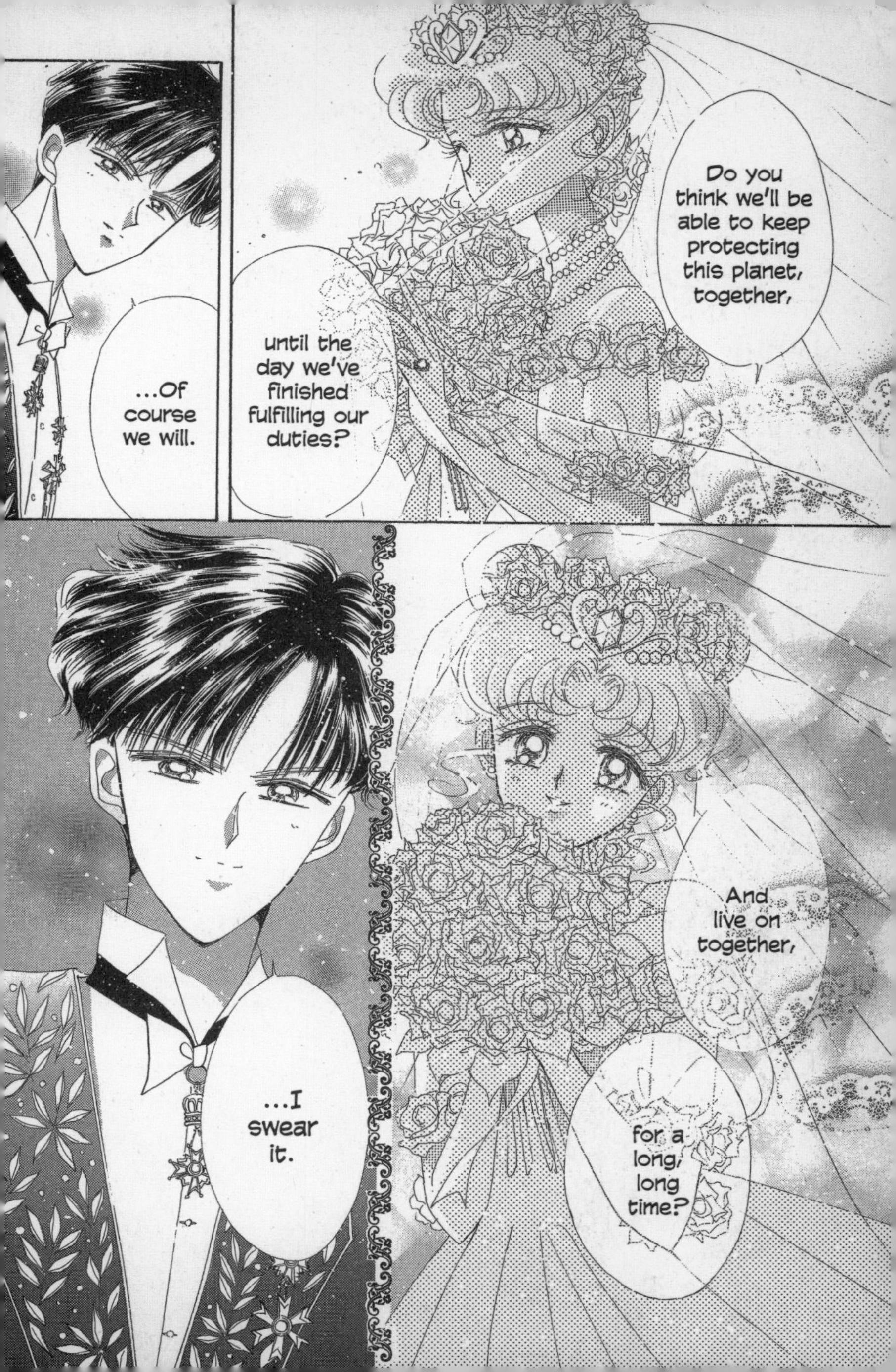
Do you think we'll be able to keep protecting this planet, together,
until the day we've finished fulfilling our duties?
...Of course we will.
And live on together,
for a long, long time?
...I swear it.

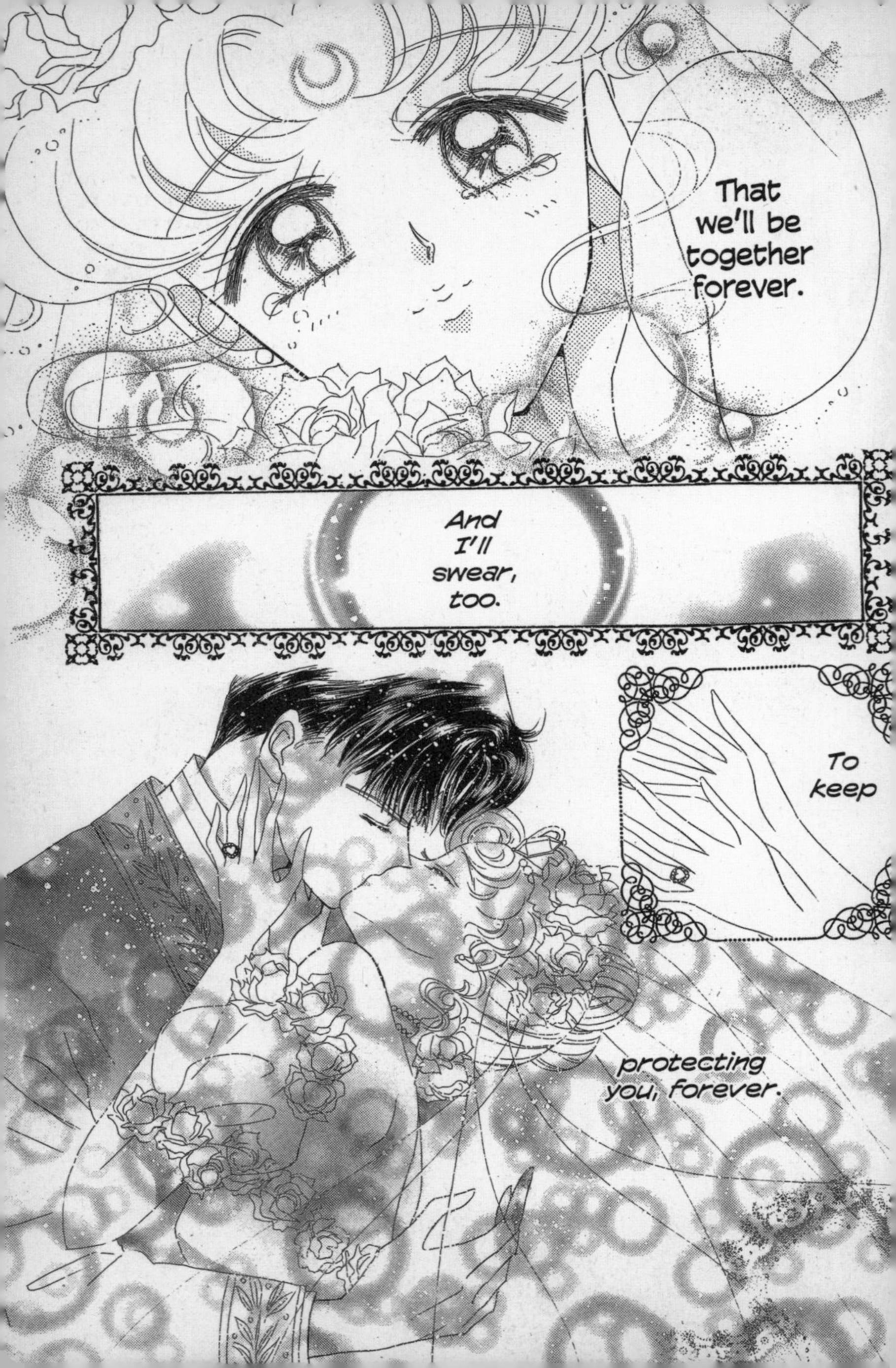
That we'll be together forever.
And I'll swear, too.
To keep
protecting you, forever.

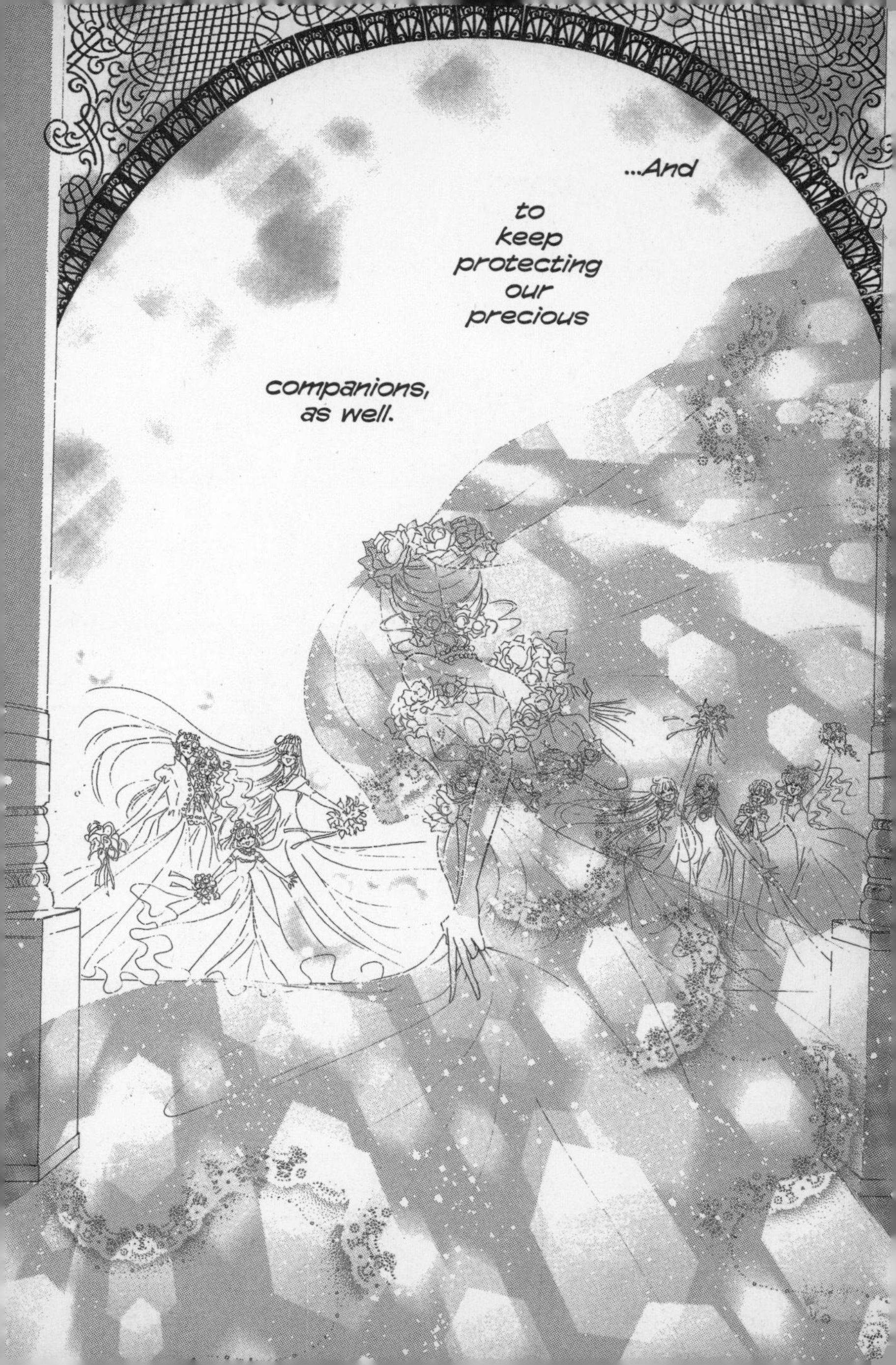
...And
to keep protecting our precious
companions, as well.

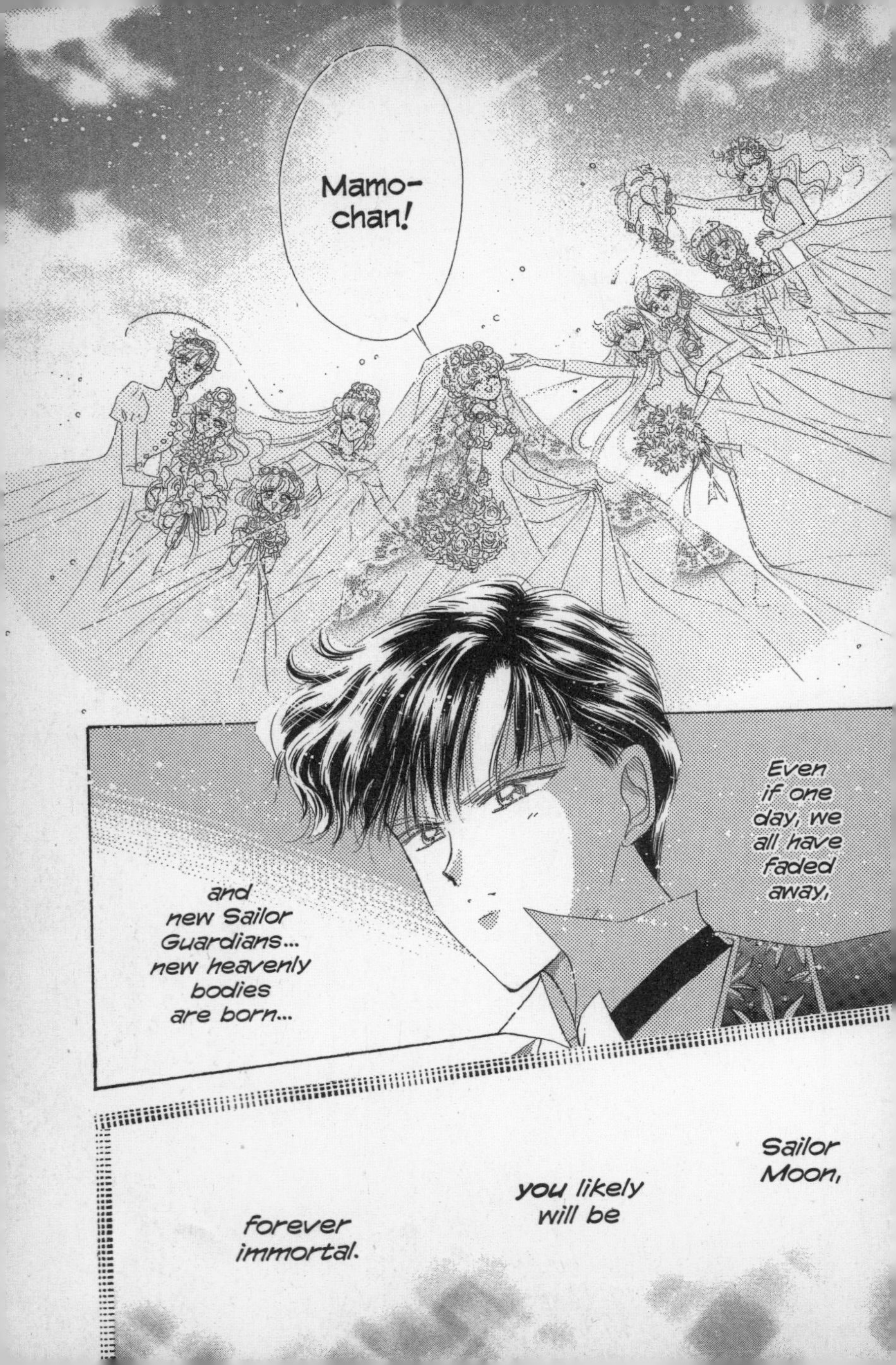
Mamo-chan!
Even if one day, we all have faded away,
and new Sailor Guardians... new heavenly bodies are born...
Sailor Moon,
you likely will be
forever immortal.

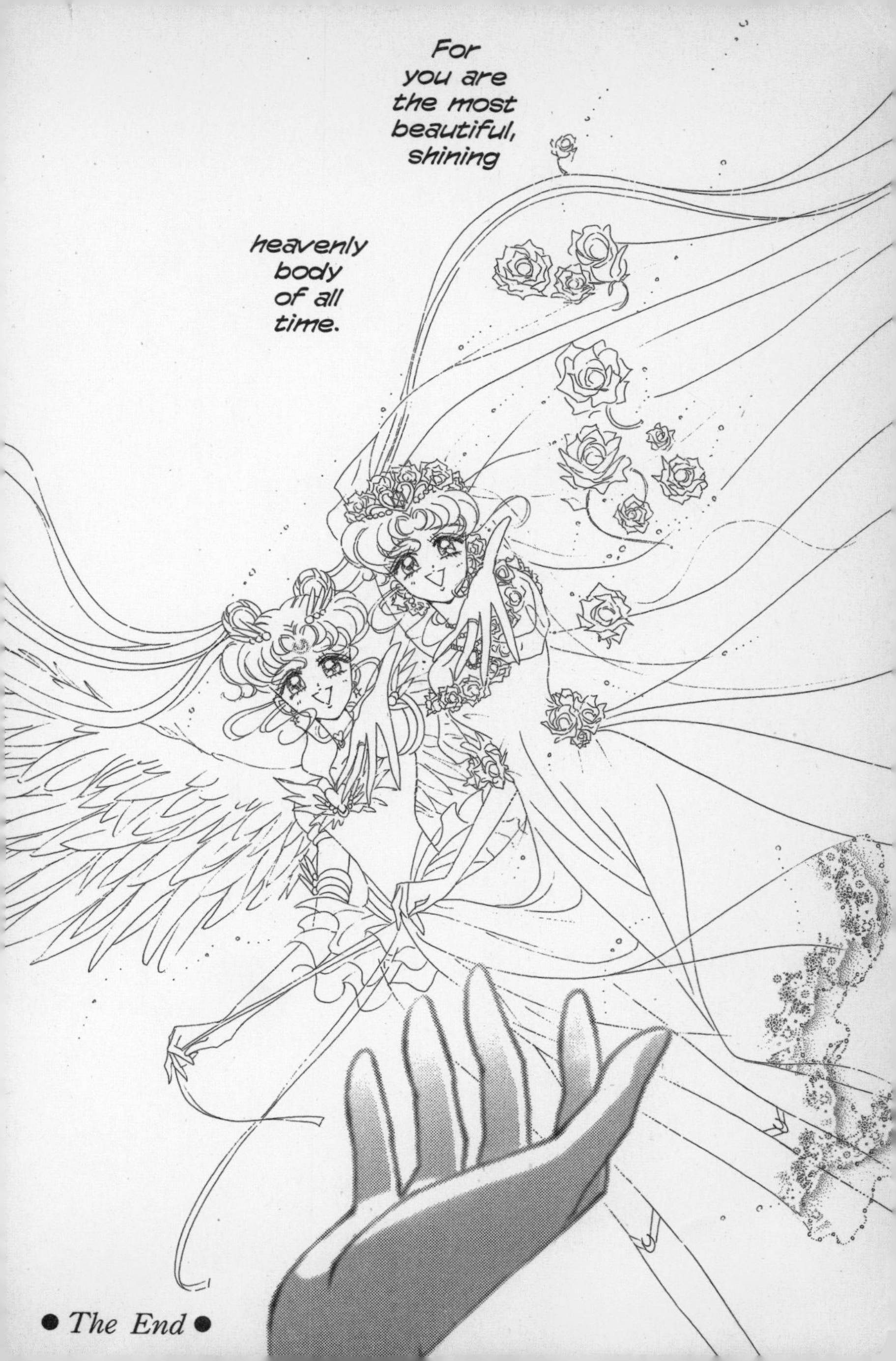
For you are the most beautiful, shining
heavenly body of all time.

• The End •

Translation Notes

Japanese is a tricky language for most Westerners, and translation is often more art than science. For your edification and reading pleasure, here are notes on some of the places where we could have gone in a different direction with our translation of the work, or where a Japanese cultural reference is used.

Nyanko Suzu (page 23)

"Nyanko" is a fictional girl's name created by adding the common Japanese girl's given name ender "-ko" ("child") to "nyan," the Japanese onomatopoeia for a cat's meow. The wordplay is extended further with the character's last name "Suzu," which with the kanji spelling used in this series means "bell," referring to the little bell Japanese people often put on their cat's collar so that the cat cannot sneak up on them or songbirds, but with a different kanji spelling can also mean "tin," which is Nyanko's Anima Mate chemical element.

Sagittarius Zero-star, Sagittarius Alpha-star (page 20, 50-51)

While Sagittarius Zero-star and Sagittarius Alpha-star appear to be fictional astronomical locations or objects created by the author, Sagittarius A-star *is* an actual radio source that is thought to be the site of a supermassive black hole at the center of the Milky Way Galaxy. It is named thus because it is located within the Sagittarius constellation and is part of a larger astronomical feature called Sagittarius A. One must take care not to confuse Sagittarius A-star with Alpha or Alpha Sagittarii, which is one of the stars in the Sagittarius constellation.

Galactica Mysotis Alpestnis (page 72)

The name of Sailor Lethe's attack appears to be an homage to the flower *Myosotis alpestris,* which is more commonly known as the Forget-me-not. However, it is not clear what the significance of the spelling change is.

Kinmokusei (Sweet osmanthus) (page 122)
Osmanthus fragrans, also known as sweet osmanthus, sweet olive, tea olive, and fragrant olive, is a species of flowering shrubs and small trees mostly native to Asia. Princess Kakyu's headdress is decorated with sweet osmanthus blossoms, and the trace scent of sweet osmanthus is what helps Seiya locate her hiding place. However, two other parts of the author's wordplay are lost in translation. The first is where the third and last kanji used to write the Japanese name for sweet osmanthus, "kinmokusei," is replaced with the kanji that means "star" or "planet" to denote the Princess and Three Lights' home planet, Planet Kinmoku. The second is the name of Kakyu's kingdom, "Tankei," which is written using the kanji for one spelling of "sweet osmanthus" in Chinese.

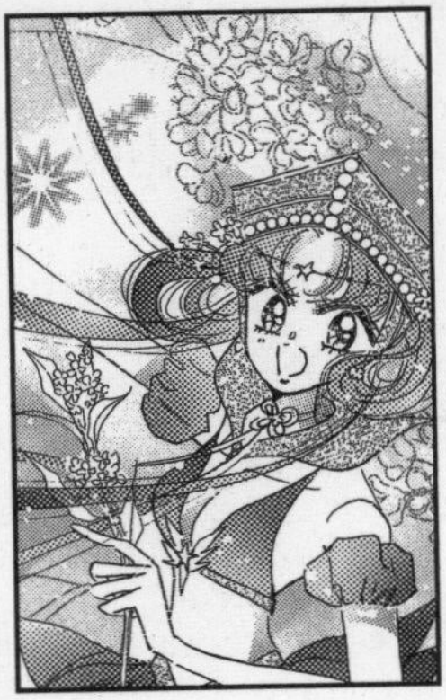

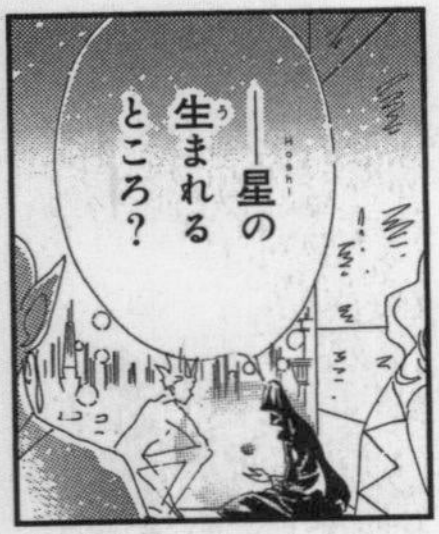
――星の生まれるところ？

Hoshi
The word "hoshi" in Japanese can sometimes be difficult to translate, as it can refer to either a planet or a star, or even one of several other astronomical light-emitting or light-reflecting heavenly bodies. Therefore, to be all-inclusive and as concise as possible, the translator has decided to use "heavenly body" unless it is absolutely clear which (English) term the author is using.

The Pretty Guardians are back!

★

Kodansha Comics is proud to present *Sailor Moon* with all new translations.

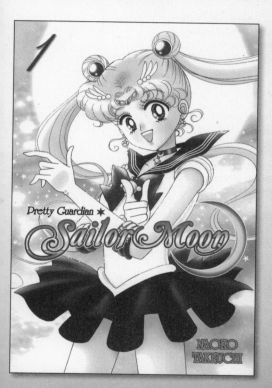

For more information, go to **www.kodanshacomics.com**

Pretty Guardian Sailor Moon volume 12 is a work of fiction. Names, characters, places, and incidents are the products of the author's imagination or are used fictitiously. Any resemblance to actual events, locales, or persons, living or dead, is entirely coincidental.

A Kodansha Trade Paperback Original.

Published in the United States by Kodansha Comics, an imprint of Kodansha USA Publishing, LLC, New York.

Publication rights for this English edition arranged through Kodansha Ltd., Tokyo.

First published in Japan in 2004 by Kodansha Ltd., Tokyo, as *Bishoujosenshi Sailor Moon Shinsoban*, volume 12.

ISBN 978-1-61262-008-4

Printed in Canada

www.kodanshacomics.com

9 8 7 6 5 4 3 2 1

Translator/Adapter: Mari Morimoto
Lettering: Jennifer Skarupa

TOMARE! STOP

You're going the wrong way!

Manga is a completely different type of reading experience.

To start at the beginning,
Go to the end!

That's right! Authentic manga is read the traditional Japanese way—from right to left, exactly the opposite of how American books are read. It's easy to follow: Just go to the other end of the book and read each page—and each panel—from right side to left side, starting at the top right. Now you're experiencing manga as it was meant to be!